Microsoft®
Excel 2000 Bible

Microsoft®
Excel 2000 Bible

John Walkenbach

IDG Books Worldwide, Inc.
An International Data Group Company

Foster City, CA ✦ Chicago, IL ✦ Indianapolis, IN ✦ New York, NY

Microsoft® Excel 2000 Bible

Published by
IDG Books Worldwide, Inc.
An International Data Group Company
919 E. Hillsdale Blvd., Suite 400
Foster City, CA 94404
www.idgbooks.com (IDG Books Worldwide Web site)

Library of Congress Catalog Card Number: 98-75379

ISBN: 0-7645-3259-6

Printed in the United States of America

10 9 8 7 6 5 4 3

1B/SU/QT/ZZ/FC

Distributed in the United States by IDG Books Worldwide, Inc.

Distributed by CDG Books Canada Inc. for Canada; by Transworld Publishers Limited in the United Kingdom; by IDG Norge Books for Norway; by IDG Sweden Books for Sweden; by Woodslane Pty. Ltd. for Australia; by Woodslane (NZ) Ltd. for New Zealand; by TransQuest Publishers Pte Ltd. for Singapore, Malaysia, Thailand, Indonesia, and Hong Kong; by ICG Muse, Inc. for Japan; by Norma Comunicaciones S.A. for Colombia; by Intersoft for South Africa; by Le Monde en Tique for France; by International Thomson Publishing for Germany, Austria and Switzerland; by Distribuidora Cuspide for Argentina; by Livraria Cultura for Brazil; by Ediciones ZETA S.C.R. Ltda. for Peru; by WS Computer Publishing Corporation, Inc., for the Philippines; by Contemporanea de Ediciones for Venezuela; by Express Computer Distributors for the Caribbean and West Indies; by Micronesia Media Distributor, Inc. for Micronesia; by Grupo Editorial Norma S.A. for Guatemala; by Chips Computadoras S.A. de C.V. for Mexico; by Editorial Norma de Panama S.A. for Panama; by American Bookshops for Finland. Authorized Sales Agent: Anthony Rudkin Associates for the Middle East and North Africa.

For general information on IDG Books Worldwide's books in the U.S., please call our Consumer Customer Service department at 800-762-2974. For reseller information, including discounts and premium sales, please call our Reseller Customer Service department at 800-434-3422.

For information on where to purchase IDG Books Worldwide's books outside the U.S., please contact our International Sales department at 317-596-5530 or fax 317-596-5692.

For consumer information on foreign language translations, please contact our Customer Service department at 800-434-3422, fax 317-596-5692, or e-mail rights@idgbooks.com.

For information on licensing foreign or domestic rights, please phone +1-650-655-3109.

For sales inquiries and special prices for bulk quantities, please contact our Sales department at 650-655-3200 or write to the address above.

For information on using IDG Books Worldwide's books in the classroom or for ordering examination copies, please contact our Educational Sales department at 800-434-2086 or fax 317-596-5499.

For press review copies, author interviews, or other publicity information, please contact our Public Relations department at 650-655-3000 or fax 650-655-3299.

For authorization to photocopy items for corporate, personal, or educational use, please contact Copyright Clearance Center, 222 Rosewood Drive, Danvers, MA 01923, or fax 978-750-4470.

is registered trademark or trademark under exclusive license to IDG Books Worldwide, Inc., from International Data Group, Inc., in the United States and/or other countries

ABOUT IDG BOOKS WORLDWIDE

Welcome to the world of IDG Books Worldwide.

IDG Books Worldwide, Inc., is a subsidiary of International Data Group, the world's largest publisher of computer-related information and the leading global provider of information services on information technology. IDG was founded more than 30 years ago by Patrick J. McGovern and now employs more than 9,000 people worldwide. IDG publishes more than 290 computer publications in over 75 countries. More than 90 million people read one or more IDG publications each month.

Launched in 1990, IDG Books Worldwide is today the #1 publisher of best-selling computer books in the United States. We are proud to have received eight awards from the Computer Press Association in recognition of editorial excellence and three from Computer Currents' First Annual Readers' Choice Awards. Our best-selling ...For Dummies® series has more than 50 million copies in print with translations in 31 languages. IDG Books Worldwide, through a joint venture with IDG's Hi-Tech Beijing, became the first U.S. publisher to publish a computer book in the People's Republic of China. In record time, IDG Books Worldwide has become the first choice for millions of readers around the world who want to learn how to better manage their businesses.

Our mission is simple: Every one of our books is designed to bring extra value and skill-building instructions to the reader. Our books are written by experts who understand and care about our readers. The knowledge base of our editorial staff comes from years of experience in publishing, education, and journalism — experience we use to produce books to carry us into the new millennium. In short, we care about books, so we attract the best people. We devote special attention to details such as audience, interior design, use of icons, and illustrations. And because we use an efficient process of authoring, editing, and desktop publishing our books electronically, we can spend more time ensuring superior content and less time on the technicalities of making books.

You can count on our commitment to deliver high-quality books at competitive prices on topics you want to read about. At IDG Books Worldwide, we continue in the IDG tradition of delivering quality for more than 30 years. You'll find no better book on a subject than one from IDG Books Worldwide.

John Kilcullen
Chairman and CEO
IDG Books Worldwide, Inc.

Steven Berkowitz
President and Publisher
IDG Books Worldwide, Inc.

Eighth Annual Computer Press Awards ≥1992

Ninth Annual Computer Press Awards ≥1993

Tenth Annual Computer Press Awards ≥1994

Eleventh Annual Computer Press Awards ≥1995

IDG is the world's leading IT media, research and exposition company. Founded in 1964, IDG had 1997 revenues of $2.05 billion and has more than 9,000 employees worldwide. IDG offers the widest range of media options that reach IT buyers in 75 countries representing 95% of worldwide IT spending. IDG's diverse product and services portfolio spans six key areas including print publishing, online publishing, expositions and conferences, market research, education and training, and global marketing services. More than 90 million people read one or more of IDG's 290 magazines and newspapers, including IDG's leading global brands — Computerworld, PC World, Network World, Macworld and the Channel World family of publications. IDG Books Worldwide is one of the fastest-growing computer book publishers in the world, with more than 700 titles in 36 languages. The "...For Dummies®" series alone has more than 50 million copies in print. IDG offers online users the largest network of technology-specific Web sites around the world through IDG.net (http://www.idg.net), which comprises more than 225 targeted Web sites in 55 countries worldwide. International Data Corporation (IDC) is the world's largest provider of information technology data, analysis and consulting, with research centers in over 41 countries and more than 400 research analysts worldwide. IDG World Expo is a leading producer of more than 168 globally branded conferences and expositions in 35 countries including E3 (Electronic Entertainment Expo), Macworld Expo, ComNet, Windows World Expo, ICE (Internet Commerce Expo), Agenda, DEMO, and Spotlight. IDG's training subsidiary, ExecuTrain, is the world's largest computer training company, with more than 230 locations worldwide and 785 training courses. IDG Marketing Services helps industry-leading IT companies build international brand recognition by developing global integrated marketing programs via IDG's print, online and exposition products worldwide. Further information about the company can be found at www.idg.com.   1/24/99

Credits

Acquisitions Editor
David Mayhew

Development Editors
Tracy Brown
Valerie Perry
Kenyon Brown

Technical Editor
Bill Karow

Copy Editors
Anne Friedman
Bill McManus

Cover Design
Murder By Design

Production
Foster City Production Department

Proofreading and Indexing
York Production Services

About the Author

John Walkenbach is one of the country's leading authorities on spreadsheet software. He holds a Ph.D. from the University of Montana and has worked as an instructor, programmer, and market research manager. He finally found a job he's good at: principal of JWalk and Associates Inc., a one-person San Diego-based consulting firm that specializes in spreadsheet application development. John is also a shareware developer, and his most popular product is the award-winning Power Utility Pak add-in for Excel — which is used by thousands of people throughout the world. John started writing about spreadsheets in 1984, and he has since written more than 250 articles and reviews for publications such as *PC World*, *InfoWorld*, *Windows* magazine, and *PC/Computing*. In addition, he's the author of a dozen other spreadsheet books, including *Excel 2000 Power Programming Techniques*, *Excel Programming For Dummies*, and *Excel 2000 For Windows For Dummies Quick Reference* (all from IDG Books Worldwide). In his spare time, John enjoys digital photography and composing and playing music in a variety of styles. John also maintains "The Spreadsheet Page" on the Web. Pay him a visit at http://www.j-walk.com.

To VaRene

Preface

Thanks for purchasing the *Microsoft Excel 2000 Bible* — your complete guide to a powerful and easy-to-use spreadsheet product.

I think that Excel 2000 is the best spreadsheet program on the market (trust me — I've used them all). Excel has been around in various incarnations for almost a decade, and each subsequent release pushes the spreadsheet envelope a bit further — in some cases, a *lot* further. My goal in writing this book is to share with you some of what I know about Excel, and in the process make you more efficient on the job.

The book contains everything that you need to know to learn the basics of Excel and then move on to more advanced topics at your own pace. You find many useful examples as well as some of the tips and slick techniques that I've accumulated over the years.

Is This Book for You?

The Bible series from IDG Books Worldwide is designed for beginning, intermediate, and advanced users. This book covers all the essential components of Excel and provides clear and practical examples that you can adapt to your own needs.

Excel can be used at many levels — from the simple to the extremely complex. I've drawn a good balance here, focusing on the topics that are most useful to most users. The following answers whether this book is for you:

Yes — If you have no spreadsheet experience

If you're new to the world of spreadsheets, welcome to the fold. This book has everything that you need to get started with Excel and then advance to other topics as the need arises.

Yes — If you have used previous versions of Excel

If you've used Excel 97, you're going to feel right at home with Excel 2000. If you're skipping a few upgrades and moving up from Excel 5 or Excel 95, you have lots to learn, because Microsoft has made many improvements in the past few years. In any case, this book can get you up to speed quickly.

Yes — If you have used Excel for the Macintosh

The Macintosh versions of Excel are very similar to the Windows versions. If you're moving over from the Mac platform, you'll find some good background information as well as specific details to make your transition as smooth as possible.

Yes — If you have used DOS versions of 1-2-3 or Quattro Pro

If you're abandoning a text-based spreadsheet such as 1-2-3 or Corel's Quattro Pro in favor of a more modern graphical product, this book can serve you well. You have a head start, because you already know what spreadsheets are all about, and you'll discover some great new ways of doing things.

Yes — If you have used Windows versions of 1-2-3 or Quattro Pro

If you've tried the other versions and are convinced that Excel is the way to go, this book quickly teaches you what Excel is all about and why it has such a great reputation. Because you're already familiar with Windows *and* spreadsheets, you can breeze through many introductory topics.

Software Versions

This book is written for Excel 2000 (also known as Excel 9), but much of the information also applies to Excel 97, Excel 95, and Excel 5. If you use any version of Excel prior to Version 5, be aware that the earlier versions are drastically different from the current version.

Conventions Used in This Book

Take a minute to scan this section to learn some of the typographical conventions that are used in this book.

Named Ranges and Your Input

Input that you type from the keyboard appears in **bold**. Named ranges may appear in a code font. Lengthy input usually appears on a separate line. For instance, I may instruct you to enter a formula such as the following:

```
="Part Name: " &VLOOKUP(PartNumber,PartList,2)
```

Key Names

Names of the keys on your keyboard appear in normal type. When two keys should be pressed simultaneously, they are connected with a plus sign, like this: Press Alt+E to select the Edit menu. Here are the key names as I refer to them in the book:

Alt	down arrow	Num Lock	right arrow
Backspace	End	Pause	Scroll Lock
Caps Lock	Home	PgDn	Shift
Ctrl	Insert	PgUp	Tab
Delete	left arrow	Print Screen	up arrow

Functions

Excel's built-in worksheet functions appear in uppercase, like this: Enter a SUM formula in cell C20.

Mouse Conventions

I assume that you're using a mouse or some other pointing device. You come across some of the following mouse-related terms:

✦ **Mouse pointer:** The small graphic figure that moves onscreen when you move your mouse. The mouse pointer is usually an arrow, but it changes shape when you move to certain areas of the screen or when you're performing certain actions.

✦ **Point:** Move the mouse so that the mouse pointer is on a specific item. For example, "Point to the Save button on the toolbar."

✦ **Press:** Press the left-mouse button once and keep it pressed. Normally, this is used when dragging.

✦ **Click:** Press the left mouse button once and release it immediately.

✦ **Right-click:** Press the right-mouse button once and release it immediately. The right-mouse button is used in Excel to pop up shortcut menus that are appropriate for whatever is currently selected.

✦ **Double-click:** Press the left-mouse button twice in rapid succession. If your double-clicking doesn't seem to be working, you can adjust the double-click sensitivity by using the Windows Control Panel icon.

✦ **Drag:** Press the left-mouse button and keep it pressed while you move the mouse. Dragging is often used to select a range of cells or to change the size of an object.

What the Icons Mean

Throughout the book, you see special graphic symbols, or *icons,* in the left margin. These call your attention to points that are particularly important or relevant to a specific group of readers. The icons in this book are as follows:

 This symbol denotes features that are new to Excel 2000.

 This icon signals the fact that something is important or worth noting. This may alert you to a concept that helps you to master the task at hand, or it may denote something that is fundamental to understanding subsequent material.

 This icon marks a more efficient way of doing something that may not be obvious.

 This indicates that the material uses an example file located on this book's companion CD-ROM.

 I use this symbol when there is a possibility that the operation I'm describing could cause problems if you're not careful.

 This icon indicates that a related topic is discussed elsewhere in this book.

How This Book Is Organized

Notice that the book is divided into six main parts, followed by four appendixes.

Part I: Getting Started — This part consists of three chapters that provide background about Excel. Chapter 2 describes the new features in Excel 2000. Chapter 3 is a hands-on guided tour of Excel, which gives new users an opportunity to get their feet wet immediately.

Part II: Introductory Concepts — The chapters in Part II cover the basic concepts with which all Excel users should be familiar.

Part III: Advanced Features — This part consists of six chapters dealing with topics that are sometimes considered advanced. Many beginning and intermediate users may find this information useful, as well.

Part IV: Analyzing Data — The broad topic of data analysis is the focus of the chapters in Part IV. Users of all levels will find some of these chapters of interest.

Part V: Other Topics—This part consists of three chapters that didn't quite fit into any other part. The chapters deal with using Excel with other applications, auditing and proofing your work, and exploring the fun side of Excel (yes, Excel *does* have a fun side).

Part VI: Customizing Excel—Part VI is for those who want to customize Excel for their own use or who are designing workbooks or add-ins that are to be used by others. It's a good introduction to Visual Basic for Applications (VBA).

Appendixes—The appendixes consist of supplemental and reference material that may be useful to you.

How to Use This Book

This book is not intended to be read cover to cover. Rather, it's a reference book that you can consult when:

+ You're stuck while trying to do something.

+ You need to do something that you've never done before.

+ You have some time on your hands, and you're interested in learning something new.

The index is quite comprehensive, and each chapter typically focuses on a single broad topic. If you're just starting out with Excel, I recommend that you read the first three chapters to gain a basic understanding of the product, and then do some experimenting on your own. After you've become familiar with Excel's environment, you can refer to the chapters that interest you the most. Some users, however, may prefer to follow the chapters in order. Part II is designed with these users in mind.

Don't be discouraged if some of the material is over your head. Most users get by just fine using only a small subset of Excel's total capabilities. In fact, the 80/20 rule applies here: 80 percent of Excel users use only 20 percent of its features. However, using only 20 percent of Excel's features still gives you *lots* of power at your fingertips.

About the CD-ROM

You'll find that my writing style emphasizes examples. I know that I learn more from a well-thought-out example than from reading a dozen pages. I've found that this is true for many other people. Consequently, I spent a lot of time developing the examples in this book. These example files are available on the companion CD-ROM.

Appendix D describes the material on the CD-ROM.

Power Utility Pak Coupon

Toward the back of the book, you'll find a coupon that you can redeem for a copy of my Power Utility Pak software — a collection of useful Excel utilities and new worksheet functions. This product normally sells for $39.95, but I'm making it available to readers of this book for only $9.95, plus shipping and handling. I developed this package by using VBA exclusively, and the complete source files are also available for those who want to learn slick VBA techniques.

I think that the Power Utility Pak is extremely useful in your day-to-day work with Excel, and I urge you to take advantage of this offer.

Contacting the Author

I'm always happy to hear from readers of my books. The best way to contact me is by e-mail at the following Internet address:

    john@j-walk.com

I get lots of e-mail, so I can't promise a personal reply.

Visit "The Spreadsheet Page"

For even more information on Excel, be sure to check out "The Spreadsheet Page" on the World Wide Web. The URL is:

    http://www.j-walk.com/ss/

Acknowledgments

Thanks to everyone at IDG Books Worldwide who played a part in getting this book into your hands. Especially, thanks to Tracy Brown and Valerie Perry; without their able assistance, I'd still be pounding away at my keyboard.

Thanks also to all the people throughout the world who have taken the time to let me know that my books have made an impact. My goal is to write books that go well beyond the material found in competing books. Based on the feedback that I've received, I think I'm succeeding. Writing software books may not be the most glamorous job — but I can't think of anything else I'd rather be doing.

Contents at a Glance

Contents

Part II: Introductory Concepts   41

Chapter 4: Navigating Through Excel 43

Chapter 5: Working with Files and Workbooks 71

Chapter 26: Performing Spreadsheet What-If Analysis 595

Chapter 27: Analyzing Data Using Goal Seeking and Solver 617

Part VI: Customizing Excel   729

Chapter 33: Customizing Toolbars and Menus 731

Chapter 34: Using and Creating Templates 747

Chapter 35: Using Visual Basic for Applications 755

Chapter 36: Creating Custom Worksheet Functions 785

Getting Started

✦ ✦ ✦ ✦

✦ ✦ ✦ ✦

A Bit of Background

Every book has to start somewhere. This chapter starts from square one by introducing you to the concept of a spreadsheet. Also included is a lot of interesting background information about Excel and Windows.

What Is Excel?

Excel is a software product that falls into the general category of spreadsheets. Excel is one of several spreadsheet products that you can run on your PC. Others include 1-2-3 and Quattro Pro.

A *spreadsheet* (including Excel) is a highly interactive computer program that consists of a collection of rows and columns displayed onscreen in a scrollable window. The intersection of each row and column is called a *cell*, which can hold a number, a text string, or a formula that performs a calculation by using one or more other cells. Copying and moving cells and modifying formulas is easy with a spreadsheet.

A spreadsheet can be saved in a file for later use or discarded after it has served its intended purpose. The cells in a spreadsheet can be formatted in various ways and printed for hard-copy reference. In addition, groups of numerical cells can be used to generate charts and maps.

The most significant advantage of an electronic spreadsheet is that the formulas recalculate their results if you change any of the cells that they use. As a result, after you set up your spreadsheet by defining formulas, you can use this "model" to explore different possibilities, with very little additional effort. Excel is currently the best-selling Windows spreadsheet — and I hope to explain why in this book.

The Evolution of Excel

Excel 2000 is actually Excel 9 in disguise.

A bit of rational thinking might lead you to think that this is the ninth version of Excel. Think again! Microsoft may be a successful company, but its version-naming techniques can be quite confusing. As you'll see, Excel 2000 actually is the seventh version of Excel.

Excel 2

Excel 2 was the original version of Excel for Windows, which first appeared in late 1987. It was labeled Version 2 to correspond to the Macintosh version, which was the original Excel. Because Windows wasn't in widespread use at the time, Version 2 included a *run-time* version of Windows — a special version with just enough features to run Excel and nothing else. This version was quite crude by today's standards and was actually quite ugly.

Excel 3

At the end of 1990, Microsoft released Excel 3 for Windows. This was a significant improvement in both appearance and features. It included toolbars, drawing capabilities, worksheet outlining, add-in support, 3D charts, workgroup editing, and lots more.

Excel 4

Excel 4 hit the streets in the spring of 1992. This version made quite an impact in the marketplace, because Windows was becoming more popular. It had lots of new features, many of which made it easier for beginners to get up to speed quickly.

Excel 5

In early 1994, Excel 5 appeared on the scene. This version introduced tons of new features, including multisheet workbooks and the new Visual Basic for Applications (VBA) macro language. Like its predecessor, Excel 5 took top honors in just about every spreadsheet comparison that was published in the trade magazines.

Excel 7

Technically, this version was called Excel for Windows 95 (there was no Excel 6). It began shipping in the summer of 1995. On the surface, this version wasn't that much different from Excel 5, and included only a few major new features. But Excel 7 was significant, because it was the first version to use the more advanced 32-bit code. Excel 7 and Excel 5 used the same file format.

Excel 8

Excel 8 (officially known as Excel 97) was probably the most significant Excel upgrade ever. The toolbars and menus had a great new look, online help took a dramatic step forward, and the number of rows available in a worksheet quadrupled. Developers were pleased to discover that Excel's programming language (VBA) improved significantly in Excel 97.

Excel 9

Excel 9 (better known as Excel 2000) is the topic of this book (although most of the material is also relevant to Excel 97). Excel 2000 has quite a few enhancements, but its most significant advancement is the capability to use HTML as a standard file format. Chapter 2 provides a list of all the new features in Excel 2000.

Excel's Competitors

Although Excel is usually considered the best spreadsheet available, it does have competitors, the two main ones being 1-2-3 and Quattro Pro.

The three leading spreadsheets are similar in their basic capabilities. For example, they all let you work with multiple worksheets in a single file; they all support a wide variety of charts; and they all have macro capabilities to help you automate or customize your work.

Many users, myself included, find that Excel is superior to the other products in both power and ease of use.

What Excel Has to Offer

Excel is a feature-rich product that can be used at many different levels. Chances are good that you won't need all of Excel's features, but you should become generally familiar with what they can do. Otherwise, you could seek another software product to accomplish a particular task, and not even realize that Excel has a feature that can accomplish it. Or, you could spend lots of time performing a task manually that Excel can handle automatically.

The following is a quick overview of what Excel can do for you. All of these topics are discussed in subsequent chapters of this book.

Multisheet Files

Excel's files (called *workbooks*) can consist of any number of separate sheets, and you access these sheets by clicking a notebook-like tab. The sheets can be worksheets or chart sheets. This feature makes organizing your work easy. For example, you can keep all of your budgeting spreadsheets in a single workbook.

Multiple Document Interface

Excel enables you to work with many files simultaneously; you don't have to close a file to consult another file (see Figure 1-1). This capability enables you to transfer information easily between worksheets in different workbooks.

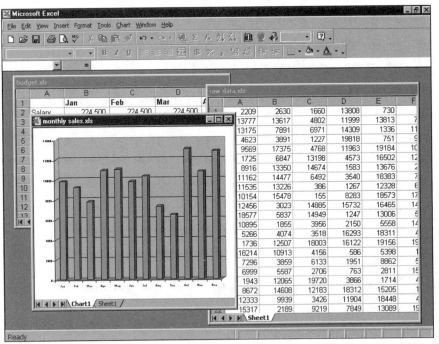

Figure 1-1: Excel enables you to work with as many different files as you need.

File Compatibility

Excel has its own file format, identifiable by the XLS file extension. In addition, Excel can read files produced by other spreadsheet programs (such as 1-2-3 and Quattro Pro), and it can read text files, dBASE files, and HTML documents.

Interactive Help

Computer documentation keeps getting better. In the past, users were lucky if the manual that accompanied a software product accurately covered all the features. Nowadays, the trend is away from written manuals and toward online help. Almost all applications, including Excel, emphasize *online help* — in other words, you can get help onscreen while working in Excel. Excel's online help is excellent and extremely detailed.

Figure 1-2 shows the Office Assistant, which serves several purposes, including:

✦ It observes your actions and stores up a series of tips, which can save you time. You can choose to view these tips whenever you want.

✦ It provides specific help with certain aspects of the program (for example, creating charts).

✦ If you enter an invalid formula, it will often make a suggestion on how to correct it.

✦ It provides an easy way to search for help on a particular topic. Just enter your question in natural language, and the Office Assistant displays a list of relevant help topics.

Easy-to-Use Features

Excel may well be the easiest-to-use spreadsheet available. It includes many features designed specifically to make commonly performed tasks straightforward and fast for both beginners and experts. The program walks you step by step through several procedures, and basic editing and formatting commands are intuitive and efficient. For example, a single dialog box enables you to change any aspect of formatting for a cell or range, and right-clicking anything brings up a context-sensitive shortcut menu.

List Management

Among Excel's most significant strengths is how well it works with lists stored in a worksheet. This feature makes it easy to sort, filter, summarize, and manipulate data stored in your worksheet.

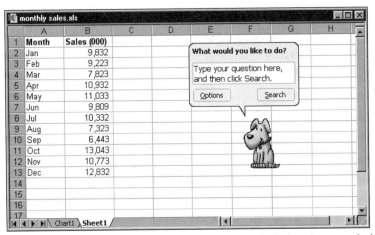

Figure 1-2: The Office Assistant pops up to provide help when needed.

Built-in Functions

Excel includes an enormous collection of built-in functions that you can use in your formulas. In addition to common functions, such as SUM and AVERAGE, you can choose functions that perform sophisticated operations that otherwise are difficult or impossible to do. For example, the CORREL function calculates the correlation coefficient for two sets of data. You also can develop other functions by using the VBA macro language (it's not as difficult as you may think).

Customizable Toolbars

Excel's *toolbars* — groups of buttons representing commands — are real time-savers, enabling you to perform common commands without using the menu. You can customize your toolbars by adding buttons for tasks that you do most often. To find out what a button does, drag the mouse over a toolbar button and pause for a second. Excel pops up a brief description of the button.

Beginning with Excel 97, the menu bar at the top of the screen is actually a toolbar. As such, you can easily customize it or even move it to a different location on the screen.

Flexible Text Handling

Although Excel's forte is number crunching, it's not too shabby at handling text. You can format or orient text that you put in cells. You also can insert text boxes (which you can move and resize) anywhere on your worksheet.

Rich Text Formatting

Excel is the only spreadsheet that enables you easily to format individual characters within a cell. For example, if a cell contains text, you can make one letter bold or a different color.

Great Charts

Excel's charting features — among the best available in any spreadsheet — enable you to modify and augment a wide assortment of graph types. You can insert a chart anywhere in a worksheet or place it on a special chart sheet.

Integrated Mapping

Excel's mapping feature lets you display your data in the form of a geographic map (see Figure 1-3). For example, you can easily create an attractive map that shows your company's sales volume by state.

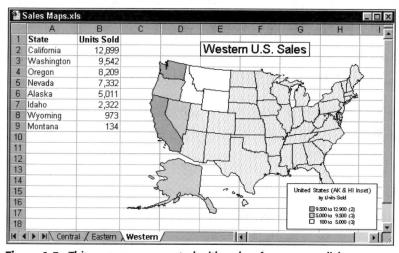

Figure 1-3: This map was generated with only a few mouse clicks.

Drawing Tools

Excel includes an excellent set of drawing tools that enables you to create attractive diagrams and basic drawings directly on your worksheet or chart. For example, you can include a simple flow diagram along with your numerical analysis.

Worksheet Outlining

Spreadsheet outlining enables you to collapse hierarchical information to show any level of detail. People who work with multilevel budgets will find this feature particularly valuable.

Pivot Tables

A pivot table makes it easy to change how you view a table of data. A pivot table can quickly summarize a list or database, and you can use drag-and-drop techniques to change the layout of the table. If you work with multidimensional data, you should check out this powerful feature — which I consider to be one of Excel's major strengths.

Advanced Analytical Tools

Analytical types will be particularly excited about Excel's unique *array* feature, which enables you to do things that are impossible in other spreadsheets. Excel also includes goal seeking, a powerful Solver feature, and the Analysis ToolPak add-in, which provides extensive statistical, financial, engineering, and scientific functions and procedures.

Flexible Printing and Print Preview

When you are ready to put your work on paper, you'll be pleased to see how easy it is. Besides normal WYSIWYG (*What You See Is What You Get*) formatting, Excel provides a handy print preview feature. From the preview window, you can easily make last-minute adjustments, including new column widths and margins. In addition, a Page Break Preview mode lets you adjust the page breaks by using simple dragging techniques.

Worksheet Auditing and Annotation

No one's perfect, but Excel can help you get closer to that goal. Excel provides a variety of auditing tools to help you track down errors and potential errors in your worksheet formulas.

A feature in Excel automatically displays comments attached to cells when the user drags the mouse over a cell that contains a comment. This is an excellent way to remind others (or yourself) what a particular cell represents.

Scenario Management

Spreadsheets are often used for *what-if analysis*—change one or more assumptions and observe the effects on dependent formulas. Excel simplifies this process with its scenario manager.

You can name scenarios, switch among scenarios (with just a few mouse clicks), and generate reports that summarize the results of your scenarios.

Spell Checking and AutoCorrect

An integrated spell checker spots spelling errors in your worksheets and charts, so you need never again display a chart titled "Bugdet Review" in a crowded boardroom.

Excel has borrowed a handy feature, AutoCorrect, from Microsoft Word. This corrects many types of input errors as you type. For example, if you enter *BUdget* into a cell, Excel automatically changes the second letter to a lowercase *u*. You can also use this feature to develop your own shorthand. For example, you can instruct Excel to replace IWC with International Widget Corporation.

Templates

If your work tends to fall into a few specific categories, it may be worth your time to set up custom spreadsheet *templates*, which are preconfigured shells that include text, row, and column headings, as well as formats, column widths, macros, and so on. You can use these templates to help create similar spreadsheets.

Excel has a Template Wizard that walks you through the steps required to create a custom template. Excel also includes a few handy templates that you may find useful. An example of such a template is shown in Figure 1-4.

Database Management

You can work with spreadsheet data as if Excel were a database. Excel features all the standard database commands and enables you to work with databases that are stored in external files.

XLM Macro Compatibility

In older versions of Excel, you could create macros by using special macro functions in XLM documents. Although Visual Basic for Applications is a much better macro language, Excel 2000 still supports XLM macros. This means that you can continue to run macros that were developed for older versions of Excel (Excel 4 and earlier).

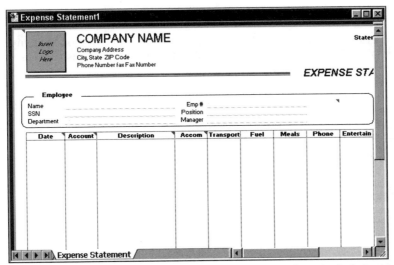

Figure 1-4: Expense Statement1 is one of several templates included with Excel 2000.

Visual Basic for Applications (VBA)

VBA is a powerful programming language that is built right into Excel (as well as several other Microsoft products). After you learn VBA's ropes, you can do magic with your Excel workbooks.

Custom Dialog Boxes

Excel makes it very easy to create custom dialog boxes (also known as user forms). Custom dialog boxes usually are used in conjunction with VBA macros that you write.

Worksheet Controls

With Excel, you can insert functional "dialog box" controls (such as buttons, scrollbars, list boxes, and check boxes) directly on your worksheet. You can even link these controls to cells without using macros. Figure 1-5 shows an example of such controls.

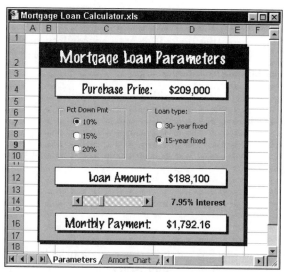

Figure 1-5: You can add functional controls, such as buttons, scrollbars, list and check boxes, directly to your worksheet to make it easier to use.

Protection Options

If you need to keep others (or yourself) from modifying your worksheet, you'll find that Excel offers a variety of protection techniques. For example, you can protect cells that contain formulas, to eliminate the possibility of accidentally deleting an important formula.

Add-In Capability

Excel supports add-ins — a feature that lets you enhance the program's functionality. Excel includes several add-ins, and you can use VBA to create your own add-ins.

OLE Support

Excel supports Microsoft's Object Linking and Embedding (OLE) technology, which makes data sharing easier than ever. For example, you can embed a Word for Windows document in a worksheet and then access all of the features of Word right in your worksheet.

Internet Support

Excel 2000 includes a variety of features that make it easy to access Internet documents, save and retrieve documents stored in HTML format, and create hyperlinks directly in your spreadsheet documents.

Cross-Platform Consistency

Excel runs on the Macintosh and the PC (in Windows); in fact, the versions are very similar across the two platforms. If you learn the Windows version, you can move to a Mac and feel right at home.

Summary

This chapter introduces the concept of a spreadsheet, presents a brief history of Excel, and examines Excel's evolution within the Microsoft environment. The bulk of the chapter provides an overview of Excel's key features—all of which are covered in subsequent chapters.

✦   ✦   ✦

What's New in Excel 2000?

Every new release of Excel is a big event for Excel fans, and Excel 2000 is certainly no exception. Although it doesn't add too many new features (compared to Excel 97), it's by far the best version yet. In this chapter I provide an overview of what's new, what's gone, and what's changed compared to Excel 97.

Installation Improvements

If you've installed previous versions of Excel, you'll notice that Excel 2000 provides a new "intelligent" installation wizard. If you have a previous version installed, you'll get a choice to perform either a similar install or a standard installation. If you choose the former, all of your previous settings will be transferred to Excel 2000.

You also have quite a bit more flexibility in selecting which features to install. Even if you omit a few key features during the intial installation, they will still appear on the menus. If you attempt to access an uninstalled component, you'll get a prompt asking you if you want to install it. Even better, if your installation somehow gets messed up—a critical file gets deleted, for example— the new self-repair feature will detect that fact and re-install the missing file.

New Internet Features

Most of the new features in Excel 2000 deal with the Internet.

✦ **HTML file format:** If you like, you can use HTML as a "native" file format for your Excel work. In other words, you can save a workbook as an HTML file and then re-open it without losing anything. Unless your work needs to be on a corporate intranet, you're much better off sticking with the normal XLS format.

✦ **Save to a server:** Excel 2000 makes it very easy to save a workbook directly to an intranet or an ISP host. In fact, if the server is running Microsoft's FrontPage Server Extensions, it's as easy as saving to a local or network drive. If end users are running Internet Explorer 4.0 or a later version, they can manipulate Excel data (for example, pivot tables, charts, and worksheets) within the browser.

✦ **Web discussions:** Use the Discussion toolbar to insert and navigate between comments. You can create discussions about the document, or online discussions specific to a paragraph. You can reply, edit, or delete from a right-clicked context menu. Comments are indented as in the threaded discussion model common on the Internet, and are threaded with the contributor's name, date, and time stamp.

✦ **Web subscription and notification:** This lets you configure documents and folders to trigger e-mail or Internet Explorer channel updates when a document or related discussion is added, changed, or deleted. You can set notification as daily, weekly, or "within a few minutes." The message provides the date and time, the name of the editor, the document's URL, and a link you can click to cancel further notifications. New comments and replies to remote documents are tracked, but you can't subscribe to e-mail updates on the remote documents and folders themselves.

Cross-Reference I discuss these features in Chapter 30.

New File Dialog Boxes

The dialog boxes that are displayed when you select File ➪ Save or File ➪ Open have been redesigned so you can see more files at one time and access them more quickly. You can use the icons in the new "Look in" bar along the left side to get to the folders and locations you use the most. Click the History icon to see the last 20–50 documents and folders you have worked with, and then click the Back button to easily return to folders you have recently visited.

PivotTable Enhancements

Excel's PivotTable feature is an extremely useful tool for summarizing data. Excel 2000 adds some new twists:

✦ **Streamlined PivotTable Wizard:** Creating pivot tables is faster than ever. The new PivotTable toolbar displays the file names, and you can simply drag them to your pivot table.

✦ **PivotChart:** Pivot tables can also now be charted. PivotChart dynamic views are linked to PivotTable.

Automatic Formula Adjustment

Excel 2000 will automatically adjust formulas when you insert a new row directly above the formula. For example, assume you have the following formula in cell A5, which sums the values in A1:A4:

```
=SUM(A1:A4)
```

If you insert a new row directly above row 5 and enter a value into cell A5, the formula adjusts automatically to:

```
=SUM(A1:A5)
```

Caution   In most cases, automatic formula adjustment is exactly what you want. In other cases, however, this can cause the formula to display an incorrect result.

See-Through Cell Selection

A common complaint among Excel users has been the fact that selecting a cell or range obscures the colors in the cells. Excel 2000 finally addresses that complaint, and now uses a different way of highlighting selected ranges. Now you can still see the colors when you select a range.

Personalized Menus

In an attempt to simplify your life, Excel 2000 is capable of adjusting its menus to your work habits. It does so by displaying only the menu items you use most frequently. You still have access to all commands, of course. At the bottom of the drop-down menu are arrows that can be clicked open to reveal additional menu choices.

Over time, Excel will learn which application features you use most often and then display them higher on the menu list. Less commonly used features are demoted and eventually disappear.

Although some users may see this as a usability enhancement, I think moving the menu commands around is bound to cause confusion. Fortunately, you can turn this feature off. Select View ➪ Toolbars ➪ Customize, then click the Options tab. Remove the checkmark from the option labeled Menus show recently used commands first.

Easier Toolbar Customization

Excel, of course, is big on toolbars. If you find that you never use some of the buttons on a particular toolbar, it's very easy to remove them. Toolbars now have a small down-pointing arrow button that, when clicked, displays a button labeled Add or Remove Buttons. Click this button to reveal a list of buttons in the toolbar (see Figure 2-1). Simply remove the checkmark to hide a button.

Figure 2-1: Excel 2000 makes it very easy to customize toolbars by showing only the buttons you need.

Documents on the Windows Taskbar

If you use Windows 98, each Excel document appears as a separate task in the Windows taskbar.

Enhanced Clipboard

Excel 2000 (along with the other members of Office 2000) uses a special Office clipboard. This enhanced clipboard supports a feature known as "collect and paste" — the ability to store information from several sources and then selectively paste it to a new location.

The Clipboard toolbar (see Figure 2-2) displays icons for each item copied. Unfortunately, this enhanced clipboard only works with the Office applications.

Figure 2-2: Excel 2000 lets you store up to 12 separate items on a special enhanced clipboard.

Euro Currency Symbol

Additional number formats are available with the Euro currency symbol.

New Image Import Options

Excel 2000 lets you import an image directly from a digital camera or scanner. It's no longer necessary to capture the image to a file and then import the file.

A New Help System

Online help in Excel 2000 sports a new look. Microsoft abandoned the traditional Windows help system in favor of a new "HTML Help" system. The system works pretty much like the old one. By default, the help display appears along side of Excel.

Cross-Reference For more information about Excel's online help system, refer to Appendix A.

Office Assistant

The Office Assistant, which debuted in Excel 97, makes an appearance in Excel 2000. I've found that people either love this feature or hate it (I'm in the latter group).

The Office Assistant is a bit less obtrusive in Excel 97 and (finally!) it can be configured in such a way that you never see it again (unless you want to). When you install Excel 2000, there is an option to omit the Office Assistant feature.

For more information about the Office Assistant, refer to Appendix A.

Multilingual Features

Multilingual users should have it a bit easier with Excel 2000. Excel 2000 can change the language used in its interface (the text in menus, dialog boxes, and so on) on the fly. Doing so is as easy as purchasing the Office language pack. Excel automatically detects the language you're typing in and switches among spelling checker, AutoCorrect, and other proofing tools accordingly.

ModeLess UserForms

Finally, macro programmers will welcome a new feature that lets you display custom dialog boxes (UserForms) in a "modeless" manner. In previous versions, everything ground to a halt while a custom dialog box was displayed. In Excel 2000, a macro programmer can keep the dialog box displayed while the user continues working — perfect for displaying status information.

Summary

This chapter provides a brief overview of the new features in Excel 2000.

✦   ✦   ✦

Getting Acquainted with Excel

New users sometimes are overwhelmed when they first fire up Excel. They're greeted with an empty workbook, lots of strange buttons, and unfamiliar commands on the menus. This chapter helps you to feel more at home with Excel, explains its main parts, and gives you a chance to do a few things to get better acquainted with it.

Starting Excel

Before you can use Excel, it must be installed on your system. And before you can install Excel, Microsoft Windows must be installed on your system. Excel 2000 requires a 32-bit operating system, such as Windows 95, Windows 98, or Windows NT. With any luck, Excel is already installed and ready to run. If not, you need to run the Setup program on the Office 2000 CD-ROM.

Excel's Parts

When Excel starts, your screen looks something like Figure 3-1. This figure identifies the major parts of Excel's window, which are explained in the following paragraphs.

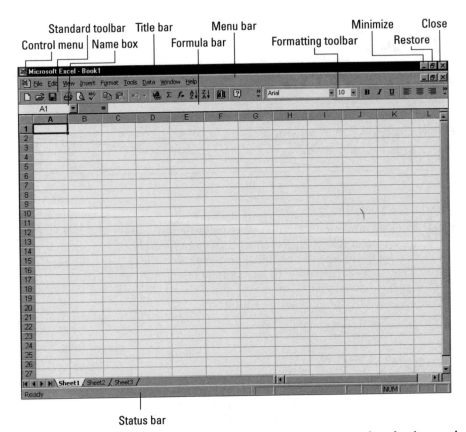

Figure 3-1: Excel runs in a window, which in this case is maximized so that it occupies the full screen.

Figure 3-1 shows Excel running in VGA mode (800 x 600 pixels). Your screen may look different if you're running Windows in a different video mode that displays more or fewer pixels onscreen.

Title Bar

All Windows programs have a title bar, which displays the name of the program and holds some control buttons that you can use to modify the window.

Window Control Menu Button

This button is actually Excel's icon. When you click it, you get a menu that lets you manipulate Excel's window.

Minimize Button

Clicking this button minimizes Excel's window and displays it in the Windows taskbar.

Restore Button

Clicking this button "unmaximizes" Excel's window so that it no longer fills the entire screen. If Excel isn't maximized, this button is replaced by a Maximize button.

Close Button

Clicking this button closes Excel. If you have any unsaved files, you're prompted to save them.

Menu Bar

This is Excel's main menu. Clicking a word on the menu drops down a list of menu items, which is one way for you to issue a command to Excel.

The menu bar in Excel 2000 is not fixed in place. In fact, it's actually a toolbar. You can drag it to any side of the window or even make it free-floating if you like.

Toolbars

The toolbars hold buttons that you click to issue commands to Excel. Some of the buttons expand to show additional buttons or commands.

Formula Bar

When you enter information or formulas into Excel, they appear in this line.

Name Box

This box displays the name of the active cell in the current workbook. When you click the arrow, the list drops down to display all named cells and named ranges (if any) in the active workbook. Select a name to activate the range or cell. You also can use the Name box to name the selected cell or range.

The Name box also displays the name of a selected object, such as a chart or drawing object. However, you cannot use the Name box to select an object or change the name of an object.

Status Bar

This bar displays various messages, as well as the status of the Num Lock, Caps Lock, and Scroll Lock keys on your keyboard.

Parts of a Workbook Window

When you work with Excel, your work is stored in workbooks. Each workbook appears in a separate window within Excel's workspace.

Figure 3-2 shows a typical workbook window with its major parts identified. These parts are described in the following paragraphs. Notice that a workbook window has many parts in common with Excel's window.

Title Bar

The title bar shows the name of the workbook and holds some control buttons that you can use to modify the window.

Window Control Menu Button

Clicking this button (actually an icon) displays a menu that lets you manipulate the workbook window.

Minimize Button

Clicking this button reduces the workbook window so that only the title bar shows.

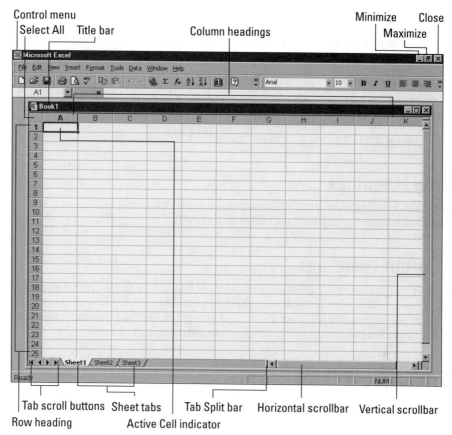

Figure 3-2: An empty Excel workbook, named Book1.

Maximize Button

Clicking this button increases the workbook window's size to fill Excel's complete workspace. If the window is already maximized, a Restore button appears in its place.

Close Button

Clicking this button closes the workbook. If you haven't saved the workbook, Excel prompts you to save it.

Select All Button

Clicking the intersection of the row and column headers selects all cells on the active worksheet of the active window.

Active Cell Indicator

This dark outline indicates the currently active cell (one of the 16,777,216 cells on each worksheet).

Row Headings

Numbers ranging from 1 to 65,536 — one for each row in the worksheet. You can click a row heading to select an entire row of cells.

Column Headings

Letters ranging from A to IV — one for each of the 256 columns in the worksheet. After column Z comes column AA, which is followed by AB, AC, and so on. After column AZ comes BA, BB, and so on until you get to the last column, labeled IV. You can click a column heading to select an entire column of cells.

Tab Scroll Buttons

These buttons let you scroll the sheet tabs to display tabs that aren't visible.

Sheet Tabs

Each of these notebook-like tabs represents a different sheet in the workbook. A workbook can have any number of sheets, and each sheet has its name displayed in a sheet tab. By default, each new workbook that you create contains three sheets.

Tab Split Bar

This bar enables you to increase or decrease the area devoted to displaying sheet tabs. When you show more sheet tabs, the horizontal scrollbar's size is reduced.

Horizontal Scrollbar

Allows you to scroll the sheet horizontally.

Vertical Scrollbar

Lets you scroll the sheet vertically.

If you have a Microsoft IntelliMouse, you can use the mouse wheel to scroll vertically.

A Hands-on Excel Session

The remainder of this chapter consists of an introductory session with Excel. If you've never used Excel, you may want to follow along on your computer to get a feel for how this program works.

On the CD-ROM

The end result of this hands-on session is available on the companion CD-ROM.

This example assumes that you've been asked to prepare a one-page report that shows your company's quarterly sales, broken down by the two sales regions (North and South). This section walks you through the steps required to do the following:

✦ Enter a table of data (the sales figures) into a worksheet

✦ Create and copy a formula (to calculate totals)

✦ Format the data so that it looks good

✦ Create a chart from the data

✦ Save the workbook to a file

✦ Print the data and chart (the one-page report)

When you're finished, you'll have a worksheet that looks like the one shown in Figure 3-3.

Note

This section is quite detailed and provides every step that you need to reproduce the worksheet shown in Figure 3-3. If you already have experience with a spreadsheet, you may find this section to be a bit *too* detailed. Don't worry. You'll find that the pace picks up in the remainder of the book.

Getting Ready

As a first stage, you start Excel and maximize its window to fill the entire screen. Then you maximize the blank workbook named Book1.

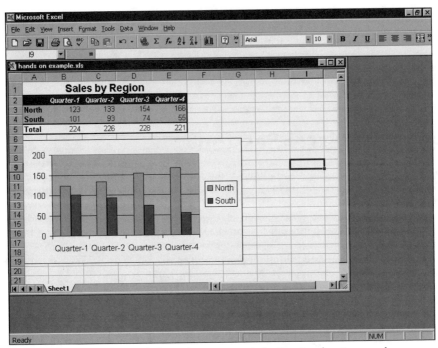

Figure 3-3: This is the worksheet that you create in the step-by-step session.

1. If Excel isn't running, start it. You're greeted with a blank window named Book1. If Excel is already running, click its Close button to exit Excel and then restart it so that you see the empty window named Book1.

2. If Excel doesn't fill the entire screen, maximize Excel's window by clicking the Maximize button in Excel's title bar.

3. Maximize the workbook window, so that you can see as much of the workbook as possible. Do this by clicking the Maximize button in Book1's title bar.

Entering the Headings

In this stage, you enter the row and column headings into the worksheet named Sheet1 in Book1. After you finish the following steps, the worksheet will look like Figure 3-4.

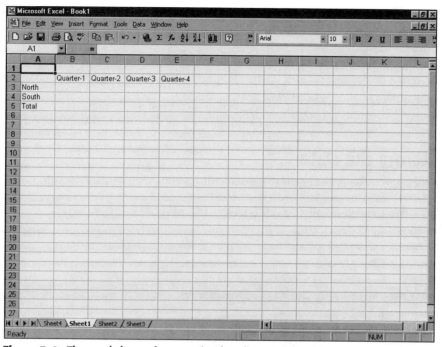

Figure 3-4: The worksheet after entering headings for the data.

1. Move the cell pointer to cell A3 by using the direction keys. The Name box displays the cell's address.

2. Enter **North** into cell A3. Just type the text and then press Enter. Depending on your setup, Excel either moves the cell pointer down to cell A4 or the pointer remains in cell A3.

3. Move the cell pointer to cell A4, type **South**, and press Enter.

4. Move the cell pointer to cell A5, type **Total**, and press Enter.

5. Move the cell pointer to cell B2, type **Quarter 1**, and press Enter.

   At this point, you could enter the other three headings manually, but let Excel do the work instead.

6. Move the cell pointer to cell B2 (if it's not already there). Notice the small square at the lower-right corner of the cell pointer. This is called the *fill handle*. When you move the mouse pointer over the fill handle, the mouse pointer changes to a dark cross.

If the cell doesn't have a fill handle, select the Tools ⇨ Options command and then click the Edit tab in the Options dialog box. Place a check mark next to the option labeled Allow cell drag and drop. Then click OK to close the Options dialog box.

7. Move the mouse pointer to the fill handle until the mouse pointer changes to a cross. Then click and drag to the right until you select the three cells to the right (C2, C3, and C4). Release the mouse button and you'll see that Excel filled in the three remaining headings for you. This is an example of AutoFill.

Entering the Data

In this stage, you simply enter the values for each quarter in each region.

1. Move the cell pointer to cell B3, type **123**, and press Enter.

2. Move to the remaining cells and enter additional data until your worksheet looks like Figure 3-5.

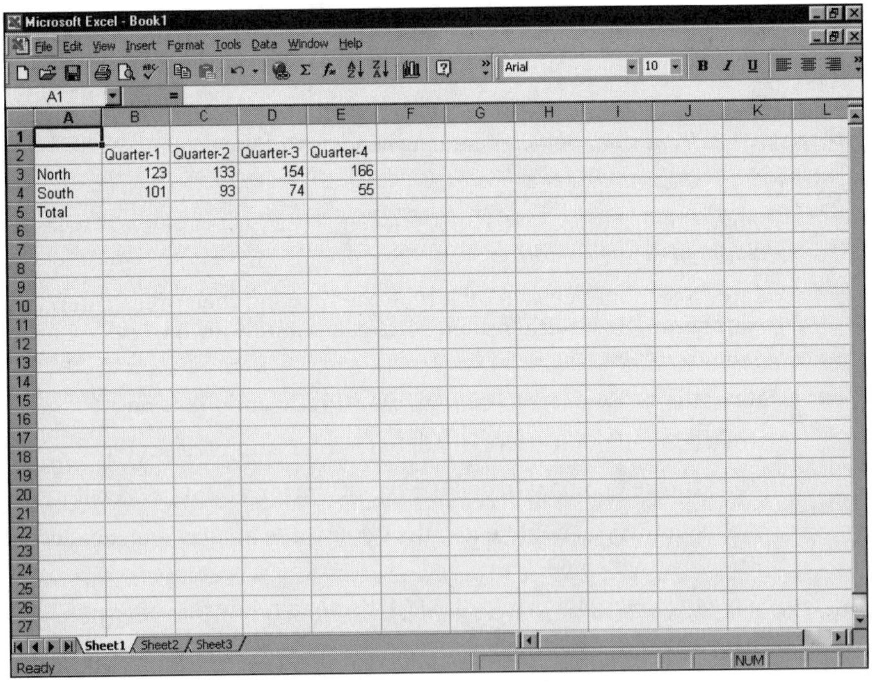

Figure 3-5: The worksheet after entering the sales data.

Creating a Formula

So far, what you've done has been fairly mundane. In fact, you could accomplish the same effect with any word processor. In this stage, you take advantage of the power feature of a spreadsheet: formulas. You create formulas to calculate the total for each region.

1. Move the cell pointer to cell B5.

2. Locate the AutoSum button on the toolbar below the menu and click it once. The AutoSum button has a Greek sigma on it. The toolbar below the menu is called the Standard toolbar. Notice that Excel inserts the following into the cell:

   `=SUM(B3:B4)`

   This is a formula that calculates the sum of the values in the range B3 through B4.

3. Because this formula is exactly what you want (Excel guessed correctly), press Enter to accept the formula. You see that the sum of the two values is displayed in the cell. You could repeat this step for the remaining three quarters, but it's much easier to copy the formula to the three cells to the right.

4. Move the cell pointer to cell B5 (if it's not already there).

5. Move the mouse pointer to the fill handle. When it changes to a cross, click and drag three cells to the right. Release the mouse button and you'll see that Excel copied the formula to the cells that you selected.

At this point, your worksheet should look like Figure 3-6. To demonstrate that these are actual "live" formulas, try changing one or two of the values in rows 3 or 4. You'll see that the cells with the formulas change also. In other words, the formulas are recalculating and displaying new results using the modified data.

Formatting the Table

The table looks fine, but it could look even better. In this stage, you use Excel's automatic formatting feature to spiff up the table a bit.

1. Move the cell pointer to any cell in the table (it doesn't matter which one because Excel will figure out that table's boundaries).

2. Click the Format menu; it drops down to display its menu items.

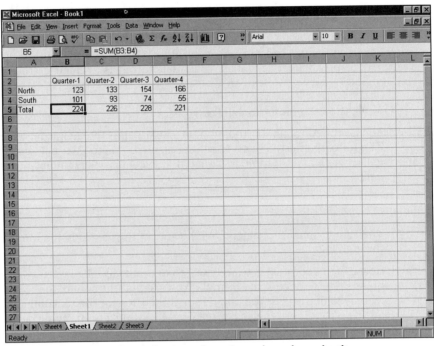

Figure 3-6: The worksheet after inserting a formula and copying it.

3. Select AutoFormat from the list of menu items. Two things happen: Excel determines the table boundaries and highlights the entire table, and it displays the AutoFormat dialog box. Figure 3-7 shows how this looks.

4. The AutoFormat dialog box has 16 "canned" formats from which to choose. Click the table format that you want to apply; this example uses Classic 3.

5. Click the OK button. Excel applies the formats to your table.

Your worksheet should look similar to Figure 3-8.

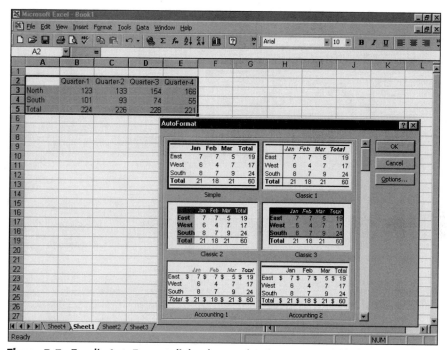

Figure 3-7: Excel's AutoFormat dialog box makes it easy to quickly format a table.

Note that Excel automatically made the following formatting changes for you:

✦ It changed some of the cell background colors

✦ It changed some of the cell foreground colors

✦ It made the column headings italic

✦ It made the row labels bold

✦ It added borders

You could have performed all of these formatting operations yourself, but it probably would have taken several minutes. The AutoFormat feature can save you lots of time.

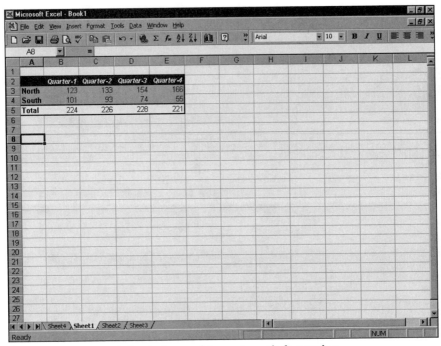

Figure 3-8: Your worksheet after applying automatic formatting.

Adding a Title

In this stage, you add a title to the table, make the title bold, and adjust it so that it's centered across the five columns of the table.

1. Move the cell pointer to cell A1.

2. Enter **Sales by Region** and then press Enter.

3. Move the cell pointer back to cell A1 (if it's not there already) and then click the Bold button on the Formatting toolbar (the Bold button has a large *B*). This makes the text bold.

4. Open the Font Size list box (see Figure 3-9) on the Formatting toolbar and select 14 from the list, to make the text larger.

5. Click in cell A1 and drag to the right until you select A1, B1, C1, D1, and E1 (that is, the range A1:E1). Don't drag the cell's fill handle. You want to select the cells — not make a copy of cell A1.

6. Click the Merge and Center button on the Formatting toolbar (refer to Figure 3-9). Excel centers the text in cell A1 across the selected cells. In fact, clicking the Merge and Center button merges the five cells into one larger cell.

Font Size list box   Merge and Center button

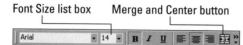

Figure 3-9: The Font Size list box and the Merge and Center button appear on the Formatting toolbar.

Your worksheet should look like Figure 3-10.

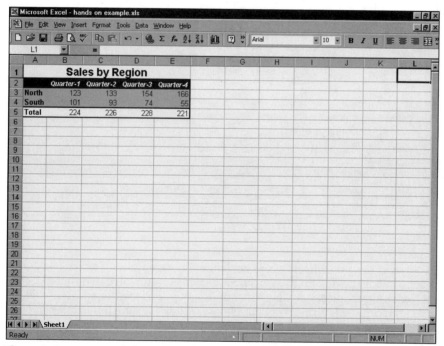

Figure 3-10: Your worksheet after adding a title and formatting it.

Creating a Chart

In this stage, you create a chart from the data in the table and place it on the worksheet directly below the table.

1. Move the cell pointer to cell A2.

2. Click and drag until you've selected all the cells in the rectangle encompassing A2 at the upper left and E4 at the lower right (15 cells in all). Notice that you're not selecting the cells in the row that displays the totals; you don't want the totals to appear in the chart.

3. With the range A2:E4 selected, click the Chart Wizard button on the Standard toolbar (the Chart Wizard button has an image of a column chart). Excel displays the Office Assistant, which offers you help with charting, and the first in a series of dialog boxes that will help you create the chart that you want (refer to Figure 3-11).

Figure 3-11: The first of four Chart Wizard dialog boxes that help you create a chart.

4. First, choose the chart type. The default chart, a Column chart, is a good choice for the data in the workbook. At this point, you can either click the Next button and specify lots of additional options for the chart or click Finish and accept all of Excel's default choices. Click the Finish button.

Excel creates the chart and displays it on the worksheet. It also displays its Chart toolbar, just in case you want to modify the chart. To get rid of the toolbar, just click the X in its title bar. Your worksheet should look like Figure 3-12.

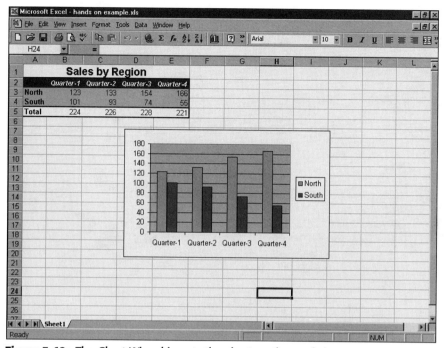

Figure 3-12: The Chart Wizard inserts the chart on the worksheet.

If you want, you can do the following:

✦ Resize the chart by dragging any of the eight handles on its borders (the handles appear only when the chart is selected)

✦ Move the chart by clicking and dragging any of its borders

Saving the Workbook

Until now, everything that you've done has occurred in your computer's memory. If the power should fail, all would be lost, so it's time to save your work to a file. Call this workbook **My first workbook**.

1. Click the Save button on the Standard toolbar. The Save button looks like a disk. Excel responds with the Save As dialog box (see Figure 3-13).

2. In the box labeled File name, enter **My first workbook** and then either click Save or press Enter.

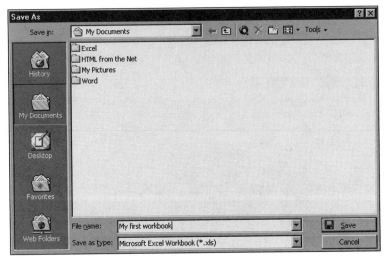

Figure 3-13: Excel's Save As dialog box.

Excel saves the workbook as a file. The workbook remains open so that you can work with it some more.

Printing the Report

As the final step, you print this report, assuming that you have a printer attached and that it works properly. To print the worksheet, just click the Print button on the Standard toolbar (this button has an image of a printer on it). The worksheet (including the chart) is printed using the default settings.

Quitting Excel

Click the Close button in Excel's title bar to exit Excel. Because no changes were made to the workbook since it was last saved, Excel closes without asking whether you want to save the file.

Summary

If this was your first time using Excel, you probably have lots of questions about what you just did in the preceding exercise. Those questions are answered in the following chapters.

If you're the adventurous type, you may have answered some of your own questions by trying out various buttons or menu items. If so, congratulations! Experimenting is the best way to get to know Excel. Just remember, the worst thing that can happen is that you mess up a workbook file. And if you do your experimentation using unimportant files, you have absolutely nothing to lose. And, don't forget about the Office Assistant. You can click the Office Assistant at any time and type a question (using natural language). Your chances are excellent that the Assistant will steer you to a help topic that answers your question.

✦   ✦   ✦

Introductory Concepts

✦ ✦ ✦ ✦

In This Part

✦ ✦ ✦ ✦

CHAPTER 4

Navigating Through Excel

Because you'll spend lots of time working in Excel, you need to understand the basics of navigating through workbooks and how best to use Excel's user interface. If you're an experienced Windows user, some of this information may already be familiar to you, so this is your chance to learn even more.

If you're new to Excel, some of the information in this chapter may seem confusing. It will become clearer as you progress through the other chapters, however.

Working with Excel's Windows

The files that Excel uses are known as *workbooks*. A workbook can hold any number of sheets, and these sheets can be either worksheets (a sheet consisting of rows and columns) or chart sheets (a sheet that holds a single chart). A *worksheet* is what people usually think of when they think of a spreadsheet.

Figure 4-1 shows Excel with four workbooks open, each in a separate window. One of the windows is minimized and appears near the top-right corner of the screen (when a workbook is minimized, only its title bar is visible).

Worksheet windows can overlap so that the title bar of one window is a different color. That's the window that contains the *active workbook*.

The workbook windows that Excel uses work much like the windows in any other Windows program. Excel's windows can be in one of the following states:

◆ **Maximized:** Fills Excel's entire workspace. A maximized window does not have a title bar, and the worksheet's name appears in Excel's title bar. To maximize a window, click its Maximize button.

✦ **Minimized:** Appears as a small window with only a title bar. To minimize a window, click its Minimize button.

✦ **Restored:** A nonmaximized size. To restore a maximized or minimized window, click its Restore button. If you work with more than one workbook simultaneously (which is quite common), you have to learn how to move, resize, and switch among the workbook windows.

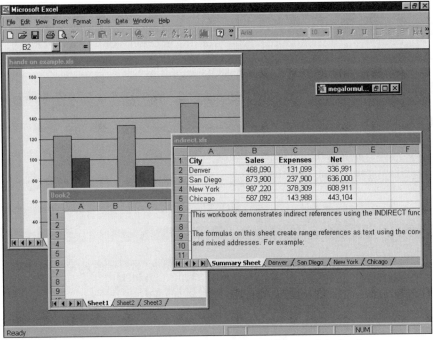

Figure 4-1: Excel with four workbooks open, one of them minimized.

As you're probably aware, Excel itself is contained in a window. Excel's window also can be maximized, minimized, or displayed in a nonmaximized size. When Excel's window is maximized, it fills the entire screen. You can activate other programs by using the Windows taskbar (usually located at the bottom of your screen).

Moving and Resizing Windows

You *cannot* move or resize a workbook window if it is maximized. You *can* move a minimized window, but doing so has no effect on its position when it is subsequently restored.

To move a window, click and drag its title bar with your mouse. Note that the windows can extend offscreen in any direction, if you want them to.

To resize a window, click and drag any of its borders until it's the size that you want it to be. When you position the mouse pointer on a window's border, the mouse pointer changes shape, which lets you know that you can now click and drag to resize the window. To resize a window horizontally and vertically at the same time, click and drag any of its corners.

If you want all of your workbook windows to be visible (that is, not obscured by another window), you can fiddle around by moving and resizing the windows manually, or you can let Excel do it for you. The Window ⇨ Arrange command displays the Arrange Windows dialog box, shown in Figure 4-2. This dialog box has four window-arrangement options. Just select the one that you want and click OK.

Figure 4-2: The Arrange Windows dialog box makes it easy to arrange the windows of all open workbooks.

Switching Among Windows

As previously mentioned, at any given time, one (and only one) workbook window is the active window. This is the window that accepts your input, and it is the window on which your commands work. The active window's title bar is a different color, and the window appears at the top of the stack of windows.

The following are several ways to make a different window the active workbook:

✦ Click another window, if it's visible. The window you click moves to the top and becomes the active window.

✦ Press Ctrl+Tab to cycle through all open windows until the window that you want to work with appears on top as the active window. Shift+Ctrl+Tab cycles through the windows in the opposite direction.

✦ Click the Window menu and select the window that you want from the bottom part of the pull-down menu. The active window has a check mark next to it, as shown in Figure 4-3. This window can display up to nine windows. If you have more than nine workbook windows open, choose More Windows (which appears below the nine window names).

EXCEL 2000

Excel 2000 offers another way to make a different window the active workbook: Click the icon in the Windows taskbar that represents the workbook window that you want to view. This feature works only with Windows 98.

Choose one

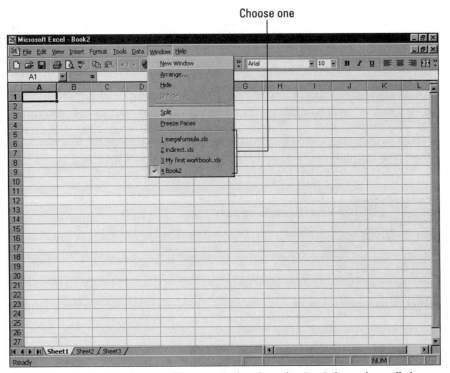

Figure 4-3: You can activate a different window by selecting it from the pull-down Window menu.

Many users (myself included) prefer to do most of their work with maximized workbook windows. This enables you to see more cells and eliminates the distraction of other workbook windows getting in the way. And besides, it's easy to activate another workbook window when you need to use it.

When you maximize one window, all the other windows are maximized, too (but you can't see them). Therefore, if the active window is maximized and you activate a different window, the new active window is also maximized. If the active workbook window is maximized, you can't select another window by clicking it (because other windows aren't visible). You must use either Ctrl+Tab, the Windows taskbar, or the Window menu to activate another window.

When would you *not* want to work exclusively with maximized worksheet windows? Excel also has some handy drag-and-drop features. For example, you can drag a range of cells from one workbook window to another. To do this type of drag and drop, both windows must be visible (that is, not maximized).

Cross-Reference   Chapter 8 discusses Excel's drag-and-drop features.

You also can display a single workbook in more than one window. For example, if you have a workbook with two worksheets, you may want to display each worksheet in a separate window. All the window-manipulation procedures described previously still apply.

Closing Windows

When you close a workbook window, Excel checks whether you have made any changes since the last time you saved the file. If not, the window closes without a prompt from Excel. If you've made any changes, Excel prompts you to save the file, before it closes the window.

 Cross-Reference You learn more about working with files in Chapter 5.

To close a window, simply click the Close button on the title bar.

Mouseless Window Manipulation

Although using a mouse to manipulate Excel's windows is usually the most efficient route, you also can perform these actions by using the keyboard. Table 4-1 summarizes the key combinations that manipulate workbook windows.

Table 4-1 Keystrokes Used to Manipulate Windows	
Key Combination	*Action*
Ctrl+F4	Close a window
Ctrl+F5	Restore a window
Ctrl+F6	Activate the next window
Ctrl+Shift+F6	Activate the previous window
Ctrl+Tab	Activate the next window
Ctrl+Shift+Tab	Activate the previous window
Ctrl+F7	Move a window*
Ctrl+F8	Resize a window*
Ctrl+F9	Minimize a window
Ctrl+F10	Maximize a window
Alt+W[n]	Activate the *n*th window

* Use the direction keys to make the change, and then press Enter.

Moving Around a Worksheet

You'll be spending a lot of time moving around your worksheets, so it pays to learn all the tricks.

Every worksheet consists of rows (numbered 1 through 65,536) and columns (labeled A through IV). After column Z comes column AA; after column AZ comes column BA, and so on. The intersection of a row and a column is a single cell. At any given time, one cell is the *active cell*. You can identify the active cell by its darker border, as shown in Figure 4-4. Its *address* (its column letter and row number) appears in the Name box. Depending on the technique that you use to navigate through a workbook, you may or may not change the active cell when you navigate.

The row and column headings of the active cell are displayed in bold — making it easy to identify the active cell.

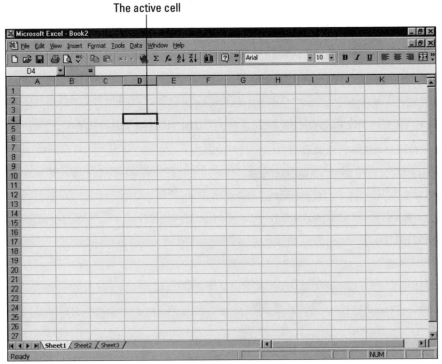

Figure 4-4: The active cell is the cell with the dark border; in this case, cell D4.

How Big Is a Worksheet?

Consider how big a worksheet really is. It has 256 columns and 65,536 rows. Do the arithmetic and you'll find that this works out to 16,777,216 cells. Remember, this is in just one worksheet. A single workbook can hold more than one worksheet—hundreds, if necessary.

If you're using the standard SVGA video mode with the default row heights and column widths, you can see 12 columns and 27 rows (or 324 cells) at a time. This works out to less than 0.001 percent of the entire worksheet. Put another way, more than 100,000 full screens of information are in a single worksheet.

If you started entering a single digit into each cell at a relatively rapid clip of one cell per second, you would take about 194 days, nonstop, to fill a worksheet. Printing the results of your effort would require more than 36,000 sheets of paper.

By the way, don't even think about actually using all the cells in a worksheet. Unless your system is equipped with an unusually large amount of memory, things will slow to a crawl as Windows churns away, swapping information to disk.

Using the Keyboard

As you probably already know, you can use the standard navigational keys on your keyboard to move around a worksheet. These keys work just as you would expect: the down arrow moves the active cell down one row, the right arrow moves it one column to the right, and so on. PgUp and PgDn move the active cell up or down one full window (the actual number of rows moved depends on the number of rows displayed in the window).

Tip

When you turn on Scroll Lock, you can scroll through the worksheet without changing the active cell. This can be useful if you need to view another area of your worksheet and then quickly return to your original location. Just press Scroll Lock and then use the direction keys to scroll through the worksheet. When you want to return to the original position (the active cell), press Ctrl+Backspace. Then, press Scroll Lock again to turn it off. When Scroll Lock is turned on, Excel displays SCRL in the status bar at the bottom of the window.

The Num Lock key on your keyboard controls how the keys on the numeric keypad behave. When Num Lock is on, Excel displays NUM in the status bar, and the keys on your numeric keypad generate numbers. Most keyboards have a separate set of navigational keys located to the left of the numeric keypad. These keys are not affected by the state of the Num Lock key.

Table 4-2 summarizes all the worksheet movement keys available in Excel.

Table 4-2
Excel's Worksheet Movement Keys

Key	Action
Up arrow	Moves the active cell up one row
Down arrow	Moves the active cell down one row
Left arrow	Moves the active cell one column to the left
Right arrow	Moves the active cell one column to the right
PgUp	Moves the active cell up one screen
PgDn	Moves the active cell down one screen
Alt+PgDn	Moves the active cell right one screen
Alt+PgUp	Moves the active cell left one screen
Ctrl+Backspace	Scrolls to display the active cell
Up arrow*	Scrolls the screen up one row (active cell does not change)
Down arrow*	Scrolls the screen down one row (active cell does not change)
Left arrow*	Scrolls the screen left one column (active cell does not change)
Right arrow*	Scrolls the screen right one column (active cell does not change)

* With Scroll Lock on

The actions for some of the keys in the preceding table may be different, depending on the transition options that you've set. Select Tools ⇨ Options and then click the Transition tab in the Options dialog box. If the Transition Navigation Keys option is checked, the navigation keys correspond to those used in older versions of Lotus 1-2-3. Generally, using the standard Excel navigation keys is better than using those for 1-2-3.

Tip   If you know either the cell address or the name of the cell that you want to activate, you can get there quickly by pressing F5 (the shortcut key for Edit ⇨ Go To). This command displays the Go To dialog box.

Just enter the cell address in the Reference box (or choose a named cell from the list), press Enter, and you're there.

Using a Mouse

Navigating through a worksheet with a mouse also works as you would expect it to work. To change the active cell by using the mouse, click another cell; it becomes the active cell. If the cell that you want to activate is not visible in the workbook window, you can use the scrollbars to scroll the window in any direction. To scroll one cell, click either of the arrows on the scrollbar. To scroll by a complete screen, click either side of the scrollbar's scroll box. You also can drag the scroll box for faster scrolling. Working with the scrollbars is more difficult to describe than to do, so if scrollbars are new to you, I urge you to experiment with them for a few minutes. You'll have it figured out in no time.

When you drag the scrollbar's scroll box, a small yellow box appears that tells you which row or column you will scroll to when you release the mouse button.

If you have a Microsoft IntelliMouse (or a compatible wheel mouse), you can use the mouse wheel to scroll vertically. The wheel scrolls three lines per click at the default rate. Also, if you click the wheel and move the mouse in any direction, the worksheet scrolls automatically in that direction. The more you move the mouse, the faster the scrolling. If you prefer to use the mouse wheel to zoom the work- sheet, select Tools ➪ Options, click the General tab, and then place a check mark next to the option labeled Zoom on roll with IntelliMouse.

Using the scrollbars or scrolling with the IntelliMouse doesn't change the active cell. It simply scrolls the worksheet. To change the active cell, you must click a new cell after scrolling.

Notice that only the active workbook window has scrollbars. When you activate a different window, the scrollbars appear.

Giving Commands to Excel

Excel is designed to take orders from you. You give these orders by issuing commands. You can give commands to Excel by using the following methods:

✦ Menus

✦ Shortcut menus

✦ Toolbar buttons

✦ Shortcut key combinations

In many cases, you can choose how to issue a particular command. For example, if you want to save your workbook to disk, you can use the menu (the File ➪ Save command), a shortcut menu (right-click the workbook's title bar and click Save), a toolbar button (the Save button on the Standard toolbar), or a shortcut key combination (Ctrl+S). The particular method you use is up to you.

The following sections provide an overview of the four methods of issuing com- mands to Excel.

Using Excel's Menus

Excel, like all other Windows programs, has a menu bar located directly below the title bar (see Figure 4-5). This menu bar is always available and ready for your command.

Excel's menus change, depending on what you're doing. For example, if you're working with a chart, Excel's menus change to give you options that are appropriate for a chart. This all happens automatically, so you don't even have to think about it.

Figure 4-5: Excel's menu bar displays different options, depending on the nature of your task.

Technically, Excel 2000's menu bar is just another toolbar. In Excel 2000, toolbars and menu bars are functionally identical. However, I'll continue to discuss menu bars as if they are something different.

Using a Mouse

Opening the menu with a mouse is quite straightforward. Click the menu that you want to open and it drops down to display menu items, also called *commands*, as shown in Figure 4-6. Click the menu item to issue the command.

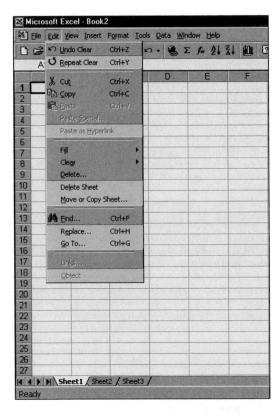

Figure 4-6: Opening Excel's Edit menu displays its menu items.

Changing Your Mind

When you issue a command to Excel by using any of the available methods, Excel carries out your command. However, just about every command can be reversed by using the Edit ➪ Undo command. Select this command after issuing a command, and it's as if you never issued the command.

Beginning with Excel 97, the Undo feature became much more useful. Excel 97 and later supports up to 16 levels of Undo. This means that you can reverse the effects of the last 16 commands that you executed! You may not fully appreciate this feature until you someday make a major error (such as deleting a column of formulas) and don't discover it until quite a bit later. You can use Edit ➪ Undo repeatedly (up to 16 times) until your worksheet reverts to the state that it was in before you made your error.

Rather than use Edit ➪ Undo, you may prefer to use the Undo button on the Standard toolbar. If you click the arrow on the right side of the button, you can see a description of the commands that are "undoable" (see the accompanying figure). The Redo button performs in the opposite direction of the Undo button: Redo repeats commands that have been undone.

So, as you're working away in Excel, don't forget about Undo. It can be a real lifesaver.

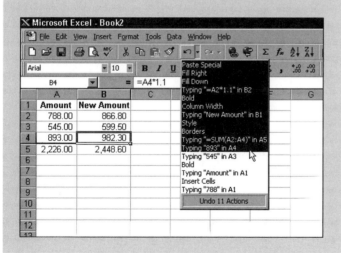

Some menu items lead to an additional *submenu;* when you click the menu item, the submenu appears to its right. Menu items that have a submenu display a small triangle. For example, the Edit ➪ Clear command has a submenu, shown in Figure 4-7. Excel's designers incorporated submenus primarily to keep the menus from becoming too lengthy and overwhelming to users.

Some menu items also have shortcut keys associated with them. The ones that do usually display the key combination next to the menu item. For example, the Edit ➪ Find command's shortcut key combination is Ctrl+F.

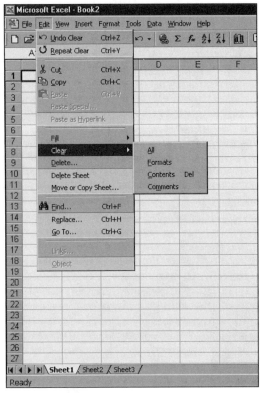

Figure 4-7: The submenu of the Edit ➪ Clear command.

Sometimes, you'll notice that a menu item appears *grayed out*. This simply means that the menu item isn't appropriate for what you're doing. Nothing happens if you select such a menu item.

Menu items that are followed by an ellipsis (three dots) always display a dialog box. Menu commands that don't have an ellipsis are executed immediately. For example, the Insert ➪ Cells command results in a dialog box, because Excel needs more information about the command. The Insert ➪ Rows command doesn't need a dialog box, so Excel performs this command immediately.

In Excel 2000, your menus may behave differently than they did in previous versions of Excel. When you open a menu, you may see the most recently used commands first. After a few moments, or if you click the arrow at the bottom of the menu, you'll see the rest of the commands for that menu. After you choose a command by clicking the arrow at the bottom of the menu, Excel leaves that command in the list of "recently used" commands; that is, you'll see it immediately among the available commands the next time that you open the menu. To find it again, you won't need to click the arrow at the bottom of the menu or wait until all the commands appear.

Personally, I think this "automatic menu customization" is one of the worst ideas ever — and is practically guaranteed to cause confusion among beginners. I highly recommend that you turn this feature off immediately. Choose Tools ➪ Customize and click the Options tab. Then, remove the check from the check box titled Menus show recently used commands first (see Figure 4-8). Note: Changing this behavior in Excel changes the behavior for *all* Office applications.

Click here

Figure 4-8: Change menu behavior to show all commands by clearing this check box.

Using the Keyboard

You can issue menu commands by using the mouse or the keyboard. Although most users tend to prefer a mouse, others find that accessing the menus with the keyboard is more efficient. This is especially true if you're entering data into a worksheet. Using a mouse means that you have to move your hand from the keyboard, locate the mouse, move it, click it, and then move your hand back to the keyboard. Although this takes only a few seconds, those seconds add up.

To issue a menu command from the keyboard, press Alt and then the menu's *hot key*. The hot key is the underlined letter in the menu; for example E is the hot key of the Edit menu. After you open the menu, you can press the appropriate hot key for a command on the menu. For example, to issue the Data ➪ Sort command, press Alt, press D, and then press S.

You also can press Alt alone, or F10. This selects the first menu (the File menu). Next, you use the direction keys to highlight the menu that you want, and then press Enter. In the menu, use the direction keys to choose the appropriate menu item, and press Enter again.

Moving the Menu

In Excel 2000, a menu bar is the same as a toolbar. Because the menu bar is a toolbar, you can move the menu to a new location, if you prefer. To move the menu, just click and drag it to its new location. This can be a bit tricky, because you must click the menu in a location that doesn't contain a menu item, such as to the right of the Help menu. You can drag the menu to any of the window borders or leave it free-floating. Figure 4-9 shows the menu after relocating it to the left side of the window.

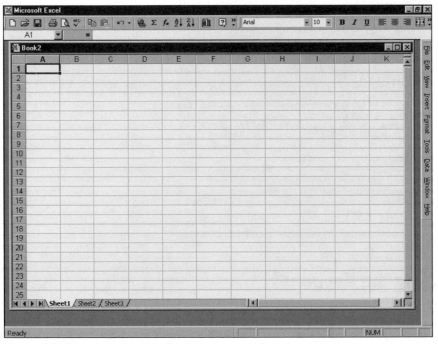

Figure 4-9: You can move Excel's menu to a new location.

Cross-Reference Learn how to customize Excel's menus (and toolbars) in Chapter 33.

Using Shortcut Menus

Besides the omnipresent menu bar, discussed in the preceding section, Excel features a slew of *shortcut menus*. A shortcut menu is context-sensitive—its contents depend on what you're doing at the time. Shortcut menus don't contain *all* the relevant commands, just those that are most commonly used for whatever is selected. You can display a shortcut menu by right-clicking just about anything in Excel.

As an example, examine Figure 4-10, which shows the shortcut menu (also called a *context menu*) that appears when you right-click a cell. The shortcut menu appears at the mouse-pointer position, which makes selecting a command fast and efficient.

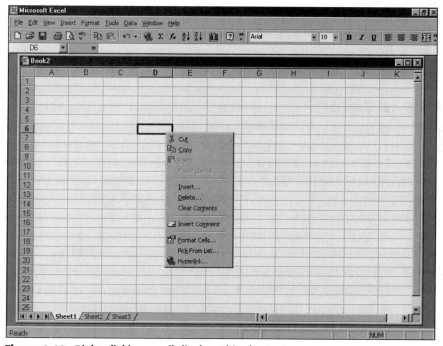

Figure 4-10: Right-clicking a cell displays this shortcut menu.

The shortcut menu that appears depends on what is currently selected. For example, if you're working with a chart, the shortcut menu that appears when you right-click a chart part contains commands that are pertinent to what is selected.

Instant Help for Commands

Excel's toolbars can be a bit daunting at times, especially for newcomers. One approach — the best approach, in my opinion — is simply to try out things to see what happens (and don't forget about the Edit ➪ Undo command). If you're not that adventurous, an easy way exists to determine the function of a particular menu command or toolbar button.

Drag the mouse pointer over a toolbar button (but don't click it). A small box appears that tells you the name of the button. Often, this provides enough information for you to determine whether the button is what you want.

For context-sensitive help on a menu command or toolbar button, choose the Help ➪ What's This? command (or, press Shift+F1). The mouse pointer turns into an arrow with a question mark beside it. Now, select any menu command or toolbar button, and Excel displays a description of the item. Note that the command itself won't be issued when you click a menu item or toolbar button.

Tip   Although shortcut menus were invented with mouse users in mind, you also can display a shortcut menu by pressing Shift+F10.

Excel's Toolbars

Excel, like all leading applications, includes convenient graphical toolbars. Clicking a button on a toolbar is just another way of issuing commands to Excel. In many cases, a toolbar button is simply a substitute for a menu command. For example, the Copy button is a substitute for Edit ➪ Copy. Some toolbar buttons, however, don't have any menu equivalent. One example is the AutoSum button, which automatically inserts a formula to calculate the sum of a range of cells. Toolbars can be customized to include menu commands as well as buttons.

By default, Excel displays two toolbars (named *Standard* and *Formatting*). Technically, it displays three toolbars, because the menu bar is actually a toolbar named *Worksheet menu bar*. All told, Excel 2000 has 23 built-in toolbars, plus the menu bar. You have complete control over which toolbars are displayed and where they are located. In addition, you can create custom toolbars, made up of buttons that you find most useful.

Cross-Reference   Learn how to customize toolbars and create new toolbars in Chapter 33.

In Excel 2000, the Standard and Formatting toolbars may appear side by side just below the menu bar. In prior versions, these toolbars appeared separately. Because the toolbars appear side by side, you can't see all the tools on either toolbar; Excel displays those tools on each toolbar that you are most likely to use frequently. If you want to use one of the "missing tools," you must click the arrow that appears at the edge of the toolbar to display all the tools available on that toolbar (see Figure 4-11). After you choose a tool from the "missing tools," Excel continues to display that tool, because you recently used it.

If you prefer to see all the tools on a toolbar, you can drag one of the toolbars to a different location. If you want to display one below the other (as previous versions of Excel did), drag one below the other or choose Tools ➪ Customize. Click the Options tab and remove the check from the check box labeled Standard and Formatting toolbars share one row. This check box *is not* available if either toolbar is hidden or both toolbars are floating (you'll learn more about "floating toolbars" later in this chapter). Changing this behavior in Excel affects only Excel.

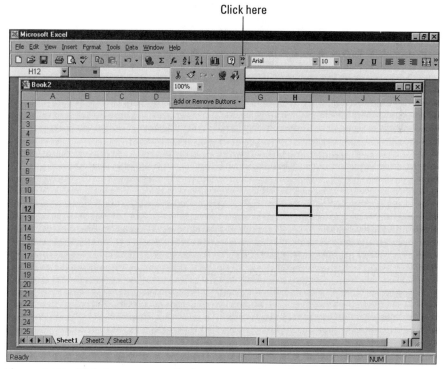

Figure 4-11: Click the arrow to display more tools on the Standard toolbar.

Table 4-3 lists all of Excel's built-in toolbars.

Table 4-3
Excel's Built-in Toolbars

Toolbar	Use
Standard	Issue commonly used commands
Formatting	Change how your worksheet or chart looks
Pivot Table	Work with pivot tables
Chart	Manipulate charts
Reviewing	Tools to use workbooks in groups
Clipboard	Tools to copy and paste multiple Clipboard selections between Office applications
Forms	Add controls (buttons, spinners, and so on) to a worksheet
Stop Recording	Record macros
External Data	Perform queries on external database files
Auditing	Identify errors in your worksheet
Full Screen	Toggle in and out of full-screen view (one tool only)
Circular Reference	Obtain assistance in identifying circular references in formulas
Visual Basic	Write macros in Visual Basic for Applications
Web	Access the Internet from Excel
Control Toolbox	Add ActiveX controls to a workbook or form
Exit Design Mode	Toggle in and out of design mode (one tool only)
Worksheet Menu Bar	The menu that appears when a worksheet is active
Chart Menu Bar	The menu that appears when a chart is selected
Drawing	Insert or edit drawings on a worksheet
Word Art	Insert or edit a picture composed of words
Picture	Insert or edit graphic images
Shadow Settings	Insert or edit shadows that appear behind objects
3D Settings	Add 3D effects to objects

EXCEL 2000

The Clipboard toolbar (and the way the Clipboard functions in Office 2000 applications) is new in Excel 2000.

Cross-Reference   See Chapter 8 for more information on the Clipboard.

Sometimes, Excel automatically pops up a toolbar to help you with a particular task. For example, if you're working with a chart, Excel displays its Chart toolbar.

Hiding or Showing Toolbars

To hide or display a particular toolbar, choose View ➪ Toolbars, or right-click any toolbar. Either of these actions displays a list of common toolbars (but not all toolbars). The toolbars that have a check mark next to them are currently visible. To hide a toolbar, click it to remove the check mark. To display a toolbar, click it to add a check mark.

If the toolbar that you want to hide or show does not appear on the menu list, select View ➪ Toolbars ➪ Customize (or select Customize from the shortcut menu that appears when you right-click a toolbar). Excel displays its Customize dialog box, shown in Figure 4-12. The Toolbars tab of this dialog box shows a list of all toolbars that are available — the built-in toolbars, plus any custom toolbars. The toolbars that have a check mark next to them are currently visible. To hide a toolbar, click it to remove the check mark. To display a toolbar, click it to add a check mark. When you're finished, click the Close button.

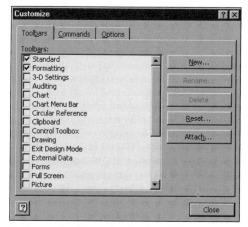

Figure 4-12: Choose which toolbars to display in the Customize dialog box.

The Customize dialog box has some other options with which you may want to experiment. Click the Options tab to display these options (see Figure 4-13). The check boxes at the top of the Options tab were discussed earlier in the chapter. The button labeled Reset my usage data, in the middle of Figure 4-13, works in conjunction with the check box titled Menus show recently used commands first.

Excel determines the commands to show based on the commands that you use most often. Clicking the Reset my usage data tells Excel to ignore your past usage and reset the menu commands to the defaults that shipped with the product. If you leave the check in the Menus show recently used commands first check box after resetting usage, Excel starts the "monitoring" process over again to determine which commands you're using most often.

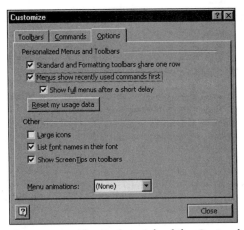

Figure 4-13: The Options tab of the Customize dialog box provides some options for toolbars.

Chapter 33 discusses the Commands tab of the Customize dialog box.

If you prefer larger buttons, check the Large icons check box. By default, when you open the Font list box, font names provide a sample of the font (see Figure 4-14). This is useful, but it also slows things down quite a bit. For a faster font list, remove the check from the check box titled List font names in their font. And if you find those pop-up screen tips distracting, uncheck the Show ScreenTips on toolbars check box. You can also specify what type of animation you prefer for the menus.

Moving Toolbars

Toolbars can be moved to any of the four sides of Excel's window, or can be free-floating. A free-floating toolbar can be dragged onscreen anywhere that you want. You also can change a toolbar's size simply by dragging any of its borders. To hide a free-floating toolbar, click its Close button.

Because Excel 2000 menu bars are actually toolbars, this discussion also applies to the menu bars.

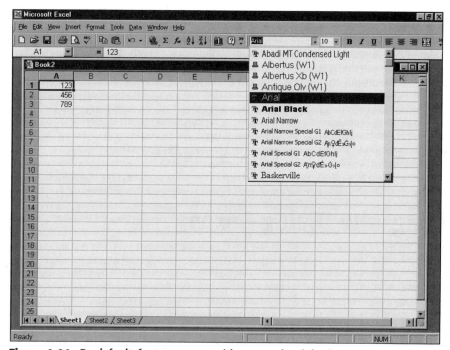

Figure 4-14: By default, font names provide a sample of the font.

When a toolbar isn't free-floating, it's said to be *docked*. A docked toolbar is stuck to the edge of Excel's window and doesn't have a title bar. Therefore, a docked toolbar can't be resized.

To move a toolbar (docked or free-floating), click and drag anywhere on the background of the toolbar (that is, anywhere except on a button). When you drag it toward the window's edge, it automatically docks itself there. When a toolbar is docked, its shape changes to a single row or single column.

Learning More About Toolbars

Describing all the toolbar buttons available would take many pages, so I won't even try. You are charged with discovering this handy feature on your own. But, throughout the rest of the book, I point out toolbar buttons that may be useful in particular situations.

Cross-Reference Chapter 33 discusses toolbars in more detail, including how to customize toolbars.

Shortcut Keys

This chapter mentioned earlier that some menu commands have equivalent shortcut keys. Usually, the shortcut key combination is displayed next to the menu item — providing a built-in way for you to learn the shortcuts as you select the commands.

Throughout the book, shortcut keys are examined that are relevant to any particular topic.

Appendix C lists all the shortcut keys available in Excel.

Working with Dialog Boxes

As previously stated, menu items that end with an ellipsis (three dots) result in a dialog box. All Windows programs use dialog boxes, so you may already be familiar with the concept.

About Dialog Boxes

You can think of a dialog box as Excel's way of getting more information from you about the command that you selected. For example, if you choose View ⇨ Zoom (which changes the magnification of the worksheet), Excel can't carry out the command until it finds out from you what magnification level you want. Dialog boxes can be simple or much more complicated. Dialog boxes are made up of several items, known as *controls*.

When a dialog box appears in response to your command, you make additional choices in the dialog box by manipulating the controls. When you're finished, click the OK button (or press Enter) to continue. If you change your mind, click the Cancel button (or press Escape) and nothing further happens — it's as if the dialog box never appeared.

If a dialog box obscures an area of your worksheet that you need to see, simply click the dialog box's title bar and drag the box to another location. The title bar in a dialog box has two controls: a Help button (Question-mark icon) and a Close button. When you click the Help button, the mouse pointer displays a question mark. You can click any part of the dialog box to get a description of that part's purpose. Clicking the Close button is the same as clicking the Cancel button or pressing Escape.

Although a dialog box looks like just another window, it works a little differently. When a dialog box appears, you can't do anything in the workbook until the dialog box is closed. In other words, you must dismiss the dialog box before you can do anything.

Navigating Dialog Boxes by Using the Keyboard

Although dialog boxes were designed with mouse users in mind, some users prefer to use the keyboard. With a bit of practice, you'll find that navigating a dialog box directly from the keyboard may be more efficient in some cases.

Every dialog box control has text associated with it, and this text always has one underlined letter (a *hot key* or *accelerator key*). You can access the control from the keyboard by pressing the Alt key and then the underlined letter. You also can use Tab to cycle through all the controls on a dialog box. Shift+Tab cycles through the controls in reverse order.

When a control is selected, it appears with a darker outline. You can use the spacebar to activate a selected control.

Dialog Box Controls

Most people find working with dialog boxes to be quite straightforward and natural. The controls usually work just as you would expect, and they can be manipulated either with your mouse or directly from the keyboard.

The following sections describe the most common dialog box controls and show some examples.

Buttons

A button control is about as simple as it gets. Just click it and it does its thing. Most dialog boxes have at least two buttons. The OK button closes the dialog box and executes the command. The Cancel button closes the dialog box without making any changes. If an ellipsis appears after the text on a button, clicking the button leads to another dialog box.

Pressing the Alt key and the button's underlined letter is equivalent to clicking the button. Pressing Enter is the same as clicking the OK button, and pressing Esc is the same as clicking the Cancel button.

Option buttons

Option buttons are sometimes known as *radio* buttons, because they work like the preset station buttons on an old-fashioned car radio. Like these car radios, only one option button at a time can be "pressed." Choosing an option button is like choosing a single item on a computerized multiple-choice test. When you click an option button, the previously selected option button is unselected.

Option buttons usually are enclosed in a group box, and a single dialog box can have several sets of option buttons. Figure 4-15 shows an example of a dialog box with option buttons.

Figure 4-15: This dialog box has seven option buttons.

Check boxes

A check box control is used to indicate whether an option is on or off. This is similar to responding to an item on a True/False test. Figure 4-16 shows a dialog box with several check boxes. Unlike option buttons, each check box is independent of the others. Clicking a check box toggles on and off the check mark.

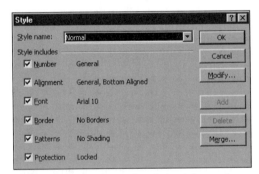

Figure 4-16: An example of check boxes in a dialog box.

Range selection boxes

A range selection box enables you to specify a worksheet range by dragging inside the worksheet. A range selection box has a small button that, when clicked, collapses the dialog box, to make it easier for you to select the range by dragging in the worksheet. After you select the range, click the button again to restore the dialog box. Figure 4-17 shows a dialog box with two range selection box controls. The control in the middle is a standard edit box.

Spinners

A spinner control makes specifying a number easy. You can click the arrows to increment or decrement the displayed value. A spinner is almost always paired with an edit box. You can either enter the value directly into the edit box or use the spinner to change it to the desired value. Figure 4-18 shows a dialog box with several spinner controls.

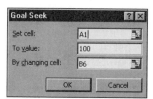

Figure 4-17: A range selection box enables you to specify a worksheet range by dragging in the worksheet.

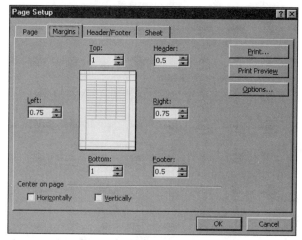

Figure 4-18: This dialog box has several spinner controls.

List boxes

A list box control contains a list of options from which you can choose. If the list is longer than will fit in the list box, you can use its vertical scrollbar to scroll through the list. Figure 4-19 shows an example of a dialog box that contains two list box controls.

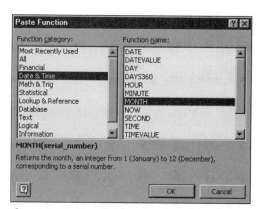

Figure 4-19: Two list box controls in a dialog box.

Drop-down boxes

Drop-down boxes are similar to list boxes, but they show only a single option at a time. When you click the arrow on a drop-down box, the list drops down to display additional choices. Figure 4-20 shows an open drop-down box control.

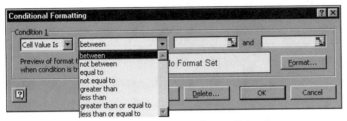

Figure 4-20: A drop-down box control in a dialog box.

Tabbed Dialog Boxes

Many of Excel's dialog boxes are "tabbed" dialog boxes. A tabbed dialog box includes notebook-like tabs, each of which is associated with a different panel. When you click a tab, the dialog box changes to display a new panel containing a new set of controls. The Format Cells dialog box, which appears in response to the Format ➪ Cells command, is a good example. This dialog box is shown in Figure 4-21. Notice that it has six tabs, which makes it functionally equivalent to six different dialog boxes.

Tabbed dialog boxes are quite convenient, because you can make several changes in a single dialog box. After you make all of your setting changes, click OK or press Enter.

Figure 4-21: The Format Cells dialog box is an example of a tabbed dialog box.

Tip   To select a tab by using the keyboard, use Ctrl+PgUp or Ctrl+PgDn, or simply press the first letter of the tab that you want to activate.

Summary

This chapter covers background information that is essential to using Excel efficiently. It discusses methods to manipulate windows (which hold workbooks), as well as several techniques used to move around within a worksheet by using the mouse or the keyboard. It also discusses the various methods used to issue commands to Excel: menus, shortcut menus, toolbar buttons, and shortcut key combinations. This chapter concludes with a general discussion of dialog boxes — an element common to all Windows programs.

✦   ✦   ✦

Working with Files and Workbooks

Computer users won't get too far without understanding
the concept of files. Every computer program uses files,
and a good understanding of how to manage files stored on
your hard drive will make your job easier. This chapter discusses how Excel uses files and what you need to know about
files to use Excel.

Some Background on Files

A *file* is an entity that stores information a disk. A hard disk is
usually organized into directories (or folders) to facilitate the
organization of files. For example, all the files that comprise
Excel are stored in a separate folder on your computer. And,
your system probably has a directory named Personal (located
in your Windows directory) that is used as the default location
for storing Excel workbooks.

Files can be manipulated in several ways. They can be copied,
renamed, deleted, or moved to another disk or folder. These
types of file operations are usually performed by using the tools
in Windows (although you also can perform these operations
without leaving Excel).

Computer programs are stored in files, and programs also store
information that they use in files. Some programs (such as
Excel) use files by loading them into memory. Others (such as
database programs) access selective parts of a file directly from
the disk and don't read the entire file into memory.

Windows makes it easy to access *properties* of files. Properties
include information such as file type, size, date created, its
read-only status, and so on. Excel enables you access some
additional custom properties of files that can help you to

locate and categorize your files. For example, you can store information that enables you quickly to locate all workbook files that apply to a particular client.

How Excel Uses Files

When you installed Excel (or the entire Microsoft Office suite) on your system, the Setup program copied many files to your hard disk and created several new folders to hold the files. These files consist of the files that are needed to run Excel, plus some sample files and Help files. The Setup program also made (or modified) some entries in the Windows *Registry*. The Registry is a master database of sorts that keeps track of all configuration information for the operating system and the software installed on your system, and also associates Excel's data files with Excel.

Excel's Data Files

Excel's primary file type is called a *workbook* file. When you open a workbook in Excel, the entire file is loaded into memory, and any changes that you make occur only in the copy of the file that's in memory. If the workbook is large, your system may not have enough memory to hold the file. In such a case, Windows uses disk-based virtual memory to simulate actual memory (this slows things down considerably). When you save the workbook, Excel saves the copy in memory to your disk, overwriting the previous copy of the file.

Table 5-1 lists the various types of files that Excel supports directly.

Table 5-1 Data Files Used by Excel	
File Type	**Description**
BAK	Backup file
XLA	Excel add-in file (several add-ins are supplied with Excel, and you can create your own add-ins)
XLB	Excel toolbar configuration file
XLC	Excel 4 chart file*
XLL	Excel link library file
XLM	Excel 4 macro file*
XLS	Excel workbook file
XLT	Excel template file
XLW	Excel workspace file

* These files became obsolete beginning with Excel 5. However, Excel can still read these files for compatibility with previous versions.

Foreign File Formats Supported

Although Excel's default file format is an XLS workbook file, it also can open files generated by several other applications. In addition, Excel can save workbooks in several different formats. Table 5-2 contains a list of file formats that Excel can read and write.

Cross-Reference   Chapter 22 covers file importing and exporting in detail.

Table 5-2
File Formats Supported by Excel

File Type	Description
WKS	1-2-3 Release 1 spreadsheet format**
WK1	1-2-3 Release 2 spreadsheet format***
WK3	1-2-3 Release 3 spreadsheet format***
WK4	1-2-3 for Windows spreadsheet format
WQ1	Quattro Pro for DOS spreadsheet format
WB1	Quattro Pro for Windows spreadsheet format**
DBF	dBASE database format
SLK	SYLK spreadsheet format
WB1	Quattro Pro for Windows spreadsheet format
HTM, HTML	Hypertext Markup Language files
CSV	Comma-separated value text file format
TXT	Text file format
PRN	Text file format
DIF	Data interchange format

** Excel can open files in this format, but not save them.

*** When you open one of these files, Excel searches for the associated formatting file (either FMT or FM3) and attempts to translate the formatting.

EXCEL 2000   Excel 2000 lets you use HTML as a "native" file format. HTML is the file format used by Web browsers. You can save and retrieve files using this format, with no loss of information.

Cross-Reference   This new HTML feature is discussed in Chapter 30.

Essential Workbook File Operations

This section describes the operations that you perform with workbook files: opening, saving, closing, deleting, and so on. As you read through this section, keep in mind that you can have any number of workbooks open simultaneously, and that at any given time, only one workbook is the active workbook. The workbook's name is displayed in its title bar (or in Excel's title bar if the workbook is maximized).

Creating a New Workbook

When you start Excel, it automatically creates a new (empty) workbook called Book1. This workbook exists only in memory and has not been saved to disk. By default, this workbook consists of three worksheets named Sheet1, Sheet2, and Sheet3. If you're starting a new project from scratch, you can use this blank workbook.

You can always create another new workbook in either of three ways:

✦ Use the File ⇨ New command

✦ Click the New Workbook button on the Standard toolbar (this button has an image of a sheet of paper)

✦ Press the Ctrl+N shortcut key combination

If you choose the File ⇨ New command, you're greeted with a dialog box named New (see Figure 5-1). This is a tabbed dialog box that enables you to choose a template for the new workbook. If you don't have any custom templates defined, the General tab displays only one option: Workbook. Clicking this gives you a plain workbook. Templates that are included with Excel are listed in the Spreadsheet Solutions tab. If you choose one of these templates, your new workbook is based on the selected template file.

Cross-Reference
Templates are discussed later in this chapter, and Chapter 33 discusses this topic in detail.

Pressing Ctrl+N or clicking the New button on the Standard toolbar bypasses the New dialog box and creates a new default workbook immediately. If you want to create a new workbook based on a template, you must use the File ⇨ New command.

Tip
If you find that you almost always end up closing the default Book1 workbook that appears when you start Excel, you can set things up so that Excel starts without an empty workbook. To do so, you need to edit the command line that you use to start Excel. For example, if you start Excel by using a shortcut on your Windows desktop, right-click the shortcut icon and choose Properties from the menu. Click the Shortcut tab and add **/e** after the command line listed in the Target field. The following is an example of a command line modified in this manner (the actual drive and path may vary on your system):

```
C:\Program Files\Microsoft Office\Office\excel.exe /e
```

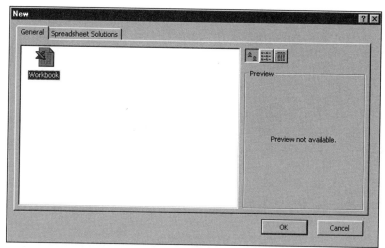

Figure 5-1: The New dialog box enables you to choose a template upon which to base the new workbook.

Opening an Existing Workbook

The following are the ways to open a workbook that has been saved on your disk:

✦ Use the File ➪ Open command

✦ Click the Open button on the Standard toolbar (the Open button has an image of a file folder opening)

✦ Press the Ctrl+O shortcut key combination

All of these methods result in the Open dialog box, shown in Figure 5-2.

You also can open an Excel workbook by double-clicking its icon in any folder window. If Excel isn't running, it starts automatically. Or, you can drag a workbook icon into the Excel window to load the workbook.

If you want to open a file that you've used recently, it may be listed at the bottom of the drop-down File menu. This menu shows a list of files that you've worked on recently. Just click the filename and the workbook opens for you (bypassing the Open dialog box).

Tip

You select the number of files to display in the recent file list—from zero up to nine. To change this setting, use Tool ➪ Options. In the Options dialog box, click the General tab and make the change to the Recently used file list setting.

EXCEL 2000

The Open dialog box has a new look in Excel 2000. It provides icons along the left side so that you can quickly activate certain folders. For example, clicking the Desktop icon activates your Windows\Desktop directory—which contains the file and shortcuts displayed on your desktop.

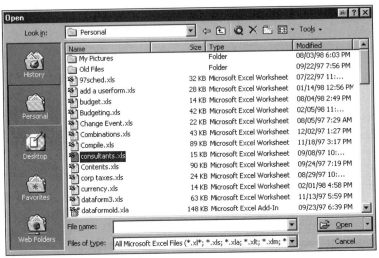

Figure 5-2: The Open dialog box.

To open a workbook from the Open dialog box, you must provide two pieces of information: the name of the workbook file (specified in the File name field) and its folder (specified in the Look in field).

This dialog box may be a bit overwhelming at first. You can ignore most of it, because many of the controls deal with locating files. If you know what folder the file is in, you simply specify the folder and then select the filename (and don't forget about the new icons on the left side of the Open dialog box). Click Open and the file opens. You also can just double-click the filename to open it.

In Excel 2000, the Open button is actually a drop-down list. Click the arrow and you see the additional options:

✦ **Open:** Opens the file normally.

✦ **Open Read Only:** Opens the selected file in read-only mode. When a file is opened in this mode, changes cannot be saved to the original filename.

✦ **Open as Copy:** Opens a copy of the selected file. If the file is named budget.xls, the workbook that opens is named copy of budget.xls.

✦ **Open in Browser:** Opens the file in your default Web browser.

Tip   You can hold down the Ctrl key and select multiple workbooks. When you click OK, all the selected workbook files will open.

Right-clicking a filename in the Open dialog box displays a shortcut menu with many extra choices. For example, you can copy the file, delete it, modify its properties, and so on.

Specifying a folder

The Look in field is actually a drop-down box. Click the arrow and the box expands to show your system components. You can select a different drive or directory from this list. The Up One Level icon (a file folder with an upward arrow) moves up one level in the folder hierarchy.

As noted previously, you can also click any of the following icons to activate a particular directory:

Icon	Folder
History	c:\windows\recent
Personal	c:\windows\personal
Desktop	c:\windows\desktop
Favorites	c:\windows\favorites
Web Folders	c:\windows\web folders

Filtering by file type

At the bottom of the Open dialog box, the drop-down list is labeled Files of type. When this dialog box is displayed, it shows All Microsoft Excel Files (*.xl*, *.xls, *.xla, *.xlt, *.xlw). This means that the files displayed are filtered, and you see only files that have an extension beginning with the letters XL. In other words, you see only standard Excel files: workbooks, add-ins, templates, and workspace files.

If you want to open a file of a different type, click the arrow in the drop-down list and select the file type that you want to open. This changes the filtering and displays only files of the type that you specify.

File display preferences

The Open dialog box can display your workbook filenames in four different styles:

- ✦ **List:** As a list of filenames only, displayed in multiple columns
- ✦ **Details:** As a list of filenames, with details about each file (its size, file type, and when it was last modified)
- ✦ **Properties:** As a list of filenames, with file properties displayed in a separate panel for the selected file
- ✦ **Preview:** As a list of filenames, with a preview screen displayed in a separate panel for the selected file

You control the style by clicking the View icon and then selecting from the drop-down list. The View icon is located in the upper-right section of the Open dialog box (see Figure 5-3). The style that you choose is entirely up to you.

Tip

If you display the files by using the Details style, you can sort the file list by any of the columns displayed (name, size, type, or date). To sort the file list, click the appropriate column heading.

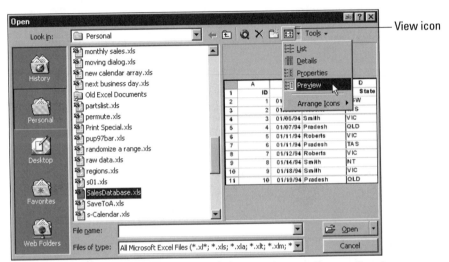

    — View icon

Figure 5-3: The View icon enables you to change the way files are listed in the Open dialog box.

The Tools menu

Clicking the Tools menu, listed last in the upper-right section of the Open dialog box, displays a shortcut menu. The following are the menu items displayed and what they do:

✦ **Find:** Opens a new dialog box that enables you to search for a particular file. See the sidebar "Finding Lost Workbooks" in Excel 2000.

✦ **Delete**: Deletes the selected file(s).

✦ **Rename**: Enables you to rename the selected file.

✦ **Print**: Opens the selected file, prints it, and then closes it.

✦ **Add to Favorites**: Adds to your Favorites directory a shortcut to the selected file.

✦ **Map Network Drive**: Displays a dialog box that enables you to map a network directory to a drive designator.

✦ **Properties**: Displays the Properties dialog box for the selected file. This enables you to examine or modify the file's properties without actually opening it.

Finding Lost Workbooks in Excel 2000

A common problem among computer users is "losing" a file. You know that you saved a file, but you don't remember the folder that you saved it in. Fortunately, Excel makes it fairly easy to locate such lost files by using the Open dialog box.

The procedure for finding files is much different in Excel 2000 — and also much easier. Select File ➪ Open, and then click Tools ➪ Find (or just press Ctl+F).You'll see the Find dialog box

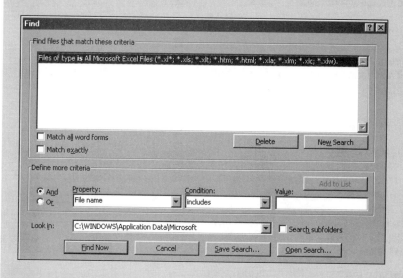

Although this dialog box looks a bit complicated, its purpose is to collect two pieces of information from you:

✦ Search criteria (what to look for)

✦ Where to look (the search scope)

You can search for files based on virtually any criteria (or combination of criteria) you can think of, including name, size, file type, contents, and so on. And after you define a search, you can save it, so that you can search later by the same criteria. When searching for a file, your search scope can be very broad (a complete hard drive) or very narrow (a specific folder).

If your searches aren't very complex, you may find it faster to use the Windows Find feature. You can search by filename, date, size, and even contents. Click the Windows Start button and then select Find ➪ Files or Folders. Enter your search criteria and click Find Now. A list of matching files will be displayed. To open a file in Excel, just double-click it.

Opening Workbooks Automatically

Many people find that they work on the same workbooks day after day. If this describes you, you'll be happy to know that you can have Excel open specific workbook files automatically whenever you start Excel.

The XLStart folder is located within the Microsoft Office folder. Any workbook files (excluding template files) that are stored in this folder open automatically when Excel starts. If one or more files open automatically from this folder, Excel won't start up with a blank workbook.

Tip

You can specify an alternate startup folder in addition to the XLStart folder. Choose Tools ➪ Options and select the General tab. Enter a new folder name in the field labeled Alternate Startup File Location. After you do that, when you start Excel, it automatically opens all workbook files in both the XLStart folder and the alternate folder that you specified.

Saving Workbooks

When you're working on a workbook, it's vulnerable to day-ruining events, such as power failures and system crashes. Therefore, you should save your work to disk often. Saving a file takes only a few seconds, but re-creating four hours of lost work takes about four hours.

Excel provides four ways to save your workbook:

✦ Use the File ➪ Save command

✦ Click the Save button on the Standard toolbar

✦ Press the Ctrl+S shortcut key combination

✦ Press the Shift+F12 shortcut key combination

If your workbook has already been saved, it's saved again using the same filename. If you want to save the workbook to a new file, use the File ➪ Save As command (or press F12).

If your workbook has never been saved, its title bar displays a name such as Book1 or Book2. Although Excel enables you to use these generic workbook names for file-names, it's not recommended. Therefore, the first time that you save a new worbook, Excel displays the Save As dialog box (see Figure 5-4) to let you provide a more mean-ingful name.

The Save As dialog box is somewhat similar to the Open dialog box. Again, you need to specify two pieces of information: the workbook's name and the folder in which to store it. If you want to save the file to a different folder, select the desired folder in the Save in field. If you want to create a new folder, click the Create New Folder icon in the Save As dialog box. The new folder is created within the folder that's displayed in the Save in field.

After you select the folder, enter the filename in the File name field. You don't need to specify a file extension—Excel adds it automatically, based on the file type specified in the Save as type field.

If a file with the same name already exists in the folder that you specify, Excel asks whether you want to overwrite that file with the new file. Be careful with this, because you can't recover the previous file if you overwrite it.

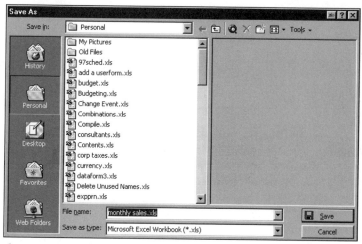

Figure 5-4: The Save As dialog box.

Caution

Remember, saving a file *overwrites* the previous version of the file on disk. If you open a workbook and then completely mess it up, don't save the file! Instead, close the workbook without saving it, and then open the good copy on disk.

File Naming Rules

Excel's workbook files are subject to the same rules that apply to other Windows 95 (or later) files. A filename can be up to 255 characters, including spaces. This enables you (finally) to give meaningful names to your files. You can't, however, use any of the following characters in your filenames:

\ (slash)

? (question mark)

: (colon)

* (asterisk)

" (quote)

< (less than)

> (greater than)

| (vertical bar)

You can use uppercase and lowercase letters in your names to improve readability. The filenames aren't case-sensitive, however. If you have a file named My 1999 Budget and try to save another file with the name MY 1999 BUDGET, Excel asks whether you want to overwrite the original file.

If you plan to share your files with others who use Excel 5 or earlier, you should make sure that the filename is no longer than eight characters, with no spaces. Otherwise, the filename will appear rather strange. For example, a file named My 1999 Budget will appear as MY1999~1.XLS, because Windows assigns every file an eight-character filename to be compatible with pre-Windows 95 operating systems.

The default file location

When you save a workbook file for the first time, the Save As dialog box proposes a folder in which to save it. Normally, this is the Personal folder (located within your \Windows folder). If you want, you can change the default file location. To do so, choose Tools ➪ Options and click the General tab in the Options dialog box. Then, enter the folder's path into the field labeled Default File Location. After doing so, the Save As dialog box defaults to this folder.

Note, however, that if you override the default folder in the Save As dialog box, the new folder becomes the default folder for the current Excel session. So, if you use the File ➪ Save As command to save another workbook, Excel proposes the new default folder.

File saving options

The Save As dialog box has a drop-down menu labeled Tools. When you click this menu, one of the options displayed is labeled General Options. Selecting this item displays the Save Options dialog box, shown in Figure 5-5. This dialog box enables you to set the following options:

✦ **Always create backup:** If this option is set, the existing version of the workbook is renamed as a BAK file before the workbook is saved. Doing this enables you to go back to the previously saved version of your workbook. Some users like to use this option because it adds another level of safety. Just be aware that your worksheet files will take up about twice as much disk space, so it's a good idea to delete the backup files occasionally.

✦ **Password to open:** If you enter a password, the password is required before anyone can open the workbook. You're asked to enter the password a second time to confirm it. Passwords can be up to 15 characters long and are case-sensitive. Be careful with this option, because it is impossible to open the workbook (using normal methods) if you forget the password.

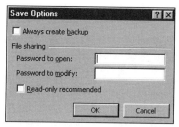

Figure 5-5: The Save Options dialog box.

✦ **Password to modify:** This option enables you to specify a password that will be required before changes to the workbook can be saved under the same filename. Use this option if you want to make sure that changes aren't made to the original version of the workbook. In other words, the workbook can be saved with a new name, but a password is required to overwrite the original version.

✦ **Read-only recommended:** If this option is checked, the file can't be saved under its original name. This is another way to ensure that a workbook file isn't overwritten.

Caution

File security is not one of Excel's strong points. Saving a workbook with a password is not a foolproof method of protecting your work. Several utilities exist that are designed to "crack" passwords in Excel files. Therefore, if you need to keep your work absolutely confidential, Excel is not your best software choice.

Saving Your Work Automatically

If you're the type who gets so wrapped up in your work that you forget to save your file, you may be interested in Excel's AutoSave feature. AutoSave automatically saves your workbooks at a prespecified interval. Using this feature requires that you load an add-in file. This add-in is included with Excel, but normally it's not installed. To load the AutoSave add-in, select Tools ➪ Add-Ins. This displays a dialog box. Click AutoSave in the list of add-ins and then click OK. The add-in will be loaded every time that you run Excel. If you no longer want to use AutoSave, repeat the process and uncheck the AutoSave add-in.

When AutoSave is loaded, the Tools menu has a new menu item: AutoSave. Selecting Tools ➪ AutoSave displays the dialog box shown in the accompanying figure.

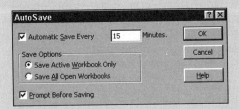

The AutoSave dialog box enables you to specify the time interval for saving. In general, you should specify a time interval equal to the maximum amount of time that you're willing to lose. For example, if you don't mind losing 15 minutes of work, set the interval for 15 minutes.

Option buttons let you choose between saving all open workbooks or just the active workbook. Another option enables you to specify whether you want to be prompted before the save takes place. If you choose to be prompted, you have the opportunity to cancel the save if you're in the middle of something important.

Caution   Using AutoSave can be helpful, but it can also be risky. When an Excel workbook is saved, the Undo stack is reset. Therefore, if you make a mistake (such as deleting a range of data) and AutoSave kicks in and saves your file, you won't be able to use Undo to reverse your mistake.

Workbook summary information

When you save a file for the first time by closing the Save As dialog box, Excel may prompt you for summary information by displaying the Properties dialog box, shown in Figure 5-6. This dialog box enables you to specify lots of descriptive information about the workbook, and also displays some details about the file.

The Properties dialog box may or may not appear, depending on how Excel is configured. To specify whether to display the Properties dialog box automatically, select Tools ➪ Options, click the General tab, and adjust the setting of the Prompt for File Properties check box.

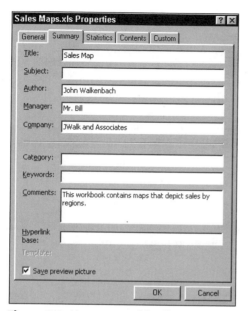

Figure 5-6: You can provide all sorts of information about your workbook in the Properties dialog box.

The Properties dialog box has the following five tabs:

✦ **General:** Displays general information about the file—its name, size, location, date created, and so on. You can't change any of the information in this panel.

✦ **Summary:** Appears by default when you first save the file. It contains nine fields of information that you can enter and modify. You can use the information in this panel to locate workbooks quickly that meet certain criteria. This is discussed later in the chapter.

✦ **Statistics:** Shows additional information about the file, and can't be changed.

✦ **Contents:** Displays the names of the sheets in the workbook, arranged by sheet type.

✦ **Custom:** Can be quite useful if you use it consistently. Basically, it enables you to store in a sort of database a variety of information about the file. For example, if the workbook deals with a client named Smith and Jones Corp., you can keep track of this bit of information and use it to help locate the file later.

You also can access the Properties dialog box for the active workbook at any time by selecting File ➪ Properties from the menu. In addition, you can view the properties of a workbook from the Open dialog box. Right-click the file in which you're interested and choose Properties from the shortcut menu.

Saving files in older formats

If your colleagues also use Excel, you may find yourself exchanging workbook files. If so, it's important that you know which version of Excel they use. Excel 97 and Excel 2000 use the same file format, but previous versions of Excel use different file formats. Generally, newer versions of Excel can open files created in older versions, but older versions of Excel cannot open files created in newer versions.

If you send a workbook to someone who uses a version of Excel prior to Excel 97, you must remember to save the file in a format that the earlier version can read.

 Caution   Even though Excel 97 and Excel 2000 use a common file format, this does not ensure complete compatibility. If your workbook makes use of any features new to Excel 2000, these features won't be available if the file is opened in Excel 97.

Excel 5 was the first version to use multisheet workbooks. Prior to Excel 5, worksheets, chart sheets, and macro sheets were stored in separate files. Consequently, if you share a multisheet workbook with someone who still uses one of these older versions, you must save each sheet separately—and in the proper format.

The Save As dialog box has a field labeled Save as type that enables you to choose the format in which to save the file. The Excel file formats are listed in Table 5-3.

 EXCEL 2000   Excel 2000 has an option that enables you to specify the default format for saved workbooks. To change the default setting, select Tools ➪ Options, click the Transition tab, and then choose the file type from the drop-down list labeled Save Excel files as.

This is improved over the Excel 97 version of the same feature, which prompts users on every file save if this option is enabled.

Table 5-3 **Excel File Formats**	
Format	**What It Does**
Microsoft Excel Workbook	Saves the file in the standard Excel 2000 file format (which is identical to the Excel 97 file format)
Microsoft Excel 97-9 & 5.0/95 Workbook	Saves the file in a format that can be read by Excel 5 through Excel 2000
Microsoft Excel 5/95 Workbook	Saves the file in a format that can be read by both Excel 5 and Excel 95
Microsoft Excel 4.0 Worksheet*	Saves the file in a format that can be read by Excel 4
Microsoft Excel 3.0 Worksheet*	Saves the file in a format that can be read by Excel 3
Microsoft Excel 2.1 Worksheet*	Saves the file in a format that can be read by Excel 2.1

* These file formats do not support multisheet workbooks.

If you need to send a workbook with three worksheets in it to a colleague who uses Excel 4, you must save it as three separate files and make sure that you select the Microsoft Excel 4.0 Worksheet option from the Save as type drop-down box (see Figure 5-7).

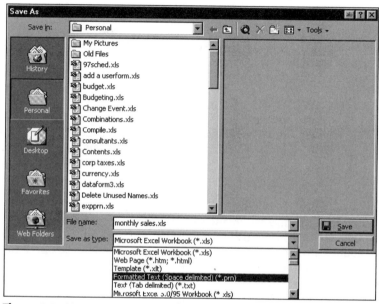

Figure 5-7: You can save an Excel workbook in a format that is readable by previous versions of Excel.

Closing Workbooks

When you're finished with a workbook, you should close it to free the memory that it uses. You can close a workbook by using any of the following methods:

✦ Use the File ➪ Close command

✦ Click the Close button in the workbook's title bar

✦ Double-click the Control icon in the workbook's title bar

✦ Press the Ctrl+F4 shortcut key

✦ Press the Ctrl+W shortcut key

If you've made any changes to your workbook since it was last saved, Excel asks whether you want to save the workbook before closing it.

Tip   To close all open workbooks, press the Shift key and choose File ➪ Close All. This command appears only when you hold down the Shift key while you click the File menu. Excel closes each workbook, prompting you for each unsaved workbook.

Using Workspace Files

As you know, you can work with any number of workbook files at a time. For example, you may have a project that uses two workbooks, and you like to arrange the windows in a certain way to make it easy to access them both. Fortunately, Excel enables you to save your entire workspace to a file. *Workspace,* as used here, means all the workbooks and their screen positions and window sizes — sort of a snapshot of Excel's current state. Then, you can open the workspace file, and Excel is set up exactly as it was when you saved your workspace.

To save your workspace, use the File ➪ Save Workspace command. Excel proposes the name resume.xlw for the workspace file. You can use this name or enter a different name in the File name field. Click the Save button, and the workspace will be saved to disk.

Caution   You need to understand that a workspace file doesn't include the workbook files themselves. It includes only the information needed to recreate the workspace. The workbooks in the workspace are saved in standard workbook files. Therefore, if you distribute a workspace file to a coworker, make sure that you also include the workbook files to which the workspace file refers.

Tip   If you save your workspace file in the XLStart folder, Excel opens the workspace file automatically when it starts up. This is handy if you tend to work with the same files every day, because essentially you can pick up where you left off the previous day.

Sharing Workbooks with Others

If your system is connected to a network, you should be aware of some other issues related to workbook files.

Cross-Reference   Chapter 21 is devoted entirety to workgroup issues.

Using Template Files

You may be able to save yourself a lot of work by using a template instead of creating a new workbook from scratch. A *template* basically is a worksheet that's all set up with formulas, ready for you to enter data.

The templates distributed with Excel are nicely formatted and relatively easy to customize. When you open a new workbook based on the template, you save the workbook to a new file. In other words, you don't overwrite the template.

Figure 5-8 shows one of the Spreadsheet Solutions templates.

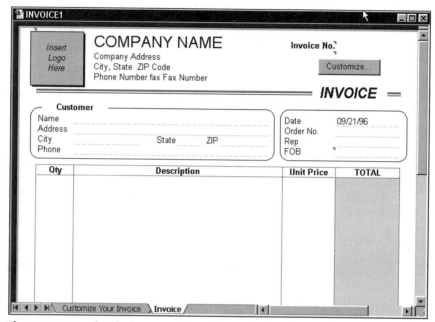

Figure 5-8: Excel includes several templates, designed to perform common tasks. This figure shows the Invoice1 template.

Excel 2000 includes three templates:

✦ **Expense Statement:** Helps you create expense report forms and a log to track them

✦ **Invoice:** Helps you create invoices

✦ **Purchase Order:** Helps you create purchase orders to send to vendors

Another template, named Village, is also available. This isn't really a template. It describes how to purchase additional templates from Village Software.

Tip   You can download additional templates from Microsoft's Web site:

    http://officeupdate.microsoft.com/

The Spreadsheet Solutions templates are handy, but be aware that they include a lot of overhead — several worksheets, dialog sheets, and a custom toolbar. Consequently, the workbooks that you generate by using these templates may be larger than you would expect. On the positive side, studying how these templates are designed can provide advanced users with some great tips.

Chapter 33 discusses templates in more detail and describes how to create your own template files.

Protecting Your Work

The final topic in this chapter offers a few words on backing up your work to protect yourself from disaster—or at least save yourself the inconvenience of repeating your work. Earlier in the chapter, you learned how to make Excel create a backup copy of your workbook when you save the file. That's a good idea, but it certainly isn't the only backup protection you should use.

If you've been around computers for a while, you probably know that hard disks aren't perfect. I've seen many hard disks fail for no apparent reason and with absolutely no advance warning. In addition, files can get corrupted—which usually makes them unreadable and essentially worthless. If a file is truly important, you need to take extra steps to ensure its safety. The following are several backup options for ensuring the safety of individual files:

✦ **Keep a backup copy of the file on the same drive.** This is essentially what happens when you select the Always create a backup option when you save a workbook file. Although this offers some protection if you create a mess of the worksheet, it won't do you any good if the entire hard drive crashes.

✦ **Keep a backup copy on a different hard drive.** This assumes, of course, that your system has more than one hard drive. This offers more protection than the preceding method, because the likelihood that both hard drives will fail is remote. If the entire system is destroyed or stolen, however, you're out of luck.

✦ **Keep a backup copy on a network server.** This assumes that your system is connected to a server on which you can write files. This method is fairly safe. If the network server is located in the same building, however, you're at risk if the entire building burns down or is otherwise destroyed.

✦ **Keep a backup copy on a removable medium.** This is the safest method. Using a removable medium, such as a floppy disk or tape, enables you physically to take the backup to another location. So, if your system (or the entire building) is damaged, your backup copy remains intact.

Most people with good backup habits acquired them because they've been burned in the past (myself included).

Windows comes with software that you can use to back up your entire system. Consult your Windows manual or online help for details.

Summary

This chapter covers the rather broad topic of files. It starts with an overview of how computers use files and narrows the scope to cover how Excel uses files. The chapter includes a discussion of the essential file operations that you perform from Excel, including creating new workbook files, opening existing files, saving files, and closing files. The chapter concludes with an introduction to the template files that are included with Excel.

✦   ✦   ✦

Entering and Editing Worksheet Data

People use spreadsheets primarily to store data and perform calculations. This chapter discusses the various types of data that you can enter into Excel.

Types of Worksheet Data

As you know, an Excel workbook can hold any number of worksheets, and each worksheet is made up of cells. A cell can hold any of three types of data:

- ✦ Values
- ✦ Text
- ✦ Formulas

A worksheet also can hold charts, maps, drawings, pictures, buttons, and other objects. These objects actually reside on the worksheet's *draw layer,* which is an invisible layer on top of each worksheet.

 Cross-Reference The draw layer is discussed in Chapter 14. This chapter is concerned only with data that you enter into worksheet cells.

Values

Values, also known as numbers, represent a quantity of some type: sales, number of employees, atomic weights, test scores, and so on. Values that you enter into cells can be used in formulas or can be used to provide the data that is used to create a chart. Values also can be dates (such as 6/9/2019) or times (such as 3:24 a.m.), and you'll see that you can manipulate these types of values quite efficiently.

Figure 6-1 shows a worksheet with some values entered in it.

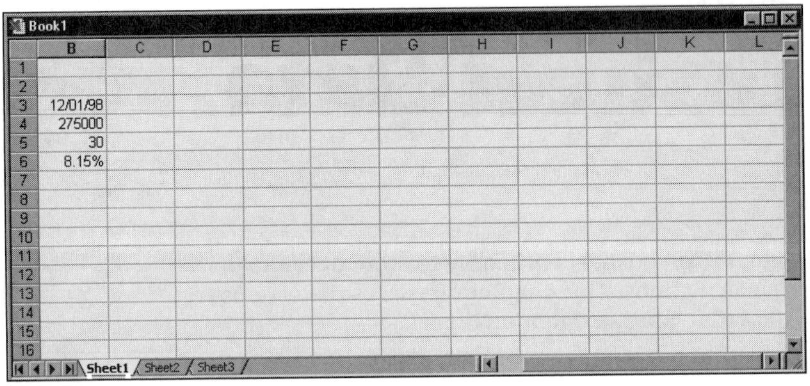

Figure 6-1: Values entered in a worksheet.

Text

Most worksheets also include non-numeric text in some of their cells. You can insert text to serve as labels for values, headings for columns, or instructions about the worksheet. Text that begins with a number is still considered text. For example, if you enter an address such as **1425 Main St.** into a cell, Excel considers this to be text rather than a value.

Figure 6-2 shows a worksheet with text in some of the cells. In this case, the text is used to clarify what the values mean.

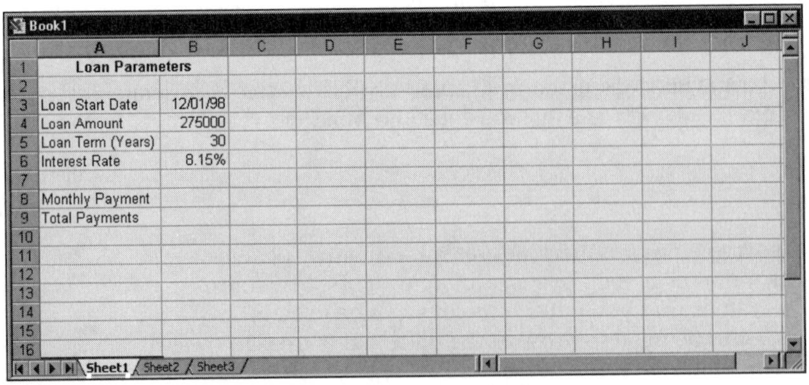

Figure 6-2: This worksheet consists of text and values.

Formulas

Formulas are what make a spreadsheet a spreadsheet — otherwise, you'd just have a strange word processor that is good at working with tables. Excel enables you to enter powerful formulas that use the values (or even text) in cells to calculate a result. When you enter a formula into a cell, the formula's result appears in the cell. If you change any of the values used by a formula, the formula recalculates and shows the new result. Figure 6-3 shows a worksheet with values, text, and formulas.

Cross-Reference
Chapter 9 discusses formulas in detail.

	A	B
1	Loan Parameters	
2		
3	Loan Start Date	12/01/98
4	Loan Amount	275000
5	Loan Term (Years)	30
6	Interest Rate	8.15%
7		
8	Monthly Payment	$ 2,046.68
9	Total Payments	$736,805.66

Figure 6-3: Cells B8 and B9 contain formulas that use the other values.

Excel's Numerical Limitations

New users often are curious about the types of values that Excel can handle. In other words, how large can numbers be? And how accurate are large numbers?

Excel's numbers are precise up to 15 digits. For example, if you enter a large value, such as 123,123,123,123,123,123 (18 digits), Excel actually stores it with only 15 digits of precision: 123,123,123,123,123,000. This may seem quite limiting, but in practice, it rarely causes any problems.

Here are some of Excel's other numerical limits:

Largest positive number: 9.9E+307

Smallest negative number: −9.9E+307

Smallest positive number: 1E-307

Largest negative number: −1E-307

These numbers are expressed in scientific notation. For example, the largest positive number is "9.9 times 10 to the 307th power."

Entering Values

Entering values into a cell is quite easy. Just move the cell pointer to the appropriate cell to make it the active cell, enter the value, and then press Enter. The value is displayed in the cell and also appears in Excel's formula bar. You can, of course, include decimal points and dollar signs when entering values and dollar signs, along with plus signs, minus signs, and commas. If you precede a value with a minus sign or enclose it in parentheses, Excel considers it to be a negative number.

Note   Sometimes, the value that you enter won't be displayed exactly as you enter it. More specifically, if you enter a large number, it may be converted to scientific notation. Notice, however, that the formula bar displays the value that you entered originally. Excel simply reformatted the value so that it would fit into the cell. If you make the column wider, the number is displayed as you entered it.

The section "Formatting values," later in this chapter, discusses the various ways to format values so that they appear differently.

Entering Text

Entering text into a cell is just as easy as entering a value: activate the cell, type the text, and then press Enter. A cell can contain a maximum of about 32,000 characters. To give you an idea of how much text can fit into a single cell, consider the fact that this entire chapter has approximately 32,000 characters.

Caution   Even though a cell can hold a huge number of characters, you'll find that it's not possible to actually display all of them.

If you type an exceptionally long text entry into a cell, the characters appear to wrap around when they reach the right edge of the window, and the formula bar expands so that the text wraps around.

What happens when you enter text that's longer than its column's current width? If the cells to the immediate right are blank, Excel displays the text in its entirety, appearing to spill the entry into adjacent cells. If an adjacent cell is not blank, Excel displays as much of the text as possible (the full text is contained in the cell; it's just not displayed). If you need to display a long text string in a cell that's adjacent to a nonblank cell, you can take one of several actions:

✦ Edit your text to make it shorter

✦ Increase the width of the column

✦ Use a smaller font

✦ Wrap the text within the cell so that it occupies more than one line

✦ Use Excel's "shrink to fit" option (see Chapter 11 for details)

Dates and Times

Often, you need to enter dates and times into your worksheet. To Excel, a date or a time is simply treated as a value — but it's formatted to appear as a date or a time.

Working with Date Values

If you work with dates and times, you need to understand Excel's date and time system. Excel handles dates by using a serial number system. The earliest date that Excel understands is January 1, 1900. This date has a serial number of 1. January 2, 1900, has a serial number of 2, and so on. This system makes it easy to deal with dates in formulas. For example, you can enter a formula to calculate the number of days between two dates.

Most of the time, you don't have to be concerned with Excel's serial number date system. You can simply enter a date in a familiar date format, and Excel takes care of the details behind the scenes. For example, if you need to enter June 1, 1999, you can simply enter the date by typing **June 1, 1999** (or use any of several different date formats). Excel interprets your entry and stores the value 36312 — which is the date serial number for that date.

Here is a sampling of the date formats that Excel recognizes. After entering a date, you can format it to appear in a different date format.

Entered into a Cell	Excel's Interpretation
6-1-99	June 1, 1999
6-1-1999	June 1, 1999
6/1/99	June 1, 1999
6/1/1999	June 1, 1999
6-1/99	June 1, 1999
June 1, 1999	June 1, 1999
Jun 1	June 1 of the current year
June 1	June 1 of the current year
6/1	June 1 of the current year
6-1	June 1 of the current year

Tip

After you enter a date, check the formula bar. If the formula bar displays exactly what you entered, Excel didn't interpret the date that you entered as a date. If the formula bar displays your entry in a format like *mm/dd/yyyy*, Excel correctly interpreted your entry as a date.

Avoid Year 2000 Surprises

Be careful when entering dates by using two digits for the year. Excel has a rather arbitrary decision point in interpreting your entries. Two-digit years between 00 and 29 are interpreted as 21st-century dates. Two-digit years between 30 and 99 are interpreted as 20th-century dates. For example, if you enter 12/5/28, Excel interprets your entry as December 5, 2028. But if you enter 12/5/30, Excel sees it as December 5, 1930. To avoid any surprises, it's a good practice to simply enter years using all four digits.

Caution   As you can see, Excel is rather smart when it comes to recognizing dates that you enter into a cell. It's not perfect, however. For example, Excel does *not* recognize any of the following entries as dates: June 1 1999, Jun-1 1999, and Jun-1/1999. Rather, it interprets these entries as text. If you plan to use dates in formulas, make sure that the date you enter is actually recognized as a date; otherwise, your formulas will produce incorrect results.

Working with Time Values

When you work with times, you simply extend Excel's date serial number system to include decimals. In other words, Excel works with times by using fractional days. For example, the date serial number for June 1, 1999, is 36312. Noon (halfway through the day) is represented internally as 36312.5.

Again, you normally don't have to be concerned with these serial numbers (or fractional serial numbers, for times). Just enter the time into a cell in a recognized format.

Here are some examples of time formats that Excel recognizes:

Entered into a Cell	Excel's Interpretation
11:30:00 am	11:30 a.m.
11:30:00 AM	11:30 a.m.
11:30 pm	11:30 p.m.
11:30	11:30 a.m.

The preceding samples don't have a day associated with them. You also can combine dates and times, however, as follows:

Entered into a Cell	Excel's Interpretation
6/1/99 11:30	11:30 a.m. on June 1, 1999

Changing or Erasing Values and Text

Not surprisingly, you can change the contents of a cell after the fact. After you enter a value or text into a cell, you can modify it in several ways:

✦ Erase the cell's contents

✦ Replace the cell's contents with something else

✦ Edit the cell's contents

Erasing the Contents of a Cell

To erase the value, text, or formula in a cell, just click the cell and press Delete. To erase more than one cell, select all the cells that you want to erase, and then press Delete. Pressing Delete removes the cell's contents, but doesn't remove any formatting (such as bold, italic, or a different number format) that you may have applied to the cell.

For more control over what gets deleted, you can use the Edit ➪ Clear command. This menu item has a submenu with four additional choices (see Figure 6-4), which are described as follows:

✦ **All:** Clears everything from the cell

✦ **Formats:** Clears only the formatting and leaves the value, text, or formula

✦ **Contents:** Clears only the cell's contents and leaves the formatting

✦ **Comments:** Clears the comment (if one exists) attached to the cell

Replacing the Contents of a Cell

To replace the contents of a cell with something else, just click the cell and type your new entry, which replaces the previous contents. Any formatting that you applied to the cell remains.

Editing the Contents of a Cell

If the cell contains only a few characters, replacing its contents by typing new data usually is easiest. But if the cell contains lengthy text or a complex formula, and you need to make only a slight modification, you probably want to edit the cell rather than reenter information.

When you want to edit the contents of a cell, you can use one of the following ways to get into cell-edit mode:

✦ **Double-click the cell.** This enables you to edit the cell contents directly in the cell.

✦ **Press F2.** This enables you to edit the cell contents directly in the cell.

✦ **Activate the cell that you want to edit and then click inside the formula bar.**
This enables you to edit the cell contents in the formula bar.

Figure 6-4: Excel provides several options for
clearing cells.

You can use whichever method you prefer. Some people find it easier to edit directly
in the cell; others prefer to use the formula bar to edit a cell. All of these methods
cause the formula bar to display two new icons, as shown in Figure 6-5. The X icon
cancels editing, without changing the cell's contents (Esc has the same effect). The
Check Mark icon completes the editing and enters the modified contents into the
cell (Enter has the same effect).

Tip   If the cell contains a formula, you can edit the formula by using any of the techniques listed previously. Or, you can take advantage of the Formula Palette. To activate the Formula Palette, click the = icon in the formula bar.

Cross-Reference The Formula Palette is explained in detail in Chapter 9.

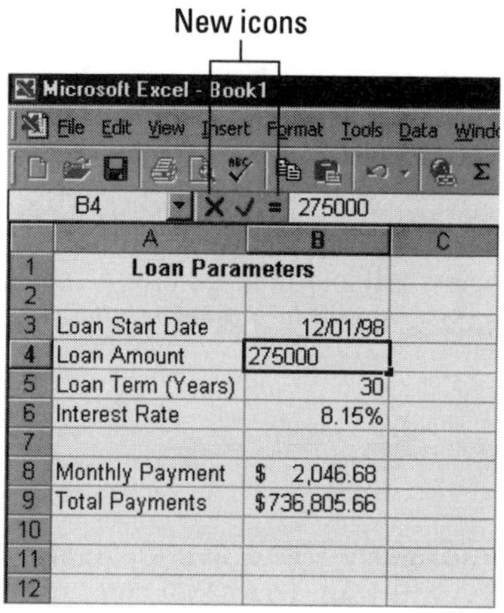

New icons

Figure 6-5: The formula bar displays two new icons when you begin editing a cell.

Editing a cell's contents works pretty much as you might expect. When you begin editing a cell, the insertion point appears as a vertical bar, and you can move the insertion point by using the direction keys. You can add new characters at the location of the insertion point. After you're in edit mode, you can use any of the following keys to move through the cell contents:

✦ **Left/right arrow:** The left- and right-arrow keys move the insertion point left or right one character, respectively, without deleting any characters.

✦ **Ctrl+left/right arrow:** Moves the insertion point one group of characters to the left or right, respectively. A group of characters is defined by a space character.

✦ **Backspace:** Erases the character to the immediate left of the insertion point.

✦ **Delete:** Erases the character to the right of the insertion point, or all selected characters.

✦ **Insert:** When you're editing, pressing the Insert key places Excel in OVR (Overwrite) mode. Rather than add characters to the cell, you *overwrite*, or replace, existing characters with new ones.

✦ **Home:** Moves the insertion point to the beginning of the cell entry.

✦ **End:** Moves the insertion point to the end of the cell entry.

✦ **Enter:** Accepts the edited data.

While editing a cell, you can use the following key combinations to select characters in the cell:

✦ **Shift+left/right arrow:** Selects characters to the left or right, respectively, of the insertion point.

✦ **Shift+Home:** Selects all characters from the insertion point to the beginning of the cell.

✦ **Shift+End:** Selects all characters from the insertion point to the end of the cell.

Tip You also can use the mouse to select characters while you're editing a cell. Just click and drag the mouse pointer over the characters that you want to select.

Formatting Values

Values that you enter into cells normally are unformatted. In other words, they simply consist of a string of numerals. Typically, you want to format the numbers so that they are easier to read or are more consistent in terms of the number of decimal places shown.

Figure 6-6 shows two columns of values. The first column consists of unformatted values. The cells in the second column have been formatted to make the values easier to read. If you move the cell pointer to a cell that has a formatted value, you find that the formula bar displays the value in its unformatted state. This is because the formatting affects only how the value is displayed in the cell.

	A	B	C
1	Unformatted Values	Formatted Values	
2	143	$143.00	
3	14533.45	14,533	
4	0.078	7.80%	
5	3.33899E+11	333,898,832,312	
6			
7	123.44	$ 123.44	
8	3982.31	$ 3,982.31	
9	-983.32	$ (983.32)	
10			
11	0.0875	1/8	
12	6195551212	(619) 555-1212	
13			
14			
15			

Figure 6-6: Unformatted values (left column) and the same values formatted.

Automatic Number Formatting

Excel is smart enough to perform some formatting for you automatically. For example, if you enter **12.2%** into a cell, Excel knows that you want to use a percentage format and applies it for you automatically. If you use commas to separate thousands (such as **123,456**), Excel applies comma formatting for you. And, if you precede your value with a dollar sign, the cell will be formatted for currency.

 A new feature in Excel 2000 makes it easier to enter values into cells formatted as a percentage. Select Tools ⇨ Options, and click the Edit tab in the Options dialog box. If the checkbox labeled Enable automatic percent entry is checked, you can simply enter a normal value into a cell formatted as a percent (for example, 12.5 for 12.5%). If this checkbox is not checked, you must enter the value as a decimal (for example, .125 for 12.5%).

Formatting Numbers Using the Toolbar

The Formatting toolbar, which is displayed, by default, to the right of the Standard toolbar, contains several buttons that let you quickly apply common number formats. When you click one of these buttons, the active cell takes on the specified number format. You also can select a range of cells (or even an entire row or column) before clicking these buttons. If you select more than one cell, Excel applies the number format to all the selected cells. Table 6-1 summarizes the formats that these Formatting toolbar buttons perform. Remember to click the arrow at the right end of the Formatting toolbar to see all of these buttons.

Table 6-1	
Number-Formatting Buttons on the Formatting Toolbar	
Button Name	*Formatting Applied*
Currency Style	Adds a dollar sign to the left, separates thousands with a comma, and displays the value with two digits to the right of the decimal point
Percent Style	Displays the value as a percentage, with no decimal places
Comma Style	Separates thousands with a comma and displays the value with two digits to the right of the decimal place
Increase Decimal	Increases the number of digits to the right of the decimal point by one
Decrease Decimal	Decreases the number of digits to the right of the decimal point by one

These five toolbar buttons actually apply predefined "styles" to the selected cells. These styles are similar to those used in word processing programs.

Cross-Reference Chapter 11 describes how to modify existing styles and create new styles.

Formatting Numbers by Using Shortcut Keys

Table 6-2 summarizes some shortcut key combinations that you can use to apply common number formatting to the selected cells or range.

Table 6-2	
Number-Formatting Keyboard Shortcuts	
Key Combination	**Formatting Applied**
Ctrl+Shift+~	General number format (that is, unformatted values)
Ctrl+Shift+$	Currency format with two decimal places (negative numbers appear in parentheses)
Ctrl+Shift+%	Percentage format, with no decimal places
Ctrl+Shift+^	Scientific notation number format, with two decimal places
Ctrl+Shift+#	Date format with the day, month, and year
Ctrl+Shift+@	Time format with the hour, minute, and a.m. or p.m.
Ctrl+Shift+!	Two decimal places, 1000 separator, and a hyphen for negative values

Other Number Formats

In some cases, the number formats that are accessible from the Formatting toolbar (or by using the shortcut key combination) are just fine. More often, however, you want more control over how your values appear. Excel offers a great deal of control over number formats.

Figure 6-7 shows Excel's Format Cells dialog box. This is a tabbed dialog box. For formatting numbers, you need to use the tab labeled Number.

Several ways exist to bring up the Format Cells dialog box. Start by selecting the cell or cells that you want to format and then do the following:

✦ Select the Format ⇨ Cells command.

✦ Right-click and choose Format Cells from the shortcut menu.

✦ Press the Ctrl+1 shortcut key.

Figure 6-7: The Number tab of the Format Cells dialog box enables you to format numbers in just about any way imaginable.

The Number tab of the Format Cells dialog box displays 12 categories of number formats from which to choose. When you select a category from the list box, the right side of the tab changes to display appropriate options. For example, Figure 6-8 shows how the dialog box looks when you click the Number category.

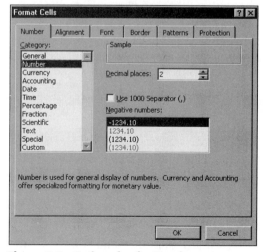

Figure 6-8: Options for the Number category.

When Numbers Appear to Add Up Incorrectly

You need to understand that applying a number format to a cell doesn't change the value — formatting changes only how the value looks. For example, if a cell contains .874543, you might format it to appear as 87%. If that cell is used in a formula, the formula uses the full value (.874543), not the displayed value (.87).

In some situations, formatting may cause Excel to display calculation results that appear incorrect, such as when totaling numbers with decimal places (see the accompanying figure). In this example, the values are formatted to display two decimal places. This formatting displays the values after they are rounded. But because Excel uses the full precision of the values in its formula, the sum of these two values appears to be incorrect (10.00 + 10.10 = 20.11). The actual values that are summed are 10.004 and 10.103.

Several solutions to this problem are available. You can format the cells to display more decimal places. Or, you can use the ROUND function on individual numbers and specify the number of decimal places Excel should round to. ROUND and other built-in functions are discussed in Chapter 10.

As another solution, you can instruct Excel to change the worksheet values to match their displayed format. To do this, choose Tools ➪ Options, select the Calculation tab, and then check the Precision as Displayed check box. Excel warns you that the underlying numbers will be permanently changed to match their appearance onscreen. If you want to select this option, backing up the worksheet on disk first is a good idea, in case you change your mind.

The Number category has three options that you can control: the number of decimal places displayed, whether to use a comma for the thousand separator, and how you want negative numbers displayed. Notice that the Negative numbers list box has four choices (two of which display negative values in red), and the choices change depending on the number of decimal places and whether you choose to use a comma to separate thousands. Also, notice that the top of the tab displays a sample of how the active cell will appear with the selected number format. After you make your choices, click OK to apply the number format to all the selected cells.

Tip

The best way to learn about number formats is to experiment. Enter some values on a worksheet and practice applying number formats.

The following are the number-format categories, along with some general comments:

✦ **General:** The default format; it displays numbers as integers, decimals, or in scientific notation if the value is too wide to fit in the cell.

✦ **Number:** Enables you to specify the number of decimal places, whether to use a comma to separate thousands, and how to display negative numbers (with a minus sign, in red, in parentheses, or in red and in parentheses).

✦ **Currency:** Enables you to specify the number of decimal places, whether to use a dollar sign, and how to display negative numbers (with a minus sign, in red, in parentheses, or in red and in parentheses). This format always uses a comma to separate thousands.

✦ **Accounting:** Differs from the Currency format in that the dollar signs always line up vertically.

✦ **Date:** Enables you to choose from 15 date formats.

✦ **Time:** Enables you to choose from eight time formats.

✦ **Percentage:** Enables you to choose the number of decimal places and always displays a percent sign.

✦ **Fraction:** Enables you to choose from among nine fraction formats.

✦ **Scientific:** Displays numbers in exponential notation (with an E): 2.00E+05 = 200,000. 2.05E+05 = 205,000. You can choose the number of decimal places to display to the left of E.

✦ **Text:** When applied to a value, causes Excel to treat the value as text (even if it looks like a value). This feature is useful for items such as part numbers.

✦ **Special:** Contains four additional number formats (Zip Code, Zip Code +4, Phone Number, and Social Security Number).

✦ **Custom:** Enables you to define custom number formats that aren't included in any of the other categories. Custom number formats are described in the next section.

Figure 6-9 shows an example from each category.

Note

If the cell displays a series of pound signs (such as ########), it means that the column is not wide enough to display the value by using the number format that you selected. Either make the column wider or change the number format.

You won't see this condition too often, because Excel usually adjusts column widths automatically to accommodate entries as you make them.

Preformatting Cells

Usually, you'll apply number formats to cells that already contain values. You also can format cells with a specific number format *before* you make an entry. Then, when you enter information, it takes on the format that you specified. You can preformat specific cells, entire rows or columns, or even the entire worksheet.

Rather than preformat an entire worksheet, however, a better idea is to change the number format for the Normal style (unless you specify otherwise, all cells use the Normal style). You can change the Normal style by selecting Format ⇨ Style. In the Style dialog box, click the Modify button and then choose the new number format for the Normal style.

Cross-Reference   Refer to Chapter 11 for more information about styles.

	A	B	C	D
1	Number Format Category	Example		
2	General	36122.8		
3	Number	36122.80		
4	Currency	$36,122.80		
5	Accounting	$ 36,122.80		
6	Date	November 23, 1998		
7	Time	7:12 PM		
8	Percentage	7.25%		
9	Fraction	1 1/2		
10	Scientific	3.61E+04		
11	Text	36122.8		
12	Special	000-03-6123		
13	Custom	Number 1234		
14				
15				
16				

Figure 6-9: Examples of values with various number formats.

Custom Number Formats

As mentioned in the previous section, the custom number format category enables you to create number formats that aren't included in any of the other categories. Excel gives you much flexibility in creating custom number formats, but doing so can be rather tricky. You construct a number format by specifying a series of codes. You enter this code sequence in the Type field after you select the Custom category on the Number tab of the Format Cells dialog box. Here's an example of a simple number format code:

```
0.000
```

This code consists of placeholders and a decimal point and tells Excel to display the value with three digits to the right of the decimal place. Here's another example:

```
00000
```

This custom number format has five placeholders and displays the value with five digits (no decimal point). This is a good format to use when the cell will hold a ZIP code (in fact, this is the code actually used by the ZIP Code format in the Special category). When you format the cell with this number format and then enter a ZIP code such as 06604 (Bridgeport, CT), the value is displayed with the leading zero. If you enter this number into a cell with the General number format, it displays as 6604 (no leading zero).

If you scroll through the list of number formats in the Custom category in the Format Cells dialog box, you see many more examples. Most of the time, you can use one of these codes as a starting point, and only slight customization will be needed.

Excel also enables you to specify different format codes for positive numbers, negative numbers, zero values, and text. You do so by separating the codes with a semicolon. The codes are arranged in the following structure:

```
Positive format; Negative format; Zero format; Text format
```

The following is an example of a custom number format that specifies a different format for each of these types:

```
[Green]General;[Red]General;[Black]General;[Blue]General
```

This example takes advantage of the fact that colors have special codes. A cell formatted with this custom number format displays its contents in a different color, depending on the value. In this case, positive numbers are green, negative numbers are red, zero is black, and text is blue.

Cross-Reference If you want to apply cell formatting automatically, such as text or background color, based on the cell's contents, a better solution is to use Excel's Conditional Formatting feature. This feature is discussed in Chapter 11.

The following number format (three semicolons) consists of no format codes for each part of the format structure—essentially hiding the contents of the cell:

```
;;;
```

Table 6-3 lists the formatting codes available for custom formats, along with brief descriptions. These codes are described further in Excel's online help.

Note Custom number formats are stored with the worksheet. To make the custom format available in a different workbook, you must copy a cell that uses the custom format to the other workbook.

Table 6-3
Codes Used to Create Custom Number Formats

Code	Comments
General	Displays the number in General format
#	Digit placeholder
0 (zero)	Digit placeholder
?	Digit placeholder
.	Decimal point
%	Percentage
,	Thousands separator
E- E+ e− e+	Scientific notation
$ − + / ( ) : space	Displays this character
\	Displays the next character in the format
*	Repeats the next character, to fill the column width
_	Skips the width of the next character
"text"	Displays the text inside the double quotation marks
@	Text placeholder
[color]	Displays the characters in the color specified
[COLOR n]	Displays the corresponding color in the color palette, where n is a number from 0 to 56
[condition value]	Enables you to set your own criteria for each section of a number format

Table 6-4 lists the codes that are used to create custom formats for dates and times.

Table 6-4
Codes Used in Creating Custom Formats for Dates and Times

Code	Comments
m	Displays the month as a number without leading zeros (1 − 12)
mm	Displays the month as a number with leading zeros (01 − 12)
mmm	Displays the month as an abbreviation (Jan − Dec)
mmmm	Displays the month as a full name (January − December)
d	Displays the day as a number without leading zeros (1 − 31)

Code	Comments
dd	Displays the day as a number with leading zeros (01–31)
ddd	Displays the day as an abbreviation (Sun–Sat)
dddd	Displays the day as a full name (Sunday–Saturday)
yy or yyyy	Displays the year as a two-digit number (00–99), or as a four-digit number (1900–2078)
h or hh	Displays the hour as a number without leading zeros (0–23), or as a number with leading zeros (00–23)
m or mm	Displays the minute as a number without leading zeros (0–59), or as a number with leading zeros (00–59)
s or ss	Displays the second as a number without leading zeros (0–59), or as a number with leading zeros (00–59)
[]	Displays hours greater than 24, or minutes or seconds greater than 60
AM/am/A/a/PM/pm/P/p	Displays the hour using a 12-hour clock; if no AM/PM indicator is used, the hour uses a 24-hour clock

On the CD-ROM

Figure 6-10 shows several examples of custom number formats, and the workbook is available at this book's Web site.

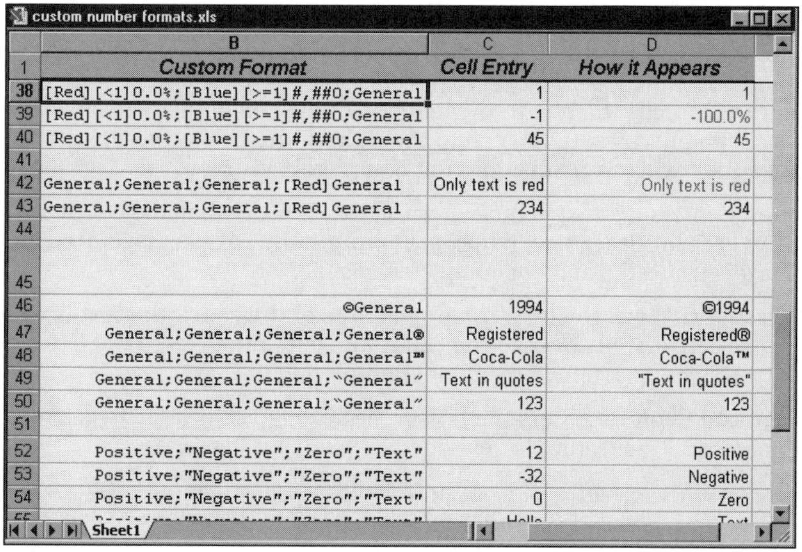

Figure 6-10: Examples of custom number formats.

Studying these examples will help you understand the concept and may give you some ideas for your own custom number formats.

Basic Cell Formatting

Whereas the preceding section discusses number formatting, this section discusses some of the basic *stylistic* formatting options available to you. These formatting techniques apply to values, text, and formulas. The options discussed in this section are available from the Formatting toolbar. Complete formatting options are available in the Format Cells dialog box, which appears when you choose Format ➪ Cells (or press Ctrl+1).

Note If you display the Standard toolbar and the Formatting toolbar side by side, you may not see many of the tools discussed in this section unless you click the arrow at the right edge of the Formatting toolbar.

Remember that the formatting you apply works with the selected cell or cells. Therefore, you need to select the cell (or range of cells) before applying the formatting.

Cross-Reference The concept of worksheet stylistic formatting is discussed in detail in Chapter 11.

Alignment

When you enter text in a cell, Excel aligns the text with the left edge of the cell. Values, on the other hand, are displayed right-aligned in the cell.

To change the alignment of a cell's contents, select the cell and then click the appropriate button on the Formatting toolbar. The relevant buttons are as follows:

✦ **Align Left:** Aligns the text to the left side of the cell. If the text is wider than the cell, it spills over to the cell to the right. If the cell to the right is not empty, the text is truncated and not completely visible.

✦ **Center:** Centers the text in the cell. If the text is wider than the cell, it spills over to cells on either side, if they are empty. If the adjacent cells aren't empty, the text is truncated and not completely visible.

✦ **Align Right:** Aligns the text to the right side of the cell. If the text is wider than the cell, it spills over to the cell to the left. If the cell to the left is not empty, the text is truncated and not completely visible.

✦ **Merge and Center:** Centers the text in the selected cells and merges the cells into one cell. This feature is described in detail in Chapter 11.

Font and Text Size

To change the font and the size of the contents of a cell or range, select the cells and then use the Font and Font Size tools on the Formatting toolbar. These tools are drop-down lists. Click the arrow on the tool to display a list of fonts or font sizes (see Figure 6-11). Then, choose the font or size that you want.

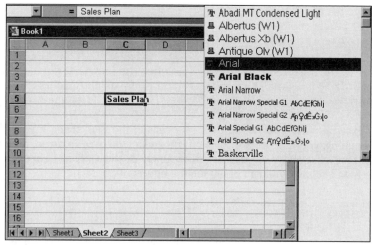

Figure 6-11: Selecting a font from the Font list.

EXCEL 2000

In Excel 2000, fonts in the Font list provide examples of the font they represent, making it easier for you to select the correct font. You can change this default behavior so that the Font list displays all fonts in Arial, as earlier versions of Excel did. Choose Tools ⇨ Customer and then click the Options tab. Remove the check from the check box labeled List font names in their font.

Attributes

The Formatting toolbar also has buttons that enable you to make the selected cells bold, italic, or underlined. As you might expect, clicking the appropriate tool makes the change. These buttons actually are toggles, so if the cell is already bold, clicking the Bold button removes the bold.

Borders

Applying a border is another type of formatting. Borders are lines drawn around all or part of selected cells or ranges. When you click the Borders button on the

Formatting toolbar, it expands to display 12 border choices in a miniature toolbar. To find the Borders tool, you may need to click the arrow at the right edge of the Formatting toolbar, to display the palette of extra tools (see Figure 6-12). You can drag the toolbar's title bar and move it anywhere you want.

 Figure 6-12: The Borders tool on the Formatting toolbar opens to display 12 border choices.

To add a border to the selected cell or cells, just click the icon that corresponds to the type of border you want. The upper-left icon removes all borders from the selected cells.

Note

Normally, Excel displays gridlines to delineate cells in the worksheet. If you add border formatting, you may want to turn off the gridline display. To do so, choose Tools ⇨ Options, click the View tab, and then uncheck the Gridlines check box. When you hide gridlines, you can easily see the effects of borders.

Colors

The Fill Color tool lets you quickly change the background color of the cell, and the Font Color tool lets you change the text color. These tools are similar to the Borders tool and also can be moved to a different location.

Data Entry Tips

This chapter wraps up with some useful tips and techniques that can make your data entry more efficient.

Validating Data Entry

In Excel 2000, you can specify the type of data that a cell or range should hold. For example, you might develop a spreadsheet that will be used by others. Assume that the worksheet has an input cell that is used in a formula. This particular cell might require a value between 1 and 12 to produce valid results in the formula. You can use the data-validation feature to display a message if the user enters a value that does not fall between 1 and 12.

To set up data validation, select the cell or range of cells that you want validated, and then choose Data ⇨ Validation. Excel displays the Data Validation dialog box, with its three tabs (see Figure 6-13).

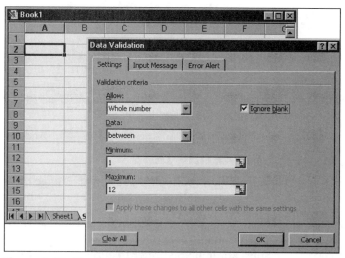

Figure 6-13: The Data Validation dialog box enables you to specify the type of data that will be entered in a cell.

✦ Click the Settings tab and specify the type of data that the cell should contain. The dialog box changes, depending on your choice in the Allow box.

✦ Click the Input Message tab and specify a message that will appear when the cell is selected (optional). The message appears from the Office Assistant (if it's displayed) or in a small pop-up box.

✦ Click the Error Alert tab and specify the message that will appear in a dialog box if invalid data is entered (optional).

You can set up data validation for as many cells as you want.

Caution   This technique isn't foolproof. The validation does not occur if the user pastes invalid data into a cell that is set up for validation.

Move the Cell Pointer After Entering Data?

Depending on how you configure Excel, pressing the Enter key after entering data into a cell may automatically move the cell pointer to another cell. Some users (like myself) find this annoying; others like it. To change this setting, choose Tools ➪ Options and click the Edit tab. The check box that controls this behavior is labeled Move Selection after Enter. You can also specify the direction in which the cell pointer moves (down, left, up, or right).

Use Arrows Instead of Enter

This chapter mentions several times that you use the Enter key when you're finished making a cell entry. Well, that's only part of the story. You also can use any of the direction keys instead of Enter. And, not surprisingly, these direction keys send you in the direction that you indicate. For example, if you're entering data in a row, press the right-arrow key rather than Enter. The other arrow keys work as expected, and you can even use PgUp and PgDn.

Selecting Cells Before Entering Data

Here's a tip that most Excel users don't know about: If you select a range of cells, Excel automatically moves the cell pointer to the next cell in the range when you press Enter. If the selection consists of multiple rows, Excel moves down the column; when it reaches the end of the selection in the column, it moves to the first selected cell in next column. To skip a cell, just press Enter without entering anything. To go backward, use Shift+Enter. If you prefer to enter the data by rows rather than by columns, use Tab rather than Enter.

If you have lots of data to enter, this technique can save you a few keystrokes — and ensure that the data you enter winds up in the proper place.

Use Ctrl+Enter for Repeated Information

If you need to enter the same data into multiple cells, your first inclination may be to enter it once and then copy it to the remaining cells. Here's a better way: Select all the cells that you want to contain the data, enter the value, text, or formula, and then press Ctrl+Enter. The single entry will be inserted into each cell in the selection.

Automatic Decimal Points

If you need to enter lots of numbers with a fixed number of decimal places, Excel has a useful tool that works like some adding machines. Select Tools ➪ Options and click the Edit tab. Check the check box labeled Fixed Decimal and make sure that it's set for two decimal places. When the Fixed Decimal option is set, Excel supplies the decimal points for you automatically. For example, if you enter **12345** into a cell, Excel interprets it as 123.45 (it adds the decimal point). To restore things back to normal, just uncheck the Fixed Decimal check box in the Options dialog box.

Note   Changing this setting doesn't affect any values that you have already entered.

Using AutoFill

Excel's AutoFill feature makes it easy to insert a series of values or text items in a range of cells. It uses the AutoFill handle (the small box at the lower left of the active cell). You can drag the AutoFill handle to copy the cell or automatically complete a series.

Cross-Reference

Chapter 7 discusses AutoFill in detail.

Using AutoComplete

With AutoComplete, you type the first few letters of a text entry into a cell, and Excel automatically completes the entry, based on other entries that you've already made in the column. If your data entry task involves repetitious text, this feature is for you.

Here's how it works. Suppose that you're entering product information in a column. One of your products is named *Widgets*. The first time that you enter *Widgets* into a cell, Excel remembers it. Later, when you start typing *Widgets* in that same column, Excel recognizes it by the first few letters and finishes typing it for you. Just press Enter and you're done. It also changes the case of letters for you automatically. If you start entering *widget* (with a lowercase *w*) in the second entry, Excel makes the *w* uppercase, to be consistent with the previous entry in the column.

Besides reducing typing, this feature also ensures that your entries are spelled correctly and are consistent.

Tip

You also can access a mouse-oriented version of this feature by right-clicking the cell and selecting Pick from List from the shortcut menu. With this method, Excel displays a drop-down box that has all the entries in the current column; just click the one that you want.

If you find the AutoComplete feature distracting, you can turn it off on the Edit tab of the Options dialog box. Remove the check mark from the check box labeled Enable AutoComplete for Cell Values.

Entering the Current Date or Time into a Cell

Sometimes, you need to date-stamp or time-stamp your worksheet. Excel provides two shortcut keys that do this for you:

✦ **Current date:** Ctrl+; (semicolon)
✦ **Current time:** Ctrl+Shift+; (semicolon)

Forcing a New Line in a Cell

If you have lengthy text in a cell, you can force Excel to display it in multiple lines within the cell. Use Alt+Enter to start a new line in a cell. Figure 6-14 shows an example of text in a cell that is displayed in multiple lines. When you add a line break, Excel automatically changes the cell's format to Wrap Text.

Cross-Reference   Learn more about the Wrap Text formatting feature in Chapter 11.

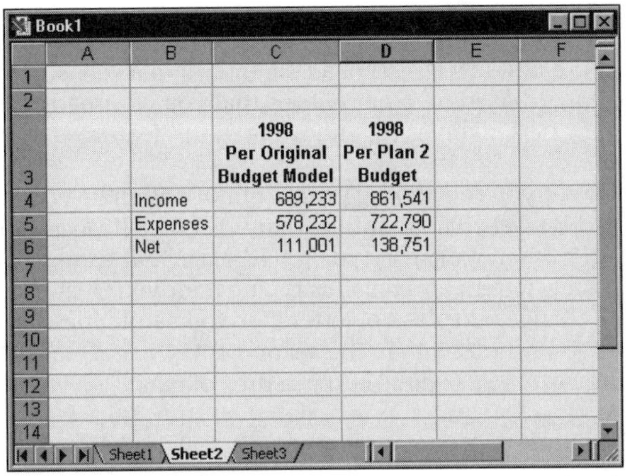

		1998 Per Original Budget Model	1998 Per Plan 2 Budget		
Income		689,233	861,541		
Expenses		578,232	722,790		
Net		111,001	138,751		

Figure 6-14: Alt+Enter enables you to force a line break in a cell.

Entering Fractions

If you want Excel to enter a fraction into a cell, leave a space between the whole number and the fraction. For example, to enter the decimal equivalent of $6\frac{7}{8}$, enter **6 7/8** and then press Enter. When you select the cell, 6.875 appears in the formula bar, and the cell entry appears as a fraction. If you have a fraction only (for example, $\frac{1}{8}$), you must enter a zero first, like this: **0 1/8**. When you select the cell and look at the formula bar, you see 0.125. In the cell, you see $\frac{1}{8}$.

Using a Data Entry Form

If you're entering data that is arranged in rows, you may find it easier to use Excel's built-in data form for data entry. Figure 6-15 shows an example of this.

Start by defining headings for the columns in the first row of your data entry range. You can always erase these entries later if you don't need them. Excel needs headings for this command to work, however. Select any cell in the header row and choose Data ⇨ Form. Excel asks whether you want to use that row for headers (choose OK). Excel then displays a dialog box similar to the one shown in Figure 6-15. You can use Tab to move between the text boxes and supply information. When you complete the data form, click the New button. Excel dumps the data into a row in the worksheet and clears the dialog box for the next row of data.

Cross-Reference

This data form feature has many other useful buttons, which are discussed further in Chapter 23.

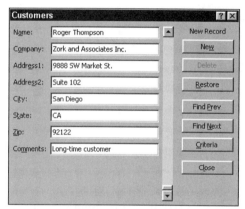

Figure 6-15: Excel's built-in data form can simplify many data entry tasks.

Using AutoCorrect for Data Entry

You can use Excel's AutoCorrect feature to create shortcuts for commonly used words or phrases. For example, if you work for a company named Consolidated Data Processing Corporation, you can create an AutoCorrect entry for an abbreviation, such as cdp. Then, whenever you type *cdp*, Excel automatically changes it to *Consolidated Data Processing Corporation*.

You can customize the AutoCorrect feature by using the Tools ⇨ AutoCorrect command. Check the option labeled Replace text as you type, and then enter your custom entries (Figure 6-16 shows an example). You can set up as many custom entries as you like.

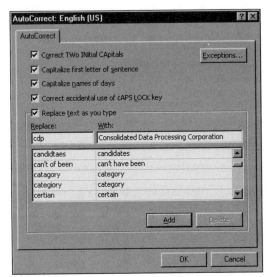

Figure 6-16: You can use Excel's AutoCorrect
feature to set up keyboard shortcuts.

Summary

A worksheet cell can contain a value, text, or a formula. This chapter focuses on
the task of entering values and formulas. It explains Excel's method of dealing with
dates and times and introduces the concept of number formatting—which makes
numbers appear differently, but doesn't affect their actual value. This chapter also
discusses common editing techniques and basic stylistic formatting, and
concludes with a series of general data entry tips.

✦   ✦   ✦

Essential Spreadsheet Operations

This chapter discusses the common spreadsheet operations that you need to know. A thorough knowledge of these procedures will help you to work more efficiently.

Working with Worksheets

When you open a new workbook in Excel, the workbook has a designated number of worksheets in it. You can specify how many sheets each new workbook will contain. By default, this number of worksheets is three. Although empty worksheets really don't use much additional memory or disk storage space, they just get in the way. And besides, adding a new worksheet when you need one is easy. I strongly recommend that you change the default value to one worksheet. To do so, select Tools ➪ Options, select the General tab, and then change the Sheets in new workbook setting to one. After doing this, all new workbooks will have a single worksheet.

You may find it helpful to think of a workbook as a notebook and worksheets as pages in the notebook. As with a notebook, you can activate a particular sheet, add new sheets, remove sheets, copy sheets, and so on. The remainder of this section discusses the operations that you can perform with worksheets.

Activating Worksheets

At any given time, one workbook is the active workbook, and one sheet is the active sheet in the active workbook. To activate a different sheet, just click its sheet tab, located at the bottom of the workbook window. You also can use the following shortcut keys to activate a different sheet:

✦ **Ctrl+PgUp:** Activates the previous sheet, if there is one

✦ **Ctrl+PgDn:** Activates the next sheet, if there is one

If your workbook has several sheets, all tabs may not be visible. You can use the tab-scrolling buttons (see Figure 7-1) to scroll the sheet tabs.

Figure 7-1: The tab-scrolling buttons let you scroll the sheet tabs to display tabs that are not visible.

The sheet tabs share space with the worksheet's horizontal scrollbar. You also can drag the tab split box (see Figure 7-2) to display more or fewer tabs. Dragging the tab split box simultaneously changes the number of tabs and the size of the horizontal scrollbar.

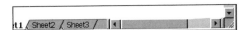

Figure 7-2: Dragging the tab split box enables you to see more (or fewer) sheet tabs.

Tip   When you right-click any of the tab-scrolling buttons, Excel displays a list of all sheets in the workbook. You can quickly activate a sheet by selecting it from the list.

Adding a New Worksheet

The following are three ways to add a new worksheet to a workbook:

✦ Select the Insert ➪ Worksheet command

✦ Press Shift+F11

✦ Right-click a sheet tab, choose the Insert command from the shortcut menu, and then select Worksheet from the Insert dialog box.

Use any of these methods, and Excel inserts a new worksheet before the active worksheet; the new worksheet becomes the active worksheet. The new worksheet, of course, has a sheet tab that displays its name.

Tip To add additional worksheets after inserting a worksheet, press Ctrl+Y (the shortcut for the Edit ➪ Repeat command) once for each additional sheet that you want to add.

Cross-Reference Chapter 34 discusses how to create and use worksheet templates. This feature enables you to add specially formatted or customized worksheets to an existing workbook.

Deleting a Worksheet

If you no longer need a worksheet, or if you want to get rid of an empty worksheet in a workbook, you can delete it in either of two ways:

✦ Select the Edit ➪ Delete Sheet command

✦ Right-click the sheet tab and choose the Delete command from the shortcut menu

Excel asks you to confirm that you want to delete the sheet.

Tip You can delete multiple sheets with a single command by selecting the sheets that you want to delete. To select multiple sheets, press Ctrl while you click the sheet tabs that you want to delete. Then, use either of the preceding methods to delete the selected sheets.

To select a group of contiguous sheets, click the first sheet tab, press Shift, and then click the last sheet tab.

Caution When you delete a worksheet, it's gone for good. This is one of the few operations in Excel that can't be undone.

Changing the Name of a Worksheet

Excel uses default names for worksheets: Sheet1, Sheet2, and so on. Providing more meaningful names for your worksheets is usually a good idea. To change a sheet's name, use any of the following methods:

✦ Choose Format ➪ sheet ➪ Rename

✦ Double-click the sheet tab

✦ Right-click the sheet tab and choose the Rename command from the shortcut menu

In any of these cases, Excel highlights the name on the sheet tab so that you can edit the name or replace it with a new name.

Sheet names can be up to 31 characters, and spaces are allowed. However, you can't use the following characters in sheet names:

:	colon
/	slash
\	backslash
?	question mark
*	asterisk

Caution   Although Excel allows you to use square brackets in a worksheet name, you should avoid doing so because it can cause problems with formulas that use external links.

Remember that the name you provide appears on the tab, and that a longer name results in a wider tab. Therefore, if you use lengthy sheet names, you won't be able to see very many sheet tabs without having to scroll.

Moving a Worksheet

Sometimes, you may want to rearrange the order of worksheets in a workbook. If you have a separate worksheet for each sales region, for example, arranging the worksheets in alphabetical order or by total sales might be helpful. You also may want to move a worksheet from one workbook to another (to move a worksheet to a different workbook, both workbooks must be open).You can move a worksheet in either of two ways:

✦ Select the Edit ⇨ Move or Copy Sheet command. This command is also available when you right-click a sheet tab.

✦ Click the sheet tab and drag it to its desired location (either in the same workbook or in a different workbook). When you drag, the mouse pointer changes to a small sheet and a small arrow guides you.

Dragging is often the easiest method, but if the workbook has many sheets, you may prefer to use the menu command. This command displays the dialog box shown in Figure 7-3, which enables you to select the workbook and the new location.

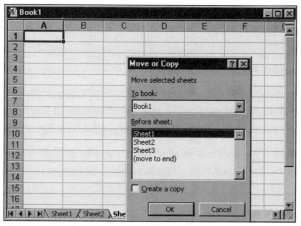

Figure 7-3: The Move or Copy dialog box.

If you move a worksheet to a workbook that already has a sheet with the same name, Excel changes the name to make it unique. For example, Sheet1 becomes Sheet1 (2).

Tip   You also can move multiple sheets at once by selecting them. Press Ctrl while you click the sheet tabs that you want to move.

Copying a Worksheet

You can make an exact copy of a worksheet — either in its original workbook or in a different workbook. The procedures are similar to those for moving a workbook:

✦ Select the Edit ➪ Move or Copy Sheet command. Select the location for the copy and make sure that the check box labeled Create a copy is checked. (The Move or Copy command is also available when you right-click a sheet tab.)

✦ Click the sheet tab, press Ctrl, and then drag it to its desired location (either in the same workbook or in a different workbook). When you drag, the mouse pointer changes to a small sheet with a plus sign on it.

If necessary, Excel changes the name of the copied sheet to make it unique within the workbook.

Note   When you copy a worksheet to a different workbook, any defined names and custom formats also get copied to the new workbook.

Hiding and Unhiding a Worksheet

In some cases, you may want to hide a worksheet. Hiding a worksheet is useful if you don't want others to see it or just want to get it out of the way. When a sheet is hidden, its sheet tab is hidden also.

To hide a worksheet, choose Format ➪ Sheet ➪ Hide. The active worksheet (or selected worksheets) will be hidden from view. Every workbook must have at least one visible sheet, so Excel won't allow you to hide all the sheets in a workbook.

To unhide a hidden worksheet, choose Format ➪ Sheet ➪ Unhide. Excel opens a dialog box that lists all hidden sheets. Choose the sheet that you want to redisplay and click OK. You can't select multiple sheets from this dialog box, so you need to repeat the command for each sheet that you want to redisplay.

Zooming Worksheets

Excel enables you to scale the size of your worksheets. Normally, everything you see onscreen is displayed at 100 percent. You can change the "zoom percentage" from 10 percent (very tiny) to 400 percent (huge). Using a small zoom percentage can help you to get a bird's-eye view of your worksheet, to see how it's laid out. Zooming in is useful if your eyesight isn't quite what it used to be and you have trouble deciphering those 8-point sales figures. Figure 7-4 shows a window zoomed to 10 percent and a window zoomed to 400 percent.

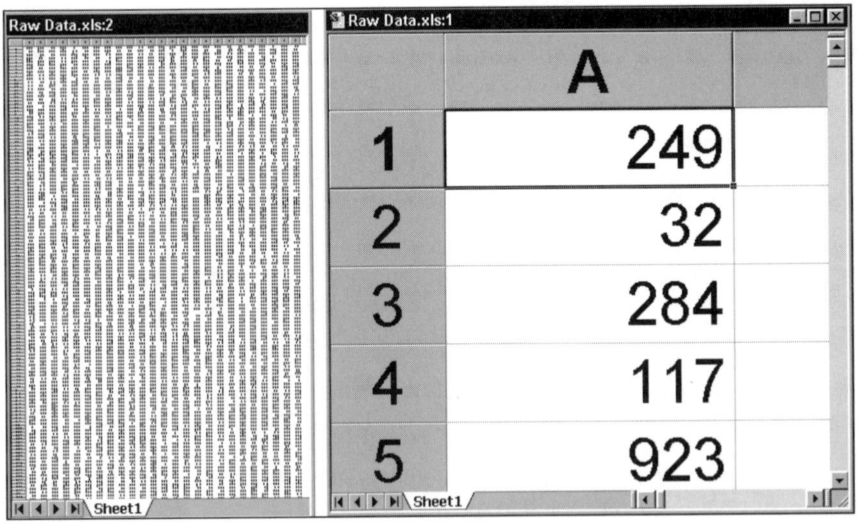

Figure 7-4: A window zoomed to 10 percent and a window zoomed to 400 percent.

You can easily change the zoom factor of the active worksheet by using the Zoom tool on the Standard toolbar. Just click the arrow and select the desired zoom factor (see Figure 7-5). Your screen transforms immediately. You can also type a zoom percentage directly into the Zoom tool box. If you choose Selection from the list, Excel zooms the worksheet to display only the selected cells (useful if you want to view only a particular range).

Figure 7-5: The Zoom tool.

Zooming affects only the active worksheet, so you can use different zoom factors for different worksheets.

If the Standard toolbar isn't displayed, you can set the zoom percentage by using the View ➪ Zoom command. This command displays the dialog box shown in Figure 7-6. You can select an option or enter a value between 10 and 400 into the edit box next to the Custom option.

Figure 7-6: The Zoom dialog box.

Note   The zoom factor affects only how Excel displays the worksheet onscreen. Zooming has no effect on how the worksheet appears when you print it.

Cross-Reference   Excel contains separate options for changing the size of your printed output (use the File ➪ Page Setup command). See Chapter 12 for details.

Cross-Reference If your worksheet uses named ranges (refer to Chapter 8), you'll find that zooming your worksheet to 39 percent or less displays the name of the range overlaid on the cells. This is useful for getting an overview of how a worksheet is laid out.

If you're using a Microsoft IntelliMouse (or a compatible wheel mouse), you can change the zoom factor by pressing Ctrl while you spin the mouse wheel. Each spin changes the zoom factor by 15 percent (but you can't zoom out more than 100 percent). If you find that you do a lot of zooming in, you can change the default behavior for the mouse wheel from scrolling to zooming. To change the default, select Tools ➪ Options, click the General tab, and then select the Zoom on roll with IntelliMouse check box. After you make this change, you can zoom by spinning the wheel and you won't have to press Ctrl.

Views, Split Sheets, and Frozen Panes

As you add more information to a worksheet, you may find that it gets more difficult to navigate and locate what you want. Excel includes a few options that enable you to view your sheet, and sometimes multiple sheets, more efficiently. This section discusses a few additional worksheet options at your disposal.

Multiple Views

Sometimes, you may want to view two different parts of a worksheet simultaneously. Or, you may want to examine more than one sheet in the same workbook simultaneously. You can accomplish either of these actions by opening a new view to the workbook, using one or more additional windows.

To create a new view of the active workbook, choose Window ➪ New Window. Excel displays a new window with the active workbook, similar to Figure 7-7. Notice the text in the windows' title bars: Budget.xls:1 and Budget.xls:2.

To help you keep track of the windows, Excel appends a colon and a number to each window.

A single workbook can have as many views (that is, separate windows) as you want. Each window is independent of the others. In other words, scrolling to a new location in one window doesn't cause scrolling in the other window(s). This also enables you to display a different worksheet in a separate window. Figure 7-8 shows three views in the same workbook. Each view displays a different worksheet.

As Chapter 8 explains, displaying multiple windows for a workbook also makes it easier to copy information from one worksheet to another. You can use Excel's drag-and-drop procedures to do this.

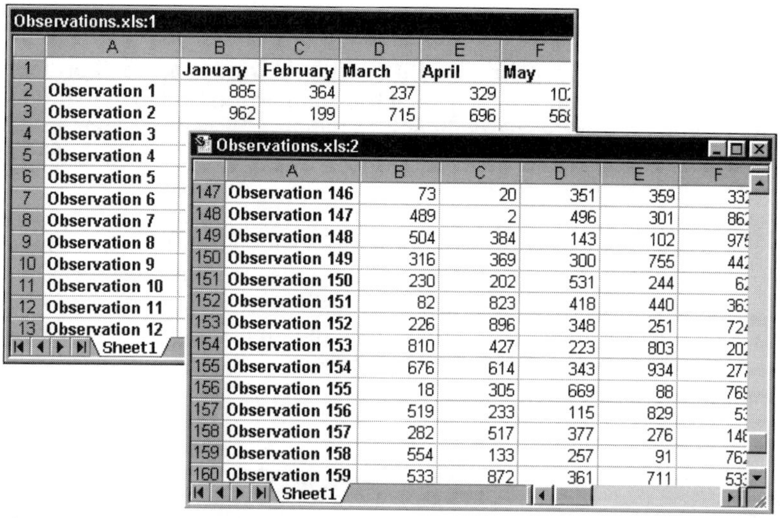

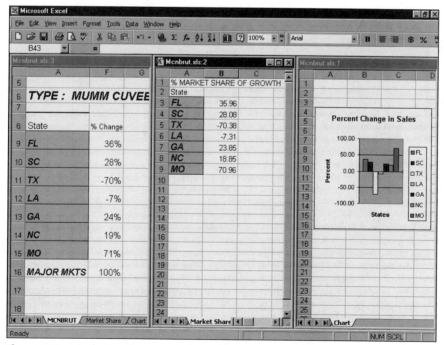

Figure 7-7: Two views of the same workbook.

Figure 7-8: Displaying three worksheets in the same workbook.

Splitting Panes

If you prefer not to clutter your screen with additional windows, Excel provides another option for viewing multiple parts of the same worksheet. The Window ⇨ Split command splits the active worksheet into two or four separate panes. The split occurs at the location of the cell pointer. You can use the mouse to drag the individual panes to resize them.

Figure 7-9 shows a worksheet split into four panes. Notice that row numbers and column letters aren't continuous. In other words, splitting panes enables you to display in a single window widely separated areas of a worksheet. The two top-to-bottom stacked panes always have the same column headings, and the two side-by-side panes always have the same row headings. To remove the split panes, choose Window ⇨ Remove Split.

	A	B	C	D	K	L	M
		January	February	March	October	November	December
2	Observation 1	885	364		425	110	689
3	Observation 2	962	199		657	980	400
4	Observation 3	351	148		836	178	472
5	Observation 4	41	396		87	676	499
6	Observation 5	627	383		871	81	775
7	Observation 6	980	826		242	438	968
8	Observation 7	796	714		29	895	85
9	Observation 8	930	654		907	420	621
10	Observation 9	67	790		76	843	197
11	Observation 10	381	436		336	680	202
62	Observation 61	986	155		942	418	56
63	Observation 62	851	879		66	429	963
64	Observation 63	539	763		932	5	374
65	Observation 64	997	762		101	617	561
66	Observation 65	80	167		125	778	768
67	Observation 66	22	825		728	43	374
68	Observation 67	202	651		224	337	500
69	Observation 68	744	381		525	762	403
70	Observation 69	33	384		80	290	292
71	Observation 70	828	861		983	334	238

Observations.xls — Sheet1

Figure 7-9: This worksheet is split into four panes.

Tip   Another way to split and unsplit panes is to drag either the vertical or horizontal split bar; when you move the mouse pointer over a split bar, the mouse point changes to a pair of parallel lines with arrows pointing outward from each line. Figure 7-10 shows where these split bars are located. To remove split panes by using the mouse, drag the pane separator all the way to the edge of the window, or just double-click it.

Split bars

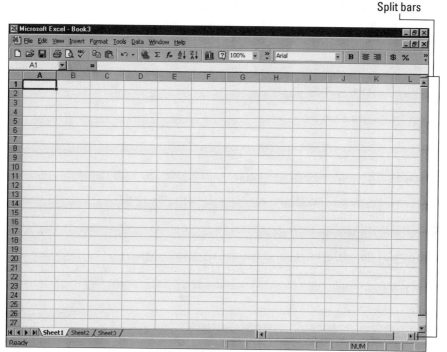

Figure 7-10: Drag these split bars to create panes.

Freezing Panes

Many worksheets, such as the one shown in Figure 7-11, are set up with row and column headings. When you scroll through such a worksheet, you can easily get lost when the row and column headings scroll out of view, as demonstrated in Figure 7-12. Excel provides a handy solution to this problem: freezing panes.

	A	B	C	D	E	F	
1		January	February	March	April	May	Jun
2	Branch 1	885	364	237	329	102	
3	Branch 2	962	199	715	696	568	
4	Branch 3	351	148	289	40	177	
5	Branch 4	41	396	72	30	908	
6	Branch 5	627	383	858	717	835	
7	Branch 6	980	826	921	171	177	
8	Branch 7	796	714	626	515	778	
9	Branch 8	930	654	911	6	107	
10	Branch 9	67	790	931	186	443	
11	Branch 10	381	436	943	208	910	
12	Branch 11	422	652	461	405	716	
13	Branch 12	818	507	586	145	809	
14	Branch 13	965	510	5	720	509	

Figure 7-11: A worksheet with row and column headings.

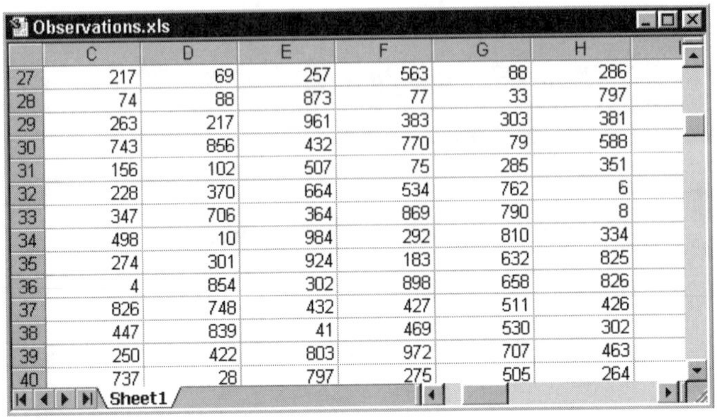

Observations.xls

	C	D	E	F	G	H
27	217	69	257	563	88	286
28	74	88	873	77	33	797
29	263	217	961	383	303	381
30	743	856	432	770	79	588
31	156	102	507	75	285	351
32	228	370	664	534	762	6
33	347	706	364	869	790	8
34	498	10	984	292	810	334
35	274	301	924	183	632	825
36	4	854	302	898	658	826
37	826	748	432	427	511	426
38	447	839	41	469	530	302
39	250	422	803	972	707	463
40	737	28	797	275	505	264

Sheet1

Figure 7-12: You can easily lose your bearings when the row and column headers scroll out of view.

Figure 7-13 shows the worksheet from the previous figure, but with frozen panes. In this case, row 1 and column A are frozen in place. This keeps the headings visible while you are scrolling through the worksheet.

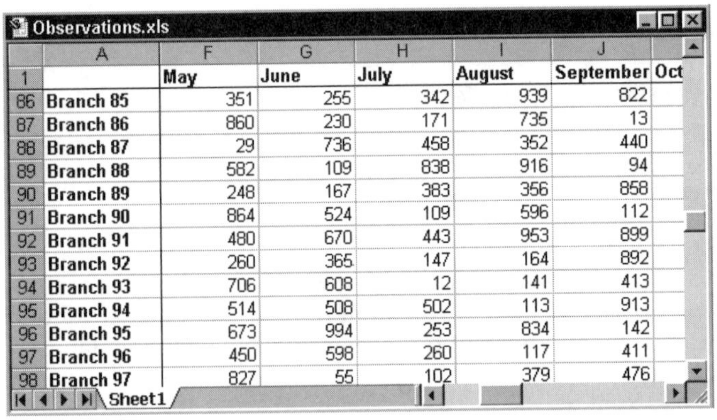

Observations.xls

	A	F	G	H	I	J
1		May	June	July	August	September Oct
86	Branch 85	351	255	342	939	822
87	Branch 86	860	230	171	735	13
88	Branch 87	29	736	458	352	440
89	Branch 88	582	109	838	916	94
90	Branch 89	248	167	383	356	858
91	Branch 90	864	524	109	596	112
92	Branch 91	480	670	443	953	899
93	Branch 92	260	365	147	164	892
94	Branch 93	706	608	12	141	413
95	Branch 94	514	508	502	113	913
96	Branch 95	673	994	253	834	142
97	Branch 96	450	598	260	117	411
98	Branch 97	827	55	102	379	476

Sheet1

Figure 7-13: A worksheet with the row and column headings frozen in place.

To freeze panes, start by moving the cell pointer to the cell below the row that you want to freeze and to the right of the column that you want to freeze. Then, select Window ➪ Freeze Panes. Excel inserts dark lines to indicate the frozen rows and columns. You'll find that the frozen row and column remain visible as you scroll throughout the worksheet. To remove the frozen panes, select Window ➪ Unfreeze Panes.

Naming Views

Some users may be interested in a feature called *named views*, which enables you to name various views of your worksheet and to switch quickly among these named views. A view includes settings for window size and position, frozen panes or titles, outlining, zoom factor, the active cell, print area, and many of the settings in the Options dialog box. Optionally, a view can include hidden print settings and hidden rows and columns. If you find that you're constantly fiddling with these settings and then changing them back, using named views can save you lots of effort.

When you select View ⇨ Custom Views, you get the dialog box shown in the accompanying figure.

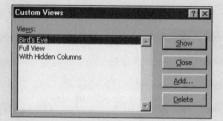

The Custom Views dialog box displays a list of all named views. To select a particular view, just select it from the list and click the Show button. To add a view, click the Add button and provide a name. To delete a named view from the list, click the Delete button.

Working with Rows and Columns

Every worksheet has exactly 65,536 rows and 256 columns. A nice feature would be the capability to specify the number of rows and columns for each worksheet, but these values are fixed and you can't change them. This section discusses some worksheet operations that involve rows and columns.

Inserting Rows and Columns

Although the number of rows and columns in a worksheet is fixed, you can still insert and delete rows and columns. These operations don't change the number of rows or columns. Rather, inserting a new row moves down the other rows to accommodate the new row. The last row is simply removed from the worksheet, if it is empty. Inserting a new column shifts the columns to the right, and the last column is removed, if it's empty.

Note
If the last row (row 65,536) is not empty, you can't insert a new row. Similarly, if the last column (column IV) contains information, Excel won't let you insert a new column. You can use this to your advantage, however. For example, if you want to ensure that no one adds new rows or columns to your worksheet, simply enter something (anything) into cell IV65536. Attempting to add a row or column displays the dialog box shown in Figure 7-14.

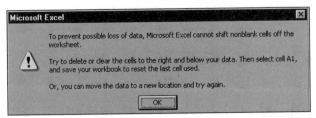

Figure 7-14: Excel's way of telling you that you can't add a new row or column.

To insert a new row or rows, you can use any of the following techniques:

✦ Select an entire row or multiple rows by clicking the row numbers in the worksheet border. Select the Insert ➪ Rows command.

✦ Select an entire row or multiple rows by clicking the row numbers in the worksheet border. Right-click and choose Insert from the shortcut menu.

✦ Move the cell pointer to the row that you want to insert and then select Insert ➪ Rows. If you select multiple cells in the column, Excel inserts additional rows that correspond to the number of cells selected in the column.

The procedure for inserting a new column or columns is the same, but you use the Insert ➪ Column command.

You also can insert cells, rather than just rows or columns. Select the range into which you want to add new cells and then select Insert ➪ Cells. To insert cells, the other cells must be shifted to the right or shifted down. Therefore, Excel displays the dialog box shown in Figure 7-15 to find out the direction in which you want to shift the cells.

Figure 7-15: When you insert cells, Excel needs to know in which direction to shift the cells to make room.

Caution

Shifting cells around may cause problems in other places in your worksheet, so use caution with the Insert ⇨ Cells command. Better yet, avoid it if you can and insert entire rows or columns. In fact, I've *never* used this command.

Deleting Rows and Columns

To delete a row or rows, use any of the following methods:

✦ Select an entire row or multiple rows by clicking the row numbers in the worksheet border and then select Edit ⇨ Delete.

✦ Select an entire row or multiple rows by clicking the row numbers in the worksheet border. Right-click and choose Delete from the shortcut menu.

✦ Move the cell pointer to the row that you want to delete and then select Edit ⇨ Delete. In the dialog box that appears, choose the Entire row option. If you select multiple cells in the column, Excel deletes all selected rows.

Deleting columns works the same way. If you discover that you accidentally deleted a row or column, select Edit ⇨ Undo (or Ctrl+Z) to undo the action.

Changing Column Widths and Row Heights

Excel provides several different ways to change the widths of columns and the height of rows.

Changing column widths

Column width is measured in terms of the number of characters that will fit into the cell's width. By default, each column's width is 8.43. This is actually a rather meaningless measurement, because in most fonts, the width of individual characters varies — the letter *i* is much narrower than the letter *W*, for example.

Tip

If pound signs (#) fill a cell, the column's width isn't wide enough to accommodate the information in the cell. Widen the column to solve the problem. For the most part, Excel automatically adjusts column width as you enter information.

You can change the width of a column or columns in several different ways, which are listed next. Before you change the width, you can select multiple columns, so that the width will be the same for all selected columns. To select multiple columns, either click and drag in the column border or press Ctrl while you select individual columns. To select all columns, click the Select All button in the upper-left corner of the worksheet border (or press Ctrl+Shift+spacebar).

✦ Drag the right-column border with the mouse until the column is the desired width.

✦ Choose Format ⇨ column ⇨ Width and enter a value in the Column Width dialog box.

✦ Choose Format ➪ column ➪ AutoFit Selection. This adjusts the width of the selected column so that the widest entry in the column fits. If you want, you can just select cells in the column, and the column is adjusted based on the widest entry in your selection.

✦ Double-click the right border of a column to set the column width automatically to the widest entry in the column.

Tip To change the default width of all columns, use the Format ➪ Column ➪ Standard Width command. This displays a dialog box into which you enter the new default column width. All columns that haven't been previously adjusted take on the new column width.

Changing row heights

Row height is measured in points (a standard unit of measurement in the printing trade). The default row height depends on the font defined in the Normal style. Excel adjusts row heights automatically to accommodate the tallest font in the row. So, if you change the font size of a cell to 20 points, for example, Excel makes the column taller so that the entire text is visible.

You can set the row height manually, however, by using any of the following techniques. As with columns, you can select multiple rows.

✦ Drag the lower row border with the mouse until the row is the desired height.

✦ Choose Format ➪ row ➪ Height and enter a value (in points) in the Row Height dialog box.

✦ Double-click the bottom border of a row to set the row height automatically to the tallest entry in the row. You also can use the Format ➪ Row ➪ AutoFit command for this.

Changing the row height is useful for spacing out rows and is preferable to inserting empty rows between lines of data. Figure 7-16 shows a simple report that uses taller rows to produce a double-spaced effect.

Hiding Rows and Columns

Excel lets you hide rows and columns. This may be useful if you don't want users to see particular information.

Tip You can also hide the rows and columns that aren't used in your worksheet — effectively making your worksheet appear smaller.

Select the row or rows that you want to hide and then choose Format ➪ RowHide. Or, select the column or columns that you want to hide and then choose Format ➪ column ➪ Hide.

You also can drag the row or column's border to hide the row or column. Drag the bottom border of a row upward or the border of a column to the left.

	A	B	C	D
1		Seminar Costs	% of Budget	
2	Printing	$1,309	19%	
3	Postage	$1,031	15%	
4	List Purchases	$1,000	14%	
5	Meeting Room Space	$544	8%	
6	Food and Beverages	$568	8%	
7	Promotion Logistics	$559	8%	
8	Marketing Materials	$554	8%	
9	Technical Services	$357	5%	
10	O&M Fees	$350	5%	
11	Market Research	$272	4%	
12	Other	$516	7%	
13	**Total**	**$7,060**	**100%**	

Budget.xls — Accounts / Seminar / Budget

Figure 7-16: Changing row heights is the best way to space out the rows in a report.

A hidden row is actually a row with its height set to zero. Similarly, a hidden column has a column width of zero. When you use the arrow keys to move the cell pointer, cells in hidden rows or columns are skipped. In other words, you can't use the arrow keys to move to a cell in a hidden row or column.

Unhiding a hidden row or column can be a bit tricky, because selecting a row or column that's hidden is difficult. The solution is to select the columns or rows that are adjacent to the hidden column or row (select at least one column or row on either side). Then, select Format ➪ Row ➪ Unhide or Format ➪ Column ➪ Unhide. Another method is to select Edit ➪ Go To (or its F5 equivalent) to activate a cell in a hidden row or column. For example, if column A is hidden, you can press F5 and specify cell A1 (or any other cell in column A) to move the cell pointer to the hidden column. Then, you can use the appropriate command to unhide the column.

Summary

This chapter delves into some important operations that all Excel users should know. It covers topics dealing with adding and removing worksheets, renaming worksheets, and moving and copying worksheets. It also discusses topics that help you control the view of your worksheet: freezing panes and splitting panes. This chapter concludes with a discussion of operations that involve entire rows or columns.

✦ ✦ ✦

Working with Cells and Ranges

This chapter discusses a variety of techniques that you use to work with cells and ranges.

Cells and Ranges

A cell is a single element in a worksheet that can hold a value, text, or a formula. A cell is identified by its *address*, which consists of its column letter and row number. For example, cell D12 is the cell in the fourth column and the twelfth row.

A group of cells is called a *range*. You designate a range address by specifying its upper-left cell address and its lower-right cell address, separated by a colon.

Here are some examples of range addresses:

A1:B1	Two cells that occupy one row and two columns
C24	A range that consists of a single cell
A1:A100	100 cells in column A
A1:D416	Cells (four rows by four columns)
C1:C65536	An entire column of cells; this range also can be expressed as C:C
A6:IV6	An entire row of cells; this range also can be expressed as 6:6
A1:IV65536	All cells in a worksheet

Alternate Cell Addresses

Typically, you reference cells by their column letter and row number (cell D16 for the cell at the intersection of the fourth column and sixteenth row, for example). You may not know it, but Excel gives you a choice in this matter. You can select Tools ➪ Options (General tab) and then choose the R1C1 reference style option. After selecting this option, the column borders in your worksheets are displayed as numbers rather than letters. Furthermore, all cell references in your formulas use this different notation.

If you find RC notation confusing, you're not alone. RC notation isn't too bad when you're dealing with absolute references. But, when relative references are involved, the brackets can drive you batty.

The numbers in the brackets refer to the relative position of the reference. For example, R[−5]C[−3] specifies the cell that's five rows above and three columns to the left. On the other hand, R[5]C[3] references the cell that's five rows *below* and three columns to the *right*. If the brackets are omitted, it specifies the same row or column: R[5]C refers to the cell five rows below in the same column.

See the following table for examples of how normal formulas translate to RC notation. These formulas are in cell B1 (otherwise known as R1C2).

Formulas Using Column Letters and Row Number	Formulas Using RC Notation
=$A$1	=R1C1
=A1+A2+A3	=RC[-1]+R[1]C[-1]+R[2]C[-1]
=(A1+A2)/$A$3	=(RC[-1]+R[1]C[-1])/R3C1

Note   When you're simply navigating through a worksheet or formatting cells, you don't really need to know the range address with which you're working. Understanding cell addresses is most important when you are creating formulas, as you'll see in the next chapter.

Selecting Ranges

To perform an operation on a range of cells in a worksheet, you must select the range of cells first. For example, if you want to make the text bold for a range of cells, you must select the range and then click the Bold button on the Formatting toolbar (or, use any of several other methods to make the text bold).

When you select a range, the cells appear highlighted in light blue-gray. The exception is the active cell, which remains its normal color. Figure 8-1 shows an example of a selected range in a worksheet.

Displaying a selected range in light blue-gray is a departure from the behavior of prior versions of Excel, in which the shading of selected cells was black. Microsoft calls this new behavior "See-through View," and it makes it easier to see the actual color formatting of selected cells.

	A	B	C	D	E	F	G	H
1								
2		Jan	Feb	Mar	Apr	May	Jun	
3		$27,540	$27,540	$28,547	$27,540	$28,547	$29,750	
4		$1,234	$9,825	$8,875	$9,825	$8,875	$9,520	
5		$3,570	$3,304	$3,425	$3,304	$3,425	$3,570	
6								
7								
8								

Budget.xls

Seminar ∖ **Budget** ∕ Income ∕ Repor

Figure 8-1: When you select a range, it appears highlighted, but the active cell within the range is not highlighted.

You can select a range in several ways:

✦ Use the mouse to drag, highlighting the range. If you drag to the end of the screen, the worksheet will scroll.

✦ Press the Shift key while you use the direction keys to select a range.

✦ Press F8 and then move the cell pointer with the direction keys to highlight the range. Press F8 again to return the direction keys to normal movement.

✦ Use the Edit ➪ Go To command (or press F5) and enter a range's address manually into the Go To dialog box. When you click OK, Excel selects the cells in the range that you specified.

Tip

As you're selecting a range, Excel displays the number of rows and columns in your selection in the Name box (located on the left side of the formula bar).

Selecting Complete Rows and Columns

You can select entire rows and columns in much the same manner as you select ranges, as follows:

✦ Click the row or column border to select a single row or column.

✦ To select multiple adjacent rows or columns, click a row or column border and drag to highlight additional rows or columns.

✦ To select multiple (nonadjacent) rows or columns, press Ctrl while you click the rows or columns that you want.

✦ Press Ctrl+spacebar to select a column. The column of the active cell (or columns of the selected cells) will be highlighted.

✦ Press Shift+spacebar to select a row. The row of the active cell (or rows of the selected cells) will be highlighted.

✦ Click the Select All button (or Ctrl+Shift+spacebar) to select all rows. Selecting all rows is the same as selecting all columns, which is the same as selecting all cells.

Selecting Noncontiguous Ranges

Most of the time, the ranges that you select will be *contiguous* — a single rectangle of cells. Excel also enables you to work with *noncontiguous ranges*, which consist of two or more ranges (or single cells) that are not necessarily next to each other. This is also known as a *multiple selection*. If you want to apply the same formatting to cells in different areas of your worksheet, one approach is to make a multiple selection. When the appropriate cells or ranges are selected, the formatting that you select is applied to them all. Figure 8-2 shows a noncontiguous range selected in a worksheet.

	A	B	C	D	E	F	J	N
1	Annual Sales Report							
2			Jan	Feb	Mar	Qtr 1	Qtr 2	Qtr 3
3								
4	Cars	Compact	31,735	11,566	71,639	114,940	126,076	150,046
5		Midsize	63,074	20,519	12,828	96,421	152,211	135,438
6		Full-size	45,696	77,739	76,476	199,911	178,082	90,148
7		Total Cars	140,505	109,824	160,943	411,272	456,369	375,632
8								
9	Trucks	Minivans	90,196	85,310	24,513	200,019	128,240	200,375
10		Full vans	80,260	18,206	66,115	164,581	125,146	148,991
11		Pickups	63,075	82,701	51,812	197,588	168,595	207,990
12		Total Trucks	233,531	186,217	142,440	562,188	421,981	557,356
13								
14		Total Sales	374,036	296,041	303,383	973,460	878,350	932,988
15								
16								

Figure 8-2: Excel enables you to select noncontiguous ranges, as shown here.

You can select a noncontiguous range in several ways:

✦ Hold down Ctrl while you drag the mouse to highlight the individual cells or ranges.

✦ From the keyboard, select a range as described previously (using F8 or the Shift key). Then, press Shift+F8 to select another range without canceling the previous range selections.

✦ Select Edit ➪ Go To and then enter a range's address manually into the Go To dialog box. Separate the different ranges with a comma. When you click OK, Excel selects the cells in the ranges that you specified (see Figure 8-3).

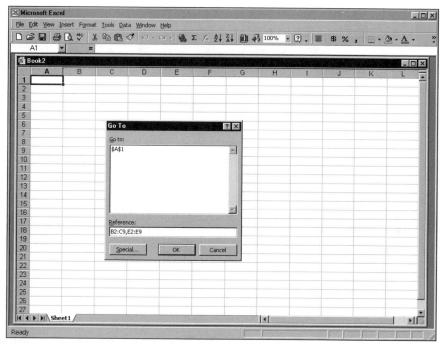

Figure 8-3: Enter a noncontiguous range by separating the ranges with a comma. This example selects a noncontiguous range made up of two ranges: B2:C9 and E2:E9.

Selecting Multisheet Ranges

So far, this discussion has focused on ranges on a single worksheet. As you know, an Excel workbook can contain more than one worksheet. And, as you might expect, ranges can extend across multiple worksheets. You can think of these as three-dimensional ranges.

Suppose that you have a workbook set up to track expenses by department. A common approach is to use a separate worksheet for each department, making it easy to organize the data. You can click a sheet tab to view the information for a particular department.

Figure 8-4 shows a workbook that has four sheets, named Total, Marketing, Operations, and Manufacturing. The sheets are laid out identically. The only difference is the values. The Total sheet contains formulas that compute the sum of the corresponding items in the three departmental worksheets.

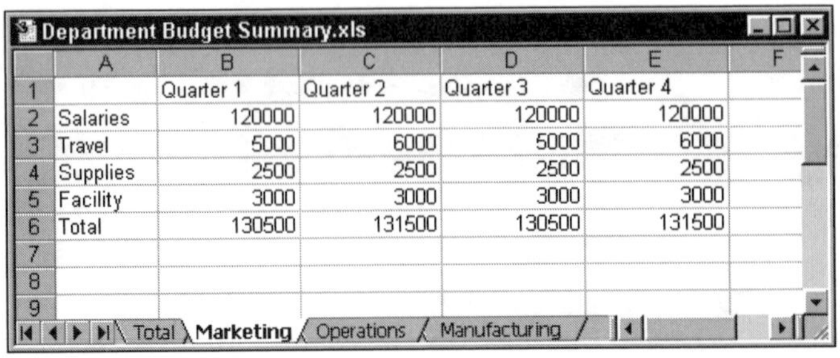

Department Budget Summary.xls

	A	B	C	D	E	F
1		Quarter 1	Quarter 2	Quarter 3	Quarter 4	
2	Salaries	120000	120000	120000	120000	
3	Travel	5000	6000	5000	6000	
4	Supplies	2500	2500	2500	2500	
5	Facility	3000	3000	3000	3000	
6	Total	130500	131500	130500	131500	
7						
8						
9						

Total | Marketing | Operations | Manufacturing

Figure 8-4: A sample workbook that uses multiple worksheets.

The worksheets in the Department Budget Summary workbook aren't formatted in any way. If you want to apply number formats, for example, one (not so efficient) approach is simply to format the values in each worksheet separately. A better technique is to select a multisheet range and format the cells in all the sheets simultaneously. The following is a step-by-step example of multisheet formatting, using the workbook shown in Figure 8-4.

1. Activate the Total worksheet.
2. Select the range B2:E6.
3. Press Shift and click the sheet tab labeled Manufacturing. This selects all worksheets between the active worksheet (Totals) and the sheet tab that you click—in essence, a three-dimensional range of cells (see Figure 8-5). Notice that the workbook window's title bar displays [Group]. This is a reminder that you've selected a group of sheets and that you're in Group edit mode.
4. Click the Comma Style button on the Formatting toolbar. This applies comma formatting to the selected cells.
5. Click one of the other sheet tabs. This selects the sheet and also cancels Group mode; [Group] is no longer displayed in the title bar.

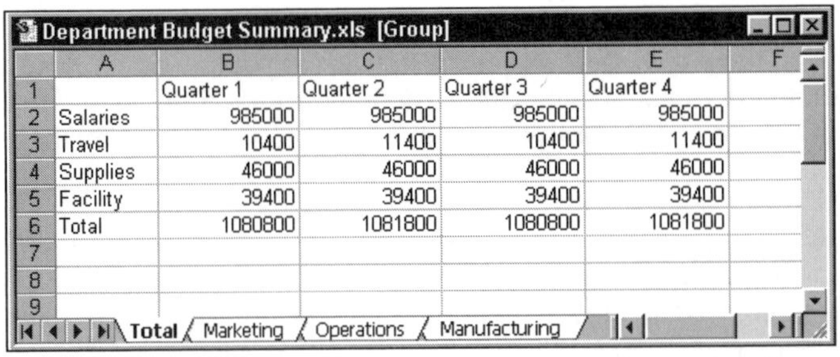

Department Budget Summary.xls [Group]

	A	B	C	D	E	F
1		Quarter 1	Quarter 2	Quarter 3	Quarter 4	
2	Salaries	985000	985000	985000	985000	
3	Travel	10400	11400	10400	11400	
4	Supplies	46000	46000	46000	46000	
5	Facility	39400	39400	39400	39400	
6	Total	1080800	1081800	1080800	1081800	
7						
8						
9						

Total | Marketing | Operations | Manufacturing

Figure 8-5: Excel in Group mode, with a three-dimensional range of cells selected.

Excel applied comma formatting to all of the values in the selected sheets.

In general, selecting a multisheet range is a simple two-step process: select the range in one sheet and then select the worksheets to include in the range. To select a group of contiguous worksheets, you can press Shift and click the sheet tab of the last worksheet that you want to include in the selection. To select individual worksheets, hold down Ctrl and click the sheet tab of each worksheet that you want to select. If all the worksheets in a workbook aren't laid out the same, you can skip the sheets that you don't want to format. When you make the selection, the sheet tabs of the selected sheets appear in reverse video, and Excel displays [Group] in the title bar.

Tip

To select all sheets in a workbook, right-click any sheet tab and choose Select All Sheets from the shortcut menu.

Special Selections

The Edit ➪ Go To command (or F5) was mentioned earlier as a way to select (or go to) a cell or range. Excel also provides a way to select only "special" cells in the workbook or in a selected range. You do this by choosing Edit ➪ Go To, which brings up the Go To dialog box. Clicking the Special button displays the Go To Special dialog box, shown in Figure 8-6.

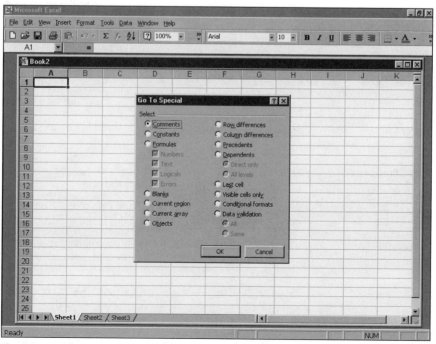

Figure 8-6: The Go To Special dialog box enables you to select specific types of cells.

After you make your choice in the dialog box, Excel selects the qualifying subset of cells in the current selection. Usually, this results in a multiple selection. If no cells qualify, Excel lets you know.

Note   If you bring up the Go To Special dialog box with only one cell selected, Excel bases its selection on the entire active area of the worksheet.

Table 8-1 offers a description of the options available in the Go To Special dialog box. Some of the options can be quite useful.

Table 8-1	
Select Special Options	
Option	**What It Does**
Comments	Selects only the cells that contain cell comments (see the next section). Ctrl+Shift+? is the shortcut.
Constants	Selects all nonempty cells that don't contain formulas. This option is useful if you have a model set up and want to clear out all input cells and enter new values. The formulas remain intact.
Formulas	Selects cells that contain formulas. Qualify this by selecting the type of result: numbers, text, logical values (TRUE or FALSE), or errors. These terms are described in the next chapter.
Blanks	Selects all empty cells.
Current Region	Selects a rectangular range of cells around the active cell. This range is determined by surrounding blank rows and columns. Ctrl+* is the shortcut.
Current Array	Selects the entire array. Arrays are covered in Chapter 20.
Objects	Selects all graphic objects on the worksheet.
Row Differences	Analyzes the selection and selects cells that are different from other cells in each row. Ctrl+\ is the shortcut.
Column Differences	Analyzes the selection and selects the cells that are different from other cells in each column. Ctrl+Shift+| is the shortcut.
Precedents	Selects cells that are referred to in the formulas in the active cell or selection. You can select either direct precedents or precedents at any level.
Dependents	Selects cells with formulas that refer to the active cell or selection. You can select either direct dependents or dependents at any level.
Last Cell	Selects the bottom-right cell in the worksheet that contains data or formatting. Ctrl+End is the shortcut.

Option	What It Does
Visible Cells Only	Selects only visible cells in the selection. This option is useful when dealing with outlines or an autofiltered list.
Conditional Formats	Selects cells that have a conditional format applied (using the Format ⇨ Conditional Formatting command).
Data Validation	Selects cells that are set up for data entry validation (using the Data ⇨ Validation command). The All option selects all such cells. The Same option selects only the cells that have the same validation rules as the active cell.

Annotating a Cell

Excel's cell-comment feature enables you to attach a comment to a cell. This feature is useful when you need to document a particular value. It's also useful to help you remember what a formula does.

Note In versions of Excel prior to Excel 97, cell comments were known as *cell notes*.

To add a comment to a cell, select the cell and then choose Insert ⇨ Comment (or Shift+F2). Excel inserts a comment that points to the active cell, as shown in Figure 8-7. Initially, the comment consists of your name. Enter the text for the cell comment and then click anywhere in the worksheet to hide the comment.

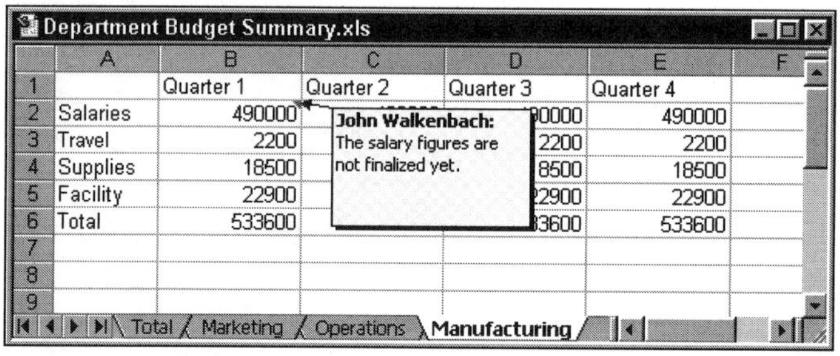

Figure 8-7: Excel enables you to add a descriptive note to a cell.

Cells that have a comment attached display a small red triangle in the upper-right corner. When you move the mouse pointer over a cell that contains a comment, the comment becomes visible.

Note Select Tools ⇨ Options (View tab) to control how cell comment indicators are displayed. You can turn off these indicators if you like.

If you want all cell comments to be visible (regardless of the location of the cell pointer), select View ➪ Comments. This command is a toggle; select it again to hide all cell comments. To edit a comment, activate the cell, right-click, and then choose Edit Comment from the shortcut menu.

To delete a cell comment, activate the cell that contains the comment, right-click, and then choose Delete Comment from the shortcut menu.

Deleting Cell Contents

To erase cells by using only the mouse, select the cell or range to be deleted. Then, click the fill handle — the small square to the lower right of the selection indicator (see Figure 8-8). When you move the mouse pointer over the fill handle, the pointer changes to a cross. As you drag up, Excel grays out the selection. Release the mouse button to erase the contents of the grayed selection.

Tip   To erase the contents of a cell or range, select the cell or range and press Delete. Or, you can select Edit ➪ Clear, which provides additional options.

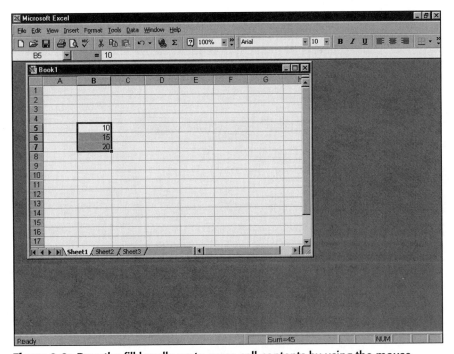

Figure 8-8: Drag the fill handle up to erase cell contents by using the mouse.

Copying a Range

Copying the contents of a cell is a very common operation. You can do any of the following:

✦ Copy a cell to another cell.

✦ Copy a cell to a range of cells. The source cell is copied to every cell in the destination range.

✦ Copy a range to another range. Both ranges must be the same size.

Note Copying a cell normally copies the cell contents, any formatting that is applied to the original cell (including conditional formatting and data validation), and the cell comment (if it has one). When you copy a cell that contains a formula, the cell references in the copied formulas are changed automatically to be relative to their new destination. More on this in the next chapter.

Copying consists of two steps (although shortcut methods exist, as you'll see later):

1. Select the cell or range to copy (the source range) and copy it to the Clipboard.

2. Move the cell pointer to the range that will hold the copy (the destination range) and paste the Clipboard contents.

When you paste information, Excel overwrites — without warning — any cells that get in the way. If you find that pasting overwrote some essential cells, choose Edit ➪ Undo (or press Ctrl+Z).

Because copying is used so often, Excel provides many different methods. I discuss each method in the following sections.

Copying by Using Toolbar Buttons

The Standard toolbar has two buttons that are relevant to copying: the Copy button and the Paste button. Clicking the Copy button transfers a copy of the selected cell or range to the Windows Clipboard and the Office Clipboard. After performing the copy part of this operation, select the cell that will hold the copy and click the Paste button.

If you're copying a range, you don't need to select an entire range before clicking the Paste button. You need only activate the upper-left cell in the destination range.

Note If you click the Copy button more than once before you click the Paste button, Excel automatically displays the Office Clipboard toolbar.

Windows Clipboard Versus Office Clipboard

The Clipboard is mentioned several times throughout this chapter. Starting with Office 2000, Windows 95 and Windows 98 have two clipboards. The original Windows Clipboard remains; whenever you cut or copy information from a Windows program, Windows stores the information on the Windows Clipboard, which is an area of memory. Each time that you cut or copy information, Windows replaces the information previously stored on the Clipboard with the new information that you cut or copied. The Windows Clipboard can store data in a variety of formats. Because information on the Clipboard is managed by Windows, it can be pasted to other Windows applications, regardless of where it originated (Chapter 29 discusses the topic of interapplication copying and pasting). Normally, you can't see information stored on the Windows Clipboard (nor would you want to).

For Windows programs other than Office programs, you can run the Clipboard Viewer program, which comes with Windows, to view the contents of the Windows Clipboard. The Clipboard Viewer may or may not be installed on your system (it is not installed, by default). The accompanying figure shows an example of this program running.

If you open the Clipboard Viewer while working in Excel, by default, you see a row/column reference rather than the actual information you copied. You can use the Clipboard Viewer's Display menu to view the data in different formats, such as the Text format shown in the accompanying figure. You also can save the Clipboard contents in a file, which you can then open at a later time.

Chapter 22 contains more information about Clipboard Viewer formats and Excel.

Office 2000 presents a new clipboard, the Office Clipboard, which is available only in Office programs. Whenever you cut or copy information in an Office program, such as Excel, the program places the information on both the Windows Clipboard and the Office Clipboard. However, the program treats information on the Office Clipboard differently than it treats information on the Windows Clipboard. Instead of replacing information on the Office Clipboard, the program appends the information to the Office Clipboard. With multiple items stored on the Clipboard, you can then paste the items either individually or as a group. You'll learn how the Office Clipboard works later in this chapter.

Copying by Using Menu Commands

If you prefer, you can use the following menu commands for copying and pasting:

✦ **Edit ➪ Copy:** Copies the selected cells to the Windows Clipboard and the Office Clipboard

✦ **Edit ➪ Paste:** Pastes the Windows Clipboard contents to the selected cell or range

You'll learn more about pasting the contents of the Office Clipboard later in this chapter.

Copying by Using Shortcut Menus

You also can use the Copy and Paste commands on the shortcut menu, as shown in Figure 8-9. The Copy command on the shortcut menu places information on both the Windows and Office Clipboards. Select the cell or range to copy, right-click, and then choose Copy from the shortcut menu. Then, select the cell in which you want the copy to appear, right-click, and choose Paste from the shortcut menu.

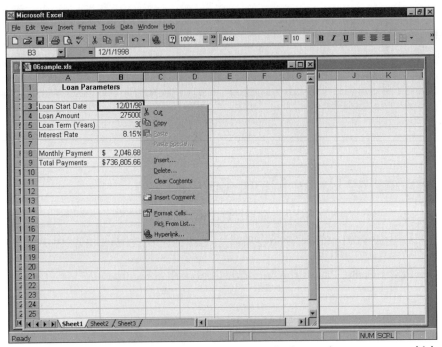

Figure 8-9: Right-clicking anywhere on the screen displays a shortcut menu, which contains Copy and Paste commands.

Copying by Using Shortcut Keys

The copy and paste operations also have shortcut keys associated with them:

✦ **Ctrl+C:** Copies the selected cells to both the Windows and Office Clipboards

✦ **Ctrl+V:** Pastes the Windows Clipboard contents to the selected cell or range

Note These shortcut keys also are used by most other Windows applications.

Copying by Using Drag and Drop

Excel also enables you to copy a cell or range by dragging. Be aware, however, that dragging and dropping *does not* place any information on either the Windows Clipboard or the Office Clipboard. Select the cell or range that you want to copy and then move the mouse pointer to one of its four borders. When the mouse pointer turns into an arrow pointing up and to the left, press Ctrl; the mouse pointer is augmented with a small plus sign. Then, simply drag the selection to its new location, while you continue to press the Ctrl key. The original selection remains behind, and Excel makes a new copy when you release the mouse button.

Note If the mouse pointer doesn't turn into an arrow when you point to the border of a cell or range, you need to make a change to your settings. Select Tools ➪ Options, click the Edit tab, and place a check mark on the option labeled Allow cell drag and drop.

Copying to Adjacent Cells

Often, you'll find that you need to copy a cell to an adjacent cell or range. This type of copying is quite common when working with formulas. For example, if you're working on a budget, you might create a formula to add the values in column B. You can use the same formula to add the values in the other columns. Rather than reenter the formula, you'll want to copy it to the adjacent cells.

Excel provides some additional options on its Edit menu for copying to adjacent cells. To use these commands, select the cell that you're copying and the cells that you are copying to (see Figure 8-10). Then, issue the appropriate command from the following list for one-step copying:

✦ **Edit ➪ Fill ➪ Down (or Ctrl+D):** Copies the cell to the selected range below

✦ **Edit ➪ Fill ➪ Right (or Ctrl+R):** Copies the cell to the selected range to the right

✦ **Edit ➪ Fill ➪ Up:** Copies the cell to the selected range above

✦ **Edit ➪ Fill ➪ Left:** Copies the cell to the selected range to the left

Note None of these commands places information on either the Windows Clipboard or the Office Clipboard.

	A	B	C	D	E	F
		Quarter 1	Quarter 2	Quarter 3	Quarter 4	
1						
2	Salaries	375000	375000	375000	375000	
3	Travel	3200	3200	3200	3200	
4	Supplies	25000	25000	25000	25000	
5	Facility	13500	13500	13500	13500	
6	Total	416700				

Department Budget Summary.xls

Total / Marketing \ Operations / Manufacturing

Figure 8-10: To copy to adjacent cells, start by selecting the cell to copy plus the cells in which you want the copy to appear.

You also can use AutoFill to copy to adjacent cells by dragging the selection's fill handle. Excel copies the original selection to the cells that you highlight while dragging. AutoFill doesn't place any information on either the Windows Clipboard or the Office Clipboard.

Cross-Reference   Chapter 9 discusses more uses for AutoFill.

Copying a Range to Other Sheets

The copy procedures described previously also work to copy a cell or range to another worksheet, even if the worksheet is in a different workbook. You must, of course, activate the other worksheet before you select the location to which you want to copy.

Excel offers a quicker way to copy a cell or range and paste it to other worksheets in the same workbook. Start by selecting the range to copy. Then, press Ctrl and click the sheet tabs for the worksheets to which you want to copy the information (Excel displays [Group] in the workbook's title bar). Select Edit ➪ Fill ➪ Across Worksheets, and a dialog box appears that asks what you want to copy (All, Contents, or Formats). Make your choice and then click OK. Excel copies the selected range to the selected worksheets; the new copy will occupy the same cells in the selected worksheets as the original occupies in the initial worksheet.

Caution   Be careful with this command, because Excel doesn't warn you if the destination cells contain information. You can quickly overwrite lots of information with this command and not even realize it.

Moving a Cell or Range

Copying a cell or range doesn't modify the cell or range that you copied. If you want to relocate a cell or range to another location, you'll find that Excel is also quite accommodating.

Recall that the Edit ➪ Copy command makes a copy of the selected cell or range and puts the copy on the Windows Clipboard and the Office Clipboard. The Edit ➪ Cut command also places the selection on both Clipboards, but the Edit ➪ Cut command also removes the contents of the selection from its original location. To move a cell or range, therefore, requires two steps:

1. Select the cell or range to cut (the source range) and "cut" it to both of the Clipboards.

2. Select the cell that will hold the moved cell or range (the destination range) and paste the contents of one of the Clipboards. The destination range can be on the same worksheet or in a different worksheet — or in a different workbook.

You also can move a cell or range by dragging it. Select the cell or range that you want to move and then slide the mouse pointer to any of the selection's four borders. The mouse pointer turns into an arrow pointing up and to the left. Drag the selection to its new location and release the mouse button. This option is similar to copying a cell, except that you don't press Ctrl while dragging; when you drag by moving, you don't place any information on either the Windows Clipboard or the Office Clipboard.

Other Cell and Range Operations

As you know, the Edit ➪ Copy command and the Edit ➪ Cut command place information on both Clipboards. Similarly, the Edit ➪ Paste command transfers the contents of the Windows Clipboard to the selected location in your worksheet.

Excel contains two more versatile ways to paste information. You can use the Office Clipboard to copy and paste multiple items, or you can use the Paste Special dialog box to paste information in distinctive ways.

Using the Office 2000 Clipboard to Paste

As mentioned earlier in this chapter, Office 2000 presents a new clipboard, the Office Clipboard, which is available only in Office programs. Whenever you cut or copy information in an Office program, such as Excel, the program places the information on both the Windows Clipboard and the Office Clipboard. However, the program treats information on the Office Clipboard differently than it treats information on the Windows Clipboard. Instead of *replacing* information on the Office Clipboard, the program *appends* the information to the Office Clipboard. With multiple items stored on the Clipboard, you can then paste the items either individually or as a group.

So far in this chapter, you've seen many ways to copy and cut information to both clipboards. Each of these techniques, however, pastes information from the Windows Clipboard, not the Office Clipboard. When would you use the Office Clipboard? When you want to store multiple items on the Office Clipboard and selectively paste them. Or, when you want to store multiple items on the Office Clipboard and paste them all simultaneously.

Note   The Office toolbar is available in *all* Office programs. Suppose that you have stored some items from Excel, Access, Outlook, PowerPoint, and Word on the Office Clipboard. You can switch to Excel and paste some or all the items from Access. And, you can switch to Word and paste some or all the items from both PowerPoint and Excel.

Suppose that you've created a worksheet like the one shown in Figure 8-11. You have sales, expense, and net information for each individual city stored on the "city" sheets (Denver, San Diego, New York, and Chicago). You want to copy the information from the "city" sheets to the summary sheet, so that you can total the information. In earlier versions of Excel, this task would have been quite tedious. With the Office Clipboard, the task is easy.

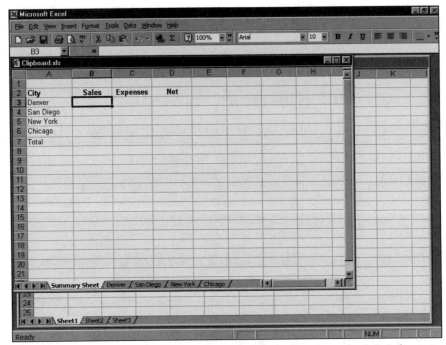

Figure 8-11: Use the Office Clipboard to copy information from the "city" sheets to the summary sheet.

The process still consists of two basic steps: copy a selection and then paste it. However, when you use the Office Clipboard, you copy several times before you paste.

Select the first cell or range that you want to copy to the Office Clipboard and copy it by using any of the techniques described earlier in this chapter: Click the Copy tool on the Standard toolbar; choose Edit ➪ Copy; press Ctrl+C; or right-click to choose Copy from the shortcut menu.

Repeat this process, selecting the next cell or range that you want to copy. As soon as you copy the information, the Office Clipboard toolbar appears, showing you the number of items that you've copied (see Figure 8-12). The Office Clipboard will hold up to 12 items; when you try to add a thirteenth item, you'll see a message asking whether you want to remove the first item that you copied or cancel copying the thirteenth item. Each item stored on the Office Clipboard toolbar contains the symbol for the program from which you copied it; if you point at one of the icons, you'll see a toolbar tip showing you a sample of the information that the item contains.

Note You can display the Office Clipboard toolbar either by clicking the Copy tool twice, without pasting, or by choosing View ➪ Toolbars ➪ Clipboard.

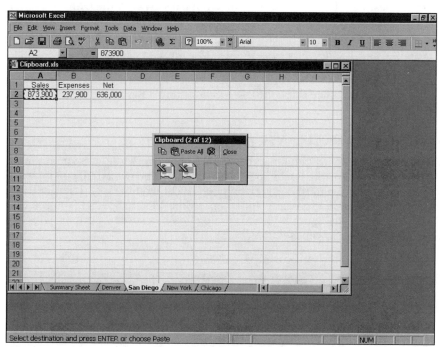

Figure 8-12: The Office Clipboard toolbar displays icons representing each item that you copy.

If necessary, continue copying information. If you want, you can use the Copy tool on the Office Clipboard toolbar; it serves the same purpose and functions in the same way as the Copy tool on the Standard toolbar.

When you're ready to paste information, select the cell into which you want to copy information. To paste an individual item, click its icon on the Office Clipboard toolbar. To paste all the items that you've copied, click the Paste All button on the Office Clipboard toolbar.

Tip Although the items appear "across" the Office Clipboard, Excel pastes them down a column when you click Paste All — even if you select a range before you click Paste All.

You can clear the contents of the Office Clipboard by clicking the Clear Clipboard tool.

Some special notes about the Office Clipboard and its functioning:

✦ Excel pastes the contents of the Windows Clipboard when you paste either by clicking the Paste tool on the Standard toolbar, by choosing Edit ➪ Paste, by pressing Ctrl+V, or by right-clicking to choose Paste from the shortcut menu.

✦ The last item that you cut or copied appears on both the Office Clipboard and the Windows Clipboard.

✦ Pasting from the Office Clipboard places that item on the Windows Clipboard. If you choose Paste All from the Office Clipboard toolbar, you paste all items stored on the Office Clipboard onto the Windows Clipboard as a single item.

✦ Clearing the Office Clipboard also clears the Windows Clipboard.

Pasting in Special Ways

The Edit ➪ Paste Special command is a much more versatile version of the Edit ➪ Paste command. For the Paste Special command to be available, you need to copy a cell or range to the Clipboards (using Edit ➪ Cut won't work). Then, select the cell in which you want to paste, and choose Edit ➪ Paste Special. You see the dialog box shown in Figure 8-13. This dialog box has several options, which are explained in the following sections.

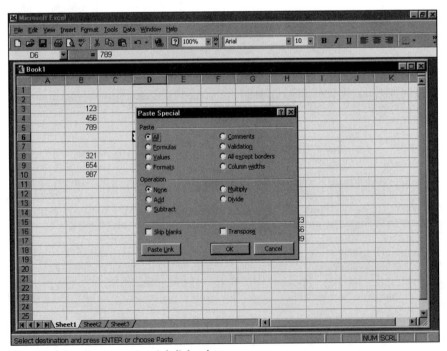

Figure 8-13: The Paste Special dialog box.

Pasting all

Selecting the All option in the Paste Special dialog box is equivalent to using the Edit ⇨ Paste command. It copies the cell's contents, formats, and data validation from the Windows Clipboard.

Pasting formulas as values

Normally, when you copy a range that contains formulas, Excel copies the formulas and automatically adjusts the cell references. The Values option in the Paste Special dialog box enables you to copy the *results* of formulas. The destination for the copy can be a new range or the original range. In the latter case, Excel replaces the original formulas by their current values.

Pasting cell formats only

If you've applied formatting to a cell or range, you can copy only the formatting and paste it to another cell or range. If you've applied lots of formatting to a cell and want to duplicate the formatting elsewhere, use the Formats option in the Paste Special dialog box to save a great deal of time.

Pasting cell comments

If you want to copy only the cell comments from a cell or range, use the Comments option in the Paste Special dialog box. This option doesn't copy cell contents or formatting.

Pasting validation criteria

If you've created validation criteria for a particular cell (by using the Data ⇨ Validation command), you can copy the validation criteria to another cell or range. Use the Validation option in the Paste Special dialog box.

Skipping borders when pasting

Often, you'll want to avoid copying borders around a cell. For example, if you have a table with a border around it, copying a cell from one of the outer cells in the table will also copy the border. To avoid pasting the border, choose the All except borders option in the Paste Special dialog box.

Pasting column widths

You can copy column width information from one column to another. Copy any cell in the column that is set at the width that you want to copy. Select a cell in the column whose width you want to set. In the Paste Special dialog box, choose the Column widths option button.

Performing mathematical operations without Formulas

The option buttons in the Operation section of the Paste Special dialog box let you perform an arithmetic operation. For example, you can copy a range to another range and select the Multiply operation. Excel multiplies the corresponding values in the source range and the destination range and replaces the destination range with the new values.

Figure 8-14 shows another example of using a mathematical operation with the Paste Special dialog box. The objective of this example is to increase the values in B4:B10 by ten percent (without using formulas). First, the contents of cell B1 were copied to the Clipboard. Then, B4:B10 was selected and the Edit ⇨ Paste Special command was issued. Choosing the Multiply operation causes each cell in B4:B10 to be multiplied by the value on the Clipboard, effectively increasing the cell values by ten percent. You also need to select the Value option—otherwise, the cells take on the formatting of the pasted cell.

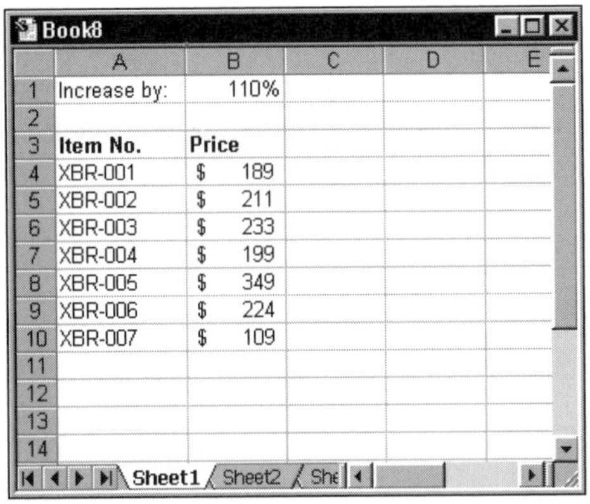

Figure 8-14: Using the Paste Special command to increase the values in a range by ten percent.

Skipping blanks when pasting

The Skip Blanks option in the Paste Special dialog box prevents Excel from overwriting cell contents in your paste area with blank cells from the copied range. This option is useful if you're copying a range to another area, but don't want the blank cells in the copied range to overwrite existing data.

Transposing a range

The Transpose option in the Paste Special dialog box changes the orientation of the copied range. Rows become columns and columns become rows. Any formulas in the copied range are adjusted so that they work properly when transposed. Note that this check box can be used with the other options in the Paste Special dialog box. Figure 8-15 shows an example of a horizontal range that was transposed to a vertical range.

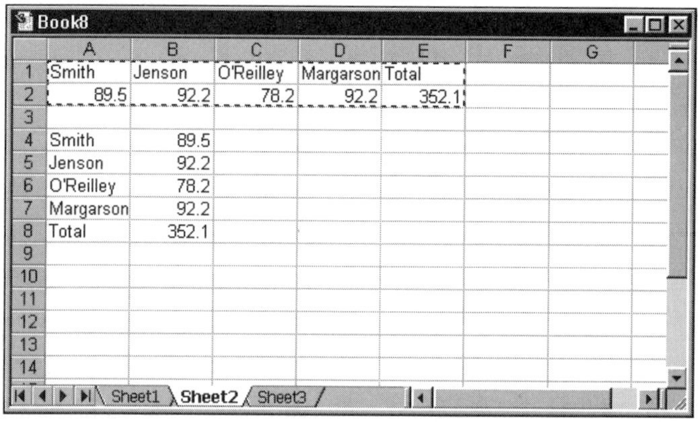

Figure 8-15: The range in A1:E2 was transposed to A4:B8.

Naming Cells and Ranges: The Basics

Dealing with cryptic cell and range addresses can sometimes be confusing (this becomes even more apparent when you deal with formulas, which are covered in the next chapter). Fortunately, Excel enables you to assign descriptive names to cells and ranges. For example, you can give a cell a name such as Interest_Rate, or you can name a range JulySales. Working with these names (rather than cell or range addresses) has several advantages, which are described next.

Advantages of Using Names

The following are a few advantages of using names:

✦ A meaningful range name (such as Total_Income) is much easier to remember than a cell address (such as AC21).

✦ Entering a name is less error-prone than entering a cell or range address.

✦ You can quickly move to areas of your worksheet either by using the Name box, located at the left side of the formula bar (click the arrow to drop down a list of defined names) or by choosing Edit ➪ Go To (or F5) and specifying the range name.

✦ When you select a named cell or range, the name appears in the Name box.

✦ Creating formulas is easier. You can paste a cell or range name into a formula either by using the Insert ➪ Name ➪ Paste command or by selecting a name from the Name box.

✦ Names make your formulas more understandable and easier to use. A formula such as =Income–Taxes is more intuitive than =D20–D40.

✦ Macros are easier to create and maintain when you use range names rather than cell addresses.

✦ You can give a name to a value or formula — even when the value or formula doesn't exist on the worksheet. For example, you can create the name Interest_Rate for a value of .075. Then, you can use this name in your formulas (more about this in the next chapter).

Valid Names

Although Excel is quite flexible about the names that you can define, it does have some rules:

✦ Names can't contain any spaces. You might want to use an underscore or a period character to simulate a space (such as Annual_Total or Annual.Total).

✦ You can use any combination of letters and numbers, but the name must begin with a letter. A name can't begin with a number (such as 3rdQuarter) or look like a cell reference (such as Q3).

✦ Symbols, except for underscores and periods, aren't allowed. Although it's not documented, I've found that Excel also allows a backslash (\ ) and question mark (?).

✦ Names are limited to 255 characters. Trust me — using a name anywhere near this length is not a good idea; in fact, it defeats the purpose of naming ranges.

✦ You can use single letters (except for R or C), but this is generally not recommended because, again, it defeats the purpose of using meaningful names.

Excel also uses a few names internally for its own use. Although you can create names that override Excel's internal names, you should avoid doing so. To be on the safe side, avoid using the following for names: Print_Area, Print_Titles, Consolidate_Area, and Sheet_Title.

Cross-Reference

You can use labels that appear as row and column headings as names; when you do, you don't actually have to define the names. This feature is most useful when you use formulas, so it is discussed in detail in Chapter 9.

Creating Names Manually

Several ways exist to create names. This section discusses two methods to create names manually.

Using the Define Name dialog box

To create a range name, start by selecting the cell or range that you want to name. Then, select Insert ➪ Name ➪ Define (or press Ctrl+F3). Excel displays the Define Name dialog box, shown in Figure 8-16.

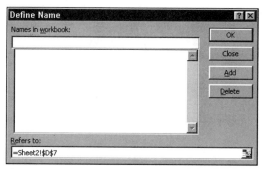

Figure 8-16: Create names for cells or ranges by using the Define Name dialog box.

Type a name in the box labeled Names in workbook (or use the name that Excel proposes, if any). The active or selected cell or range address appears in the Refers to box. Verify that the address listed is correct and then click OK to add the name to your worksheet and close the dialog box. Or, you can click the Add button to continue adding names to your worksheet. If you do this, you must specify the Refers to range either by typing an address (make sure to begin with an equal sign) or by pointing to it in the worksheet. Each name appears in the list box.

Using the Name box

A faster way to create a name is to use the Name box. Select the cell or range to name and then click the Name box and type the name. Press Enter to create the name. If a name already exists, you can't use the Name box to change the range to which that name refers. Attempting to do so simply selects the range.

Note   When you enter a name in the Name box, you *must* press Enter to actually record the name. If you type a name and then click in the worksheet, Excel won't create the name.

The Name box is a drop-down list and shows all names in the workbook (see Figure 8-17). To choose a named cell or range, click the Name box and choose the name. The name appears in the Name box, and Excel selects the named cell or range in the worksheet. Oddly enough, you can't open the Name box by using the keyboard; you must use a mouse. After you click the Name box, however, you can use the direction keys and Enter to choose a name.

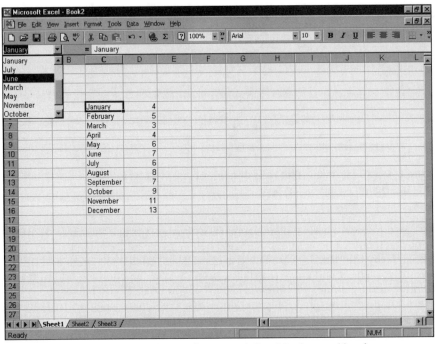

Figure 8-17: The Name box shows all names defined in the workbook.

Creating Names Automatically

You may have a worksheet that contains text that you want to use for names for adjacent cells or ranges. Figure 8-18 shows an example of such a worksheet. In this case, you might want to use the text in column A to create names for the corresponding values in column B. Excel makes this very easy to do.

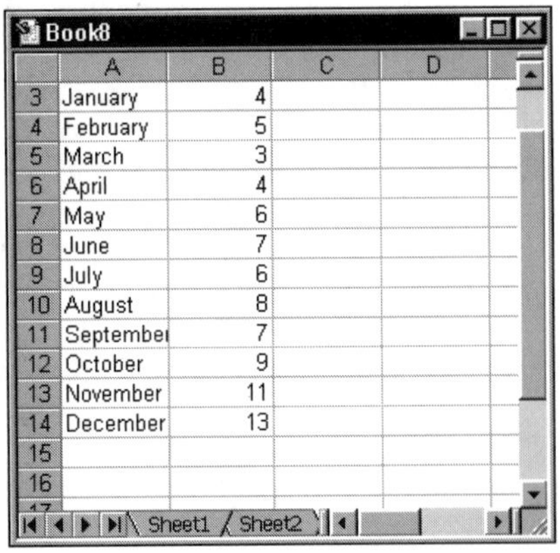

Figure 8-18: Excel makes it easy to create names by using text in adjacent cells.

To create names by using adjacent text, start by selecting the name text and the cells that you want to name (these can be individual cells or ranges of cells). The names must be adjacent to the cells that you're naming (a multiple selection is allowed). Then, choose Insert ➪ Name ➪ Create (or Ctrl+Shift+F3). Excel displays the Create Names dialog box, shown in Figure 8-19. The check marks in this dialog box are based on Excel's analysis of the selected range. For example, if Excel finds text in the first row of the selection, it proposes that you create names based on the top row. If Excel didn't guess correctly, you can change the check boxes. Click OK and Excel creates the names.

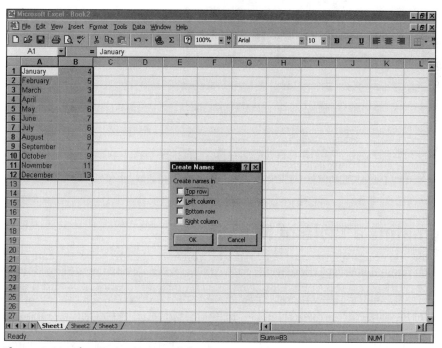

Figure 8-19: The Create Names dialog box.

Note   If the text contained in a cell would result in an invalid name, Excel modifies the name to make it valid. For example, if a cell contains the text *Net Income* (which is invalid for a name because it contains a space), Excel converts the space to an underscore character. If Excel encounters a value or a formula where text should be, however, it doesn't convert it to a valid name. It simply doesn't create a name.

Caution   You should double-check the names that Excel creates. Sometimes, the Insert ➪ Name ➪ Create command works counterintuitively.

Figure 8-20 shows a small table of text and values. If you select the entire table, choose InsertName ⇨ Create, and accept Excel's suggestions (Top Row and Left Column options), you'll find that the name Products doesn't refer to A2:A5, as you would expect, but instead refers to B2:C5. If the upper-left cell of the selection contains text and you choose the Top Row and Left Column options, Excel uses that text for the name of the entire data — excluding the top row and left column. So, before you accept the names that Excel creates, take a minute to make sure that they refer to the correct ranges.

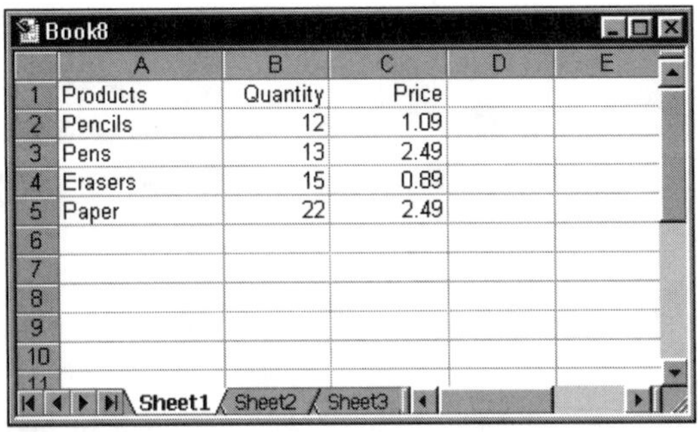

Figure 8-20: Creating names from the data in this table may produce unexpected results.

Creating a Table of Names

After you create a large number of names, you may need to know the ranges that each name defines, particularly if you're trying to track down errors or document your work. Excel lets you create a list of all names in the workbook and their corresponding addresses. To create a table of names, first move the cell pointer to an empty area of your worksheet — the table is created at the active cell position and will overwrite any information at that location. Use the Insert ⇨ Name ⇨ Paste command (or F3). Excel displays the Paste Name dialog box, shown in Figure 8-21, which lists all the defined names. To paste a list of names, click the Paste List button.

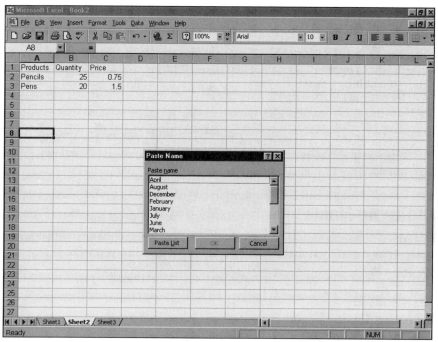

Figure 8-21: The Paste Name dialog box.

Deleting Names

If you no longer need a defined name, you can delete it. Deleting a range name *does not* delete information in the range; it can, however, make formulas in your workbook invalid.

Choose Insert ➪ Name ➪ Define to display the Define Name dialog box. Choose the name that you want to delete from the list and then click the Delete button.

Caution   Be extra careful when deleting names. If the name is used in a formula, deleting the name causes the formula to become invalid (it will display #NAME?). However, deleting a name can be undone, so if you find that formulas return #NAME? after you delete a name, select Edit ➪ Undo to get the name back.

If you delete the rows or columns that contain named cells or ranges, the names contain an invalid reference. For example, if cell A1 on Sheet1 is named Interest and you delete row 1 or column A, Interest then refers to =Sheet1!#REF! (that is, an erroneous reference). If you use Interest in a formula, the formula displays #REF.

Redefining Names

After you define a name, you may want to change the cell or range to which it refers. Select Insert ➪ Name ➪ Define to display the Define Name dialog box. Click the name that you want to change and then edit the cell or range address in the Refers to edit box. If you want to, you can click the edit box and select a new cell or range by pointing in the worksheet.

Note   Excel automatically adjusts the cells to which your names refer. For example, assume that cell A10 is named Summary. If you delete a row above row 10, Summary then refers to cell A9. This is just what you would expect to happen, so you don't need to be concerned about it.

Changing Names

Excel doesn't have a simple way to change a name once you create the name. If you create a name and then realize that it's not the name that you want — or, perhaps, that you spelled it incorrectly — you must create the new name and then delete the old name.

Learning More About Names

Excel offers some additional features with respect to using names — features unmatched in any of its competitors.

Cross-Reference   These advanced naming features are most useful when working with formulas and therefore are discussed in Chapter 9.

Summary

This chapter discusses the basic worksheet operations that involve cells and ranges. These operations include selecting, copying, moving, deleting, and working with ranges that extend across multiple worksheets in a workbook. This chapter also introduces the topic of names, an important concept that can make your worksheets more readable and easier to maintain.

✦   ✦   ✦

Creating and Using Formulas

Formulas are what make a spreadsheet so useful. Without formulas, a spreadsheet would be little more than a word processor with a very powerful table feature. A worksheet without formulas is essentially dead. Using formulas adds life and lets you calculate results from the data stored in the worksheet. This chapter introduces formulas and helps you get up to speed with these important elements.

Introducing Formulas

To add a formula to a worksheet, you enter it into a cell. You can delete, move, and copy formulas just like any other item of data. Formulas use arithmetic operators to work with values, text, worksheet functions, and other formulas to calculate a value in the cell. Values and text can be located in other cells, which makes changing data easy and gives worksheets their dynamic nature. For example, Excel recalculates formulas if the value in a cell used by the formula changes. In essence, you can see multiple scenarios quickly by changing the data in a worksheet and letting formulas do the work.

A formula entered into a cell can consist of any of the following elements:

- ✦ Operators such as + (for addition) and * (for multiplication)
- ✦ Cell references (including named cells and ranges)
- ✦ Values or text
- ✦ Worksheet functions (such as SUM or AVERAGE)

A formula can consist of up to 1,024 characters. After you enter a formula into a cell, the cell displays the result of the formula. The formula itself appears in the formula bar when you select the cell, however.

Here are a few examples of formulas:

=150*.05	Multiplies 150 times .05. This formula uses only values and isn't all that useful.
=A1+A2	Adds the values in cells A1 and A2.
=Income–Expenses	Subtracts the cell named Expenses from the cell named Income.
=SUM(A1:A12)	Adds the values in the range A1:A12.
=A1=C12	Compares cell A1 with cell C12. If they are identical, the formula returns TRUE; otherwise, it returns FALSE.

Note   Notice that formulas always begin with an equal sign so that Excel can distinguish formulas from text.

Operators Used in Formulas

Excel lets you use a variety of operators in your formulas. Table 9-1 lists the operators that Excel recognizes. In addition to these, Excel has many built-in functions that enable you to perform more operations.

Cross-Reference   These functions are discussed in detail in Chapter 10.

Table 9-1	
Operators Used in Formulas	
Operator	**Name**
+	Addition
-	Subtraction
*	Multiplication
/	Division
^	Exponentiation
&	Concatenation
=	Logical comparison (equal to)
>	Logical comparison (greater than)
<	Logical comparison (less than)
>=	Logical comparison (greater than or equal to)
<=	Logical comparison (less than or equal to)
<>	Logical comparison (not equal to)

You can, of course, use as many operators as you need (formulas can be quite complex). Figure 9-1 shows a worksheet with a formula in cell B5. The formula is as follows:

```
=(B2-B3)*B4
```

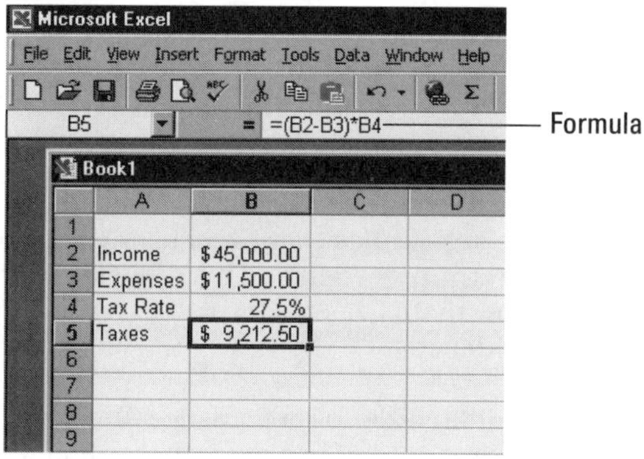

Figure 9-1: A formula that uses two operators.

In this example, the formula subtracts the value in B3 from the value in B2 and then multiplies the result by the value in B4. If the worksheet had names defined for these cells, the formula would be a lot more readable. Here's the same formula after naming the cells:

```
=(Income-Expenses)*TaxRate
```

Now, are you beginning to understand the importance of naming ranges? The following are some additional examples of formulas that use various operators.

="Part-"&"23A"	Joins *(concatenates)* the two text strings to produce *Part-23A.*
=A1&A2	Concatenates the contents of cell A1 with cell A2. Concatenation works with values as well as text. If cell A1 contains 123 and cell A2 contains 456, this formula would return the value 123456.
=6^3	Raises 6 to the third power (216).
=216^(1/3)	Returns the cube root of 216 (6).
=A1<A2	Returns TRUE if the value in cell A1 is less than the value in cell A2. Otherwise, it returns FALSE. Logical comparison operators also work with text. If A1 contained Bill and A2 contained Julia, the formula would return TRUE, because Bill comes before Julia in alphabetical order.
=A1<=A2	Returns TRUE if the value in cell A1 is less than or equal to the value in cell A2. Otherwise, it returns FALSE.

=A1<>A2   Returns TRUE if the value in cell A1 isn't equal to the value
                 in cell A2. Otherwise, it returns FALSE.

Operator Precedence

In an earlier example, parentheses are used in the formula, to control the order in which the calculations occur. The formula without parentheses looks like this:

```
=Income-Expenses*TaxRate
```

If you enter the formula without the parentheses, Excel computes the wrong answer. To understand why this occurs, you need to understand a concept called *operator precedence,* which basically is the set of rules that Excel uses to perform its calculations. Table 9-2 lists Excel's operator precedence. This table shows that exponentiation has the highest precedence (that is, it's performed first), and logical comparisons have the lowest precedence.

You use parentheses to override Excel's built-in order of precedence. Returning to the previous example, the formula that follows doesn't use parentheses and, therefore, is evaluated using Excel's standard operator precedence. Because multiplication has a higher precedence, the Expense cell is multiplied by the TaxRate cell. Then, this result is subtracted from Income. This isn't what was intended.

The correct formula, which follows, uses parentheses to control the order of operations. Expressions within parentheses are always evaluated first. In this case, Expenses is subtracted from Income and the result is multiplied by TaxRate.

```
=(Income-Expenses)*TaxRate
```

Table 9-2
Operator Precedence in Excel Formulas

Symbol	Operator	Precedence
^	Exponentiation	1
*	Multiplication	2
/	Division	2
+	Addition	3
-	Subtraction	3
&	Concatenation	4
=	Equal to	5
<	Less than	5
>	Greater than	5

You can also *nest* parentheses in formulas, which means putting parentheses inside of parentheses. If you do so, Excel evaluates the most deeply nested expressions first and works its way out. Figure 9-2 shows an example of a formula that uses nested parentheses.

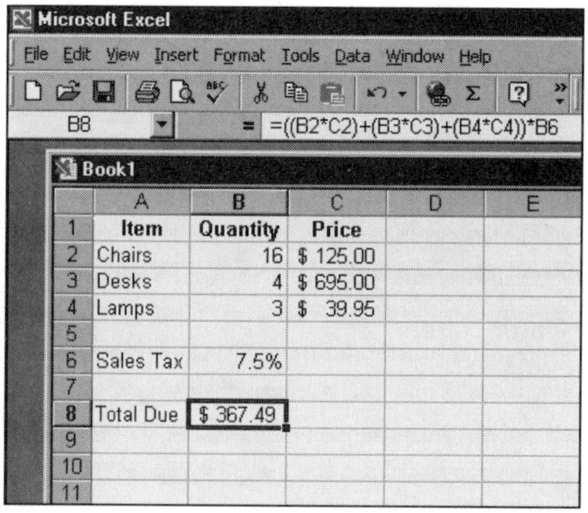

Figure 9-2: A formula with nested parentheses.

```
=((B2*C2)+(B3*C3)+(B4*C4))*B6
```

This formula has four sets of parentheses — three sets are nested inside the fourth set. Excel evaluates each nested set of parentheses and then adds up the three results. This sum is then multiplied by the value in B6.

Using parentheses liberally in your formulas is a good idea. I often use parentheses even when they aren't necessary, to clarify the order of operations and make the formula easier to read. For example, if you want to add 1 to the product of two cells, the following formula will do it:

```
=1+A1*A2
```

I find it much clearer, however, to use the following formula (with superfluous parentheses):

```
=1+(A1*A2)
```

Every left parenthesis, of course, must have a matching right parenthesis. If you have many levels of nested parentheses, it can sometimes be difficult to keep them straight. If the parentheses don't match, Excel displays a message explaining the problem and won't let you enter the formula. Fortunately, Excel lends a hand in helping you match parentheses. When you enter or edit a formula that has parentheses, pay attention to the text. When the insertion point moves over a parenthesis, Excel momentarily bolds it and its matching parenthesis. This lasts for less than a second, so be alert.

In some cases, if your formula contains mismatched parentheses, Excel may propose a correction to your formula. Figure 9-3 shows an example of the Formula AutoCorrect feature. You may be tempted simply to accept the proposed correction, but be careful — in many cases, the proposed formula, although syntactically correct, isn't the formula that you want.

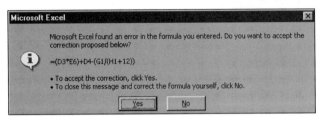

Figure 9-3: Excel's Formula AutoCorrect feature often suggests a correction to an erroneous formula.

Excel's Built-in Functions

Excel provides a bewildering number of built-in worksheet functions that you can use in your formulas. These include common functions (such as SUM, AVERAGE, and SQRT) as well as functions designed for special purposes, such as statistics or engineering. Functions can greatly enhance the power of your formulas. They can simplify your formulas and make them easier to read; in many cases, functions enable you to perform calculations that would not be possible otherwise. If you can't find a worksheet function that you need, Excel even lets you create your own custom functions.

Cross-Reference

Excel's built-in functions are discussed in the next chapter, and Chapter 35 covers the basics of creating custom functions by using VBA.

Entering Formulas

As mentioned earlier, a formula must begin with an equal sign to inform Excel that the cell contains a formula rather than text. Basically, two ways exist to enter a formula into a cell: enter it manually or enter it by pointing to cell references. Each of these methods is discussed in the following sections.

Entering Formulas Manually

Entering a formula manually involves, well, entering a formula manually. You simply type an equal sign (=), followed by the formula. As you type, the characters appear in the cell and in the formula bar. You can, of course, use all the normal editing keys when entering a formula.

Entering Formulas by Pointing

The other method of entering a formula still involves some manual typing, but you can simply point to the cell references instead of entering them manually. For example, to enter the formula =A1+A2 into cell A3, follow these steps:

1. Move the cell pointer to cell A3.

2. Type an equal sign (=) to begin the formula. Notice that Excel displays Enter in the status bar.

3. Press the up arrow twice. As you press this key, notice that Excel displays a faint moving border around the cell and that the cell reference appears in cell A3 and in the formula bar. Also notice that Excel displays Point in the status bar.

4. Type a plus sign (+). The faint border disappears and Enter reappears in the status bar.

5. Press the up arrow one more time. A2 is added to the formula.

6. Press Enter to end the formula.

Pointing to cell addresses rather than entering them manually is usually more accurate and less tedious.

 Tip　When you create a formula that refers to other cells, the cell that contains the formula has the same number format as the first cell it refers to.

Excel includes the Formula Palette feature that you can use when you enter or edit formulas. To display the Formula Palette, click the Edit Formula button in the Formula bar (the Edit Formula button looks like an equal sign). The Formula Palette lets you enter formulas manually or use the pointing techniques described previously. The Formula Palette, shown in Figure 9-4, displays the result of the formula as it's being entered. The Formula Palette usually appears directly below the edit line, but you can drag it to any convenient location (as you can see in the figure).

Edit Formula button

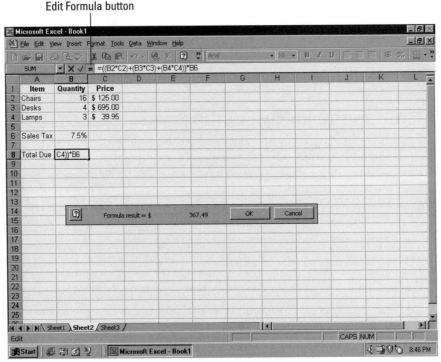

Figure 9-4: The Formula Palette displays the result of the formula as it's being entered.

Pasting Names

If your formula uses named cells or ranges, you can either type the name in place of the address or choose the name from a list and have Excel insert the name for you automatically. You have two ways available to insert a name into a formula:

✦ **Select Insert ➪ Name ➪ Paste:** Excel displays its Paste Name dialog box with all the names listed (see Figure 9-5). Select the name and click OK. Or, you can double-click the name, which inserts the name and closes the dialog box.

✦ **Press F3:** This also displays the Paste Name dialog box.

Figure 9-5: The Paste Name dialog box lets you insert a name into a formula.

Referencing Cells Outside the Worksheet

Formulas can refer to cells in other worksheets — and the worksheets don't even have to be in the same workbook. Excel uses a special type of notation to handle these types of references.

Cells in Other Worksheets

To use a reference to a cell in another worksheet in the same workbook, use the following format:

```
SheetName!CellAddress
```

In other words, precede the cell address with the worksheet name, followed by an exclamation point. Here's an example of a formula that uses a cell on the Sheet2 worksheet:

```
=A1*Sheet2!A1
```

This formula multiplies the value in cell A1 on the current worksheet by the value in cell A1 on Sheet2.

Note

If the worksheet name in the reference includes one or more spaces, you must enclose it in single quotation marks. For example, here's a formula that refers to a cell on a sheet named All Depts:

```
=A1*'All Depts'!A1
```

Cells in Other Workbooks

To refer to a cell in a different workbook, use this format:

```
=[WorkbookName]SheetName!CellAddress
```

In this case, the workbook name (in square brackets), the worksheet name, and an exclamation point precede the cell address. The following is an example of a formula that uses a cell reference in the Sheet1 worksheet in a workbook named Budget:

```
=[Budget.xls]Sheet1!A1
```

If the workbook name in the reference includes one or more spaces, you must enclose it (and the sheet name) in single quotation marks. For example, here's a formula that refers to a cell on Sheet1 in a workbook named Budget For 1999:

```
=A1*'[Budget For 1999]Sheet1'!A1
```

When a formula refers to cells in a different workbook, the other workbook doesn't need to be open. If the workbook is closed, you must add the complete path to the reference. Here's an example:

```
=A1*'C:\ MSOffice\Excel\[Budget For 1999]Sheet1'!A1
```

Cross-Reference   File linking is covered in detail in Chapter 19.

Entering References to Cells Outside the Worksheet

To create formulas that refer to cells not in the current worksheet, use the pointing technique described earlier (refer to the section "Entering Formulas by Pointing"). Excel takes care of the details regarding the workbook and worksheet references. The workbook that you're using in your formula must be open to use the pointing method.

Note   If you point to a different worksheet or workbook when creating a formula, you'll notice that Excel always inserts absolute cell references. Therefore, if you plan to copy the formula to other cells, make sure that you change the cell references to relative. This concept of absolute versus relative cell references is discussed in the following section.

Absolute Versus Relative References

You need to be able to distinguish between *relative* and *absolute cell references*. By default, Excel creates relative cell references in formulas except when the formula includes cells in different worksheets or workbooks. The distinction becomes apparent when you copy a formula to another cell.

Relative References

Figure 9-5 shows a worksheet with a formula in cell D2. The formula, which uses the default relative references, is as follows:

```
=B2*C2
```

When you copy this formula to the two cells below it, Excel doesn't produce an exact copy of the formula; rather, it generates these formulas:

✦ **Cell D3:** =B3*C3

✦ **Cell D4:** =B4*C4

Excel adjusts the cell references to refer to the cells that are relative to the new formula. Think of it like this: The original formula contained instructions to multiply the value two cells to the left by the value one cell to the left. When you copy the cell, these *instructions* get copied, not the actual contents of the cell. Usually, this is exactly what you want. You certainly don't want to copy the formula verbatim; if you did, the new formulas would produce the same value as the original formula.

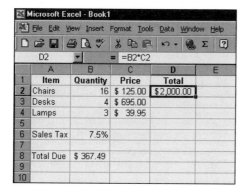

Figure 9-6: The formula in cell D2 will be copied to the cell below.

Note When you cut and paste a formula (move it to another location), the cell references in the formula aren't adjusted. Again, this is what you usually want to happen. When you move a formula, you generally want it to continue to refer to the original cells.

Absolute References

Sometimes, however, you *do* want a cell reference to be copied verbatim. Figure 9-6 shows an example of a formula that contains an absolute reference. In this example, cell B6 contains a sales tax rate. The formula in cell D2 is as follows:

```
=(B2*C2)*$B$6
```

Notice that the reference to cell B6 has dollar signs preceding the column letter and the row number. These dollar signs indicate to Excel that you want to use an absolute cell reference. When you copy this formula to the two cells below, Excel generates the following formulas:

✦ **Cell D3:** =(B3*C3)*$B$6

✦ **Cell D4:** =(B4*C4)*$B$6

In this case, the relative cell references were changed, but the reference to cell B6 wasn't changed, because it's an absolute reference.

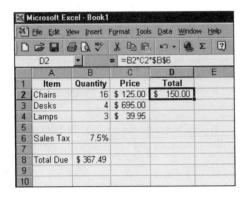

Figure 9-7: A formula that uses an absolute cell reference.

Mixed References

An absolute reference uses two dollar signs in its address: one for the column letter and one for the row number. Excel also allows mixed references in which only one of the address parts is absolute. Table 9-3 summarizes all the possible types of cell references.

When would you use a mixed reference? Figure 9-7 shows an example of a situation in which a mixed reference is appropriate. This worksheet will contain a table of values in which each cell consists of the value in column A multiplied by the value in row 1. The formula in cell B2 is as follows:

```
=B$1*$A2
```

Table 9-3 Types of Cell References	
Example	*Type*
A1	Relative reference
$A$1	Absolute reference
$A1	Mixed reference (column letter is absolute)
A$1	Mixed reference (row number is absolute)

This formula contains two mixed cell references. In the B$1 reference, the row number is absolute, but the column letter is relative. In the $A2 reference, the row number is relative, but the column letter is absolute. You can copy this formula to the range B2:E5 and each cell will contain the correct formula. For example, the formula in cell E5 would be as follows:

```
=E$1*$A5
```

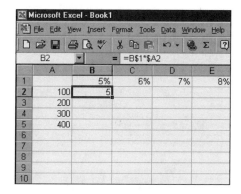

Figure 9-8: This formula uses a mixed reference.

Entering Nonrelative References

You can enter nonrelative references (absolute or mixed) manually by inserting dollar signs in the appropriate positions. Or, you can use a handy shortcut: the F4 key. When you're entering a cell reference — either manually or by pointing — you can press F4 repeatedly to have Excel cycle through all four reference types.

For example, if you enter **=A1** to start a formula, pressing F4 converts the cell reference to =$A$1. Pressing F4 again converts it to =A$1. Pressing it again displays =$A1. Pressing it one more time returns to the original =A1. Keep pressing F4 until Excel displays the type of reference that you want.

Note When you name a cell or range, Excel (by default) uses an absolute reference for the name. For example, if you give the name SalesForecast to A1:A12, the Refers to box in the Define Name dialog box lists the reference as $A$1:$A$12. This is almost always what you want. If you copy a cell that has a named reference in its formula, the copied formula contains a reference to the original name.

When a Formula Returns an Error

Sometimes when you enter a formula, Excel displays a value that begins with a pound sign (#). This is a signal that the formula is returning an error value. You'll have to correct the formula (or correct a cell that the formula references) to get rid of the error display.

As noted previously in this chapter, Excel often suggests a correction for an erroneous formula.

Note If the entire cell is filled with pound characters, this means that the column isn't wide enough to display the value. You can either widen the column or change the number format of the cell.

Table 9-4 lists the types of error values that may appear in a cell that has a formula. Formulas may return an error value if a cell to which they refer has an error value. This is known as the ripple effect — a single error value can make its way into lots of other cells that contain formulas that depend on the cell.

Table 9-4 Excel Error Values	
Error Value	**Explanation**
#DIV/0!	The formula is trying to divide by zero (an operation that's not allowed on this planet). This also occurs when the formula attempts to divide by a cell that is empty.
#NAME?	The formula uses a name that Excel doesn't recognize. This can happen if you delete a name that's used in the formula or if you have unmatched quotes when using text.
#N/A	The formula is referring (directly or indirectly) to a cell that uses the NA function to signal that data is not available.
#NULL!	The formula uses an intersection of two ranges that don't intersect (this concept is described later in the chapter).
#NUM!	A problem with a value exists; for example, you specified a negative number where a positive number is expected.
#REF!	The formula refers to a cell that isn't valid. This can happen if the cell has been deleted from the worksheet.
#VALUE!	The formula includes an argument or operand of the wrong type. An *operand* is a value or cell reference that a formula uses to calculate a result.

Editing Formulas

You can edit your formulas just like you can edit any other cell. You might need to edit a formula if you make some changes to your worksheet and need to adjust the formula to accommodate the changes. Or, the formula may return one of the error values described in the previous section, and you need to edit the formula to correct the error.

The following are the four ways to get into cell-edit mode:

✦ Double-click the cell, which enables you to edit the cell contents directly in the cell.

✦ Press F2, which enables you to edit the cell contents directly in the cell.

✦ Select the cell that you want to edit, and then click in the formula bar. This enables you to edit the cell contents in the formula bar.

✦ Click the Edit Formula button in the Formula bar to access the Formula Palette.

Cross-Reference   Chapter 6 also discusses these methods.

While you're editing a formula, you can select multiple characters either by dragging the mouse over them or by holding down Shift while you use the direction keys.

You might have a lengthy formula that you can't seem to edit correctly — and Excel won't let you enter it because of the error. In this case, you can convert the formula to text and tackle it again later. To convert a formula to text, just remove the initial equal sign (=). When you're ready to try again, insert the initial equal sign to convert the cell contents back to a formula.

Changing When Formulas Are Calculated

You've probably noticed that Excel calculates the formulas in your worksheet immediately. If you change any cells that the formula uses, Excel displays the formula's new result, with no effort on your part. All this happens when Excel's Calculation mode is set to Automatic. In Automatic Calculation mode (which is the default mode), Excel follows these rules when calculating your worksheet:

✦ When you make a change — enter or edit data or formulas, for example — Excel calculates immediately those formulas that depend on new or edited data.

✦ If Excel is in the middle of a lengthy calculation, it temporarily suspends the calculation when you need to perform other worksheet tasks; it resumes when you're finished.

✦ Formulas are evaluated in a natural sequence. In other words, if a formula in cell D12 depends on the result of a formula in cell D11, Excel calculates cell D11 before calculating D12.

Sometimes, however, you may want to control when Excel calculates formulas. For example, if you create a worksheet with thousands of complex formulas, you'll find that things can slow to a snail's pace while Excel does its thing. In such a case, set Excel's calculation mode to Manual, which you can do in the Calculation tab of the Options dialog box (see Figure 9-9).

To select Manual calculation mode, click the Manual option button. When you switch to Manual calculation mode, Excel automatically places a check in the Recalculate before save check box. You can remove the check if you want to speed up file saving operations.

If your worksheet uses any data tables (described in Chapter 26), you may want to select the Automatic except tables option. Large data tables calculate notoriously slowly.

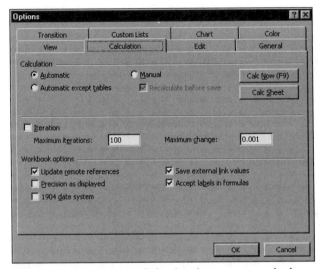

Figure 9-9: The Options dialog box lets you control when Excel calculates formulas.

When you're working in Manual calculation mode, Excel displays Calculate in the status bar when you have any uncalculated formulas. You can use the following shortcut keys to recalculate the formulas:

  ✦ **F9:** Calculates the formulas in all open workbooks

  ✦ **Shift+F9:** Calculates only the formulas in the active worksheet. Other worksheets in the same workbook aren't calculated.

  ✦ **Ctrl+Alt+F9:** This keyboard shortcut combination isn't documented. It forces a complete recalculation. This shortcut became popular when several recalculation bugs in Excel 97 surfaced.

Note   Excel's Calculation mode isn't specific to a particular worksheet. When you change Excel's Calculation mode, it affects all open workbooks, not just the active workbook.

Handling Circular References

When you're entering formulas, you may occasionally see a message from Excel like the one shown in Figure 9-9, indicating that the formula you just entered will result in a *circular reference*. A circular reference occurs when a formula refers to its own value—either directly or indirectly. For example, you create a circular reference if you enter =**A1+A2+A3** into cell A3, because the formula in cell A3 refers to cell A3. Every time the formula in A3 is calculated, it must be calculated again because A3 has changed. The calculation would go on forever—in other words, the answer will never be resolved.

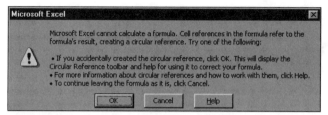

Figure 9-10: Excel's way of telling you that your formula contains a circular reference.

When you get the circular reference message after entering a formula, Excel gives you two options:

✦ Click OK to attempt to locate the circular reference

✦ Click Cancel to enter the formula as-is

Usually, you want to correct any circular references, so you should choose OK. When you do so, Excel displays the Help topic on circular references and the Circular Reference toolbar (see Figure 9-11). On the Circular Reference toolbar, click the first cell in the Navigate Circular Reference drop-down list box, and then examine the cell's formula. If you cannot determine whether the cell is the cause of the circular reference, click the next cell in the Navigate Circular Reference box. Continue to review the formulas until the status bar no longer displays Circular.

If you ignore the circular reference message (by clicking Cancel), Excel lets you enter the formula, and displays a message in the status bar to remind you that a circular reference exists. In this case, the message reads Circular: A3. If you activate a different workbook, the message simply displays Circular (without the cell reference).

Note   Excel won't tell you about a circular reference if the Iteration setting is on. You can check this in the Options dialog box (in the Calculation tab). If Iteration is on, Excel performs the circular calculation the number of times specified in the Maximum iterations field (or until the value changes by less than .001 — or whatever value is in the Maximum change field). In a few situations, you may use a circular reference intentionally (explained in a following section). In these cases, the Iteration setting must be on. However, keeping the Iteration setting turned off is best, so that you are warned of circular references. Most of the time, a circular reference indicates an error that you must correct.

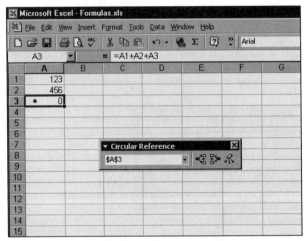

Figure 9-11: The Circular Reference toolbar.

Indirect Circular References

Usually, a circular reference is quite obvious and, therefore, easy to identify and correct. Sometimes, however, circular references are indirect. In other words, a formula may refer to a formula that refers to a formula that refers back to the original formula. In some cases, it may require a bit of detective work to get to the problem.

Cross-Reference

You may be able to get some assistance identifying a formula's dependents and precedents by using the tools on the Circular Reference toolbar, which are discussed in Chapter 31.

Intentional Circular References

As mentioned previously, you can use a circular reference to your advantage in some situations. Figure 9-12 shows a simple example.

In this example, a company has a policy of contributing five percent of its net profit to charity. The contribution itself, however, is considered an expense and is therefore subtracted from the net profit figure. This produces a circular reference—but this circular reference can be resolved if the Excel's Iteration setting is turned on.

On the CD-ROM

This workbook is available on the companion CD-ROM.

Using AutoFill Rather Than Formulas

Chapter 8 discusses AutoFill as a quick way to copy a cell to adjacent cells. AutoFill also has some other uses, which may even substitute for formulas in some cases. I'm surprised to find that many experienced Excel users don't take advantage of the AutoFill feature — which can be a real time-saver.

Besides being a shortcut way to copy cells, AutoFill can quickly create a series of incremental values. For example, if you need a list of values from 1 to 100 to appear in A1:A100, you can do it with formulas. You enter **1** in cell A1, the formula **=A1+1** into cell A2, and then copy the formula to the 98 cells below.

You also can use AutoFill to create the series for you without using a formula. To do so, enter **1** into cell A1 and **2** into cell A2. Select A1:A2 and drag the fill handle down to cell A100. When you use AutoFill in this manner, Excel analyzes the selected cells and uses this information to complete the series. If cell A1 contained 1 and cell A2 contained 3, Excel recognizes this pattern and fills in 5, 7, 9, and so on. This also works with decreasing series (10, 9, 8, and so on) and dates. If no pattern is discernible in the selected cells, Excel performs a linear regression and fills in values on the calculated trend line.

Excel also recognizes common series names, such as days and months. If you enter Monday into a cell and then drag its fill handle, Excel fills in the successive days of the week. You also can create custom AutoFill lists by using the Custom Lists tab of the Options dialog box. Finally, if you drag the fill handle with the right-mouse button, Excel displays a shortcut menu to let you select an AutoFill option.

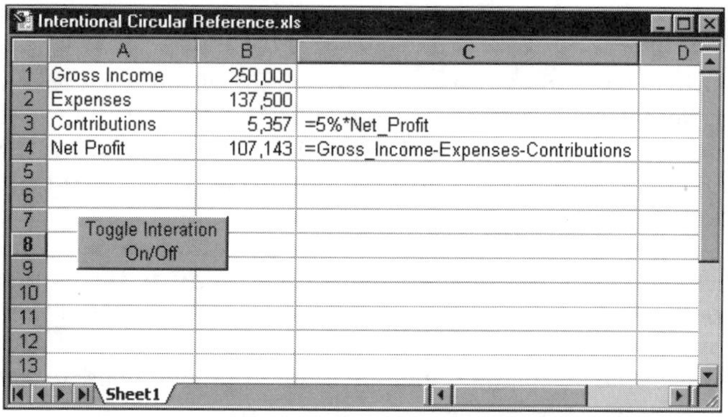

Figure 9-12: An example of an intentional circular reference.

The Contributions cell contains the following formula:

```
=5%*Net_Profit
```

The Net Profit cell contains the following formula:

```
=Gross_Income-Expenses-Contributions
```

These formulas produce a resolvable circular reference. Excel keeps calculating until the formula results don't change anymore. To get a feel for how this works, substitute various values for Gross Income and Expenses. If the Iteration setting is off, Excel displays its Circular Reference message and won't display the correct result. If the Iteration setting is on, Excel keeps calculating until the Contributions value is, indeed, five percent of Net Profit. In other words, the result becomes increasingly more accurate until it converges on the final solution. For your convenience, I include a button on the worksheet that toggles the Iteration setting on and off by using a simple macro.

Note Depending on your application, you may need to adjust the settings in the Maximum iterations field or the Maximum change field in the Options dialog box. For example, to increase accuracy, you can make the Maximum change field smaller. If the result doesn't converge after 100 iterations, you can increase the Maximum iterations field.

Advanced Naming Techniques

As promised in the preceding chapter, this section describes some additional techniques that involve names.

Sheet-Level Names

Usually, you can use a range name that you create anywhere within the workbook. In other words, names, by default, are "workbook level" names rather than "sheet level" names. But what if you have several worksheets in a workbook and you want to use the same name (such as Dept_Total) on each sheet? In this case, you need to create sheet-level names.

To define the name Dept_Total in more than one worksheet, activate the worksheet in which you want to define the name, choose Insert ➪ Name ➪ Define, and then, in the Names in workbook box, precede the name with the worksheet name and an exclamation point. For example, to define the name Dept_Total on Sheet2, activate Sheet2 and enter the following in the Define Name dialog box:

```
Sheet2!Dept_Total
```

If the worksheet name contains at least one space, enclose the worksheet name in single quotation marks, like this:

```
'Adv Dept'!Dept_Total
```

You also can create a sheet-level name by using the Name box (located at the left side of the formula bar). Select the cell or range, click in the Name box, and enter the name, preceded by the sheet's name and an exclamation point (as shown previously). Press Enter to create the name.

When you write a formula that uses a sheet-level name on the sheet in which it's defined, you don't need to include the worksheet name in the range name (the Name box won't display the worksheet name either). If you use the name in a formula on a different worksheet, however, you must use the entire name (sheet name, exclamation point, and name).

Note   Only the sheet-level names on the current sheet appear in the Name box. Similarly, only sheet-level names in the current sheet appear in the list when you open the Paste Name or Define Name dialog boxes.

Using sheet-level names can become complicated if you have an identical book-level name and sheet-level name (yes, Excel does allow this). In such a case, the sheet-level name takes precedence over the book-level name — but only in the worksheet in which you defined the sheet-level name. For example, you might have defined a book-level name of Total for a cell on Sheet1. You also can define a sheet-level name of Total (in, say Sheet2). When Sheet2 is active, Total refers to the sheet-level name. When any other sheet is active, Total refers to the book-level name. You can refer to a sheet-level name in a different worksheet, however, by preceding the name with the worksheet name and an exclamation point (such as Sheet1!Total). To make your life easier, just avoid using the same name at the book level and sheet level.

Using Multisheet Names

Names even can extend into the third dimension; that is, they can extend across multiple worksheets in a workbook. You can't simply select the multisheet range and enter a name in the Name box, however. Excel makes you do a little additional work to define a multisheet name.

You must use the Define Name dialog box to create a multisheet name, and you must enter the reference in the Refers to box manually. The format for a multisheet reference is as follows:

```
FirstSheet:LastSheet!RangeReference
```

In Figure 9-13, a multisheet name is being defined for A1:C12 that extends across Sheet1, Sheet2, and Sheet3.

After the name is defined, you can use it in formulas. This name won't appear in the Name box, however, or in the Go To dialog box. In other words, Excel lets you define the name, but it doesn't give you a way to select automatically the cells to which the name refers.

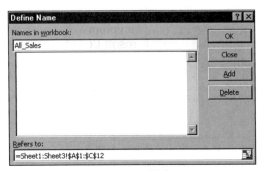

Figure 9-13: Creating a multisheet name.

Naming Constants

Even many advanced Excel users don't realize that you can give a name to an item that doesn't even appear in a cell. For example, if formulas in your worksheet use a sales tax rate, you would probably insert the tax rate value into a cell and use this cell reference in your formulas. To make things easier, you would probably also name this cell something like SalesTax.

Here's another way to do it: Choose Insert ➪ Name ➪ Define (or press Ctrl+F3) to bring up the Define Name dialog box. Enter the name (in this case, **SalesTax**) into the Names in workbook field. Then, click the Refers to box, delete its contents, and replace it with a value such as **.075** (see Figure 9-14). Don't precede the constant with an equal sign. Click OK to close the dialog box.

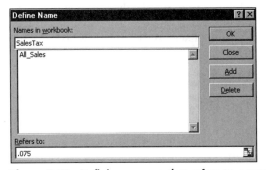

Figure 9-14: Defining a name that refers to a constant.

You just created a name that refers to a constant rather than a cell or range. If you type =**SalesTax** into a cell, this simple formula returns .075 — the constant that you defined. You also can use this constant in a formula such as =A1*SalesTax.

As with all names, named constants are stored with the workbook. They can be used on any worksheet in the workbook.

In the preceding example, the constant was a value. A constant also can be text, however. For example, you can define a constant for your company's name. If you work for Microsoft, you can define the name MS for Microsoft Corporation.

Note Named constants don't appear in the Name box or in the Go To dialog box—which makes sense, because these constants don't reside anywhere tangible. They do appear in the Paste Names dialog box, however, which *does* make sense, because you'll use these names in formulas.

As you might expect, you can change the value of the constant by accessing the Define Name dialog box and simply changing the value in the Refers to box. When you close the dialog box, Excel uses the new value to recalculate the formulas that use this name.

Although this technique is useful in many situations, the value is rather difficult to change. Having a constant located in a cell makes it much easier to modify. If the value is truly a "constant," however, you won't need to change it.

Naming Formulas

This section takes the preceding section to the next logical level: naming formulas. Figure 9-15 shows an example of this. In this case, the name MonthlyRate refers to the following formula:

```
=Sheet3!$B$1/12
```

When you use the name MonthlyRate in a formula, it uses the value in B1 divided by 12. Notice that the cell reference is an absolute reference.

Naming formulas gets more interesting when you use relative references rather than absolute references. When you use the pointing technique to create a formula in the Refers to box, Excel always uses absolute cell references, which is unlike its behavior when you create a formula in a cell.

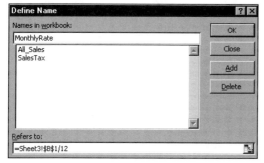

Figure 9-15: Excel lets you give a name to a formula that doesn't exist in the worksheet.

Figure 9-16 shows a name, Power, being created for the following formula:

```
=Sheet1!A1^Sheet1!B1
```

Notice that cell C1 is the active cell, which is very important. When you use this named formula in a worksheet, the cell references are always relative to the cell that contains the name. For example, if you enter **=POWER** into cell D12, cell D12 displays the result of B12 raised to the power of the value contained in cell C12.

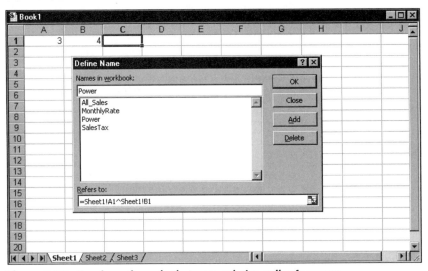

Figure 9-16: Naming a formula that uses relative cell references.

Range Intersections

This section describes an interesting concept that is unique to Excel: *range intersections*. Excel uses an intersection operator — a space — to determine the overlapping references in two ranges. Figure 9-17 shows a simple example. The formula in cell G5 is

```
=B1:B7 A4:E4
```

and returns 180, the value in cell B4 — that is, the value at the intersection of the two ranges.

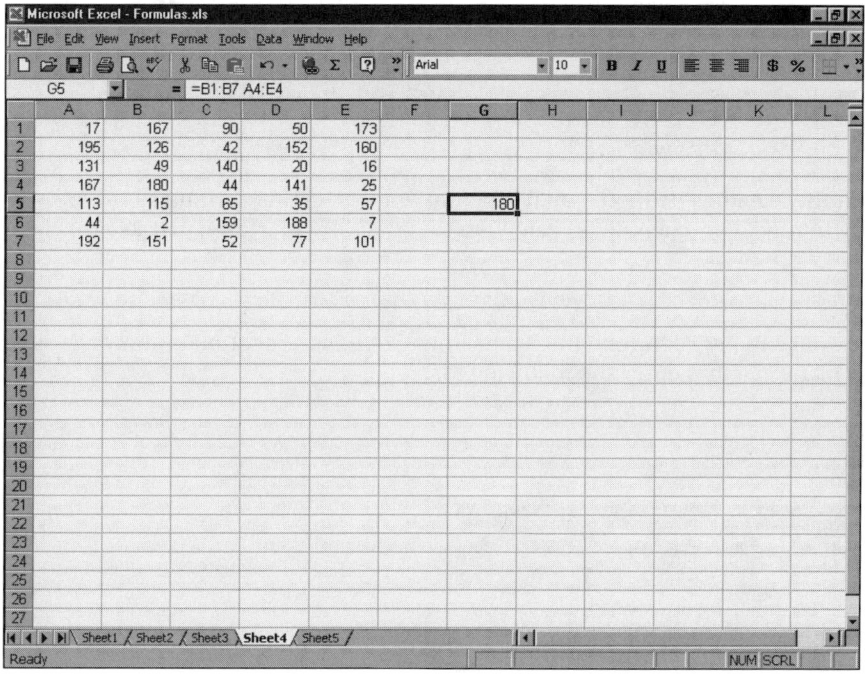

Figure 9-17: An example of an intersecting range.

The intersection operator is one of three *reference* operators for ranges. Table 9-5 lists these operators.

Table 9-5		
Reference Operators for Ranges		
Operator	**What It Does**	
: (colon)	Specifies a range	
, (comma)	Specifies the union of two ranges	
(space)	Specifies the intersection of two ranges	

The real value of knowing about range intersections is apparent when you use names. Examine Figure 9-18, which shows a table of values. I selected the entire table and then used the Insert ⇨ name ⇨ Create command to create names automatically. Excel created the following names:

North	=Sheet1!$B$2:$E$2	Qtr1	=Sheet1!$B$2:$B$5
South	=Sheet1!$B$3:$E$3	Qtr2	=Sheet1!$C$2:$C$5
West	=Sheet1!$B$4:$E$4	Qtr3	=Sheet1!$D$2:$D$5
East	=Sheet1!$B$5:$E$5	Qtr4	=Sheet1!$E$2:$E$5

With these names defined, you'll find that you can create formulas that are very easy to read. For example, to calculate the total for Quarter 4, just use this formula:

```
=SUM(Qtr4)
```

But things really get interesting when you use the intersection operator. Move to any blank cell and enter the following formula:

```
=Qtr1 West
```

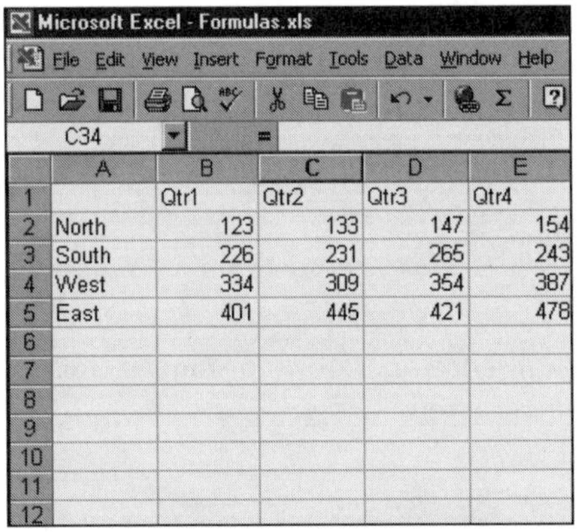

Figure 9-18: This table demonstrates how to use range intersections.

This formula returns the value for the first quarter for the West region. In other words, it returns the value where the Qtr1 range intersects with the West range. Naming ranges in this manner can help you create very readable formulas.

Applying Names to Existing References

When you create a new name for a cell or a range, Excel doesn't automatically use the name in place of existing references in your formulas. For example, assume that you have the following formula in cell F10: =A1–A2.

If you define a name Income for A1 and Expenses for A2, Excel won't automatically change your formula to =Income–Expenses. Replacing cell or range references with their corresponding names is fairly easy, however.

Using Row and Column Headings As "Names"

Beginning with Excel 97, you have access to a feature that lets you use "names" without actually defining them. To understand how this feature works, refer to the accompanying figure, which shows a typical table with row and column headers. Excel lets you use the row and column headers as names in your formulas (and you don't have to define the names). For example, to refer to the cell that holds February sales for the South region, use the following formula:

```
=Feb South
```

In other words, the formula returns the cell that intersects the Feb column and the South row. You can also use this technique with functions. Here's a formula that returns the total sales for March:

```
=SUM(March)
```

Excel handles all the details for you. If you change a row or column heading, all the formulas change automatically to use the new label.

	A	B	C	D	E	F
1		Jan	Feb	Mar	Total	
2	North	11	14	15	40	
3	South	31	34	44	109	
4	West	43	32	56	131	
5	East	109	89	65	263	
6						
7						
8						
9						

This technique has a few limitations. The labels are not "real" names—they don't appear in the Define Name dialog box, nor do they appear in the Name box. For this reason, you can use this method only when the formula refers to cells on the same sheet. The real problem, however, is the inability to document the names. In other words, you can never tell for sure exactly what a name refers to. For that reason, I don't recommend using this feature. Rather, take a few extra seconds and create a "real" range name.

To apply names to cell references in formulas after the fact, start by selecting the range that you want to modify. Then, choose Insert ➪ Name ➪ Apply. Excel displays the Apply Names dialog box, shown in Figure 9-19 Select the names that you want to apply by clicking them and then click OK. Excel replaces the range references with the names in the selected cells.

The Apply Names dialog box has some options. If you click the Options button, the dialog box expands to display even more options. Most of the time, the defaults work just fine. For more control over the names that you apply, however, you may want to use one or more of its options. These are described in Excel's online Help.

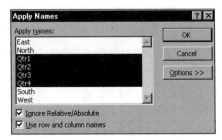

Figure 9-19: The Apply Names dialog box lets you replace cell or range references with names.

Tips for Working with Formulas

This chapter concludes with a few additional tips and pointers relevant to formulas.

Don't "Hard Code" Values

When you create a formula, think twice before using a value in the formula. For example, if your formula calculates sales tax (which is 6.5 percent), you may be tempted to enter a formula such as the following:

```
+A1*.065
```

A better approach is to insert the sales tax rate in a cell and use the cell reference. Or, you can define it as a named constant by using the technique presented earlier in this chapter. Doing so makes modifying and maintaining your worksheet easier. For example, if the sales tax rate changed to 6.75 percent, you would have to modify every formula that uses the old value. If the tax rate is stored in a cell, you simply change one cell and Excel updates all the formulas.

Using the Formula Bar As a Calculator

If you simply need to perform a calculation, you can use the formula bar as a calculator. For example, enter the following formula—but don't press Enter:

```
=(145*1.05)/12
```

If you press Enter, Excel enters the formula into the cell. But because this formula always returns the same result, you might prefer to store the formula's result rather than the formula. To do so, press F9, and then press Enter. Excel stores the formula's result (12.6875) rather than the formula. This also works if the formula uses cell references.

This is most useful when you use worksheet functions. For example, to enter the square root of 221 into a cell, enter **=SQRT(221)**, press F9, and then press Enter. Excel enters the result: 14.8660687473185. You also can use this technique to evaluate only part of a formula. Consider this formula:

```
=(145*1.05)/A1
```

If you want to convert to a value just the part in the parentheses, select the part of the formula that you want to evaluate (that is, select 145*1.05). Then, press F9, followed by Enter. Excel converts the formula to the following:

```
=152.25/A1
```

Making an Exact Copy of a Formula

As you know, when you copy a formula, Excel adjusts its cell references when you paste the formula to a different location. Sometimes, you may want to make an exact copy of the formula. One way to do this is to convert the cell references to absolute values, but this isn't always desirable. A better approach is to select the formula in edit mode and then copy it to the Clipboards as text. You can do this in several ways. Here's a step-by-step example of how to make an exact copy of the formula in A1 and copy it to A2:

1. Double-click A1 to get into edit mode.

2. Drag the mouse to select the entire formula. You can drag from left to right or from right to left.

3. Click the Copy button on the Standard toolbar. This copies the selected text to the Clipboards.

4. Press Enter to end edit mode.

5. Select cell A2.

6. Click the Paste button to paste the text into cell A2.

You also can use this technique to copy just *part* of a formula, to use that part in another formula. Just select the part of the formula that you want to copy by dragging the mouse; then, use any of the available techniques to copy the selection to the Clipboard. You can then paste the text to another cell.

Formulas (or parts of formulas) copied in this manner won't have their cell references adjusted when they are pasted to a new cell, because the formulas are being copied as text, not as actual formulas.

Converting Formulas to Values

If you have a range of formulas that will always produce the same result (that is, dead formulas), you may want to convert them to values. As discussed in the previous chapter, you can use the Edit ⇨ Paste Special command to do this. Assume that range A1:A20 contains formulas that have calculated results that will never change or that you don't want to change. For example, if you use the @RAND function to create a set of random numbers, and you don't want Excel to recalculate the random numbers each time that you press Enter, convert the formulas to values. To convert these formulas to values:

1. Select A1:A20.

2. Click the Copy button.

3. Select Edit ➪ Paste Special. Excel displays its Paste Special dialog box.

4. Click the Values option button and then click OK.

5. Press Enter or Esc to cancel paste mode.

Array Formulas

Excel supports another type of formula called an *array formula*. Array formulas can be extremely powerful, because they let you work with complete ranges of cells rather than individual cells. You'll find that you can perform some amazing feats by using array formulas. This is a rather advanced concept, which is covered in Chapter 20.

Summary

This chapter introduces the concept of formulas. Formulas are entered into cells and use values found in other cells to return a result. This chapter explains how to enter and edit formulas, when to use absolute cell references, how to identify errors in your formulas, and how to handle circular references (either accidental or intentional). It also explains how to set Excel to Manual recalculation mode — and why you would need to do so. The chapter continues by discussing some additional naming techniques that can make your formulas even more powerful. This chapter concludes with a series of tips that can help you get the most out of formulas.

✦　　✦　　✦

Using Worksheet Functions

The preceding chapter discussed formulas. This chapter continues with coverage of Excel's built-in worksheet functions.

What Is a Function?

Functions, in essence, are built-in tools that you use in formulas. They can make your formulas perform powerful feats and save you a lot of time. Functions can do the following:

+ Simplify your formulas

+ Allow formulas to perform calculations that are otherwise impossible

+ Speed up some editing tasks

+ Allow "conditional" execution of formulas — giving them rudimentary decision-making capability

Function Examples

A built-in function can simplify a formula significantly. To calculate the average of the values in ten cells (A1:A10) without using a function, you need to construct a formula like this:

```
=(A1+A2+A3+A4+A5+A6+A7+A8+A9+A10)/10
```

Not very pretty, is it? Even worse, you would need to edit this formula if you added another cell to the range. You can replace this formula with a much simpler one that uses one of Excel's built-in worksheet functions:

```
=AVERAGE(A1:A10)
```

Next, look at how using a function can enable you to perform calculations that would not be possible otherwise. What if you need to determine the largest value in a range? A formula can't tell you the answer without using a function. Here's a simple formula that returns the largest value in the range A1:D100:

```
=MAX(A1:D100)
```

Functions also can sometimes eliminate manual editing. Assume that you have a worksheet that contains 1,000 names in cells A1:A1000, and all the names appear in all capital letters. Your boss sees the listing and informs you that the names will be mail-merged with a form letter and that all-uppercase is not acceptable; for example, JOHN F. CRANE must appear as John F. Crane. You *could* spend the next several hours reentering the list — or you could use a formula like the following, which uses a function to convert the text in cell A1 to proper case:

```
=PROPER(A1)
```

Enter this formula once in cell B1 and then copy it down to the next 999 rows. Then, select B1:B1000 and use the Edit ⇨ Paste Special command (with the Values option) to convert the formulas to values. Delete the original column, and you've just accomplished several hours of work in less than a minute.

One last example should convince you of the power of functions. Suppose that you have a worksheet that calculates sales commissions. If the salesperson sold more than $100,000 of product, the commission rate is 7.5 percent; otherwise, the commission rate is 5.0 percent. Without using a function, you would have to create two different formulas and make sure that you use the correct formula for each sales amount. Here's a formula that uses the IF function to ensure that you calculate the correct commission, regardless of the sales amount:

```
=IF(A1<100000,A1*5%,A1*7.5%)
```

More About Functions

All told, Excel includes more than 300 functions. And if that's not enough, you can purchase additional specialized functions from third-party suppliers, and even create your own custom functions (using VBA), if you're so inclined.

You can easily be overwhelmed by the sheer number of functions, but you'll probably find that you use only a dozen or so of the functions on a regular basis. And as you'll see, Excel's Paste Function dialog box (described later in this chapter) makes it easy to locate and insert a function, even if it's not one that you use frequently.

Cross-Reference

Appendix B contains a complete listing of Excel's worksheet functions, with a brief description of each.

Function Arguments

In the preceding examples, you may have noticed that all the functions used parentheses. The information inside the parentheses is called an *argument*. Functions vary in how they use arguments. Depending on the function, a function may use:

✦ No arguments

✦ One argument

✦ A fixed number of arguments

✦ An indeterminate number of arguments

✦ Optional arguments

The RAND function, which returns a random number between 0 and 1, doesn't use an argument. Even if a function doesn't use an argument, however, you must still provide a set of empty parentheses, like this:

```
=RAND()
```

If a function uses more than one argument, you must separate each argument by a comma. The examples at the beginning of the chapter used cell references for arguments. Excel is quite flexible when it comes to function arguments, however. An argument can consist of a cell reference, literal values, literal text strings, or expressions.

Accommodating Former 1-2-3 Users

If you've ever used any of the 1-2-3 spreadsheets (or any versions of Quattro Pro), you'll recall that these products require you to type an "at" sign (@) before a function name. Excel is smart enough to distinguish functions without you having to flag them with a symbol.

Because old habits die hard, however, Excel accepts @ symbols when you type functions in your formulas — but it removes them as soon as you enter the formula.

These competing products also use two dots (..) as a range operator — for example, A1..A10. Excel also lets you use this notation when you type formulas, but Excel replaces the notation with its own range operator, a colon (:).

This accommodation goes only so far, however. Excel still insists that you use the standard Excel function names, and it doesn't recognize or translate the function names used in other spreadsheets. For example, if you enter the 1-2-3 @AVG function, Excel flags it as an error (Excel's name for this function is AVERAGE).

Using Names As Arguments

As you've seen, functions can use cell or range references for their arguments. When Excel calculates the formula, it simply uses the current contents of the cell or range to perform its calculations. The SUM function returns the sum of its argument(s). To calculate the sum of the values in A1:D20, you can use:

```
=SUM(A1:A20)
```

And, not surprisingly, if you've defined a name for A1:A20 (such as Sales), you can use the name in place of the reference:

```
=SUM(Sales)
```

In some cases, you may find it useful to use an entire column or row as an argument. For example, the formula that follows sums all values in column B:

```
=SUM(B:B)
```

This technique is particularly useful if the range that you're summing changes (if you're continually adding new sales figures, for instance). If you do use an entire row or column, just make sure that the row or column doesn't contain extraneous information that you don't want included in the sum. You might think that using such a large range (a column consists of 65,536 cells) might slow down calculation time — this isn't true. Excel's recalculation engine is quite efficient.

Literal Arguments

A *literal argument* is a value or text string that you enter into a function. For example, the SQRT function takes one argument. In the following example, the formula uses a literal value for the function's argument:

```
=SQRT(225)
```

Using a literal argument with a simple function like this one defeats the purpose of using a formula. This formula always returns the same value, so it could just as easily be replaced with the value 15. Using literal arguments makes more sense with formulas that use more than one argument. For example, the LEFT function (which takes two arguments) returns characters from the beginning of its first argument; the second argument specifies the number of characters. If cell A1 contains the text Budget, the following formula returns the first letter, or *B:*

```
=LEFT(A1,1)
```

Expressions As Arguments

Excel also lets you use *expressions* as arguments. Think of an expression as a formula within a formula. When Excel encounters an expression as a function's argument, it evaluates the expression and then uses the result as the argument's value. Here's an example:

```
=SQRT((A1^2)+(A2^2))
```

This formula uses the SQRT function, and its single argument is the following expression:

```
(A1^2)+(A2^2)
```

When Excel evaluates the formula, it starts by evaluating the expression in the argument and then computes the square root of the result.

Other Functions As Arguments

Because Excel can evaluate expressions as arguments, you shouldn't be surprised that these expressions can include other functions. Writing formulas that have functions within functions is sometimes known as *nesting* functions. Excel starts by evaluating the most deeply nested expression and works its way out. Here's an example of a nested function:

```
=SIN(RADIANS(B9))
```

The RADIANS function converts degrees to radians — which is the unit used by all of Excel's trigonometric functions. If cell B9 contains an angle in degrees, the RADIANS function converts it to radians, and then the SIN function computes the sine of the angle.

With a few exception, you can nest functions as deeply as you need, as long as you don't exceed the 1,024-character limit for a formula.

Ways to Enter a Function

You have two ways available to enter a function into a formula: manually or by using the Paste Function dialog box.

Entering a Function Manually

If you're familiar with a particular function — you know how many arguments it takes and the types of arguments — you may choose simply to type the function and its arguments into your formula. Often, this method is the most efficient.

Changeable Range References in Excel 2000

Many functions contain a range reference as an argument. For example, the function that follows uses the range A10:A20:

```
=SUM(A10:A20)
```

If you add a new row between rows 10 and 20, Excel expands the formula's range reference for you automatically. If you add a new row between rows 12 and 13, the formula changes to the following:

```
=SUM(A10:A21)
```

In most cases, this is exactly what you want to happen.

In prior versions of Excel, if you inserted a new row at row 10, however, Excel would *not* include the new row in the range reference; that is, Excel wouldn't automatically expand the argument range reference to include rows that you add at the top or bottom of the range. Because this behavior often confused new users, Microsoft changed Excel's behavior in Excel 2000. In Excel 2000, when you add a row at any place in a referenced range, Excel changes the function that referenced the original range to include the new row automatically.

Tip
When you enter a function, Excel always converts the function's name to upper-case. Thus, always using lowercase when you type functions is a good idea: if Excel doesn't convert it to uppercase when you press Enter, then Excel doesn't recognize your entry as a function—which means that you spelled it incorrectly.

If you omit the closing parenthesis, Excel adds it for you automatically. For example, if you type =**SUM(A1:C12** and press Enter, Excel corrects the formula by adding the right parenthesis.

Pasting a Function

Formula Palette assists you by providing a way to enter a function and its arguments in a semiautomated manner. Using the Formula Palette ensures that the function is spelled correctly and has the proper number of arguments in the correct order.

To insert a function, start by selecting the function from the Paste Function dialog box, shown in Figure 10-1. You can open this dialog box by using any of the following methods:

✦ Choose the Insert ⇨ Function command from the menu

✦ Click the Paste Function button on the Standard toolbar

✦ Press Shift+F3

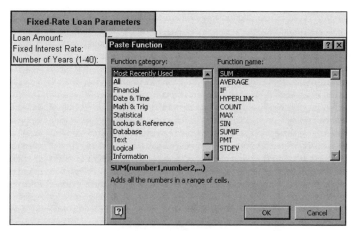

Figure 10-1: The Paste Function dialog box.

The Paste Function dialog box shows the Function category list on the left side of the dialog box. When you select a category, the Function name list box displays the functions in the selected category.

The Most Recently Used category lists the functions that you've used most recently. The All category lists all the functions available across all categories. Use this if you know a function's name, but aren't sure of its category.

Tip   To select a function quickly in the Most Recently Used category, click the Edit Formula icon in the formula bar and then select the function from the function list (which occupies the space usually used by the Name box).

When you select a function in the Function name list box, notice that Excel displays the function (and its argument names) in the dialog box, along with a brief description of what the function does.

When you locate the function that you want to use, click OK. Excel's Formula Palette appears, as in Figure 10-2, and the Name box changes to the Formula List box. Use the Formula Palette to specify the arguments for the function. You can easily specify a range argument by clicking the Collapse Dialog button (the icon at the right edge of each box in the Formula Palette). Excel temporarily collapses the Formula Palette to a thin box, so that you can select a range in the worksheet. When you want to redisplay the Formula Palette, click the button again.

The Formula Palette usually appears directly below the formula bar, but you can move it to any other location by dragging it.

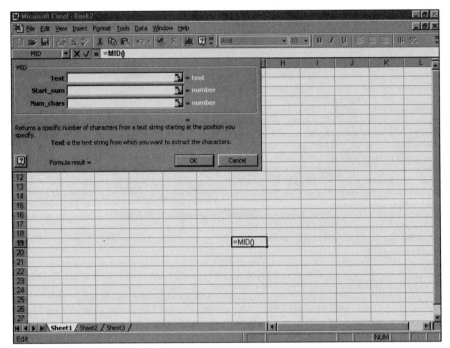

Figure 10-2: The Formula Palette.

Inserting a function: An example

This section presents a step-by-step example that explains how to insert a function into a formula. The formula uses the AVERAGE function to compute the average of a range of cells. To insert a function into a formula, proceed as follows:

1. Open a new workbook and enter values into H1:H6 (any values will do).

2. Select cell H7. This cell will contain the formula.

3. Click the Insert Function button on the Standard toolbar. Excel displays its Paste Function dialog box.

4. Because the AVERAGE function is in the Statistical category, click Statistical in the Function category list box. The Function name list box displays the statistical functions.

5. Click AVERAGE in the Function name list box. The dialog box shows the function and its list of arguments. It also displays a brief description of the function.

6. Click the OK button. Excel closes the Paste Function dialog box and displays the Formula Palette (see Figure 10-3) to prompt you for the function's arguments.

Tip   You may not need to complete Steps 7, 8, and 9 if Excel suggests the correct range when the Formula Palette appears.

7. Click the Collapse Dialog button at the right edge of the box labeled Number1 to collapse the Formula Palette temporarily and shift to the worksheet, so that you can select a range.

8. Select the range H1:H6 in the worksheet. This range address appears in the collapsed box, and the formula bar shows the result.

9. Click the Collapse Dialog button again to redisplay the Formula Palette, which shows the formula result.

10. Because you're finding the average of only one range, you don't need to enter any additional arguments. Click the OK button.

Cell H7 now contains the following formula, which returns the average of the values in H1:H6:

```
=AVERAGE(H1:H6)
```

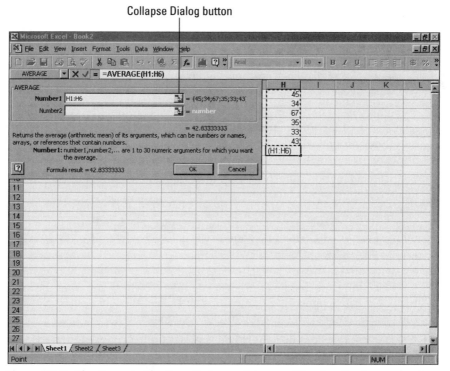

Figure 10-3: The Formula Palette, offering assistance with a function's arguments.

More about entering functions

The following are some additional tips to keep in mind when you use the Formula Palette to enter functions:

✦ Click the Help button (or press F1) at any time to get help about the function that you selected.

✦ If you're starting a new formula, the Formula Palette automatically provides the initial equal sign for you.

✦ If the active cell is not empty when you invoke the Formula Palette, you will be able to edit the formula.

✦ You can use the Paste Function dialog box to insert a function into an existing formula. Just edit the formula and move the insertion point to the location where you want to insert the function. Then, open the Paste Function dialog box and select the function.

✦ If you change your mind about entering a function, click the Cancel button.

✦ The number of boxes that you see in the Formula Palette is determined by the number of arguments used by the function that you selected. If a function uses no arguments, you won't see any boxes. If the function uses a variable number of arguments (such as the AVERAGE function), Excel adds a new box every time that you enter an optional argument.

✦ On the right side of each box, you'll see the current value for each argument.

✦ A few functions, such as INDEX, have more than one form. If you choose such a function, Excel displays another dialog box that lets you choose which form you want to use.

✦ If you only need help remembering a function's arguments, type an equal sign and the function's name, and then press Ctrl+Shift+A. Excel inserts the function with placeholders for the arguments. You need to replace these placeholders with actual arguments.

✦ To locate a function quickly in the Function name list that appears in the Paste Function dialog box, open the list box, type the first letter of the function name, and then scroll to the desired function. For example, if you have selected the All category and want to insert the SIN function, click anywhere on the Function name list box and press S. Excel selects the first function that begins with S — very close to SIN.

✦ If you're using the Formula Palette and want to use a function as the argument for a function (a nested function), click in the box where you want the argument to appear. Then, open the Function List and select the function. Excel will insert the nested function and prompt you for its arguments.

✦ If the active cell contains a formula that uses one or more functions, the Formula Palette lets you edit each function. In the formula bar, click the function that you want to edit. Figure 10-4 shows a formula with multiple functions.

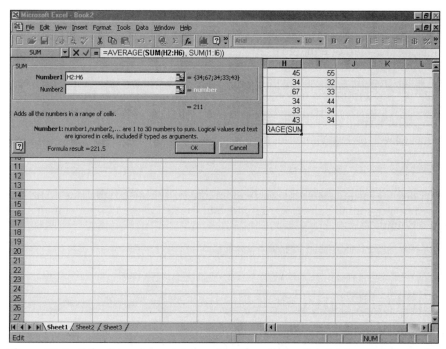

Figure 10-4: If the formula contains multiple functions, click the function in the formula bar to edit it.

Function Examples

This section presents examples of formulas that use functions. It covers all categories listed in the Paste Function dialog box, but not every available function. For more information about a particular function, consult the online Help. For a list of all functions by category, use the Paste Function dialog box.

Cross-Reference   You can also look at Appendix B for more functions by category.

Mathematical and trigonometric functions

Excel provides 50 functions in this category, more than enough to do some serious number crunching. The category includes common functions, such as SUM and INT, as well as plenty of esoteric functions.

INT

The INT function returns the integer (non-decimal) portion of a number by truncating all digits after the decimal point. The example that follows returns 412:

```
=INT(412.98)
```

RAND

The RAND function, which takes no arguments, returns a uniform random number that is greater than or equal to 0 and less than 1. "Uniform" means that all numbers have an equal chance of being generated. This function often is used in worksheets, to simulate events that aren't completely predictable — such as winning lottery numbers — and returns a new result whenever Excel calculates the worksheet.

In the example that follows, the formula returns a random number between 0 and 12 (but 12 will never be generated):

```
=RAND()*12
```

The following formula generates a random integer between two values. The cell named Lower contains the lower bound, and the cell named Upper contains the upper bound:

```
=INT((Upper-Lower+1)*RAND()+Lower)
```

Volatile Functions

Some Excel functions belong to a special class of functions called *volatile.* No, these aren't functions that cause your worksheet to explode. Rather, Excel recalculates a volatile function whenever it recalculates the workbook — even if the formula that contains the function is not involved in the recalculation.

The RAND function is an example of a volatile function, because it generates a new random number every time Excel calculates the worksheet. Other volatile functions are as follows:

AREAS	INDEX	OFFSET
CELL	INDIRECT	ROWS
COLUMNS	NOW	TODAY

A side effect of using these volatile functions is that Excel always prompts you to save the workbook — even if you made no changes. For example, if you open a workbook that contains any of these volatile functions, scroll around a bit (but don't change anything), and then close the file, Excel asks whether you want to save the workbook.

You can circumvent this behavior by using Manual Recalculation mode, with the Recalculate before Save option turned off.

ROMAN

The ROMAN function converts a value to its Roman-numeral equivalent (hey, I never said *all* the functions were useful). Unfortunately for old-movie buffs, no function exists to convert in the opposite direction. The function that follows returns MCMXCVIII:

```
=ROMAN(1998)
```

ROUND

The ROUND function rounds a value to a specified digit to the left or right of the decimal point. This function is often used to control the precision of your calculation. ROUND takes two arguments: the first is the value to be rounded; the second is the digit. If the second argument is negative, the rounding occurs to the left of the decimal point. Table 10-1 demonstrates, with some examples, how this works.

Table 10-1
Examples of Using the ROUND Function

Function	Result
=ROUND(123.457,2)	123.46
=ROUND(123.457,1)	123.50
=ROUND(123.457,0)	123.00
=ROUND(123.457,-1)	120.00
=ROUND(123.457,-2)	100.00
=ROUND(123.457,-3)	0.00

Caution   Don't confuse rounding a value with number formatting applied to a value. When a formula references a cell that has been rounded with the ROUND function, the formula uses the rounded value. If a number has been formatted to *appear* rounded, formulas that refer to that cell use the actual value stored.

Note   If your work involves rounding, also check out the ROUNDUP and ROUNDDOWN functions. In addition, the FLOOR and CEILING functions let you round to a specific multiple — for example, you can use FLOOR to round a value down to the nearest multiple of 10 (124.5 would be rounded to 130).

PI

The PI function returns the value of π significant to 14 decimal places. It doesn't take any arguments and is simply a shortcut for the value 3.14159265358979. In the example that follows, the formula calculates the area of a circle (the radius is stored in a cell named Radius):

```
=PI()*(Radius^2)
```

SIN

The SIN function returns the sine of an angle. The *sine* is defined as the ratio between the opposite side and the hypotenuse of a triangle. SIN takes one argument — the angle expressed in radians. To convert degrees to radians, use the RADIANS function (a DEGREES function also exists to do the opposite conversion). For example, if cell F21 contains an angle expressed in degrees, the formula that follows returns the sine:

```
=SIN(RADIANS(F21))
```

Excel contains the full complement of trigonometric functions. Consult the online Help for details.

SQRT

The SQRT function returns the square root of its argument. If the argument is negative, this function returns an error. The example that follows returns 32:

```
=SQRT(1024)
```

To compute a cube root, raise the value to the $1/3$ power. The example that follows returns the cube root of 32768 — which is 32. Other roots can be calculated in a similar manner.

```
=32768^(1/3)
```

SUM

If you analyze a random sample of workbooks, you'll likely discover that SUM is the most widely used function. It's also among the simplest. The SUM function takes from 1 to 30 arguments. To calculate the sum of three ranges (A1:A10, C1:10, and E1:E10), you use three arguments, like this:

```
=SUM(A1:A10,C1:10,E1:E10)
```

The arguments don't have to be all the same type. For example, you can mix and match single cell references, range references, and literals, as follows:

```
=SUM(A1,C1:10,125)
```

Because the SUM function is so popular, the Excel designers made it very accessible — automatic, in fact. To insert a formula that uses the SUM function, just click the AutoSum button on the Standard toolbar. Excel analyzes the context and suggests a range for an argument. If it suggests correctly (which it usually does), press Enter or click the AutoSum button again. If Excel's guess is incorrect, just drag the mouse and make the selection yourself. To insert a series of SUM formulas — to add several columns of numbers, for example — select the entire range and then click AutoSum. In this case, Excel knows exactly what you want, so it doesn't ask you to confirm it.

SUMIF

The SUMIF function is useful for calculating conditional sums. Figure 10-5 displays a worksheet with a table that shows sales by month and by region. The SUMIF function is used in the formulas in column F. For example, the formula in F2 is as follows:

```
=SUMIF(B:B,E2,C:C)
```

	A	B	C	D	E	F	G	H
1	**Month**	**Region**	**Sales**		**Regional Summary**			
2	Jan	North	16,491		North	54,485		
3	Jan	South	14,557		South	55,089		
4	Jan	West	3,522		West	45,668		
5	Jan	East	22,041		East	61,846		
6	Feb	North	2,061		**TOTAL**	**217,088**		
7	Feb	South	21,813					
8	Feb	West	1,169		**Monthly Summary**			
9	Feb	East	12,486		Jan	56,611		
10	Mar	North	33,956		Feb	37,529		
11	Mar	South	18,318		Mar	79,155		
12	Mar	West	13,500		Apr	43,793		
13	Mar	East	13,381		**TOTAL**	**217,088**		
14	Apr	North	1,977					
15	Apr	South	401					
16	Apr	West	27,477					
17	Apr	East	13,938					
18								
19								

Regional Sales.xls — Sheet1

Figure 10-5: The SUMIF function returns the sum of values if the values meet specified criteria.

SUMIF takes three arguments. The first argument is the range that you're using in the selection criteria — in this case, the entire column B. The second argument is the selection criteria, a region name in the example. The third argument is the range of values to sum if the criteria are met. In this example, the formula in F2 adds the values in column C only if the corresponding text in column B matches the region in column E.

The figure also shows the data summarized by month. The formula in F9 is the following:

```
=SUMIF(A:A,E9,C:C)
```

You also can use Excel's pivot table feature to perform these operations.

Cross-Reference   Pivot tables are covered in Chapter 25.

Text Functions

Although Excel is primarily known for its numerical prowess, it has 23 built-in functions that are designed to manipulate text, a few of which are demonstrated in this section.

CHAR

The CHAR function returns a single character that corresponds to the ANSI code specified in its argument (these codes range from 1 to 255). The CODE function performs the opposite conversion. The formula that follows returns the letter *A*:

```
=CHAR(65)
```

This function is most useful for returning symbols that are difficult or impossible to enter from the keyboard. For example, the formula that follows returns the copyright symbol (©):

```
=CHAR(169)
```

Figure 10-6 shows the characters returned by the CHAR function for arguments from 1 to 255 (using the Arial font).

Note   Not all codes produce printable characters, and the characters may vary depending on the font used.

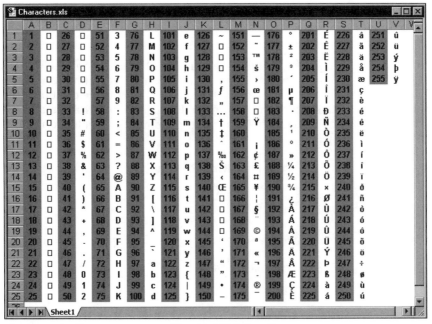

Figure 10-6: Characters returned by the CHAR function.

LEFT

The LEFT function returns a string of characters of a specified length from another string, beginning at the leftmost position. This function uses two arguments. The first argument is the string and the second argument (optional) is the number of characters. If the second argument is omitted, Excel extracts the first character from the text. In the example that follows, the formula returns the letter *B*:

```
=LEFT("B.B. King")
```

The formula that follows returns the string *Alber*:

```
=LEFT("Albert King",5)
```

Note   Excel also has a RIGHT function that extracts characters from the right of a string of characters and a MID function (described after the next section) that extracts characters from any position.

LEN

The LEN function returns the number of characters in a string of text. For example, the following formula returns 12:

```
=LEN("Stratocaster")
```

If you don't want to count leading or trailing spaces, use the LEN function with a nested TRIM function. For example, if you want to know the number of characters in the text in cell A1 without counting spaces, use this formula:

```
=LEN(TRIM(A1))
```

MID

The MID function returns characters from a text string. It takes three arguments. The first argument is the text string. The second argument is the position at which you want to begin extracting. The third argument is the number of characters that you want to extract. If cell A1 contains the text *Joe Louis Walker,* the formula that follows returns *Louis*:

```
=MID(A1,5,5)
```

REPLACE

The REPLACE function replaces characters with other characters. The first argument is the text containing the string that you're replacing. The second argument is the character position at which you want to start replacing. The third argument is the number of characters to replace. The fourth argument is the new text that will replace the existing text. In the example that follows, the formula returns *Albert Collins*:

```
=REPLACE("Albert King",8,4,"Collins")
```

SEARCH

The SEARCH function lets you identify the position in a string of text in which another string occurs. The function takes three arguments. The first argument is the text for which you're searching. The second argument is the string that you want to search. The third argument (optional) is the position at which you want to start searching. If you omit the third argument, Excel starts searching from the beginning of the text.

In the example that follows, assume that cell A1 contains the text *John Lee Hooker.* The formula searches for a space and returns 5, because the first space character was found at the fifth character position.

```
=SEARCH(" ",A1,1)
```

To find the second space in the text, use a nested SEARCH function that uses the result of the first search (incremented by one character) as the third argument:

```
=SEARCH(" ",A1,SEARCH(" ",A1,1)+1)
```

The following formula uses the LEFT function to return the characters to the left of the first space in the text in cell A1. For example, if A1 contains *Jimmy Dawkins,* the formula would return the first name *Jimmy*:

```
=LEFT(A1,SEARCH(" ",A1))
```

The preceding formula has a slight flaw: if the text in cell A1 contains no spaces, the formula results in an error. Here's an improved version that returns the entire string in A1 if it doesn't contains a space:

```
=IF(ISERROR(SEARCH(" ",A1)),A1,LEFT(A1,SEARCH(" ",A1)))
```

UPPER

The UPPER function converts characters to uppercase. If cell A1 contains the text *Lucille*, the formula that follows returns *LUCILLE*:

```
=UPPER(A1)
```

Note　　Excel also has a LOWER function (to convert to lowercase) and a PROPER function (to convert to proper case). In proper case, the first letter of each word is capitalized.

Logical Functions

The Logical category contains only six functions (although several other functions could, arguably, be placed in this category). This section discusses three of these functions: IF, AND, and OR.

IF

The IF function is one of the most important of all functions. This function can give your formulas decision-making capability.

The IF function takes three arguments. The first argument is a logical test that must return either TRUE or FALSE. The second argument is the result that you want the formula to display if the first argument is TRUE. The third argument is the result that you want the formula to display if the first argument is FALSE.

In the example that follows, the formula returns Positive if the value in cell A1 is greater than zero, and returns Negative otherwise:

```
=IF(A1>0,"Positive","Negative")
```

Notice that the first argument (A1>0) evaluates to logical TRUE or FALSE. This formula has a problem in that it returns the text Negative if the cell is blank or contains 0. The solution is to use a nested IF function to perform another logical test. The revised formula is as follows:

```
=IF(A1>0,"Positive",IF(A1<0,"Negative","Zero"))
```

The formula looks complicated, but when you break it down, you see that it's rather simple. Here's how the logic works. If A1 is greater than 0, the formula displays Positive, and nothing else is evaluated. If A1 is not greater than zero, however, the second argument is evaluated. The second argument is as follows:

```
IF(A1<0,"Negative","Zero")
```

This is simply another IF statement that performs the test on A1 again. If it's less than 0, the formula returns Negative. Otherwise, it returns Zero. You can nest IF statements as deeply as you need to—although it can get very confusing after three or four levels.

Using nested IF functions is quite common, so understanding how this concept works is in your best interest. Mastering IF will definitely help you to create more powerful formulas.

Figure 10-7 shows an example of using the IF function to calculate sales commissions. In this example, the usual commission rate is 5.5 percent of sales. If the total sales of a sales rep exceeds the sales goal, the commission rate is 6.25 percent. The formula in cell C6, shown next, uses the IF function to make a decision regarding which commission rate to use based on the sales amount:

```
=IF(B6>=SalesGoal,B6*BonusRate,B6*CommissionRate)
```

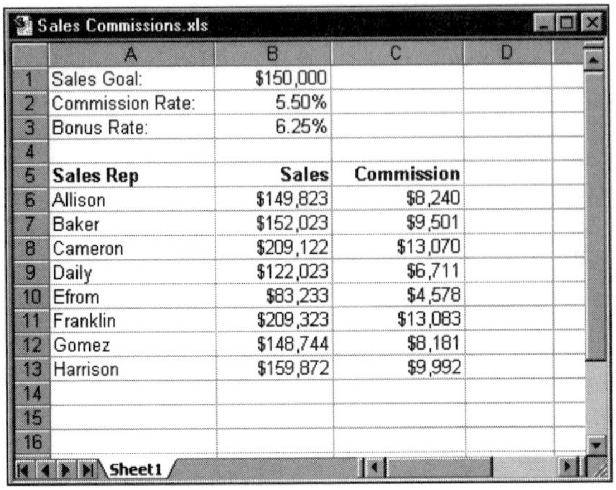

Sales Commissions.xls

	A	B	C	D
1	Sales Goal:	$150,000		
2	Commission Rate:	5.50%		
3	Bonus Rate:	6.25%		
4				
5	**Sales Rep**	**Sales**	**Commission**	
6	Allison	$149,823	$8,240	
7	Baker	$152,023	$9,501	
8	Cameron	$209,122	$13,070	
9	Daily	$122,023	$6,711	
10	Efrom	$83,233	$4,578	
11	Franklin	$209,323	$13,083	
12	Gomez	$148,744	$8,181	
13	Harrison	$159,872	$9,992	
14				
15				
16				

Sheet1

Figure 10-7: Using the IF statement to calculate sales commissions.

AND

The AND function returns a logical value (TRUE or FALSE) depending on the logical value of its arguments. If all its arguments return TRUE, the AND function returns TRUE. If at least one of its arguments returns FALSE, AND returns FALSE.

In the example that follows, the formula returns TRUE if the values in cells A1:A3 are all negative:

```
=AND(A1<0,A2<0,A3<0)
```

The formula that follows uses the AND function as the first argument for an IF function. If all three cells in A1:A3 are negative, this formula displays All Negative. If at least one is not negative, the formula returns Not All Negative:

```
=IF(AND(A1<0,A2<0,A3<0),"All Negative","Not All Negative")
```

OR

The OR function is similar to the AND function, but it returns TRUE if at least one of its arguments is TRUE; otherwise, it returns FALSE. In the example that follows, the formula returns TRUE if the value in any of the cells—A1, A2, or A3—is negative:

```
=OR(A1<0,A2<0,A3<0)
```

Information Functions

Excel's 15 functions in the Information category return a variety of information about cells. Many of these functions return a logical TRUE or FALSE.

CELL

The CELL function returns information about a particular cell. It takes two arguments. The first argument is a code for the type of information to display. The second argument is the address of the cell in which you're interested.

The example that follows uses the `"type"` code, which returns information about the type of data in the cell. It returns *b* if the cell is blank, *l* if it contains text (a label), or *v* if the cell contains a value or formula. For example, if cell A1 contains text, the following formula returns *l*:

```
=CELL("type",A1)
```

If the second argument contains a range reference, Excel uses the upper-left cell in the range.

Note   Excel has other functions that let you determine the type of data in a cell. The following functions may be more useful: ISBLANK, ISERR, ISERROR, ISLOGICAL, ISNA, ISNONTEXT, ISNUMBER, ISREF, ISTEXT, and TYPE.

Table 10-2 lists the possible values for the first argument of the CELL function. When using the CELL function, make sure that you enclose the first argument in quotation marks.

Table 10-2
Codes for the CELL Function Info_Type Argument

Type	What It Returns
address	The cell's address
col	Column number of the cell
color	1 if the cell is formatted in color for negative values — otherwise, 0
contents	The contents of the cell
filename	Name and path of the file that contains the cell (returns empty text if the workbook has not been saved)
format	Text value corresponding to the number format of the cell
prefix	Text value corresponding to the label prefix of the cell; this is provided for 1-2-3 compatibility
protect	0 if the cell is not locked; 1 if the cell is locked
row	Row number of the cell
type	Text value corresponding to the type of data in the cell
width	Column width of the cell, rounded off to an integer

INFO

The INFO function takes one argument — a code for information about the operating environment. In the example that follows, the formula returns the path of the current folder (that is, the folder that Excel displays when you choose File ⇨ Open):

```
=INFO("directory")
```

Table 10-3 lists the valid codes for the INFO function. The codes must be enclosed in quotation marks.

Table 10-3 Codes for the INFO Function	
Code	**What It Returns**
directory	Path of the current folder
memavail	Amount of memory available, in bytes
memused	Amount of memory being used, in bytes
numfile	Number of worksheets in all open workbooks (including hidden workbooks and add-ins)
origin	Returns the cell reference of the top- and leftmost cell visible in the window, based on the current scrolling position
osversion	Current operating system version, as text
recalc	Current recalculation mode — Automatic or Manual
release	Version of Excel
system	Name of the operating environment — mac (for Macintosh) or pcdos (for Windows)
totmem	Total memory available on the system, in bytes

ISERROR

The ISERROR function returns TRUE if its argument returns an error value. Otherwise, it returns FALSE. This function is useful for controlling the display of errors in a worksheet.

Figure 10-8 shows a worksheet that is set up to track monthly sales. Each month, the worksheet is updated with two figures: the number of sales reps on staff and the total sales for the month. Formulas in columns E and F, respectively, calculate the percentage of the sales goal (Actual Sales divided by Sales Goal) and the average sales per sales rep. Notice that the formulas in column F display an error when the data is missing. Cell F2 contains a simple formula:

```
=D2/C2
```

To avoid displaying an error for missing data, change the formula to the following formula and copy it to the cells that follow. If the division results in an error, the formula displays nothing. Otherwise, it displays the result.

```
=IF(ISERROR(D2/C2),"",D2/C2)
```

Month	Sales Goal	Sales Reps	Actual Sales	Pct. Of Goal	Avg. Per Rep
January	500,000	9	510,233	102%	56,693
February	525,000	10	518,733	99%	51,873
March	550,000	10	569,844	104%	56,984
April	575,000	10	560,923	98%	56,092
May	600,000	11	601,923	100%	54,720
June	625,000			0%	#DIV/0!
July	650,000			0%	#DIV/0!
August	675,000			0%	#DIV/0!
September	700,000			0%	#DIV/0!
October	725,000			0%	#DIV/0!
November	750,000			0%	#DIV/0!
December	775,000			0%	#DIV/0!

Figure 10-8: This worksheet is displaying an error for formulas that refer to missing data.

Note

Excel offers several other functions that let you trap error values: ERROR.TYPE, ISERR, and ISNA. Also, note that the preceding formula could have used the ISBLANK function to test for missing data.

Date and Time Functions

If you use dates or times in your worksheets, you owe it to yourself to check out Excel's 14 functions that work with these types of values. This section demonstrates a few of these functions.

Cross-Reference

To work with dates and times, you should be familiar with Excel's serial number date-and-time system. Refer to Chapter 6.

TODAY

The TODAY function takes no argument. It returns a date that corresponds to the current date — that is, the date set in the system. If you enter the following formula into a cell on June 16, 1998, the formula returns 6/16/98:

```
=TODAY()
```

Note Excel also has a NOW function that returns the current system date and the current system time.

DATE

The DATE function displays a date based on its three arguments: year, month, and day. This function is useful if you want to create a date based on information in your worksheet. For example, if cell A1 contains 1998, cell B1 contains 12, and cell C1 contains 25, the following formula returns the date for December 25, 1998:

```
=DATE(A1,B1,C1)
```

DAY

The DAY function returns the day of the month for a date. If cell A1 contains the date 12/25/98, the following formula returns 25:

```
=DAY(A1)
```

Note Excel also includes the YEAR and MONTH functions that extract from a date the year part and month part, respectively.

WEEKDAY

The WEEKDAY function returns the day of the week for a date. It takes two arguments: the date and a code that specifies the type of result (the second argument is optional). The codes are listed in Table 10-4.

Table 10-4 Codes for the WEEKDAY Function	
Code	**What It Returns**
1 or omitted	Numbers 1-7, corresponding to Sunday through Saturday
2	Numbers 1-7, corresponding to Monday through Sunday
3	Numbers 0-6, corresponding to Monday through Sunday

If cell A1 contains 12/25/98, the formula that follows returns 6 — which indicates that this date is a Friday:

```
=WEEKDAY(A1)
```

Tip You also can format cells that contain dates to display the day of the week as part of the format. Use a custom format code of ddd (for abbreviated days of the week) or dddd (for fully spelled days of the week).

TIME

The TIME function displays a time based on its three arguments: hour, minute, and second. This function is useful if you want to create a time based on information in your worksheet. For example, if cell A1 contains 8, cell B1 contains 15, and cell C1 contains 0, the following formula returns 8:15:00 AM:

```
=TIME(A1,B1,C1)
```

HOUR

The HOUR function returns the hour for a time. If cell A1 contains the time 8:15:00 AM, the following formula returns 8:

```
=HOUR(A1)
```

Note   Excel also includes the MINUTE and SECOND functions, which extract the minute part and second part, respectively, from a time.

Financial Functions

The Financial function category includes 16 functions that are designed to perform calculations that involve money.

Depreciation functions

Excel offers five functions to calculate depreciation of an asset over time. The function that you choose depends on the type of depreciation that you use. Figure 10-9 shows a chart that depicts how an asset is depreciated over time, using each of the five depreciation functions.

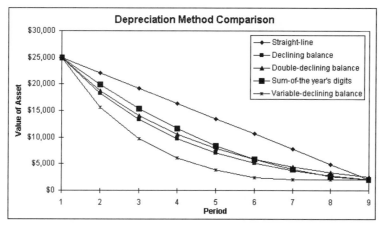

Figure 10-9: A comparison of Excel's five depreciation functions.

Table 10-5 summarizes the depreciation functions and the arguments used by each. For complete details, consult the online Help system.

Table 10-5 Excel's Depreciation Functions		
Function	**Depreciation Method**	**Arguments***
SLN	Straight-line	Cost, Salvage, Life
DB	Declining balance	Cost, Salvage, Life, Period, [Month]
DDB	Double-declining balance	Cost, Salvage, Life, Period, Month, [Factor]
SYD	Sum-of-the year's digits	Cost, Salvage, Life, Period
VDB	Variable-declining balance	Cost, Salvage, Life, Start Period, End Period, [Factor], [No Switch]

* Arguments in brackets are optional

The arguments for the depreciation functions are described as follows:

✦ **Cost:** Original cost of the asset.

✦ **Salvage:** Salvage cost of the asset after it has been fully depreciated.

✦ **Life:** Number of periods over which the asset will be depreciated.

✦ **Period:** Period in the Life for which the calculation is being made.

✦ **Month:** Number of months in the first year; if omitted, Excel uses 12.

✦ **Factor:** Rate at which the balance declines; if omitted, it is assumed to be 2 (that is, double-declining).

✦ **Rate:** Interest rate per period. If payments are made monthly, for example, you must divide the annual interest rate by 12.

Loan and annuity functions

Table 10-6 lists the functions that can help you perform calculations related to loans and annuities.

Notice that these functions all use pretty much the same arguments — although the exact arguments that are used depend on the function. To use these functions successfully, you must understand how to specify the arguments correctly. The following list explains these arguments:

✦ **Nper:** Total number of payment periods. For a 30-year mortgage loan with monthly payments, Nper is 360.

✦ **Per:** Period in the loan for which the calculation is being made; it must be a number between 1 and Nper.

✦ **Pmt:** Fixed payment made each period for an annuity or a loan. This usually includes principal and interest (but not fees or taxes).

✦ **FV:** Future value (or a cash balance) after the last payment is made. The future value for a loan is 0. If FV is omitted, Excel uses 0.

✦ **Type:** Either 0 or 1, and indicates when payments are due. Use 0 if the payments are due at the end of the period, and 1 if they are due at the beginning of the period.

✦ **Guess:** Used only for the RATE function. It's your best guess of the internal rate of return. The closer your guess, the faster Excel can calculate the exact result.

Table 10-6
Loan and Annuity Functions

Function	Calculation	Arguments*
FV	Future value	Rate, Nper, Pmt, [PV], [Type]
PV	Present value	Rate, Nper, Pmt, [FV], [Type]
PMT	Payment	Rate, Nper, PV, [FV], [Type]
PPMT	Principal payment	Rate, Per, Nper, PV, [FV], [Type]
IPMT	Interest payment	Rate, Per, Nper, PV, [FV], [Type]
ISPMT	Payment interest	Rate, Per, Nper, PV
RATE	Interest rate per period	Nper, Pmt, PV, [FV], [Type], [Guess]
NPER	Number of periods	Rate, Pmt, PV, [FV], [Type]

* Arguments in brackets are optional

This book's CD-ROM contains an example workbook that demonstrates the use of the PMT, PPMT, and IPMT functions to calculate a fixed-interest amortization schedule.

Lookup and Reference Functions

The 17 functions in the Lookup and Reference category, some of which are demonstrated in this section, are used to perform table lookups and obtain other types of information.

VLOOKUP

The VLOOKUP function can be quite useful when you need to use a value from a table, such as a table of tax rates. This function retrieves text or a value from a table, based on a specific key in the first column of the table. The retrieved result is at a specified horizontal offset from the first row of the table.

Figure 10-10 shows an example of a lookup table (named PartsList) in range D2:F9. The worksheet is designed so that a user can enter a part number into cell B2 (which is named Part), and formulas in cells B4 and B5 return the appropriate information for the part by using the lookup table. The formulas are as follows:

✦ **Cell B4:** =VLOOKUP(Part,PartsList,2,FALSE)

✦ **Cell B5:** =VLOOKUP(Part,PartsList,3,FALSE)

	A	B	C	D	E	F	
	Part Lookup.xls						
1							
2	Enter Part No. -->	225		Part Number	Name	Unit Cost	
3				145	Mesh Rod	$5.95	
4	Name:	Toe Bolt		155	Puddle Joint	$12.95	
5	Unit Cost:	$0.49		187	Penguin Bold	$1.29	
6				205	Finger Nut	$0.98	
7				225	Toe Bolt	$0.49	
8				319	Piano Nail	$0.99	
9				377	Mule Pip	$9.95	
10							
11							
12							

Figure 10-10: A vertical lookup table.

The formula in B4 looks up the value in the cell named Part in the first column of the table named PartsList. It returns the value in the column that corresponds to its third argument (column 2). The fourth argument tells Excel that it must find an exact match. If the fourth argument is TRUE (or omitted), Excel returns the next largest value that is less than the lookup value (the values in the first column must be in ascending order). Using an inexact match is useful for income tax tables, in which a line doesn't exist for every possible income.

If you enter a value that doesn't appear in the table, the formula returns #N/A. You can change the formula to produce a more user-friendly error message by using the ISNA function. The revised formula is as follows:

```
=IF(ISNA(VLOOKUP(Part,PartsList,2,FALSE)),"NotFound",VLOOKUP(Pa
rt,PartsList,2,FALSE))
```

If you enter a part that is not in the list, this formula returns Not Found rather than #N/A.

Note   The HLOOKUP function works exactly like VLOOKUP except that it looks up the value horizontally in the table's first row.

MATCH

The MATCH function searches a range for a value or text and returns the relative row or column in which the item was found. Figure 10-11 shows a simple example. The worksheet contains the month names in A1:A12. Cell D2 contains the following formula:

```
=MATCH(D1,A1:A12,0)
```

The formula returns 7, because cell D1 contains July, and July is the seventh element in the range A1:A12.

The third argument for the MATCH function specifies the type of match that you want (0 means an exact match). Use the values of 1 and –1 when you are willing to accept an inexact match.

	A	B	C	D	E
1	January		Enter a month -->	July	
2	February		Result:	7	
3	March				
4	April				
5	May				
6	June				
7	July				
8	August				
9	September				
10	October				
11	November				
12	December				
13					

Figure 10-11: Using the MATCH function to return a relative position in a range.

INDEX

The INDEX function returns a value from a range using a row index (for a vertical range), column index (for a horizontal range), or both (for a two-dimensional range). The formula that follows returns the value in A1:J10 that is in its fifth row and third column:

```
=INDEX(A1:J10,5,3)
```

On the CD-ROM, you'll find a workbook that demonstrates the INDEX and MATCH functions. The workbook, shown in Figure 10-12, displays the mileage between selected U.S. cities.

The OFFSET function performs a similar function.

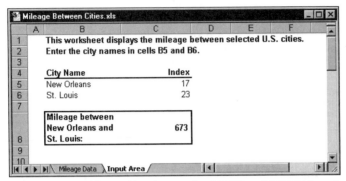

Figure 10-12: This workbook uses the INDEX and MATCH functions to look up the mileage between selected U.S. cities.

INDIRECT

The INDIRECT function returns the value in a cell specified by its text argument. For example, the following formula returns the value (or text) in cell A1:

```
=INDIRECT("A1")
```

This function is most useful when you use a reference as its argument (not a literal, as shown previously). For example, suppose cell C9 contains the text Sales and, in your worksheet, you have defined the name Sales for cell A1; A1 (or Sales) contains the value 46. The following formula returns 46, the value in the cell named Sales:

```
=INDIRECT(C9)
```

This concept can be a bit difficult to grasp, but after you master it, you can put it to good use. Figure 10-13 shows a multisheet workbook with formulas that use the INDIRECT function to summarize the information in the other worksheets in the workbook. Cell B2 contains the following formula, which was copied to the other cells:

```
=INDIRECT("'"&$A2&"'"&"!"&B$1)
```

This formula builds a cell reference by using text in row 1 and column A. Excel evaluates the argument as follows:

```
'Denver'!Sales
```

The Denver sheet has a range named Sales. Therefore, the indirect function returns the value in the cell named Sales on the Denver worksheet.

This file is available on the book's CD-ROM.

Figure 10-13: These formulas use the INDIRECT function to summarize values contained in the other workbooks.

Statistical Functions

The Statistical category contains a whopping 80 functions that perform various calculations. Many of these are quite specialized, but several are useful for nonstatisticians.

AVERAGE

The AVERAGE function returns the average (arithmetic mean) of a range of values. The *average* is the sum of the range divided by the number of values in the range. The formula that follows returns the average of the values in the range A1:A100:

```
=AVERAGE(A1:A100)
```

If the range argument contains blanks or text, Excel doesn't include these cells in the average calculation. As with the SUM formula, you can supply any number of arguments.

> **Note**   Excel also provides the MEDIAN function (which returns the middle-most value in a range) and the MODE function (which returns the value that appears most frequently in a range).

COUNTIF

The COUNTIF function is useful if you want to count the number of times that a specific value occurs in a range. This function takes two arguments: the range that contains the value to count and a criterion used to determine what to count. Figure 10-14 shows a worksheet set up with student grades. The COUNTIF function is used in the formulas in column E. For example, the formula in E2 is as follows:

```
=COUNTIF(B:B,D2)
```

Notice that the first argument consists of a range reference for the entire column B, enabling you to insert new names easily without having to change the formulas.

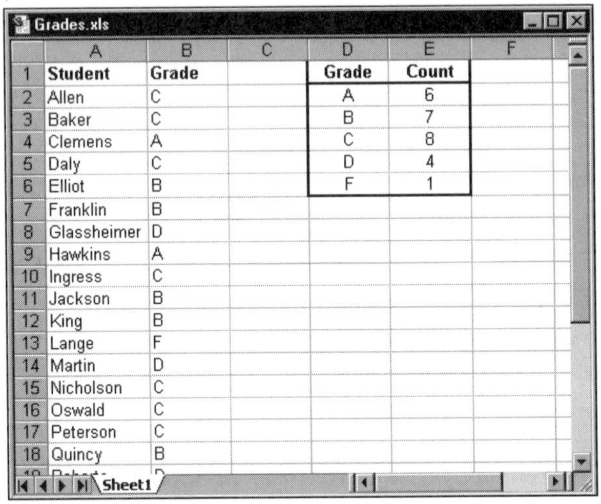

Figure 10-14: Using the COUNTIF function to create a distribution of grades.

Cross-Reference   You also can use the Analysis ToolPak add-in to create frequency distributions. See Chapter 28 for details.

COUNT, COUNTA, COUNTBLANK, and COUNTIF

The COUNT function returns the number of values in a range. The COUNTA function returns the number of nonblank cells in a range. For example, the following formula returns the number of nonempty cells in column A:

```
=COUNTA("A:A")
```

COUNTBLANK counts the number of blank cells in a range, and COUNTIF counts the number of cells within a range that meet the criteria that you specify in the argument.

MAX and MIN

Use the MAX function to return the largest value in a range, and the MIN function to return the smallest value in a range. Both MAX and MIN ignore logical values and text. The following formula displays the largest and smallest values in a range named Data; using the concatenation operator causes the result to appear in a single cell:

```
="Smallest: "&MIN(Data)&" Largest: "&MAX(Data)
```

For example, if the values in Data range from 12 to 156, this formula returns Smallest: 12 Largest: 156.

MAXA and MINA are new to Excel 2000. These functions work like MAX and MIN, respectively, but MAXA and MINA don't ignore logical values and text.

LARGE and SMALL

The LARGE function returns the *n*th-largest value in a range. For example, to display the second-largest value in a range named Data, use the following formula:

```
=LARGE(Data,2)
```

The SMALL function works just as you would expect; it returns the *n*th-smallest value in a range.

Database Functions

Excel's Database function category consists of a dozen functions that you use when working with database tables (also known as lists) stored in a worksheet. These functions all begin with the letter *D*, and they all have non-database equivalents. For example, the DSUM function is a special version of the SUM function that returns the sum of values in a database that meet a specified criterion. A database table is a rectangular range with field names in the top row. Each subsequent row is considered a record in the database.

To use a database function, you must specify a special criteria range in the worksheet. This type of criteria range is the same one that you use with Excel's Data ➪ Filter ➪ Advanced Filter command.

Cross-Reference   This topic is discussed in Chapter 23.

The DSUM function calculates the sum of the values in a specified field, filtered by the criteria table. For example, to calculate the total sales for the North region, enter **North** under the Region field in the criteria range. Then, enter the following formula into any cell (this assumes that the database table is named Data and that the criteria range is named Criteria):

```
=DSUM(Data,"Sales",Criteria)
```

The formula returns the sum of the Sales field, but only for the records that meet the criteria in the range named Criteria. You can change the criteria, and the formula displays the new result. For example, to calculate the sales for January, enter **Jan** under the Month field in the Criteria range (and delete any other entries).

If you want to use several DSUM formulas, you can have each of them refer to a different criteria range (you can use as many criteria ranges as you need).

Excel's other database functions work exactly like the DSUM function.

Analysis ToolPak Functions

When you begin to feel familiar with Excel's worksheet functions, you can explore those that are available when you load the Analysis ToolPak. This add-in provides you with dozens of additional worksheet functions.

When you load this add-in, the Paste Function dialog box displays a new category, Engineering. It also adds new functions to the following function categories: Financial, Date & Time, Math & Trig, and Information.

Cross-Reference   The Analysis ToolPak is discussed in Chapter 28. See Appendix B for a summary of the Analysis ToolPak function.

Creating Megaformulas

Often, spreadsheets require intermediate formulas to produce a desired result. After you get the formulas working correctly, you often can eliminate the intermediate formulas and use a single *megaformula* instead (this term is my own—no official name exists for such a formula). The advantages? You use fewer cells (less clutter) and recalculation takes less time. Besides, people in the know will be impressed with your formula-building abilities. The disadvantage? The formula may be impossible to decipher or modify.

Imagine a worksheet with a column of people's names. And suppose that you've been asked to remove all middle names and middle initials from the names—but not all of the names have a middle name or initial. Editing the cells manually would take hours, so you opt for a formula-based solution. Although this task is not a difficult one, it normally involves several intermediate formulas. Also assume that you want to use as few cells as possible in the solution.

Figure 10-15 shows the solution, which requires six intermediate formulas. The names are in column A; the end result is in column H. Columns B through G hold the intermediate formulas. Table 10-7 shows the formulas used in this worksheet, along with a brief description of each.

	A	B	C	D	E	F	G	H
1	Bob Smith	Bob Smith	4	#VALUE!	4	Bob	Smith	Bob Smith
2	Mike A. Jones	Mike A. Jones	5	8	8	Mike	Jones	Mike Jones
3	Jim Ray Johnson	Jim Ray Johnson	4	8	8	Jim	Johnson	Jim Johnson
4	Tom Alvin Jacobs	Tom Alvin Jacobs	4	10	10	Tom	Jacobs	Tom Jacobs
5	Mr. Fred Kingsley	Mr. Fred Kingsley	4	9	9	Mr.	Kingsley	Mr. Kingsley
6	J.P. Smithers	J.P. Smithers	5	#VALUE!	5	J.P.	Smithers	J.P. Smithers
7								
8								
9								
10								

megaformula.xls — Sheet1

Figure 10-15: Removing the middle names and initials requires six intermediate formulas.

Table 10-7
Intermediate Formulas

Cell	Intermediate Formula	What It Does
B1	=TRIM(A1)	Removes excess spaces
C1	=FIND(" ",B1,1)	Locates first space
D1	=FIND(" ",B1,C1+1)	Locates second space (returns an error if no second space exists)
E1	=IF(ISERROR(D1),C1,D1)	Uses the first space if no second space
F1	=LEFT(B1,C1)	Extracts the first name
G1	=RIGHT(B1,LEN(B1)-E1)	Extracts the last name
H1	=F1&G1	Concatenates the two names

You can eliminate all the intermediate formulas by creating a huge formula (what I call a megaformula). You do so by starting with the end result and then replacing each cell reference with a copy of the formula in the cell referred to (but don't copy the equal sign). Fortunately, you can use the Clipboard to copy and paste. Keep repeating this process until cell H1 contains nothing but references to cell A1. You end up with the following megaformula in one cell:

```
=LEFT(TRIM(A1),FIND("",TRIM(A1),1))&RIGHT(TRIM(A1),LEN(TRIM(A1)
)-IF(ISERROR(FIND(" ",TRIM(A1),FIND(" ",TRIM(A1),1)+1)),FIND("
",TRIM(A1),1),FIND(" ",TRIM(A1),FIND(" ",TRIM(A1),1)+1)))
```

When you're satisfied that the megaformula is working, you can delete the columns that hold the intermediate formulas, because they are no longer used.

The megaformula performs exactly the same task as all the intermediate formulas — although it's virtually impossible for anyone (even the original author) to figure out. If you decide to use megaformulas, make sure that the intermediate formulas are performing correctly before you start building a megaformula. Even better, keep a copy of the intermediate formulas somewhere, in case you discover an error or need to make a change.

Your only limitation is that Excel's formulas can be no more than 1,024 characters. Because a megaformula is so complex, you may think that using one would slow down recalculation. Actually, the opposite is true. As a test, I created a worksheet that used a megaformula 20,000 times. Then, I created another worksheet that used six intermediate formulas rather than the megaformula. As you can see in Table 10-8, the megaformula recalculated faster and also resulted in a much smaller file.

This workbook is available on the CD-ROM.

Table 10-8 Intermediate Formulas Versus Megaformula		
Method	Recalc Time (seconds)	File Size
Intermediate formulas	9.2	7.1MB
Megaformula	5.1	2.5MB

Creating Custom Functions

Although Excel offers more functions than you'll ever need, you may eventually search for a function that you need and not be able to find it. The solution is to create your own.

If you don't have the skills to create your own functions, you may be able to purchase custom Excel functions from a third-party provider that specializes in your industry. Or, you can hire a consultant to develop functions that meet your needs.

To create a custom function, you must be well-versed in Visual Basic for Applications (VBA). When you create a custom function, you can use it in your worksheet, just like the built-in functions.

 Cross-Reference   Custom worksheet functions are covered in Chapter 36.

Learning More About Functions

This chapter has just barely skimmed the surface. Excel has hundreds of functions that I haven't mentioned. To learn more about the functions available to you, I suggest that you browse through them by using the Paste Function dialog box and click the Help button when you see something that looks useful. The functions are thoroughly described in Excel's online Help system.

Summary

This chapter discusses the built-in worksheet functions available in Excel. These functions are arranged by category, and you can enter them into your formulas either manually (by typing them) or by using the Paste Function dialog box and the Formula Palette. Many examples of functions across the various categories are also discussed.

✦   ✦   ✦

Worksheet Formatting

Chapter 6 discussed number formatting, which enables you to change the way that Excel displays values in their cells. This chapter covers what I refer to as *stylistic* formatting, which is purely cosmetic.

Overview of Stylistic Formatting

The stylistic formatting that you apply to worksheet cells doesn't affect the actual content of the cells. Rather, you should use stylistic formatting with the goal of making your work easier to read or more attractive. In this chapter, you'll learn about the following types of formatting:

+ Using different type fonts, sizes, and attributes
+ Changing the way the contents of cells are aligned within cells
+ Using colors in the background or foreground of cells
+ Using patterns for cell background
+ Using borders around cells
+ Using a graphic background for your worksheet

On the CD-ROM This book's CD-ROM contains a file that demonstrates many of the techniques used in this chapter.

Why Bother Formatting?

Some users tend to shy away from formatting. After all, it doesn't do anything to make the worksheet more accurate, and formatting just takes valuable time.

I'll be the first to admit that stylistic formatting isn't essential for every workbook that you develop. If no one except you will ever see your workbook, you may not want to bother. If anyone else will use your workbook, however, I strongly suggest that you spend some time applying simple formatting. Figure 11-1 shows how even simple formatting can significantly improve a worksheet's readability.

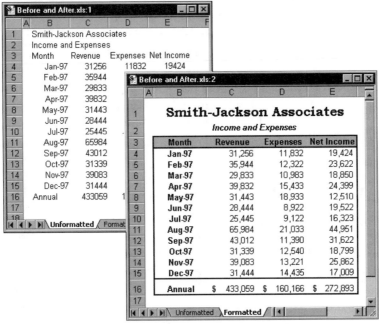

Figure 11-1: Before and after applying simple stylistic formatting.

On the other hand, some users go overboard with formatting. I've downloaded many Excel worksheets from the Internet and online services, such as CompuServe. Some of these worksheets are hideous and don't convey a professional image. You disguise your work and make it difficult to read and understand if you use too many different fonts, font sizes, colors, and borders.

Eventually, you'll strike a happy medium with your stylistic formatting: not too much, but enough to clarify what you're trying to accomplish with your worksheet.

When to Format

When you're developing a worksheet, you can apply stylistic formatting at any time. Some people prefer to format their work as they go along (I'm in this group). Others wait until the workbook is set up and then apply the formatting as the final step (the icing on the cake). The choice is yours.

The Formatting Toolbar

Chapter 6 introduced the Formatting toolbar, shown in Figure 11-2, which you use to apply simple stylistic formatting quickly.

Figure 11-2: The Formatting toolbar contains many tools to apply formats.

In many cases, this toolbar may contain all the formatting tools that you need. But some types of formatting require that you use the Format Cells dialog box. This chapter covers the finer points of stylistic formatting, including options not available on the Formatting toolbar.

The Format Cells Dialog Box

This chapter refers repeatedly to the Format Cells dialog box. This is a tabbed dialog box from which you can apply nearly any type of stylistic formatting (as well as number formatting). The formats that you choose in the Format Cells dialog box apply to the cells that you have selected at the time.

After selecting the cell or range to format, you can display the Format Cells dialog box by using any of the following methods:

✦ Choose the Format ➪ Cells command

✦ Press Ctrl+1

✦ Right-click the selected cell or range and choose Format Cells from the shortcut menu

The Format Cells dialog box contains six tabs. When you first open this dialog box, you see the Number tab. You can choose another tab by clicking any of the other tabs. When you open this dialog box again, Excel displays the tab that you used last.

Working with Fonts

Fonts are one of the elements that distinguish a *graphical user interface* (GUI), such as Windows, from a character-based interface (such as plain-old DOS). A GUI can display different fonts in different sizes and with different attributes (bold, italic, underline). A character-based display typically shows one font of the same size and may be capable of handling different font attributes.

Tip   You can use different fonts, sizes, or attributes in your worksheets to make various parts stand out, such as the headers for a table. You also can adjust the font size to make more information appear on a single page.

Reducing the font size so that your report fits on a certain number of pages isn't always necessary.

Cross-Reference   Excel has a handy option that automatically scales your printed output to fit on a specified number of pages, which is discussed in Chapter 12.

About Fonts

When you select a font, Excel displays only the fonts that are installed on your system. Windows includes several fonts, and Microsoft Office 2000 includes many additional fonts that you can install on your system. You can acquire fonts from a variety of other sources, too, such as the Internet and online services. For best results, you should use TrueType fonts. You can display and print these fonts in any size, without the "jaggies" (jagged edges) that characterize nonscalable fonts.

Caution   Although you can obtain fonts from many different locations, remember that fonts take up space on your hard drive and use memory. In addition, using too many fonts in a workbook can confuse the reader. You may not ever need any fonts other than those that come with Windows.

If you plan to distribute a workbook to other users, you should stick with the fonts that are included with Windows. If you open a workbook and your system doesn't have the font with which the workbook was created, Windows attempts to use a similar font. Sometimes this works, and sometimes it doesn't. To be on the safe side, use the following fonts only if you plan to share your workbook with others:

- ✦ Arial
- ✦ Courier New
- ✦ Symbol
- ✦ Times New Roman
- ✦ Wingdings

The Default Font

By default, the information that you enter into an Excel worksheet uses the 10-point Arial font. A font is described by its typeface (Arial, Times New Roman, Courier New, and so on) as well as by its size, measured in points (there are 72 points in one inch). Excel's row height, by default, is 12.75 points. Therefore, 10-point type entered into 12.75-point rows leaves a small amount of blank space between the characters in adjacent rows.

Note   If you have not manually changed a row's height, Excel automatically adjusts the row height based on the tallest text that you enter into the row. You can, of course, override this adjustment and change the row height to any size that you like by using 0.25-point increments. For example, if you enter a row height of 15.35, Excel makes the row 15.5 points high (it always rounds up).

The default font is the font specified by the Normal style for the workbook. All cells use the Normal style unless you specifically apply a different style. If you want to change the font for all cells that use the Normal style, you simply change the font used in the Normal style by using these steps:

1. Choose the Format ➪ Style command. Excels displays the Style dialog box.

2. Make sure that Normal appears in the *Style name* drop-down box and click the Modify button. Excel displays the Format Cells dialog box.

3. Click the Font tab and choose the font and size that you want as the default.

4. Click OK to return to the Style dialog box.

5. Click OK again to close the Style dialog box.

The font for all cells that use the Normal style changes to the font that you specified. You can change the font for the Normal style at any time. Excel's style feature is discussed later in this chapter.

Cross-Reference   If you want to change the default font permanently, create a template named book.xlt that uses a different font for the Normal style. Templates are covered in Chapter 34.

Changing Fonts in Excel 2000

Use the Font and Font Size tools on the Formatting toolbar to change the font or size for selected cells. Just select the cells, click the appropriate tool, and then choose the font or size from the drop-down list. In Excel 2000, you can see samples of the fonts when you open the Font list box on the Formatting toolbar (see Figure 11-3). If you prefer the behavior of earlier versions of Excel, in which you don't see font samples when you open this list box, you can change this behavior in the Options dialog box.

You also can use the Font tab in the Format Cells dialog box, as shown in Figure 11-4. This tab enables you to control several other attributes of the font—from a single dialog box—and preview the font before you select it. Notice that you also can change the font style (bold, italic), underlining, color, and effects (strikethrough, superscript, or subscript). If you click the check box labeled Normal Font, Excel displays the selections for the font defined for the Normal style.

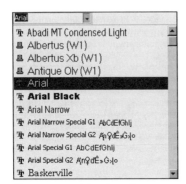

Figure 11-3: The Font list on the Formatting toolbar shows samples as well as choices.

Note

Notice in Figure 11-5 that Excel provides four different underlining styles. In the two accounting underline styles, dollar signs and percent signs aren't underlined. In the two nonaccounting underline styles, the entire cell contents are always underlined.

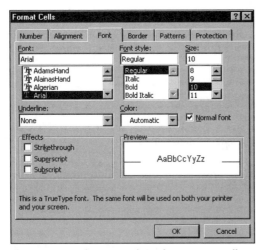

Figure 11-4: The Font tab in the Format Cells dialog box.

Figure 11-5 shows examples of font formatting.

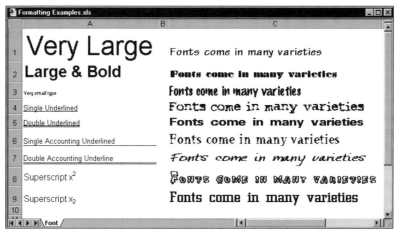

Figure 11-5: Examples of font formatting.

Using Multiple Formatting in One Cell

If a cell contains text (not a formula or a value), Excel also enables you to format individual characters in the cell. To do so, switch into edit mode (double-click the cell) and then select the characters that you want to format. You can select characters either by dragging the mouse over them or by holding down the Shift key as you press the left- or right-arrow key. Then, use any of the standard formatting techniques. The changes apply to only the selected characters in the cell. This technique doesn't work with cells that contain values or formulas.

Figure 11-6 shows a few examples of using different fonts, sizes, and attributes in a cell.

Selecting Fonts and Attributes with Shortcut Keys

If you prefer to keep your hands on the keyboard, you can use the following shortcut keys to format a selected range quickly:

Ctrl+B	Bold
Ctrl+I	Italic
Ctrl+U	Underline
Ctrl+5	Strikethrough

These shortcut keys act as a toggle. For example, you can turn on and off bold by repeatedly pressing Ctrl+B.

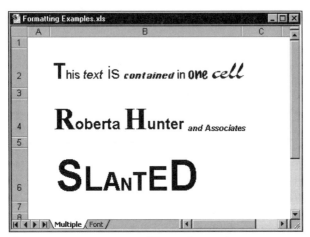

Figure 11-6: You can use different fonts, sizes, or attributes for selected characters in text.

Changing Cell Alignment

Cell alignment refers to how a cell's contents are situated in the cell. The contents of a cell can be aligned both vertically and horizontally. The effect that you see depends on the cell's height and width. For example, if the row uses standard height, you may not notice any changes in the cell's vertical alignment (but if you increase the row's height, these effects are apparent).

Note   Excel also enables you to display text at a specified orientation — you choose the angle.

Figure 11-7 shows some examples of cells formatted with the various horizontal and vertical alignment options.

Horizontal Alignment Options

You can apply most of the horizontal alignment options by using the tools on the Formatting toolbar. Or, you can use the Alignment tab in the Format Cells dialog box, as shown in Figure 11-8.

The horizontal alignment options are as follows:

✦ **General:** Aligns numbers to the right, aligns text to the left, and centers logical and error values. This option is the default alignment.

✦ **Left:** Aligns the cell contents to the left side of the cell. If the text is wider than the cell, it spills over to the cell to the right. If the cell to the right is not empty, the text is truncated and not completely visible.

✦ **Center:** Centers the cell contents in the cell. If the text is wider than the cell, it spills over to cells on either side, if they are empty. If the adjacent cells aren't empty, the text is truncated and not completely visible.

✦ **Right:** Aligns the cell contents to the right side of the cell. If the text is wider than the cell, it spills over to the cell to the left. If the cell to the left isn't empty, the text is truncated and not completely visible.

✦ **Fill:** Repeats the contents of the cell until the cell's width is filled. If cells to the right also are formatted with Fill alignment, they also are filled.

✦ **Justify:** Justifies the text to the left and right of the cell. This option is applicable only if the cell is formatted as wrapped text and uses more than one line.

✦ **Center across selection:** Centers the text over the selected columns. This option is useful for precisely centering a heading over a number of columns.

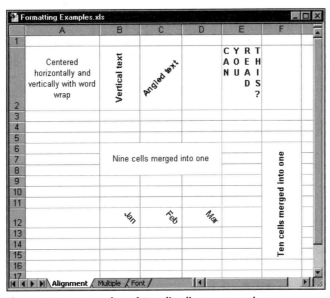

Figure 11-7: Examples of Excel's alignment options.

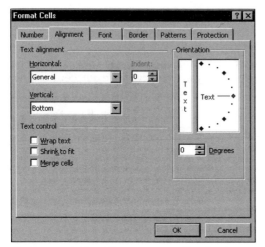

Figure 11-8: The Alignment panel in the Format Cells dialog box.

Vertical Alignment Options

To change the vertical alignment, you must use the Alignment tab of the Format Cells dialog box (these options are not available on the Formatting toolbar). The vertical alignment options are as follows:

- ✦ **Top:** Aligns the cell contents to the top of the cell
- ✦ **Center:** Centers the cell contents vertically in the cell
- ✦ **Bottom:** Aligns the cell contents to the bottom of the cell
- ✦ **Justify:** Justifies the text vertically in the cell; this option is applicable only if the cell is formatted as wrapped text and uses more than one line

Text Control Options

The Alignment tab of the Format Cells dialog box offers three additional options, which are discussed in the following sections.

Wrap Text

The Wrap text option displays the text on multiple lines in the cell, if necessary. Use this option to display lengthy headings without having to make the columns too wide.

Shrink to Fit

Excel includes a Shrink to fit option, which reduces the size of the text so that it fits into the cell without spilling over to the next cell.

If you apply wrap text formatting to a cell, you can't use the shrink-to-fit formatting.

Merging Cells

When you merge cells, you don't combine the contents of cells. Rather, you combine a group of cells that occupy the same space into a single cell. Figure 11-9 shows two sets of merged cells. Range C3:G3 has been merged into a single cell that holds the table's title. Range B5:B9 has also been merged to hold a title for the table's rows.

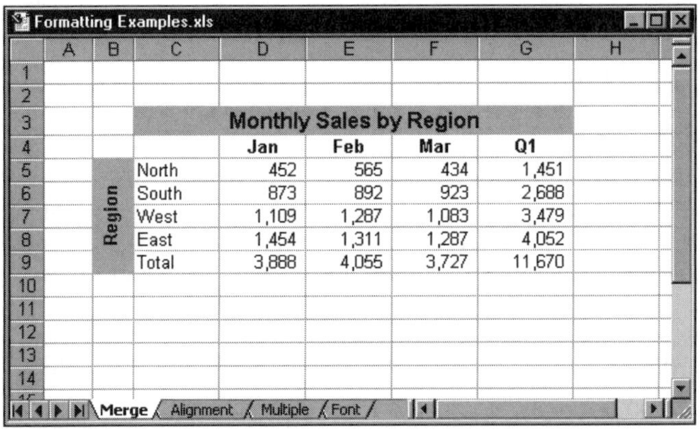

Figure 11-9: The titles for this table appear in merged cells.

You can merge any number of cells, occupying any number of rows and columns. However, the range that you intend to merge should be empty, except for the upper-left cell. If any of the other cells that you intend to merge are not empty, Excel displays a warning.

To merge cells, select the cells that you want to merge and then click the Merge and Center tool on the Formatting toolbar. The only way to "unmerge" cells is to use the Format Cells dialog box. Select the merged cell(s), open the Format Cells dialog box, and, on the Alignment tab, remove the check from the Merge cells box.

Changing a Cell's Orientation

You can display text horizontally, vertically, or specify an angle. To change the orientation, select the cell or range, open the Format Cells dialog box, and select the Alignment tab. Use the gauge to specify an angle between –90 and +90 degrees.

Figure 11-10 shows an example of text displayed at a 45-degree angle.

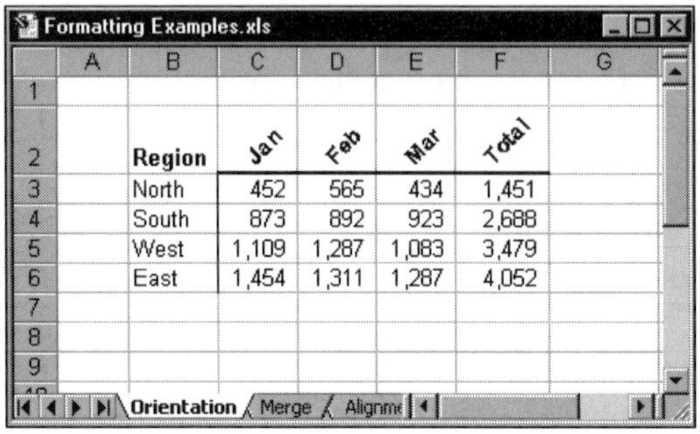

Figure 11-10: An example of rotated text.

Colors and Shading

Excel provides the tools to create some very colorful worksheets. I've known people who avoid using color because they are uncertain of how the colors will translate when printed on a black-and-white printer. With Excel, that's not a valid concern. You can instruct Excel to ignore the colors when you print. Choose File ➪ Page Setup to display the Page Setup dialog box. Click the Sheet tab and place a check in the Black and White check box.

You control the color of the cell's text in the Font tab of the Format Cells dialog box, and you control the cell's background color in the Patterns tab. You can also use tools on the Formatting toolbar (Font Color and Fill Color) to change the color of these items.

A cell's background can be solid (one color) or consist of a pattern that uses two colors. To select a pattern, click the Pattern drop-down list in the Format Cells dialog box. It expands as shown in Figure 11-11. Choose a pattern from the top part of the box and a second color from the bottom part. The first pattern in the list is "None" — use this option if you want a solid background. The Sample box to the right shows how the colors and pattern will look. If you plan to print the worksheet, you need to experiment to see how the color patterns translate to your printer.

Another Type of Justification

Excel provides another way to justify text, using its Edit ⇨ Fill ⇨ Justify command. This command has nothing to do with the alignment options discussed in this chapter. The Edit ⇨ Fill ⇨ Justify command is useful for rearranging text in cells so that it fits in a specified range. For example, you may import a text file that has very long lines of text.

You easily can justify this text so that it's displayed in narrower lines. The accompanying figure shows a range of text before and after using the Edit ⇨ Fill ⇨ Justify command.

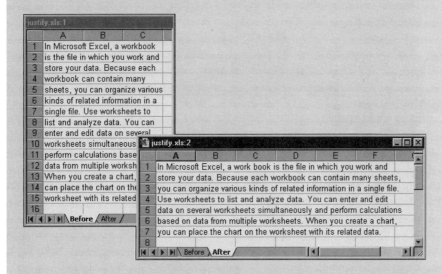

This command works with text in a single column. It essentially redistributes the text in the cells so that it fits into a specified range. You can make the text either wider (so that it uses fewer rows) or narrower (so that it uses more rows).

Select the cells that you want to justify (all in one column) and then extend the selection to the right so that the selection is as wide as you want the end result to be. Choose Edit ⇨ Fill ⇨ Justify, and Excel redistributes the text.

Blank rows serve as paragraph markers. If the range that you select isn't large enough to hold all the text, Excel warns you and allows you to continue or abort. Be careful, because justified text overwrites anything that gets in its way.

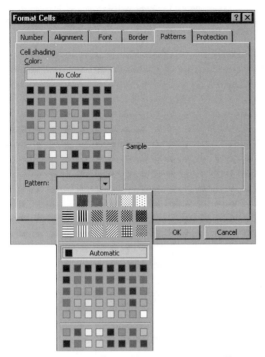

Figure 11-11: Choosing a pattern for a cell background.

You might want to use a background color to make a large table of data easier to read. You probably are familiar with computer printer paper that has alternating green-and-white horizontal shading (often referred to as "green bar"). You can use background colors to simulate this effect in Excel. See Figure 11-12 for an example.

Tip   Here's a quick way to apply shading to every other row. This technique assumes that you want to shade every odd-numbered row in the range A1:F100. Start by shading A1:F1 with the color that you want. Then, select A1:F2 (row 1 is shaded and row 2 is not) and copy the range to the Clipboard. Next, select A3:F100 and choose Edit ➪ Paste Special (with the Formats option).

To hide quickly the contents of a cell, make the background color the same as the font text color. The cell contents are still visible in the formula bar when you select the cell, however.

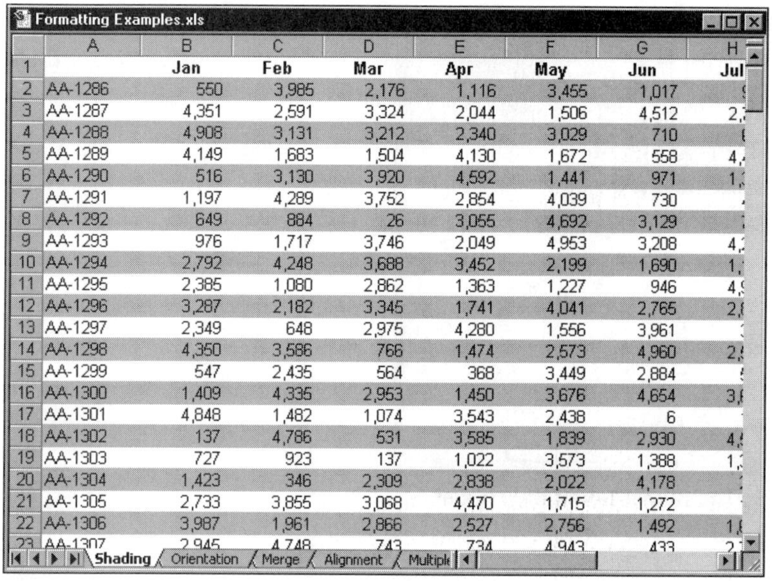

	A	B	C	D	E	F	G	H
1		Jan	Feb	Mar	Apr	May	Jun	Jul
2	AA-1286	550	3,985	2,176	1,116	3,455	1,017	
3	AA-1287	4,351	2,591	3,324	2,044	1,506	4,512	2,
4	AA-1288	4,908	3,131	3,212	2,340	3,029	710	
5	AA-1289	4,149	1,683	1,504	4,130	1,672	558	4,
6	AA-1290	516	3,130	3,920	4,592	1,441	971	1,
7	AA-1291	1,197	4,289	3,752	2,854	4,039	730	
8	AA-1292	649	884	26	3,055	4,692	3,129	
9	AA-1293	976	1,717	3,746	2,049	4,953	3,208	4,
10	AA-1294	2,792	4,248	3,688	3,452	2,199	1,690	1,
11	AA-1295	2,385	1,080	2,862	1,363	1,227	946	4,
12	AA-1296	3,287	2,182	3,345	1,741	4,041	2,765	2,
13	AA-1297	2,349	648	2,975	4,280	1,556	3,961	
14	AA-1298	4,350	3,586	766	1,474	2,573	4,960	2,
15	AA-1299	547	2,435	564	368	3,449	2,884	
16	AA-1300	1,409	4,335	2,953	1,450	3,676	4,654	3,
17	AA-1301	4,848	1,482	1,074	3,543	2,438	6	
18	AA-1302	137	4,786	531	3,585	1,839	2,930	4,
19	AA-1303	727	923	137	1,022	3,573	1,388	1,
20	AA-1304	1,423	346	2,309	2,838	2,022	4,178	
21	AA-1305	2,733	3,855	3,068	4,470	1,715	1,272	
22	AA-1306	3,987	1,961	2,866	2,527	2,756	1,492	1,
23	AA-1307	2,945	4,748	743	734	4,943	433	2,

Figure 11-12: Shading alternate lines can make a lengthy table easier to read.

Borders and Lines

Borders often are used to group a range of similar cells or simply to delineate rows or columns. Excel offers 13 different styles of borders, as you can see on the Border tab in the Format Cells dialog box (see Figure 11-13). This dialog box works with the selected cell or range and enables you to specify which border style to use for each border of the selection.

Before you open this dialog box, select the cell or range to which you want to add borders. First, choose a line style and then choose the border position for the line style by clicking one of the icons.

Notice that the Border tab has three "presets," which can save you some clicking. If you want to remove all borders from the selection, click None. To put an outline around the selection, choose Outline preset. To put borders inside the selection, click Inside preset.

Excel displays the selected border style in the dialog box. You can choose different styles for different border positions and choose a color for the border. Using this dialog box may require some trial and error, but you'll get the hang of it. Figure 11-14 shows examples of borders in a worksheet.

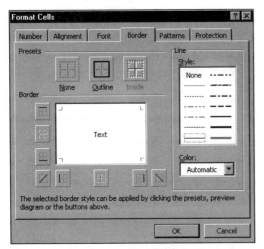

Figure 11-13: The Border tab of the Format Cells dialog box.

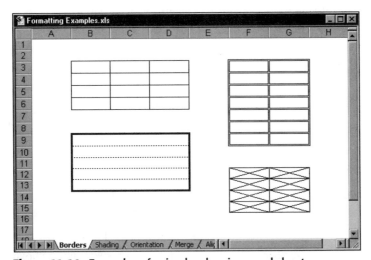

Figure 11-14: Examples of using borders in a worksheet.

When you apply diagonal lines to a cell or range, the selection looks like it has been crossed out.

Tip   If you use border formatting in your worksheet, you might want to turn off the grid display, to make the borders more pronounced. Use the View tab of the Options dialog box to do this.

About the Color Palette

Excel gives you 56 colors from which to choose. These colors are known as the *palette*. You can examine the colors in the palette by clicking the Color or Font Color tool on the Formatting toolbar. You may notice that these colors aren't necessarily unique (some are repeated).

Chances are, you're running Windows in a video mode that supports at least 256 colors. So, why can you use only 56 colors in Excel? Good question. That's just the way Excel was designed.

However, you're not limited to the 56 colors that some unknown techie in Redmond came up with. You can change the colors in the palette to whatever colors you like. To do so, open the Options dialog box and click the Color tab, as shown in the accompanying figure.

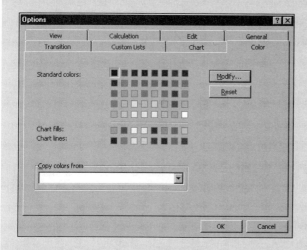

You'll see that the choice of colors for the palette seems to have some rationale. For example, the first 40 colors are designated standard colors. These are followed by 8 chart-fill colors and 8 chart-line colors.

If you want to change a color, select it and click the Modify button. Excel responds with a dialog box named Colors. This dialog box has two tabs: Standard and Custom. Use either tab to select a new color (you have many more choices in the Custom tab). After you select the color, click OK, and the color that you selected replaces the previous color.

If your worksheet uses the replaced color, the new color takes over where that color appeared. If your system is using a video driver that supports only 16 colors, the system creates some of the colors by blending two colors (*dithering*). Dithered colors can be used for cell backgrounds, but text and lines are displayed using the nearest solid color. If you want to revert back to Excel's standard colors, click the Reset button.

Each workbook stores its own copy of the color palette, and you even can copy color palettes from another workbook (which must be open). Use the Options dialog box's drop-down box labeled Copy Colors From.

Producing 3D Effects

You can use a combination of borders and background shading to produce attractive 3D effects on your worksheet. These 3D effects resemble raised or depressed tabs, as shown in the accompanying figure.

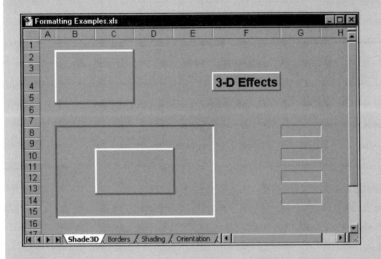

For the best results, use a light-gray background color. To produce a raised effect, apply a white border to the top and left side of the range, and a dark-gray border on the bottom and right side.

To produce a sunken effect, use a dark-gray border on the top and left side, and a white border on the bottom and right side. You can vary the line thickness to produce different effects.

You'll find the 3D Shading utility, which is part of the Power Utility Pak, on this book's CD-ROM.

Adding a Worksheet Background

Excel also enables you to choose a graphics file to serve as a background for a worksheet—similar to the wallpaper that you may display on your Windows desktop. The image that you choose is repeated, so that it tiles the entire worksheet.

Tip

Thousands of background graphics files are available on the World Wide Web. Many Web sites use graphics files for backgrounds, and these files are designed to tile nicely. In addition, these files are usually very small. If you encounter a Web site that uses a good graphic as a background, you can save the file to your hard drive and use it in your Excel workbooks.

To add a background to a worksheet, choose FormatSheet ➪ Background. Excel displays a dialog box that enables you to choose a graphics file. When you locate a file, click OK. Excel tiles your worksheet with the graphic. Some backgrounds make viewing text difficult, so you may want to use a solid background color for cells that contain text (see Figure 11-15). You'll also want to turn off the gridline display, because the gridlines show through the graphic.

Note   The graphic background on a worksheet is for display only — it isn't printed when you print the worksheet.

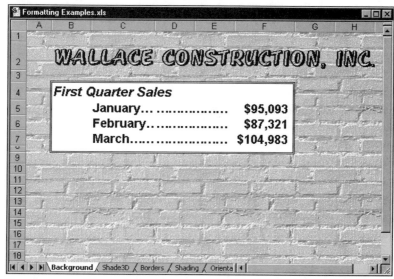

Figure 11-15: This worksheet has a graphic background, but cells that contain text use a white background, which overrides the graphic.

AutoFormatting

So far, this chapter has described the individual formatting commands and tools at your disposal. Excel also has an *AutoFormatting* feature that can automatically perform many types of formatting for you. Figure 11-16 shows an unformatted table in a worksheet (left side) and the same table formatted using one of Excel's AutoFormats.

EXCEL 2000   You also can apply AutoFormatting to PivotTables; see Chapter 25.

Copying Formats by Painting

If you want to copy the formats from one cell to another cell or range, you can select Edit ⇨ Paste Special and then click the Formats option. Or, use the Format Painter button on the Standard toolbar (the button with the paintbrush image).

Start by selecting the cell or range that has the formatting attributes you want to copy. Then, click the Format Painter button. Notice that the mouse pointer changes to include a paintbrush. Next, select the cells to which you want to apply the formats. Release the mouse button, and Excel completes the painting (and you don't have to clean the brush).

If you double-click the Format Painter button, you can paint multiple areas of the worksheet with the same formats. Excel applies the formats that you copy to each cell or range that you select. To get out of paint mode, click the Format Painter button again (or press Esc).

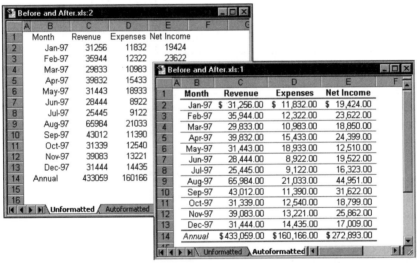

Figure 11-16: A worksheet table before and after using AutoFormat.

Using AutoFormats

To apply an AutoFormat, move the cell pointer anywhere within a table that you want to format; Excel determines the table's boundaries automatically. Then, choose Format ⇨ AutoFormat. Excel responds with the dialog box shown in Figure 11-17. Choose one of the 17 AutoFormats from the list and click OK. Excel formats the table for you.

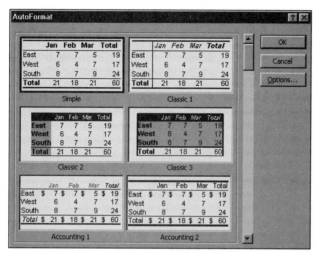

Figure 11-17: The AutoFormat dialog box.

Excel applies AutoFormatting rather intelligently. For example, Excel analyzes the data contained in the table and then formats the table to handle items such as subtotals. Figure 11-18 shows an example of a table that contains a subtotal line for each department. When I applied an AutoFormat, Excel took these subtotals into account and produced an attractive table in about one second.

	Region	State	Sales
2	Region	State	Sales
3	West	California	872,982.00
4	West	Washington	498,232.00
5	West	Oregon	198,355.00
6	West Total		1,569,569.00
7	East	New York	733,209.00
8	East	New Jersey	507,816.00
9	East	Massachusetts	450,982.00
10	East Total		1,692,007.00
11	Midwest	Missouri	322,484.00
12	Midwest	Illinois	598,329.00
13	Midwest Total		920,813.00
14	Grand Total		4,182,389.00

Figure 11-18: AutoFormatting even accommodates subtotals in a table.

Controlling AutoFormats

Although you can't define your own AutoFormats, you can control the type of formatting that is applied. When you click the Options button in the AutoFormat dialog box, the dialog box expands to show six options (see Figure 11-19).

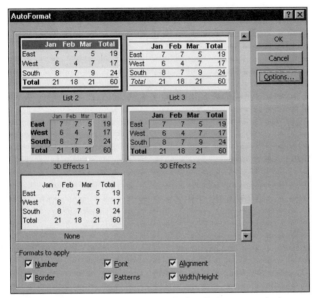

Figure 11-19: The AutoFormat dialog box, expanded to show its options.

Initially, the six check boxes are all checked—which means that Excel will apply formatting from all six categories. If you want it to skip one or more categories, just remove the check from the appropriate box before you click OK. For example, when I use AutoFormats, I hardly ever want Excel to change the column widths, so I turn off the Width/Height option. If you've already formatted the numbers, you may want to turn off the Number option.

Using Conditional Formatting

Excel's conditional formatting feature changes cell formats based on the contents of the cell. For example, if the cell contains a negative number, the cell appears bold with a red background. To apply conditional formatting to a cell or range, select the range and then choose Format ➪ Conditional Formatting. You'll see the dialog box shown in Figure 11-20, which enables you to specify up to three conditions for the selected cells.

Figure 11-20: Excel enables you to specify formats based on the cell's value.

The condition can be based on either the cell's value or a formula that you specify (the formula must be a logical formula and return either True or False). Follow these steps to apply conditional formatting:

1. In the first drop-down list, choose either Cell Value Is or Formula Is.

2. If you chose Cell Value Is in Step 1, specify the conditions by using the controls in the dialog box. For example, you can specify between 0 and 100. You can enter values or cell references.

3. If you chose Formula Is in Step 1, specify a reference to the formula. Remember, the formula must return either True or False.

4. Click the Format button and specify the formatting that will be used when the condition is true.

5. If you want to specify another conditional format for the selection, click the Add button. The dialog box expands so that you can repeat Steps 1 through 4 for another condition.

6. When you finish, click OK.

Note Conditional formatting is a great feature, but it's not foolproof. If you copy a value and paste it into a cell that has conditional formatting, the formatting will not be applied. In fact, copying a value to a cell that has conditional formatting wipes out the conditional formatting information. In other words, the feature works only for data that is entered into a cell manually or calculated by a formula.

Using Named Styles

The *named style* feature — borrowed from word processing — is, perhaps, one of the most underutilized features in Excel (named styles may also be the most underutilized feature in word processors).

If you find that you continually are applying the same combination of fonts, lines, and shading in your worksheets, you can save time and effort if you create and use named styles. Named styles apply, in a single step, the formats that you specify, helping you to apply consistent formats across your worksheets.

The real power of styles lies in what happens when you change a component of a style; in this case, all the cells that use that named style automatically incorporate the change. Suppose that you apply a particular style to a dozen cells scattered throughout your worksheet. Later, you realize that these cells should have a font size of 14 points rather than 12 points. Rather than change each cell, simply edit the style. All cells with that particular style change automatically.

A style can consist of settings for six different attributes, although a style doesn't have to use all the attributes. You may recognize these attributes; they correspond to the six tabs in the Format Cells dialog box. The attributes that make up a style are the following:

✦ Number format

✦ Font (type, size, and color)

✦ Alignment (vertical and horizontal)

✦ Borders

✦ Pattern

✦ Protection (locked and hidden)

By default, all cells have the Normal style. In addition, Excel provides five other built-in styles—all of which control only the cell's number format. The styles that are available in every workbook are listed in Table 11-1. If these styles don't meet your needs (and they probably don't), you can easily create new styles.

Table 11-1
Excel's Built-In Styles

Style Name	Description	Number Format Example
Normal	Excel's default style	1234
Comma*	Comma with two decimal places	1,234.00
Comma[0]	Comma with no decimal places	1,234
Currency*	Left-aligned dollar sign with two decimal places	$1,234.00
Currency[0]	Left-aligned dollar sign with no decimal places	$1,234
Percent*	Percent with no decimal places	12%

* This style can be applied by clicking a button the Standard toolbar.

Applying Styles

This section discusses the methods that you can use to apply existing styles to cells or ranges.

Toolbar Buttons

As mentioned in the preceding section, you can use three buttons on the Standard toolbar to attach a particular style to a cell or range. You need to understand that when you use these buttons to format a value, you're really changing the cell's style. Consequently, if you later want to change the Normal style, cells formatted with any of these buttons won't be affected by the change.

Using the Style Tool

If you plan to work with named styles, you might want to make an addition to one of your toolbars. In fact, I strongly suggest that you do so. Excel has a handy Style tool available. However, this tool (oddly) is not on any of the built-in toolbars — maybe this is why the named style feature is underutilized. To add the Style tool to a toolbar (the Formatting toolbar is a good choice), follow these steps:

1. Right-click any toolbar and choose Customize from the shortcut menu. Excel displays its Customize dialog box.

2. Click the Commands tab.

3. In the Categories list box, click Formatting. The Buttons box displays all available tools in the Formatting category.

4. Click the Style tool (it's a list box labeled *Style*) and drag it to your Formatting toolbar. If you drag the Style tool to the middle of the toolbar, the other tools scoot over to make room for it.

5. Click the Close button in the Customize dialog box.

The new Style tool displays the style of the selected cell and also lets you quickly apply a style — or even create a new style. To apply a style by using the Style tool, select the cell or range, open the Style list box, and then choose the style that you want to apply.

Using the Format ⇨ Style Command

You also can apply a style by using the Format ⇨ Style command, which prompts Excel to display its Style dialog box. Just choose the style that you want to apply from the Style Name drop-down list. However, using the Style tool, as described in the previous section, is a much quicker way to apply a style.

The CD-ROM for this book contains a workbook that defines several styles. You may want to open this workbook and experiment.

Creating New Styles

Two ways are available to create a new style: use the Format ⇨ Style command or use the Style tool. To create a new style, first select a cell and apply all the formatting that you want to include in the new style. You can use any of the formatting that is available in the Format Cells dialog box.

After you format the cell to your liking, choose Format ⇨ Style. Excel displays its Style dialog box, shown in Figure 11-21. Excel displays the name of the current style of the cell (probably Normal) in the Style Name drop-down. This box is highlighted, so that you can simply enter a new style name by typing it. When you do so, Excel displays the words *By Example* to indicate that it's basing the style on the current cell.

The check boxes display the current formats for the cell. By default, all check boxes are checked. If you don't want the style to include one or more format categories, remove the check(s) from the appropriate box(es). Click OK to create the style.

You also can create a style from scratch in the Style dialog box. Just enter a style name and then click the Modify button to select the formatting.

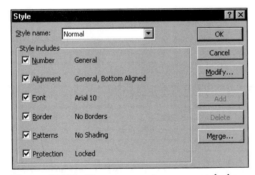

Figure 11-21: You can create a new style by using the Style dialog box.

Tip   If you added the Style tool to one of your toolbars, you can create a new style without using the Style dialog box. Just format a cell, click inside the Style tool list box, and then type the name. Using this method, you can't specify which formatting categories to omit from the style, but, as you learn next, you can easily modify an existing style.

Overriding a Style

After you apply a style to a cell, you can apply additional formatting to it by using any formatting method discussed in this chapter. Formatting modifications that you make to the cell don't affect other cells that use the same style.

Modifying a Style

To change an existing file, open the Style dialog box. From the Style name drop-down box, choose the style that you want to modify. You can make changes to the check boxes to include or exclude any of the format categories, or you can click the Modify button to display the familiar Format Cells dialog box. Make the changes that you want and click OK. Click OK again to close the Style dialog box. Excel modifies all the cells formatted with the selected style by applying the new formatting.

Tip
You also can use the Style tool to change a style. Start by modifying the formatting of a cell that uses the style. Then, click inside the Style tool list box, select the style name, and press Enter. Excel asks whether you want to redefine the style based on the selection. Respond in the affirmative to change the style—and all of the cells that use the style.

Deleting a Style

If you no longer need a style, you can delete it. To do so, open the Style dialog box, choose the style from the list, and then click Delete. All the cells that had the style revert back to the Normal style.

Suppose that you applied a style to a cell and then applied additional formatting. If you delete the style, the cell retains all of its additional formatting.

Merging Styles from Other Workbooks

You may create one or more styles that you use frequently. Although you could go through the motions and create these styles for every new workbook, a better approach is to merge the styles from a workbook in which you previously created them.

To merge styles from another workbook, open both the workbook that contains the styles that you want to merge *and* the workbook into which you want to merge styles. From the workbook *into which* you want to merge styles, choose Format ➪ Style and click the Merge button. Excel displays a list of all open workbooks, as shown in Figure 11-22. Select the workbook that contains the styles you want to merge and click OK. Excel copies styles from the workbook that you selected into the active workbook.

When you're merging styles, colors are based on the palette stored with the workbook in which you use the style. Therefore, if the two workbooks involved in the merge use different color palettes, the colors used in the styles may not look the same in each workbook.

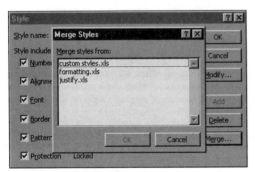

Figure 11-22: Merging styles from another workbook is a good way to make your workbooks look consistent.

Controlling Styles with Templates

When you start Excel, it loads with several default settings, including the settings for stylistic formatting. If you spend a lot of time changing the default elements, you should know about templates.

Here's an example. You may prefer to use 12-point Arial rather than 10-point Arial as the default font. And maybe you prefer Wrap Text to be the default setting for alignment. Templates provide an easy way to change defaults.

The trick is to create a workbook with the Normal style modified to the way that you want it. Then, save the workbook as a template in your XLStart folder. After doing so, you can select File ➪ New to display a dialog box from which you can choose the template for the new workbook. Template files also can store other named styles, providing you with an excellent way to give your workbooks a consistent look.

Cross-Reference　Chapter 34 discusses templates in detail.

Summary

This chapter explores all topics related to stylistic formatting: different fonts and sizes, alignment options, applying colors and shading, and using borders and lines. It discusses Excel's AutoFormat feature, which can format a table of data automatically. The chapter concludes with a discussion of named styles, an important concept that can save you time and make your worksheets look more consistent.

✦　　✦　　✦

Printing Your Work

Many of the worksheets that you develop with Excel are designed to serve as printed reports. You'll find that printing from Excel is quite easy, and you can generate attractive, well-formatted reports with minimal effort. But, as you'll see, Excel has plenty of options that provide you with a great deal of control over the printed page. These options are explained in this chapter.

One-Step Printing

The Print button on the Standard toolbar is a quick way to print the current worksheet, using the default settings. Just click the button, and Excel sends the worksheet to the printer. If you've changed any of the default print settings, Excel uses the new settings; otherwise, it uses the following default settings:

+ Prints the active worksheet (or all selected worksheets), including any embedded charts or drawing objects

+ Prints one copy

+ Prints the entire worksheet

+ Prints in portrait mode

+ Doesn't scale the printed output

+ Uses 1-inch margins for the top and bottom and .75-inch margins for the left and right

+ Prints with no headers or footers

+ For wide worksheets that span multiple pages, it prints down and then across

As you might suspect, you can change any of these default print settings.

When you print a worksheet, Excel prints only the *active area* of the worksheet. In other words, it won't print all four million cells — just those that have data in them. If the worksheet contains any embedded charts or drawing objects, they also are printed (unless you have modified the Print Object property of the object).

 If you create a workbook based on a template, the template may contain different default print settings. Templates are discussed in Chapter 34.

Adjusting Your Print Settings

You adjust Excel's various print settings in two different dialog boxes:

✦ The Print dialog box (accessed either with the File ➪ Print command or Ctrl+P).

✦ The Page Setup dialog box (accessed with the File ➪ Page Setup command). This is a tabbed dialog box with four tabs.

Both of these dialog boxes have a Print Preview button that previews the printed output onscreen.

Settings in the Print Dialog Box

You actually start the printing process from the Print dialog box, unless you use the Print button on the Standard toolbar. After you select your print settings, click OK from the Print dialog box to print your work.

Selecting a Printer

Before printing, make sure that you have selected the correct printer (applicable only if you have access to more than one printer) by using the Print dialog box, shown in Figure 12-1. You can select the printer from the Printer drop-down list. This dialog box also lists information about the selected printer, such as its status and where it's connected.

 Clicking the Properties button displays a property box for the selected printer. The exact dialog box that you see depends on the printer. The Properties dialog box lets you adjust printer-specific settings. In most cases, you won't have to change any of these settings, but you should be familiar with the settings that you can change.

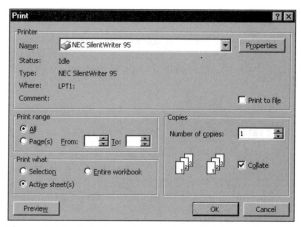

Figure 12-1: Select a printer in the Print dialog box.

If you check the Print to file check box, Excel stores the output in a file, prompting you for a filename before printing. The resulting file will *not* be a standard text file. Rather, it will include all the printer codes that are required to print your worksheet. Printing to a file is useful if you don't have immediate access to a printer. You can save the output to a file and then send this file to your printer at a later time.

Tip   If you want to save your workbook as a text file, use the File ➪ Save As command, and select one of the text file formats from the drop-down list labeled Save as type.

Before printing, you might want to view your worksheets in Page Break Preview mode. To enter this mode, choose the View ➪ Page Break Preview command. The worksheet display changes, and you can see exactly what will be printed and where the page breaks occur. To change the print range, drag any of the dark borders. This feature is discussed in more detail later in this chapter.

After you print a worksheet (or view it in Page Break Preview mode), Excel displays dashed lines to indicate where the page breaks occur. This is a useful feature, because the display adjusts dynamically. For example, if you find that your printed output is too wide to fit on a single page, you can adjust the column widths (keeping an eye on the page-break display) until they are narrow enough to print on one page.

Tip   If you don't want to see the page breaks displayed in your worksheet, open the Options dialog box, click the View tab, and remove the check mark from the Automatic Page Breaks check box.

Printing Selected Pages

If your printed output uses multiple pages, you can select which pages to print, in the Print dialog box. In the Page range section, indicate the number of the first and last pages to print. You can either use the spinner controls or type the page numbers in the edit boxes.

Specifying What to Print

The Print what section of the Print dialog box lets you specify what to print. You have three options:

✦ **Selection:** Prints only the range that you selected before issuing the File ➪ Print command.

✦ **Selected sheet(s):** Prints the active sheet or sheets that you selected. You can select multiple sheets by pressing Ctrl and clicking the sheet tabs. If you select multiple sheets, Excel begins printing each sheet on a new page.

✦ **Entire workbook:** Prints the entire workbook, including chart sheets.

Tip   You can also select File ➪ Print Area ➪ Set Print Area to specify the range or ranges to print. Before you choose this command, select the range or ranges that you want to print. To clear the print area, select File ➪ Print Area ➪ Clear Print Area.

Printing Multiple Copies

The Print dialog box also enables you to select the number of copies to print. The upper limit is 32,767 copies — not that anyone would ever need that many. You also can specify that you want the copies collated. If you choose this option, Excel prints the pages in order for each set of output. If you're printing only one page, Excel ignores the Collate setting.

Settings in the Page Setup Dialog Box

Using the Page Setup dialog box, you can control page settings and margins, create headers and footers, and adjust sheet settings. Choose File ➪ Page Setup to open the Page Setup dialog box; in Figure 12-2, you see the Page tab of the Page Setup dialog box.

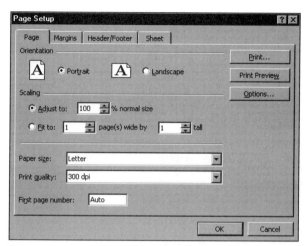

Figure 12-2: You control page settings in the Page tab of the Page Setup dialog box.

Controlling Page Settings

The Page tab of the Page Setup dialog box enables you to control the following settings:

✦ **Orientation:** Choose either Portrait (tall pages) or Landscape (wide pages). Landscape orientation might be useful if you have a wide range that doesn't fit on a vertically oriented page.

✦ **Scaling:** You can set a scaling factor manually or let Excel scale the output automatically to fit on the number of pages that you specify. Scaling can range from 10 percent to 400 percent of normal size. If you want to return to normal scaling, enter 100 in the box labeled % normal size.

✦ **Paper size:** This setting enables you to select the paper size that you're using. Click the box and see the choices.

✦ **Print quality:** If the installed printer supports it, you can change the printer's resolution—which is expressed in dots per inch (dpi). Higher numbers represent better print quality, but higher resolutions take longer to print.

✦ **First page number:** You can specify a page number for the first page. This is useful if the pages that you're printing will be part of a larger document and you want the page numbering to be consecutive. Use Auto if you want the beginning page number to be 1—or to correspond to the pages that you selected in the Print dialog box. If you're not printing page numbers in your header or footer, this setting is irrelevant.

Adjusting Margins

A margin is the blank space on the side of the page. Wider margins leave less space available for printing. You can control all four page margins from the Margins tab of the Page Setup dialog box, shown in Figure 12-3.

To change a margin, click the appropriate spinner (or you can enter a value directly).

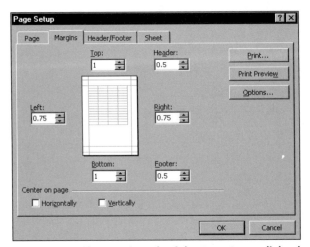

Figure 12-3: The Margins tab of the Page Setup dialog box.

Note   The Preview box in the center of the dialog box is a bit deceiving, because it doesn't really show you how your changes look in relation to the page. Rather, it simply displays a darker line to let you know which margin you're adjusting.

In addition to the page margins, you can adjust the distance of the header from the top of the page and the distance of the footer from the bottom of the page. These settings should be less than the corresponding margin; otherwise, the header or footer may overlap with the printed output.

Normally, Excel aligns the printed page at the top and left margins. If you would like the output to be centered vertically or horizontally, check the appropriate check box.

You also can change the margins while you're previewing your output — ideal for last-minute adjustments before printing. Previewing is explained later in the chapter.

Changing the Header or Footer

A *header* is a line of information that appears at the top of each printed page. A *footer* is a line of information that appears at the bottom of each printed page. You can align information in headers and footers at the left margin, in the center of the header or footer, and at the right margin. For example, you can create a header that prints your name at the left margin, the worksheet name centered in the header, and the page number at the right margin. By default, new workbooks do not have any headers or footers.

The Header/Footer tab of the Page Setup dialog box appears in Figure 12-4. This dialog box displays the current header and footer and gives you other header and footer options in the drop-down lists labeled Header and Footer.

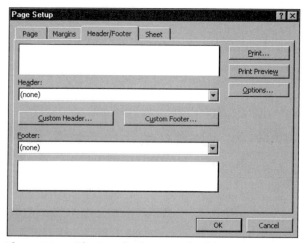

Figure 12-4: The Header/Footer tab of the Page Setup dialog box.

When you click the Header (or Footer) drop-down list, Excel displays a list of predefined headers (or footers). If you see one that you like, select it. You then can see how it looks in context — which part is left-justified, centered, or right-justified. If you don't want a header or footer, choose the option labeled (none) for both the Header and Footer drop-down list boxes.

If you don't find a predefined header or footer that is exactly what you want, you can define a custom header or footer. Start by selecting a header or footer that's similar to the one that you want to create (you'll use the selected header or footer as the basis for the customized one). Click the Custom Header or Custom Footer button, and Excel displays a dialog box like the one shown in Figure 12-5.

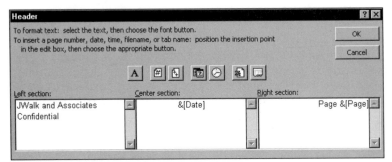

Figure 12-5: If none of the predefined headers or footers is satisfactory, you can define a custom header or custom footer.

This dialog box enables you to enter text or codes in each of the three sections. To enter text, just click in the section and enter the text. To enter variable information, such as the current date or the page number, you can click one of the buttons. Clicking the button inserts a special code. The buttons and their functions are listed in Table 12-1.

Table 12-1		
Custom Header/Footer Buttons and Their Functions		
Button	**Code**	**Function**
Font	Not applicable	Lets you choose a font for the selected text
Page Number	&[Page]	Inserts the page number
Total Pages	&[Pages]	Inserts the total number of pages to be printed
Date	&[Date]	Inserts the current date
Time	&[Time]	Inserts the current time
File	&[File]	Inserts the workbook name
Sheet	&[Tab]	Inserts the sheet's name

You can combine text and codes and insert as many codes as you like into each section. If the text that you enter uses an ampersand (&), you must enter the ampersand twice (because Excel uses an ampersand to signal a code). For example, to enter the text *Research & Development* into a section of a header or footer, enter **Research && Development**.

You also can use different fonts and sizes in your headers and footers. Just select the text that you want to change and then click the Font button. Excel displays its Fonts dialog box so that you can make your choice. If you don't change the font, Excel uses the font defined for the Normal style.

Tip You can use as many lines as you like. Use Alt+Enter to force a line break for multiline headers or footers.

After you define a custom header or footer, it appears at the bottom of the appropriate drop-down list on the Header/Footer tab of the Page Setup dialog box. You can have only one custom header and one custom footer in a workbook. So, if you edit a custom header, for example, it replaces the existing custom header in the drop-down list.

Unfortunately, you can't print the contents of a specific cell in a header or footer. For example, you might want Excel to use the contents of cell A1 as part of a header. To do so, you need to enter the cell's contents manually — or write a macro to perform this operation.

On the CD-ROM Excel 2000 still doesn't implement one of the most requested features: the ability to print a workbook's full path and filename in a header or footer. You can print the file name, but you find an option to print the path. The companion CD-ROM contains an add-in that I developed that adds this feature to Excel.

Controlling Sheet Options

The Sheet tab of the Page Setup dialog box (shown in Figure 12-6) contains several additional options. Each is described in the sections that follow.

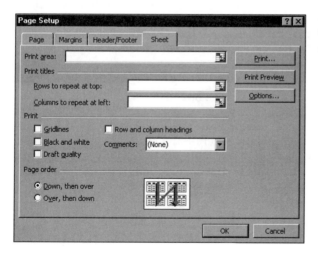

Figure 12-6: The Sheet tab of the Page Setup dialog box.

Print area

The Print area box lists the range defined as the print area. If you select a range of cells and choose the Selection option in the Print dialog box, the selected range address appears in this box. Excel also defines this as the reference for the Print_Area name.

If the Print area box is blank, Excel prints the entire worksheet. You can activate this box and select a range (Excel will modify its definition of Print_Area), or you can enter a previously defined range name into the box.

Print titles

Many worksheets are set up with titles in the first row and descriptive names in the first column. If such a worksheet requires more than one page, reading subsequent pages may be difficult, because the text in the first row and first column won't be printed on subsequent pages. Excel offers a simple solution: *print titles*.

Caution   Don't confuse print titles with headers; these are two different concepts. Headers appear at the top of each page and contain information such as the worksheet name, date, or page number. Print titles describe the data being printed, such as field names in a database table or list.

You can specify particular rows to repeat at the top of every printed page, or particular columns to repeat at the left of every printed page. To do so, just activate the appropriate box and select the rows or columns in the worksheet. Or, you can enter these references manually. For example, to specify rows 1 and 2 as repeating rows, enter **1:2**.

In the old days, users often were surprised to discover that print titles appeared twice on the first page of their printouts. This occurred because they defined a print area that included the print titles. Excel now handles this automatically, however, and doesn't print titles twice if they are part of the print area.

Tip   You can specify different print titles for each worksheet in the workbook. Excel remembers print titles by creating sheet-level names (Print_Titles).

Print

The section labeled Print contains five check boxes:

- ✦ **Gridlines:** If checked, Excel prints the gridlines to delineate cells. If you turn off the gridline display in the worksheet (in the View tab of the Options dialog box), Excel automatically removes the check from this box for you. In other words, the default setting for this option is determined by the gridline display in your worksheet.

- ✦ **Black and white:** If checked, Excel ignores any colors in the worksheet and prints everything in black and white. By taking advantage of this option, you can format your worksheet for viewing on your monitor and still get readable print output.

- ✦ **Draft quality:** If checked, Excel prints in draft mode. In draft mode, Excel doesn't print embedded charts or drawing objects, cell gridlines, or borders, which reduces the printing time.

- ✦ **Row and column headings:** If checked, Excel prints the row and column headings on the printout, enabling you to identify easily specific cells from a printout.

✦ **Comments:** If checked, Excel prints cell notes by using the option that you specify: either At the end of the sheet or As displayed on sheet.

Printer-Specific Options

The Print dialog box has a button labeled Options (refer to Figure 2-2). Clicking this button displays another dialog box that enables you to adjust properties that are specific to the selected printer. See Figure 12-7 for an example. You can also open this dialog box from the Page Setup dialog box (click the Options button).

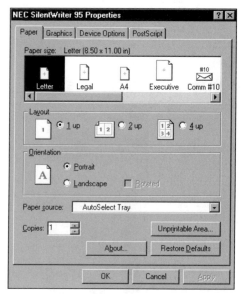

Figure 12-7: The Page Setup dialog box lets you set printer-specific options.

Some of the printer settings can be set directly from Excel. Other settings may not be accessible from Excel, and you can change them in this dialog box. For example, if your printer uses multiple paper trays, you can select which tray to use.

Using Print Preview

Excel's print preview feature displays an image of the printed output on your screen. This is a handy feature that enables you to see the result of the options that you set, before you actually send the job to the printer. It'll save you lots of time—not to mention printing supplies.

Accessing Print Preview

Several ways exist to preview your document:

✦ Select the File ➪ Print Preview command.

✦ Click the Print Preview button on the Standard toolbar. Or, you can press Shift and click the Print button on the Standard toolbar (the Print button serves a dual purpose).

✦ Click the Print Preview button in the Print dialog box.

✦ Click the Print Preview button in the Page Setup dialog box.

Any one of these methods changes Excel's window to a preview window, as shown in Figure 12-8.

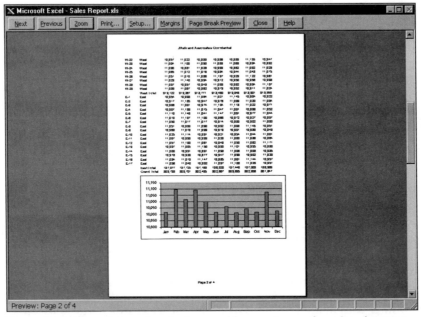

Figure 12-8: The print preview feature enables you to see the printed output before you send it to the printer.

The preview window has several buttons along the top:

✦ **Next:** Displays an image of the next page.

✦ **Previous:** Displays an image of the previous page.

✦ **Zoom:** Zooms the display in or out. This button toggles between the two levels of zooming that are available. You also can simply click the preview image to toggle between zoom modes.

✦ **Print:** Sends the job to the printer.

✦ **Setup:** Displays the Page Setup dialog box, so that you can adjust some settings. When you close the dialog box, you return to the preview screen, so that you can see the effects of your changes.

✦ **Margins:** Displays adjustable columns and margins, described in the next section.

✦ **Page Break Preview:** Displays the worksheet in Page Break Preview mode.

✦ **Close:** Closes the preview window.

✦ **Help:** Displays help for the preview window.

Making Changes While Previewing

When you click the Margins button in the preview window, Excel adds markers to the preview that indicate column borders and margins (see Figure 12-9). You can drag the column or margin markers to make changes that appear onscreen.

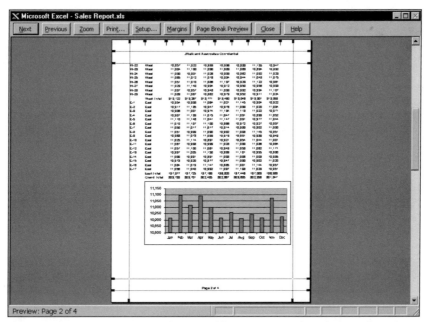

Figure 12-9: You can adjust column widths or margins directly from the print preview window.

For example, if you print a worksheet and discover that Excel is printing the last column on a second page, you can adjust the column widths or margins in the preview window to force all the columns to print on a single page. After you drag one of these markers, Excel updates the display so that you can see what effect it had.

When you make changes to the column widths in the preview window, these changes also are made to your worksheet. Similarly, changing the margins in the preview window changes the settings that appear in the Margins tab of the Page Setup dialog box.

Dealing with Page Breaks

If you print lengthy reports, you know that it's often important to have control over the page breaks. For example, you normally wouldn't want a row to print on a page by itself. Fortunately, Excel gives you superb control over page breaks.

As you may have discovered, Excel handles page breaks automatically. After you print or preview your worksheet, it even displays dashed lines to indicate where page breaks occur. Sometimes, however, you'll want to force a page break — either a vertical or a horizontal one. For example, if your worksheet consists of several distinct areas, you may want to print each area on a separate sheet of paper.

Inserting a Page Break

To insert a vertical manual page break, move the cell pointer to the cell that will begin the new page, but make sure that you place the pointer in column A; otherwise, you'll insert a vertical page break and a horizontal page break. For example, if you want row 14 to be the first row of a new page, select cell A14. Then, choose Insert ⇨ Page Break. Excel displays a dashed line to indicate the page break. The dashed line for manual page breaks is slightly thinner than the lines for natural page breaks.

To insert a horizontal page break, move the cell pointer to the cell that will begin the new page, but in this case, make sure that you place the pointer in row one. Select Insert ⇨ Page Break to create the page break.

Removing a Page Break

To remove a vertical manual page break, move the cell pointer anywhere in the first row beneath the manual page break and then select Insert ⇨ Remove Page Break (this command appears only when you place the cell pointer in the first row following a manual page break).

To remove a horizontal manual page break, perform the same procedure, but position the cell pointer anywhere in the first column following a horizontal page break.

Tip   To remove all manual page breaks in the worksheet, click the Select All button (or press Ctrl+A); then, choose Insert ⇨ Remove Page Break.

Using Page Break Preview

Page Break Preview mode makes dealing with page breaks easy. To use Page Break Preview, choose View ⇨ Page Break Preview. The screen changes, as shown in Figure 12-10.

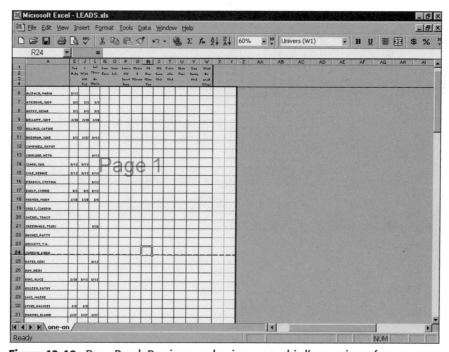

Figure 12-10: Page Break Preview mode gives you a bird's-eye view of your worksheet and shows exactly where the page breaks occur.

When you enter Page Break Preview mode, Excel does the following:

✦ Changes the zoom factor so that you can see more of the worksheet

✦ Displays the page numbers overlaid on the pages

✦ Displays the current print range with a white background; nonprinting data appears with a gray background

✦ Displays all page breaks

When you're in Page Break Preview mode, you can drag the borders to change the print range or the page breaks. When you change the page breaks, Excel automatically adjusts the scaling so that the information fits on the pages, per your specifications.

Note In Page Break Preview mode, you still have access to all of Excel's commands. You can change the zoom factor if you find the text to be too small.

To return to normal viewing, select the View ➪ Normal command.

Using Custom Views

Workbooks commonly are used to store a variety of information, and often, several different reports are printed from such workbooks. If this sounds familiar, you need to know about Excel's custom views feature.

The custom views feature enables you to give names to various views of your worksheet, and you can quickly switch among these named views. A view includes settings for the following:

✦ Print settings, as specified in the Page Setup dialog box (optional)

✦ Hidden rows and columns (optional)

✦ Display settings, as specified in the Options Display dialog box

✦ Selected cells and ranges

✦ The active cell

✦ Window sizes and positions

✦ Frozen panes

For example, you might define a view that hides a few columns of numbers, another view with a print range defined as a summary range only, another view with the page setup set to landscape, and so on.

To create a named custom view, first set up your worksheet with the settings that you want to include in the view. These settings can include any of the settings listed previously. For example, you might create a view that has a specific range of cells defined as the print range. Then, select View ➪ Custom Views, and Excel displays a dialog box that lists all named views. Initially, this list is empty, but you can click the Add button to add a view in the Add View dialog box, shown in Figure 12-11.

Enter a name for the view and make any adjustments to the check boxes. Click OK, and Excel saves the view. You can add as many views as you want and easily switch among them — just highlight the custom view that you want to display from the Custom Views dialog box and then click the Show button.

Figure 12-11: Use the Add View dialog box to supply a name for a new custom view.

More About Printing

A few issues related to printing just don't fit anywhere other than a "miscellaneous" section. This section serves as that "miscellaneous" section and provides some additional information regarding printing.

Problems with Fonts (When WYS Isn't WYG)

Sometimes, you may find that the printed output doesn't match what you see onscreen. You almost always can trace this problem to the fonts that you use. If your printer doesn't have a font that you use to display your worksheet, Windows attempts to match the font as best as it can. Often, the match just isn't good enough.

Simply using TrueType fonts almost always solves this problem; these scalable fonts are designed for both screen viewing and printing.

Printing Noncontiguous Ranges on a Single Page

You may have discovered that Excel lets you specify a print area that consists of noncontiguous ranges (a multiple selection). For example, if you need to print, say, A1:C50, D20:F24, and M11:P16, you can press Ctrl while you select these ranges and then issue the File ➪ Print command and choose the Selection option. Better yet, give this multiple selection a range name so that you can quickly choose the same ranges the next time.

Printing multiple ranges is a handy feature, but you may not like the fact that Excel prints each range on a new sheet of paper — and this behavior can't be changed.

You might consider creating live *snapshots* of the three ranges and pasting these snapshots to an empty area of the worksheet. Then, you can print this new area that consists of the snapshots, and Excel won't skip to a new page for each range.

To create a live snapshot of a range, select the range and copy it to the Clipboard. Then, to paste a live link (see the Note that follows), select the cell in which you want to paste the snapshot (an empty worksheet is a good choice), press and hold the Shift key, and choose Edit ➪ Paste Picture Link. Repeat this procedure for the other ranges. After you paste them, you can rearrange the snapshots any way you like. Notice that these are truly live links: change a cell in the original range and the change appears in the linked picture. Figure 12-12 shows an example of snapshots made from several ranges.

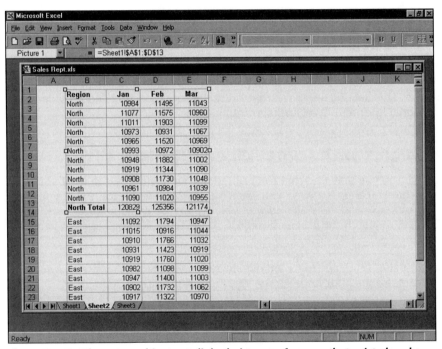

Figure 12-12: These two objects are linked pictures of ranges that exist elsewhere in the workbook, which enables you to print nonadjacent ranges on a single sheet.

Hiding Cells Before Printing

You may have a worksheet that contains confidential information. You may want to print the worksheet, but not the confidential parts. Several techniques prevent certain parts of a worksheet from printing:

✦ When you hide rows or columns, the hidden rows aren't printed.

✦ You can effectively hide cells or ranges by making the text color the same color as the background color.

✦ You can hide cells by using a custom number format that consists of three semicolons (;;;).

✦ You can mask off a confidential area of a worksheet by covering it with a rectangle object. Click the Rectangle tool on the Drawing toolbar and drag the rectangle to the proper size. For best results, you can make the rectangle white with no border.

✦ You can use a text box object, available by using the Text Box tool on the Drawing toolbar, to mask off a range. The advantage to using a text box is that you can add text to it with information about the concealed data (see Figure 12-13).

	A	B	C	D	E	F
1	Name	Department	Date Hired	Salary	Supervisor	
2	Bill Jones	Marketing	03/06/91		Rudolph	
3	Julia Richardson	Sales	05/12/94		Winkler	
4	Hank Snow	Operations	11/30/95	Confidential	Kingsley	
5	Marley Robins	Operations	01/04/89		Kingsley	
6	Ted Smith	Sales	03/04/94		Winkler	
7	Francine Snerd	Maintenance	12/15/93		Martinsdale	
8	Lucille King	Administration	11/21/90		Wu	
9						
10						
11						
12						
13						

Sheet1

Figure 12-13: You can use a text box to hide confidential data so that it won't print.

If you find that you must regularly hide data before you print certain reports, consider using the custom views feature to create a named view that doesn't show the confidential information.

Using a Template to Change Printing Defaults

If you are never satisfied with Excel's default print settings, you may want to create a template with the print settings that you use most often. After doing so, you can create a new workbook based on the template, and the workbook will have your own print settings for defaults.

Cross-Reference   Chapter 34 discusses template files.

Summary

This chapter presents the basics — and some finer points — of printing in Excel. You learn how to use the Print dialog box and the Page Setup dialog box to control what gets printed and how it is printed. You also learn about the print preview feature that shows how the printed output will look before it hits the paper. The chapter covers features such as manual page breaks, custom views, Page Break Preview mode, tips on printing noncontiguous ranges on a single sheet, and hiding cells that contain confidential information.

✦   ✦   ✦

Chart-Making Basics

Charts — also known as graphs — have been an integral part of spreadsheets since the early days of Lotus 1-2-3. Charting features have improved significantly over the years, and you'll find that Excel provides you with the tools to create a wide variety of highly customizable charts. In fact, Excel has so much capability in this area that *two* chapters are needed to present the information. This chapter presents the basic information that you need to know to create charts and make simple modifications to them. Chapter 16 continues with a discussion of advanced options and a slew of chart-making tricks and techniques.

Overview of Charts

Basically, a *chart* presents a table of numbers visually. Displaying data in a well-conceived chart can make the data more understandable, and you often can make your point more quickly as a result. Because a chart presents a picture, charts are particularly useful for understanding a lengthy series of numbers and their interrelationships. Making a chart helps you to spot trends and patterns that would be nearly impossible to identify when examining a range of numbers.

You create charts from numbers that appear in a worksheet. Before you can create a chart, you must enter some numbers in a worksheet. Normally, the data that is used by a chart resides in a single worksheet, within one file — but that's not a strict requirement. A single chart can use data from any number of worksheets or even from different workbooks.

When you create a chart in Excel, you have two options for where to place the chart:

✦ Insert the chart directly into a worksheet as an object. A chart like the one that appears in Figure 13-1 is known as an *embedded* chart.

✦ Create the chart as a new chart sheet in your workbook (see Figure 13-2). A chart sheet differs from a worksheet in that a chart sheet can hold a single chart and doesn't have cells.

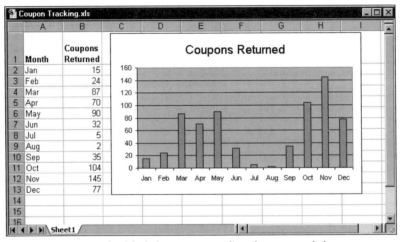

Figure 13-1: An embedded chart appears directly on a worksheet.

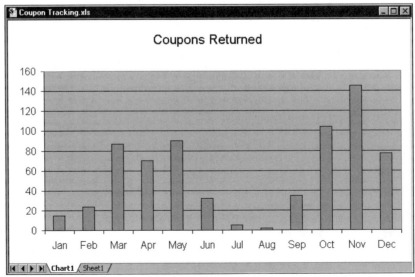

Figure 13-2: This chart appears on a separate chart sheet.

Each method has its advantages, as you'll discover later in this chapter. Regardless of the chart-making option that you choose, you have complete control over the chart's appearance. You can change the colors, move the legend, format the numbers on the scales, add gridlines, and so on.

Converting a range of numbers into a chart is quite easy, and many people find this aspect of Excel to be rather fun. You can experiment with different chart types to determine the best way to make your case. If that isn't enough, you can make a variety of adjustments to your charts, such as adding annotations, clip art, and other bells and whistles. The real beauty of Excel's charts, however, lies in their connection to worksheet data — if the numbers in your worksheet change, the charts reflect those changes instantly.

Chart Types

You're probably aware of the many types of charts: bar charts, line charts, pie charts, and so on. Excel enables you to create all the basic chart types, and even some esoteric chart types, such as radar charts and doughnut charts. Table 13-1 lists Excel's chart types and the number of subtypes associated with each.

Table 13-1 Excel Chart Types	
Chart Type	**Subtypes**
Area	6
Bar	6
Column	7
Combination	6
Line	7
Pie	6
Doughnut	2
Radar	3
XY (Scatter)	5
Surface	4
Bubble	2
Stock	4
Cylinder	7
Cone	7
Pyramid	7

See the "Reference: Excel's Chart Types" section later in this chapter for a complete listing of Excel's chart types.

Which Chart Type to Use?

Beginning chart makers commonly ask how to determine the most appropriate chart type for the data. No good answer exists to this question, and I'm not aware of any hard-and-fast rules for determining which chart type is best for your data. Perhaps the best rule is to use the chart type that gets your message across in the simplest way.

Figures 13-3, 13-4, and 13-5 show the same data plotted using three different chart types. Although all three charts represent the same information, they look quite different.

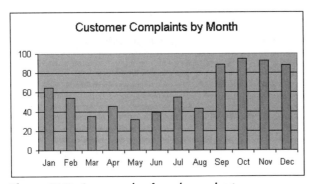

Figure 13-3: An example of a column chart.

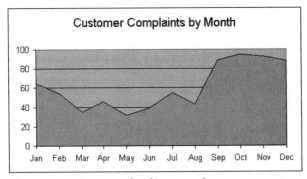

Figure 13-4: An example of an area chart.

Figure 13-5: An example of a pie chart.

The column chart is probably the best choice for this particular set of data, because it clearly shows the information for each month in discrete units. The area chart may not be appropriate, because it seems to imply that the data (Excel calls each set of data that you chart a *data series*) is continuous — that points exist in between the 12 actual data points (this same argument could be made against using a line chart). The pie chart is simply too confusing. Pie charts are most appropriate for a data series in which you want to emphasize proportions. If you have too many data points, a pie chart can be impossible to interpret.

Fortunately, Excel makes changing a chart's type after you create the chart an easy procedure. Experiment with various chart types until you find the one that represents your data accurately and clearly — and as simply as possible.

The Chart Wizard

You use the Chart Wizard to create a chart. The Chart Wizard consists of a series of dialog boxes that guide you through the process of creating the exact chart that you need. Figure 13-6 shows the first of four Chart Wizard dialog boxes.

Cross-Reference

Chapter 3 presented a step-by-step introductory example that created a simple chart by using the Chart Wizard. If you're new to chart making, you may want to work through that example. The Chart Wizard is explained in detail later in this chapter.

Figure 13-6: One of several dialog boxes displayed by the Chart Wizard.

Creating a Chart with One Keystroke

For a quick demonstration of how easily you can create a chart, follow these instructions. This example bypasses the Chart Wizard and creates a chart on a separate chart sheet.

1. Enter data to be charted into a worksheet. Figure 13-7 shows an example of data that's appropriate for a chart.

2. Select the range of data that you entered in Step 1, including the row and column titles. For example, if you entered the data shown in Figure 13-7, select A1:C4.

3. Press F11. Excel inserts a new chart sheet (named Chart1) and displays the chart, based on the selected data. Figure 13-8 shows the result.

	A	B	C	D	E
1		Region 1	Region 2		
2	January	89	85		
3	February	93	74		
4	March	75	31		
5					
6					
7					
8					

Figure 13-7: This data would make a good chart.

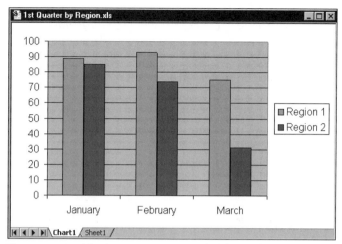

Figure 13-8: This chart was generated with one keystroke.

In this simple example, Excel created its default chart type (which is a two-dimensional column chart) by using the default settings. For more control over the chart-making process, you'll want to use the Chart Wizard.

How Excel Handles Charts

A chart is essentially an object that Excel creates. This object consists of one or more data series, displayed graphically; the appearance of the data series depends on the selected chart type. For example, if you create a line chart that uses two data series, the chart contains two lines — each representing one data series. You can distinguish each of the lines by its thickness, color, and data markers. The data series in the chart are linked to cells in the worksheet.

You can include a maximum of 255 data series in most charts; the exception is a standard pie chart, which can display only one data series. If your chart uses more than one data series, you may want to use a legend to help the reader identify each series. Excel also places a limit on the number of categories (or data points) in a data series: 32,000 (4,000 for 3D charts). Most users never run up against this limit.

Charts can use different numbers of axes:

✦ Common charts, such as column, line, and area charts, have a category axis and a value axis. The *category* axis normally is the horizontal axis, and the *value* axis normally is the vertical axis (this is reversed for bar charts, in which the bars extend from the left of the chart rather than from the bottom).

✦ Pie charts and doughnut charts have no axes (but they do have calories). A pie chart can display only one data series. A doughnut chart can display multiple data series.

✦ A radar chart is a special chart that has one axis for each point in the data series. The axes extend from the center of the chart.

✦ True 3D charts have three axes: a category axis, a value axis, and a series axis that extends into the third dimension. Refer to the upcoming sidebar, "3D or Not 3D? That Is the Question," for a discussion about Excel's 3D charts.

A chart is not stagnant. You can always change its type, add custom formatting, add new data series to it, or change an existing data series so that it uses data in a different range.

Before you create a chart, you need to determine whether you want it to be an embedded chart or a chart that resides on a chart sheet.

3D or Not 3D? That Is the Question

Some of Excel's charts are referred to as *3D charts*. This terminology can be a bit confusing, because some of these so-called 3D charts aren't technically 3D charts. Rather, they are 2D charts with a perspective look to them; that is, they appear to have some depth. The accompanying figure shows two "3D" charts.

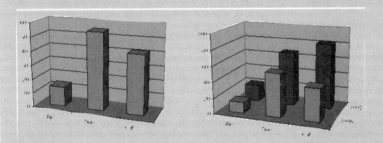

The chart on the left isn't a true 3D chart. It's simply a 2D chart that uses perspective to add depth to the columns. The chart on the right is a true 3D chart, because the data series extend into the third dimension.

A true 3D chart has three axes: a value axis (the height dimension), a category axis (the width dimension), and a series axis (the depth dimension).

Embedded Charts

An embedded chart basically floats on top of a worksheet, on the worksheet's draw layer. As with other drawing objects (such as a text box or a rectangle), you can move an embedded chart, resize it, change its proportions, adjust its borders, and perform other operations.

Chapter 14 discusses Excel's drawing objects and the draw layer.

To make any changes to the actual chart in an embedded chart object, you must click it to select the chart; Excel's menus, which swap places with the toolbars when you select a chart, include commands that are appropriate for working with charts. In addition, a Chart menu replaces the Data menu. Using embedded charts enables you to print the chart next to the data that it uses.

Figure 13-9 shows an example of a report with a chart embedded.

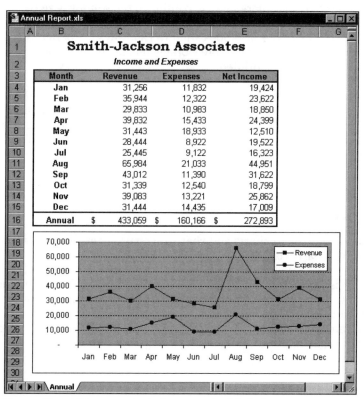

Figure 13-9: This report includes an embedded chart.

Chart Sheets

When you create a chart on a chart sheet, the chart occupies the entire sheet. If you plan to print a chart on a page by itself, using a chart sheet is your best choice. If you have many charts to create, you may want to create each one on a separate chart sheet, to avoid cluttering your worksheet. This technique also makes locating a particular chart easier, because you can change the names of the chart sheets' tabs to correspond to the chart that it contains.

Excel's menus change when a chart sheet is active, similar to the way that they change when you select an embedded chart. The Chart menu replaces the Data menu, and other menus include commands that are appropriate for working with charts.

Excel displays a chart in a chart sheet in WYSIWYG mode: the printed chart looks just like the image on the chart sheet. If the chart doesn't fit in the window, you can use the scrollbars to scroll it or adjust the zoom factor.

You also can size the chart in a chart sheet according to the window size by using the View ➪ Sized with Window command. When this setting is enabled, the chart adjusts itself when you resize the workbook window (it always fits perfectly in the window). In this mode, the chart that you're working on may or may not correspond to how it looks when printed.

If you create a chart on a chart sheet, you can easily convert it to an embedded chart. Choose Chart ➪ Location and then select the worksheet that holds the embedded chart from the As object in list box. Excel deletes the chart sheet and moves the chart to the sheet that you specify. This operation also works in the opposite direction: You can relocate an embedded chart to a new chart sheet.

Creating Charts

You can create both embedded charts and charts on chart sheets with or without the assistance of the Chart Wizard.

Note   Excel always has a default chart type. Normally, the default is a column chart (but you can change this type, as you'll see later). If you create a chart without using the Chart Wizard, Excel creates the chart by using the default chart type. If you use the Chart Wizard, Excel prompts you for the chart type, so the default chart type becomes irrelevant.

Creating an Embedded Chart with Chart Wizard

To invoke the Chart Wizard to create an embedded chart:

1. Select the data to be charted (optional).
2. Choose Insert ⇨ Chart (or, click the Chart Wizard tool on the Standard toolbar).
3. Make your choices in Steps 1 through 3 of the Chart Wizard.
4. In Step 4 of the Chart Wizard, select the option labeled As object in.

The Chart Wizard is explained in detail later in this chapter.

Creating an Embedded Chart Directly

To create an embedded chart without using the Chart Wizard:

1. Make sure that the Chart toolbar is displayed.
2. Select the data to be charted.
3. Click the Chart Type tool on the Chart toolbar and then select a chart type from the displayed icons.

Excel adds the chart to the worksheet by using the default settings.

Note The Chart Type tool on the Chart toolbar displays an icon for the last selected chart. However, this tool works like a list box; you can expand it to display all 18 chart types (see Figure 13-10). Just click the arrow to display the additional chart types.

Figure 13-10: The Chart Type tool expands so that you can create the type of chart you want.

The Chart Toolbar

The Chart toolbar appears when you click an embedded chart, activate a chart sheet, or choose View ➪ Toolbars ➪ Chart. This toolbar, shown in the accompanying figure, includes nine tools. You can use these tools to make some common chart changes:

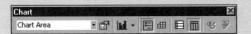

✦ **Chart Objects:** When a chart is activated, you can select a particular chart element by using this drop-down list.

✦ **Format Selected Object:** Displays the Format dialog box for the selected chart element.

✦ **Chart Type:** Expands to display 18 chart types when you click the arrow. After it's expanded, you can drag this tool to a new location — creating, in effect, a miniature floating toolbar.

✦ **Legend:** Toggles the legend display in the selected chart.

✦ **Data Table:** Toggles the display of the data table in a chart.

✦ **By Row:** Plots the data by rows.

✦ **By Column:** Plots the data by columns.

✦ **Angle Text (Downward):** Displays the selected text at a −45-degree angle.

✦ **Angle Text (Upward):** Displays the selected text at a +45-degree angle.

If you press Shift while you click either of the Angle Text tools, Excel no longer angles the selected text.

Excel includes several other chart-related tools that aren't on the Chart toolbar. You can customize the toolbar to include these additional tools, which are located in the Charting category in the Customize dialog box.

In addition, several tools on the other toolbars work with charts, including the Color, Font Color, Bold, Italic, and Font tools.

Creating a Chart on a Chart Sheet with the Chart Wizard

To start the Chart Wizard and create an embedded chart:

1. Select the data that you want to chart (optional).

2. Choose Insert ➪ Chart (or click the Chart Wizard tool on the Standard toolbar).

3. Make your choices in Steps 1 through 3 of the Chart Wizard.

4. In Step 4 of the Chart Wizard, select the option labeled As new sheet.

To create a new chart on a chart sheet by using the default chart type, select the data to be charted and then press the F11 key. This command inserts a new chart sheet. The chart is created from the selected range, without accessing the Chart Wizard.

Creating a Chart with the Chart Wizard

The Chart Wizard consists of four dialog boxes that prompt you for various settings for the chart. By the time that you reach the last dialog box, the chart is usually just what you need.

Selecting the Data

Before you start the Chart Wizard, select the data that you want to include in the chart. This step isn't necessary, but it makes creating the chart easier for you. If you don't select the data before invoking the Chart Wizard, you can select it in the second Chart Wizard dialog box.

When you select the data, include items such as labels and series identifiers (row and column headings). Figure 13-11 shows a worksheet with a range of data set up for a chart. This data consists of monthly sales for two regions. You would select the entire range for this worksheet, including the month names and region names.

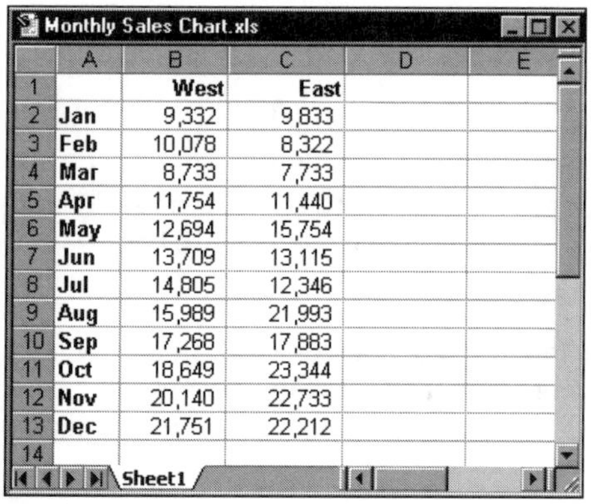

	A	B	C	D	E
1		West	East		
2	Jan	9,332	9,833		
3	Feb	10,078	8,322		
4	Mar	8,733	7,733		
5	Apr	11,754	11,440		
6	May	12,694	15,754		
7	Jun	13,709	13,115		
8	Jul	14,805	12,346		
9	Aug	15,989	21,993		
10	Sep	17,268	17,883		
11	Oct	18,649	23,344		
12	Nov	20,140	22,733		
13	Dec	21,751	22,212		
14					

Figure 13-11: Data to be charted.

The data that you plot doesn't have to be contiguous. You can press Ctrl and make a multiple selection. Figure 13-12 shows an example of how to select noncontiguous ranges for a chart. In this case, Excel uses only the selected cells for the chart.

Monthly Sales Chart.xls					
	A	B	C	D	E	F
1		West	East	Combined		
2	Jan	9,332	9,833	19,165		
3	Feb	10,078	8,322	18,400		
4	Mar	8,733	7,733	16,466		
5	Apr	11,754	11,440	23,194		
6	May	12,694	15,754	28,448		
7	Jun	13,709	13,115	26,824		
8	Jul	14,805	12,346	27,151		
9	Aug	15,989	21,993	37,982		
10	Sep	17,268	17,883	35,151		
11	Oct	18,649	23,344	41,993		
12	Nov	20,140	22,733	42,873		
13	Dec	21,751	22,212	43,963		
14						
15						

Figure 13-12: Selecting noncontiguous ranges to be charted.

After you select the data, start the Chart Wizard, either by clicking the Chart Wizard button on the Standard toolbar or by selecting Insert ➪ Chart. Excel displays the first of four Chart Wizard dialog boxes.

At any time while using the Chart Wizard, you can go back to the preceding step by clicking the Back button. Or, you can click Finish to close the Chart Wizard. If you close the Chart Wizard early, Excel creates the chart by using the information that you provided up to that point.

Don't be too concerned about creating the perfect chart. You later can change, at any time, every choice that you make in the Chart Wizard.

Chart Wizard – Step 1 of 4

Figure 13-13 shows the first Chart Wizard dialog box, in which you select the chart type. This dialog box has two tabs: Standard Types and Custom Types. The Standard Types tab displays the 14 basic chart types and the subtypes for each. The Custom Types tab displays some customized charts (including user-defined custom charts).

Tip   When you work in the Custom Types tab, the dialog box shows a preview of your data with the selected chart type. In the Standard Types tab, you get a preview by clicking the button labeled Click and Hold to View Sample. When you click this button, keep the mouse button pressed.

When you decide on a chart type and subtype, click the Next button to move to the next step.

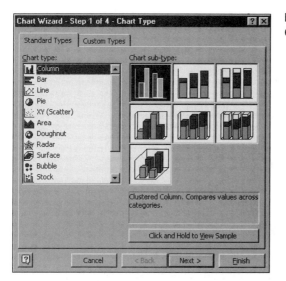

Figure 13-13: The first of four Chart Wizard dialog boxes.

Chart Wizard — Step 2 of 4

In the second step of the Chart Wizard (shown in Figure 13-14), you verify the data ranges and specify the orientation of the data (whether it's arranged in rows or columns). The orientation of the data has a drastic effect on the look of your chart. Usually, Excel guesses the orientation correctly — but not always.

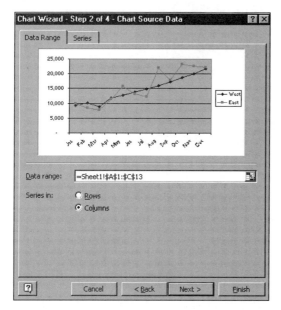

Figure 13-14: In the second Chart Wizard dialog box, you verify the range and specify whether to plot by columns or rows.

If you select the Series tab, you can verify or change the data that is used for each series of the chart. Click the Next button to advance to the next dialog box.

Chart Wizard — Step 3 of 4

In the third Chart Wizard dialog box, shown in Figure 13-15, you specify most of the options for the chart. This dialog box has six tabs:

✦ **Titles:** Add titles to the chart.

✦ **Axes:** Turn on or off axes display and specify the type of axes.

✦ **Gridlines:** Specify gridlines, if any.

✦ **Legend:** Specify whether to include a legend and where to place it.

✦ **Data Labels:** Specify whether to show data labels and what type of labels.

✦ **Data Table:** Specify whether to display a table of the data.

Note   The options available depend on the type of chart that you selected in Step 1 of the Chart Wizard.

After you select the chart options, click Next to move to the final dialog box.

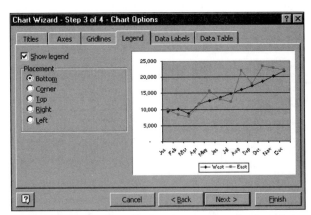

Figure 13-15: You specify the chart options in the third Chart Wizard dialog box.

Chart Wizard — Step 4 of 4

Step 4 of the Chart Wizard, shown in Figure 13-16, lets you specify where to place the chart. Make your choice and click Finish.

Excel creates and displays the chart. If you place the chart on a worksheet, Excel centers it in the worksheet window and selects it.

Figure 13-16: Step 4 of the Chart Wizard asks you where to put the chart.

Basic Chart Modifications

After you create a chart, you can modify it at any time. The modifications that you can make to a chart are extensive. This section covers some of the more common chart modifications:

✦ Moving and resizing the chart

✦ Changing a chart's location

✦ Changing the chart type

✦ Moving chart elements

✦ Deleting chart elements

Other types of chart modifications are discussed in Chapter 16.

Activating a Chart

Before you can modify a chart, it must be activated. To activate an embedded chart, click it, which also activates the element that you click. To activate a chart on a chart sheet, just click its sheet tab.

Moving and Resizing a Chart

If your chart is on a chart sheet, you can't move or resize it. You can, however, change the way that it's displayed by selecting View ➪ Sized with Window.

If you embedded the chart, you can freely move and resize it. Click the chart's border to select the chart; eight handles (small black squares) appear on the chart's border. Drag the chart to move it, or drag any of the handles to resize the chart.

Changing a Chart's Location

Use the Chart ➪ Location command to relocate an embedded chart to a chart sheet, or convert a chart on a chart sheet to an embedded chart. This command displays the Chart Location dialog box.

Tip   If you select an embedded chart and choose an existing chart sheet as its new location, Excel will ask if you'd like to embed the chart on the chart sheet. If you respond Yes, the chart sheet will contain an additional chart. This is a way to overcome the normal limit of one chart per chart sheet. Even better, you can delete the original chart on the chart sheet and then rearrange your embedded charts on a single chart sheet.

Changing the Chart Type

To change the chart type of the active chart, use either of the following methods:

✦ Click the Chart Type button's drop-down arrow on the Chart toolbar. The button expands to show 18 basic chart types.

✦ Choose the Chart ➪ Chart Type command.

The Chart ➪ Chart Type command displays the dialog box shown in Figure 13-17. You may recognize this dialog box as the first of the Chart Wizard dialog boxes. Click the Standard Types tab to select one of the standard chart types (and a subtype), or click the Custom Types tab to select a customized chart. After you select a chart type, click OK; the selected chart will be changed to the type that you selected.

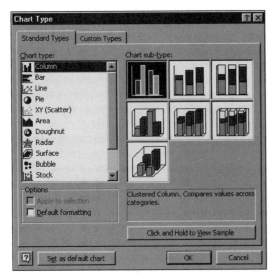

Figure 13-17: The Chart Type dialog box enables you to change the chart's type.

If you've customized some aspects of your chart, choosing a new chart type from the Custom Types tab may override some or all the changes that you've made. For example, if you've added gridlines to the chart and then select a custom chart type that doesn't use gridlines, your gridlines disappear. Therefore, you should make sure that you're satisfied with the chart before you make too many custom changes to it. However, you can always use Edit ⇨ Undo to reverse your actions.

In the Custom Types tab, if you click the User-defined option, the list box displays the name of any user-defined custom formats. If you haven't defined any custom formats, this box shows Default, referring to the default chart type. Changing the default chart type is discussed later in this chapter.

Chapter 16 explains how to create custom formats.

Moving and Deleting Chart Elements

Some of the chart parts can be moved (any of the titles, the legend, or data labels). To move a chart element, simply click it to select it and then drag it to the desired location in the chart. To delete a chart element, select it and then press Delete.

Other Modifications

When a chart is activated, you can select various parts of the chart to change. Modifying a chart is similar to everything else you do in Excel. First, you make a selection (in this case, select a chart part). Then, you issue a command to do something with the selection.

You can use the Fill Color tool on the Formatting toolbar to change colors. For example, if you want to change the color of a series, select the series and choose the color that you want from the Fill Color tool. You'll find that many other toolbar tools work with charts. For example, you can select the chart's legend and then click the Bold tool to make the legend text bold.

When you double-click a chart element (or press Ctrl+1 after selecting it), its Formatting dialog box appears, which varies, depending on the item selected. In most cases, the dialog box is of the tabbed variety. Many modifications are self-evident — for example, changing the font used in a title. Others, however, are a bit trickier.

Chapter 16 discusses these chart modifications in detail.

Changing the Default Chart Type

The default chart type is mentioned many times in this chapter. Excel's default chart type is a 2D column chart with a light-gray plot area, a legend on the right, and horizontal gridlines.

If you don't like the looks of this chart or if you typically use a different type of chart, you can easily change the default chart in the following manner:

1. Select the Chart ⇨ Chart Type command.

2. Choose the chart type that you want to use as the default chart. This can be a chart from either the Standard Types tab or the Custom Types tab.

3. Click the button labeled Set as default chart type. You are asked to verify your choice.

Tip If you have many charts of the same type to create, changing the default chart format to the chart type with which you're working is much more efficient than separately formatting each chart. Then, you can create all of your charts without having to select the chart type.

Printing Charts

Printing embedded charts is nothing special; you print them the same way that you print a worksheet (see Chapter 12). As long as you include the embedded chart in the range that you want to print, Excel prints the chart as it appears onscreen.

Tip If you select an embedded chart and then choose File ⇨ Print (or click the Print button), Excel prints the chart on a page by itself and does *not* print the worksheet.

If you print in Draft mode, Excel doesn't print embedded charts. Also, if you don't want a particular embedded chart to appear on your printout, right-click the chart and choose Format Chart Area from the shortcut menu. Click the Properties tab in the Format Chart Area dialog box and remove the check mark from the Print Object check box.

If you created the chart on a chart sheet, Excel prints the chart on a page by itself. If you open Excel's Page Setup dialog box when the chart sheet is active, the Sheet tab is replaced with a tab named Chart. Figure 13-18 shows the Chart tab of the Page Setup dialog box.

This dialog box has several options:

✦ **Use full page:** Excel prints the chart to the full width and height of the page margins. This usually isn't a good choice, because the chart's relative proportions change and you lose the WYSIWYG advantage.

✦ **Scale to fit page:** Expands the chart proportionally in both dimensions until one dimension fills the space between the margins. This option usually results in the best printout.

✦ **Custom:** Prints the chart as it appears on your screen. Select View ⇨ Sized with Window to make the chart correspond to the window size and proportions. The chart prints at the current window size and proportions.

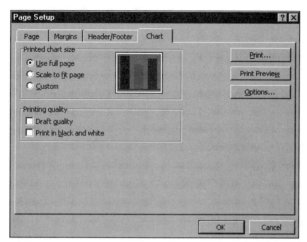

Figure 13-18: The Chart tab of the Page Setup dialog box.

The Printing quality options work just like those for worksheet pages. If you choose the Draft quality option for a chart sheet, Excel prints the chart, but its quality may not be high (the actual effect depends on your printer). Choosing the Print in black and white option prints the data series with black-and-white patterns rather than colors.

Tip   Because charts usually take longer to print than text, using the print preview feature before you print a chart is an especially good idea. This feature enables you to see what the printed output will look like, so that you can avoid surprises.

Reference: Excel's Chart Types

For your reference, this chapter concludes with a discussion of Excel's chart types and a listing of the subtypes for each. This section may help you determine which chart type is best for your data.

Column Charts

Column charts are one of the most common chart types. This type of chart is useful for displaying discrete data (as opposed to continuous data). You can have any number of data series, and the columns can be stacked on top of each other. Figure 13-19 shows an example of a column chart.

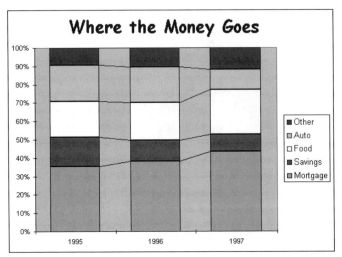

Figure 13-19: This stacked column chart displays each series as a percentage of the total. It may substitute for several pie charts.

Table 13-2 lists Excel's seven column chart subtypes.

	Table 13-2 **Column Chart Subtypes**	
Chart Type	*Description*	
Clustered Column	Standard column chart.	
Stacked Column	Column chart with data series stacked.	
100% Stacked Column	Column chart with data series stacked and expressed as percentages.	
3-D Clustered Column	Standard column chart with a perspective look.	
3-D Stacked Column	Column chart with a perspective look. Data series are stacked and expressed as percentages.	
3-D 100% Stacked Column	Column chart with a perspective look. Excel stacks the data series and expresses them as percentages.	
3-D Column	A true 3D column chart with a third axis.	

Bar Charts

A *bar chart* is essentially a column chart that has been rotated 90 degrees to the left. The advantage in using a bar chart is that the category labels may be easier to read (see Figure 13-20 for an example). You can include any number of data series in a bar chart. In addition, the bars can be stacked from left to right. Table 13-3 lists Excel's six bar chart subtypes.

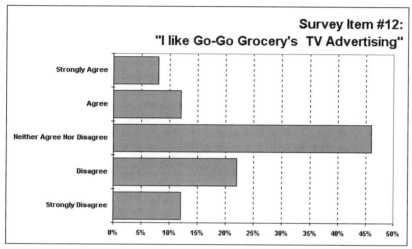

Figure 13-20: If you have lengthy category labels, a bar chart may be a good choice.

Table 13-3 lists Excel's six bar chart subtypes.

Table 13-3	
Bar Chart Subtypes	
Chart Type	*Description*
Clustered Bar	Standard bar chart.
Stacked Bar	Bar chart with data series stacked.
100% Stacked Bar	Bar chart with data series stacked and expressed as percentages.
3-D Clustered Bar	Standard bar chart with a perspective look.
3-D Stacked Bar	Bar chart with a perspective look. Excel stacks data series and expresses them as percentages.
3-D 100% Stacked Bar	Bar chart with a perspective look. Excel stacks data series and expresses them as percentages.

Line Charts

Line charts are frequently used to plot data that is continuous rather than discrete. For example, plotting daily sales as a line chart may let you spot trends over time. See Figure 13-21 for an example.

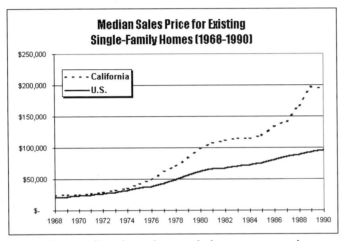

Figure 13-21: A line chart often can help you spot trends in your data.

Table 13-4 lists Excel's seven line chart subtypes.

	Table 13-4
	Line Chart Subtypes

Chart Type	Description
Line	Standard line chart.
Stacked Line	Line chart with stacked data series.
100% Stacked Line	Line chart with stacked data series expressed as percentages.
Line with Data Markers	Line chart with data markers.
Stacked Line with Data Markers	Line chart with stacked data series and data markers.
100% Stacked Line with Data Markers	Line chart with stacked data series and line markers, expressed as percentages.
3-D Line	A true 3D line chart with a third axis.

Pie Charts

A *pie chart* is useful when you want to show relative proportions or contributions to a whole. Figure 13-22 shows an example of a pie chart. Generally, a pie chart should use no more than five or six data points; otherwise, it's difficult to interpret. A pie chart can use only one data series.

You can explode a slice of a pie chart. Activate the chart and select the slice that you want to explode. Then, drag it away from the center.

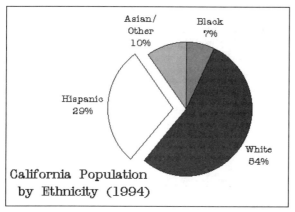

Figure 13-22: A pie chart with one slice exploded.

Table 13-5 lists Excel's six pie chart subtypes.

Table 13-5 Pie Chart Subtypes	
Chart Type	**Description**
Pie	Standard pie chart.
3-D Pie	Pie chart with perspective look.
Pie of Pie	Pie chart with one slice broken into another pie.
Exploded Pie	Pie chart with one or more slices exploded.
Exploded 3-D Pie	Pie chart with perspective look, with one or more slices exploded.
Bar of Pie	Pie chart with one slice broken into a column.

Cross-Reference The Pie of Pie and Bar of Pie chart types enable you to display a second chart that clarifies one of the pie slices. You can use the Options tab of the Format Data Series dialog box to specify which data is assigned to the second chart. Refer to Chapter 16 for details.

XY (Scatter) Charts

Another common chart type is *XY (Scatter) charts* (also known as *scattergrams*). An XY chart differs from the other chart types in that both axes display values (there is no category axis).

This type of chart often is used to show the relationship between two variables. Figure 13-23 shows an example of an XY chart that plots the relationship between sales calls and sales. The chart shows that these two variables are positively related: months in which more calls were made typically had higher sales volumes.

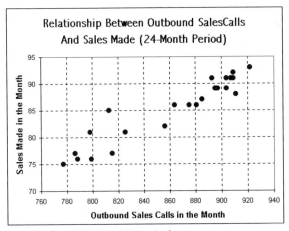

Figure 13-23: An XY (Scatter) chart.

Table 13-6 lists Excel's five XY (Scatter) chart subtypes.

Table 13-6	
XY (Scatter) Chart Subtypes	
Chart Type	**Description**
Scatter	XY chart with markers and no lines.
Scatter with Smoothed Lines	XY chart with markers and smoothed lines.
Scatter with Smoothed Lines and No Data Markers	XY chart with smoothed lines and no markers.

Chart Type	Description
Scatter with Lines	XY chart with lines and markers.
Scatter with Lines and No Data Markers	XY chart with lines and no markers.

Area Charts

Think of an *area chart* as a line chart that has been colored in. Figure 13-24 shows an example of a stacked area chart. Stacking the data series enables you to see clearly the total plus the contribution by each series.

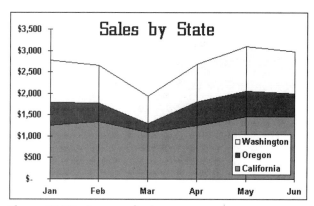

Figure 13-24: An area chart.

Table 13-7 lists Excel's six area chart subtypes.

Table 13-7 Area Chart Subtypes	
Chart Type	**Description**
Area	Standard area chart.
Stacked Area	Area chart, data series stacked.
100% Stacked Area	Area chart, expressed as percentages.
3-D Area	A true 3D area chart with a third axis.
3-D Stacked Area	Area chart with a perspective look, data series stacked.
3-D 100% Stacked Area	Area chart with a perspective look, expressed as percentages.

Doughnut Charts

A *doughnut chart* is similar to a pie chart, except that it has a hole in the middle. Unlike a pie chart, a doughnut chart can display more than one series of data. Figure 13-25 shows an example of a doughnut chart (the arrow and series descriptions were added manually; these items aren't part of a doughnut chart).

Notice that Excel displays the data series as concentric rings. As you can see, a doughnut chart with more than one series to chart can be difficult to interpret. Sometimes, a stacked column chart for such comparisons expresses your meaning better than a doughnut chart.

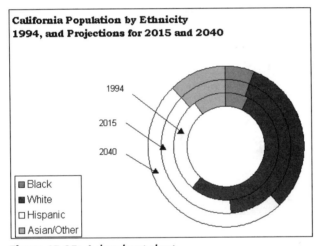

Figure 13-25: A doughnut chart.

Table 13-8 lists Excel's two doughnut chart subtypes.

Table 13-8 Doughnut Chart Subtypes	
Chart Type	**Subtype**
Doughnut	Standard doughnut chart.
Exploded Doughnut	Doughnut chart with all slices exploded.

Radar Charts

You may not be familiar with radar charts. A *radar chart* has a separate axis for each category, and the axes extend from the center. The value of the data point is plotted on the appropriate axis. If all data points in a series have an identical value, it produces a perfect circle. See Figure 13-26 for an example of a radar chart.

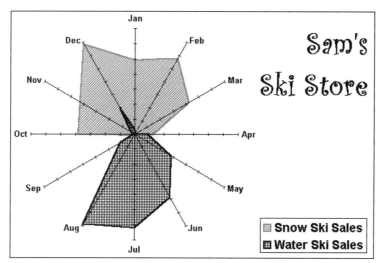

Figure 13-26: A radar chart.

Table 13-9 lists Excel's three radar chart subtypes.

Table 13-9 Radar Chart Subtypes	
Chart Type	**Subtype**
Radar	Standard radar chart (lines only).
Radar with Data Markers	Radar chart with lines data markers.
Filled Radar	Radar chart with lines colored in.

Surface Charts

Surface charts display two or more data series on a surface. As Figure 13-27 shows, these charts can be quite interesting. Unlike other charts, Excel uses color to distinguish values, not to distinguish the data series. You can change these colors only by modifying the workbook's color palette, using the Color tab in the Options dialog box.

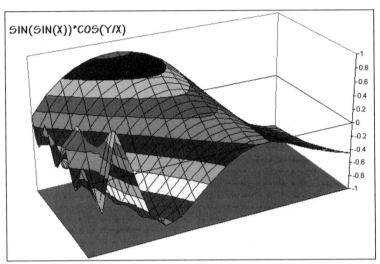

SIN(SIN(X))*COS(Y/X)

Figure 13-27: A surface chart.

Table 13-10 lists Excel's four 3D surface chart subtypes.

Table 13-10
Surface Chart Subtypes

Chart Type	Description
3-D Surface	Standard 3D surface chart.
3-D Surface (wireframe)	3D surface chart with no colors.
Surface (top view)	3D surface chart, as viewed from above.
Surface (top view wireframe)	3D surface chart, as viewed from above, no color.

Bubble Charts

Think of a bubble chart as an XY (Scatter) chart that can display an additional data series. That additional data series is represented by the size of the bubbles.

Figure 13-28 shows an example of a bubble chart. In this case, the chart displays the results of a weight-loss program. The *x* axis represents the original weight, the *y* axis shows the length of time in the program, and the size of the bubbles represents the amount of weight lost.

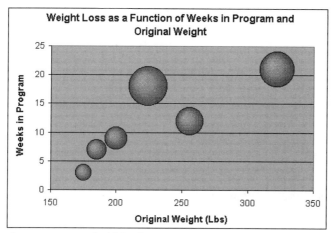

Figure 13-28: A bubble chart.

Table 13-11 lists Excel's two bubble chart subtypes.

Table 13-11	
Bubble Chart Subtypes	
Chart Type	*Subtype*
Bubble Chart	Standard bubble chart.
Bubble with 3-D effect	Bubble chart with 3D bubbles.

Stock Charts

Stock charts are most useful for displaying stock market information. These charts require three to five data series, depending on the subtype.

Figure 13-29 shows an example of a stock chart. This chart uses the High-Low-Close subtype that requires three data series.

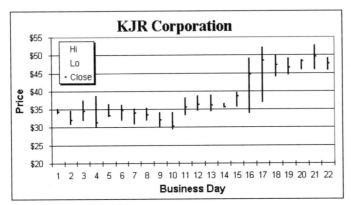

Figure 13-29: A stock chart.

Table 13-12 lists Excel's four stock chart subtypes.

	Table 13-12
	Stock Chart Subtypes
Chart Type	**Subtype**
High-Low-Close	Displays the stock's high, low, and closing prices.
Open-High-Low-Close	Displays the stock's opening, high, low, and closing prices.
Volume-High-Low-Close	Displays the stock's volume, high, low, and closing prices.
Volume-Open-High-Low-Close	Displays the stock's volume, open, high, low, and closing prices.

Cylinder, Cone, and Pyramid Charts

These three chart types are essentially the same—except for the shapes that are used. You usually can use these charts in place of a bar or column chart.

Figure 13-30 shows an example of a pyramid chart.

Each of these chart types has seven subtypes, which are described in Table 13-13.

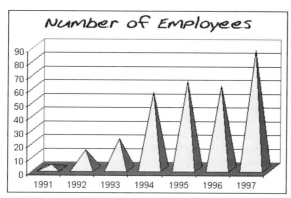

Figure 13-30: A pyramid chart.

Table 13-13	
Cylinder, Cone, and Pyramid Chart Subtypes	
Chart Type	**Subtype**
Clustered Column	Standard column chart.
Stacked Column	Column chart with data series stacked.
100% Stacked Column	Column chart with data series stacked and expressed as percentages.
Clustered Bar	Standard bar chart.
Stacked Bar	Bar chart with data series stacked.
100% Stacked Bar	Bar chart with data series stacked and expressed as percentages.
3-D Column	A true 3D column chart with a third axis.

Summary

This chapter introduces Excel's chart-making feature. Charts can be embedded on a worksheet or created in a separate chart sheet. You can either use the Chart Wizard to walk you through the chart-making process or create a default chart in a single step. This chapter also describes how to change the default chart type.

After a chart is created, you can make many types of modifications. A few simple modifications are discussed; Chapter 16 presents additional chart information.

Printing charts works much like printing worksheets, although you should be familiar with the page setup options when you're printing chart sheets. The chapter concludes with a complete listing and description of Excel's chart types and subtypes.

✦   ✦   ✦

Enhancing Your Work with Pictures and Drawings

In Chapter 13, you learned how to create charts from the numbers in your worksheet. This chapter continues in the same vein by discussing pictures and drawings. Like charts, these objects can be placed on a worksheet's draw layer to add pizzazz to an otherwise boring report. (See the sidebar, "A Word About the Draw Layer," later in this chapter.)

This chapter discusses three major types of images:

✦ Bitmap and line-art graphics imported directly into a workbook or copied from the Clipboard

✦ Objects created by using Excel's drawing tools

✦ Objects inserted by using other Microsoft Office tools, such as WordArt and Organization Chart

Cross-Reference Excel also can create another type of graphic image: maps. But that's the topic of Chapter 17.

Importing Graphics Files

Excel can import a wide variety of graphics files into a worksheet. You have several choices:

✦ Use the Microsoft Clip Gallery to locate and insert an image

✦ Directly import a graphic file

✦ Copy and paste the image by using the Windows Clipboard

✦ Import the image from a digital camera or scanner

Using the Clip Gallery

The Clip Gallery is a shared application that is also accessible from other Microsoft Office products.

Note

Besides providing an easy way to locate and insert images, the Clip Gallery enables you to insert sound and video files.

EXCEL 2000

The Clip Gallery is available in both Excel 97 and Excel 2000, but the feature works a bit differently in Excel 2000. In addition, Excel 2000 gives you direct access to Microsoft's Clip Gallery Live on the Web.

You access the Clip Gallery by selecting the Insert ➪ Picture ➪ Clip Art command. This displays the Insert ClipArt dialog box, shown in Figure 14-1. Click the Pictures tab and then click a category, and the images in that category appear. Locate the image that you want and click it. A graphic menu pops up from which you can choose to insert the image, preview the image, add the image to your "favorites," or find similar images. You can also search for clip art by keyword — just enter some text in the Search for clips box, and the matching images are displayed.

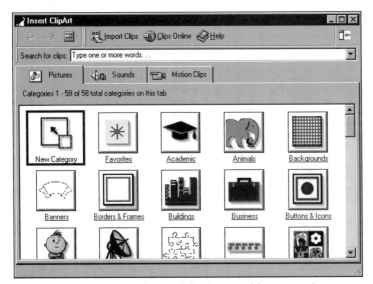

Figure 14-1: The Insert ClipArt dialog box enables you to insert pictures, sounds, or video.

If you select the insert option, the image is embedded in your worksheet. You can then either select additional images from the Clip Gallery or close the Insert ClipArt dialog box.

When an image is selected, Excel displays its Picture toolbar, which contains tools that enable you to adjust the image.

Tip You also can add new files to the Clip Gallery. You might want to do this if you tend to insert a particular graphic file into your worksheets (such as your company logo). Use the Import Clips button to select the file and specify the category for the image.

EXCEL 2000 If you can't find a suitable image, you can go online and browse through the clip art at Microsoft's Web site. In the Insert ClipArt dialog box, click the Clips Online button. Your Web browser will be activated, and you can view the images (or listen to the sounds) and download those that you want. Figure 14-2 shows Microsoft's online Clip Gallery

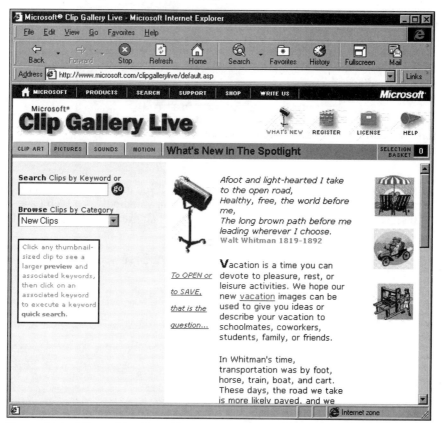

Figure 14-2: Microsoft's Clip Gallery Live enables you to download additional clip art.

Importing Graphics Files

If the graphic image that you want to insert is available in a file, you can easily import the file into your worksheet by choosing Insert ⇨ Picture ⇨ From File. Excel displays the Insert Picture dialog box, shown in Figure 14-3. This dialog box works just like the Open dialog box. By default, it displays only the graphics files that Excel can import. If you choose the Preview option, Excel displays a preview of the selected file in the right panel of the dialog box.

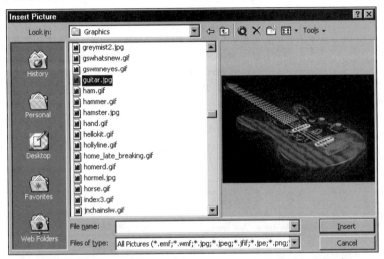

Figure 14-3: The Insert Picture dialog box enables you to embed a picture in a worksheet.

EXCEL 2000   Excel 2000 supports animated GIF files — sort of. If you insert an animated GIF file, the image will be animated only if you save your workbook as a Web page and then view it in a Web browser. Figure 14-4 shows an example of a graphics file in a worksheet.

Figure 14-4 shows an example of a graphic image in a worksheet.

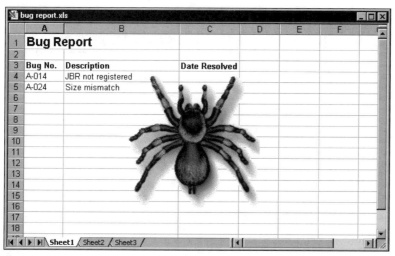

Figure 14-4: An example of a graphics file embedded in a worksheet.

About Graphics Files

Graphics files come in two main categories: *bitmap* and *vector* (picture). Bitmap images are made up of discrete dots. They usually look pretty good at their original size, but often lose clarity if you increase or decrease the size. Vector-based images, on the other hand, retain their crispness, regardless of their size. Examples of common bitmap file formats include BMP, PCX, DIB, JPG, and GIF. Examples of common vector file formats include CGM, WMF, EPS, and DRW.

Bitmap files vary in the number of colors that they use (even black-and-white images use multiple colors, because these are usually gray-scale images). If you view a high-color bitmap graphic by using a video mode that displays only 16 or 256 colors, the image usually doesn't look very good.

You can find thousands of graphics files free for the taking on the Internet and online services such as CompuServe, America Online, and Prodigy.

Caution   Using bitmap graphics in a worksheet can dramatically increase the size of your workbook, resulting in more memory usage and longer load and save times.

Table 14-1 lists the graphics file types that Excel can import. The most common graphics file formats are GIF, JPG, and BMP.

Table 14-1	
Graphics File Formats Supported by Excel	
File Type	**Description**
BMP	Windows bitmap
CDR	CorelDRAW graphics
CGM	Computer Graphics Metafiles
DIB	Windows bitmap
DRW	Micrografx Designer/Draw
DXF	AutoCAD format 2D
EMF	Windows Enhanced Metafile
EPS	Encapsulated PostScript
GIF	Graphic Interchange Format
HGL	HP Graphics Language
JPG	JPEG File Interchange Format
PCT	Macintosh graphics
PCD	Kodak Photo CD
PCX	Bitmap graphics
PNG	Portable Network Graphics
RLE	Windows bitmap
TGA	Targa graphics format
TIF	Tagged Interchange Format
WMF	Windows metafile
WPG	WordPerfect graphics

Tip   If you want to use a graphic image for a worksheet's background (similar to wallpaper on the Windows desktop), select Format ⇨ Sheet ⇨ Background and then select a graphics file. The selected graphics file is tiled on the worksheet. It won't be printed, however.

Copying Graphics by Using the Clipboard

In some cases, you may want to use a graphic image that is not stored in a separate file or that is in a file that Excel can't import. For example, you may have a drawing program that uses a file format that Excel doesn't support. You may be able to export the file to a supported format, but it may be easier to load the file into the drawing program and copy the image to the Clipboard. Then, you can activate Excel and paste the image to the draw layer. (See the sidebar, "A Word About the Draw Layer," later in this chapter.)

This capability also is useful if you don't want to copy an entire image. For example, a drawing may consist of several components, and you may want to use only one element in Excel. In this case, using the Clipboard is the only route.

Suppose that you see a graphic displayed onscreen but you can't select it — it may be part of a program's logo, for example. In this case, you can copy the entire screen to the Clipboard and then paste it into Excel. Most of the time, you don't want the entire screen — just a portion of it. The solution is to capture the entire screen (or window), copy it to the Windows Paint program, and then copy just the part that you want (or crop out what you don't want) and paste it to your Excel worksheet. Figure 14-5 demonstrates this technique using Paint. In this case, a window was copied and pasted to Paint.

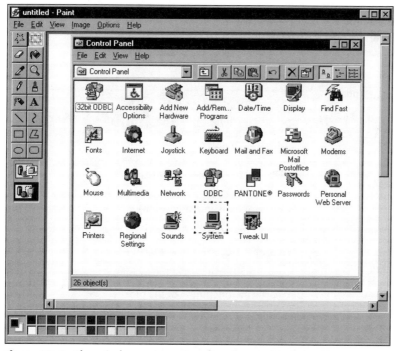

Figure 14-5: The window was captured and pasted to Paint. You can copy the part that you want and paste it to Excel.

Use the following keyboard commands, as needed:

PrintScreen: Copies the entire screen to the Clipboard

Alt+PrintScreen: Copies the active window to the Clipboard

Importing from a Digital Camera or Scanner

You can bring in an image directly from a digital camera or a scanner. To use this feature, make sure that your device is connected and set up properly. Then, choose Insert ⇨ Picture ⇨ From Scanner or Camera. The exact procedure varies, depending on your camera or scanner. In most cases, the image appears in Microsoft Photo Editor. You can adjust the image, if necessary, and then select File ⇨ Exit and Return to Excel.

 Importing images from a digital camera or scanner is a new feature in Excel 2000.

Modifying Pictures

When you insert a picture on a worksheet, you can modify the picture in various ways by using the Picture toolbar, shown in Figure 14-6. This toolbar appears automatically when you select a picture object. The tools are described in Table 14-2, in left-to-right order on the toolbar.

Figure 14-6: The Picture toolbar enables you to adjust a picture.

Table 14-2
The Tools on the Picture Toolbar

Tool Name	What the Tool Does
Insert Picture from File	Displays the Insert Picture dialog box.
Image Control	Enables you to change a picture to gray-scale, black and white, or a watermark (semitransparent).
More Contrast	Increases the contrast of the picture.
Less Contrast	Decreases the contrast of the picture.
More Brightness	Increases the brightness of the picture.
Less Brightness	Decreases the brightness of the picture.
Crop	Crops the picture. After clicking this tool, drag any of the picture's handles to make the picture smaller.
Line Style	Selects a border for the picture.
Format Picture	Displays the Format Picture dialog box.
Set Transparent Color	Selects a color that will be transparent. Underlying cell contents appear through the selected transparent color. This option is not available for all types of pictures.
Reset Picture	Returns the picture to its original state.

A Word About the Draw Layer

Every worksheet and chart sheet has a *draw layer,* an invisible surface that is completely independent of the cells on a worksheet (or the chart on a chart sheet). The draw layer can hold graphic images, drawings, embedded charts, OLE objects, and so on.

Objects placed on the draw layer can be moved, resized, copied, and deleted — with no effect on any other elements in the worksheet. Objects on the draw layer have properties that relate to how they are moved and sized when underlying cells are moved and sized. When you right-click a graphic object and choose Format Object from the shortcut menu, you get a tabbed dialog box (see the accompanying figure). Click the Properties tab to adjust how the object moves or resizes with its underlying cells. Your choices are as follows:

◆ **Move and size with cells:** If this option is selected, the object appears to be attached to the cells beneath it. For example, if you insert rows above the object, the object moves down. If you increase the column width, the object gets wider.

◆ **Move but don't size with cells:** If this option is checked, the object moves if rows or columns are inserted, but it never changes its size if you change row heights or column widths.

◆ **Don't move or size with cells:** This option makes the object completely independent of the underlying cells.

The preceding options control how an object is moved or sized with respect to the underlying cells. Excel also enables you to "attach" an object to a cell. In the Edit panel of the Options dialog box, place a check mark next to the check box labeled Cut, copy, and sort objects with cells. After you do so, graphic objects on the draw layer are attached to the underlying cells.

Because a chart sheet doesn't have cells, objects placed on a chart sheet don't have these options. Such objects do have a property, however, that relates to how the object is sized if the chart size is changed.

Using Excel's Drawing Tools

The discussion so far has focused on using graphic images from other sources. If your needs involve simple (or not so simple) graphic shapes, you can use the drawing tools built into Excel to create a variety of graphics.

Beginning with Excel 97, the drawing features have been improved significantly. These tools also are available in the other Microsoft Office applications.

The Drawing Toolbar

Excel's drawing tools are available from the Drawing toolbar, shown in Figure 14.7. The drawing objects feature is one of the few features in Excel that's not available from the menus. Notice that the Standard toolbar has a tool named Drawing. Clicking this tool toggles the Drawing toolbar on and off. Normally, the Drawing toolbar appears at the bottom of Excel's window, but (as with all toolbars) you can place it anywhere that you like. As you'll see, this toolbar includes more than meets the eye.

Figure 14-7: Display the Drawing toolbar to create and modify drawings.

Table 14-3 describes the tools in the Drawing toolbar. The tools are listed in the order in which they appear, from left to right.

Table 14-3 **The Tools on the Drawing Toolbar**	
Tool Name	**What the Tool Does**
Draw	Displays a menu with choices that enable you to manipulate drawn objects.
Select Objects	Selects one or more graphic objects. If you have several objects and you want to select a group of them, use this tool to drag the outline so that it surrounds all the objects. Click the button again to return to normal selection mode.
Free Rotate	Lets you freely rotate a drawn object.
AutoShapes	Displays a menu of seven categories of shapes. Drag this menu to create an AutoShapes toolbar. You also can display the AutoShapes toolbar with the Insert ➪ Picture ➪ AutoShapes command.
Line	Inserts a line.
Arrow	Inserts an arrow.
Rectangle	Inserts a rectangle or a square.
Oval	Inserts an oval or a circle.
Text Box	Inserts a free-floating box into which you type text.
WordArt	Displays the WordArt Gallery dialog box, which enables you to create attractive titles using text. You also can display this dialog box by selecting Insert ➪ Picture ➪ WordArt.
Insert Clip Art	Displays the Insert ClipArt dialog box . You can also display this dialog box with the Insert ➪ Picture ➪ Clip Art command.
Fill Color	Select a fill color or fill effect for an object.
Line Color	Select the line color for an object.

Tool Name	What the Tool Does
Font Color	Select a font color for text objects.
Line Style	Specify the width of the lines in an object.
Dash Style	Specify the style of the lines in an object.
Arrow Style	Specify the arrow style for arrows.
Shadows	Specify the type of shadow for an object and settings for the shadow.
3-D	Specify the type of perspective effect for an object and settings for the effect.

 Insert Clip Art and Line Color are two new tools of Excel 2000.

Drawing AutoShapes

Drawing objects with the AutoShapes tool is quite intuitive. The AutoShapes tool expands to display the following shape categories:

- ✦ **Lines:** Six styles of lines, including arrows and freehand-drawing capabilities.

- ✦ **Connectors:** Nine styles of lines designed to indicate connections between other objects. These objects automatically "snap to" other objects.

- ✦ **Basic Shapes:** Thirty-two basic shapes, including standard shapes, such as boxes and circles, and nonstandard shapes, such as a smiley face and a heart.

- ✦ **Block Arrows:** Twenty-eight arrow shapes.

- ✦ **Flowchart:** Twenty-seven shapes suitable for flowchart diagrams.

- ✦ **Stars and Banners:** Sixteen stars and banners. Stars are handy for drawing attention to a particular cell.

- ✦ **Callouts:** Twenty callouts, suitable for annotating cells.

- ✦ **More AutoShapes:** In Excel 2000, you can get even more AutoShapes. Clicking this button brings up a dialog box named More AutoShapes — which contains several additional shapes (actually, these are clip art images).

 More AutoShapes is a new feature of Excel 2000.

Click a tool and then drag in the worksheet to create the shape (the mouse pointer changes shape, reminding you that you're in draw mode). When you release the mouse button, the object is selected and its name appears in the Name box (see Figure 14-8).

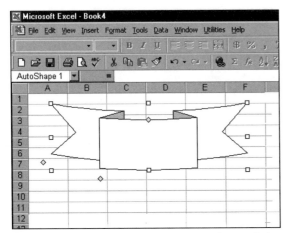

Figure 14-8: This shape was drawn on the worksheet. Its name, AutoShape1, appears in the Name box.

Formatting AutoShape Objects

You can format the AutoShape objects at any time. First, you must select the object. If the object is filled with a color or pattern, you can click anywhere on the object to select it. If the object is not filled, you must click the object's border.

You can make some modifications by using the toolbar buttons — for example, change the fill color. Other modifications require that you use the Format AutoShape dialog box. After selecting one or more objects, you can bring up this dialog box by using any of the following techniques:

✦ Choose the Format ➪ AutoShape command

✦ Press Ctrl+1

✦ Double-click the object

✦ Right-click the object and choose Format AutoShape from the shortcut menu

The Format AutoShape dialog box has several tabs, the number of which depends on the type of object and whether it contains text. Each of these tabs is discussed in the following sections.

The Colors and Lines tab

Select the Colors and Lines tab to adjust the colors, lines, and arrow used in the object.

This dialog box contains more than meets the eye, and it can lead to other dialog boxes. For example, click the Color drop-down list and you can select Fill Effects —

which brings up another multitabbed dialog box that enables you to specify a wide variety of fill effects.

Beginning with Excel 97, you'll find many new types of fill effects. Spend some time experimenting with these effects, and I'm sure that you'll be impressed.

The Size panel

The Size tab of the Format AutoShape dialog box (shown in Figure 14-9) enables you to adjust the size, rotation, and scale of the object. If the object is a picture, you can use the Reset button to return the object to its original dimensions and rotation.

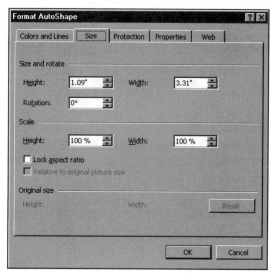

Figure 14-9: The size tab of the Format AutoShape dialog box.

Note   Contrary to what you might expect, if you rotate an object that contains text, the text *will not* rotate along with the object. You can also change the object's size directly by dragging the object. You can change the rotation directly by clicking the Free Rotate tool on the Drawing toolbar.

The Protection tab

The Protection tab determines whether the object is "locked." Locking has no effect, however, unless the worksheet is protected and the Objects option is in effect. You can protect the worksheet with the Tools ➪ Protection ➪ Protect Sheet command.

Tip   Locking an object prevents the object from being moved or resized. After you format all of your objects to your satisfaction, you should lock all objects and protect the sheet.

The Properties tab

The Properties tab of the Format AutoShape dialog box determines how an object is moved and sized with respect to the underlying cells. (See the sidebar "A Word About the Draw Layer," earlier in this chapter.)

The Font tab

The Font tab appears only if the shape contains text. It should be familiar, because its options are the same as for formatting cells.

The Alignment tab

The Alignment tab appears only if the shape contains text. You can specify the vertical and horizontal alignment of the text, and choose the orientation. Unlike text that is contained in cells, you cannot specify an angle for the orientation (you're limited to 90 degrees).

If you click the Automatic size option, the shape's size adjusts to fit the text that it contains.

The Margins tab

The Margins tab appears only if the shape contains text. Use the controls in this panel to adjust the amount of space along the sides of the text.

The Web tab

If you plan to save your worksheet as a Web page, you can specify some alternative text for the object in this tab. The alternative text appears when the user hovers the mouse pointer over the image in a Web browser.

 EXCEL 2000   The Web tab is a new feature of Excel 2000.

Changing the Stack Order of Objects

As you add drawing objects to the draw layer of a worksheet, you'll find that objects are "stacked" on top of each other in the order in which you add them. New objects are stacked on top of older objects. Figure 14-10 shows an example of drawing objects stacked on top of one another.

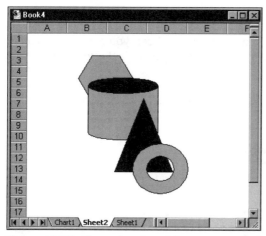

Figure 14-10: These drawing objects are stacked on top of one another.

If you find that an object is obscuring part of another, you can change the order in this stack. Right-click the object and select Order from the shortcut menu. This leads to a submenu with the following choices:

✦ **Bring to Front:** Brings the object to the top of the stack.

✦ **Send to Back:** Sends the object to the bottom of the stack.

✦ **Bring Forward:** Brings the object one step higher toward the top of the stack.

✦ **Send Backward:** Sends the object one step lower toward the bottom of the stack.

Grouping Objects

Excel enables you to combine two or more drawing objects into a single object, which is known as *grouping*. For example, if you create a design that uses four separate drawing objects, you can combine them into a group. Then, you can manipulate this group as a single object (move it, resize it, and so on).

To group two or more objects, select all the objects and then right-click. Choose Grouping ➪ Group from the shortcut menu.

Later, if you need to modify one of the objects in the group, you can ungroup them by right-clicking and selecting Grouping ➪ Ungroup from the shortcut menu. This breaks the object into its original components.

Aligning Objects

When you have several drawing objects on a worksheet, you may want to align these objects with each other. You can either drag the objects (which isn't very precise) or use the automatic alignment options.

Figure 14-11 shows objects before and after they were aligned to the left.

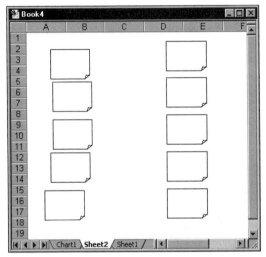

Figure 14-11: The objects on the left are not aligned. Those on the right are aligned to the left.

To align objects, start by selecting them. Then, click the Draw tool on the Drawing toolbar. This tool expands to show a menu. Select the Align or Distribute menu option, followed by any of the six alignment options: Align Left, Align Center, Align Right, Align Top, Align Middle, or Align Bottom.

Note   Unfortunately, you can't specify which object is used as the basis for the alignment. When you're aligning objects to the left, they are always aligned with the leftmost object. When you're aligning objects to the top, they are always aligned with the topmost object. Alignment in other directions works the same way.

Spacing Objects Evenly

Excel can also "distribute" three or more objects such that they are equally spaced, horizontally or vertically. Select the objects and then click the Draw tool on the Drawing toolbar. This tool expands to show a menu. Select the Align or Distribute menu option, followed by either Distribute Horizontally or Distribute Vertically.

Changing the AutoShape Defaults

You can change the default settings for the AutoShapes that you draw. For example, if you prefer a particular text color or fill color, you can set these as the defaults for all new AutoShapes that you draw.

To change the default settings, create an object and format it as you like. You can change colors, fill effects, line widths and styles, and shadow or 3D effects. Then, select the formatted object, right-click, and select Set AutoShape Defaults from the shortcut menu. You can also access this command from the Draw tool on the Drawing toolbar (this tool expands to show a menu).

Adding Shadows and 3D Effects

You can apply attractive shadow and 3D effects to AutoShapes (except for those in the Line and Connectors categories). Use the Shadow and 3D tools on the Drawing toolbar to apply these effects.

Shadows and 3D effects are mutually exclusive. In other words, you can apply either a shadow or a 3D effect to an AutoShape — not both.

To apply either of these effects, select an AutoShape that you've drawn on a worksheet and then click either the Shadow or the 3D tool. The tool expands to show a list of options (see Figure 14-12). Select an option, and it's applied to the selected shape.

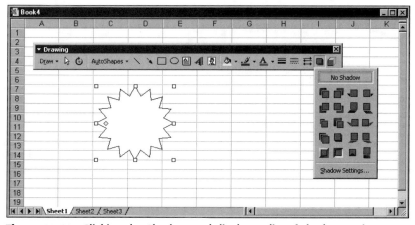

Figure 14-12: Clicking the Shadow tool displays a list of shadow options.

You can adjust the Shadow or 3D settings by clicking the appropriate tool and then selecting the Shadow Settings or 3D Settings option. Both of these options display a toolbar that enables you to fine-tune the effect. You'll find that *lots* of options are available, and they're all quite straightforward. The best way to become familiar with these effects is to experiment.

Using WordArt

WordArt is an application that's included with Microsoft Office. You can insert a WordArt image either by using the WordArt tool on the Drawing toolbar or by selecting Insert ➪ Picture ➪ WordArt. Either method displays the WordArt Gallery dialog box (see Figure 14-13). Select a style and then enter your text in the next dialog box. Click OK, and the image is inserted in the worksheet.

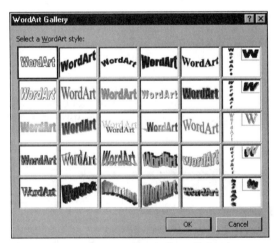

Figure 14-13: The WordArt Gallery dialog box enables you to select a general style for your image.

When you select a WordArt image, Excel displays the WordArt toolbar. Use these tools to modify the WordArt image. You'll find that you have *lots* of flexibility with these tools. In addition, you can use the Shadow and 3D tools to further manipulate the image. Figure 14-14 shows an example of a WordArt image inserted on a worksheet.

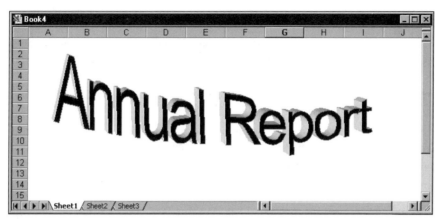

Figure 14-14: An example of WordArt.

Drawing Tips

Although drawing objects is quite intuitive, several tips can make this task easier. This section lists some tips and techniques that you should know:

✦ To create an object with the same height and width, press Shift while you draw the object.

✦ To constrain a line or arrow object to angles that are divisible by 15 degrees, press Shift while you draw the object.

✦ To make an object snap to the worksheet row and column gridlines, press the Alt key while you draw the object.

✦ If you press Alt while moving an object, its upper-left corner snaps to the row and column gridlines.

✦ To select multiple objects, press Ctrl while you click them. Or, use the Select Objects tool on the Drawing toolbar to select objects by "lassoing" them.

✦ To select all objects on a worksheet, select Edit ➪ Go To (or press F5) and then click the Special button in the Go To dialog box. Choose the Objects option button and click OK. All objects are selected. Use this technique if you want to delete all objects (select them all and then press Delete).

✦ You can insert text into most of the AutoShapes (the exceptions are the shapes in the Connectors and Lines categories). To add text to a shape, right-click it and select Add Text from the shortcut menu.

✦ You might find that working with drawing objects is easier if you turn off the worksheet grid line. The snap-to-gridline features work, even if the grid lines aren't visible.

✦ You can control how objects appear onscreen by using the View tab of the Options dialog box. Normally, the Show All option is selected. You can hide all objects by choosing Hide All, or display objects as placeholders by choosing Show Placeholders (this may speed up things if you have complex objects that take a long time to redraw).

✦ To copy an object with the mouse, single-click it to select it and then press Ctrl while you drag it.

✦ If an object contains text, you can rotate the text 90 degrees by using the Alignment tab on the Format Object dialog box.

✦ By default, drawn objects are printed along with the worksheet. If you don't want the objects to print, access the Sheet panel of the Page Setup dialog box and select the Draft option. Or, right-click the object, select Format from the shortcut menu, and then uncheck the Print Object check box in the Properties panel.

✦ If you want the underlying cell contents to show through a drawn object, access the Colors and Lines tab in the Format dialog box and then set the Fill option to No Fill. You can also select the Semi-transparent option, which enables you to choose a fill color *and* have the cell contents show.

✦ If you save your file as a Web page, each drawn object is stored as a separate GIF file.

A Gallery of Drawing Examples

This section provides you with some examples of using Excel's drawing tools. Perhaps these examples will get your own creative juices flowing.

Calling Attention to a Cell

The AutoShapes in the Stars and Banners category are useful for calling attention to a particular cell or range to make it stand out from the others. Figure 14-15 shows two examples (one subtle, one more flamboyant) of how you can make one cell's value jump out.

Creating Shapes with Shadow and 3D Effects

Figure 14-16 shows a sample of several objects that have various shadow and 3D effects applied. As you can see, the effects can be quite varied.

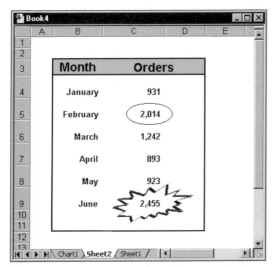

Figure 14-15: Two ways of making a particular cell stand out.

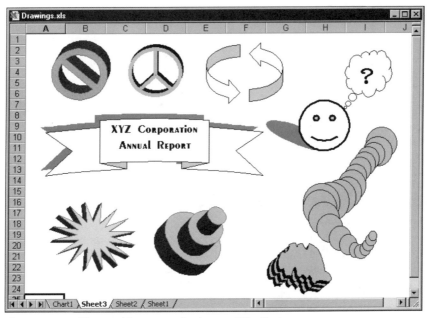

Figure 14-16: These objects use shadow or 3D effects.

Creating Organizational Charts

Figure 14-17 shows a simple organizational chart that was created with the AutoShape drawing tools. The shapes in the Connectors and Flowchart categories were used and then 3D effects were added. To make the box size consistent, one box was created and then copied several times.

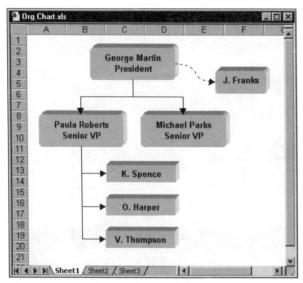

Figure 14-17: This organizational chart was created with Excel's drawing tools.

You can also create an organizational chart by selecting Insert ➪ Picture ➪ Organization Chart. This starts the Microsoft Organization Chart application that inserts an OLE object into the worksheet.

Changing the Look of Cell Comments

If a cell contains a cell comment, you can replace the normal comment box with any of the AutoShapes in the Callouts category. Select the cell comment and then click the Draw tool on the Drawing toolbar. This tool expands to show a menu. Select Change AutoShape ➪ Callouts, followed by the desired callout shape. Figure 14-18 shows an example of cell comments that use different AutoShapes.

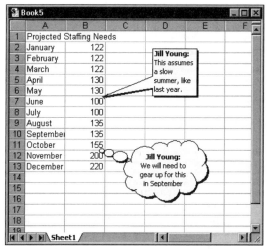

Figure 14-18: These cell comments use different AutoShapes.

Linking Text in an Object to a Cell

As an alternative to typing text directly into an object, consider creating a link to a cell. After doing so, the text displayed in the object reflects the current contents of the linked cell. Figure 14-19 shows an AutoShape that is linked to a cell. The shape is selected; notice that the edit line displays a formula.

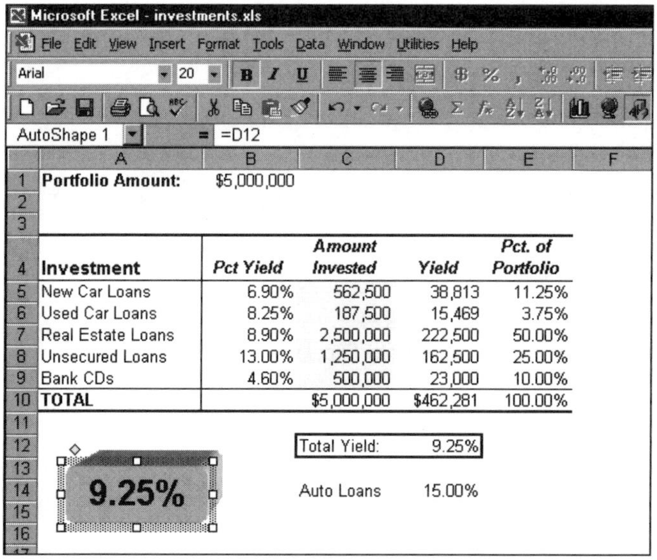

Figure 14-19: The text in the AutoShape is linked to cell D12.

To link an AutoShape to a cell, select the object and then click in the edit line. Enter a simple cell reference, such as =A1, and press Enter. You can format the text in the shape independent of the format of the cell. For best results, access the shape's Format dialog box and change the following settings:

✦ Automatic margins (Margins tab)

✦ Automatic size (Alignment tab)

✦ Center Horizontal alignment and Center Vertical alignment (Alignment tab)

Creating Flow Diagrams

You also can create flow diagrams by using the drawing tools. The shapes in the Connectors and Flowchart categories are most useful. This capability often is useful to describe how a process or system works. Figure 14-20 shows an example of a flow diagram. After creating the diagram, all the objects were selected and grouped together so that the diagram could be moved as a single unit.

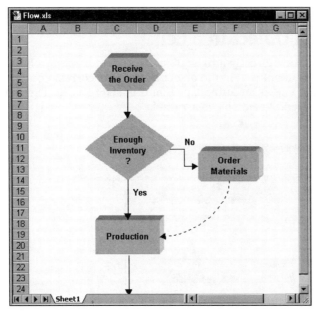

Figure 14-20: This flow diagram was created with Excel's drawing tools.

Annotating a Chart

One of the most common uses of the drawing tools is to annotate a chart. For example, you can add descriptive text with an arrow, to call attention to a certain data point. This technique works for both embedded charts and charts on chart sheets. Figure 14-21 shows an example of an embedded chart that has been annotated.

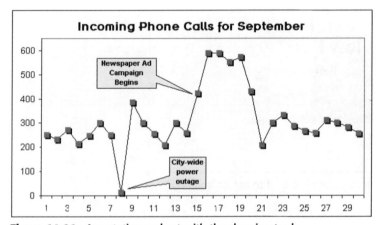

Figure 14-21: Annotating a chart with the drawing tools.

Pasting Pictures of Cells

One of Excel's best-kept secrets is its ability to copy and paste pictures of cells. You can copy a cell or range and then paste a picture of the cell or range on any work-sheet. The picture can be static or linked. With a linked picture, the link is to the cells. In other words, if you change the contents of a cell that's in a picture, the picture changes.

To create a picture of a cell or range, select a range and choose Edit ➪ Copy. Then press Shift and click the Edit menu (pressing Shift is essential). Choose Paste Picture to create a static picture, or choose Paste Picture Link to paste a linked picture of the selection.

If you don't hold down Shift when you select the Edit menu, the Paste Picture and Paste Picture Link commands do not appear.

Figure 14-22 shows an example of a linked picture, with some additional formatting to the picture object (fill color and a shadow). Notice that the picture displays a cell reference in the formula bar.

Figure showing Microsoft Excel - Book5 with two columns of month data. The left column shows a selected picture object "Picture 3" with formula =Lb:$I$1, displaying:

	A	B	C	D	E	F	G
1							
2							
3	January		321				
4	February		344				
5	March		433				
6	April		509		January	321	
7	May		589		February	344	
8	June		618		March	433	
9	July		584		April	509	
10	August		449		May	589	
11	September		698		June	618	
12	October		721		July	584	
13	November		982		August	449	
14	December		789		September	698	
15					October	721	
16					November	982	
17					December	789	
18							
19							

Figure 14-22: This picture is linked to the cells in E6:F17.

Cross-Reference

Using linked pictures is particularly useful for printing noncontiguous ranges. See "Printing Noncontiguous Ranges on a Single Page" in Chapter 12 for more information.

Summary

This chapter covers several types of graphic information that you can add to a worksheet's draw layer: imported graphic images, objects that you draw by using Excel's drawing tools, and other objects, such as WordArt or an OLE object, from Microsoft's Organization Chart application. Several examples demonstrate some ways that you can use these objects in your workbooks.

✦   ✦   ✦

Putting It All Together

The preceding chapters present basic information about how Excel works. But you probably already realize that simply knowing the commands and shortcuts won't help you create successful workbooks. This chapter helps you to tie everything together, and provides some pointers and examples to help you develop workbooks that do what you want them to do.

The Audience for Spreadsheets

Before you get too far into this chapter, pause and think about spreadsheets in general. Spreadsheets can be classified in many ways, but the following two broad categories provide a useful place to start:

- ◆ Spreadsheets that you develop for your own use
- ◆ Spreadsheets that others will use

As you'll see, the way in which you develop your spreadsheet — and the amount of time and effort that you put into it — often depends on who is the ultimate user (you alone or others).

Developing Spreadsheets for Yourself

If you're the only person who will use a particular spreadsheet, you should be less concerned with issues such as security, ease of use, and error handling than you would be if you were creating the spreadsheet for others. After all, you develop the spreadsheet and thus know how it is designed. If an error occurs, you can simply track down the source and correct the problem.

Quick-and-dirty spreadsheets

Chances are good that many of the spreadsheets you develop for your own use are "quick-and-dirty" — usually fairly small and developed to solve a problem or answer a question quickly. For example, you're about to buy a new car and want to figure out your monthly payment for various loan amounts. Or, you need to generate a chart that shows your company's monthly sales, so you quickly enter 12 values, whip off a chart, and paste it into your word processing document.

In these examples, you don't really care what the spreadsheet looks like, as long as it gives you the correct answer (or in the case of the second example, produces a nice-looking chart). You can probably input the entire model in a few minutes, and you certainly won't take the time to document your work. In many cases, you won't even bother to save the file.

For-your-eyes-only spreadsheets

As the name implies, this category includes spreadsheets created by you that no one else will ever see or use. One example is a file in which you keep information that is relevant to your income taxes. You open the file whenever a check comes in the mail, you incur an expense that can be justified as business-related, you buy tax-deductible Girl Scout cookies, and so on. Another example is a spreadsheet that you use to keep track of your employees' time records (sick leave, vacation, and such).

Spreadsheets that are for your eyes only differ from the quick-and-dirty ones in that you use them more than once; therefore, you save these spreadsheets to files. Again, though, these are spreadsheets that are not worth spending a great deal of time on — you may apply some simple formatting, but that's about it (after all, you don't really need to impress yourself — or do you?). Like the quick-and-dirty kind, this type of spreadsheet lacks any type of error detection, because you already understand how the formulas are set up and, thus, know enough to avoid inputting data that produces erroneous results. If an error does crop up, you probably immediately know what caused it.

Spreadsheets in this category sometimes increase in sophistication over time. For example, I have an Excel workbook that I use to track my income by source. This workbook was simple when I first set it up, but I tend to add accoutrements to it nearly every time I use it: more summary formulas, better formatting, and even a chart that displays income by month. My latest modification was to add a trend line to the chart to project income based on past trends.

Developing Spreadsheets for Others

If others will use a spreadsheet that you are developing, you need to pay a lot more attention to minor details. Because of this, such a spreadsheet usually takes longer to create than one that only you will see. The amount of extra effort depends, in large part, on the experience level of the other users. A spreadsheet that will be utilized by an inexperienced computer user is often the most difficult to develop, simply because you need to make sure that it's "bulletproof." In other words, you don't want the user to mess things up (erase a formula, for example). In addition, you have to make perfectly clear how the spreadsheet should be used. This often means adding more formatting and instructions for the user.

As you'll discover in later chapters, you can use Excel as a complete application-development environment and create sophisticated applications that may not even look like a normal spreadsheet. Doing so almost always requires using macros and custom interface elements, such as buttons, custom toolbars, and custom menus.

Characteristics of a Successful Spreadsheet

You create a spreadsheet to accomplish some end result, which could be any of thousands of things. If the spreadsheet is successful, it meets most or all of the following criteria (some of which are appropriate only if the spreadsheet is used by others):

✦ It enables the end user to perform a task that he or she probably would not be able to do otherwise—or a task that would take *much* longer to do manually.

✦ It's the appropriate solution to the problem.

Using a spreadsheet isn't always the most suitable approach. For example, you can create an organizational chart with Excel, but if you create organizational charts for a living, you're better off with a software product designed specifically for that task.

✦ It accomplishes its goal.

This may seem like an obvious prerequisite, but I've seen many spreadsheets that fail to meet this test.

✦ It produces accurate results.

As you may have discovered by now, creating formulas that produce the wrong results is quite easy. In most cases, returning no answer is better than returning an incorrect one.

✦ It doesn't let the user accidentally (or intentionally) delete or modify important components.

Excel has built-in features to help in this area (see "Applying Appropriate Protection," later in this chapter).

✦ It doesn't let the user enter inappropriate data.

Excel data-validation features make this type of checking easier than ever.

✦ It's laid out clearly so that the user always knows how to proceed.

I've opened far too many spreadsheets and not had a clue as to how to proceed — or even what the purpose of the spreadsheet was.

✦ Its formulas and macros are well documented so that, if necessary, they can be changed.

✦ It is designed so that it can be modified in simple ways without making major changes.

You can create spreadsheets at many different levels, ranging from simple fill-in-the-blank templates to extremely complex applications that utilize custom menus and dialog boxes, and that may not even look like spreadsheets. The remainder of this chapter focuses on relatively simple spreadsheets — those that can be produced by using only the information presented in Parts I and II of this book.

Uses for Spreadsheets

Millions of spreadsheets are in daily use throughout the world. Many fit into the quick-and-dirty or for-your-eyes-only classifications described previously. Of the spreadsheets with lasting value, however, the majority probably fit into one or more of the following broad categories:

✦ Financial or data-analysis models

✦ Reports and presentations

✦ List-management worksheets

✦ Workbooks that enable database access

These types of spreadsheets are discussed in the following sections.

Financial or Data-Analysis Models

Before the days of personal computers, large companies relied on mainframe systems to do their financial analysis. Smaller companies used sheets of accounting paper. But things have changed dramatically over the past decade, and now companies of all sizes can use personal computers to perform sophisticated analyses, in the blink of an eye.

This category of spreadsheets covers a wide variety of applications, including budgeting, investment analysis, modeling, and statistical data analysis. These applications can range from simple tables of numbers to sophisticated mathematical models designed for "what-if" analyses.

One common type of spreadsheet is a *budget spreadsheet*, which typically has months along the top and budget categories along the left. Each intersecting cell contains a projected expense—for example, telephone expenses for June. Budgets use SUM formulas (and maybe SUBTOTAL formulas) to calculate annual totals and totals for each category. Excel's multisheet feature enables you to store on separate sheets the budgets for different departments or divisions.

Budget categories often are arranged hierarchically. For example, you could have a category called Personnel that consists of subcategories such as Salary, Benefits, Bonus, and so on (see Figure 15-1). In such a case, you could create additional formulas to calculate category totals.

Cross-Reference

Excel's outlining feature is ideal for creating formulas to calculate category totals, which is the topic of Chapter 18.

		Jan	Feb	Mar	Q1	Apr	Ma
1							
2	**Marketing**						
3	Salaries	35,000	35,000	35,000	105,000	35,000	35,000
4	Benefits	7,350	7,350	7,350	22,050	7,350	7,350
5	Bonus	0	0	0	0	0	0
6	**Total Personnel**	**42,350**	**42,350**	**42,350**	**127,050**	**42,350**	**42,350**
7	Office	2,250	2,250	2,250	6,750	2,250	2,250
8	Computer	900	900	900	2,700	900	900
9	**Total Supplies**	**3,150**	**3,150**	**3,150**	**9,450**	**3,150**	**3,150**
10	Transportation	3,000	3,000	3,000	9,000	5,500	3,000
11	Hotel	1,050	1,050	1,050	3,150	3,400	1,050
12	Meals	500	500	500	1,500	1,250	500
13	**Total Travel**	**4,550**	**4,550**	**4,550**	**13,650**	**10,150**	**4,550**
14	Computers	4,500	4,500	4,500	13,500	4,500	4,500
15	Copiers	1,100	1,100	1,100	3,300	1,100	1,100
16	Other	950	950	950	2,850	950	950
17	**Total Equipment**	**6,550**	**6,550**	**6,550**	**19,650**	**6,550**	**6,550**
18	Lease	2,000	2,000	2,000	6,000	2,500	2,500
19	Utilities	450	450	450	1,350	450	450
20	Taxes	540	540	540	1,620	540	540
21	Other	1,200	1,200	1,200	3,600	1,200	1,200
22	Telephone	875	875	875	2,625	875	875
23	Postage	250	250	250	750	250	250
24	**Total Facility**	**5,315**	**5,315**	**5,315**	**15,945**	**5,815**	**5,815**
25	**Total Marketing**	**61,915**	**61,915**	**61,915**	**185,745**	**68,015**	**62,415**
26	**Operations**						
27	Salaries	210,000	210,000	210,000	630,000	215,000	215,000
28	Benefits	44,100	44,100	44,100	132,300	45,150	45,150

Outlined Budget.xls

Figure 15-1: This budget worksheet uses formulas to calculate subtotals within each category.

Another type of financial application is a *what-if model*. A what-if model calculates formulas by using assumptions that are specified in a series of input cells. For example, you can create an amortization spreadsheet that calculates details for a loan, based on the loan amount, the interest rate, and the term of the loan. This model would have three input cells. Excel's Scenario Manager is designed to make this type of model easier to handle.

Chapter 26 discusses various ways to set up what-if models.

Reports and Presentations

Some spreadsheets are designed primarily for their end result: printed output. These spreadsheets take advantage of Excel's formatting and chart-making features to produce attractive, boardroom-quality output.

Of course, any spreadsheet can produce good, quality reports, so spreadsheets in this category often fall into another category, as well.

Nowadays, instead of printing your work, you may display it in the form of a Web page, either on the Internet or on your corporate intranet. The new HTML features in Excel 2000 make this task easier than ever.

List Management

Another common use for spreadsheets is *list management,* in which a list is essentially a database table stored in a worksheet. A database table consists of field names in the top row and records in the rows below. Beginning with Excel 97, worksheets have 65,536 rows — which means that the potential for list-management applications has improved dramatically.

Excel has some handy tools that enable you to manipulate lists in a variety of ways (see Figure 15-2).

List management is the topic of Chapter 23.

Database Access

Another category of spreadsheets works with data stored in external databases. You can use Excel to query external databases and bring in a subset of the data that meets criteria that you specify. Then, you can do what you want with this data, independent of the original database.

Spreadsheets that use external databases are covered in Chapter 24.

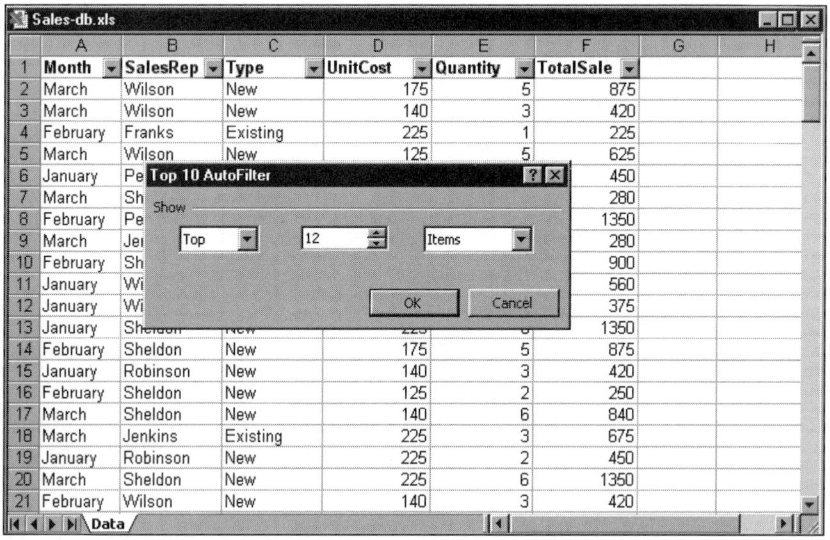

Figure 15-2: Excel makes working with lists of data easy.

Turnkey Applications

A *turnkey application* refers to a spreadsheet solution that is programmed to work as a standalone application. Such an application always requires macros, and may involve creating custom menus and custom toolbars.

These applications are large-scale projects that are designed to be used by many people or for a long time. They often interact with other systems (such as a corporate database) and must be very stable. Although this book touches on some elements of developing such applications, they are beyond this book's scope.

Steps in Creating a Spreadsheet

This section discusses the basic steps that you may follow to create a spreadsheet. This discussion assumes that you're creating a workbook that others may use, so you may skip some of these steps if the spreadsheet is for you only. These steps are for relatively simple spreadsheets — those that don't use macros, custom toolbars, or other advanced features. And, of course, these are only basic guidelines. Everyone eventually develops his or her own style, and you may find a method that works better for you. The basic steps are as follows:

1. Think about what you want to accomplish.

2. Consider the audience.

3. Design the workbook layout.

4. Enter data and formulas.

5. Apply appropriate formatting.

6. Test your spreadsheet.

7. Apply protection as necessary.

8. Document your work.

Each of these steps is discussed in the following sections.

Developing a Plan

If you're like me, when you set out to create a new spreadsheet, you may have a tendency to jump right in and get to work. Tempting as it may be to create something concrete as quickly as possible, try to restrain yourself. The end product is almost always better if you take some time to determine exactly what you're trying to accomplish and come up with a plan of action. The time that you spend at this stage usually saves you more time later in the project.

Developing a plan for a spreadsheet may involve answering the following questions and collecting the necessary information that is involved:

✦ How is the problem currently being addressed? And what's wrong with the current solution?

✦ Is a spreadsheet really the best solution to the problem?

✦ How long will the spreadsheet be used?

✦ How many people will be using it?

✦ What type of output, if any, will be required?

✦ Does data already exist that can be imported?

✦ Will the requirements for this project change over time?

The point here is to attempt to learn as much as possible about the project that you're developing. With that information, you can determine a plan of action — which may even mean *not* using a spreadsheet for the solution.

Considering the Audience

If you'll be the only user of the workbook that you're developing, you can skip this step. But if others will be using your workbook, take some time to find out about these people. Answering the following questions often prevents having to make changes later:

✦ **How experienced are the users?** Can they perform basic operations, such as copying, inserting rows, and so on? Don't assume that everyone knows as much as you do.

✦ **What software will they be using?** For example, if you develop your spreadsheet by using Excel 2000, you need to be aware that it can't be loaded into Excel 95 or earlier versions unless you first save the file in the older format. Users with older versions won't be able to take advantage of the newer features.

✦ **What hardware will they be using?** If your spreadsheet takes 3 minutes to calculate on your Pentium-based system, it may well take 20 minutes on a slower 486 system. Also, be aware of different video modes. If you develop your spreadsheet by using a 1024 X 768 video mode, users with an 800 X 600 or 640 X 480 display will have a much smaller viewing area.

✦ **Do you want to allow changes?** Often, you want to make sure that your formulas don't get modified. If so, you'll need to perform some basic protection (see "Applying Appropriate Protection," later in this chapter).

Designing the Workbook Layout

An important consideration is how you want to lay out the workbook. Before the days of multisheet workbooks, this was a lot more difficult than it is today. When your file has only a single worksheet, you have to plan it carefully to ensure that making a change doesn't affect something else.

Spreadsheets often consist of distinct blocks of information. In the old days, spreadsheet designers often used a layout like the one shown in Figure 15-3. This example is for a spreadsheet that has three main blocks: an input area, a calculation area, and a report area. This *offset block layout* minimizes the possibility of damage. For example, deleting a column or changing its width affects only one area. If the areas were laid out vertically, this would not be the case.

Because Excel uses multiple worksheets in a file, however, this type of layout is rarely necessary. Using a separate worksheet for each block is much easier and more efficient. An added advantage is that you can access the various blocks simply by clicking the tab (which can be named appropriately).

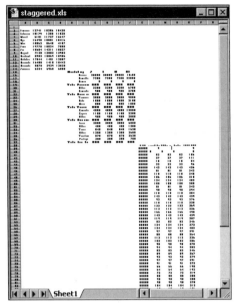

Figure 15-3: This offset block layout is one way to organize a worksheet.

Entering Data and Formulas

This phase of the spreadsheet development process is often where people begin. But if you've thought through the problem, considered the users, and created an appropriate layout, this phase should go more smoothly than if you jumped right in without the preliminary steps.

The more that you know about Excel, the easier this phase is. Formulas are just one part of a spreadsheet. Sometimes, you may need to incorporate one or more of the following features (all of which are discussed later in the book):

- ✦ Workbook consolidation
- ✦ List management
- ✦ External databases
- ✦ Outlining
- ✦ Data validation
- ✦ Conditional formatting
- ✦ Hyperlinks

✦ Statistical analysis

✦ Pivot tables

✦ Scenario management

✦ Solver

✦ Mapping

✦ Interaction with other applications

✦ Custom menus or toolbars (which require macros)

Applying Appropriate Formatting

Many people prefer to format their work as they go along. If that's not your style, this step must be performed before you unleash your efforts to the end-users. As I mentioned in Chapter 11, almost all worksheets benefit from some stylistic formatting. At the very least, you need to adjust the number formats so that the values appear correctly. If the worksheet will be used by others, make sure that any color combinations you use will be visible for those running on a monochrome system (such as a notebook computer).

Of all the basic steps in creating a spreadsheet, formatting is the one with the most variety. Although beauty may be in the eye of the beholder, there are some guidelines that you might want to consider:

✦ **Preformat all numeric cells.** Use number formats that are appropriate for the numbers and make sure that the columns are wide enough to handle the maximum values. For example, if a cell is designed to hold an interest rate, format it with a percent sign. And if you create an amortization schedule, make sure that the columns are wide enough to handle large amounts.

✦ **Use only basic fonts.** If others will be using your workbook, stick to the basic TrueType fonts that come with Windows. Otherwise, the fonts may not translate well, and the user may see a string of asterisks rather than a value.

✦ **Don't go overboard with fonts.** As a rule of thumb, never use more than two different typefaces in a single workbook. Usually, one works just fine (Arial is a good choice). If you use different font sizes, do so sparingly.

✦ **Be careful with color.** Colored text or cell backgrounds can make your workbook much easier to use. For example, if you use a lookup table, you can use color to clarify where the table's boundaries are. Or, you may want to color-code the cells that will accept user input. Overuse of colors makes your spreadsheet look gaudy and unprofessional, however. Also, make sure that color combinations will work if the workbook is opened on a monochrome notebook computer.

✦ **Consider identifying the active area.** Many spreadsheets are set up using only a few cells—the active area. Inexperienced users often scroll away from the active area and get lost. One technique is to hide all rows and columns that aren't used. Or, you can apply a color background (such as light gray) to all unused cells. This makes the cells in use very clear.

✦ **Remove extraneous elements.** In some cases, you can simplify things significantly by removing elements that might get in the way or cause the screen to appear more confusing than it is. These elements include automatic page breaks, gridlines, row and column headers, and sheet tabs. These options, which you set in the View panel of the Options dialog box, are saved with the worksheet.

Testing the Spreadsheet

Before you actually use your newly created spreadsheet for real work, you should test it thoroughly. This is even more critical if others will be using your spreadsheet. If you've distributed 20 copies of your file and then discover a major error in a formula, you'll have to do a "recall" and send out a corrected copy. Obviously, catching the errors before you send out a spreadsheet is much easier.

Testing basically is the process of ensuring that the formulas produce correct results under all possible circumstances. I don't know of any specific rules for testing a worksheet, so you're pretty much on your own here. I can, however, offer a few guidelines:

✦ **Test with all potential versions.** If some of your end-users are using older versions of Excel, it's critical that you test your work using all the other versions. Saving your file in an older format means that others can open your file with an older version of Excel. It does *not* guarantee that everything will still work correctly!

✦ **Try extreme input values.** If your worksheet is set up to perform calculations using input cells, spend some time and enter very large or very small numbers and observe the effects on the formulas. If the user should enter a percentage, see what happens if you enter a large value. If a positive number is expected, try entering a negative number. This also is a good way to ensure that your columns are wide enough.

✦ **Provide data validation.** Although you can't expect your formulas to yield usable results for invalid entries (garbage in, garbage out), you may want to use Excel's data validation features to ensure that data entered is of the proper type.

✦ **Use dummy data.** If you have a budget application, for example, try entering 1 into each nonformula cell. This is a good way to make sure that all of your SUM formulas refer to the correct ranges. An incorrect formula usually stands out from the others.

✦ **Familiarize yourself with Excel's auditing tools.** Excel has several useful tools that can help you track down erroneous formulas.

Excel's auditing tools are discussed in Chapter 31.

Applying Appropriate Protection

A spreadsheet can be quite fragile. Deleting a single formula often has a ripple effect and causes other formulas to produce an error value or, even worse, incorrect results. I've seen cases in which an inexperienced user deleted a critical formula, panicked, and cemented the mistake by saving the file and reopening it — only to discover, of course, that the original (good) version had been overwritten.

You can circumvent such problems by using the protection features built into Excel. The following are the two general types of protection:

+ Sheet protection
+ Workbook protection

Protecting Sheets

The Tools ➪ Protection ➪ Protect Sheet command displays the dialog box shown in Figure 15-4.

Figure 15-4: The Protect Sheet dialog box.

This dialog box has three check boxes:

+ **Contents:** Cells that have their Locked property turned on can't be changed.

+ **Objects:** Drawing objects (including embedded charts) that have their Locked property turned on can't be selected.

+ **Scenarios:** Defined scenarios that have their Prevent Changes property turned on can't be changed (see Chapter 26 for a discussion of scenario management).

You may provide a password in the Protect Sheet dialog box. If you enter a password, the password must be reentered before the sheet can be unprotected. If you don't supply a password, anyone can unprotect the sheet.

By default, all cells have their Locked property turned on. Before protecting a worksheet, you'll normally want to turn off the Locked property for input cells.

You can change the Locked property of a cell or object by accessing its Format dialog box and clicking the Protection tab. Cells have an additional property: Hidden. This name is a bit misleading, because it doesn't actually hide the cell. Rather, it prevents the cell contents from being displayed in the formula bar. You can use the Hidden property to prevent others from seeing your formulas.

Note You can't change a cell's Locked property while the sheet is protected. You must unprotect the sheet to make any changes, and then protect it again.

Note Protection isn't just for worksheets that others will be using. Many people protect worksheets to prevent themselves from accidentally deleting cells.

Protecting Workbooks

The second type of protection is workbook protection. The Tools ⇨ Protection ⇨ Protect Workbook command displays the dialog box shown in Figure 15-5.

Figure 15-5: The Protect Workbook dialog box.

This dialog box has two check boxes:

✦ **Structure:** Protects the workbook window from being moved or resized.

✦ **Windows:** Prevents any of the following changes to a workbook: adding a sheet, deleting a sheet, moving a sheet, renaming a sheet, hiding a sheet, or unhiding a sheet.

Again, you can determine whether to supply a password, depending on the level of protection that you need.

Documenting Your Work

The final step in the spreadsheet-creation process is documenting your work. Making some notes about your spreadsheet is always a good idea. After all, you may need to modify the spreadsheet later. The elegant formula that you create today may be completely meaningless when you need to change it in six months. The following sections provide some general tips on documenting your spreadsheets.

Use the Properties Dialog Box

The File ➪ Properties command displays the Properties dialog box (the Summary tab is shown in Figure 15-6). You may want to take a few minutes to fill in the missing information and enter some comments in the Comments box.

Use Cell Comments

As you know, you can document individual cells by using the Insert ➪ Comment command. The comment appears when you move the mouse pointer over the cell. If you don't like the idea of seeing the cell comments appear, adjust this setting in the View tab of the Options dialog box. Unfortunately, this setting applies to all workbooks, so if you turn off the note indicator for one workbook, you turn it off for all of them.

Use a Separate Worksheet

Perhaps the best way to document a workbook is to insert a new worksheet and store your comments there. Some people also like to keep a running tally of any modifications that they make. You can hide the worksheet so that others can't see it.

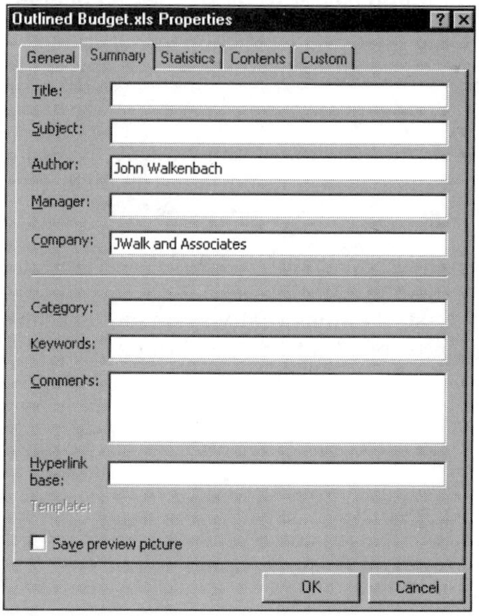

Figure 15-6: The Summary tab of the Properties dialog box.

A Workbook That's Easy to Maintain

One of the cardinal rules of "spreadsheeting" is that things change. You may have a sales-tracking spreadsheet that you've been using for years, and it works perfectly well. But then you're informed that the company has bought out one of your competitors, and the sales regions will be restructured. Your sales-tracking workbook suddenly no longer applies.

You often can save yourself lots of time by planning for the inevitable changes. You can do a few things to make your worksheets as modifiable as possible:

✦ **Avoid hard-coding values in formulas**. For example, assume that you have formulas that calculate sales commissions by using a commission rate of 12.5 percent. Rather than use the value .125 in the formulas, enter it into a cell and use the cell reference. Or, use the technique described in Chapter 9 (see "Naming constants") to create a named constant.

✦ **Use names whenever possible.** Cell and range names make your formulas easier to read and more understandable. When the time comes to modify your formulas, you may be able to modify just the range to which a name refers.

✦ **Use simplified formulas.** Beginning users sometimes create formulas that are more complicated than they need to be. Often, this is because they don't know about a particular built-in function. As you gain more experience with Excel, be on the lookout for useful functions that can make your formulas simple and clear. Such formulas are much easier to modify, when needed.

✦ **Use a flexible layout.** Rather than try to cram everything into a single worksheet, use multiple worksheets. You'll find that this makes expanding much easier, should the need arise.

✦ **Use named styles.** Using named styles makes obtaining consistent formatting much easier if you need to add new data to accommodate a change. This feature is discussed in Chapter 11 (see "Using Named Styles").

✦ **Keep it clean.** Keeping your workbooks clean and free of extraneous information is also a good idea. For example, if the workbook has empty worksheets, remove them. If you created names that you no longer use, delete them. If you no longer need a range of cells that you used to perform a quick calculation, delete the range.

When Things Go Wrong

Many types of errors can occur when you work with Excel (or any spreadsheet, for that matter). These errors range from inconvenient errors that can be easily corrected to disastrous, irreparable errors.

For example, a formula may return an error value when a certain cell that it uses contains a zero. Normally, you can isolate the problem and correct the formula, so that the error doesn't appear anymore (this is an example of an easily corrected error). A potentially disastrous error is when you open a worksheet and Excel reports that it can't read the file. Figure 15-7 shows the message that you get. Unless you made a recent backup, you could be in deep trouble. Unfortunately, this type of error (a corrupted file) occurs more often than you might think.

Figure 15-7: When you see an error message like this, you better have a recent backup available.

Good testing helps you to avoid problems with your formulas. Making modifications to your work, however, may result in a formula that no longer works. For example, you may add a new column to the worksheet, and the formulas don't pick up the expanded cell reference. This is an example of when using names could eliminate the need to adjust the formulas.

You will encounter cases in which a formula just doesn't work as it should. When this happens, try to isolate the problem as simply as possible. I've found that a good way to deal with such formulas is to create a new workbook with a very simplified example of what I'm trying to accomplish. Sometimes, looking at the problem in a different context can shed new light on it.

The only way to prevent disasters — such as a corrupt file — is to develop good backup habits. If a file is important, you should never have only one copy of it. You should get in the habit of making a daily backup on a different storage medium.

Where to Go from Here

This chapter concludes Part II. If you're following the book in sequential-chapter order, you now have enough knowledge to put Excel to good use.

Excel has many more features that may interest you, however, which are covered in the remaining chapters. Even if you're satisfied with what you already know about Excel, I strongly suggest that you at least browse through the remaining chapters. You may see something that can save you hours.

Summary

This chapter distinguishes two general categories of spreadsheets: those that you create for yourself only and those that others will use. The approach that you take depends on the end-user. This chapter also covers the characteristics of a successful spreadsheet, basic types of spreadsheets, basic steps that you may follow to create a spreadsheet, and features in Excel that let you protect various parts of your work. The chapter concludes with some tips on how to make your spreadsheets easier to maintain and how to handle some common types of errors.

✦   ✦   ✦

Advanced Features

Advanced Charting

Chapter 13 introduces charting. This chapter takes the topic to the next level. You learn how to customize your charts to the maximum, so that they look exactly as you want. I also share some slick charting tricks that I've picked up over the years.

Chart Customization: An Overview

Often, the basic chart that Excel creates is sufficient for your needs. If you're using a chart to get a quick visual impression of your data, a chart that's based on one of the standard chart types usually does just fine. But, if you want to create the most effective chart possible, you probably want to take advantage of the additional customization techniques available in Excel.

Customizing a chart involves changing its appearance, as well as possibly adding new elements to it. These changes can be purely cosmetic (such as changing colors or modifying line widths) or quite substantial (such as changing the axis scales or rotating a 3D chart). New elements that you might add include features such as a data table, a trendline, or error bars.

Note   Before you can customize a chart, you must activate it on a chart sheet, by clicking its sheet tab. To activate an embedded chart, click the chart's border. To deactivate an embedded chart, just click anywhere in the worksheet.

Tip   In some cases, you may prefer to work with an embedded chart in a separate window. For example, if the embedded chart is larger than the workbook window, working with it in its own window is much easier. To display an embedded chart in a window, right-click the chart's border and select Chart Window from the shortcut menu.

Here's a partial list of the customizations that you can make to a chart:

✦ Change any colors, patterns, line widths, marker styles, and fonts.

✦ Change the data ranges that the chart uses, add a new chart series, or delete an existing series.

✦ Choose which gridlines to display.

✦ Determine the size and placement of the legend (or delete it altogether).

✦ Determine where the axes cross.

✦ Adjust the axis scales by specifying a maximum and minimum, changing the tick marks and labels, and so on. You also can specify that a scale be represented in logarithmic units.

✦ Add titles for the chart and axes, as well as free-floating text anywhere in the chart.

✦ Add error bars and trendlines to a data series.

✦ Display the data points in reverse order.

✦ Rotate a 3D chart to get a better view or to add impact.

✦ Replace line-chart markers with bitmaps.

Note   You can easily become overwhelmed with all the chart customization options. However, the more that you work with charts, the easier it becomes. Even advanced users tend to experiment a great deal with chart customization, and they rely heavily on trial and error — a technique that I strongly recommend.

Elements of a Chart

Before chart modifications are discussed, a brief digression is necessary to discuss the various elements of a chart. The number and type of elements in a chart varies with the type of chart — for example, pie charts don't have axes, and only 3D charts have walls and floors.

When a chart is activated, you can select various parts of the chart with which to work. Modifying a chart is similar to everything else that you do in Excel: First you make a selection (in this case, select a chart element) and then you issue a command to do something with the selection. Unlike a worksheet selection, with a chart selection, you can select only one chart element at a time. The exceptions are elements that consist of multiple parts, such as gridlines. Selecting one gridline selects them all.

You select a chart element by clicking it. The name of the selected item appears in the Name box. When a chart is activated, you can't access the Name box; it's simply a convenient place for Excel to display the chart element's name.

The Chart toolbar, which is displayed when you select a chart, contains a tool called Chart Objects (see Figure 16-1). This is a drop-down list of all the named elements in a chart. Rather than selecting a chart element by clicking it, you can use this list to select the chart element that you want to work with.

Figure 16-1: The Chart Objects tool in the Chart toolbar provides another way to select a chart element.

Tip Yet another way to select a chart element is to use the keyboard. When a chart is activated, press the up arrow or down arrow to cycle through all parts in the chart. When a data series is selected, press the right arrow or left arrow to select individual points in the series.

Table 16-1 lists the various elements of a chart (not all of these parts appear in every chart). You might want to create a chart and practice selecting some of these parts — or use the Chart Objects tool in the Chart toolbar to examine the element names.

Using the Format Dialog Box

When a chart element is selected, you can access the element's Format dialog box to format or set options for the element. Each chart element has a unique Format dialog box. You can access this dialog box by using any of the following methods:

✦ Select the Format ⇨ Selected Part Name command (the Format menu displays the actual name of the selected part)

✦ Double-click a chart part

✦ Select the chart element and press Ctrl+1

✦ Right-click the chart element and choose the Format command from the shortcut menu

Any of these methods displays a tabbed Format dialog box that enables you to make many changes to the selected chart element. For example, Figure 16-2 shows the dialog box that appears when the chart's title is selected.

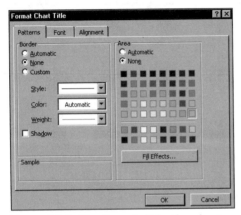

Figure 16-2: The Format dialog box for a chart's title. Each chart element has its own Format dialog box.

In the following sections, the details of the various types of chart modifications are discussed in depth.

Table 16-1	
Chart Elements	
Part	**Description**
Category Axis	The axis that represents the chart's categories.
Category Title	The title for the category axis.
Chart Area	The chart's background.
Chart Title	The chart's title.
Corners	The corners of 3D charts (except 3D pie charts). Select the corners if you want to rotate a 3D chart by using a mouse.
Data Label	A data label for a point in a series. The name is preceded by the series and the point. Example: Series 1 Point 1 Data Label.

Part	Description
Data Labels	Data labels for a series. The name is preceded by the series. Example: Series 1 Data Labels.
Data Table	The chart's data table.
Down-Bars	Down-bars in a stock market chart.
Dropline	A dropline that extends from the data point downward to the axis.
Error Bars	Error bars for a series. The name is preceded by the series. Example: Series 1 Error Bars.
Floor	The floor of a 3D chart.
Gridlines	A chart can have major and minor gridlines for each axis. The element is named using the axis and the type of gridlines. Example: Value Axis Major Gridlines.
High-Low Lines	High-low lines in a stock market chart.
Legend Entry	One of the text entries inside of a legend.
Legend Key	One of the keys inside of a legend.
Legend	The chart's legend.
Plot Area	The chart's Plot Area—the actual chart, without the legend.
Point	A point in a data series. The name is preceded by the series. Example: Series 1 Point 2.
Series Axis	The axis that represents the chart's series (3D charts only).
Series	A line that connects a series.
Trendline	A trendline for a data series.
Up-Bars	Up-bars in a stock market chart.
Value Axis Title	The title for the value axis.
Value Axis	The axis that represents the chart's values. A Secondary Value Axis may also exist.
Walls	The walls of a 3D chart only (except 3D pie charts).

Chart Background Elements

As mentioned in the preceding section, a chart consists of many elements. This section discusses two of those elements: the Chart Area and the Plot Area. These chart items provide a background for other elements in the chart.

The Chart Area

The Chart Area is an object that contains all other elements in the chart. You can think of it as a chart's master background. You can't change the size of the Chart Area. For an embedded chart, it's always the same size as the embedded chart object. For a chart sheet, the Chart Area is always the entire sheet.

The following are the three tabs of the Chart Area dialog box and some key points about each:

✦ **Patterns tab:** Enables you to change the Chart Area's color and patterns (including fill effects) and add a border, if you like.

✦ **Font tab:** Enables you to change the properties of *all fonts used in the chart*. Changing the font doesn't affect fonts that you have previously changed, however. For example, if you make the chart's title 20-point Arial and then change the font to 8-point Arial in the Format Chart Area dialog box, the title's font is not affected.

✦ **Properties tab:** Enables you to specify how the chart is moved and sized with respect to the underlying cells. You also can set the Locked property and specify whether the chart will be printed.

Note　If you delete the Chart Area, you delete the entire chart.

Note　Prior to Excel 97, clicking an embedded chart selected the chart object. You could then adjust its properties. To activate the chart, you actually had to double-click it. Beginning with Excel 97, clicking an embedded chart activates the chart contained inside the chart object. You can adjust the chart object's properties by using the Properties tab of the Format dialog box. To select the chart object itself, press Ctrl while you click the chart. You might want to select the chart object to change its name by using the Name box.

The Plot Area

The Chart Area of a chart contains the Plot Area, which is the part of the chart that contains the actual chart. The Plot Area is unlike the Chart Area in that you can resize and reposition the Plot Area. The Format Plot Area dialog box has only one tab: Patterns. This tab enables you to change the color and pattern of the Plot Area and adjust its borders.

Tip When you select a chart element, you'll find that many of the toolbar buttons that you normally use for worksheet formatting also work with the selected chart element. For example, if you select the chart's Plot Area, you can change its color by using the Fill Color tool on the Formatting toolbar. If you select an element that contains text, you can use the Font Color tool to change the color of the text.

Working with Chart Titles

A chart can have as many as five different titles:

✦ Chart title

✦ Category (X) axis title

✦ Value (Y) axis title

✦ Second category (X) axis title

✦ Second value (Y) axis title

The number of titles that you can use depends on the chart type. For example, a pie chart supports only a chart title, because it has no axes.

To add titles to a chart, activate the chart and use the Chart ➪ Options command. Excel displays the Chart Options dialog box. Click the Titles tab and enter text for the title or titles (see Figure 16-3).

 Tip The titles that Excel adds are placed in the appropriate position, but you can drag them anywhere.

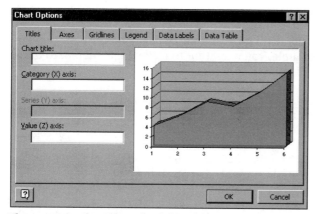

Figure 16-3: The Titles tab of the Chart Options dialog box lets you add titles to a chart.

To modify a chart title's properties, access its Format dialog box. This dialog box has tabs for the following:

✦ **Patterns:** Change the background color and borders

✦ **Font:** Change the font, size, color, and attributes

✦ **Alignment:** Adjust the vertical and horizontal alignment and orientation

Text in a chart is not limited to titles. In fact, you can add free-floating text anywhere that you want. To do so, select any part of the chart except a title or data label. Then, type the text in the formula bar and press Enter. Excel adds a Text Box AutoShape that contains the text. You can move the Text Box wherever you want it and format it to your liking.

Working with the Legend

If you create your chart with the Chart Wizard, you have an option (in Step 3) to include a legend. If you change your mind, you can easily delete the legend or add one if it doesn't exist.

To add a legend to your chart, use the Chart ⇨ Options command and then click the Legend tab in the Chart Options dialog box. Place a check mark in the Show legend check box. You also can specify where to place the legend by using the Placement option buttons.

The quickest way to remove a legend is to select the legend and then press Delete. To move a legend, click and drag it to the desired location. Or, you can use the legend's Format dialog box to position the legend (using the Placement tab).

A chart's legend consists of text and keys. A *key* is a small graphic that corresponds to the chart's series. You can select individual text items within a legend and format them separately by using the Format Legend Entry dialog box (which has only a single panel: Font). For example, you may want to make the text bold, to draw attention to a particular data series.

You can't use the Chart toolbar's Select Object drop-down list to select a legend entry or legend key. You must either click the item or select the legend itself, and then press the right arrow until the element that you want is selected.

The Legend tool in the Chart toolbar acts as a toggle. Use this button to add a legend, if one doesn't exist, and to remove the legend, if one exists.

After you move a legend from its default position, you may want to change the size of the Plot Area to fill in the gap left by the legend. Just select the Plot Area and drag a border to make it the desired size.

If you didn't include legend text when you originally selected the cells to create the chart, Excel displays *Series 1, Series 2,* and so on in the legend. To add series names, choose Chart ➪ Source Data and then select the Series tab in the Source Data dialog box (refer to Figure 16-4). Select a series from the Series list box, activate the Name box, and then either specify a cell reference that contains the label or directly enter the series name.

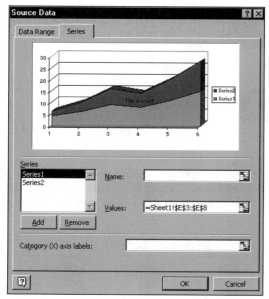

Figure 16-4: Use the Series tab of the Source Data dialog box to change the name of a data series.

Changing Gridlines

Gridlines can help you to determine what the chart series represents numerically. Gridlines simply extend the tick marks on the axes. Some charts look better with gridlines; others appear more cluttered. You can decide whether gridlines can enhance your chart. Sometimes, horizontal gridlines alone are enough, although XY charts often benefit from both horizontal and vertical gridlines.

To add or remove gridlines, choose Chart ➪ Options and then select the Gridlines tab. This Chart Options dialog box is shown in Figure 16-5.

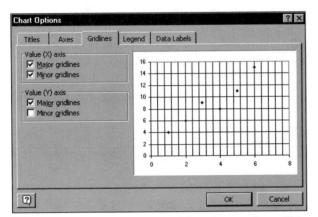

Figure 16-5: The Gridlines tab of the Chart Options dialog box lets you add or remove gridlines from the chart.

Each axis has two sets of gridlines: major and minor. *Major* units display a label. *Minor* units are located between the labels. You can choose which to add or remove by checking or unchecking the appropriate check boxes. If you're working with a true 3D chart, the dialog box has options for three sets of gridlines.

To modify the properties of a set of gridlines, select one gridline in the set and access the Format Gridlines dialog box. This dialog has two tabs:

✦ **Patterns:** Changes the line style, width, and color

✦ **Scale:** Adjusts the scale used on the axis

The next section presents an in-depth discussion of scaling.

Modifying the Axes

Charts vary in the number of axes that they use. Pie and doughnut charts have no axes. All 2D charts have two axes (three, if you use a secondary-value axis; four, if you use a secondary-category axis in an *XY* chart). True 3D charts have three axes. Excel gives you a lot of control over these axes. To modify any aspect of an axis, access its Format Axis dialog box, which has five tabs:

✦ **Patterns:** Change the axis line width, tick marks, and placement of tick mark labels

✦ **Scale:** Adjust the minimum and maximum axis values, units for major and minor gridlines, and other properties

✦ **Font:** Adjust the font used for the axis labels

✦ **Number:** Adjust the number format for the axis labels

✦ **Alignment:** Specify the orientation for the axis labels

Because the axes' properties can dramatically affect the chart's look, the Patterns and Scale dialog box tabs are discussed separately, in the following sections.

Axes Patterns

Figure 16-6 shows the Patterns tab of the Format Axis dialog box.

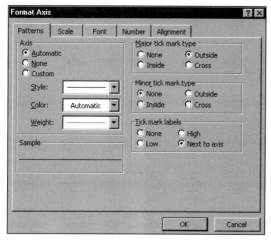

Figure 16-6: The Patterns tab of the Format Axis dialog box.

This tab has four sections:

✦ **Axis:** Controls the line characteristics of the axis (the style, color, and weight of the line).

✦ **Major tick mark type:** Controls how the major tick marks appear. You can select None (no tick marks), Inside (inside the axis), Outside (outside the axis), or Cross (on both sides of the axis).

✦ **Minor tick mark type:** Controls how the minor tick marks appear. You can select None (no tick marks), Inside (inside the axis), Outside (outside the axis), or Cross (on both sides of the axis).

✦ **Tick mark labels:** Controls where the axis labels appear. Normally, the labels appear next to the axis. You can, however, specify that the labels appear High (at the top of the chart), Low (at the bottom of the chart), or not at all (None). These options are useful when the axis doesn't appear in its normal position, at the edge of the Plot Area.

Note Major tick marks are the axis tick marks that normally have labels next to them. Minor tick marks are between the major tick marks.

Axes Scales

Adjusting the scale of a value axis can dramatically affect the chart's appearance. Manipulating the scale, in some cases, can present a false picture of the data. Figure 16-7 shows two charts that use the same data; the only difference between the charts is that the Minimum value has been adjusted on the value axis scale. In the first chart, the differences are quite apparent. In the second chart, little difference is apparent between the data points.

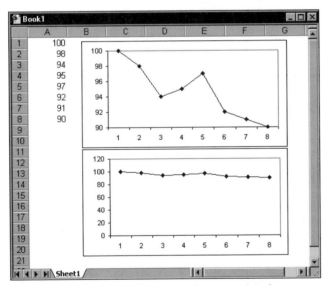

Figure 16-7: These two charts use the same data but different scales.

The actual scale that you use depends on the situation. No hard-and-fast rules exist about scale, except that you shouldn't misrepresent data by manipulating the chart to prove a point that doesn't exist.

If you're preparing several charts that use similarly scaled data, keeping the scales the same is a good idea, so that the charts can be compared more easily. The charts in Figure 16-8 show the distribution of responses for a survey. Because the same scale was not used on the value axes, however, comparing the responses across survey items is difficult. All charts in the series should have the same scale.

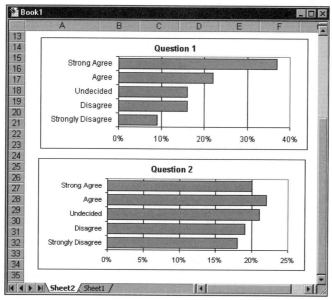

Figure 16-8: These charts use different scales on the value axis, making a comparison between the two difficult.

Excel automatically determines the scale for your charts. You can, however, override Excel's choice in the Scale tab of the Format Axis dialog box (see Figure 16-9).

Note The Scale tab varies slightly, depending on which axis is selected.

This dialog box offers the following options:

✦ **Minimum:** Enter a minimum value for the axis. If the check box is checked, Excel determines this value automatically.

✦ **Maximum:** Enter a maximum value for the axis. If the check box is checked, Excel determines this value automatically.

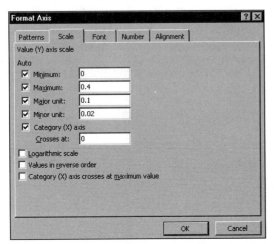

Figure 16-9: The Scale tab of the Format Axis dialog box.

✦ **Major unit:** Enter the number of units between major tick marks. If the check box is checked, Excel determines this value automatically.

✦ **Minor unit:** Enter the number of units between minor tick marks. If the check box is checked, Excel determines this value automatically.

✦ *Axis Type* **axis Crosses at:** Position the axis at a different location. By default, it's at the edge of the Plot Area. The exact wording of this option (*Axis Type*) varies, depending on which axis is selected.

✦ **Logarithmic scale**: Use a logarithmic scale for the axes. A log scale primarily is useful for scientific applications in which the values to plot have an extremely large range. You receive an error message if the scale includes 0 or negative values.

✦ **Values in reverse order:** Make the scale values extend in the opposite direction. For a value axis, for example, selecting this option displays the smallest scale value at the top and the largest at the bottom (the opposite of how it normally appears).

✦ *Axis Type* **crosses at maximum value:** Position the axes at the maximum value of the perpendicular axis (normally, the axis is positioned at the minimum value of the perpendicular axis). The exact wording of this option (*Axis Type*) varies, depending on which axis is selected.

Working with Data Series

Every chart consists of one or more data series. Each series is based on data that is stored in a worksheet. This data translates into chart columns, lines, pie slices, and so on. This section discusses most of the customizations that you can perform with a chart's data series.

To work with a data series, you must first select it. Activate the chart and then click the data series that you want to select. In a column chart, click a column; in a line chart, click a line; and so on. Make sure that you select the entire series and not just a single point. You may find it easier to select the series by using the Chart Object tool in the Chart toolbar.

When you select a data series, Excel displays the series name in the Name box (for example, Series 1, or the actual name of the series), and the SERIES formula in the formula bar. A selected data series has a small square on each element of the series. In addition, the cells used for the selected series are outlined in color.

Many customizations that you perform with a data series use the Format Data Series dialog box, which has as many as seven tabs. The number of tabs varies, depending on the type of chart. For example, a pie chart has four tabs, and a 3D column chart has four tabs. Line and column charts have six tabs, and *XY* (scatter) charts have seven tabs. The possible tabs in the Format Data Series dialog box are as follows:

  ✦ **Axis:** Specify which value axis to use for the selected data series. This is applicable only if the chart has two value axes.

  ✦ **Data Labels:** Display labels next to each data point.

  ✦ **Options:** Change options specific to the chart type.

  ✦ **Patterns:** Change the color, pattern, and border style for the data series. For line charts, change the color and style of the data marker in this tab.

  ✦ **Series Order:** Specify the order in which the data series are plotted.

  ✦ **Shape:** Specify the shape of the columns (in 3D column charts only).

  ✦ *X* **Error Bars:** Add or modify error bars for the *X* axis. This is available only for *XY* charts.

  ✦ *Y* **Error Bars**: Add or modify error bars for the *Y* axis.

The sections that follow discuss many of these dialog box options.

Deleting a Data Series

To delete a data series in a chart, select the data series and press the Delete key. The data series is removed from the chart. The data in the worksheet, of course, remains intact.

Note You can delete all data series from a chart. If you do so, the chart appears empty. It retains its settings, however. Therefore, you can add a data series to an empty chart and it again looks like a chart.

Adding a New Data Series to a Chart

A common need is to add another data series to an existing chart. You *could* re-create the chart and include the new data series, but usually adding the data to the existing chart is easier. Excel provides several ways to add a new data series to a chart:

✦ Activate the chart and select Chart ➪ Source Data. In the Source Data dialog box, click the Series tab (see Figure 16-10). Click the Add button and then specify the data range in the Values box (you can enter the range address or point to it).

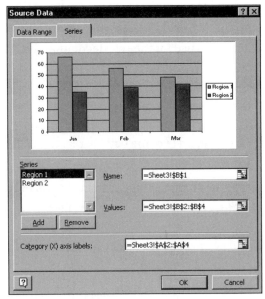

Figure 16-10: Use the Source Data dialog box to add a new data series to a chart.

✦ Select the range to add and copy it to the Clipboard. Then, activate the chart and choose Edit ➪ Paste Special. Excel responds with the dialog box shown in Figure 16-11. Complete this dialog box to correspond to the data that you selected (or just use Edit ➪ Paste and let Excel determine how the data fits into the chart).

✦ Select the range to add and drag it into the chart. When you release the mouse button, Excel updates the chart with the data that you dragged in. This technique works only if the chart is embedded on the worksheet.

Figure 16-11: Using the Paste Special dialog box is one way to add new data to a chart.

Changing Data Used by a Series

Often, you create a chart that uses a particular range of data, and then you extend the range by adding new data points in the worksheet. For example, the previous month's sales data arrives in your office, and you enter the numbers into your sales-tracking worksheet. Or, you may delete some of the data points in a range that is plotted; for example, you may not need to plot older information. In either case, you'll find that the chart doesn't update itself automatically. When you add new data to a range, it isn't included in the data series. If you delete data from a range, the chart displays the deleted data as zero values.

Cross-Reference　You can create a chart that updates automatically when you add new data to your worksheet. See "Chart-Making Tricks," later in this chapter.

The following sections describe a few different ways to change the range used by a data series.

Dragging the Range Outline

The easiest way to change the data range for a data series is to drag the range outline. This technique works only for embedded charts. When you select a series, Excel outlines the data range used by that series. You can drag the small dot in the lower-right corner of the range outline to extend or contract the data series. Figure 16-12 shows an example of how this looks. In this figure, the data series needs to be extended to include the data for July. If the chart uses a range for the category axis, you'll also need to extend that range.

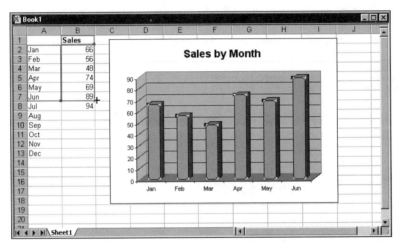

Figure 16-12: To change the range used in a chart's data series, select the data series and drag the small dot at the lower-right corner of the range outline.

You can drag the outline in either direction, so you can use this technique to expand or contract a range used in a data series.

Using the Data Source Dialog Box

To update the chart to reflect a different data range, activate the chart and select Chart ⇨ Source Data. Click the Series tab and then select the series from the Series list box. Adjust the range in the Name box (you can edit the range reference or point to the new range).

Editing the SERIES Formula

Every data series in a chart has an associated SERIES formula, which appears in the formula bar when you select a data series in a chart (see Figure 16-13). You can edit the range references in the SERIES formula directly. You can even enter a new SERIES formula manually—which adds a new series to the chart (however, easier ways to do this exist, as described previously).

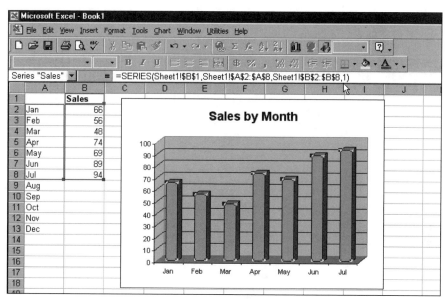

Figure 16-13: When you select a data series, its SERIES formula appears in the formula bar.

A SERIES formula consists of a SERIES function with four arguments. The syntax is as follows:

```
=SERIES(Name_ref,Categories,Values,Plot_order)
```

Excel uses absolute cell references in the SERIES function. To change the data that a series uses, edit the cell references (third argument) in the formula bar. The first and second arguments are optional and may not appear in the SERIES formula. If the series doesn't have a name, the Name_ref argument is missing and Excel uses dummy series names in the legend (Series1, Series2, and so on). If no category names exist, the Categories argument is missing, and Excel uses dummy labels (1, 2, 3, and so on).

 Caution
If the data series uses category labels, make sure that you adjust the reference for the category labels also. This is the second argument in the SERIES formula.

Using Names in SERIES Formulas

Perhaps the best way to handle data ranges that change over time is to use named ranges. Create names for the data ranges that you use in the chart and then edit the SERIES formula. Replace each range reference with the corresponding range name.

After making this change, the chart uses the named ranges. If you add new data to the range, just change the definition for the name, and the chart is updated.

Displaying Data Labels in a Chart

Sometimes, you may want your chart to display the actual data values for each point. Or, you may want to display the category label for each data point. Figure 16-14 shows an example of both of these options.

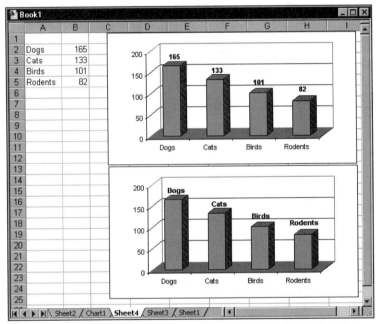

Figure 16-14: The top chart has data labels for each data point; the bottom chart has category labels for each point.

You specify data labels in the Data Labels tab of the Chart Options dialog box (see Figure 16-15). This tab has several options. Note that not all options are available for all chart types. If you select the check box labeled Show legend key next to label, each label displays its legend key next to it.

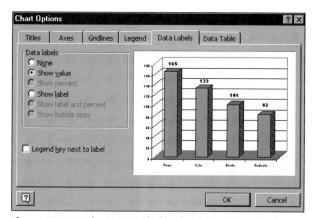

Figure 16-15: The Data Labels tab of the Chart Options dialog box.

The data labels are linked to the worksheet, so if your data changes, the labels also change. If you want to override the data label with other text, select the label and enter the new text (or even a cell reference) in the formula bar.

Often, you'll find that the data labels aren't positioned properly — for example, a label may be obscured by another data point. If you select an individual label, you can drag the label to a better location.

Tip   After you add data labels to a series, format the labels by using the Format Data Labels dialog box.

As you work with data labels, you may discover that Excel's Data Labels feature leaves a bit to be desired. For example, it would be nice to be able to specify a range of text to be used for the data labels. This would be particularly useful in *XY* charts in which you want to identify each data point with a particular text item. Unfortunately, this isn't possible. You can add data labels and then manually edit each label — or, you can use the Chart Data Labeler utility that's included with my Power Utility Pak (use the coupon in the back of the book to get your copy).

Handling Missing Data

Sometimes, data that you're charting may be missing one or more data points. Excel offers several ways to handle the missing data. You don't control this in the Format Data Series dialog box (as you might expect). Rather, you must select the chart, choose Tools ➪ Options, and then click the Chart tab, which is shown in Figure 16-16. The reason for putting this setting in the Options dialog box is known only to the Excel design team.

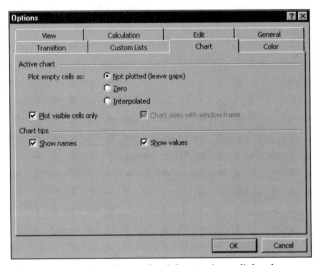

Figure 16-16: The Chart tab of the Options dialog box.

Note   A chart must be activated when you select the Tools ➪ Options command, or the options in the Chart panel are grayed.

The options that you set apply to the entire active chart, and you can't set a different option for different series in the same chart.

The following are the *options* in the Chart panel for the active chart:

✦ **Not plotted (leave gaps):** Missing data is simply ignored, and the data series will have a gap.

✦ **Zero:** Missing data is treated as zero.

✦ **Interpolated:** Missing data is calculated by using data on either side of the missing point(s). This option is available only for line charts.

Controlling a Data Series by Hiding Data

Usually, Excel doesn't plot data that is in a hidden row or column. You can sometimes use this to your advantage, because it's an easy way to control what data appears in the chart. If you're working with outlines or data filtering (both of which use hidden rows), however, you may not like the idea that hidden data is removed from your chart. To override this, activate the chart and select the Tools ➪ Options command. In the Options dialog box, click the Chart tab and remove the check mark from the check box labeled Plot visible cells only.

Note　The Plot visible cells only setting applies only to the active chart. A chart must be activated when you open the Options dialog box. Otherwise, the option is grayed. This is another example of a setting that shows up in an unexpected dialog box.

Adding Error Bars

For certain chart types, you can add error bars to your chart. Error bars often are used to indicate "plus or minus" information that reflects uncertainty in the data. Error bars are appropriate only for area, bar, column, line, and *XY* charts. Click the *Y* Error Bars tab in the Format Data Series dialog box to display the options shown in Figure 16-17.

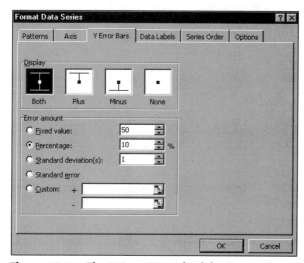

Figure 16-17: The *Y* Error Bars tab of the Format Data Series dialog box.

A data series in an *XY* chart can have error bars for both the *X* values and *Y* values. Excel enables you to specify several types of error bars:

✦ **Fixed value:** The error bars are fixed by an amount that you specify.

✦ **Percentage:** The error bars are a percentage of each value.

✦ **Standard deviation(s):** The error bars are in the number of standard-deviation units that you specify (Excel calculates the standard deviation of the data series).

✦ **Standard error:** The error bars are one standard error unit (Excel calculates the standard error of the data series).

✦ **Custom:** The error bar units for the upper or lower error bars are set by you. You can enter either a value or a range reference that holds the error values that you want to plot as error bars.

Figure 16-18 shows a chart with error bars added. After you add error bars, you can access the Format Error Bars dialog box to modify the error bars. For example, you can control the line style and color of the error bars.

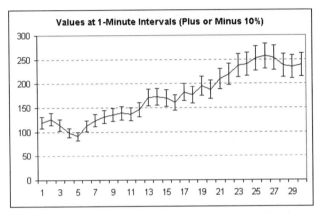

Figure 16-18: This chart has error bars added to the data series.

Adding a Trendline

When you're plotting data over time, you may want to plot a trendline that describes the data. A *trendline* points out general trends in your data. In some cases, you can forecast future data with trendlines. A single series can have more than one trendline.

Excel makes adding a trendline to a chart quite simple. Although you might expect this option to be in the Format Data Series dialog box, it's not. The place to go is the Add Trendline dialog box, shown in Figure 16-19, which you access by selecting Chart ➪ Add Trendline. This command is available only when a data series is selected.

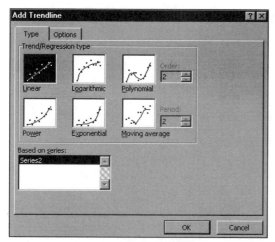

Figure 16-19: The Add Trendline dialog box offers several types of automatic trendlines.

The type of trendline that you choose depends on your data. Linear trends are most common, but some data can be described more effectively with another type. One of the options on the Type tab is Moving average, which is useful for smoothing out "noisy" data. The Moving average option enables you to specify the number of data points to include in each average. For example, if you select 5, Excel averages every five data points.

When you click the Options tab in the Add Trendline dialog box, Excel displays the options shown in Figure 16-20.

The Options tab enables you to specify a name to appear in the legend and the number of periods that you want to forecast. Additional options let you set the intercept value, specify that the equation used for the trendline should appear on the chart, and choose whether the R-squared value appears on the chart.

Figure 16-21 shows two charts. The chart on the left depicts a data series without a trendline. The chart on the right is the same chart, but a linear trendline has been added that shows the trend in the data.

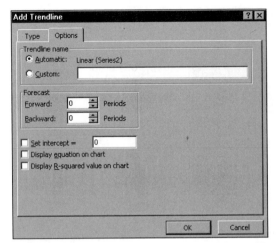

Figure 16-20: The Options tab in the Add Trendline dialog box enables you to smooth or forecast data.

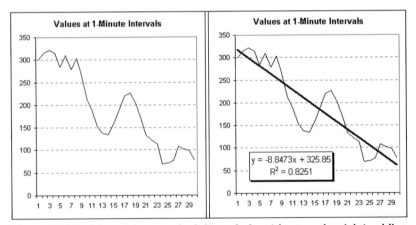

Figure 16-21: Before (chart on the left) and after (chart on the right) adding a linear trendline to a chart.

When Excel inserts a trendline, it may look like a new data series, but it's not. It's a new chart element with a name, such as Series 1 Trendline 1. You can double-click a trendline to change its formatting or its options.

Creating Combination Charts

A *combination chart* is a single chart that consists of series that use different chart types. For example, you may have a chart that shows both columns and lines. A combination chart also can use a single type (all columns, for example), but include a second value axis. A combination chart requires at least two data series.

Creating a combination chart simply involves changing one or more of the data series to a different chart type. Select the data series and then choose Chart ➪ Chart Type. In the Chart Type dialog box, select the chart type that you want to apply to the selected series. Figure 16-22 shows an example of a combination chart.

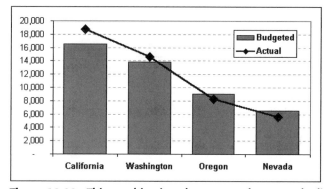

Figure 16-22: This combination chart uses columns and a line.

Note   In some cases, you can't combine chart types. For example, you can't combine a 2D chart type with a 3D chart type. If you choose an incompatible chart type for the series, Excel lets you know.

You can't create combination 3D charts, but if you use a 3D column or 3D bar chart, you can change the shape of the columns or bars. Select a series and access the Format Data Series dialog box. Click the Shape tab and then choose the shape for the selected series.

Using Secondary Axes

If you need to plot data series that have drastically different scales, you probably want to use a *secondary scale*. For example, assume that you want to create a chart that shows monthly sales, along with the average amount sold per customer. These two data series use different scales (the average sales values are much smaller than the total sales). Consequently, the average sales data range is virtually invisible in the chart.

The solution is to use a secondary axis for the second data series. Figure 16-23 shows two charts. The first uses a single value axis, and the second data series (a line) is hardly visible. The second chart uses a secondary axis for the second data series — which makes it easy to see.

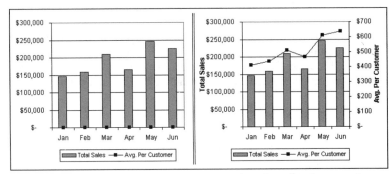

Figure 16-23: These charts show the same data, but the chart on the right uses a secondary axis for the second data series.

To specify a secondary axis, select the data series in the chart and then access the Format Data Series dialog box. Click the Axis tab and choose the Secondary axis option.

Displaying a Data Table

In some cases, you may want to display a *data table*, which displays the chart's data in tabular form, directly in the chart.

To add a data table to a chart, choose Chart ⇨ Chart Options and select the Data Table tab in the Chart Options dialog box. Place a check mark next to the option labeled Show data table. You also can choose to display the legend keys in the data table. Figure 16-24 shows a chart with a data table.

To adjust the formatting or font used in the data table, access the Format Data Table dialog box.

Creating Custom Chart Types

Excel comes with quite a few custom chart types that you can select from the Custom Types tab of the Chart Type dialog box. Each of these custom chart types is simply a standard chart that has been formatted. In fact, you can duplicate any of these custom chart types just by applying the appropriate formatting.

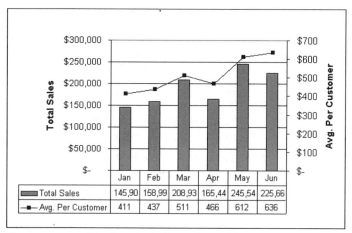

	Jan	Feb	Mar	Apr	May	Jun
Total Sales	145,90	158,99	208,93	165,44	245,54	225,66
Avg. Per Customer	411	437	511	466	612	636

Figure 16-24: This chart includes a data table.

As you might expect, you can create your own custom chart types, called *user-defined* custom chart types.

The first step in designing a custom chart type is to create a chart that's customized the way that you want. For example, you can set any of the colors, fill effects, or line styles; change the scales; modify fonts and type sizes; add gridlines; add a formatted title; and even add free-floating text or graphic images.

When you're satisfied with the chart, choose Chart ⇨ Chart Type to display the Chart Type dialog box. Click the Custom Types tab and then select the User-defined option. This displays a list of all user-defined custom chart types.

Click the Add button, which displays the Add Custom Chart Type dialog box, as shown in Figure 16-25. Enter a name for the new chart type and a description. Click OK, and your custom chart type is added to the list.

Add Custom Chart Type

This dialog allows you to make the active chart into a custom chart type.

Enter a text name for the new custom chart type.

Name: Corporate Column Chart

Enter a text description for the new custom chart type.

Description: Column chart that uses corporate colors. No legend

OK Cancel

Figure 16-25: The Custom Chart Type dialog box.

How Custom Chart Types Are Stored

The custom chart types that you can select from the Chart Types dialog box are stored in a workbook named Xl8galry.xls, located in the Excel (or Office) folder. If you open Xl8galry, you can see that it contains only chart sheets — one for each custom chart type.

Also notice that the series formulas for these charts don't refer to actual worksheet ranges. Rather, the series formulas use arrays entered directly into the series formulas. This makes the charts completely independent of any specific worksheet range.

If you create a user-defined custom chart type, it's stored in a file called xlusrgal.xls, also in the Excel folder. Each custom chart type that you create is stored as a chart sheet.

If you want your coworkers to have access to your custom chart types, simply put a copy of your xlusrgal.xls file into their Excel (or Office) folders. By copying the file, you enable everyone in your workgroup to produce consistent-looking charts.

Working with 3D Charts

One of the most interesting classes of Excel charts is its 3D charts. Certain situations benefit from the use of 3D charts, because you can depict changes over two different dimensions. Even a simple column chart commands more attention if you present it as a 3D chart. Not all charts that are labeled "3D" are true 3D charts, however. A true 3D chart has three axes. Some of Excel's 3D charts are simply 2D charts with a perspective look to them.

Modifying 3D Charts

All 3D charts have a few additional parts that you can customize. For example, most 3D charts have a *floor* and *walls,* and the true 3D charts also have an additional axis. You can select these chart elements and format them to your liking. This chapter doesn't go into the details, because the formatting options are quite straightforward. Generally, 3D formatting options work just like the other chart elements.

Rotating 3D Charts

When you start flirting with the third dimension, you have a great deal of flexibility regarding the viewpoint for your charts. Figure 16-26 shows a 3D column chart that has been rotated to show four different views.

You can rotate a 3D chart in one of the following two ways:

✦ Activate the 3D chart and choose the Chart ⇨ 3D View command. The dialog box shown in Figure 16-27 appears. You can make your rotations and perspective changes by clicking the appropriate controls. The sample that you see in the dialog box is *not* your actual chart. The displayed sample just gives you an idea of the types of changes that you're making. Make the adjustments and then choose OK to make them permanent (or click Apply to apply them to your chart without closing the dialog box).

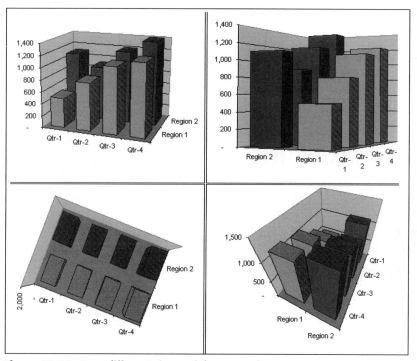

Figure 16-26: Four different views of the same chart.

✦ Rotate the chart in real time by dragging corners with the mouse. Click one of the corners of the chart. Black handles appear, and the word *Corners* appears in the Name box. You can drag one of these black handles and rotate the chart's 3D box to your satisfaction. This method definitely takes some practice. If your chart gets totally messed up, choose Chart ⇨ 3D View and then select the Default button to return to the standard 3D view.

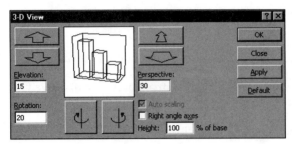

Figure 16-27: The 3D View dialog box enables you to rotate and change the perspective of a 3D chart. You also can drag the chart with the mouse.

Tip   When you rotate a 3D chart, hold down the Ctrl key while you drag, to see an outline of the entire chart — not just the axes. This technique is helpful, because when you drag only the chart's axes, you can easily lose your bearings and end up with a strange-looking chart.

Chart-Making Tricks

In this section, I share chart-making tricks that I've picked up over the years. Some use little-known features; others are undocumented, as far as I can tell. Several tricks enable you to make charts that you may have considered impossible to create.

Changing a Worksheet Value by Dragging

Excel provides an interesting chart-making feature that also can be somewhat dangerous. This feature lets you change the value in a worksheet by dragging the data markers on two-dimensional line charts, bar charts, column charts, *XY* charts, and bubble charts.

Here's how it works. Select an individual data point in a chart series (not the entire series) and then drag the point in the direction in which you want to adjust the value. As you drag the data marker, the corresponding value in the worksheet changes to correspond to the data point's new position on the chart. Figure 16-28 shows the result of dragging the data points around on an *XY* chart with five data series.

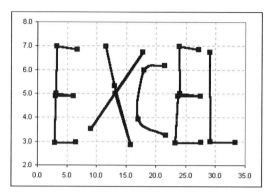

Figure 16-28: This XY chart has five data series.

If the value of a data point that you move is the result of a formula, Excel displays the Goal Seek dialog box (goal seeking is discussed in Chapter 27). Use this dialog box to specify the cell that Excel should adjust to make the formula produce the result that you pointed out on the chart. This technique is useful if you know what a chart should look like and you want to determine the values that will produce the chart. Obviously, this feature also can be dangerous, because you inadvertently can change values that you shouldn't — so be careful.

Unlinking a Chart from Its Data Range

A nice thing about charts is that they are linked to data that is stored in a worksheet. You also can unlink a data series so that it no longer relies on the worksheet data.

To unlink a data series, select the data series and then activate the formula bar. Press F9, and the series formula converts its range references to arrays that hold the values (see the formula bar in Figure 16-29). If you unlink all the series in the chart, you create a dead graph that uses no data in a worksheet. If you want, however, you can edit the individual values in the arrays.

Creating Picture Charts

Excel makes it easy to incorporate a pattern, texture, or graphic file for elements in your chart. Figure 16-30 shows an example of a column chart that displays a graphic.

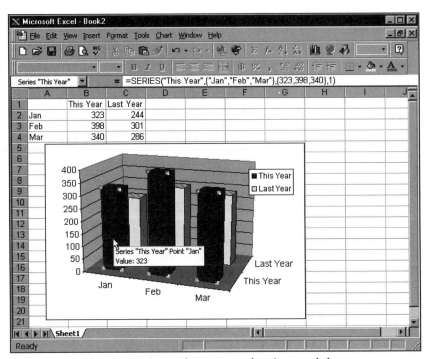

Figure 16-29: This data series no longer uses data in a worksheet.

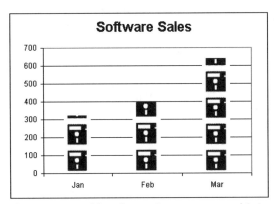

Figure 16-30: This column chart uses a graphic image.

The following sections describe how to create picture charts, using two methods.

Using a Graphic File to Create a Picture Chart

To convert a data series to pictures, start with a column or bar chart (either standard or 3D). Then, access the chart's Format Data Series dialog box and select the Patterns tab. Click the Fill Effects button to get the Fill Effects dialog box. Click the Picture tab and then click the Select Picture button to locate the graphics file that you want to use.

Note   Use the Fill Effects dialog box to specify some options for the image.

Using the Clipboard to Create a Picture Chart

This section describes another way to create a picture chart — a method for which the image that you want to use doesn't have to exist in a file. This technique works if the image can be copied to the Clipboard. It's also the only way to get pictures into the data points for a line or *XY* chart.

The first step is to locate the image that you want to use and copy it to the Clipboard. Generally, simpler images work better. You may want to paste it into Excel first, where you can adjust the size, remove the borders, and add a background color, if desired. Or you can create the image by using Excel's drawing tools. In either case, copy the image to the Clipboard.

When the image is on the Clipboard, activate the chart, select the data series, and then choose Edit ➪ Paste. Your chart is converted. You also can paste the image to a single point in the data series, rather than to the entire data series — simply select the point before you paste.

This technique also works with data markers in line charts, *XY* (scatter) charts, or bubble charts. Figure 16-31 shows an example of a line chart that uses a smiley face instead of the normal data markers. I created this graphic by using Excel's drawing tools (it's one of the AutoShapes in the Basic Shapes category).

Pasting Linked Pictures to Charts

Another useful charting technique involves pasting linked pictures to a chart. Excel doesn't let you do this directly, but this pasting is possible if you know a few tricks. The technique is useful, for example, if you want your chart to include the data that's used by the chart — but the data table feature (discussed earlier in this chapter) isn't flexible enough for you.

Figure 16-32 shows an example of a data range pasted to a chart as a linked picture. If the data changes, the changes are reflected in the chart as well as in the linked picture. Notice that the effect is similar to using a data table, but it allows more formatting options.

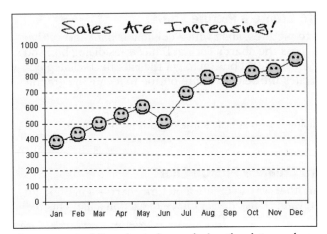

Figure 16-31: A line chart after replacing the data markers with a copied graphic image.

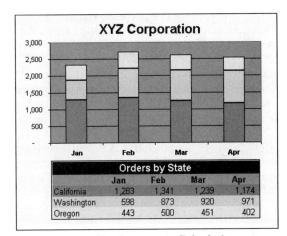

Figure 16-32: This chart uses a linked picture to display the data used in the chart series.

Here are the steps to create the linked picture:

1. Create the chart as usual and format the data range to your liking.

2. Select the data range, press Shift, and select Edit ➪ Copy Picture. Excel displays a dialog box—accept the default options. This copies the range to the Clipboard as a picture.

3. Activate the chart and paste the Clipboard contents. You'll probably have to resize the Plot Area to accommodate the pasted image.

4. The image that is pasted is a picture, but not a linked picture. To convert the image to a linked picture, select it and then enter the range reference in the formula bar (or simply point it out). For this example, I entered **=Sheet1!A1:E5**.

The picture is now a linked picture. Changing any of the cells that are used in the chart's SERIES formula is reflected immediately in the linked picture.

Simple Gantt Charts

Creating a simple Gantt chart isn't difficult when using Excel, but it does require some setup work. *Gantt charts* are used to represent the time required to perform each task in a project. Figure 16-33 shows data that was used to create the Gantt chart in Figure 16-34.

A workbook that demonstrates this technique is available on the companion CD-ROM.

	A	B	C	D	E
1	Task	Start Date	Duration	End Date	
2	Planning Meeting	12/29/98	1	12/29/98	
3	Develop Questionnaire	12/30/98	11	01/09/99	
4	Print and Mail Questionnaire	01/13/99	9	01/21/99	
5	Receive Responses	01/16/99	15	01/30/99	
6	Data Entry	01/16/99	18	02/02/99	
7	Data Analysis	02/03/99	4	02/06/99	
8	Write Report	02/09/99	12	02/20/99	
9	Distribute Draft Report	02/23/99	1	02/23/99	
10	Solicit Comments	02/24/99	4	02/27/99	
11	Finalize Report	03/02/99	5	03/06/99	
12	Distribute to Board	03/09/99	1	03/09/99	
13	Board Meeting	03/17/99	1	03/17/99	
14					

Sheet1

Figure 16-33: Data used in the Gantt chart.

Here are the steps to create this chart:

1. Enter the data as shown in Figure 16-33. The formula in cell D2, which was copied to the rows below it, is **=B2+C2-1**.

2. Use the Chart Wizard to create a stacked bar chart from the range **A2:C13**. Use the second subtype, which is labeled Stacked Bar.

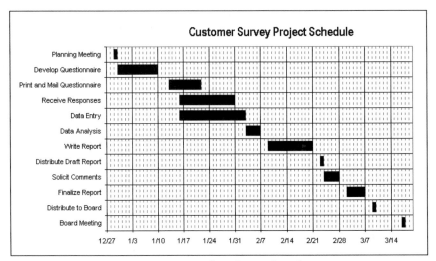

Figure 16-34: You can create a Gantt chart from a bar chart.

3. In Step 2 of the Chart Wizard, select the Columns option. Also, notice that Excel incorrectly uses the first two columns as the Category axis labels.

4. In Step 2 of the Chart Wizard, click the Series tab and add a new data series. Then, set the chart's series to the following:

   Series 1: **B2:B13**

   Series 2: **C2:C13**

   Category (*x*) axis labels: **A2:A13**

5. In Step 3 of the Chart Wizard, remove the legend and then click Finish to create an embedded chart.

6. Adjust the height of the chart so that all the axis labels are visible. You can also accomplish this by using a smaller font size.

7. Access the Format Axis dialog box for the horizontal axis. Adjust the horizontal axis Minimum and Maximum scale values to correspond to the earliest and latest dates in the data (note that you can enter a date into the Minimum or Maximum edit box). You might also want to change the date format for the axis labels.

8. Access the Format Axis dialog box for the vertical axis. In the Scale tab, select the option labeled Categories in reverse order, and also set the option labeled Value (*y*) axis crosses at maximum category.

9. Select the first data series and access the Format Data Series dialog box. In the Patterns tab, set Border to None and Area to None. This makes the first data series invisible.

10. Apply other formatting, as desired.

Comparative Histograms

With a bit of creativity, you can create charts that you may have considered impossible with Excel. For example, Figure 16-35 shows data that was used to create the comparative histogram chart shown in Figure 16-36. Such charts often display population data.

	A	B	C	D
1	Age Group	Female	Male	
2	<21	-14%	5%	
3	21-30	-23%	15%	
4	31-40	-32%	31%	
5	41-50	-18%	30%	
6	51-60	-8%	14%	
7	61-70	-3%	3%	
8	>70	-2%	2%	
9		-100%	100%	

Figure 16-35: Data used in the comparative histogram chart.

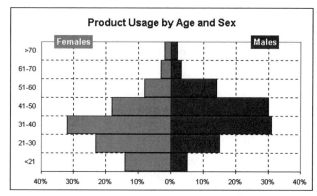

Figure 16-36: Producing this comparative histogram chart requires a few tricks.

On the CD-ROM

A workbook that demonstrates this technique is available on the companion CD-ROM.

Here's how to create the chart:

1. Enter the data as shown in Figure 16-35. Notice that the values for females are entered as negative values.

2. Select A1:C8 and create a 2D bar chart. Use the subtype labeled Clustered Bar.

3. Apply the following custom number format to the horizontal axis: **0%;0%;0%**. This custom format eliminates the negative signs in the percentages.

4. Select the vertical axis and access the Format Axis dialog box. Click the Patterns tab and remove all tick marks. Set the Tick mark labels option to Low. This keeps the axis in the center of the chart but displays the axis labels at the left side.

5. Select either of the data series and then access the Format Data Series dialog box. Click the Options tab and set the Overlap to 100 and the Gap width to 0.

6. Add two text boxes to the chart (**Females** and **Males**), to substitute for the legend.

7. Apply other formatting, as desired.

Charts That Update Automatically

Earlier in this chapter, I discussed several ways to modify the data range used by a chart series. If you have a chart that displays daily sales, for example, you probably need to change the chart's data range each day when you add new data. Although updating a chart's data range isn't difficult, you might be interested in a trick that forces Excel to update the chart's data range whenever you add new data to your worksheet.

On the CD-ROM

A workbook that demonstrates this technique is available on the companion CD-ROM.

To force Excel to update your chart automatically when you add new data, follow these steps:

1. Create the worksheet shown in Figure 16-37.

2. Select Insert ➪ Name ➪ Define to bring up the Define Name dialog box. In the Names in workbook field, enter **Date**. In the Refers to field, enter this formula:

   ```
   =OFFSET(Sheet1!$A$2,0,0,COUNTA(Sheet1! $A:$A)-1)
   ```

3. Click Add. Notice that the OFFSET function refers to the first data point (cell A2) and uses the COUNTA function to get the number of data points in the

column. Because column A has a heading in row 1, the formula subtracts 1 from the number.

4. Type **Sales** in the Names in workbook field, and in the Refers to field enter:

```
=OFFSET(Sheet1!$B$2,0,0,COUNTA(Sheet1!$B:$B)-1)
```

5. Click Add and then OK to close the dialog box.

6. Activate the chart and select the data series. In this example, the formula in the formula bar will read:

```
=SERIES(Sheet1!$B$1,Sheet1!$A$2:$A$10, Sheet1!$B$2:$B$10,1)
```

7. Replace the range references with the names that you defined in Steps 2 and 4. The formula should read:

```
=SERIES(,Sheet1!Date,Sheet1!Sales,1)
```

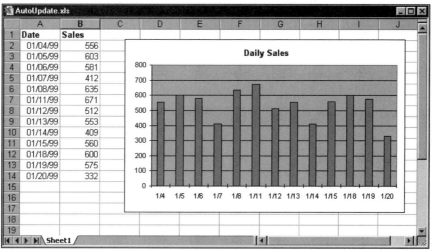

Figure 16-37: This chart is updated automatically whenever you add new data to columns A and B.

After you perform these steps, when you add data to columns A and B, the chart will be updated automatically to show the new data.

To use this technique for your own data, make sure that the first argument for the OFFSET function refers to the first data point, and that the argument for COUNTA refers to the entire column of data. Also, if the columns used for the data contain any other entries, COUNTA will return an incorrect value.

Summary

This chapter picks up where Chapter 13 left off by discussing most of the chart customization options in Excel. This chapter demonstrates how to create combination charts and your own custom chart formats — which let you apply a series of customizations with a single command. This chapter also discusses 3D charts, and concludes with several examples that use chart-making tricks.

✦   ✦   ✦

Creating Maps with Microsoft Map

In previous chapters, you saw how you can use a chart to display data in a different — and, usually, more meaningful — way. This chapter explores the topic of mapping and describes how to present geographic information in the form of a map.

The mapping feature is not actually part of Excel. Rather, this feature uses an OLE server application named *Microsoft Map*, which was developed by MapInfo Corporation. You can use this application to insert maps into other Microsoft Office applications. Because the mapping application is not part of Excel, you'll find that the user interface is quite different from that of Excel. When a map is active, Microsoft Map menus and toolbars replace Excel's menus and toolbars.

Mapping: An Overview

Mapping, like charting, is a tool that visually presents data. People use maps for a variety of purposes, but the common factor in maps is that they work with data that has a basis in geography. If you classify information by state, province, or country, chances are good that you can represent the data on a map. For example, if your company sells its products throughout the United States, showing the annual sales for each state may be useful.

A Mapping Example

Figure 17-1 shows sales data for a company, with the data categorized by state. To understand this information, you would have to spend a lot of time examining the data.

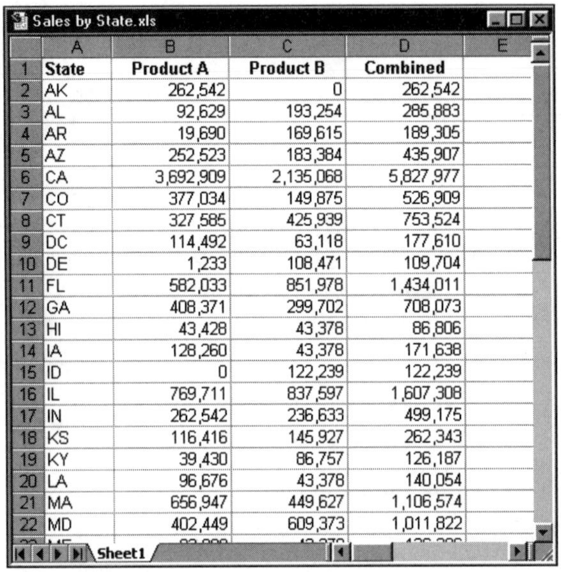

	A	B	C	D	E
1	State	Product A	Product B	Combined	
2	AK	262,542	0	262,542	
3	AL	92,629	193,254	285,883	
4	AR	19,690	169,615	189,305	
5	AZ	252,523	183,384	435,907	
6	CA	3,692,909	2,135,068	5,827,977	
7	CO	377,034	149,875	526,909	
8	CT	327,585	425,939	753,524	
9	DC	114,492	63,118	177,610	
10	DE	1,233	108,471	109,704	
11	FL	582,033	851,978	1,434,011	
12	GA	408,371	299,702	708,073	
13	HI	43,428	43,378	86,806	
14	IA	128,260	43,378	171,638	
15	ID	0	122,239	122,239	
16	IL	769,711	837,597	1,607,308	
17	IN	262,542	236,633	499,175	
18	KS	116,416	145,927	262,343	
19	KY	39,430	86,757	126,187	
20	LA	96,676	43,378	140,054	
21	MA	656,947	449,627	1,106,574	
22	MD	402,449	609,373	1,011,822	

Figure 17-1: Raw data that shows sales by state.

Figure 17-2 shows the same data displayed in a chart. Although an improvement over the raw-data table, this type of presentation doesn't really work, because it has too many data points. In addition, the chart doesn't reveal any information about sales in a particular region.

Figure 17-3 shows the sales data presented as a map (it looks even better in color). This presentation uses different colors to represent various sales ranges. Looking at the map, you can see clearly that this company performs much better in some regions than in others.

The map in Figure 17-3 might be even more revealing if the sales were represented relative to the population of each state; that is, in per capita sales. This population data is available as a sample file on the Office CD (Mapstats.xls).

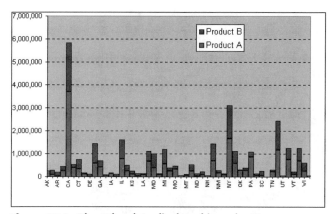

Figure 17-2: The sales data displayed in a chart.

Figure 17-4 shows the contents sheet for this workbook.

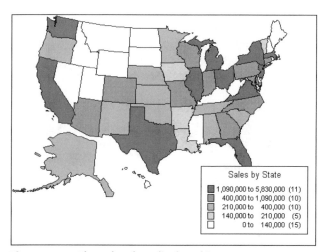

Figure 17-3: The sales data displayed in a map.

Available Maps

The Microsoft Map feature supports a good variety of maps and enables you to create maps in several different formats. A single map can display multiple sets of data, each in a different format. For example, your map can show sales by state and indicate the number of sales offices in each state. In addition, your map can display other accoutrements, such as labels and pin markers.

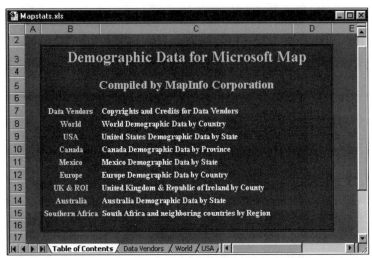

Figure 17-4: The Mapstats workbook contains population statistics that you can use in your maps.

The maps included with Microsoft Map are listed in Table 17-1. As you'll see later in this chapter, a map can be zoomed to display only a portion of it. Therefore, you can use the Europe map to zoom in on a particular region or country.

Table 17-1	
Maps Included with Microsoft Map	
Map	*Description*
Australia	The continent of Australia, by state
Canada	The country of Canada, by province
Europe	The continent of Europe, by country
Mexico	The country of Mexico, by state
North America	The countries of North America (Canada, U.S., Mexico)
U.K. Standard Regions	The countries of the United Kingdom, by region
U.S. in North America	United States (excluding Alaska and Hawaii insets), by state
U.S. with AK and HI Insets	United States (with Alaska and Hawaii insets), by state
World Countries	The world, by country

If you would like to order additional maps or data from MapInfo, you can contact the company directly or visit its Web site. For information on how to do so, activate a map and click the Help ⇨ About command.

Creating a Map

Creating a basic map with Microsoft Map is simple. In almost all cases, however, you'll want to customize the map. This section discusses the basics of mapmaking.

Setting Up Your Data

The Microsoft Map feature works with data stored in a list format (for an example, refer to Figure 17-1). The first column should contain names of map regions (such as states or countries). The columns to the right should contain data for each area. You can have any number of data columns, because you select the columns to use after the map is created.

Creating the Map

To create a map, start by selecting the data. The selection must include one column of area names and at least one column of data. If the columns have descriptive headers, include these in the selection.

Choose Insert ⇨ Map (or click the Map button on the Standard toolbar). Click and drag to specify the location and size of the map or just click to create a map of the default size. Unlike charts, maps must be embedded on a worksheet (there are no separate map sheets).

Microsoft Map analyzes the area labels and generates the appropriate map. If two or more maps are possible (or if you've developed any custom map templates), you'll see the Multiple Maps Available dialog box, shown in Figure 17-5. Select the map that you want to use from this list.

Figure 17-5: If multiple maps are available for your data, you can choose from this dialog box which map to use.

You don't have the Insert ⇨ Map command?

Excel's mapping feature is performed by an OLE server application. The mapping feature is not an integral part of Excel, and it may not be installed on your system. If you don't see a Map command on the Insert menu, you need to install the mapping feature.

To install the mapping feature, you need to rerun Excel's Setup program (or the Microsoft Office Setup program) and specify the mapping feature. Microsoft Map displays the map using the first column of data. It also displays the Microsoft Map Control dialog box, discussed later in the chapter. When the map is created, it is activated. Whenever a map is activated, Microsoft Map's menus and toolbar replace Excel's menus and toolbars. When you click outside the map, Excel's user interface reappears. You can reactivate a map by double-clicking it.

Setting the Map Format(s)

When a map first appears, the Microsoft Map Control dialog box is visible (see Figure 17-6). Use this dialog box to change the format of the selected map. You can use the Show/Hide Map Control tool to toggle the display of this dialog box.

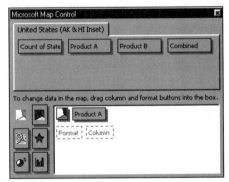

Figure 17-6: The Microsoft Map Control dialog box.

By default, you create maps by using the value-shading map format. You can change the format or display two or more formats on a single map. You use the Microsoft Map Control dialog box by dragging the items in it. The top of the dialog box displays all available data fields (which correspond to the columns that you selected when you created the map). The bottom part contains the map format information. Six format icons on the left determine the map format (described in the sections that follow). You combine a map format icon with one or more data fields by dragging the icon. For example, you can replace the default map format icon with another one simply by dragging the new icon over the existing one. Some map formats use more than one data field. In such a case, you can drag additional data fields next to the icon.

To change options for a particular map format, either double-click the format icon or use the Map menu and choose the menu command that is appropriate for the format that you want to change. In either case, you get a dialog box that's appropriate for the map format.

The following sections include descriptions (and samples) of each map format supported by Microsoft Map.

Value shading

With this map format, each map region is shaded based on the value of its data. This format is appropriate for data-quantitative information, such as sales, population, and so on. Figure 17-7 shows an example of a map formatted with value shading (this map is zoomed to show only part of the U.S.). In this example, the sales are broken down into four ranges, and each sales range is associated with different shading.

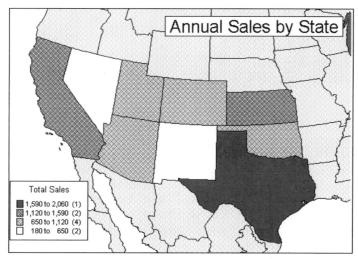

Figure 17-7: This map uses the value-shading format.

You can change the interval ranges in the Format Properties dialog box, shown in Figure 17-8.

When you're viewing a map that uses value shading, choose Map ➪ Value Shading Options, and Microsoft Map opens the value-shading version of the Format Properties dialog box. You can specify the number of value ranges and the method of defining the ranges — an equal number of areas in each range or an equal spread of values in each range. You also can select a color for the shading. The map displays different variations of the single color that you select. You can choose the summary function to use (SUM or AVERAGE). To hide the format from the map, remove the check mark from the Visible check box.

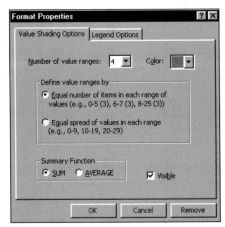

Figure 17-8: The Value Shading Options tab of the Format Properties dialog box.

Category shading

With the category-shading map format, each map region is colored based on a data value. The map legend has one entry (color) for every value of the data range. Therefore, this format is appropriate for data that has a small number of discrete values. For example, you can use the format to identify states that have a sales office, the number of sales reps in a country, and so on. A common use for this format is to identify the states that make up each sales region. Data need not be numeric. For example, the data can consist of text such as Yes and No.

Figure 17-9 shows a map that uses category shading to identify states that met the annual sales goal.

Figure 17-9: This map uses the category-shading format.

To change the colors in the categories, use the Format Properties dialog box. Again, when you're viewing a map that uses category shading, you can open this dialog box by choosing Map ⇨ Category Shading Options. Microsoft Map displays the category-shading version of the Format Options dialog box.

Dot density

The dot-density map format displays data as a series of dots. Larger values translate into more dots. The dots are placed randomly within a map region. Figure 17-10 shows an example of a map that uses the dot-density format. This map depicts population in the U.K. and Ireland. Each dot represents 100,000 people.

To change the number of units for each dot or to change the dot size, access the Dot Density Options tab of the Format Properties dialog box, which is shown in Figure 17-11.

Figure 17-10: A dot-density format map, showing the population of the U.K. and Ireland.

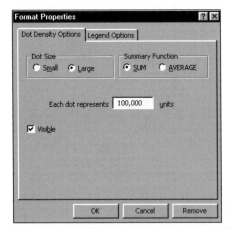

Figure 17-11: The Dot Density Options tab of the Format Properties dialog box.

Graduated symbol

The graduated-symbol map format displays a symbol, the size of which is proportional to the area's data value. Figure 17-12 shows an example of this format. I used a Wingdings font character for the symbol. To change the symbol, use the Graduated Symbol Options dialog box. You can select a font, size, and specific character.

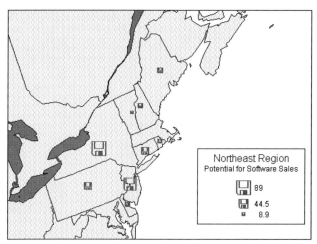

Figure 17-12: A graduated-symbol format map.

Pie chart

The pie-chart map format requires at least two columns of data. Maps with this format display a pie chart within each map region. Figure 17-13 shows an example. This map shows a pie chart that depicts the relative sales of three products for each state.

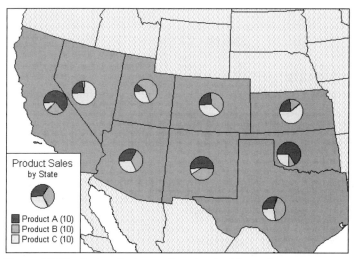

Figure 17-13: A map that uses the pie-chart format.

To change the setting for a pie-chart format map, use the Pie Chart Options tab of the Format Properties dialog box, shown in Figure 17-14. This dialog box enables you to select a color for each pie slice. If you choose the Graduated option, the size of each pie is proportional to the sum or average of the data. If you don't use the Graduated option, you also can set the diameter of the pies.

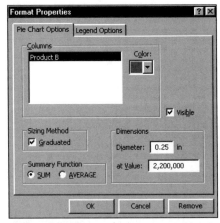

Figure 17-14: The Pie Chart Options tab of the Format Properties dialog box.

Column chart

The column-chart map format is similar to the pie-chart format — except that it displays a column chart instead of a pie chart. Figure 17-15 shows an example.

Combining map formats

As previously mentioned, a single map can include multiple formats for different data. You do this by stacking groups of icons and data fields in the Microsoft Map Control dialog box. For example, you can display sales as value shading and the number of customers as a dot-density map. Each map format has its own legend.

Overlaying multiple map types has no rules, so some experimentation usually is necessary. Unless the map is very simple, however, you're generally better off using only one or two map types per map; otherwise, the map gets so complicated that the original goal (making the data clear) is lost.

Figure 17-16 shows an example of a map that uses two formats. The value-shading format shows sales broken down into four categories. The graduated-symbol format shows the states that have a sales office.

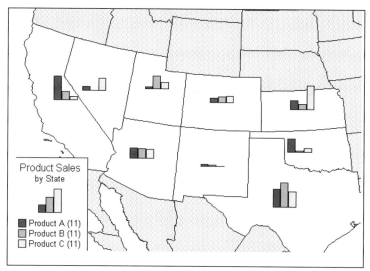

Figure 17-15: A map that uses the column-chart format.

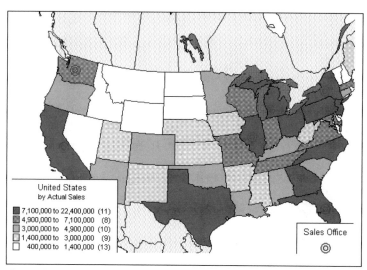

Figure 17-16: An example of a map that uses two map formats:
the value-shading format and the graduated-symbol format.

Customizing Maps

After you create a map, you have numerous customization options from which to
choose, which are described in the following sections.

Using the Microsoft Map Toolbar

Whenever a map is activated, the Microsoft Map toolbar appears (see the accompanying figure). Note that this isn't one of Excel's toolbars; rather, this is a special toolbar that appears only when a map is activated. This toolbar is handy for manipulating and customizing the map.

The tools on the Microsoft Map toolbar, from left to right, and their corresponding functions are presented in the following table.

Tool	Purpose
Select Objects	Changes mouse pointer into an arrow, to select objects in the map
Grabber	Reposition the map within the map window
Center Map	Specify the center of the map
Map Labels	Add geography labels or data values in the map
Add Text	Add free-floating text to the map
Custom Pin Map	Add pins to the map, to indicate specific locations
Display Entire	Displays the entire (unzoomed) map
Redraw Map	Redraws the map
Show/Hide Microsoft Map Control	Toggles the display of the floating Microsoft Map Control dialog box
Zoom Percentage of Map	Changes how much of the map that you view
Help	Provides help for a menu item or toolbar button

Zooming In and Out

Microsoft Map enables you to zoom your map in and out. Zooming in displays less of the map and zooming out displays more of the map (or makes the entire map smaller). Use the Zoom Percentage of Map control on the toolbar (no menu commands exist).

To zoom in, select a zoom percentage greater than 100 percent. To zoom out, select a zoom percentage less than 100 percent. Before you zoom out, you might want to specify the point that will be the center of the map (use the Center Map toolbar button).

Repositioning a Map

You'll find that, after zooming in or out, the map may not be optimally positioned within the map object rectangle. Use the Grabber tool to move the map image within the map object. Just click and drag the map to reposition it.

Adding Labels

Usually, a map doesn't have labels to identify areas. You can't automatically add labels to all areas (for example, all states in the U.S.), but you can add individual labels, one at a time. You also can insert data values that correspond to a particular map region (such as sales for West Virginia).

Use the Label tool to add labels or data values. When you click the Label tool, the dialog box shown in Figure 17-17 appears. The option button labeled Map feature names refers to labels for the various parts of the map (for example, state names in a U.S. map). When you select the Values from option, you can insert data values from a category in the list box. After closing the dialog box, you can drag the mouse pointer over the map. The label or data value appears when the mouse pointer is over a map region. Just click to place the label or data value and then repeat this procedure for each map label or data value that you want to add. Figure 17-18 shows a map that uses labels and data values.

Figure 17-17: The Map Labels dialog box enables you to add labels or data values to your map.

To move a label, click and drag it to a new location. You can change the font, size, or color of a label by double-clicking it. Stretching the label (by dragging a border) also makes the font larger or smaller.

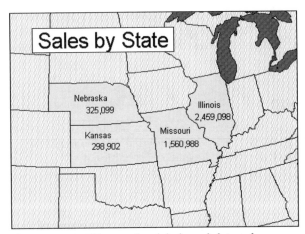

Figure 17-18: This map has labels and data values.

Adding Text

Besides the labels described in the preceding section, you can add free-floating text to your map by using the Text tool. Just click the Text tool, click the area of the map where you want to add text, and enter your text. You can manipulate text the same way that you manipulate labels.

If you don't like the fact that a map title always has a border around it (and the border can't be removed), delete the title and create your own with the Text tool.

Adding Pins to a Map

In some cases, you may want to add one or more identifier icons to your map. This is similar in concept to inserting pins in a wall map to identify various places.

Clicking the Custom Pin Map tool displays a dialog box that asks you to enter a name for a custom pin map (or choose an existing pin map). Enter a descriptive label; you'll be able to bring these same pins into another map (of the same type) later. For example, if you're identifying sales office locations, you can then add the same pins to another map.

When you close the dialog box, the mouse pointer changes to a pushpin. You can place these pins anywhere in your map. When you click the map to place a pin, you also can enter descriptive text. Double-clicking a pin enables you to change the symbol that is used to something other than a pin. Figure 17-19 shows a map with pins added to it.

Figure 17-19: This map has pins to identify specific locations.

Modifying the Legend

You have quite a bit of control over the legend in a map. Note that a map displays a separate legend for each map format that it uses. To modify a legend, double-click it to see the dialog box shown in Figure 17-20.

Figure 17-20: The Legend Options tab of the Format Properties dialog box.

You can display a legend in a compact format or in its normal format. A compact format takes up less space, but it doesn't give many details. You also can change the legend's title and subtitle (and enter a different title for a compacted legend). Other buttons enable you to adjust the font (including size and color) and edit the labels that are used in the legend.

To make other changes to the legend — such as changing the number of data ranges that are used — select the appropriate menu item on the Map menu. For example, to change the number of ranges that are used in a value-shading map format, select the Map ⇨ Value Shading Options command.

Adding and Removing Features

You can add or remove certain features of a map. When you select Map ⇨ Features, you see the Map Features dialog box (see Figure 17-21), which lists all available features for the selected map. To turn on a feature, place a check mark next to it. To turn off a feature, remove the check mark. The features available vary with the map that you're using. If a feature doesn't appear in the list, you can add it by clicking the Add button.

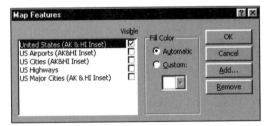

Figure 17-21: The Map Features dialog box.

Figure 17-22 shows a North America map with some features added (major cities, major highways, and world oceans) and some features removed (Canada and Mexico).

Table 17-2 lists the features available for each map. You can, however, add features from different maps — add world oceans to a North America map, for example.

In some cases, you may want your map to display only specific areas. For example, if your company does business in Missouri, Illinois, Kansas, and Nebraska, you can create a map that shows only these four states. Create a map that includes these states and then remove all features from the map by using the Map ⇨ Features command. The map then shows only those areas that have data. Figure 17-23 shows an example.

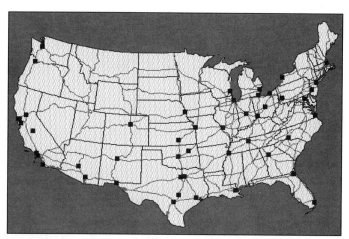

Figure 17-22: This map has features added and removed.

Table 17-2
Available Map Features

Map	Features
Australia	Airports, Cities, Highways, Major Cities
Canada	Airports, Cities, Forward Sortation Areas, Highways, Lakes, Major Cities
Europe	Airports, Cities, Highways, Major Cities
Mexico	Cities, Highways, Major Cities
U.K.	2-Digit Post Codes, Airports, Cities, Highways, Major Cities, Standard Regions
U.S. in North America	5-Digit Zip Code Centers, Highways, Major Cities, Great Lakes
U.S. (AK & HI Inset)	Airports, Cities, Major Cities
World	Capitals, Countries, Graticule, Oceans

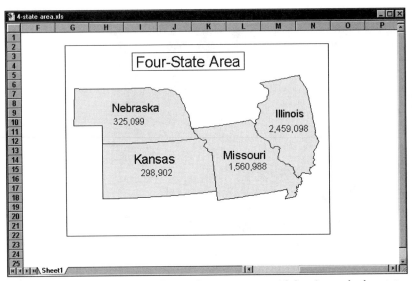

Figure 17-23: This map has all of its features removed, leaving only the states for which data is provided.

Plotting U.S. ZIP Codes

Besides recognizing geographic place names, Microsoft Map recognizes U.S. five-digit ZIP codes. If the data that you select contains more than one type of geographic data (for example, state names and ZIP codes), you need to specify which field to use in the map as the geographic data. Figure 17-24 shows the Specify Geographic Data dialog box, which warns you of the existence of more than one type of data that qualifies as geographic data.

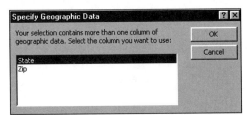

Figure 17-24: The Specify Geographic Data dialog box enables you to select the data to use as geographic data.

If you want to create a map that uses ZIP codes, make sure that your ZIP codes are formatted as values, not as text. Otherwise, Microsoft Map won't recognize them as ZIP codes.

Because ZIP codes are continually being added, Microsoft Map may not recognize all of your ZIP codes. If Microsoft Map encounters an unknown ZIP code, you receive the Resolve Unknown Geographic Data dialog box, shown in Figure 17-25. This dialog box gives you the opportunity to change the ZIP code to another one. Or, you can simply discard that item of data by clicking the Discard button.

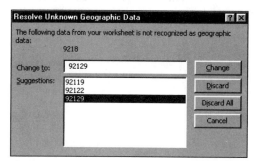

Figure 17-25: Microsoft Map displays the Resolve Unknown Geographic Data dialog box when it doesn't recognize a geographic name.

Figure 17-26 shows a map that depicts customers by their ZIP codes. This is a graduated-symbol map (the default format when ZIP codes are used as data). Note that the symbols appear on the geographic centers of the ZIP codes and don't shade the entire ZIP code areas.

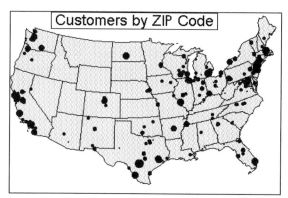

Figure 17-26: This map shows customers by ZIP code centers.

Adding More Data to a Map

After you create a map, you can add additional data to it. Use the Insert ⇨ Data command to add data from a worksheet range, or use the Insert ⇨ External Data command to add new data from a database file. Make sure that the data includes geographic labels that match the map to which you're adding data.

Map Templates

As you may have figured out by now, getting a map just right can sometimes take a lot of time. Fortunately, you can save a map template, so that you can reuse the settings for another map. To do so, create and customize the map and then choose Map ⇨ Save Map Template. You can save a template that includes the following:

✦ The features that you've added or removed

✦ A particular view (zoomed in or out)

✦ Both of the preceding items

Saved templates then appear in the Multiple Maps Available dialog box, which appears when you create a map.

Converting a Map to a Picture

You'll find that working with maps sometimes can be rather sluggish — a great deal of work goes on behind the scenes. When you finish with your map, you can convert it to a static picture that is no longer linked to the data. Click the map once to select it (don't double-click it) and then choose Edit ⇨ Copy. Then, select Edit ⇨ Paste Special and choose the Picture (Enhanced Metafile) option. This creates an unlinked picture of the map. Then, you can select the original map object and delete it.

If you convert a map to a picture, no way exists to link data back to the picture. If any of your data changes or you want to make modifications to the map, you have to re-create the map.

Learning More

The Microsoft Map feature is relatively complex, and it definitely takes time to master. The best way to master this feature is simply to create some maps and perform customizations. As previously mentioned, the user interface is different from Excel's, so you'll have to try some new techniques. Generally, you can find your way around maps by doing the following:

✦ Double-clicking objects

✦ Right-clicking objects

✦ Exploring the menus (they change somewhat, depending on the type of map)

✦ Using the Microsoft Map toolbar

Summary

This chapter covers Excel's new Microsoft Map feature—which is actually an OLE server application developed by MapInfo Corporation. Some data is more appropriate for a map than for a chart, and this chapter demonstrates the difference. This chapter also describes the basics of creating and customizing maps and provides an example of each map format.

✦   ✦   ✦

Creating and Using Worksheet Outlines

If you use a word processor, you may be familiar with the concept of an outline. Most word processors have an outline mode that lets you view only the headings and subheadings in your document. You can easily expand a heading to show the detail (that is, the text) below it. To write this book, I used the outline feature in my word processor extensively.

Excel also is capable of using outlines, and understanding this feature can make working with certain types of worksheets much easier for you.

Introducing Worksheet Outlines

You can use outlines to create summary reports in which you don't want to show all the details. You'll find that some worksheets are more suitable for outlines than others. If your worksheet uses hierarchical data with subtotals, it's probably a good candidate for an outline.

An Example

The best way to understand how worksheet outlining works is to look at an example. Figure 18-1 shows a simple budget model without an outline. Subtotals are used to calculate subtotals by region and by quarter.

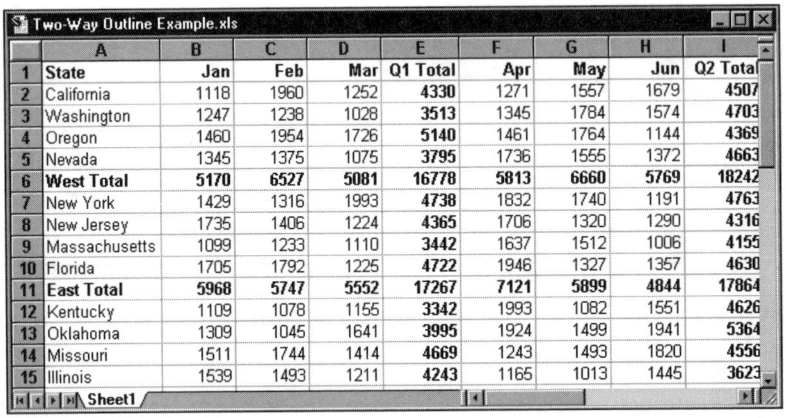

Two-Way Outline Example.xls

	A	B	C	D	E	F	G	H	I
1	State	Jan	Feb	Mar	Q1 Total	Apr	May	Jun	Q2 Total
2	California	1118	1960	1252	4330	1271	1557	1679	4507
3	Washington	1247	1238	1028	3513	1345	1784	1574	4703
4	Oregon	1460	1954	1726	5140	1461	1764	1144	4369
5	Nevada	1345	1375	1075	3795	1736	1555	1372	4663
6	West Total	5170	6527	5081	16778	5813	6660	5769	18242
7	New York	1429	1316	1993	4738	1832	1740	1191	4763
8	New Jersey	1735	1406	1224	4365	1706	1320	1290	4316
9	Massachusetts	1099	1233	1110	3442	1637	1512	1006	4155
10	Florida	1705	1792	1225	4722	1946	1327	1357	4630
11	East Total	5968	5747	5552	17267	7121	5899	4844	17864
12	Kentucky	1109	1078	1155	3342	1993	1082	1551	4626
13	Oklahoma	1309	1045	1641	3995	1924	1499	1941	5364
14	Missouri	1511	1744	1414	4669	1243	1493	1820	4556
15	Illinois	1539	1493	1211	4243	1165	1013	1445	3623

Sheet1

Figure 18-1: A typical budget model with subtotals.

Figure 18-2 shows the same worksheet after the outline was created. Notice that Excel adds a new border to the left of the screen. This border contains controls that enable you to determine which level to view. This particular outline has three levels: States, Regions (each region consists of states), and Grand Total (the sum of each region's subtotal). In Figure 18.2, the outline is fully expanded so that you can see all the data.

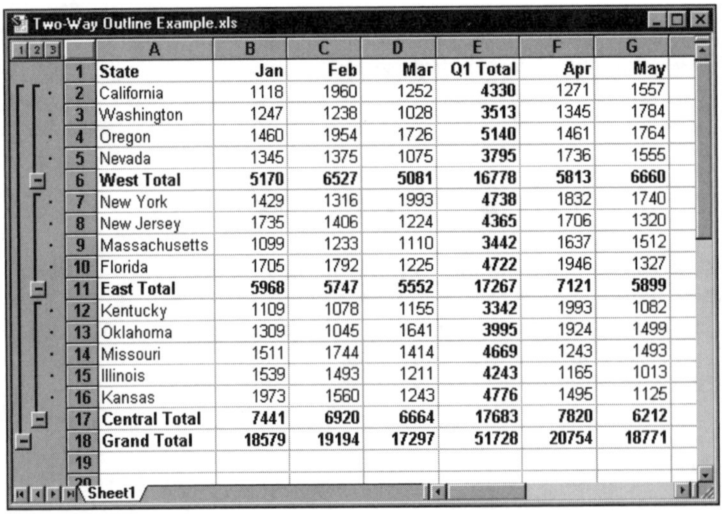

Two-Way Outline Example.xls

	A	B	C	D	E	F	G
1	State	Jan	Feb	Mar	Q1 Total	Apr	May
2	California	1118	1960	1252	4330	1271	1557
3	Washington	1247	1238	1028	3513	1345	1784
4	Oregon	1460	1954	1726	5140	1461	1764
5	Nevada	1345	1375	1075	3795	1736	1555
6	West Total	5170	6527	5081	16778	5813	6660
7	New York	1429	1316	1993	4738	1832	1740
8	New Jersey	1735	1406	1224	4365	1706	1320
9	Massachusetts	1099	1233	1110	3442	1637	1512
10	Florida	1705	1792	1225	4722	1946	1327
11	East Total	5968	5747	5552	17267	7121	5899
12	Kentucky	1109	1078	1155	3342	1993	1082
13	Oklahoma	1309	1045	1641	3995	1924	1499
14	Missouri	1511	1744	1414	4669	1243	1493
15	Illinois	1539	1493	1211	4243	1165	1013
16	Kansas	1973	1560	1243	4776	1495	1125
17	Central Total	7441	6920	6664	17683	7820	6212
18	Grand Total	18579	19194	17297	51728	20754	18771
19							

Sheet1

Figure 18-2: The budget model after creating an outline.

Figure 18-3 depicts the outline displayed at the second level. Now, the outline shows only the totals for the regions (the detail rows are hidden). You can partially expand the outline to show the detail for a particular region. Collapsing the outline to level 1 shows only the headers and the Grand Total row.

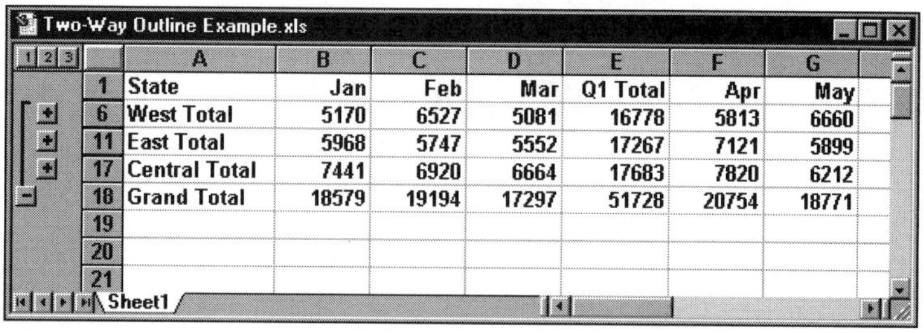

	A	B	C	D	E	F	G
1	State	Jan	Feb	Mar	Q1 Total	Apr	May
6	West Total	5170	6527	5081	16778	5813	6660
11	East Total	5968	5747	5552	17267	7121	5899
17	Central Total	7441	6920	6664	17683	7820	6212
18	Grand Total	18579	19194	17297	51728	20754	18771

Figure 18-3: The budget model after collapsing the outline to the second level.

Excel can create outlines in both directions. In the preceding examples, the outline was a row (vertical) outline. Figure 18-4 shows the same model after a column (horizontal) outline was added. Now, Excel displays another border at the top.

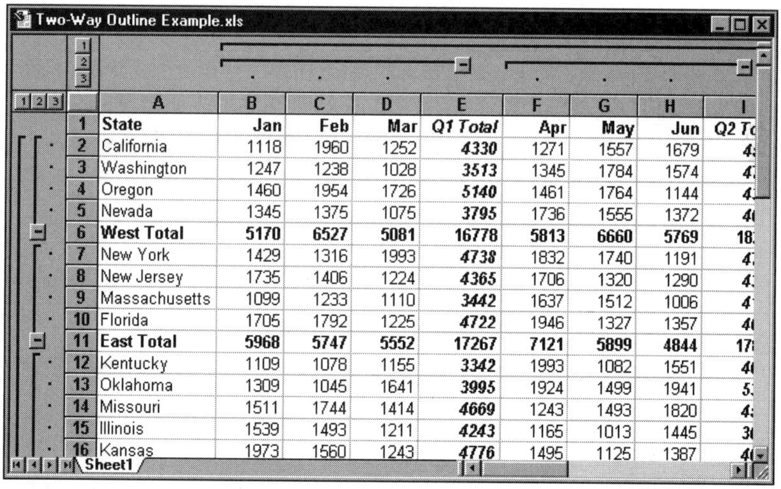

	A	B	C	D	E	F	G	H
1	State	Jan	Feb	Mar	*Q1 Total*	Apr	May	Jun
2	California	1118	1960	1252	*4330*	1271	1557	1679
3	Washington	1247	1238	1028	*3513*	1345	1784	1574
4	Oregon	1460	1954	1726	*5140*	1461	1764	1144
5	Nevada	1345	1375	1075	*3795*	1736	1555	1372
6	West Total	5170	6527	5081	16778	5813	6660	5769
7	New York	1429	1316	1993	*4738*	1832	1740	1191
8	New Jersey	1735	1406	1224	*4365*	1706	1320	1290
9	Massachusetts	1099	1233	1110	*3442*	1637	1512	1006
10	Florida	1705	1792	1225	*4722*	1946	1327	1357
11	East Total	5968	5747	5552	17267	7121	5899	4844
12	Kentucky	1109	1078	1155	*3342*	1993	1082	1551
13	Oklahoma	1309	1045	1641	*3995*	1924	1499	1941
14	Missouri	1511	1744	1414	*4669*	1243	1493	1820
15	Illinois	1539	1493	1211	*4243*	1165	1013	1445
16	Kansas	1973	1560	1243	*4776*	1495	1125	1387

Figure 18-4: The budget model after adding a column outline.

If you create both a row and a column outline in a worksheet, you can work with each outline independent of the other. For example, you can show the row outline at the second level and the column outline at the first level. Figure 18-5 shows the model with both outlines collapsed at the second level. The result is a nice summary table that gives regional totals by quarter.

You'll find the workbook used in the preceding examples on this book's CD-ROM.

	A	E	I	M	Q	R	S
1	State	Q1 Total	Q2 Total	Q3 Total	Q4 Total	Grand Total	
6	West Total	16778	18242	18314	19138	72472	
11	East Total	17267	17864	17910	18925	71966	
17	Central Total	17683	17550	17752	17357	70342	
18	Grand Total	51728	53656	53976	55420	214780	
19							
20							
21							
22							

Two-Way Outline Example.xls — Sheet1

Figure 18-5: The budget model with both outlines collapsed at the second level.

More About Outlines

The following are points to keep in mind about worksheet outlines:

✦ A single worksheet can have only one outline (row, column, or both). If you need to create more than one outline, move the data to a new worksheet.

✦ You can either create an outline manually or have Excel do it for you automatically. If you choose the latter option, you may need to do some preparation to get the worksheet in the proper format.

✦ You can create an outline for either all data on a worksheet or just a selected data range.

✦ You can remove an outline with a single command.

✦ You can hide the outline symbols (to free screen space) but retain the outline.

✦ You can have up to eight nested levels in an outline.

Worksheet outlines can be quite useful. But if your main objective is to summarize a large amount of data, you might be better off using a pivot table. A pivot table is much more flexible and doesn't require that you create the subtotal formulas; it does the summarizing for you automatically.

Cross-
Reference   Pivot tables are discussed in Chapter 25.

Creating an Outline

In this section, you learn the two ways to create an outline: automatically and manually. But, before getting into the details of those two methods, the all-important first step is examined: getting your data ready for outlining.

Preparing the Data

Before you create an outline, you need to ensure the following:

- ✦ The data is appropriate for an outline
- ✦ The formulas are set up properly

Determining appropriate data

What type of data is appropriate for an outline? Generally, the data should be arranged in a hierarchy, such as a budget that consists of an arrangement similar to the following:

Company

        Division

                Department

                        Budget Category

                                Budget Item

In this case, each budget item (for example, airfare and hotel expenses) is part of a budget category (for example, travel expenses). Each department has its own budget, and the departments are rolled up into divisions. The divisions make up the company. This type of arrangement is well-suited for a row outline — although most of your outlines probably won't have this many levels.

Once created, you can view the information at any level of detail that you want. When you need to create reports for different levels of management, try using an outline. Upper management may want to see only the Division totals. Division managers may want to see totals by department, and each department manager needs to see the full details for his or her department.

As demonstrated at the beginning of the chapter, you can include time-based information that is rolled up into larger units (such as months and quarters) in a column outline. Column outlines work just like row outlines, however, and the levels need not be time-based.

Setting up the formulas

Before you create an outline, you need to make sure that all the summary formulas are entered correctly and consistently. *Consistently* means that the formulas are in the same relative location. Generally, formulas that compute summary formulas (such as subtotals) are entered below the data to which they refer. In some cases, however, the summary formulas are entered above the referenced cells. Excel can handle either method, but you must be consistent throughout the range that you outline. If the summary formulas aren't consistent, automatic outlining won't produce the results that you want.

Note   If your summary formulas aren't consistent (that is, some are above and some are below the data), you still can create an outline, but you must do it manually.

Creating an Outline Automatically

Excel can create an outline for you automatically in a few seconds, whereas it might take you ten minutes or more to do the same thing manually.

To have Excel create an outline, move the cell pointer anywhere within the range of data that you're outlining. Then, choose Data ➪ Group and Outline ➪ Auto Outline. Excel analyzes the formulas in the range and creates the outline. Depending on the formulas that you have, Excel creates a row outline, a column outline, or both.

If the worksheet already has an outline, Excel asks whether you want to modify the existing outline. Click Yes to force Excel to remove the old outline and create a new one.

Note   Excel automatically creates an outline when you use the Data ➪ Subtotals command, which inserts subtotal formulas automatically if you set up your data as a list.

Cross-Reference   The Data ➪ Subtotals command is discussed in Chapter 23 (see the section "Creating Subtotals").

Creating an Outline Manually

Usually, letting Excel create the outline is the best approach. It's much faster and less error-prone. If the outline that Excel creates isn't what you have in mind, however, you can create an outline manually.

When Excel creates a row outline, the summary rows all must be above the data or below the data (they can't be mixed). Similarly, for a column outline, the summary columns all must be to the right of the data or to the left of the data. If your worksheet doesn't meet these requirements, you have two choices:

✦ Rearrange the worksheet so that it does meet the requirements

✦ Create the outline manually

Using an Outline for Text

If you need to present lots of textual information in a workbook—as in user instructions, for example—consider arranging the information in the form of an outline. The accompanying figure shows an example that I developed for one of my shareware products. The user manual is contained on a worksheet, and I created an outline to make locating a specific section easier. I also used a simple macro, attached to a check box, to make it easy for users to expand and collapse the outline.

The workbook shown in the figure is available on this book's CD-ROM.

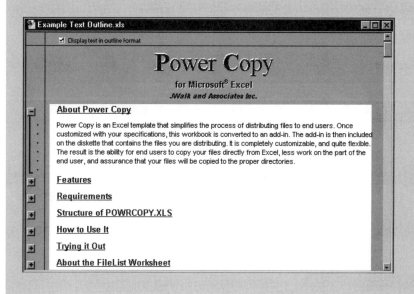

You also need to create an outline manually if the range doesn't contain any formulas. You may have imported a file and want to use an outline to display it better. Because Excel uses the formulas to determine how to create the outline, it is not able to make an outline without formulas.

Creating an outline manually consists of creating groups of rows (for row outlines) or groups of columns (for column outlines). To create a group of rows, click the row numbers for all the rows that you want to include in the group—but do not select the row that has the summary formulas. Then, choose Data ⇨ Group and Outline ⇨ Group. Excel displays outline symbols for the group. Repeat this for each group that you want to create. When you collapse the outline, Excel hides rows in the group. But the summary row, which is not in the group, remains in view.

Note   If you select a range of cells (rather than entire rows or columns) before you create a group, Excel displays a dialog box asking what you want to group. It then groups entire rows or columns based on the range that you select.

You also can select groups of groups to create multilevel outlines. When you create multilevel outlines, always start with the innermost groupings and then work your way out. If you realize that you grouped the wrong rows, you can ungroup the group by selecting Data ➪ Group and Outline ➪ Ungroup.

Excel has toolbar buttons that speed up the process of grouping and ungrouping (see the sidebar "Outlining Tools"). You also can use the following keyboard shortcuts:

✦ **Alt+Shift+right arrow:** Groups selected rows or columns

✦ **Alt+Shift+left arrow:** Ungroups selected rows or columns

Creating outlines manually can be confusing at first, but if you stick with it, you'll become a pro in no time.

Outlining Tools

Excel doesn't have a toolbar devoted exclusively to outlining, but it *does* have one that comes close. The Pivot Table toolbar (see accompanying figure) includes four tools that are handy for working with outlines.

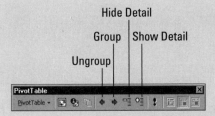

The relevant Pivot Table toolbar buttons are as follows:

Button Name	What It Does
Ungroup	Ungroups selected rows or columns
Group	Groups selected rows or columns
Show Detail	Shows details of selected summary cell
Hide Detail	Hides details of selected summary cell

Using Outlines

This section discusses the basic operations that you can perform with a worksheet outline.

Displaying Levels

To display various outline levels, click the appropriate outline symbol. These symbols consist of buttons with numbers on them (1, 2, and so on) and buttons with either a plus sign (+) or a minus sign (–).

Clicking the 1 button collapses the outline so that it displays no detail, just the highest summary level of information. Clicking the 2 button expands the outline to show one level, and so on. The number of numbered buttons depends on the number of outline levels. Choosing a level number displays the detail for that level, plus any lower levels. To display all levels — the most detail — click the highest-level number.

You can expand a particular section by clicking its + button, or you can collapse a particular section by clicking its – button. In short, you have complete control over the details that Excel exposes or hides in an outline.

If you prefer, you can use the Hide Detail and Show Detail commands on the Data ⇨ Group and Outline menu, to hide and show details, respectively. Or, you can use one of the buttons on the Pivot Table toolbar to hide or show information.

Tip   If you constantly adjust the outline to show different reports, consider using the Custom Views feature to save a particular view and give it a name. Then, you can quickly switch among the named views. Use the View ⇨ Custom Views command for this.

Applying Styles to an Outline

When you create an outline, you can have Excel automatically apply named styles to the summary rows and columns.

Cross-Reference   Chapter 11 discusses named styles.

Excel uses styles with names in the following formats (where *n* corresponds to the outline level):

✦ RowLevel_*n*

✦ ColLevel_*n*

For example, the named style that is applied to the first row level is RowLevel_1. These styles consist only of formats for the font. Using font variations makes distinguishing various parts of the outline a bit easier. You can, of course, modify the styles in any way that you want. For example, you can use the Format ⇨ Style command to change the font size or color for the RowLevel_1 style. After you do so, all the RowLevel_1 cells take on the new formatting. Figure 18-6 shows an outline with the automatic outline styles assigned.

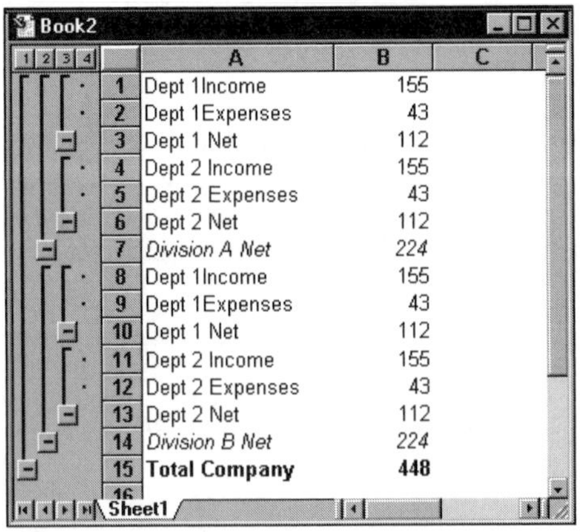

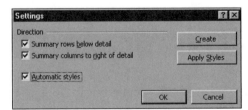

Figure 18-6: This outline has automatic styles.

You can have Excel automatically apply the styles when it creates an outline, or you can apply them after the fact. You control this in the Settings dialog box, shown in Figure 18-7. This dialog box appears when you select Data ⇨ Group and Outline ⇨ Settings.

Figure 18-7: The Settings dialog box.

If the *Automatic styles* check box contains a check when you create the outline, Excel automatically applies the styles. To apply styles to an existing outline, select the outline, choose Data ⇨ Group and Outline ⇨ Settings, and then click the Apply Styles button. Notice that you also can create an outline by using this dialog box.

You may prefer to use Excel's Format ➪ AutoFormat command to format an outline. Several of the AutoFormats use different formatting for summary cells.

Adding Data to an Outline

You may need to add additional rows or columns to an outline. In some cases, you may be able to insert new rows or columns without disturbing the outline, and the new rows or columns become part of the outline. In other cases, you'll find that the new row or column is not part of the outline. If you create the outline automatically, just select Data ➪ Group and Outline ➪ Auto Outline again. Excel makes you verify that you want to modify the existing outline. If you create the outline manually, you need to make the adjustments manually, as well.

Removing an Outline

If you no longer need an outline, you can remove it by selecting Data ➪ Group and Outline ➪ Clear Outline. Excel fully expands the outline by displaying all hidden rows and columns, and the outline symbols disappear. The outline styles remain in effect, however.

Caution You can't "undo" removing an outline, so make sure that you *really* want to remove the outline before you select this command.

Hiding the Outline Symbols

The outline symbols Excel displays when an outline is present take up quite a bit of space (the exact amount depends on the number levels). If you want to see as much as possible onscreen, you can temporarily hide these symbols, without removing the outline. The following are the two ways to do this:

✦ Open the Options dialog box, select the View tab, and remove the check from the Outline Symbols check box

✦ Press Ctrl+8

Note When you hide the outline symbols, the outline still is in effect, and the worksheet displays the data at the current outline level. That is, some rows or columns may be hidden.

To redisplay the outline symbols, either place a check mark in the Outline Symbols check box in the Options dialog box or press Ctrl+8.

The Custom Views feature, which saves named views of your outline, also saves the status of the outline symbols as part of the view, enabling you to name some views with the outline symbols and other views without them.

Creating Charts from Outlines

A worksheet outline also is a handy way to create summary charts. If you have a large table of data, creating a chart usually produces a confusing mess. But, if you create an outline first, then you can collapse the outline and select the summary data for your chart. Figure 18-8 shows an example of a chart created from a collapsed outline. When you expand an outline from which you created a chart, the chart shows the additional data.

Note   If your chart shows all the data in the outline, even when it's collapsed, remove the check from the Plot Visible Cells Only check box in the Chart tab in the Options dialog box.

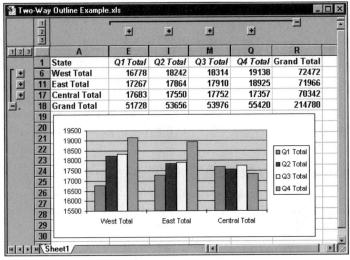

Figure 18-8: This chart was created from the summary cells in an outline.

Summary

This chapter discusses the advantages of creating an outline from worksheet data. It teaches you how to create row outlines and column outlines, either automatically or manually. It also discusses how to use an outline after it is created.

✦   ✦   ✦

Linking and Consolidating Worksheets

This chapter discusses two procedures that are common in the world of spreadsheets: linking and consolidation. *Linking* is the process of using references to cells in external workbooks to get data into your worksheet. *Consolidation* combines or summarizes information from two or more worksheets (which can be in multiple workbooks).

Linking Workbooks

When you link worksheets, you connect them together in such a way that one depends on the other. The workbook that contains the link formulas (or external reference formulas) is called the *dependent* workbook. The workbook that contains the information used in the external reference formula is called the *source* workbook. Note, importantly, that you don't need to open the source workbook when you link it to the dependent workbook.

 Cross-Reference
You also can create links to data in other applications, such as a database program or a word processor. This is a completely different procedure and is the topic of Chapter 29.

Why Link Workbooks?

When you consider linking workbooks, you might ask yourself the following question: If Workbook A needs to access data in another workbook (Workbook B), why not just enter the data into Workbook A in the first place? In some cases, you can. But the real value of linking becomes apparent when you continually update the source workbook. Creating a link in Workbook A to Workbook B means that, in Workbook A, you always have access to the most recent information in Workbook B, because Workbook A is updated whenever Workbook B changes.

Linking workbooks also can be helpful if you need to consolidate different files. For example, each regional sales manager might store data in a separate workbook. You can create a summary workbook that first uses link formulas to retrieve specific data from each manager's workbook and then calculates totals across all regions.

Linking also is useful as a way to break up a large model into smaller files. You can create smaller workbook modules that are linked together with a few key external references. Often, this approach makes your model easier to deal with and uses less memory.

Linking has its downside, however. As you'll see later, external reference formulas are somewhat fragile, and accidentally severing the links that you create is relatively easy. You can prevent this from happening if you understand how linking works. Later in the chapter, some of the problems that may arise are discussed, as well as how to avoid them (see "Potential Problems with External Reference Formulas").

Creating External Reference Formulas

The following are the ways that you can create an external reference formula:

✦ **Type the cell references manually.** These references may be lengthy, because they include workbook and sheet names (and, possibly, even drive and path information). The advantage of manually typing the cell references is that the source workbook doesn't have to be open.

✦ **Point to the cell references.** If the source workbook is open, you can use the standard pointing techniques to create formulas that use external references.

✦ **With the source workbook open, select Edit ➪ Paste Special with the Paste Link button.**

✦ **Use Excel's Data ➪ Consolidate command.** This method is discussed later in the chapter (see "Consolidating Worksheets by Using Data ➪ Consolidate").

Understanding the link formula syntax

This section discusses the concept of external references. The general syntax for an external reference formula is as follows:

```
=[WorkbookName]SheetName!CellAddress
```

Precede the cell address by the workbook name (in brackets), the worksheet name, and an exclamation point. Here's an example of a formula that uses cell A1 in the Sheet1 worksheet of a workbook named Budget:

```
=[Budget.xls]Sheet1!A1
```

If the workbook name or the sheet name in the reference includes one or more spaces, you must enclose the text in single quotation marks. For example, here's a formula that refers to cell A1 on Sheet1 in a workbook named Annual Budget:

```
='[Annual Budget]Sheet1'!A1
```

When a formula refers to cells in a different workbook, that other workbook doesn't need to be open. If the workbook is closed and not in the current folder, you must add the complete path to the reference; for example:

```
='C:\MSOffice\Excel\Budget Files\[Annual Budget]Sheet1'!A1
```

Creating a link formula by pointing

As previously mentioned, you can directly enter external reference formulas, but doing so can cause errors, because you must have every bit of information exactly correct. Instead, have Excel build the formula for you, as follows:

1. Open the source workbook.

2. Select the cell in the dependent workbook that will hold the formula.

3. Enter the formula. When you get to the part that requires the external reference, activate the source workbook and select the cell or range.

4. Finish the formula and press Enter.

You'll see that when you point to the cell or range, Excel automatically takes care of the details and creates a syntactically correct external reference. When you point to a cell reference by using the procedure outlined in the preceding steps, the cell reference is always an absolute reference (such as $A$1). If you plan to copy the formula to create additional link formulas, you can change the absolute reference to a relative reference by removing the dollar signs.

As long as the source workbook remains open, the external reference doesn't include the path to the workbook. If you close the source workbook, however, the external reference formulas change to include the full path. If you use the File ➪ Save As command to save the source workbook with a different name, Excel changes the external references to use the new filename.

Pasting links

The Paste Special command provides another way to create external reference formulas:

1. Open the source workbook.

2. Select the cell or range that you want to link and then copy it to the Clipboard.

3. Activate the dependent workbook and select the cell in which you want the link formula to appear. If you're pasting a range, just select the upper-left cell.

4. Choose Edit ➪ Paste Special and then click the Paste Link button.

Working with External Reference Formulas

You need to understand that a single workbook can contain links that refer to any number of different source workbooks. This section discusses what you need to know about working with links.

Creating links to unsaved workbooks

Excel enables you to create link formulas to unsaved workbooks, and even to nonexistent workbooks. Assume that you have two workbooks open and you haven't saved either of them (they have the names Book1 and Book2). If you create a link formula to Book1 in Book2 and then save Book2, Excel displays the dialog box shown in Figure 19-1. Generally, you should avoid this situation. Simply save the source workbook first.

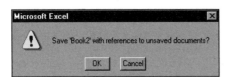

Figure 19-1: This message indicates that the workbook you're saving contains references to a workbook that you haven't yet saved.

You also can create links to documents that don't exist. You might want to do this if you'll be using a source workbook from a colleague, but the file hasn't arrived. When you enter an external reference formula that refers to a nonexistent workbook, Excel displays its File Not Found dialog box, shown in Figure 19-2. If you click Cancel, the formula retains the workbook name that you entered, but it returns an error. When the source workbook becomes available, the error goes away and the formula displays its proper value.

Opening a workbook with external reference formulas

When you open a workbook that contains one or more external reference formulas, Excel retrieves the current values from the source workbooks and calculates the formulas.

If Excel can't locate a source workbook that's referred to in a link formula, it displays its File Not Found dialog box and prompts you to supply a workbook to use for the source workbook.

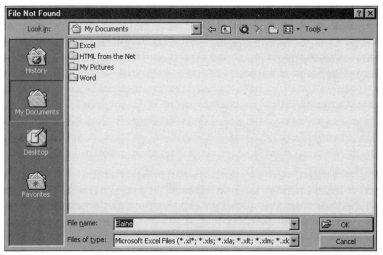

Figure 19-2: When you enter a formula that refers to a nonexistent workbook, Excel displays this dialog box to help you locate the file.

Examining links

If your workbook uses several workbook links, you might want to see a list of source workbooks. To do so, choose the Edit ➪ Links command. Excel responds with the Links dialog box, shown in Figure 19-3. This dialog box lists all source workbooks, plus other types of links to other documents.

Cross-Reference   These other types of links are explained in Chapter 29.

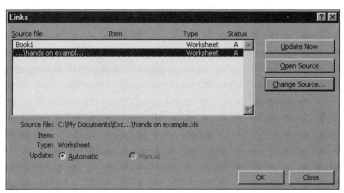

Figure 19-3: The Links dialog box lists all link sources.

Updating links

If you want to ensure that your link formulas have the latest values from their source workbooks, you can force an update. This step might be necessary if you just learned that someone made changes to the source workbook and saved the latest version to your network server.

To update linked formulas with their current value, open the Links dialog box (choose Edit ➪ Links), choose the appropriate source workbook, and then click the Update Now button. Excel updates the link formulas with the latest version of the source workbook.

Excel always sets worksheet links to the Automatic update option in the Links dialog box, and you can't change them to Manual. This means that Excel updates the links only when you open the workbook. Excel doesn't automatically update links when the source file changes.

Changing the link source

A time may come when you need to change the source workbook for your external references. For example, you might have a worksheet that has links to a workbook named Preliminary Budget, but you later receive a finalized version named Final Budget.

You *could* change all the cell links manually, or you could simply change the link source. Do this in the Links dialog box. Select the source workbook that you want to change and click the Change Source button. Excel displays a dialog box that enables you to select a new source file. After you select the file, all external reference formulas are updated.

Severing links

If you have external references in a workbook and then decide that you no longer need the links, you can convert the external reference formulas to values, thereby severing the links. To do so, follow these steps:

1. Select the range that contains the external reference formulas and copy it to the Clipboard.

2. Choose the Edit ➪ Paste Special command. Excel displays the Paste Special dialog box.

3. Select the Values option and click OK.

4. Press Esc to cancel cut-copy mode.

All formulas in the selected range are converted to their current values.

Potential Problems with External Reference Formulas

Using external reference formulas can be quite useful, but the links may be unintentionally severed. In almost every case, you'll be able to reestablish lost links. If you open the workbook and Excel can't locate the file, you're presented with a dialog box that enables you to specify the workbook and re-create the links. You also can change the source file by using the Change Source button in the Links dialog box. The following sections discuss some pointers that you must remember when you use external reference formulas.

Renaming or moving a source workbook

If you rename the source document or move it to a different folder, Excel won't be able to update the links. You need to use the Links dialog box and specify the new source document.

Using the File ⇨ Save As command

If both the source workbook and the destination workbook are open, Excel doesn't display the full path in the external reference formulas. If you use the File ⇨ Save As command to give the source workbook a new name, Excel modifies the external references to use the new workbook name. In some cases, this may be what you want. But in other cases, it may not. Bottom line? Be careful when you use the File ⇨ Save As command with a workbook that is linked to another workbook.

Modifying a source workbook

If you open a workbook that is a source workbook for another workbook, be extremely careful if you don't open the destination workbook at the same time. For example, if you add a new row to the source workbook, the cells all move down one row. When you open the destination workbook, it continues to use the old cell references — which are now invalid. You can avoid this problem in the following ways:

✦ **Open the destination workbook when you modify the source workbook.** If you do so, Excel adjusts the external references in the destination workbook when you make changes to the source workbook.

✦ **Use names rather than cell references in your link formula.** This is the safest approach.

Intermediary links

Excel doesn't place many limitations on the complexity of your network of external references. For example, Workbook A can contain external references that refer to Workbook B, which can contain an external reference that refers to Workbook C. In this case, a value in Workbook A can ultimately depend on a value in Workbook C. Workbook B is an *intermediary link*.

I don't recommend these types of links, but if you must use them, be aware that Excel doesn't update external reference formulas if the workbook isn't open. In the preceding example, assume that Workbooks A and C are open. If you change a value in Workbook C, Workbook A won't reflect the change, because you didn't open Workbook B (the intermediary link).

Consolidating Worksheets

The term *consolidation,* in the context of worksheets, refers to several operations that involve multiple worksheets or multiple workbook files. In some cases, consolidation involves creating link formulas. Here are two common examples of consolidation:

✦ The budget for each department in your company is stored in a separate worksheet in a single workbook. You need to consolidate the data and create a company-wide budget.

✦ Each department head submits his or her budget to you in a separate work-book. Your job is to consolidate these files into a company-wide budget.

These tasks can be very difficult or quite easy; the tasks are easy if the information is laid out exactly the same in each worksheet (as you'll see shortly).

If the worksheets aren't laid out identically, they may be similar enough. In the second example, some budget files submitted to you may be missing categories that aren't used by a particular department. In this case, you can use a handy feature in Excel that matches data by using row and column titles. This feature is discussed later in the chapter (see "Consolidating Worksheets by Using Data ➪ Consolidate).

If the worksheets bear little or no resemblance to each other, your best bet may be to edit the sheets so that they correspond to one another. In some cases, simply reentering the information in a standard format may be more efficient.

You can use any of the following techniques to consolidate information from multiple workbooks:

✦ Use external reference formulas

✦ Copy the data and use the Paste Special command

✦ Use Excel's Data ➪ Consolidate command

✦ Use a pivot table (discussed in Chapter 25)

Using Links to Recover Data from Corrupted Files

Sooner or later (with luck, later), it's bound to happen. You attempt to open an Excel workbook, and you get an error telling you that Excel can't access the file. Most of the time, this indicates that the file (somehow) got corrupted. If you're lucky, you have a recent backup. If you're *very* lucky, you haven't made any changes to the file since you backed it up. But assume that you fell a bit behind on your backup procedures, and the dead file is the only version you have.

Although I don't know of any method to fully recover a corrupt file, I'll share with you a method that sometimes enables you to recover at least some of the data from worksheets in the file (values, not formulas). Your actual success depends on how badly the file is corrupted.

This technique involves creating an external reference formula that refers to the corrupt file. You need to know the names of the worksheets that you want to recover. For example, assume that you have a workbook named Summary Data that you can't open. Further, assume that this workbook is stored on the C drive in a folder named Sheets. This workbook has one sheet, named Sheet1. Here's how to attempt to recover the data from this worksheet:

1. Open a new workbook.

2. In cell A1, enter the following external reference formula:

```
='C:\Sheets\[Summary Data]Sheet1'!A1
```

If you're lucky, this formula returns the value in cell A1 of Sheet1 in the corrupt file.

3. Copy down this formula and to the right to recover as many values as you can.

4. Convert the external reference formulas in the new workbook to values and then save the workbook.

If the corrupt file has additional worksheets, repeat these steps for any other worksheets in the workbook (you need to know the exact sheet names).

Consolidating Worksheets by Using Formulas

Consolidating with formulas simply involves creating formulas that use references to other worksheets or other workbooks. The primary advantages to using this method of consolidation are the following:

✦ Dynamic updating — if the values in the source worksheets change, the formulas are updated automatically.

✦ The source workbooks don't need to be open when you create the consolidation formulas.

If you are consolidating the worksheets in the same workbook—and if all the worksheets are laid out identically—the consolidation task is quite simple. You can just use standard formulas to create the consolidations. For example, to compute the total for cell A1 in worksheets named Sheet2 through Sheet10, enter the following formula:

```
=SUM(Sheet2:Sheet10!A1)
```

You can enter this formula manually or use the multisheet selection technique discussed in Chapter 8 (see "Selecting Multisheet Ranges"). You can then copy this formula to create summary formulas for other cells. Figure 19-4 shows this technique at work.

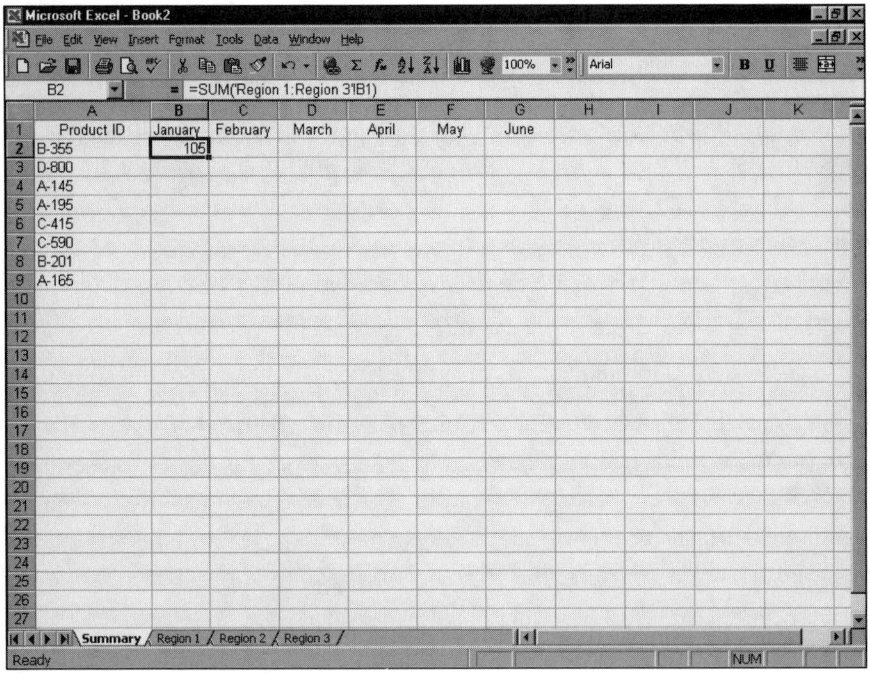

Figure 19-4: Consolidating multiple worksheets by using formulas.

If the consolidation involves other workbooks, you can use external reference formulas to perform your consolidation. For example, if you want to add the values in cell A1 from Sheet1 in two workbooks (named Region1 and Region2), you can use the following formula:

```
=[Region1.xls]Sheet1!A1+[Region2.xls]Sheet1!A1
```

You can include any number of external references in this formula, up to the 1,024-character limit for a formula. However, if you use many external references, such a formula can be quite lengthy and confusing, if you need to edit it.

Caution Remember that Excel expands the references to include the full path — which can increase the length of the formula. Therefore, this expansion may cause the formula to exceed the limit, thus creating an invalid formula.

If the worksheets that you're consolidating aren't laid out the same, you can still use formulas — but you have to ensure that each formula refers to the correct cell.

Consolidating Worksheets by Using Paste Special

Another method of consolidating information is to use the Edit ➪ Paste Special command. This method is applicable only when all the worksheets that you're consolidating are open. The disadvantage — a major disadvantage — is that the consolidation isn't dynamic. In other words, it doesn't generate a formula. So, if any data that was consolidated changes, the consolidation is no longer accurate.

This technique takes advantage of the fact that the Paste Special command can perform a mathematical operation when it pastes data from the Clipboard. Figure 19-5 shows the Paste Special dialog box.

Figure 19-5: The Paste Special dialog box.

Here's how to use this method:

1. Copy the data from the first source range.

2. Activate the destination workbook and select the cell in which you want to place the consolidation formula.

3. Select Edit ➪ Paste Special, click the Add option, and then click OK.

Repeat these steps for each source range that you want to consolidate. As you can see, this can be quite error-prone and isn't really a good method of consolidating data.

Consolidating Worksheets by Using Data ⇨ Consolidate

For the ultimate in data consolidation, use Excel's Data ⇨ Consolidate command. This method is quite flexible, and in some cases, it even works if the source worksheets aren't laid out identically. This technique can create consolidations that are static (no link formulas) or dynamic (with link formulas). The Data ⇨ Consolidate command supports the following methods of consolidation:

✦ **By position:** This method is accurate only if the worksheets are laid out identically.

✦ **By category:** Excel uses row and column labels to match data in the source worksheets. Use this option if the data is laid out differently in the source worksheets or if some source worksheets are missing rows or columns.

Figure 19-6 shows the Consolidate dialog box, which appears when you select Data ⇨ Consolidate. The following list is a description of the controls in this dialog box:

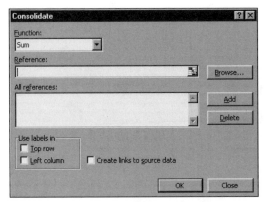

Figure 19-6: The Consolidate dialog box enables you to specify ranges to consolidate.

✦ **Function list box:** Specify the type of consolidation. Usually, you use Sum, but you also can select from ten other options: Count, Avg, Max, Min, Product, Count Nums, StdDev (standard deviation), StdDevp (population standard deviation), Var (variance), or Varp (population variance).

✦ **Reference text box:** Specify a range from a source file that you want to consolidate. You can enter the range reference manually or use any standard pointing technique (if the workbook is open). After you enter the range in this box, click the Add button to add it to the All References list. If you consolidate by position, don't include labels in the range. If you consolidate by category, *do* include labels in the range.

✦ **All references list box:** Contains the list of references that you have added with the Add button.

✦ **Use labels in check boxes:** Use to instruct Excel to perform the consolidation by examining the labels in the top row, the left column, or both positions. Use these options when you consolidate by category.

✦ **Create links to source data check box:** When you select this option, Excel creates an outline that consists of external references to the destination cells in the destination worksheet. Additionally, Excel includes summary formulas in the outline. If you don't select this option, the consolidation doesn't use formulas.

✦ **Browse button:** Displays a dialog box that enables you to select a workbook to open. It inserts the filename in the Reference box, but you have to supply the range reference.

✦ **Add button:** Adds the reference in the Reference box to the All References list.

✦ **Delete button:** Deletes the selected reference from the All References list.

An example

The simple example in this section demonstrates the power of the Data ⇨ Consolidate command. Figure 19-7 shows three single-sheet workbooks that will be consolidated. These worksheets report product sales for three months. Notice, however, that they don't all report on the same products. In addition, the products aren't even listed in the same order. In other words, these worksheets aren't laid out identically — which makes creating consolidation formulas difficult.

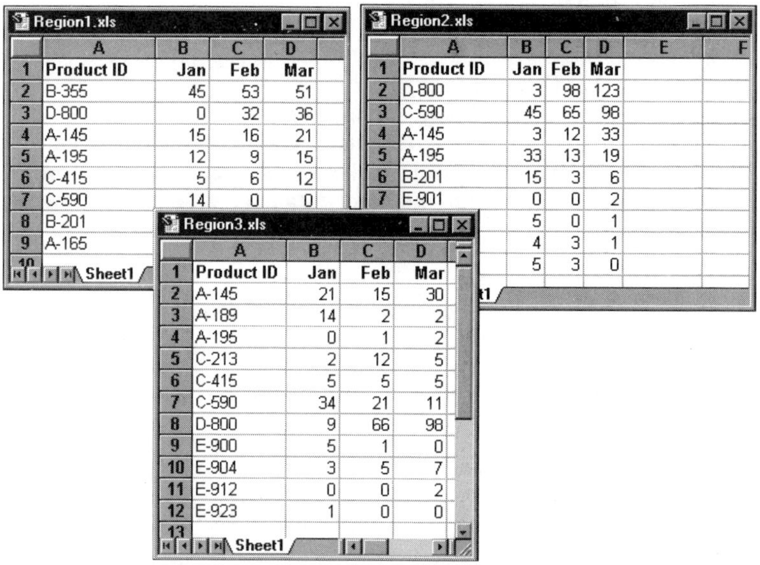

Figure 19-7: Three worksheets to be consolidated.

To consolidate this information, start with a new workbook. The source workbooks can be open or not — it doesn't matter. Follow these steps to consolidate the workbooks:

1. Select Data ➪ Consolidate. Excel displays its Consolidate dialog box.

2. Select the type of consolidation summary that you want to use. Use Sum for this example.

3. Enter the reference for the first worksheet to consolidate. If the workbook is open, you can point to the reference. If it's not open, click the Browse button to locate the file on disk. The reference must include a range. Use **A1:D100**. This range is larger than the actual range to consolidate, but using this range ensures that the consolidation still works if new rows are added to the source file. When the reference in the Reference box is correct, click Add to add it to the All References list.

4. Enter the reference for the second worksheet. You can simply edit the existing reference by changing Region1 to **Region2** and then clicking Add. This reference is added to the All References list.

5. Enter the reference for the third worksheet. Again, you can simply edit the existing reference by changing Region2 to **Region3** and then clicking Add. This final reference is added to the All References list.

6. Because the worksheets aren't laid out the same, select the Left column and Top row check boxes to force Excel to match the data by using the labels.

7. Select the Create links to source data check box to make Excel create an outline with external references.

8. Click OK to begin the consolidation.

In seconds, Excel creates the consolidation, beginning at the active cell. Figure 19-8 shows the result. Notice that Excel created an outline, which is collapsed to show only the subtotals for each product. If you expand the outline, you can see the details. Examine it further, and you'll discover that each detail cell is an external reference formula that uses the appropriate cell in the source file. Therefore, the destination range is updated automatically if any data is changed.

More about consolidation

Excel is very flexible regarding the sources that you can consolidate. You can consolidate data from the following:

✦ Workbooks that are open

✦ Workbooks that are closed (you have to enter the reference manually — but you can use the Browse button to get the filename part of the reference)

✦ The same workbook in which you're creating the consolidation

		A	B	C	D	E	F
	1			Jan	Feb	Mar	
	3	B-355		45	53	51	
	7	D-800		12	196	257	
	11	A-145		39	43	84	
	13	A-189		14	2	2	
	17	A-195		45	23	36	
	19	E-901		0	0	2	
	21	C-213		2	12	5	
	25	C-415		15	11	18	
	29	C-590		93	86	109	
	32	B-201		19	5	9	
	35	E-900		9	4	1	
	38	A-165		8	3	1	
	40	E-904		3	5	7	
	42	E-912		0	0	2	
	44	E-923		1	0	0	
	45						

Data Consolidation Example.xls — Sheet1

Figure 19-8: The result of the consolidation.

And, of course, you can mix and match any of the preceding choices in a single consolidation.

Excel remembers the references that you entered in the Consolidate dialog box and saves them with the workbook. Therefore, if you want to refresh a consolidation later, you won't have to reenter the references.

If you perform the consolidation by matching labels, be aware that the matches must be exact. For example, *Jan* does not match *January*. The matching isn't case-sensitive, however, so *April* does match *APRIL*. In addition, the labels can be in any order, and they need not be in the same order in all the source ranges.

If you don't choose the Create links to source data check box, Excel doesn't create formulas, which generates a static consolidation. If the data on any of the source worksheets changes, the consolidation doesn't update automatically. To update the summary information, you need to select the destination range and repeat the Data ⇨ Consolidate command.

Tip   If you name the destination range **Consolidate_Area**, you don't need to select it before you update the consolidation. Consolidate_Area is a name that has special meaning to Excel.

If you choose the Create links to source data check box, Excel creates an outline. This is a standard worksheet outline, and you can manipulate it by using the techniques described in Chapter 18.

Summary

This chapter discusses two important spreadsheet procedures: linking and consolidation. *Linking* is the process of referring in one worksheet to cells in external workbooks. *Consolidation* is the process of combining or summarizing information from two or more worksheets (which can be in multiple workbooks). This chapter covers various methods of linking and consolidation, and lists potential pitfalls.

✦　　✦　　✦

Creating and Using Array Formulas

This chapter introduces a concept that may be new to
you: *array formulas*. Understanding this special type of
formula may open a whole new world of analytical capability.
Working with arrays (rather than with individual cells)
requires a different type of mind-set. Some people never
quite get the hang of arrays, and others take to this concept
quickly. If you're in the former group, don't despair. Using
array formulas can be considered an optional skill.

Introducing Arrays

This chapter discusses two concepts:

✦ **Array:** A collection of cells or values that is operated on
as a group. An array can be stored in cells or can be a
named constant that consists of multiple elements.

✦ **Array formula:** A formula that uses one or more arrays
either directly or as arguments for a function. An array
formula can occupy one or more cells.

If you've ever done any computer programming, you've probably been exposed to arrays. An *array* is a collection of items.
Excel's arrays can be one-dimensional or two-dimensional.
These dimensions correspond to rows and columns. For
example, a *one-dimensional array* can be a cell range that
occupies cells in one row (a horizontal array) or one column
(a vertical array). A *two-dimensional array* occupies cells in
one or more rows and columns.

You can perform operations on arrays by using *array formulas*. For example, if you construct an array formula to multiply a five-item vertical array by another five-column vertical array, the result is another five-column vertical array that consists of each element in the first array multiplied by each corresponding element in the second array. Because Excel can fit only one value in a cell, the results of an operation such as this one occupy five cells — and the same array formula is in each of the five cells.

Figure 20-1 illustrates this example. Each cell in the range C1:C5 holds the same formula: {=A1:A5*B1:B5}. The result occupies five cells and contains each element of the first array multiplied by each corresponding element in the second array. The brackets around the formula designate it as an array formula (more about this later in "Entering an Array Formula").

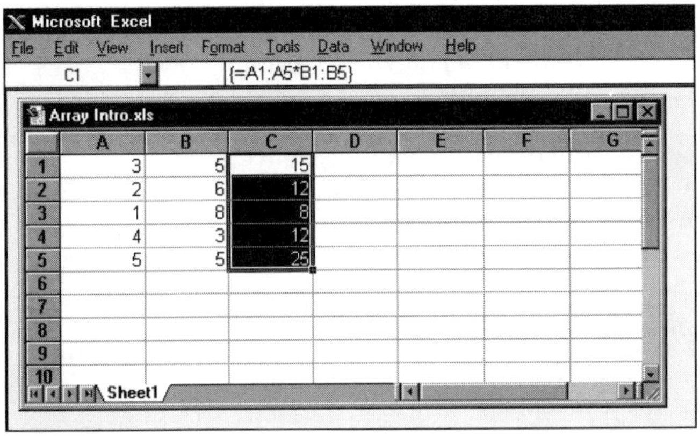

Figure 20-1: A single array formula entered in the range C1:C5 produces results in five cells.

As you will see, arrays have their pros and cons. At the very least, this feature provides an alternative way of doing some operations and is the only way to perform others.

Advantages of Array Formulas

The following are some of the advantages that may be obtained by using array formulas (as opposed to single-cell formulas):

✦ Much more efficient to work with

✦ Eliminate the need for intermediary formulas

✦ Enable you to do things that would otherwise be difficult or impossible

✦ Use less memory

Disadvantages of Array Formulas

This list shows a few disadvantages of array formulas:

✦ Some large arrays can slow your spreadsheet recalculation time to a crawl.

✦ Arrays can make your worksheets more difficult for others to understand.

✦ You must remember to enter an array formula with a special key sequence (Ctrl+Shift+Enter). Otherwise, the result isn't what you expect.

✦ Array formulas cannot be exported to other spreadsheet formats (such as Lotus 1-2-3).

Understanding Arrays

This section presents several examples to help clarify the concept of arrays. As always, you can get more from this chapter if you follow along on your own computer.

Array Formulas Versus Standard Formulas

You often can use a single array formula to substitute for a range of copied formulas. Figure 20-2 shows two examples; the upper worksheet uses standard single-result formulas. The formulas use the SQRT function to calculate the square roots of the values in column A. The formula =SQRT(A3) was entered into cell B3 and copied to the three cells below it. This example uses four different formulas to calculate the results in column B.

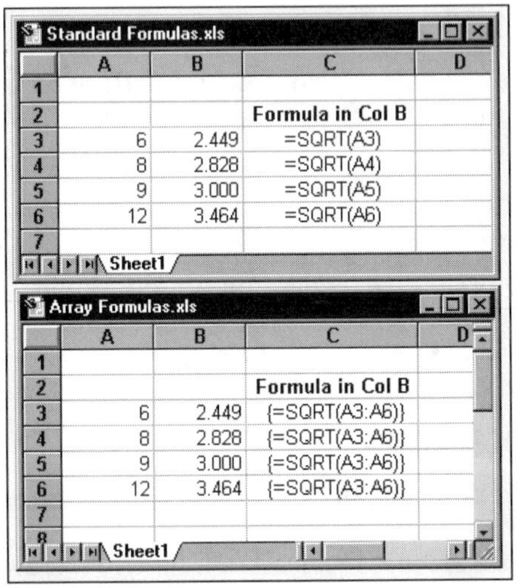

Figure 20-2: These workbooks accomplish the same result, but one uses standard formulas and the other uses an array formula.

The lower workbook uses a single array formula, which is inserted into all four cells. Use the following steps to enter this array formula:

1. Select the range B3:B6.

2. Enter **SQRT(A3:A6)**.

3. Press Ctrl+Shift+Enter to designate the formula as an array formula.

Excel enters the array formula into the three selected cells. It also adds brackets around the formula to indicate that it's an array formula. The key point here is that this example uses only one formula, but the results appear in four different cells, because the formula is operating on a four-cell array.

To further demonstrate that this is, in fact, one formula, try to edit one of the cells in B3:B6. You find that Excel doesn't let you make any changes. To modify an array formula that uses more than one cell, you must select the entire array before you edit the formula.

Virtually no advantage is gained by using an array formula in the preceding example (except perhaps to save the time that it takes to copy the formula). The real value of array formulas becomes apparent as you work through this chapter.

An Array Formula in One Cell

Figure 20-3 shows another example. The worksheet on the left uses standard formulas to calculate the average change from the pretest to the posttest. The worksheet on the right also calculates the average changes, but it uses an array formula. This array formula resides in only one cell, because the result is a single value. This is an example of how an array formula can eliminate the need for intermediary formulas. As you can see, you don't need to include an additional column to calculate the change in scores.

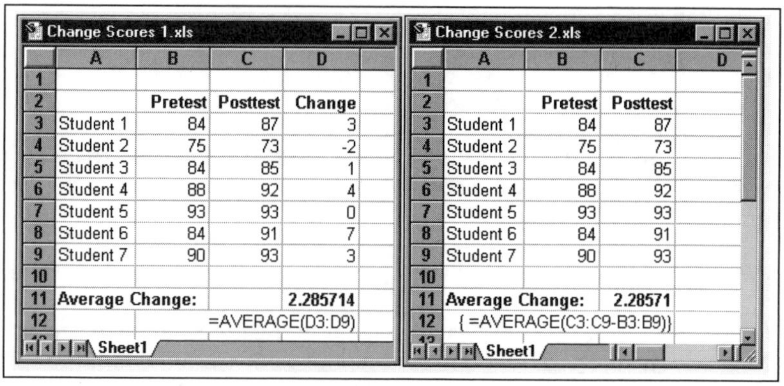

Figure 20-3: Using an array formula to eliminate intermediary formulas.

The formula in cell C11 is as follows:

```
{=AVERAGE(C3:C9-B3:B9)}
```

This array formula operates on two arrays, which are stored in cells. It subtracts each element of B3:B9 from the corresponding element in C3:C9 and produces (in memory) a new seven-element array that holds the result. The AVERAGE function computes the average of the elements in the new array, and the result is displayed in the cell.

Looping with Arrays

Excel's array feature enables you to perform individual operations on each cell in a range — in much the same way as a program language's looping feature enables you to work with elements of an array. For example, assume that you have a range of cells (named Data) that contains positive and negative values. You need to compute the average of just the positive values in the range. Figure 20-4 shows an example of this.

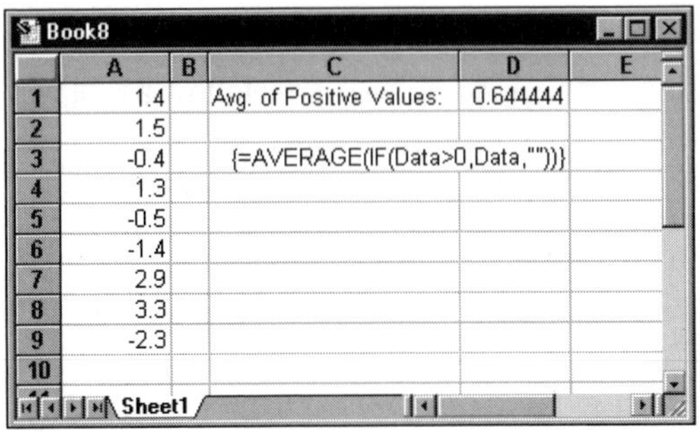

Figure 20-4: You can use an array formula to calculate the average of only the positive values in this range.

One approach is to sort the data and then use the AVERAGE function to calculate the average on only the positive values. A more efficient approach uses the following array formula:

```
={AVERAGE(IF(Data>0,Data,""))}
```

The IF function in this formula checks each element in the input range to see whether it's greater than zero. If so, the IF function returns the value from the input range; otherwise, it returns an empty string. The result is an array that's identical to the input array, except that all nonpositive values are replaced with a null string (the third argument of the IF functions). The AVERAGE function then computes the average of this new array, and the result is displayed in the cell.

The preceding problem can also be solved with the following nonarray formula:

```
=SUMIF(Data,">0",Data)/COUNTIF(Data,">0")
```

Many similar operations can't be performed with a standard formula, however. For example, to calculate the median of the positive values in a range, an array formula is the only solution.

Some more useful examples that use arrays are presented later in this chapter, but for now, some rules are provided for how to work with arrays and array formulas.

Working with Arrays

This section deals with the mechanics of selecting arrays and entering and editing array formulas. These procedures are a little different from working with ordinary ranges and formulas.

Entering an Array Formula

When you enter an array formula into a cell or range, you must follow a special procedure, so that Excel knows that you want an array formula rather than a normal formula. You enter a normal formula into a cell by pressing Enter. You enter an array formula into one or more cells by pressing Ctrl+Shift+Enter.

You can easily identify array formulas, because they are enclosed in brackets in the formula bar. For example, {=SQRT(A1:A12)} is an array formula.

Don't enter the brackets when you create an array formula; Excel inserts them for you. If the result of an array formula consists of more than one value, you must select all the cells before you enter the formula. If you fail to do this, only the first result shows.

Editing an Array Formula

If an array formula occupies multiple cells, you must edit the entire range as though it is a single cell. The key point to remember is that you can't change just one element of an array formula. If you attempt to do so, Excel displays the messages shown in Figure 20-5.

Figure 20-5: Excel's warning message reminds you that you can't edit just one cell of a multicell array.

The following rules apply to multicell array formulas. (If you try to do any of these things, Excel lets you know about it.):

✦ You can't change the contents of any cell that makes up an array formula.

✦ You can't move cells that make up part of an array formula. You can, however, move an entire array formula.

✦ You can't delete cells that form part of an array formula, but you can delete an entire array.

✦ You can't insert new cells into an array range; this rule includes inserting rows or columns that would add new cells to an array range.

To edit an array formula, select all the cells in the array range and activate the formula bar as usual (click it or press F2). Excel removes the brackets from the formula while you're editing it. Edit the formula and then press Ctrl+Shift+Enter to enter the changes. All the cells in the array now reflect your editing changes.

Selecting an Array Range

You can select an array range manually by using the normal selection procedures. Or, you can use either of the following methods:

✦ Move to any cell in the array range. Select Edit ➪ Go To (or press F5), click the Special button, and then choose the Current Array option. Click OK to close the dialog box.

✦ Move to any cell in the array range and press Ctrl+/ to select the entire array.

Formatting Arrays

Although you can't change any part of an array formula without changing all parts, you're free to apply formatting to the entire array or to only parts of it.

Using Array Constants

So far, the examples in this chapter have used cell ranges to hold arrays. You can also use constant values as an array. These constants can be entered directly into a formula or defined by using the Define Name dialog box. Array constants can be used in array formulas in place of a reference to a range of cells. To use an array constant in an array formula, type the set of values directly into the formula and enclose it in brackets. If you defined a name for the array constant, you can use the name instead.

Array constants can be either one-dimensional or two-dimensional. One-dimensional arrays can be either vertical or horizontal. The elements in a one-dimensional horizontal array are separated by commas. The following example is a one-dimensional horizontal array:

```
{1,2,3,4,5}
```

Because this array constant has five values, it requires five cells (in a row). To enter this array into a range, select a range that consists of one row and five columns. Then, enter ={1,2,3,4,5} and press Ctrl+Shift+Enter.

When you use array constants, you must enter the brackets. Excel doesn't provide them for you. The following example is another horizontal array; it has seven elements:

```
{"Sun","Mon","Tue","Wed","Thu","Fri","Sat"}
```

Figure 20-6 demonstrates how to create a named array constant by using the Define Name dialog box.

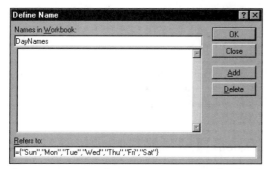

Figure 20-6: Creating an array constant in the Define Name dialog box.

The elements in a one-dimensional vertical array are separated by semicolons. The following is a six-element vertical array:

```
{10;20;30;40;50;60}
```

The following is another example of a vertical array; this one has four elements:

```
{"Widgets";"Sprockets";"Do-Dads";"Thing-A-Majigs"}
```

Two-dimensional arrays also separate the elements in a single row with commas and separate the rows with semicolons. The next example is a 3 × 4 array (three rows, each of which occupies four columns):

```
{1,2,3,4;5,6,7,8;9,10,11,12}
```

Figure 20-7 shows how this array appears in a worksheet. First, the array constant was created and named MyArray. Then, A1:D3 was selected and =MyArray was entered. The array formula was entered into the range by pressing Ctrl+Shift+Enter.

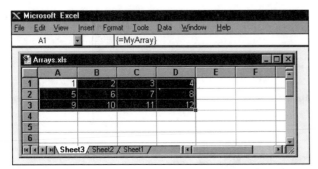

Figure 20-7: An array constant used in a formula.

You can't list cell references, names, or formulas in an array formula in the same way as you list constants. For example, {2*3,3*3,4*3} isn't valid, because it lists formulas. {A1,B1,C1} isn't valid, either, because it lists cell references. Instead, you should use a range reference, such as {A1:C1}.

You must remember an array's dimensions when you're performing operations on it. Consider the following array formula:

```
={2,3,4}*{10,11}
```

This formula multiplies a 1 × 3 array by a 1 × 2 array. Excel returns an array with three values: 20, 33, and #N/A. Because the second array wasn't large enough, Excel generated #N/A as the third element of the result.

Examples of Using Array Formulas

Perhaps the best way to learn about array formulas is by following examples and adapting them to your own needs. This section presents useful examples that give you a good idea of how you can use array formulas.

All the examples presented in this section can be found in a workbook on this book's companion CD-ROM.

Using an Array Constant

Figure 20-8 shows a practical example of an array constant.

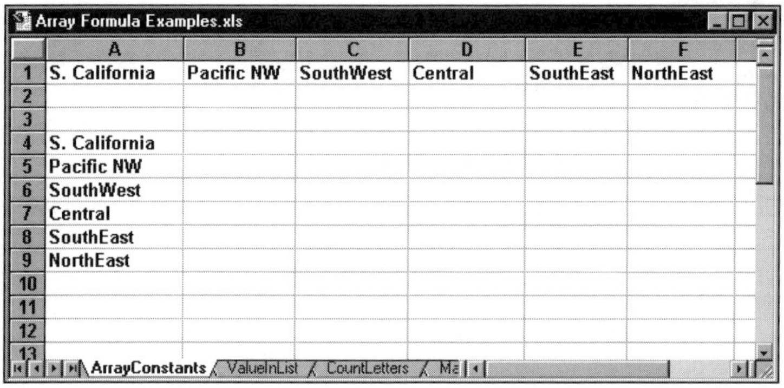

Figure 20-8: Using an array constant to enter the names of sales regions.

The following steps demonstrate how to create this example:

1. Define the following constant, named SalesRegions:

```
={"S. California";"Pacific NW";"SouthWest";"Central";"
SouthEast";" NorthEast"}
```

Because the elements are separated by semicolons, this is a vertical array.

2. Select A4:A9 and enter **=SalesRegions**.

3. Press Ctrl+Shift+Enter.

The worksheet in Figure 20-8 also shows the sales regions displayed horizontally. To do this, select A1:F1 and then enter the following formula (by pressing Ctrl+Shift +Enter):

```
{=TRANSPOSE(SalesRegions)}
```

The TRANSPOSE function converts a horizontal array to a vertical array (and vice versa).

The method just described is one of several ways to enter a stored list quickly into a range of cells. Perhaps a better approach is to create a custom list in the Custom Lists panel of the Options dialog box.

Identifying a Value in a Range

To determine whether a particular value is contained in a range, choose Edit ➪ Find. But, you also can make this determination by using an array formula. Figure 20-9 shows a worksheet with a list of names (named Names). An array formula in cell E4 checks the name that is entered into cell B1 (named TestValue). If the name exists, it displays the text Name is in the list. Otherwise, it displays Name not found.

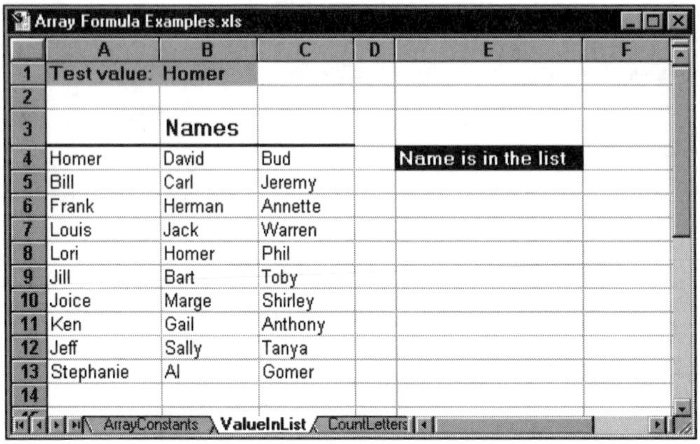

Figure 20-9: Determining whether a range contains a particular value.

The formula in cell E4 is as follows:

```
{=IF(OR(TestValue=Names),"Name is in the list","Name not
found")}
```

This formula compares TestValue to each cell in the range Names. It builds a new array that consists of logical TRUE or FALSE values. The OR function returns TRUE if any one of the values in the new array is TRUE. The IF function determines which message to display based on the result.

Counting Characters in a Range

This example demonstrates how to use nested functions in an array formula to loop through each element in the input range. Figure 20-10 shows a worksheet with text entered in a range named WordList.

The array formula in cell B1 is as follows:

```
{=SUM(LEN(WordList))}
```

This formula is quite straightforward. It creates an array that consists of the length of each word in the WordList range. Then, it uses the SUM formula to add the values in this new array. You can accomplish this without an array formula by using an additional column of formulas and then summing the results.

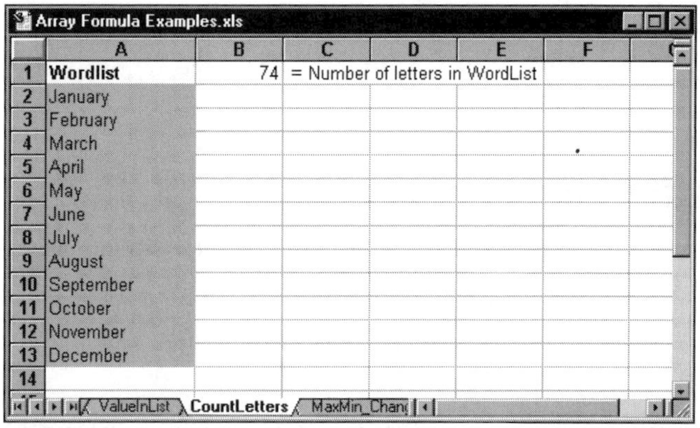

Figure 20-10: This array formula counts the number of characters in a range of text.

Computing Maximum and Minimum Changes

Figure 20-11 shows another example of how an array formula can eliminate the need for intermediary formulas. This worksheet shows two test scores for a group of students. Array formulas compare the two tests and calculate the largest decrease and the largest increase.

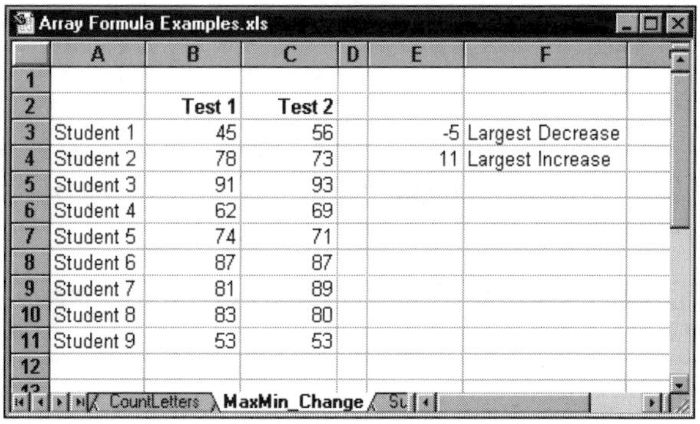

Figure 20-11: Array formulas determine the largest decrease and the largest increase in test scores.

The formulas are as follows:

```
E3:        {=MIN(C3:C11-B3:B11)}
E4:        {=MAX(C3:C11-B3:B11)}
```

Looping Through Characters in a Cell

The following array formula calculates the sum of the digits in an integer, which is stored in a cell named Number:

```
{=SUM(VALUE(MID(Number,ROW($A$1:OFFSET($A$1,LEN(Number)-
1,0)),1))))}
```

This is a rather complex formula that makes use of an interesting trick; thus, it is explained next one part at a time, so that you can see how it works. (Figure 20-12 shows an example.)

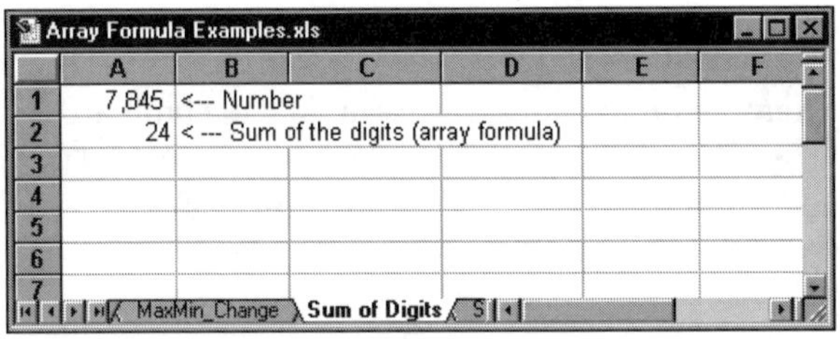

Figure 20-12: An array formula calculates the sum of the digits in a value.

You may be confused by the ROW function (this is the trick). This function is used to generate an array of consecutive integers, beginning with 1 and ending with the number of digits in the absolute value of Number.

If Number is 489, then LEN(Number) is 3. The ROW function can then be simplified as follows:

```
{=ROW($A$1:OFFSET($A$1,3-1,0))}
```

This formula generates an array with three elements: {1,2,3}, which is used as the second argument for the MID function (the third argument is 1). The MID part of the formula, simplified a bit and expressed as values, is the following:

```
{=MID(489,{1,2,3},1)}
```

This formula generates an array with three elements: {4,8,9}. By simplifying again and adding the SUM function, the formula becomes as follows:

```
{=SUM({4,8,9})}
```

This produces the result of 21.

The following is another version of this formula that also works with negative numbers. The ABS function is added to calculate the absolute value of the result:

```
{=SUM(VALUE(MID(ABS(Number),ROW($A$1:OFFSET($A$1,LEN(ABS(Number
))-1,0)),1))))}
```

Summing Every *n*th Value in a Range

The next example can be quite useful. Suppose that you have a range of values and you want to compute the sum of every third value in the list — the first, the fourth, the seventh, and so on. You can't accomplish this with a standard formula. The following array formula does the job, however. It assumes that a cell named Nth determines which values to sum, and that the range to sum is named Data.

```
{=IF(nth=0,0,SUM(IF(MOD(ROW($A$1:OFFSET($A$1,COUNT(Data)-
1,0)),nth)=0,Data,0)))}
```

The formula uses the MOD function to determine which values to sum. The first argument for the MOD function is as follows:

```
ROW($A$1:OFFSET($A$1,COUNT(Data)-1,0))
```

This expression generates an array that begins with 1 and ends with the number of cells in the Data range. If the MOD function returns 0, the value is included in the array to sum.

Notice that a special case exists for when Nth is 0 (that is, sum every cell in the range), because the MOD function returns an error when its second argument is 0.

This formula has a limitation: It works only when Data consists of a single column of values, because it uses the ROW function to determine the element in the array.

Figure 20-13 shows an example that uses the preceding array formula, plus a series of intermediary formulas to calculate the result without using an array formula.

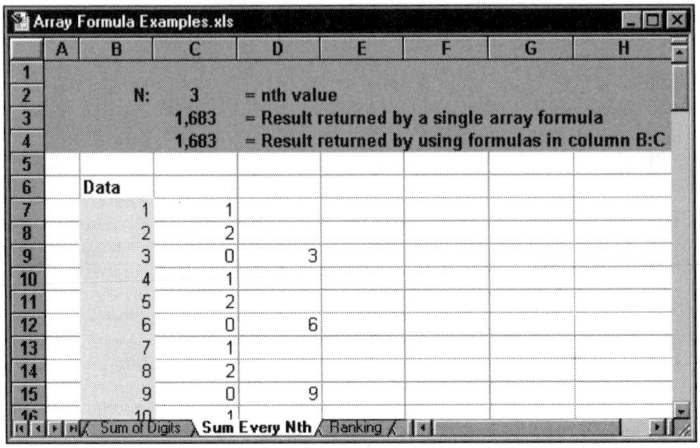

Figure 20-13: You can use an array formula to sum every nth element in a range — or use a series of intermediary formulas (a less-efficient approach).

An Alternate Method of Ranking

Often, computing rank orders for a range of data is helpful. If you have a worksheet with the annual sales figures for 20 salespeople, for example, you may want to know how each person ranks, from highest to lowest.

If you do this sort of work, you've probably discovered Excel's RANK function. You also may have noticed, however, that the ranks produced by this function don't handle ties the way that you may like. For example, if two values are tied for third place, they both receive a rank of 3. Many people prefer to assign each an average (or midpoint) of the ranks — that is, a rank of 3.5 for both values tied for third place.

Figure 20-14 shows a worksheet that uses two methods to rank a column of values (named Sales). The first method (column C) uses Excel's RANK function. Column D uses array formulas to compute the ranks.

The following is the array formula in cell D2:

```
{=IF(((SUM(IF(Sales=B2,1)))=1,(SUM(IF(Sales>=B2,1,0))),(SUM(IF(S
ales>=B2,1)))-((SUM(IF(Sales=B2,1)))-1)*0.5)}
```

This formula was entered into cell D2 and then copied to the cells below it.

The formula is rather complex, but breaking it down into parts should help you understand how it works.

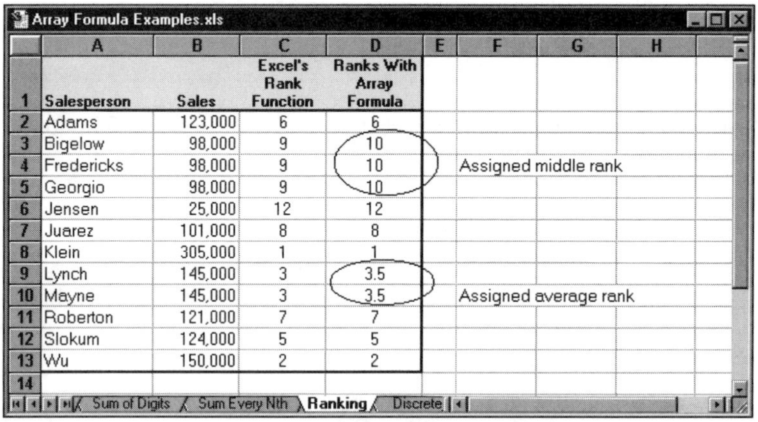

Array Formula Examples.xls

Salesperson	Sales	Excel's Rank Function	Ranks With Array Formula	
Adams	123,000	6	6	
Bigelow	98,000	9	10	
Fredericks	98,000	9	10	Assigned middle rank
Georgio	98,000	9	10	
Jensen	25,000	12	12	
Juarez	101,000	8	8	
Klein	305,000	1	1	
Lynch	145,000	3	3.5	
Mayne	145,000	3	3.5	Assigned average rank
Roberton	121,000	7	7	
Slokum	124,000	5	5	
Wu	150,000	2	2	

Sum of Digits / Sum Every Nth / Ranking / Discrete

Figure 20-14: Ranking data with Excel's RANK function and with array formulas.

Frequency Distributions

Before Excel 5, the only way to calculate frequency distributions was to use array formulas. Beginning with Excel 5, however, the COUNTIF function provides a more direct way to generate frequency distributions.

Figure 20-15 shows a worksheet with a series of scores in column A that range from 1 to 4. Column D contains array formulas to calculate the frequency of each score.

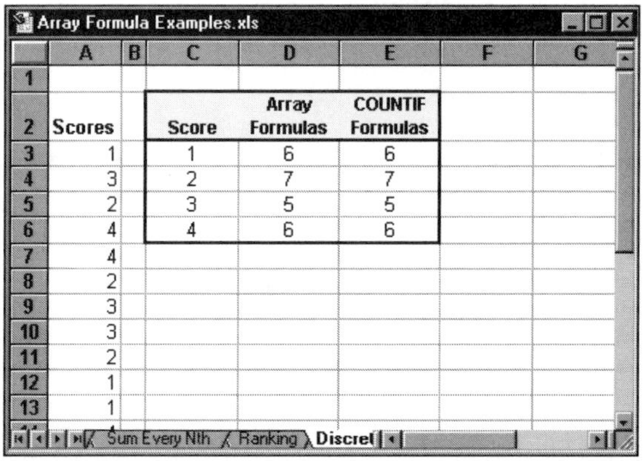

Array Formula Examples.xls

Scores	Score	Array Formulas	COUNTIF Formulas
1	1	6	6
3	2	7	7
2	3	5	5
4	4	6	6
4			
2			
3			
3			
2			
1			
1			

Sum Every Nth / Ranking / Discrete

Figure 20-15: Calculating discrete frequency distributions by using array formulas and COUNTIF functions.

The formula in D6 is as follows:

```
{=SUM(IF(Scores=C3,1)))}
```

The corresponding formulas in column E use the COUNTIF function. The following is the formula in cell E6:

```
=COUNTIF(Scores,C3)
```

Both of these methods count specific values. But what if the scores are noninteger values, as in Figure 20-16? Both types of formulas require modification to handle noninteger data.

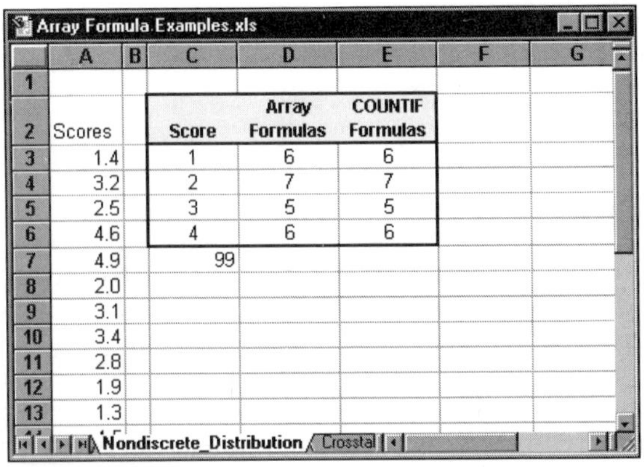

Figure 20-16: Calculating nondiscrete frequency distributions by using array formulas and COUNTIF functions.

The array formula can be modified as follows:

```
=SUM(IF(Scores>=C3,1))-SUM(IF(Scores>=C4,1))
```

The following is the revised COUNTIF formula:

```
=COUNTIF(Scores,">="&C3)-COUNTIF(Scores,">="&C4)
```

The array formula requires you to add an additional value in column C, so that the last array formula doesn't refer to an empty cell (I added a value of 99).

You also can compute distributions by using the Histogram tool in the Analysis ToolPak (see Chapter 28). An advantage to using arrays or COUNTIF functions, however, is that these procedures are dynamic and display the correct values if you change the input data.

Dynamic Crosstabs

The preceding section demonstrates that using COUNTIF is better than using array formulas to calculate frequency distributions. This section demonstrates how to extend these distributions into another dimension and create crosstabs. In this case, an array formula is the only method that can get the job done. This technique enables you to create a dynamic crosstab table that is updated automatically whenever the data is changed. Even a pivot table can't do that!

The worksheet in Figure 20-17 shows a simple expense account listing. Each item consists of the date, the expense category, and the amount spent. Each column of data is a named range, indicated in the first row.

	A	B	C	D	E	F	G	H	I
1	Dates	Categories	Amounts						
2	4-Jan	Food	23.50			Transp	Food	Lodging	
3	4-Jan	Transp	15.00		4-Jan	160.50	49.57	65.95	
4	4-Jan	Food	9.12		5-Jan	20.00	27.80	89.00	
5	4-Jan	Food	16.95		6-Jan	0.00	101.96	75.30	
6	4-Jan	Transp	145.50		7-Jan	11.50	25.00	112.00	
7	4-Jan	Lodging	65.95						
8	5-Jan	Transp	20.00						
9	5-Jan	Food	7.80						
10	5-Jan	Food	20.00						
11	5-Jan	Lodging	89.00		{=SUM(IF($E3&F$2=Dates&Categories,Amounts))}				
12	6-Jan	Food	9.00						
13	6-Jan	Food	3.50						
14	6-Jan	Food	11.02						
15	6-Jan	Food	78.44						

Figure 20-17: You can use array formulas to summarize data such as this in a dynamic crosstab table.

Array formulas were used to summarize this information into a handy table that shows the total expenses, by category, for each day. Cell F3 contains the following array formula, which was copied to the remaining 11 cells in the table:

```
{=SUM(IF($E3&F$2=DATES&CATEGORIES,AMOUNTS))}
```

These array formulas display the totals for each day, by category.

Note　This formula operates similarly to the more simple one demonstrated in the preceding section. This formula has a few new twists, however. Rather than count the number of entries, the formula adds the appropriate value in the Amounts range. It does so, however, only if the row and column names in the summary table match the corresponding entries in the DATES and CATEGORIES ranges. It does the comparison by concatenating (using the & operator) the row and column names and comparing the resulting string to the concatenation of the corresponding DATES and CATEGORIES values. If the two match, the =SUM function kicks in and adds the corresponding value in the AMOUNTS range.

This technique can be customized, of course, to hold any number of different categories and any number of dates. You can eliminate the dates, in fact, and substitute people's names, departments, regions, and so on.

You also can cross-tabulate data by creating a pivot table. But, unlike a pivot table, using the procedure described here is completely dynamic (a pivot table must be updated if the data changes).

Cross-Reference   Pivot tables are discussed in Chapter 25.

Returning the Last Value in a Column

Suppose that you have a worksheet that you update frequently and need to determine the most recently entered value in a column. The following array formula returns the contents of the last nonempty cell in the first 500 rows of column A:

```
=INDIRECT(ADDRESS(MAX((ROW(1:500)*(A1:A500<>""))),COLUMN(A:A)))
```

You can modify this formula to work with a different column, and with a different number of rows in the column. To use a different column, change the column references from A to whichever column you need. To check more than 500 rows, change the two references to row 500.

Returning the Last Value in a Row

The following array formula is similar to the previous formula, but it returns the last nonempty cell in a row (in this case, row 1):

```
=INDIRECT(ADDRESS(1,(MAX((TRANSPOSE(ROW(1:256))*(1:1<>""))))))
```

To use this formula for a different row, change the first argument for the ADDRESS function to the new ADDRESS function and the 1:1 reference to correspond to the row.

A Single-Formula Calendar

The final array formula example is perhaps the most impressive. Figure 20-18 shows a monthly calendar that is calculated using a single array formula entered in B6:H11. This workbook includes a few additional bells and whistles. For example, you can choose the month and year to display by using dialog box controls that are inserted directly on the worksheet. When you change the month or year, the calendar is updated immediately.

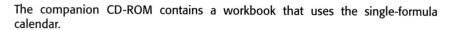

Figure 20-18: This calendar is calculated with a single array formula.

The array formula is as follows:

```
{=IF(MONTH(StartDate)<>MONTH(StartDate-StartDOW+Week*7+Weekday-
1),"",StartDate-StartDOW+Week*7+Weekday-1)}
```

This formula uses a few cell references (StartDate and StartDOW) and two named array constants, which are defined as follows:

```
Week:    ={0;1;2;3;4;5}
Weekday: ={1,2,3,4,5,6,7}
```

I leave it up to you to figure out how this works. Suffice it to say that it took more than a few minutes to develop.

On the CD-ROM

The companion CD-ROM contains a workbook that uses the single-formula calendar.

Tips for Array Formulas

If you've followed along in this chapter, you probably understand the advantages of using array formulas. As you gain more experience with arrays, you undoubtedly will discover some disadvantages.

The primary problem with array formulas is that they slow your worksheet's recalculations, especially if you use large arrays. On a faster system, this may not be a problem. But if you have a slower system and speed is of the essence, you should probably avoid using large arrays.

Array formulas are one of the least understood features of Excel. Consequently, if you plan to share a worksheet with someone who may need to make modifications, you should probably avoid using array formulas. Encountering an array formula when you don't know what it is can be confusing.

You may also discover that you can easily forget to enter an array formula by pressing Ctrl+Shift+Enter. If you edit an existing array, you still must use these keys to complete the edits. Except for logical errors, this is probably the most common problem that users have with array formulas. If you press Enter by mistake after editing an array formula, just double-click the cell to get back into Edit mode and then press Ctrl+Shift+Enter.

Summary

This chapter introduces the concept of *array formulas*, a special type of formula that operates on a group of cells. You can write an array formula by entering a single formula that performs an operation on multiple inputs and produces multiple results — with each result displayed in a separate cell. This chapter also presents several practical examples of array formulas.

✦   ✦   ✦

Using Excel in a Workgroup

If you use Excel on a standalone computer — a PC that's not connected to a network — you can skip this chapter, because it applies only to users who run Excel on a network.

Using Excel on a Network

A computer network consists of a group of PCs that are linked. A common type of network uses a *client-server model*, in which one or more PCs on the network act as dedicated *servers,* because they store files centrally and supply information, while user PCs are called *clients* (they use data in the centrally stored files on the server). Other networks are *peer-to-peer networks* that don't have a central server. Users on a network can perform the following tasks:

- ✦ Access files on other systems
- ✦ Share files with other users
- ✦ Share resources such as printers and fax modems
- ✦ Communicate with each other electronically

In many offices, networks now perform functions that formerly required a mainframe system and *dumb* terminals. Networks are usually less expensive, easier to expand, more manageable, and more flexible in terms of software availability than a mainframe system.

This chapter discusses the Excel features that are designed for network users.

File Reservations

Networks provide users with the ability to share information stored on other computer systems. Most networks have one or more file servers attached. A file server stores files that members of a workgroup share. A network's file server may contain, for example, files that store customer lists, price lists, and form letters. Keeping these files on a file server has two major advantages:

✦ It eliminates the need to have multiple copies of the files stored locally on user PCs.

✦ It ensures that the file is always up to date; for example, if everyone makes changes to the same shared copy of a customer list, there's little likelihood that the portions of the list will be correct while other portions will be obsolete.

Some software applications are *multiuser applications*. Most database software applications, for example, enable multiple users to work simultaneously on the same database files. One user may be updating customer records in the database, while another is extracting records. But what if a user is updating a customer record and another user wants to make a change to that same record? Multiuser database software contains record-locking safeguards that ensure only one user at a time can modify a particular record.

Excel is *not* a multiuser application. When you open an Excel file, the entire file is loaded into memory. If the file is accessible to other users, you wouldn't want someone else to open a file that you've opened. If Excel allowed you to open and change a file that someone else on a network has already opened, the following scenario could happen.

Assume that your company keeps its sales information in an Excel file that is stored on a network server. Elaine wants to add this week's data to the file, so she loads it from the server and begins adding new information. A few minutes later, Albert loads the file to correct some errors that he noticed last week. Elaine finishes her work and saves the file. A while later, Albert finishes his corrections and saves the file. Albert's file overwrites the copy that Elaine saved, and her additions are gone.

This scenario *can't happen,* because Excel uses a concept known as *file reservation.* When Elaine opens the sales file, she has the reservation for the file. When Albert tries to open the file, Excel informs him that Elaine is using the file. If he insists on opening it, Excel opens the file as *read-only.* In other words, Albert can open the file, but he can't save it under the same name. Figure 21-1 shows the message that Albert receives if he tries to open a file that is in use by someone else.

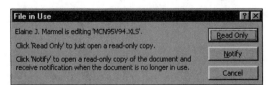

Figure 21-1: The File in Use dialog box appears if you try to open a file that someone else is using.

Albert has these three choices:

✦ **Select Cancel, wait a while, and try again.** He may call Elaine and ask her when she expects to be finished.

✦ **Select Read Only.** This lets him open the file to read it, but doesn't let him save changes to the same filename.

✦ **Select Notify, which opens the file as read-only.** Excel pops up a message when Elaine is finished using the file.

Figure 21-2 shows the message that Albert receives when the file is available.

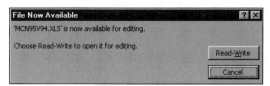

Figure 21-2: The File Now Available dialog box pops up with a new message when the file is available for editing.

Shared Workbooks

Although Excel isn't a multiuser application, it does support a feature known as *shared workbooks,* which enables multiple users to work on the same workbook simultaneously. Excel keeps track of the changes and provides appropriate prompts to handle conflict.

Appropriate Workbooks for Sharing

Although you can designate any workbook as a shared list, only certain workbooks contain information that is appropriate for sharing. The following are examples of workbooks that work well as shared lists:

✦ **Project tracking:** You may have a workbook that contains status information for projects. If multiple people are involved in the project, they can make changes and updates to the parts that are relevant.

✦ **Customer lists:** With customer lists, changes usually occur infrequently, but records are added and deleted.

✦ **Consolidations:** You may create a budget workbook in which each department manager is responsible for his or her department's budget. Usually, each department's budget appears on a separate sheet, with one sheet serving as the consolidation sheet.

Limitations of Shared Workbooks

If you plan to designate a workbook as shared, be aware that you cannot perform any of the following actions while sharing the workbook:

✦ Delete worksheets or chart sheets.

✦ Insert or delete a block of cells. However, you can insert or delete entire rows and columns.

✦ Merge cells.

✦ Define or apply conditional formats.

✦ Set up or change data-validation restrictions and messages.

✦ Insert or change charts, pictures, drawings, objects, or hyperlinks.

✦ Assign or modify a password to protect individual worksheets or the entire workbook.

✦ Create or modify pivot tables, scenarios, outlines, or data tables.

✦ Insert automatic subtotals.

✦ Make changes to dialog boxes or menus.

✦ Write, change, view, record, or assign macros. However, you can record a macro in a shared workbook that you store in another, unshared workbook.

Designating a Workbook As a Shared Workbook

To designate a workbook as a shared workbook, select Tools ➪ Share Workbook. Excel displays the dialog box that is shown in Figure 21-3. This dialog box has two tabs: Editing and Advanced. In the Editing tab, select the check box to allow changes by multiple users and then click OK. Excel then prompts you to save the workbook.

When you open a shared workbook, the window's title bar displays [Shared]. If you no longer want other users to be able to use the workbook, remove the check mark from the Share Workbook dialog box and save the workbook.

Whenever you're working with a shared workbook, you can find out whether any other users are working on the workbook. Choose Tools ➪ Share Workbook, and the Share Workbook dialog box lists the names of the other users who have the file open, as well as the time that each user opened the workbook.

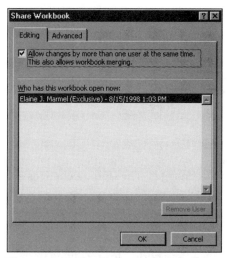

Figure 21-3: The Share Workbook dialog box lets you specify a workbook as a shared workbook.

Advanced Settings

Excel allows you to set options for shared workbooks. Select Tools ➪ Share Workbook and click the Advanced tab to access these options (see Figure 21-4).

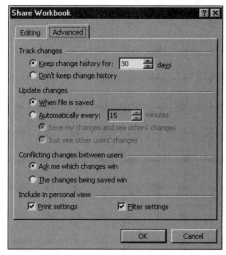

Figure 21-4: The Advanced tab of the Share Workbook dialog box.

Tracking changes

Excel can keep track of the workbook's changes — something known as *change history*. When you designate a workbook as a shared workbook, Excel automatically turns on the change history option, enabling you to view information about previous (and perhaps conflicting) changes to the workbook. You can turn off change history by selecting the option labeled Don't keep change history. You can also specify the number of days for which Excel tracks change history.

Updating changes

While you're working on a shared workbook, you can use the standard File ⇨ Save command to update the workbook with your changes. The Update changes settings determine what happens when you save a shared workbook:

✦ **When file is saved:** You receive updates from other users when you save your copy of the shared workbook.

✦ **Automatically every:** Lets you specify a time period for receiving updates from other users of the workbook. You can also specify whether Excel should save your changes automatically, too, or just show you the changes made by other users.

Conflicting changes between users

As you may expect, multiple users working on the same file can result in some conflicts. For example, assume that you're working on a shared customer database workbook, and another user also has the workbook open. If you and the other user both make a change to the same cell, a conflict occurs. You can specify the manner in which Excel resolves the conflicts by selecting one of two options in the Advanced tab of the Share Workbook dialog box:

✦ **Ask me which changes win:** If you select this option, Excel displays a dialog box to let you determine how to settle the conflict.

✦ **The changes being saved win:** If you select this option, your changes always take precedence.

Include in personal view

The final section of the Advanced tab of the Share Workbook dialog box enables you to specify settings that are specific to your view of the shared workbook. You can choose to use your own print settings and your own data-filtering settings. If you don't place checks in these check boxes, you can't save your own print and filter settings.

Mailing and Routing Workbooks

Excel provides a few additional workgroup features. To use these features, your system must have one of the following items installed:

✦ Office 2000

✦ Microsoft Exchange

✦ A mail system that is compatible with MAPI (Messaging Application Programming Interface)

✦ Lotus cc:Mail

✦ A mail system that is compatible with VIM (Vendor Independent Messaging)

The procedures vary, depending on the mail system that you have installed; for this reason, discussions in the following sections are general in nature. For specific questions, consult your network administrator.

Mailing a Workbook As an E-mail Attachment

Electronic mail, or *e-mail*, is commonplace in most offices, and is an extremely efficient means of communication. Unlike a telephone, e-mail doesn't rely on the recipient of the message being available when you want to send the message.

In addition to sending messages by e-mail, you can send complete files — including Excel workbooks. Like a growing number of software applications, Excel is *mail-enabled,* which means that you don't have to leave Excel to send a worksheet to someone by e-mail.

To send a copy of your workbook to someone on your network, select File ➪ Send To ➪ Mail Recipient (as Attachment). Excel creates an e-mail message with a copy of the workbook attached, using your default e-mail program; in Figure 21-5, Excel opened Outlook Express to send the workbook. You send this e-mail message the same way that you send any message — from your e-mail program. You also can send the message to multiple recipients, the same way that you send any e-mail message to multiple recipients.

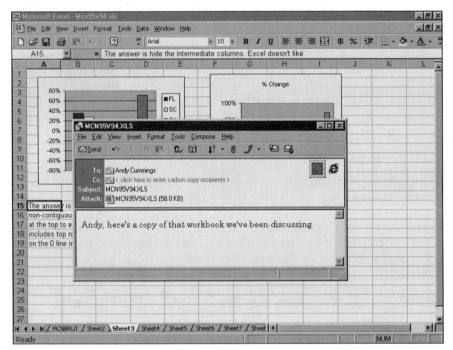

Figure 21-5: Sending a workbook as an attachment to an e-mail message.

Note   When you send any file by using an e-mail program, you send a *copy* of the file. If the recipient makes changes to the notebook, the changes do not appear in your copy of the workbook.

Routing a Workbook to Others

If you choose File ➪ Send To ➪ Routing Recipient, Excel enables you to attach a routing slip to a workbook, similar to the one you see in Figure 21-6. Routing a workbook is most useful when you want the first person in the group to review (and possibly edit) the workbook and then send it to the next person on the list. For example, if you're responsible for your department's budget, you may need input from Alice — and her input may depend on Andy's input. You can set up the workbook and then route it to the others so that they can make their respective additions. When you set up the routing slip, you can tell Excel to return the workbook to you when the routing is finished.

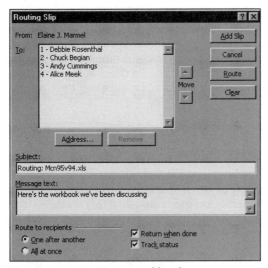

Figure 21-6: Routing a workbook.

When you route a workbook, you have the following two options:

✦ **Sequential routing:** Enables you to route the workbook sequentially to workgroup members. When the first recipient is finished, the workbook goes to the second recipient. When the second recipient is finished, the workbook goes to the third, and so on. When all recipients have received the workbook, it can be returned to you. Choose One after another at the bottom of the Routing Slip dialog box for this type of routing.

✦ **Simultaneous routing:** Enables you to route the workbook to all recipients at once. You receive a copy of the workbook from each recipient (not just one copy). This type of routing is useful if you want to solicit comments from a group of coworkers, and you want the responses back quickly (you don't want to wait until a single worksheet makes the circuit). Choose All at once at the bottom of the Routing Slip dialog box for this type of routing.

Click Route to route the workbook immediately. If you don't want to route immediately, click Add Slip. Later, when you're ready to route, choose File ➪ Send To ➪ Next Routing Recipient. Either choice places the workbook in the outgoing mail folder of your e-mail program. To actually route the workbook, open your e-mail program to send the message.

Note   Whether you route or attach a workbook to an e-mail message, Excel uses your e-mail program. Since you can send a workbook to a number of people, either as an e-mail attachment or by using a routing slip, the distinction between the two methods lies in the distinction between sequential and simultaneous routing. If you choose simultaneous routing and you *don't* place a check in the Return when done check box, routing and attaching are identical, because you can't guarantee a reply to e-mail.

Summary

This chapter presents a basic overview of using Excel in a network environment. It explains how the concept of a file reservation prevents two users from modifying a workbook simultaneously. Excel's shared workbook feature, however, lets multiple users work on a single workbook at the same time. The chapter concludes with a discussion of mailing and routing workbooks.

✦   ✦   ✦

Analyzing Data

Importing Data from Other Sources

When you get right down to it, Excel can be described as a tool that manipulates data — the numbers and text that you use in a worksheet. But before you can manipulate data, it must be present in a worksheet. This chapter describes a variety of data-importing techniques.

An Overview of Importing

The following are the six basic ways to import data into Excel:

✦ Enter the data manually by typing values and text into cells

✦ Generate data by using formulas or macros

✦ Use Query (or a pivot table) to import data from an external database

✦ Import data from an HTML document on the Internet or a corporate intranet

✦ Copy data from another application by using the Windows Clipboard

✦ Import data from another (non-Excel) file

This chapter deals primarily with the last two methods: Clipboard copying and foreign-file importing.

Cross-Reference

Chapter 29 is somewhat related to this topic. It deals with linking to and from other applications and embedding objects. Querying external databases is covered in Chapter 24, and pivot tables are covered in Chapter 25. Chapter 30 discusses how Excel works with the Internet.

A Few Words About Data

Data is a broad concept that means different things to different people. Data is basically raw information that can come in any number of forms. For example, data can be numbers, text, or a combination. Most of what you do in Excel involves manipulating data in one way or another.

As computers become more commonplace, data is increasingly available in machine-readable formats (otherwise known as *files*). Not too long ago, major data suppliers provided printed reports to their clients. Now, data suppliers commonly offer a choice of formats: paper or disk.

Data that is stored in files can be in a wide variety of formats. Common file formats for distributing data include Lotus 1-2-3 files (WKS and WK1), dBASE files (DBF), and text files (which come in several varieties). Excel's file format is rather complex, and the format tends to change with every new version of Excel. Consequently, the Excel file format is not widely used for the general distribution of data.

Note   The file format for Excel 2000 files is the same as the file format for Excel 97. However, if you use an Excel 2000 file in Excel 97, you will have access only to Excel 97 features.

As an Excel user, you need to understand the types of data that you can access either directly or indirectly.

File Formats Supported by Excel

Rarely does a computer user work with only one application or interact only with people using the same applications he or she uses. Suppose that you're developing a spreadsheet model that uses data from last year's budget, which is stored in your company's mainframe. You can request a printout of the data, of course, and manually enter it into Excel. If the amount of data isn't too large, this route may be the most efficient. But what if you have hundreds of entries to make? Your mainframe probably can't generate an Excel workbook file, but an excellent chance exists that it can send the report to a text file, which you can then import into an Excel worksheet. Potentially, you can save several hours of work and virtually eliminate data-entry errors.

As you know, Excel's native file format is an XLS file. In addition, Microsoft included the capability to read other file formats directly. For example, you can open a file that was created in several other spreadsheet products, such as Lotus 1-2-3 and Quattro Pro. Table 22-1 lists all the file formats that Excel can read (excluding its own file types).

To open any of these files, choose File ➪ Open and select the file type from the drop-down list labeled Files of type (see Figure 22-1)to display only the files of the selected type in the file list. If the file is a text file, Excel's Text Import Wizard appears, to help you interpret the file. The Text Import Wizard is discussed later in this chapter.

Table 22-1	
File Formats Supported by Excel	
File Type	*Description*
Text	Space delimited, tab delimited, and comma delimited
Lotus 1-2-3	Spreadsheet files generated by Lotus 1-2-3 for DOS Release 1.x, Release 2.x, Release 3.x, and 1-2-3 for Windows
Quattro Pro/DOS	Files generated by Novell's Quattro Pro for DOS spreadsheet
Microsoft Works 2.0	Files generated by Microsoft Works 2.0
dBASE	Database files in the DBF format
SYLK	Files generated by Microsoft's MultiPlan spreadsheet
Data Interchange Format	Files generated by the VisiCalc spreadsheet
HTML	Files developed for the World Wide Web
Quattro Pro for Windows	Files generated by Corel's Quattro Pro for Windows spreadsheet

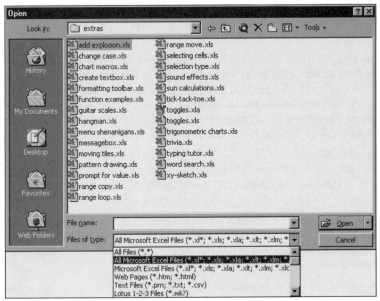

Figure 22-1: Use the Open dialog box to import a foreign file.

You should understand, however, that being able to read a file and translating it perfectly are two different matters. In some cases, you may encounter one or more of the following problems while reading a foreign file into Excel:

✦ Some formulas aren't translated correctly

✦ Unsupported functions aren't translated

✦ Formatting is incorrect

✦ Column widths are incorrect

When you open a file that wasn't produced by Excel, examine it carefully to ensure that Excel retrieved the data correctly.

The following sections discuss the various types of files that Excel can read. Each section discusses a file type and lists that file type's associated file extensions.

If a colleague sends you a file that Excel can't open, don't give up. Simply ask your colleague to save the spreadsheet in a format that Excel *can* read. For example, many applications can save files in 1-2-3 format, and most applications can export to a text file format.

Lotus 1-2-3 Spreadsheet Files

Lotus spreadsheets come in several flavors:

✦ **WKS files:** Single-sheet files used by 1-2-3 Release 1.*x* for DOS. Excel can read and write these files. If you export a workbook to a WKS file, Excel saves only the active worksheet, because 1-2-3 Release 1.*x* supports only one worksheet per workbook.

✦ **WK1 files:** Single-sheet files used by 1-2-3 Release 2.*x* for DOS. The formatting for these files is stored in ALL files (produced by the Allways add-in) or FM1 files (produced by the WYSIWYG add-in). Excel can read and write all of these file types. When you save a file to the WK1 format, you can choose which (if any) type of formatting file to generate. And, like WKS files, if you export a workbook to a WK1 file, Excel saves only the active worksheet.

✦ **WK3 files:** Multisheet (potentially) files generated by 1-2-3 Release 3.*x* for DOS, 1-2-3 Release 4.*x* for DOS, and 1-2-3 Release 1.*x* for Windows. The formatting for these files is stored in FM3 files (produced by the WYSIWYG add-in). Excel can read and write WK3 files with or without the accompanying FM3 file.

✦ **WK4 files:** Multisheet (potentially) files generated by 1-2-3 Release 4.*x* for Windows and 1-2-3 Release 5.*x* for Windows. Lotus combined formatting and data into one file, eliminating the separate formatting file. Excel can read and write these files.

✦ **1-2-3 files:** Multisheet (potentially) files generated by 1-2-3 97 (also known as Release 6) and 1-2-3 Millenium Edition (also known as Release 7). Excel can neither read nor write these files.

If you plan to import or export 1-2-3 files, I urge you to read the online Help for general guidelines and for specific types of information that may not be translated.

Excel evaluates some formulas differently from 1-2-3. To ensure complete compatibility when you work with an imported 1-2-3 file, choose Tools ⇨ Options, select the Transition tab, and then check the box labeled Transition Formula Evaluation.

Quattro Pro Spreadsheet Files

Quattro Pro files exist in several versions:

+ **WQ1 files:** Single-sheet files generated by Quattro Pro for DOS Versions 1, 2, 3, and 4. Excel can read and write these files. If you export a workbook to a WQ1 file, Excel saves only the active worksheet.

+ **WQ2 files:** Multisheet (potentially) files generated by Quattro Pro for DOS Version 5. Excel can neither read nor write this file format.

+ **WB1 files:** Multisheet (potentially) files generated by Quattro Pro for Windows Versions 1 and 5 (there are no Versions 2 through 4). Excel can read (but not write) this file format.

+ **WB2 files:** Multisheet (potentially) files generated by Quattro Pro for Windows Version 6. Excel can neither read nor write this file format.

Database File Formats

DBF files are single-table database files generated by dBASE and several other database programs. Excel can read and write DBF files up to and including dBASE 4.

If you have Microsoft Access installed on your system, you can take advantage of a feature that converts a worksheet list into an Access database file. To use this feature, you must install the Access Links add-in in Excel (you need your Office 2000 CD-ROM). Use the Data ⇨ Convert to MS Access command.

Excel can't read or write any other database file formats directly. If you install the Query add-in, however, you can use Query to access many other database file formats and then copy or link the data into an Excel worksheet.

See Chapter 24 for details on how to use Query to copy or link data from other database file formats into an Excel worksheet.

Text File Formats

Text files simply contain data—no formatting. The following relatively standard text file formats exist, although no standard file extensions exist:

✦ **Tab-delimited files:** Each line consists of fields that are separated by tabs. Excel can read these files, converting each line to a row and each field to a column. Excel also can write these files, using TXT as the default extension.

✦ **Comma-separated files:** Each line consists of fields that are separated by commas. Sometimes, text appears in quotation marks. Excel can read these files, converting each line to a row and each field to a column. Excel can also write these files, using CSV as the default extension.

✦ **Space-delimited files:** Each line consists of fields that are separated by spaces. Excel can read these files, converting each line to a row and each field to a column. Excel also can write these files, using PRN as the default extension.

If you want your exported text file to use a different extension, specify the complete filename and extension in quotation marks. For example, saving a workbook in comma-separated format normally uses the CSV extension. If you want your file to be named output.txt (with a TXT extension), enter **"output.txt"** in the File name box in the Save As dialog box.

When you attempt to load a text file into Excel, the Text Import Wizard kicks in to help you specify how you want Excel to retrieve the file (discussed in detail later in the chapter).

HTML Files

Excel can read and save files in HTML (Hypertext Markup Language) format, a file format that is used on the World Wide Web. And, through the use of XML (Extensible Markup Language), HTML files retain all document properties, including fonts and formatting.

Using Excel, you can edit any Excel document from within a Web browser. While you are viewing a page that was created in an Office application, such as Excel, click the Edit button on the browser's toolbar. Office opens the document in the application that was used to create it. You can then edit the Web page and resave it in any of the file formats that the application supports or in HTML.

Other File Formats

The following are two other types of file formats that you will rarely encounter; I haven't seen a DIF file in ages, and I've never seen a SYLK file.

✦ **Data Interchange Format (DIF):** Used by VisiCalc. Excel can read and write these files.

✦ **Symbolic Link (SYLK):** Used by MultiPlan. Excel can read and write these files.

Using the Clipboard to Get Data

Using the Windows Clipboard is a another method of importing data into your worksheet. The process involves selecting data from another application and copying the data to the Clipboard. Then, you reactivate Excel and paste the information to the worksheet. The exact results that you get can vary quite a bit, depending on the type of data that you copied and the Clipboard formats that it supports. Obviously, you must have a copy of the other application installed on your system.

Note   If you copy information from another Office application, you use the Office Clipboard, not the Windows Clipboard. The Office Clipboard supports copying and pasting of all formats used in all Office applications.

About the Clipboard

As you read in Chapter 8, Office 2000 provides Windows 95 or Windows 98 with two clipboards. The original Windows Clipboard remains; whenever you cut or copy information from a Windows program, Windows stores the information on the Windows Clipboard, which is an area of memory. Each time that you cut or copy information, Windows replaces the information previously stored on the Clipboard with the new information that you cut or copied. The Windows Clipboard can store data in a variety of formats. Because Windows manages it, information on the Windows Clipboard can be pasted to other Windows applications, regardless of where it originated. Normally, you can't see information stored on the Windows Clipboard (nor would you want to).

Note   To view the Windows Clipboard contents, you can run the Clipboard Viewer program, which comes with Windows. The Clipboard Viewer may or may not be installed on your system (it is not installed by default). You can use the Clipboard Viewer to view only the last piece of information that you copied to the Office Clipboard.

When you copy or cut data to the Clipboard, the source application places one or more formats on the Clipboard along with the data. Different applications support different Clipboard formats. When you paste Clipboard data into another application, the destination application determines which format it can handle and typically selects the format that either provides the most information or is appropriate for where you are pasting it. If you view cells copied from Excel in the Clipboard Viewer, by default, you'll see a row/column reference rather than the actual information that you copied (see Figure 22-2). In some cases, you can use the Display command in the Clipboard Viewer application to view the Clipboard data in a different format. For example, you can display a range of cells from Excel as a picture, bitmap, text, OEM text, or a DIB bitmap. Figures 22-3, 22-4, 22-5, and 22-6, show examples of the same Excel range as it appears in the Clipboard Viewer when using different Display formats.

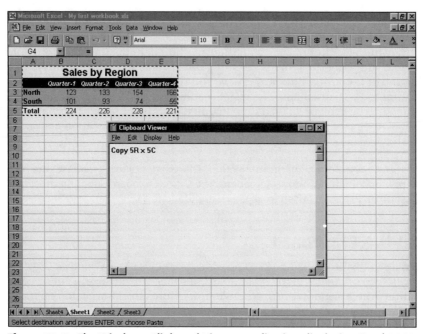

Figure 22-2: The Windows Clipboard Viewer application displaying Excel 2000 data in default format, Display Text.

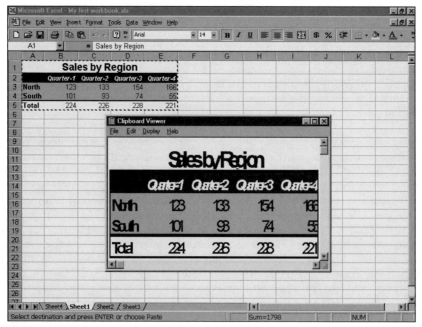

Figure 22-3: The same data in Picture format.

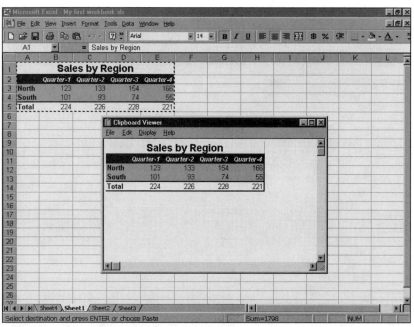

Figure 22-4: Both Bitmap and DIB Bitmap format closely resemble the formatted appearance of the data in Excel.

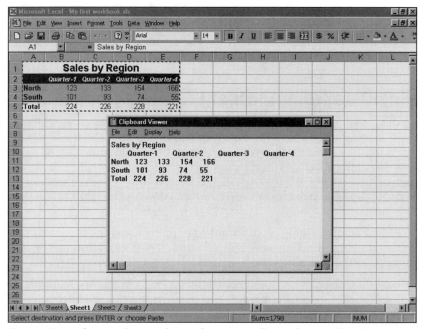

Figure 22-5: The Text format shows the text similar to the way that it appears in the Notepad.

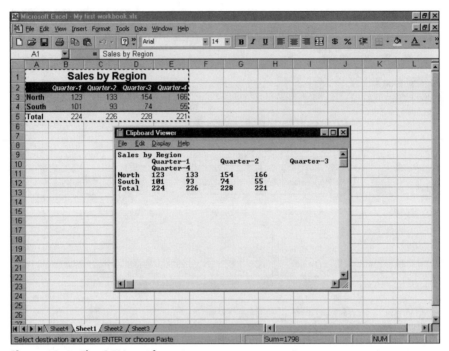

Figure 22-6: The OEM text format.

Importantly, the format that you select in the Clipboard Viewer *doesn't* affect how Excel copies the data. In some cases, however, you can use Excel's Edit ➪ Paste Special command to select alternate methods of pasting the data.

Copying Data from Another Windows Application

Copying data from one Windows application to another is quite straightforward. The *source application* contains the data that you're copying, and the *destination application* receives the data that you're copying. Use the following steps to copy data from one application into another:

1. Activate the source document window that contains the information you want to copy.

2. Select the information that you want to copy by using the mouse or the keyboard. If Excel is the source application, this information can be a cell, range, chart, or drawing object.

3. Select Edit ➪ Copy (or any available shortcut). A copy of the information is sent to the Windows Clipboard. If you're copying from an Office application, a copy of the information is also sent to the Office Clipboard.

4. Activate the destination application. If it isn't open, you can start it without affecting the contents of the Clipboard.

5. Move to the position to which you want to paste in the destination application.

6. Select Edit ⇨ Paste from the menu in the destination application. If the Clipboard contents aren't appropriate for pasting, the Paste command is grayed (not available).

In Step 3, you also can select Edit ⇨ Cut from the source application menu. This step erases the selection from the source application after it's placed on the Clipboard.

Many Windows applications use a common keyboard convention for the Clipboard commands. Generally, this technique is a bit faster than using the menus, because these keys are adjacent to each other. The shortcut keys and their equivalents are the following:

Ctrl+C   Edit ⇨ Copy

Ctrl+X   Edit ⇨ Cut

Ctrl+V   Edit ⇨ Paste

You need to understand that Windows applications vary in how they respond to data that you paste from the Clipboard. If the Edit ⇨ Paste command isn't available (it is grayed on the menu) in the destination application, the application can't accept the information from the Clipboard. If you copy a table from Word for Windows to Excel, the data translates into cells perfectly—complete with formatting. Copying data from other applications may not work as well; for example, you may lose the formatting, or you may end up with all the data in a single column rather than in separate columns. As discussed later in this chapter, you can use the Convert Text to Columns Wizard to convert this data into columns.

If you plan to do a great deal of copying and pasting between two applications, experiment until you understand how the two applications can handle each other's data.

Copying Data from a Non-Windows Application

You also can use the Windows Clipboard with non-Windows applications running in a DOS window. As you may know, you can run non-Windows programs from Windows either in a window or in full-screen mode (the application takes over the complete screen).

When you're running a non-Windows application in Windows, you can press Alt+Print Screen to copy the entire screen to the Clipboard. The screen contents can then be pasted into a Windows application (including Excel). To copy only part of the screen, you must run the application in a window: press Alt+Enter to toggle between full-screen mode and windowed mode. You can then click the Control menu, choose Edit ⇨ Mark, and select text from the window. This window may or may not have a toolbar displayed. If it does not, follow these steps:

1. Right-click the title bar and select the Toolbar option.

2. Click the Mark tool and select the text to copy.

3. Click the Copy tool to copy the selected text to the Clipboard.

4. Activate Excel.

5. Select Edit ⇨ Paste to copy the Clipboard data into your worksheet.

Figure 22-7 shows Quattro Pro running in a DOS window. Some text is selected.

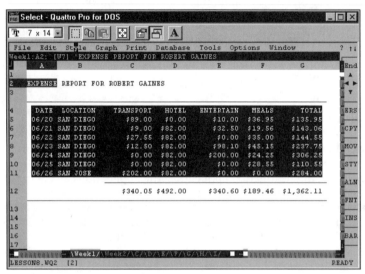

Figure 22-7: Copying data from Quattro Pro for DOS.

If you use this technique and copy to Excel, the information is pasted as text in a single column. In other words, even if you copy information from neatly formatted columns, it's all pasted into a single column in Excel. But don't fret — you can use Excel's Convert Text to Columns Wizard to convert this data into columns.

You're limited to copying one screen of information at a time — you can't scroll the DOS application while you're selecting text.

Importing Text Files

Text files (sometimes referred to as ASCII files) are usually considered to be the lowest-common-denominator file type. Such files contain only data, with no formatting. Consequently, most applications can read and write text files. So, if all else fails, you can probably use a text file to transfer data between two applications that don't support a common file format. Because text files are so commonly used, this entire section is devoted to discussing them and explaining how to use Excel's Text Import Wizard.

About Text Files

You may find it helpful to think of some text files in terms of a database table. Each line in the text file corresponds to a database record, and each record consists of a number of fields. In Excel, each line (or record) is imported to a separate row, and each field goes into a separate column. Text files come in two types: delimited and nondelimited.

Text files consist of plain text and end-of-line markers. *Delimited* text files use a special character to separate the fields on each line — typically a comma, a space, or a tab (but occasionally, you'll see other delimiters used). In addition, text is usually (but not always) enclosed in quotation marks.

Nondelimited files don't contain a special field-separator character. Often, however, each field is a fixed length, enabling you easily to break each line of text into separate columns. When you view a nondelimited file, the data often appears to be in columns.

If you use a proportional font, such as Arial or Times Roman, the fields of text file may appear to not line up, although they actually do. In proportional font sets, each character uses a different amount of horizontal space. For best results, use a non-proportional font, such as Courier New, when working with text files. Excel uses Courier New in its Text Import Wizard dialog box. Figure 22-8 shows the same text displayed in Arial and Courier New fonts.

	A	B	C	D	E	F	G	H
1	DATE LOCATION	TRANSPORT	HOTEL	ENTERTAIN	MEALS	TOTAL		
2	06/20 SAN DIEGO	$89.00	$0.00	$10.00	$36.95	$135.95		
3	06/21 SAN DIEGO	$9.00	$82.00	$32.50	$19.56	$143.06		
4	06/22 SAN DIEGO	$27.55	$82.00	$0.00	$35.00	$144.55		
5	06/23 SAN DIEGO	$12.50	$82.00	$98.10	$45.15	$237.75		
6	06/24 SAN DIEGO	$0.00	$82.00	$200.00	$24.25	$306.25		
7	06/25 SAN DIEGO	$0.00	$82.00	$0.00	$28.55	$110.55		
8	06/26 SAN JOSE	$202.00	$82.00	$0.00	$0.00	$284.00		
9								
10	DATE LOCATION	TRANSPORT	HOTEL	ENTERTAIN	MEALS	TOTAL		
11	06/20 SAN DIEGO	$89.00	$0.00	$10.00	$36.95	$135.95		
12	06/21 SAN DIEGO	$9.00	$82.00	$32.50	$19.56	$143.06		
13	06/22 SAN DIEGO	$27.55	$82.00	$0.00	$35.00	$144.55		
14	06/23 SAN DIEGO	$12.50	$82.00	$98.10	$45.15	$237.75		
15	06/24 SAN DIEGO	$0.00	$82.00	$200.00	$24.25	$306.25		
16	06/25 SAN DIEGO	$0.00	$82.00	$0.00	$28.55	$110.55		
17	06/26 SAN JOSE	$202.00	$82.00	$0.00	$0.00	$284.00		
18								

Figure 22-8: Using a proportional font may obscure columns in a text file.

Excel is quite versatile when importing text files. If each line of the text file is identically laid out, importing is usually problem-free. But if the line contains mixed information, you may need to do some additional work to make the data usable.

For example, you create text files in some programs by sending a printed report to a disk file rather than to the printer. These reports often have extra information, such as page headers and footers, titles, summary lines, and so on.

Using the Text Import Wizard

Prior versions of Excel treated importing text files differently from other types of database information. In Excel 2000, if you use the technique described in this section, you'll create a Text File Query, which you can refresh in the same way that you refresh Database and Web queries. This new feature will make easier the lives of those who need to regularly import text files, because they won't need to "set up" the import each time. When you want to update the Excel file that you create by importing a text file, choose Data ➪ Refresh Data. Highlight the text file that you originally imported and click the Import button. Excel automatically updates the Excel version of the file with any new data that may appear in the text file.

Cross-Reference
For more information on Database queries, see Chapter 24. For more information on Web queries, see Chapter 30.

To import a text file into Excel, choose Data ➪ Get External Data ➪ Import Text File. In the Import Text File dialog box, navigate to the folder containing the file that you want to import. The dialog box then displays text files that have an extension of TXT. If the text file that you're importing has a different extension, select the All Files option. Or, you can enter the filename directly into the File name box, if you know the file's name.

Excel displays its Text Import Wizard, a series of interactive dialog boxes in which you specify the information that Excel requires to break the lines of the text file into columns. You can truly appreciate this time-saving feature if, in a previous life, you struggled with the old data-parsing commands that are found in other spreadsheet programs and older versions of Excel.

Text Import Wizard: Step 1 of 3

Figure 22-9 shows the first of three Text Import Wizard dialog boxes. In the Original data type section, verify the type of data file (Excel almost always guesses correctly). You also can indicate the row that Excel should use to start importing. For example, if the file has a title in the first row, you may want to skip the first line.

Notice that you can preview the file at the bottom of the dialog box, using the scrollbars to view more of the file. If the characters in the file don't look right, you may need to change the File Origin; this determines which character set to use (in many cases, it doesn't make any difference). After you finish with this step, click the Next button to move to Step 2.

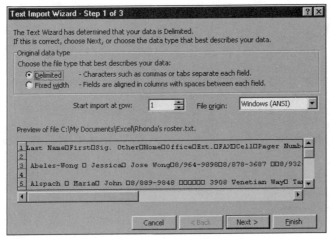

Figure 22-9: Step 1 of the Text Import Wizard.

Text Import Wizard: Step 2 of 3

The dialog box that you see for Step 2 of the Text Import Wizard varies, depending on your choice in the Original data type section in Step 1. If you selected Delimited, you see the dialog box shown in Figure 22-10. You can specify the type of delimiter, the text qualifier, and whether to treat consecutive delimiters as a single delimiter; choosing to treat consecutive delimiters as a single delimiter tells Excel to skip empty columns. The Data preview section displays vertical lines to indicate how Excel will break up the fields. The Data preview section changes as you make choices in the dialog box.

If you selected Fixed width, you see the dialog box shown in Figure 22-11. At this point, Excel attempts to identify the column breaks and displays vertical break lines to represent how it will break fields apart into columns. If Excel guesses wrong, you can move the lines, insert new ones, or delete lines that Excel proposes. You'll see instructions in the dialog box.

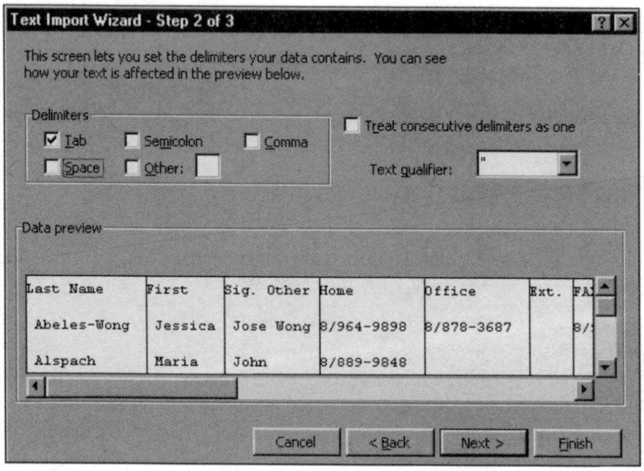

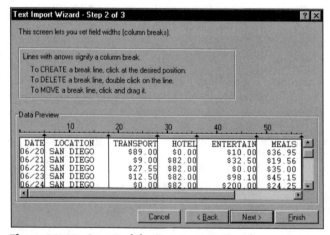

Figure 22-10: Step 2 of the Text Import Wizard
(for delimited files).

Figure 22-11: Step 2 of the Text Import Wizard
(for fixed-width files).

If you're importing a print image file that includes page headers, you can ignore
them when you specify the column indicators. Rather, base the columns on the
data. When the file is imported, you can then delete the rows that contain the
page headers.

When you're satisfied with how the column breaks look, click Next to move to the
final step. Or, you can click Back to return to Step 1 and change the file type.

Text Import Wizard: Step 3 of 3

Figure 22-12 shows the last of the three Text Import Wizard dialog boxes. In this dialog box, you can select individual columns and specify the formatting to apply (General, Text, or Data). You also can specify columns to skip—they aren't imported. If you click the Advanced button, you'll see the dialog box shown in Figure 22-13, in which you can specify characters to use as decimal and thousands separators. When you're satisfied with the results, click Finish. Excel prompts you for the starting cell location for the imported data; when you click OK, Excel imports the data and displays the External Data toolbar, which helps you to work with the imported text file (see Figure 22-14). For example, if you click the Data Range Properties tool, you see the External Data Range Properties dialog box, shown in Figure 22-15, which you can use to change how Excel treats the imported file.

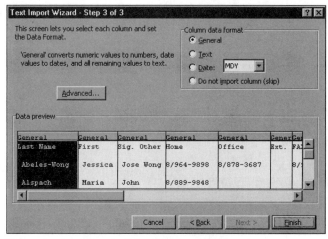

Figure 22-12: Step 3 of the Text Import Wizard.

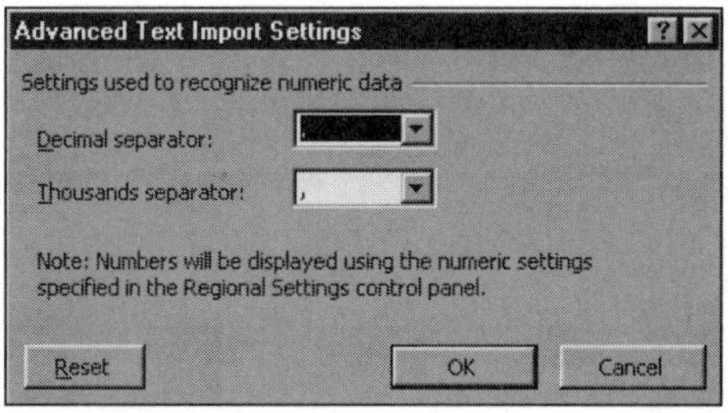

Figure 22-13: The Advanced Text Import Settings dialog box.

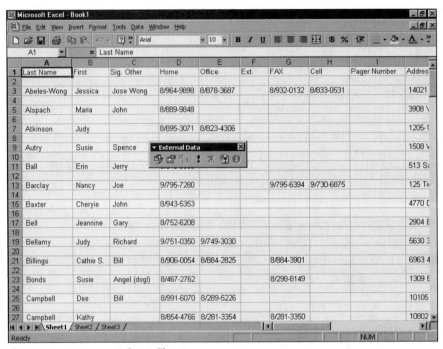

Figure 22-14: Imported text file.

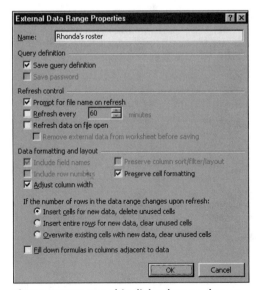

Figure 22-15: Use this dialog box to change the way that Excel treats the imported file.

If the results aren't what you expect, close the workbook and try again (text importing often involves trial and error). Don't forget that you can scroll the Data Preview window to make sure that all the data is converted properly. With some files, however, importing all the data properly is impossible. In such cases, you may want to import the file as a single column of text and then break lines into columns selectively. The procedure for doing this is discussed in the next section.

Using the Text to Columns Wizard

Excel can parse text that is stored in a column. Start by selecting the text (in a single column). Then, choose Data ➪ Text to Columns, and Excel displays the first of three Text to Columns Wizard dialog boxes. These dialog boxes are identical to those used for the Text Import Wizard, except that the title bar text is different.

Unfortunately, you can't use the Data ➪ Text to Columns command on a multiple selection; this would be quite handy for parsing imported files with several different layouts. Even worse, you can't use the Edit ➪ Repeat command to repeat the Text to Columns command.

Summary

This chapter identifies the various sources for getting data into Excel: entering data manually, generating data from formulas or macros, using Query or pivot tables, copying data using the Clipboard, and importing foreign files (including text files) into Excel. The chapter focuses on Clipboard operations and file importing.

✦   ✦   ✦

Working with Lists

CHAPTER 23

Research conducted by Microsoft indicates that Excel is frequently used to manage lists, or *worksheet databases*. This chapter covers list management and demonstrates useful techniques that involve lists.

What Is a List?

A list is essentially an organized collection of information. More specifically, a list consists of a row of headers (descriptive text), followed by additional rows of data, which can be values or text. You may recognize this as a database table — which is exactly what it is. Beginning with Excel 5, Microsoft uses the term *list* to refer to a database stored in a worksheet and the term *database* to refer to a table of information stored in an external file. To avoid confusion, I adhere to Microsoft's terminology.

Cross-Reference I cover external database files in Chapter 24.

Figure 23-1 shows an example of a list in a worksheet. This particular list has its headers in row 1 and has 10 rows of data. The list occupies four columns. Notice that the data consists of several different types: text, values, and dates. Column C contains a formula that calculates the monthly salary from the value in column B.

	A	B	C	D	E	F
		Annual	Monthly		Date	
1	Name	Salary	Salary	Location	Hired	
2	James Brackman	42,400	3,533	New York	2/1/93	
3	Michael Orenthal	28,900	2,408	Arizona	4/5/94	
4	Francis Jenkins	67,800	5,650	New York	10/12/93	
5	Peter Yolanda	19,850	1,654	Minnesota	1/4/95	
6	Walter Franklin	45,000	3,750	Arizona	2/28/90	
7	Louise Victor	52,000	4,333	New York	5/2/94	
8	Sally Rice	48,500	4,042	New York	11/21/92	
9	Charles K. Barkley	24,500	2,042	Minnesota	6/4/90	
10	Melinda Hintquest	56,400	4,700	Arizona	6/1/87	
11	Linda Harper	75,000	6,250	Minnesota	8/7/91	
12						
13						
14						

Figure 23-1: An example of a list.

People often refer to the columns in a list as *fields* and to the rows as *records*. Using this terminology, the list shown in the figure has five fields (Name, Annual Salary, Monthly Salary, Location, and Date Hired) and ten records.

The size of the lists that you develop in Excel is limited by the size of a single worksheet. In other words, a list can have no more than 256 fields and can consist of no more than 65,535 records (one row contains the field names). A list of this size would require a great deal of memory and even then may not be possible. At the other extreme, a list can consist of a single cell — not very useful, but it's still considered a list.

Note   In versions of Excel prior to Excel 97, a list was limited to 16,383 records.

What Can You Do with a List?

Excel provides several tools to help you manage and manipulate lists. Consequently, people use lists for a wide variety of purposes. For some users, a list is simply a method to keep track of information (for example, customer lists); others use lists to store data that ultimately will appear in a report. Common list operations include:

✦ Entering data into the list

✦ Filtering the list to display only the rows that meet certain criteria

✦ Sorting the list

✦ Inserting formulas to calculate subtotals

✦ Creating formulas to calculate results on the list filtered by certain criteria

✦ Creating a summary table of the data in the list (this is done using a pivot table; see Chapter 25).

With the exception of the last item, these operations are covered in this chapter.

Designing a List

Although Excel is quite accommodating when it comes to the information that is stored in a list, planning the organization of your list information will pay off. The following are some guidelines to keep in mind when creating lists:

◆ Insert descriptive labels (one for each column) in the first row of the list, called the *header row*. If you use lengthy labels, consider using the Wrap Text format so that you don't have to widen the columns.

See Chapter 11 for information on the Wrap Text format.

◆ Make sure each column contains the same type of information. For example, don't mix dates and text in a single column.

◆ You can use formulas that perform calculations on other fields in the same record. If you use formulas that refer to cells outside the list, make these absolute references; otherwise, you get unexpected results when you sort the list.

◆ Don't leave any empty rows within the list. For list operations, Excel determines the list boundaries automatically, and an empty row signals the end of the list.

◆ For best results, try to keep the list on a worksheet by itself. If you must place other information on the same worksheet as the list, place the information above or below the list. In other words, don't use the cells to the left or the right of a list.

◆ Select Window ➪ Freeze Panes to make sure that you can see the headings when you scroll the list.

◆ You can preformat entire columns to ensure that the data has the same format. For example, if a column contains dates, format the entire column with the desired date format.

Many people find working in spreadsheets most appealing because changing the layout is relatively easy. Lists behave no differently than any other kind of data in Excel; changing a list's layout is also easy. For example, you may create a list and then decide that it needs another column (field). No problem. Just insert a new column, give it a field name, and Excel expands your list. If you've ever used a database management program, you can appreciate the simplicity of this layout change.

Entering Data into a List

You can enter data into a list in three ways:

✦ Manually, using all standard data entry techniques

✦ By importing it or copying it from another file

✦ By using a dialog box

There's really nothing special about entering data into a list. You just navigate through the worksheet and enter the data into the appropriate cells.

Excel has two features that assist with repetitive data entry:

✦ **AutoComplete.** When you begin to type in a cell, Excel scans up and down the column for entries that match what you're typing. If it finds a match, Excel fills in the rest of the text automatically. Press Enter to make the entry. You can turn this feature on or off in the Edit tab of the Options dialog box.

✦ **Pick Lists.** You can right-click on a cell and select Pick from list from the shortcut menu. Excel displays a list box that shows all entries in the column (see Figure 23-2). Click on the one that you want to enter into the cell (no typing is required).

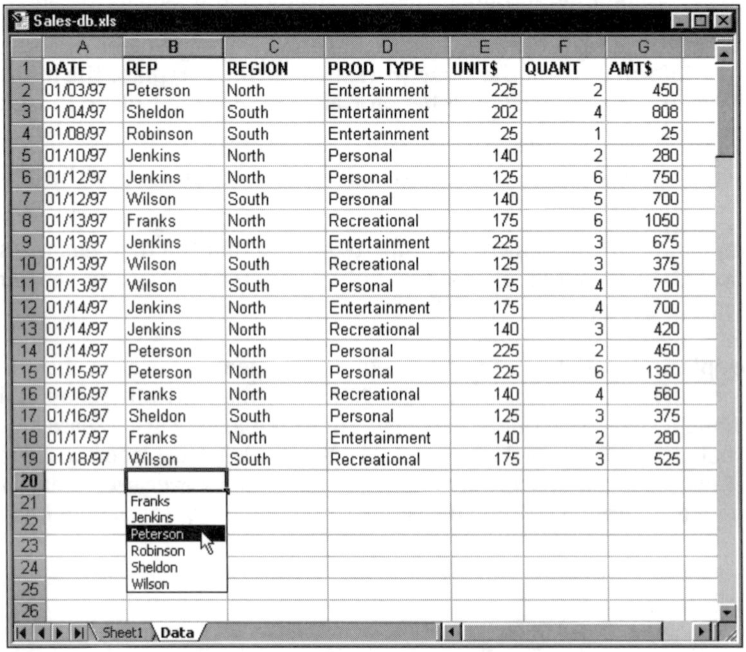

	A	B	C	D	E	F	G	
1	DATE	REP	REGION	PROD_TYPE	UNIT$	QUANT	AMT$	
2	01/03/97	Peterson	North	Entertainment	225	2	450	
3	01/04/97	Sheldon	South	Entertainment	202	4	808	
4	01/08/97	Robinson	South	Entertainment	25	1	25	
5	01/10/97	Jenkins	North	Personal	140	2	280	
6	01/12/97	Jenkins	North	Personal	125	6	750	
7	01/12/97	Wilson	South	Personal	140	5	700	
8	01/13/97	Franks	North	Recreational	175	6	1050	
9	01/13/97	Jenkins	North	Entertainment	225	3	675	
10	01/13/97	Wilson	South	Recreational	125	3	375	
11	01/13/97	Wilson	South	Personal	175	4	700	
12	01/14/97	Jenkins	North	Entertainment	175	4	700	
13	01/14/97	Jenkins	North	Recreational	140	3	420	
14	01/14/97	Peterson	North	Personal	225	2	450	
15	01/15/97	Peterson	North	Personal	225	6	1350	
16	01/16/97	Franks	North	Recreational	140	4	560	
17	01/16/97	Sheldon	South	Personal	125	3	375	
18	01/17/97	Franks	North	Entertainment	140	2	280	
19	01/18/97	Wilson	South	Recreational	175	3	525	
20								
21		Franks						
22		Jenkins						
23		Peterson						
24		Robinson						
25		Sheldon						
26		Wilson						

Sales-db.xls

Figure 23-2: Choosing the Pick from list command on the shortcut menu gives you a list of all items in the current column.

If you prefer to use a dialog box for your data entry, Excel accommodates you. To display a data entry dialog box, move the cell pointer anywhere within the list and choose Data ⇨ Form. Excel determines the boundaries of your list and displays a dialog box showing each field in the list. Figure 23-3 depicts an example of such a dialog box. Fields that have a formula don't have an edit box.

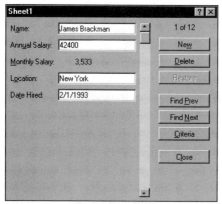

Figure 23-3: The Data ⇨ Form command gives you a handy data entry dialog box.

Note If the number of fields exceeds the limit of your display, the dialog box contains two columns of field names. If your list consists of more than 32 fields, however, the Data ⇨ Form command doesn't work. You must forego this method of data entry and enter the information directly into the cells.

Entering Data with the Data Form Dialog Box

When the data form dialog box appears, Excel displays the first record in the list. Notice the indicator in the upper-right corner of the dialog box that tells you the number of the selected record and the total number of records in the list.

To enter a new record, click on the New button to clear the fields. Then you can enter the new information into the appropriate fields. Use Tab or Shift+Tab to move among the fields. When you click on New (or Close), Excel appends the data that you entered to the bottom of the list. You also can press Enter, which is equivalent to clicking on the New button. If the list contains any formulas, Excel enters them for you automatically into the new record.

Tip If you named the range of your list Database, Excel automatically extends the range definition to include the new row(s) that you add to the list using the data form dialog box. Note that this works only if you name the list Database; any other name doesn't work.

Other Uses for the Data Form Dialog Box

You can use the data form dialog box for more than just data entry. You can edit existing data in the list, view data one record at a time, delete records, and display records that meet certain criteria.

The dialog box contains a number of additional buttons, which are described as follows:

+ **Delete:** Deletes the displayed record.

+ **Restore:** Restores any information that you edited. You must click on this button before you click on the New button.

+ **Find Prev:** Displays the previous record in the list. If you entered a criterion, this button displays the previous record that matches the criterion.

+ **Find Next:** Displays the next record in the list. If you entered a criterion, this button displays the next record that matches the criterion.

+ **Criteria:** Clears the fields and lets you enter a criterion upon which to search for records. For example, to locate records that have a salary greater than $50,000, enter **>50000** into the Salary field. Then you can use the Find Next and Find Prev buttons to display the qualifying records.

+ **Close:** Closes the dialog box (and enters the data that you were entering, if any).

Using Microsoft Access Forms for Data Entry

If you have Microsoft Access installed on your system, you can use its form creation tools to develop a data entry form for an Excel worksheet. This feature uses the Access Links add-in, which must be loaded. When the add-in is loaded, you have a new command: Data ⇨ Access Form.

Choosing this command starts Access (if it's not already running) and begins its Form Wizard. Use the Form Wizard to create the data entry form. You can then use this form to add data to your Excel worksheet. Access's Form Wizard places a button on your worksheet that contains the text View Access Form. Click on this button to use the form. Figure 23-4 shows an Access form being used to enter data into an Excel worksheet.

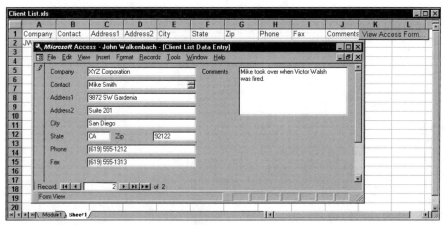

Figure 23-4: This form, developed in Microsoft Access, is being used to enter data into an Excel worksheet.

Filtering a List

Filtering a list is the process of hiding all rows in the list except those that meet some criteria that you specify. For example, if you have a list of customers, you can filter the list to show only those who live in New Jersey. Filtering is a common (and very useful) technique. Excel provides two ways to filter a list:

✦ AutoFilter, for simple filtering criteria

✦ Advance Filter, for more complex filtering

AutoFiltering

To use Excel's AutoFilter feature to filter a list, place the cell pointer anywhere within the list and then choose Data ➪ Filter ➪ AutoFilter. Excel analyzes your list and adds drop-down arrows to the field names in the header row, as shown in Figure 23-5.

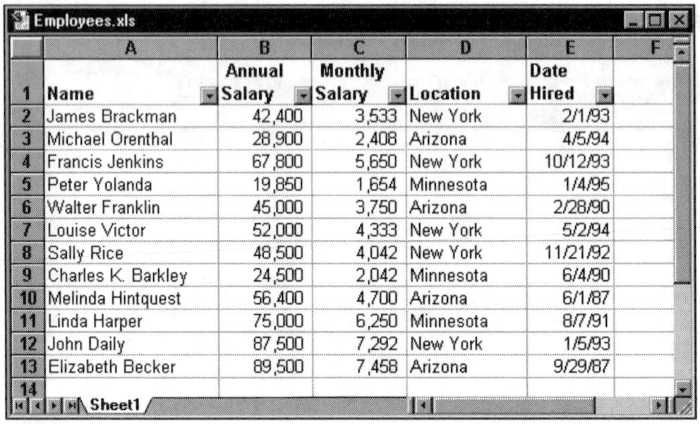

Employees.xls

	A	B	C	D	E	F
1	Name	Annual Salary	Monthly Salary	Location	Date Hired	
2	James Brackman	42,400	3,533	New York	2/1/93	
3	Michael Orenthal	28,900	2,408	Arizona	4/5/94	
4	Francis Jenkins	67,800	5,650	New York	10/12/93	
5	Peter Yolanda	19,850	1,654	Minnesota	1/4/95	
6	Walter Franklin	45,000	3,750	Arizona	2/28/90	
7	Louise Victor	52,000	4,333	New York	5/2/94	
8	Sally Rice	48,500	4,042	New York	11/21/92	
9	Charles K. Barkley	24,500	2,042	Minnesota	6/4/90	
10	Melinda Hintquest	56,400	4,700	Arizona	6/1/87	
11	Linda Harper	75,000	6,250	Minnesota	8/7/91	
12	John Daily	87,500	7,292	New York	1/5/93	
13	Elizabeth Becker	89,500	7,458	Arizona	9/29/87	
14						

Sheet1

Figure 23-5: When you choose the Data ➪ Filter ➪ AutoFilter command, Excel adds drop-down arrows to the field names in the header row.

When you click on the arrow in one of these drop-down lists, the list expands to show the unique items in that column. Select an item, and Excel hides all rows except those that include the selected item. In other words, Excel filters the list by the item that you selected.

After you filter the list, the status bar displays a message that tells you how many rows qualified. In addition, the drop-down arrow changes color to remind you that you filtered the list by a value in that column.

AutoFiltering has a limit. Only the first 999 unique items in the column appear in the drop-down list. If your list exceeds this limit, you can use advanced filtering, which is described later.

Besides showing every item in the column, the drop-down list includes five other items:

✦ **All:** Displays all items in the column. Use this to remove filtering for a column.

✦ **Top 10:** Filters to display the "top 10" items in the list; this is discussed later.

✦ **Custom:** Lets you filter the list by multiple items; this is discussed later.

✦ **Blanks:** Filters the list by showing rows that contain blanks in this column.

✦ **NonBlanks:** Filters the list by showing rows that contain non-blanks in this column.

To display the entire list again, click on the arrow and choose All — the first item in the drop-down list. Or, you can select Data ➪ Filter ➪ Show All.

To move out of Autofilter mode and remove the drop-down arrows from the field names, choose Data ⇨ Filter ⇨ AutoFilter again to remove the check mark from the AutoFilter menu item and restore the list to its normal state.

Caution   If you have any formulas that refer to data in a filtered list, be aware that the formulas don't adjust to use only the visible cells. For example, if a cell contains a formula that sums values in column C, the formula continues to show the sum for *all* the values in column C — not just those in the visible rows. To solve this problem, use database functions, which I describe later in this chapter.

Multicolumn AutoFiltering

Sometimes you may need to filter a list by values in more than one column. Figure 23-6 shows a list comprised of several fields.

	A	B	C	D	E
1	Month	State	Product	Price	From Ad
2	Jan	CA	Printer	208	Yes
3	Jan	CA	Printer	203	No
4	Jan	IL	Printer	468	No
5	Jan	IL	Printer	226	No
6	Jan	NY	Printer	484	Yes
7	Jan	NY	Printer	373	Yes
8	Jan	CA	Modem	249	Yes
9	Jan	CA	Modem	329	No
10	Jan	IL	Modem	760	Yes
11	Jan	IL	Modem	959	No
12	Jan	NY	Modem	419	No
13	Jan	NY	Modem	555	No
14	Jan	CA	HardDrive	287	Yes
15	Jan	CA	HardDrive	758	No
16	Jan	IL	HardDrive	651	Yes
17	Jan	IL	HardDrive	233	No
18	Jan	NY	HardDrive	332	Yes
19	Jan	NY	HardDrive	852	Yes
20	Jan	CA	Mouse	748	No
21	Jan	CA	Mouse	811	No

Figure 23-6: The list before filtering by multiple columns.

Assume that you want to see the records that show modems sold in February. In other words, you want to filter out all records except those in which the Month field is *Feb* and the Product field is *Modem*.

First, get into Autofilter mode. Then click on the drop-down arrow in the Month field and select *Feb* to filter the list to show only records with *Feb* in the Month field. Then click on the drop-down arrow in the Product field and select *Modem*, filtering the filtered list to show only records that contain *Modem* in the Product column — resulting in a list filtered by values in two columns. Figure 23-7 shows the result.

	Month	State	Product	Price	From Ad
38	Feb	CA	Modem	249	Yes
39	Feb	CA	Modem	329	No
40	Feb	IL	Modem	579	No
41	Feb	IL	Modem	592	Yes
42	Feb	NY	Modem	651	No
43	Feb	NY	Modem	475	Yes
218	Feb	CA	Modem	249	Yes
219	Feb	CA	Modem	329	No
220	Feb	IL	Modem	691	No
221	Feb	IL	Modem	915	No
222	Feb	NY	Modem	724	No
223	Feb	NY	Modem	266	Yes
398	Feb	CA	Modem	329	No
399	Feb	CA	Modem	329	No
400	Feb	IL	Modem	936	No
401	Feb	IL	Modem	227	No
402	Feb	NY	Modem	603	No
403	Feb	NY	Modem	889	No
578	Feb	CA	Modem	329	No
579	Feb	CA	Modem	329	No

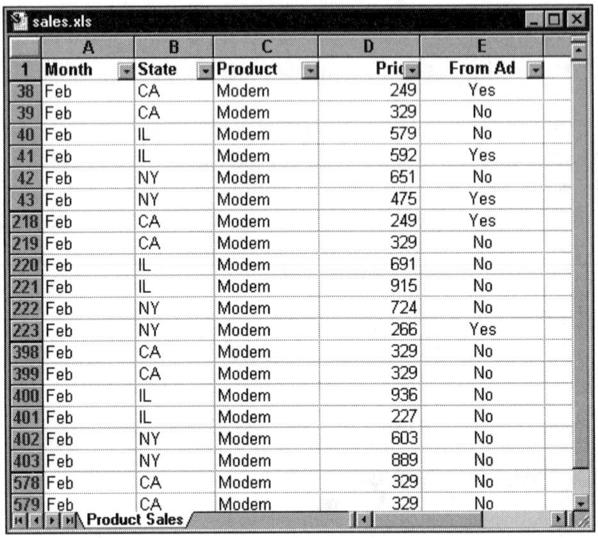

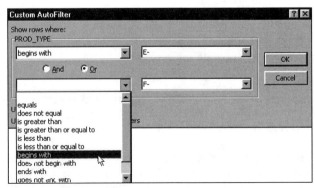

Figure 23-7: The same list filtered by values in two columns.

You can filter a list by any number of columns. Excel applies a different color to the drop-down arrows in the columns that have a filter applied.

Custom AutoFiltering

Usually, AutoFiltering involves selecting a single value for one or more columns. If you choose the Custom option in a drop-down list, you gain a bit more flexibility in filtering the list; Excel displays a dialog box like the one shown in Figure 23-8.

Figure 23-8: The Custom AutoFilter dialog box gives you more filtering options.

The Custom AutoFilter dialog box lets you filter in several ways:

✦ **Values above or below a specified value.** For example, sales amounts greater than 10,000.

✦ **Values within a range.** For example, sales amounts greater than 10,000 AND sales amounts less than 50,000.

✦ **Two discrete values.** For example, state equal to *New York* OR state equal to *New Jersey*.

✦ **Approximate matches.** You can use the * and ? wildcards to filter in a number of other ways. For example, to display only those customers whose last name begins with *B,* use **B***.

Custom AutoFiltering can be useful, but it definitely has limitations. For example, if you want to filter the list to show only three values in a field (such as New York or New Jersey or Connecticut), you can't do it by AutoFiltering. Such filtering tasks require the advanced filtering feature, which I discuss later in this chapter.

Top 10 AutoFiltering

Sometimes you may want to use a filter on numerical fields to show only the highest or lowest values in the list. For example, if you have a list of employees, you may want to identify the 12 employees with the longest tenure. You could use the custom AutoFilter option, but then you must supply a cutoff date (which you may not know). The solution is to use Top 10 AutoFiltering.

Top 10 AutoFiltering is a generic term; it doesn't limit you to the top *10* items. In fact, it doesn't even limit you to the *top* items. When you choose the Top 10 option from a drop-down list, you see dialog box that is shown in Figure 23-9.

Figure 23-9: The Top 10 AutoFilter gives you more AutoFilter options.

You can choose either Top or Bottom and specify any number. Suppose, for example, that you want to see the 12 employees with the longest tenure. Choose Bottom and 12 to filter the list and show the 12 rows with the smallest values in the Date Hired field. You also can choose Percent or Value in this dialog box. For example, you can filter the list to show the Bottom 5 percent of the records.

Charting filtered list data

You can create some interesting multipurpose charts that use data in a filtered list. The technique is useful because only the visible data appears in the chart. When you change the AutoFilter criteria, the chart updates itself to show only the visible cells.

Note   For this technique to work, select the chart and make sure that the Plot Visible Cells Only option is enabled on the Chart tab of the Options dialog box.

Figure 23-10 shows an example of a chart created with an unfiltered list. It shows sales data for three months for each of four sales regions.

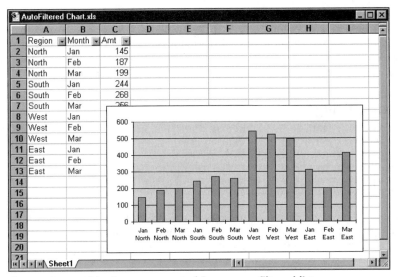

Figure 23-10: This chart was created from an unfiltered list.

Figure 23-11 shows the same chart, but the list was filtered to show only the North sales region. You can apply other filters, and the chart updates automatically. This technique lets a single chart show several different views of the data.

Advanced Filtering

In many cases, AutoFiltering does the job. But if you run up against its limitations, you need to use advanced filtering. Advanced filtering is much more flexible than AutoFiltering, but it takes a bit of up-front work to use it. Advanced filtering provides you with the following capabilities:

✦ You can specify more complex filtering criteria.

✦ You can specify computed filtering criteria.

✦ You can extract a copy of the rows that meet the criteria to another location.

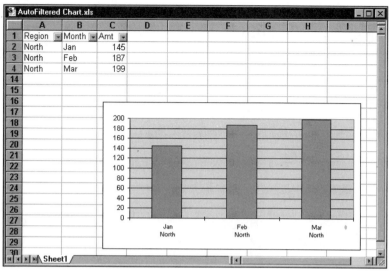

Figure 23-11: The chart from the previous figure, after filtering the list.

Setting up a criteria range

Before you can use the advanced filtering feature, you must set up a *criteria range,* a designated range on a worksheet that conforms to certain requirements. The criteria range holds the information that Excel uses to filter the list. It must conform to the following specifications:

✦ It must consist of at least two rows, and the first row must contain some or all field names from the list.

✦ The other rows of the criteria range must consist of your filtering criteria.

Although you can put the criteria range anywhere in the worksheet, it's a good idea not to put it in rows where you placed the list. Because Excel hides some of these rows when filtering the list, you may find that your criteria range is no longer visible after filtering. Therefore, you should generally place the criteria range above or below the list.

Figure 23-12 shows a criteria range, located in A1:D2, above the list that it uses. Only some field names appear in the criteria range. You don't need to include, in the criteria range, field names for fields that you don't use in the selection criteria.

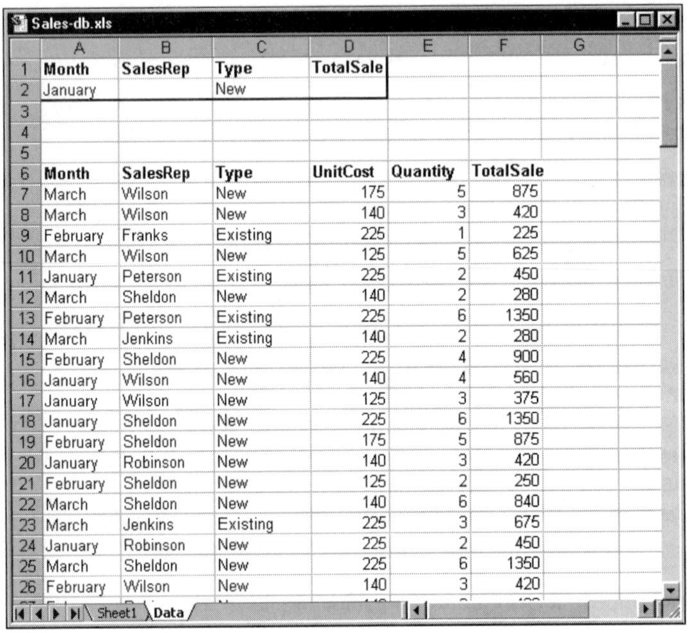

Figure 23-12: A criteria range for a list.

In this example, the criteria range has only one row of criteria. The fields in each row of the criteria range (except for the header row) are joined with an AND operator. Therefore, the filtered list shows rows in which the Month column equals *January* AND the Type column equals *New*. In other words, the list displays only sales to new customers made in January.

To perform the filtering, choose Data ⇨ Filter ⇨ Advanced filter. Excel displays the dialog box that is shown in Figure 23-13. Specify the list range and the criteria range, and make sure that you select the option labeled Filter the List in-place. Click on OK, and Excel filters the list by the criteria that you specified.

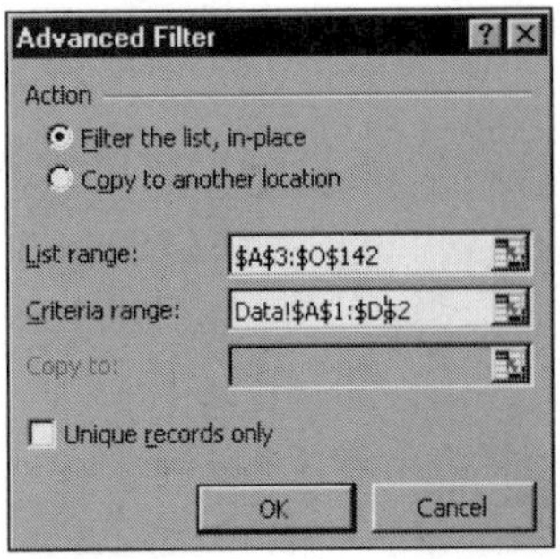

Figure 23-13: The Advanced Filter dialog box.

Multiple criteria

If you use more than one row in the criteria range, the criteria in each row are joined with an OR operator. A criteria range can have any number of rows, each of which is joined to the others with an OR operator. Figure 23-14 shows a criteria range (A1:D3) with two rows of criteria.

	A	B	C	D	E	F	G
1	Month	SalesRep	Type	TotalSale			
2	January		New				
3	February			>1000			
4							
5							
6	Month	SalesRep	Type	UnitCost	Quantity	TotalSale	
7	March	Wilson	New	175	5	875	
8	March	Wilson	New	140	3	420	
9	February	Franks	Existing	225	1	225	
10	March	Wilson	New	125	5	625	
11	January	Peterson	Existing	225	2	450	
12	March	Sheldon	New	140	2	280	
13	February	Peterson	Existing	225	6	1350	
14	March	Jenkins	Existing	140	2	280	
15	February	Sheldon	New	225	4	900	
16	January	Wilson	New	140	4	560	
17	January	Wilson	New	125	3	375	
18	January	Sheldon	New	225	6	1350	
19	February	Sheldon	New	175	5	875	
20	January	Robinson	New	140	3	420	
21	February	Sheldon	New	125	2	250	
22	March	Sheldon	New	140	6	840	
23	March	Jenkins	Existing	225	3	675	
24	January	Robinson	New	225	2	450	
25	March	Sheldon	New	225	6	1350	
26	February	Wilson	New	140	3	420	

Figure 23-14: This criteria range has two sets of criteria.

In this example, the filtered list shows rows in either of the following:

✦ *The Month field is January AND the Type field is New.*

✦ The Month field is *February* AND the Total Sale field is greater than 1000.

You cannot filter this way with AutoFiltering.

Types of criteria

The entries that you make in the criteria range can be either of the following:

✦ Text or value criteria. The filtering involves comparisons to a value or string, using operators such as equal (=), greater than (>), not equal to (<>), and so on.

✦ **Computed criteria.** The filtering involves a computation of some sort.

Text or value criteria

Table 23-1 lists the comparison operators that you can use with text or value criteria.

Table 23-1 Comparison Operators	
Operator	**Comparison Type**
=	Equal to
>	Greater than
>=	Greater than or equal to
<	Less than
<=	Less than or equal to
<>	Not equal to

Table 23-2 shows examples of criteria that use strings.

Table 23-2 Examples of String Criteria	
Criteria	**Effect**
>K	Text that begins with *L* through *Z*
<>C	All text, except text that begins with C
="January"	Text that matches January
Sm*	Text that begins with Sm
s*s	Text that begins with s and ends with s
s?s	Three-letter text that begins with *s* and ends with *s*

Note   The text comparisons are not case sensitive. For example, si* matches *Simpson* as well as *sick*.

Computed criteria

Using computed criteria can make filtering even more powerful. Computed criteria filter the list based one or more calculations. Figure 23-15 shows a simple list that consists of project numbers, start dates, end dates, and resources. Above the list, in range A1:A2, is the criteria range. Notice, however, that this criteria range does not use a field header from the list — it uses a new field header. A computed criteria essentially computes a new field for the list. Therefore, you must supply new field names in the first row of the criteria range.

	A	B	C	D	E
1	ProjLength				
2	TRUE				
3					
4	Project Number	Start Date	End Date	Resources	
5	AS-109	03/05/97	04/09/97	3,395	
6	AS-110	03/12/97	03/17/97	485	
7	AS-111	04/01/97	04/10/97	873	
8	AS-112	04/01/97	05/03/97	3,104	
9	AS-113	04/12/97	05/01/97	1,843	
10	AS-114	04/21/97	06/05/97	4,365	
11	AS-115	05/03/97	05/15/97	1,164	
12	AS-116	05/21/97	06/09/97	1,843	
13	AS-117	06/02/97	08/01/97	5,820	

Project List

Figure 23-15: This list is to be filtered using computed criteria.

Cell A2 contains the following formula:

```
=C5-B5+1>=30
```

This formula returns a logical value of either *True* or *False*. The result of the formula refers to cells in the first row of data in the list; it does *not* refer to the header row. When you filter the list by this criterion, the list shows only rows in which the project length (End Date–Start Date+1) is greater than or equal to 30 days. In other words, Excel bases the comparison on a computation.

Note   You could accomplish the same effect, without using a computed criterion, by adding a new column to the list that contains a formula to calculate the project length. Using a computed criterion, however, eliminates the need to add a new column.

To filter the list to show only the projects that use above average resources, you could use the following computed criteria formula:

```
=D5>AVERAGE(D:D)
```

This filters the list to show only the rows in which the value of the Resources field is greater than the average of the Resources field.

Keep in mind the following items when using computed criteria:

✦ Don't use a field name in the criteria range that appears in the list. Create a new field name or just leave the cell blank.

✦ You can use any number of computed criteria and mix and match them with noncomputed criteria.

✦ Don't pay attention to the values returned by formulas in the criteria range. These refer to the first row of the list.

✦ If your computed formula refers to a value outside the list, use an absolute reference rather than a relative reference. For example, use $C$1 rather than C1.

✦ Create your computed criteria formulas using the first row of data in the list (not the field names). Make these references relative, not absolute. For example, use C5 rather than $C$5.

Other advanced filtering operations

The Advanced Filter dialog box gives you two other options:

✦ Copy to Another Location

✦ Unique Records Only

Both of these advanced filtering options are discussed below.

Copying qualifying rows

If you choose the Copy to Another Location option in the Advanced Filter dialog box, Excel copies the qualifying rows to another location in the worksheet or a different worksheet. You specify the location for the copied rows in the Copy to edit box. Note that the list itself is not filtered when you use this option.

Displaying only unique rows

Choosing the option labeled Unique records only hides all duplicate rows that meet the criteria that you specify. If you don't specify a criteria range, this option hides all duplicate rows in the list.

Using Database Functions with Lists

It's important to understand that Excel's worksheet functions don't ignore hidden cells. Therefore, if you have a SUM formula that calculates the total of the values in a column of a list, the formula returns the same value when you filter the list.

To create formulas that return results based on filtering criteria, you need to use Excel's database worksheet functions. For example, you can create a formula that calculates the sum of values in a list that meets certain criteria. Set up a criteria range as described previously. Then enter a formula such as the following:

```
=DSUM(ListRange,FieldName,Criteria)
```

In this case, ListRange refers to the list, FieldName refers to the field name cell of the column that you are summing, and Criteria refers to the criteria range.

Excel's database functions are listed in Table 23-3.

	Table 23-3
	Excel's Database Worksheet Functions

Function	Description
DAVERAGE	Returns the average of selected database entries
DCOUNT	Counts the cells containing numbers from a specified database and criteria
DCOUNTA	Counts nonblank cells from a specified database and criteria
DGET	Extracts from a database a single record that matches the specified criteria
DMAX	Returns the maximum value from selected database entries
DMIN	Returns the minimum value from selected database entries
DPRODUCT	Multiplies the values in a particular field of records that match the criteria in a database
DSTDEV	Estimates the standard deviation based on a sample of selected database entries
DSTDEVP	Calculates the standard deviation based on the entire population of selected database entries
DSUM	Adds the numbers in the field column of records in the database that match the criteria
DVAR	Estimates variance based on a sample from selected database entries
DVARP	Calculates variance based on the entire population of selected database entries

Cross-Reference Refer to Chapter 10 for general information about using worksheet functions.

Sorting a List

In some cases, the order of the rows in your list doesn't matter. But in other cases, you want the rows to appear in a specific order. For example, in a price list, you may want the rows to appear in alphabetical order by product name. This makes the products easier to locate in the list. Or, if you have a list of accounts receivable information, you may want to sort the list so that the higher amounts appear at the top of the list (in descending order).

Rearranging the order of the rows in a list is called *sorting*. Excel is quite flexible when it comes to sorting lists, and you can often accomplish this task with the click of a mouse button.

Simple Sorting

To quickly sort a list in ascending order, move the cell pointer into the column that you want to sort. Then click on the Sort Ascending button the Standard toolbar. The Sort Descending button works the same way, but it sorts the list in descending order. In both cases, Excel determines the extent of your list and sorts all the rows in the list.

When you sort a filtered list, Excel sorts only the visible rows. When you remove the filtering from the list, the list is no longer sorted.

Be careful if you sort a list that contains formulas. If the formulas refer to cells in the list that are in the same row, you don't have any problems. But if the formulas refer to cells in other rows in the list or to cells outside the list, the formulas will not be correct after you sort the list. If formulas in your list refer to cells outside the list, make sure that the formulas use an absolute cell reference.

More Complex Sorting

Sometimes, you may want to sort by two or more columns. This is relevant to break ties. A tie occurs when rows with duplicate data remain unsorted. Figure 23-16 shows an example of an unsorted list. If you sort this list by Month, Excel places the rows for each month together. But you may also want to show the Sales Reps in ascending order within each month. In this case, you would need to sort by two columns (Month and Sales Rep). Figure 23-17 shows the list after sorting by these two columns.

You can use the Sort Ascending and Sort Descending buttons to do this — but you need to do two sorts. First, sort by the Sales Reps column, and then sort by the Month column. As I explain in the next section, Excel provides a way to accomplish multicolumn sorting with a single command.

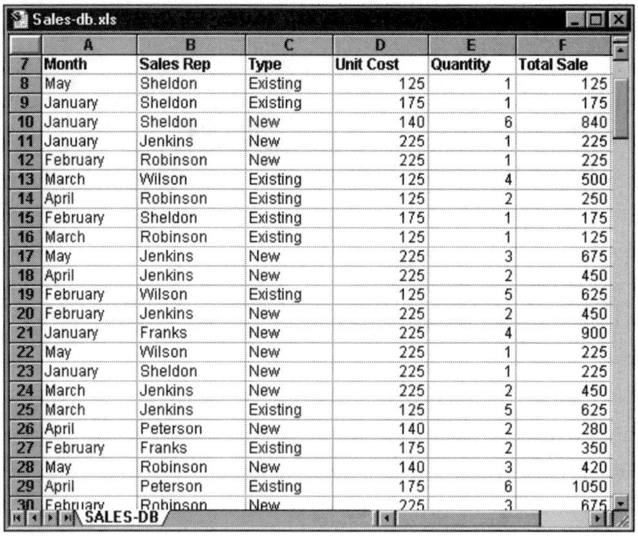

Sales-db.xls

	A	B	C	D	E	F
7	Month	Sales Rep	Type	Unit Cost	Quantity	Total Sale
8	May	Sheldon	Existing	125	1	125
9	January	Sheldon	Existing	175	1	175
10	January	Sheldon	New	140	6	840
11	January	Jenkins	New	225	1	225
12	February	Robinson	New	225	1	225
13	March	Wilson	Existing	125	4	500
14	April	Robinson	Existing	125	2	250
15	February	Sheldon	Existing	175	1	175
16	March	Robinson	Existing	125	1	125
17	May	Jenkins	New	225	3	675
18	April	Jenkins	New	225	2	450
19	February	Wilson	Existing	125	5	625
20	February	Jenkins	New	225	2	450
21	January	Franks	New	225	4	900
22	May	Wilson	New	225	1	225
23	January	Sheldon	New	225	1	225
24	March	Jenkins	New	225	2	450
25	March	Jenkins	Existing	125	5	625
26	April	Peterson	New	140	2	280
27	February	Franks	Existing	175	2	350
28	May	Robinson	New	140	3	420
29	April	Peterson	Existing	175	6	1050
30	February	Robinson	New	225	3	675

SALES-DB

Figure 23-16: This list is unsorted.

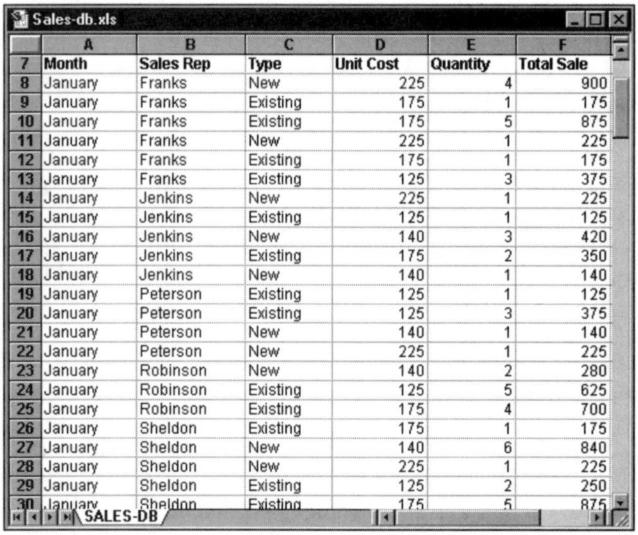

Sales-db.xls

	A	B	C	D	E	F
7	Month	Sales Rep	Type	Unit Cost	Quantity	Total Sale
8	January	Franks	New	225	4	900
9	January	Franks	Existing	175	1	175
10	January	Franks	Existing	175	5	875
11	January	Franks	New	225	1	225
12	January	Franks	Existing	175	1	175
13	January	Franks	Existing	125	3	375
14	January	Jenkins	New	225	1	225
15	January	Jenkins	Existing	125	1	125
16	January	Jenkins	New	140	3	420
17	January	Jenkins	Existing	175	2	350
18	January	Jenkins	New	140	1	140
19	January	Peterson	Existing	125	1	125
20	January	Peterson	Existing	125	3	375
21	January	Peterson	New	140	1	140
22	January	Peterson	New	225	1	225
23	January	Robinson	New	140	2	280
24	January	Robinson	Existing	125	5	625
25	January	Robinson	Existing	175	4	700
26	January	Sheldon	Existing	175	1	175
27	January	Sheldon	New	140	6	840
28	January	Sheldon	New	225	1	225
29	January	Sheldon	Existing	125	2	250
30	January	Sheldon	Existing	175	5	875

SALES-DB

Figure 23-17: The list after sorting on two fields.

Excel's Sorting Rules

Because cells can contain different types of information, you may be curious about how Excel sorts this information. For an ascending sort, the information appears in the following order:

1. Values: Excel sorts numbers from smallest negative to largest positive, and treats dates and times as values. In all cases, Excel sorts using the actual values in cells (not their formatted appearance).

2. Text: In alphabetical order, as follows: 0 1 2 3 4 5 6 7 8 9 (space) ! " # $ % & ' ( ) * + , - . / : ; < = > ? @ [\ ] ^ _ ` { | } ~ A B C D E F G H I J K L M N O P Q R S T U V W X Y Z.

   By default, sorting is not case sensitive. You can change this behavior, however, in the Sort Options dialog box (described in this chapter).

3. Logical values: False comes before True.

4. Error values: Error values (such as #VALUE! and #NA) appear in their original order; Excel does not sort them by error type.

5. Blank cells: Blanks cells always appear last.

Sorting in descending order reverses this sequence — except that blank cells *still* appear last.

The Sort dialog box

If you want to sort by more than one field, choose Data ➪ Sort. Excel displays the dialog box that is shown in Figure 23-18. Simply select the first sort field from the drop-down list labeled Sort By, and specify Ascending or Descending order. Then, do the same for the second sort field. If you want to sort by a third field, specify the field in the third section. If the Header Row option is set, the first row (field names) is not affected by the sort. Click on OK, and the list's rows rearrange in a flash.

If the sorting didn't occur as you expected, select Edit ➪ Undo (or press Ctrl+Z) to undo the sorting.

What if you need to sort your list by more than three fields? It can be done, but it takes an additional step. For example, assume that you want to sort your list by five fields: Field1, Field2, Field3, Field4, and Field5. Start by sorting by Field3, Field4, and Field5. Then re-sort the list by Field1 and Field2. In other words, sort the three "least important" fields first; they remain in sequence when you do the second sort.

Figure 23-18: The Sort dialog box
lets you sort by up to three columns.

Often, you want to keep the records in their original order but perform a temporary sort just to see how it looks. The solution is to add an additional column to the list with sequential numbers in it (don't use formulas to generate these numbers, but you can use the Fill command). Then, after you sort, you can return to the original order by resorting on the field that contains the sequential numbers. You can also use Excel's undo feature to return the list to its original order. If you use an additional column, you can perform other operations while the list is temporarily sorted (and these operations won't be undone when you undo the sort operation).

Sort options

When you click on the Options button in the Sort dialog box, Excel displays the Sort Options dialog, shown in Figure 23-19.

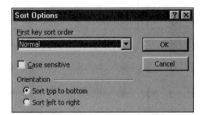

Figure 23-19: The Sort Options
dialog gives you some additional
sorting options.

These options are described as follows:

✦ **First key sort order:** Lets you specify a custom sort order for the sort (see the next section).

How Excel Identifies a Header Row

When you use the Data ➪ Sort command, there's no need to select the list before you choose the command. That's because Excel examines the active cell position and then establishes the list's boundaries for you. In addition, Excel attempts to determine whether the list contains a header row. If the list has a header row, Excel excludes this row from the sort.

How does this happen? I'm not sure exactly, but the following seems to be Excel's "thought" process:

1. Select the current region. (You can do this manually: press F5, click on the Special button, select the Current Region option, and click on OK.)

2. Examine the first row of the selection.

3. Determine whether the first row contains any blanks. If so, this list has no header row.

4. Determine whether the first row contains text. If so, check the other cells. If they also contain text, this list has no header row.

5. Determine whether the first row contains uppercase text while the list itself contains lowercase or proper case text. If so, this list has a header row.

6. Determine whether the cells in the first row are formatted differently from the other cells in the list. If so, this list has a header row.

Knowing this information can help you eliminate incorrect sorting. For example, if you want to sort a range that doesn't have a header row, you need to make sure that Excel doesn't sort the data as if it had a header row. For best results, use the Sort Ascending and Sort Descending toolbar buttons only when the data that you're sorting has headers. If your data contains no headers, select Data ➪ Sort and make sure that the No Header Row option is selected.

✦ **Case sensitive:** Makes the sorting case sensitive so that uppercase letters appear before lowercase letters in an ascending sort. Normally, sorting ignores the case of letters.

✦ **Orientation:** Enables you to sort by columns rather than by rows (the default).

Using a Custom Sort Order

Excel typically sorts either numerically or alphabetically, depending on the data being sorted. In some cases, however, you may want to sort your data in other ways. For example, if your data consists of month names, you usually want it to appear in month order rather than alphabetically. You can use the Sort Options dialog box to perform such a sort. Select the appropriate list from the drop-down list labeled First key sort order. Excel, by default, has four "custom lists," and you can define your own. Excel's custom lists are as follows:

✦ **Abbreviated days:** Sun, Mon, Tue, Wed, Thu, Fri, Sat

✦ **Days:** Sunday, Monday, Tuesday, Wednesday, Thursday, Friday, Saturday

✦ **Abbreviated months:** Jan, Feb, Mar, Apr, May, Jun, Jul, Aug, Sep, Oct, Nov, Dec

✦ **Months:** January, February, March, April, May, June, July, August, September, October, November, December

Note that the abbreviated days and months do not have periods after them. If you use periods for these abbreviations, Excel doesn't recognize them (and doesn't sort them correctly).

You may want to create a custom list. For example, your company may have several stores, and you want the stores to be listed in a particular order (not alphabetically). If you create a custom list, sorting puts the items in the order that you specify in the list. You must use the Data ➪ Sort command to sort by a custom list (click on the Options button to specify the custom list).

To create a custom list, use the Custom Lists tab of the Options dialog box, as shown in Figure 23-20. Select the NEW LIST option, and make your entries (in order) in the List Entries box. Or, you can import your custom list from a range of cells by selecting the range and then clicking the Import button.

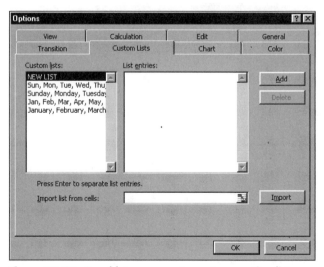

Figure 23-20: Excel lets you create custom sorting lists.

Custom lists also work with the AutoFill handle in cells. If you enter the first item of a custom list and then drag the cell's AutoFill handle, Excel fills in the remaining list items automatically.

Sorting Nonlists

You can, of course, sort any range in a worksheet — it doesn't have to be a list. You need to be aware of a few things, however. The Sort Ascending and Sort Descending toolbar buttons may assume (erroneously) that the top row is a header row and not include these cells in the sort (see the sidebar, "How Excel identifies a header row," earlier in this chapter).

Therefore, to avoid potential errors when sorting non-lists, don't use these toolbar buttons. Rather, select the entire range, and select Data ➪ Sort (making sure that you choose the No Header Row option).

Creating Subtotals

The final topic of this chapter is automatic subtotals — a handy feature that can save you a great deal of time. To use this feature, your list must be sorted, because the subtotals are inserted whenever the value in a specified field changes. Figure 23-21 shows an example of a list, sorted by the Month field, which is appropriate for subtotals.

	A	B	C	D	E	F	G
1	Month	Sales Rep	Type	Unit Cost	Quantity	Total Sale	
2	January	Franks	New	225	4	900	
3	January	Franks	Existing	175	5	875	
4	January	Franks	New	225	1	225	
5	January	Franks	Existing	175	1	175	
6	January	Jenkins	New	225	1	225	
7	January	Jenkins	Existing	125	1	125	
8	February	Franks	New	225	4	900	
9	February	Jenkins	New	225	2	450	
10	February	Jenkins	New	225	3	675	
11	February	Jenkins	New	225	3	675	
12	February	Jenkins	New	225	3	675	
13	February	Jenkins	Existing	175	1	175	
14	February	Peterson	New	225	1	225	
15	February	Peterson	New	225	2	450	
16	March	Peterson	Existing	125	2	250	
17	March	Peterson	New	225	2	450	
18	March	Robinson	Existing	125	1	125	
19	March	Robinson	Existing	125	5	625	
20	March	Robinson	New	225	4	900	
21	April	Franks	New	175	4	700	
22	April	Franks	New	175	3	525	
23	April	Jenkins	New	225	2	450	
24	April	Jenkins	New	140	3	420	

Figure 23-21: This list is a good candidate for subtotals, which are inserted at each change of the month.

To insert subtotal formulas into a list automatically, move the cell pointer anywhere in the list and choose Data ➪ Subtotals. You see the dialog box shown in Figure 23-22.

Figure 23-22: The Subtotal dialog box automatically inserts subtotal formulas into a sorted list.

This dialog box offers the following choices:

✦ **At Each Change in:** This drop-down list displays all fields in your list. You must have sorted the list by the field that you choose.

✦ **Use Function: Choose from 11 functions:** You should normally use Sum (the default).

✦ **Add Subtotal to:** This list box shows all the fields in your list. Place a check mark next to the field or fields that you want to subtotal.

✦ **Replace Current Subtotals:** If this box is checked, Excel removes any existing subtotal formulas and replaces them with the new subtotals.

✦ **Page Break Between Groups:** If this box is checked, Excel inserts a manual page break after each subtotal.

✦ **Summary Below Data:** If this box is checked, Excel places the subtotals below the data (the default). Otherwise, the subtotal formulas appear above the totals.

✦ **Remove All:** This button removes all subtotal formulas in the list.

When you click on OK, Excel analyzes the list and inserts formulas as specified — and creates an outline for you. The formulas all use the SUBTOTAL worksheet function.

When you add subtotals to a filtered list, the subtotals may no longer be accurate when the filter is removed.

Figure 23-23 shows a worksheet after adding subtotals.

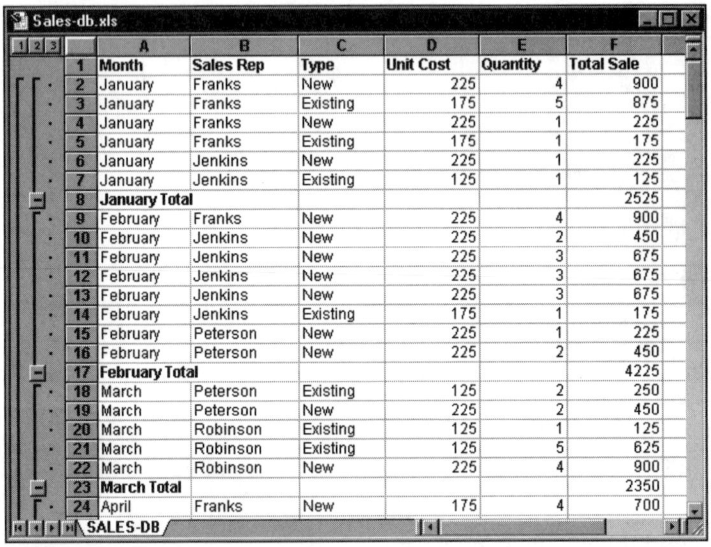

	Month	Sales Rep	Type	Unit Cost	Quantity	Total Sale
2	January	Franks	New	225	4	900
3	January	Franks	Existing	175	5	875
4	January	Franks	New	225	1	225
5	January	Franks	Existing	175	1	175
6	January	Jenkins	New	225	1	225
7	January	Jenkins	Existing	125	1	125
8	January Total					2525
9	February	Franks	New	225	4	900
10	February	Jenkins	New	225	2	450
11	February	Jenkins	New	225	3	675
12	February	Jenkins	New	225	3	675
13	February	Jenkins	New	225	3	675
14	February	Jenkins	Existing	175	1	175
15	February	Peterson	New	225	1	225
16	February	Peterson	New	225	2	450
17	February Total					4225
18	March	Peterson	Existing	125	2	250
19	March	Peterson	New	225	2	450
20	March	Robinson	Existing	125	1	125
21	March	Robinson	Existing	125	5	625
22	March	Robinson	New	225	4	900
23	March Total					2350
24	April	Franks	New	175	4	700

Figure 23-23: Excel added the subtotal formulas automatically — and even created an outline.

Summary

In this chapter, I discuss lists. A list is simply a database table that is stored on a worksheet. The first row of the list (the header row) contains field names, and subsequent rows contain data (records). I offer some pointers on data entry and discuss two ways to filter a list to show only rows that meet certain criteria. AutoFiltering is adequate for many tasks, but if your filtering needs are more complex, you need to use advanced filtering. I end the chapter with a discussion of sorting and Excel's automatic subtotal feature.

✦ ✦ ✦

Using External Database Files

The preceding chapter described how to work with lists that are stored in a worksheet. Many users find that worksheet lists are sufficient for their data tracking. Others, however, choose to take advantage of Excel's capability to access data that is stored in external database files. That's the topic of this chapter.

Why Use External Database Files?

Accessing external database files from Excel is useful when you have the following situations:

+ You need to work with a very large database.

+ You share the database with others; that is, other users have access to the database and may need to work with the data at the same time.

+ You want to work with only a subset of the data — data that meets certain criteria that you specify.

+ The database is in a format that Excel can't read.

If you need to work with external databases, you may prefer Excel to other database programs. The advantage? After you bring the data into Excel, you can manipulate and format it by using familiar tools.

As you may know, Excel can read some database files directly — specifically, those produced by various versions of dBASE (with a DBF extension). If the database has fewer than 65,535 records and no more than 255 fields, you can load the entire file into a worksheet, memory permitting. Even if you have enough memory to load such a large file, however, Excel's performance would likely be poor.

In many cases, you may not be interested in all the records or fields in the file. Instead, you may want to bring in just the data that meets certain criteria. In other words, you want to *query* the database and load into your worksheet a subset of the external database that meets the criteria. Excel makes this type of operation relatively easy.

> **Note**   To perform queries using external databases, Microsoft Query must be installed on your system. If Query is not installed, you will be prompted to install it when you select the Data ⇨ Get External Data ⇨ Create New Query command. You must rerun the Excel (or Microsoft Office) setup program and install Query.

In previous versions of Excel, using Microsoft Query required that you load an add-in. That is no longer necessary, starting with Excel 97, although the add-in is still included for compatibility purposes.

To work with an external database file from Excel, use the Query application that is included with Excel. The general procedure is as follows:

1. Activate a worksheet.

2. Choose Data ⇨ Get External Data ⇨ New Database Query. This starts Query.

3. Specify whether you want to use Query directly or use Query Wizard.

4. Specify the database that you want to use and then create a *query*—a list of criteria that specifies which records you want.

5. Specify how you want the data returned that passes your query—either to a worksheet or as a pivot table.

You can choose to save the query in a file so that you can reuse it later. This means that modifying the query or *refreshing* it (updating it with any changed values) is a simple matter. This is particularly useful when the data resides in a shared database that is continually being updated.

> **Cross-Reference**   The next chapter discusses pivot tables. You can create a pivot table using data in an external file, and use Query to retrieve data.

Using Query: An Example

The best way to become familiar with Query is to walk through an example.

The Database File

The file that is used in this example is named Budget.dbf.

> **On the CD-ROM**   If you want to try this example, you can find it on this book's CD-ROM.

This database file is a dBASE IV database with a single table that consists of 15,840 records. This file contains the following fields:

✦ **Sort:** A numeric field that holds record sequence numbers.

✦ **Division:** A text field that specifies the company division (Asia, Europe, N. America, Pacific Rim, or S. America).

✦ **Department:** A text field that specifies the department within the division. Each division is organized into the following departments: Accounting, Advertising, Data Processing, Human Resources, Operations, Public Relations, R&D, Sales, Security, Shipping, and Training.

✦ **Category:** A text field that specifies the budget category. The four categories are Compensation, Equipment, Facility, and Supplies & Services.

✦ **Item:** A text field that specifies the budget item. Each budget category has different budget items. For example, the Compensation category includes the following items: Benefits, Bonuses, Commissions, Conferences, Entertainment, Payroll Taxes, Salaries, and Training.

✦ **Month:** A text field that specifies the month (abbreviated as Jan, Feb, and so on).

✦ **Budget:** A numeric field that stores the budgeted amount.

✦ **Actual:** A numeric field that stores the actual amount spent.

✦ **Variance:** A numeric field that stores the difference between the Budget and Actual fields.

The Task

The objective of this exercise is to develop a report that shows the first quarter (January through March) actual compensation expenditures of the training department in the North American division. In other words, the query will extract records for which the following applies:

✦ The Division is N. America

✦ The Department is Training

✦ The Category is Compensation

✦ The Month is Jan, Feb, or Mar

Using Query to Get the Data

You *could* import the entire dBASE file into a worksheet and then choose Data ➪ Filter ➪ AutoFilter to filter the data as required. This approach would work, because the file has fewer than 65,535 records, which isn't always the case. Using Query, however, you import only the data that's required.

Some Database Terminology

People who spend their days working with databases seem to have their own special language. The following terms can help you hold your own among a group of database experts:

External database: A collection of data that is stored in one or more files (not Excel files). Each file of a database holds a single table, and tables are comprised of records and fields.

Field: In a database table, an element of a record that corresponds to a column.

ODBC: An acronym for Open DataBase Connectivity, a standard developed by Microsoft that uses drivers to access database files in different formats. Microsoft Query comes with drivers for Access, dBASE, FoxPro, Paradox, SQL Server, Excel workbooks, and ASCII text files. ODBC drivers for other databases are available from Microsoft and third-party providers.

Query: To search a database for records that meet specific criteria. This term is also used as a noun; you can write a query, for example.

Record: In a database table, a single element that corresponds to a row.

Refresh: To rerun a query to get the latest data. This is applicable when the database contains information that is subject to change, as in a multiuser environment.

Relational database: A database that is stored in more than one table or file. At least one common field (sometimes called the *key field*) connects the tables.

Result set: The data that is returned by a query, usually a subset of the original database. Query returns the result set to your Excel workbook or to a pivot table.

SQL: An acronym for Structured Query Language (usually pronounced *sequel*). Query uses SQL to query data that is stored in ODBC databases.

Table: A record- and field-oriented collection of data. A database consists of one or more tables.

Starting query

Begin with an empty worksheet. Select Data ➪ Get External Data ➪ New Database Query; this action launches and activates Microsoft Query, a separate application. Excel continues to run, and you can switch back and forth between Query and Excel, as needed.

Selecting a data source

When Query starts, it displays the Choose Data Source dialog box, shown in Figure 24-1. This dialog box contains three tabs:

✦ Databases: Lists the data sources that are known to Query—this tab may be empty, depending on which data sources are defined on your system.

✦ Queries: Contains a list of stored queries. Again, this may or may not be empty.

✦ OLAP Cubes: Lists OLAP databases (see sidebar) that are available for Query.

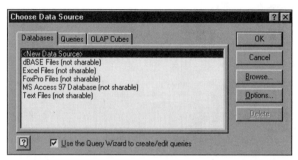

Figure 24-1: The Choose Data Source dialog box.

OLAP Databases

OLAP is an acronym for *online analytical processing*; OLAP presents a new way to organize large databases to suit the way that you analyze and manage information. In an OLAP database, data is organized by level of detail. In a business database, for example, you might want to track sales around the world for the products of a particular company. In an OLAP organization of this information, you would need to consider where and when each product was sold, as well as which product was sold. Each of these aspects of the OLAP database is called a *dimension*, and each dimension is comprised of several fields that can be organized hierarchically, by level of detail. You might call the "where" dimension the Location dimension, and it might contain, for example, fields for country, region, and city. The Time dimension, containing information about when the product was sold, might contain fields for month, date, day, and year.

Dimensions in an OLAP database combine to provide information about the intersecting points; because you can combine several dimensions, OLAP databases are called *cubes*.

You can connect Excel to an OLAP data source created with either the Microsoft DSS (Decision Support Services) Analysis server or other third-party OLAP products that provide data source drivers that are compatible with OLD-DB for OLAP. You connect to an OLAP cube the same way that you connect to other external data sources. Excel can display data that you retrieve from an OLAP cube as either a PivotTable or a PivotChart. You cannot display OLAP data as an external data range of the type discussed in this chapter.

If you've previously worked with a particular database, its name appears in the list of databases. Otherwise, you need to identify the source.

In the Databases tab, select the <New Database Source> option and click OK. This displays the Create New Data Source dialog box, shown in Figure 24-2.

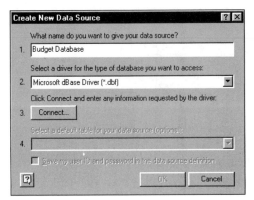

Figure 24-2: The Create New Data Source dialog box.

The Create New Data Source dialog box has the following four numbered parts:

1. Enter a descriptive name for the data source. For this example, the name is Budget Database.

2. Select a driver for the data source by selecting from the list of installed drivers. Because the database file in this example is a dBASE file, select the driver named Microsoft dBASE Driver.

3. The Connect button displays the ODBC Setup dialog box that asks for information specific to the driver that you select in Step 2. In this dialog box, you select the directory where the database is located.

4. Select the default data table that you want to use (this step is optional). If the database requires a password, you can also specify that the password be saved with the Data Source definition.

After you supply all the information in the Create New Data Source dialog box, click OK, and Excel redisplays the Choose Data Source dialog box — which now includes the data source that you created.

You have to go through these steps only once for each data source. The next time that you access Query, the Budget Database (and any other database sources that you define) appears in the Choose Data Source dialog box.

Using the ODBC Manager

Occasionally, you may need to edit data sources—for example, if you move your database files to a new location. You can do this by using the ODBC Manager utility. This program is available in the Windows Control Panel (it's called *32-bit ODBC*). This utility also lets you add new data sources and remove those that you no longer need.

Use Query Wizard?

The Choose Data Source dialog box has a check box at the bottom that lets you specify whether to use Query Wizard to create your query. Query Wizard walks you through the steps that are used to create your query, and if you use Query Wizard, you don't have to deal directly with Query. I highly recommend using Query Wizard—and the examples in this chapter use this tool.

In the Choose Data Sources dialog box, make sure that you check the Query Wizard check box at the bottom of the dialog box and then click OK to start Query Wizard.

Query Wizard: Choosing the columns

In the first step of Query Wizard (see Figure 24-3), select the database columns that you want to appear in your query.

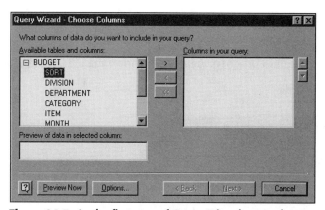

Figure 24-3: In the first step of Query Wizard, you select the columns to use in your query.

The columns that you select determine the fields from the database that Query returns to Excel. Recall that the query for this example involves selecting records based on the following fields: Division, Department, Month, Category, and Actual. You also want to add the Item field. The left tab of the dialog box shows all the available columns. To add a column to the right tab, select the column and click the > button (or, you can double-click the column name).

After you finish adding the columns, the Query Wizard dialog box looks like Figure 24-4.

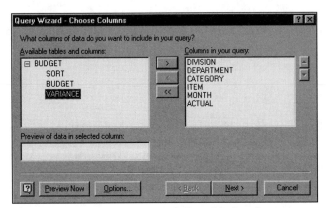

Figure 24-4: Six columns have been added to the query.

If you want to see the data for a particular column, select the column and click the Preview Now button. If you accidentally add a column that you don't need, select it in the right tab and click the < button to remove it. After you select all the columns for the query, click the Next button.

Query Wizard: Filtering data

In the second Query Wizard dialog box, you specify your record selection criteria — how you want to filter the data. This step is optional. If you want to retrieve all the data, just click the Next button to proceed. Figure 24-5 shows the Filter Data dialog box of Query Wizard.

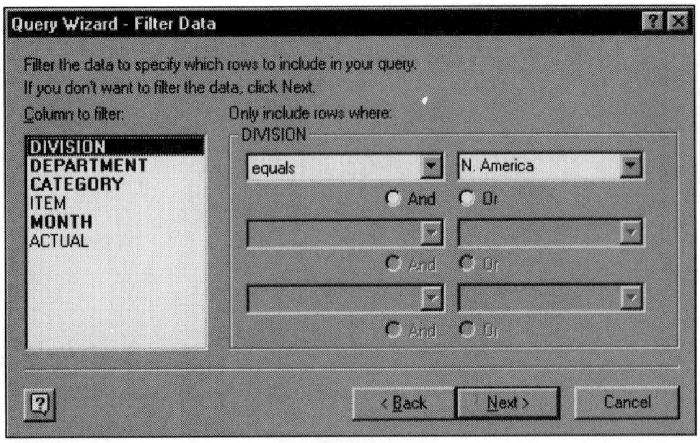

Figure 24-5: In the second step of Query Wizard, you specify how you want to filter the data.

For the example, you don't need all records. Recall that you're interested only in the records in which one of the following applies:

✦ The Division is N. America.

✦ The Department is Training.

✦ The Category is Compensation.

✦ The Month is Jan, Feb, or Mar.

You enter the criteria by column. In this case, you need to specify four criteria (one for each of four columns):

1. In the Column to filter column, select DIVISION. In the right tab, select equals from the first drop-down list, and N. America from the second drop-down list.

2. In the Column to filter column, select DEPARTMENT. In the right tab, select equals from the first drop-down list, and Training from the second drop-down list.

3. In the Column to filter column, select CATEGORY. In the right tab, select equals from the first drop-down list, and Compensation from the second drop-down list.

4. In the Column to filter column, select MONTH. In the right tab, select equals from the first drop-down list, and Jan from the second drop-down list. Because this column is filtered by multiple values, click the Or option and then select equals and Feb from the drop-down lists in the second row. Finally, select equals and Mar from the drop-down lists in the second row.

To review the criteria that you've entered, select the column from the Column to filter list. Query Wizard displays the criteria that you entered for the selected column. After you enter all the criteria, click Next.

Query Wizard: Sort order

The third step of the Query Wizard enables you to specify how you want the records to be sorted (see Figure 24-6). This step is optional, and you can click Next to move to the next step if you don't want the data sorted or prefer to sort it after it's returned to your worksheet.

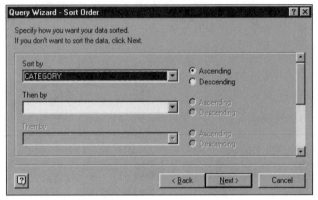

Figure 24-6: In the third step of Query Wizard, you specify the sort order.

For this example, sort by CATEGORY in Ascending order. You can specify as many sort fields as you like. Click Next to move to the next step.

Query Wizard: Finish

The final step of Query Wizard, shown in Figure 24-7, lets you do the following things:

✦ Give the query a name

✦ Save it to a file, so that it can be reused

✦ Specify what to do with the data

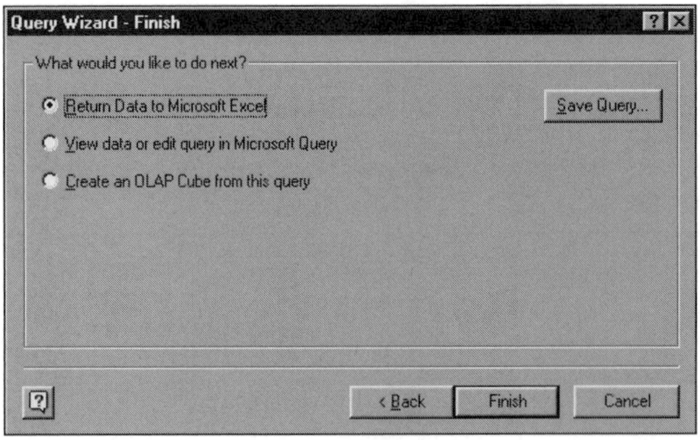

Figure 24-7: The final step of Query Wizard.

Normally, you want to return the data to Excel. If you know how to use the Microsoft Query application, you can return the data to Query and examine it, or even modify the selection criteria. Or, you can create an OLAP cube to use in a PivotTable or PivotChart report.

If you plan to reuse this query, you should save it to a file. Click the Save Query button, and you are prompted for a filename. After you make your choices, click Finish.

Query Operators

The following table lists and describes the operators that are available when you create a query. These operators give you complete control over which rows are returned.

Operator	What It Does
equals	Field is identical to value
does not equal	Field is not equal to value
is greater than	Field is greater than value
is greater than or equal to	Field is greater than or equal to value
is less than	Field is less than value
is less than or equal to	Field is less than or equal to value
is one of	Field is in a list of values, separated by commas
is not one of	Field is not in a list of values, separated by commas
is between	Field is between two values, separated by commas
is not between	Field is not between two values, separated by commas
begins with	Field begins with the value
does not begin with	Field does not begin with value
ends with	Field ends with value
does not end with	Field does not end with value
contains	Field contains value
does not contain	Field does not contain value
like	Field is like value (using * and ? wildcard characters)
not like	Field is not like value (using * and ? wildcard characters)
is Null	Field is empty
is not Null	Field is not empty

Specifying a Location for the Data

Figure 24-8 shows the Returning External Data to Microsoft Excel dialog box, which appears when you click the Finish button in the Query Wizard dialog box.

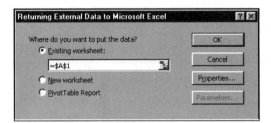

Figure 24-8: Specifying what to do with the data.

You can select from the following choices:

✦ **Existing worksheet:** You can specify the upper-left cell.

✦ **New worksheet:** Excel can insert a new worksheet and insert the data beginning in cell A1.

✦ **Pivot Table Report:** Excel can display its Pivot Table Wizard, so that you can specify the layout for a pivot table (see Chapter 25).

Figure 24-9 shows the data that is returned to a worksheet.

	A	B	C	D	E	F
1	DIVISION	DEPARTMENT	CATEGORY	ITEM	MONTH	ACTUAL
2	N. America	Training	Compensation	Payroll Taxes	Feb	3542
3	N. America	Training	Compensation	Benefits	Jan	3283
4	N. America	Training	Compensation	Bonuses	Jan	3331
5	N. America	Training	Compensation	Commissions	Jan	3143
6	N. America	Training	Compensation	Payroll Taxes	Jan	3516
7	N. America	Training	Compensation	Training	Jan	4058
8	N. America	Training	Compensation	Conferences	Jan	4281
9	N. America	Training	Compensation	Entertainment	Jan	3344
10	N. America	Training	Compensation	Salaries	Feb	3972
11	N. America	Training	Compensation	Benefits	Feb	3985
12	N. America	Training	Compensation	Salaries	Jan	4313
13	N. America	Training	Compensation	Commissions	Feb	3288
14	N. America	Training	Compensation	Entertainment	Mar	3205
15	N. America	Training	Compensation	Training	Feb	3757
16	N. America	Training	Compensation	Conferences	Feb	4055
17	N. America	Training	Compensation	Entertainment	Feb	3724
18	N. America	Training	Compensation	Salaries	Mar	3748
19	N. America	Training	Compensation	Benefits	Mar	3808
20	N. America	Training	Compensation	Bonuses	Mar	3809
21	N. America	Training	Compensation	Commissions	Mar	3271
22	N. America	Training	Compensation	Payroll Taxes	Mar	3347
23	N. America	Training	Compensation	Training	Mar	3678
24	N. America	Training	Compensation	Conferences	Mar	4146
25	N. America	Training	Compensation	Bonuses	Feb	2611

Figure 24-9: The results of the query.

Working with an External Data Range

Excel stores the data that Query returns in either a worksheet or a pivot table. When Excel stores data in a worksheet, it stores the data in a specially named range, known as an *external data range;* Excel creates the name for this range automatically.

This section describes what you can do with the data that Excel receives from Query and stores in a worksheet.

Adjusting External Data Range Properties

You can adjust various properties of the external data range by using the External Data Range Properties dialog box (see Figure 24-10).

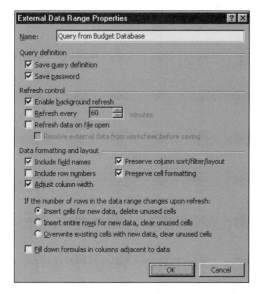

Figure 24-10: The External Data Range Properties dialog box enables you to specify various options for an external data range.

To display this dialog box, the cell pointer must be within the external data range. You can open this dialog box by using any of three methods:

- ◆ Right-click and select Data Range Properties from the shortcut menu.
- ◆ Select Data ➪ Get External Data ➪ Data Range Properties.
- ◆ Click the Data Range properties tool on the External Data toolbar (this toolbar appears automatically when you perform a query).

The following list describes the options in the External Data Range Properties dialog box:

✦ **Name:** The name of the external data range. You can change this name or use the default name that Excel creates. Excel substitutes, in the range name, the underscore character for any spaces that you see in the Name box of the External Data Range Properties box.

✦ **Query definition:** If you check Save query definition, Excel stores the query definition with the external data range, enabling you to refresh the data or edit the query, if necessary. If the database requires a password, you can also store the password so that you don't need to enter it when you refresh the query.

✦ **Refresh control:** Determines how and when Excel refreshes the data.

✦ **Data formatting and layout:** Determines the appearance of the external data range.

The External Data Range Properties dialog box has quite a few options. For specific details, click the Help icon in the title bar and then click an option in the dialog box.

You can manipulate data returned from a query just like any other worksheet range. For example, you can sort the data, format it, or create formulas that use the data.

EXCEL 2000

In prior versions of Excel, if you intend to refresh the query, you need to keep the external data range intact. That is, you can't insert new rows or columns in the external data range, because refreshing the query causes the external range to be rewritten. Similarly, you lose any formatting that you applied to the external data range when you refresh the query.

In Excel 2000, refreshing a query *does not* overwrite the external data range. You are free to format the external data range or insert rows and columns. You also can include formulas in those rows and columns that refer to other parts of the external data range. Your work *will not* be destroyed when you refresh the query.

Refreshing a Query

After performing a query, you can save the file and then retrieve it later. The file contains the data that you originally retrieved from the external database. The external database may have changed, however, in the interim.

If you checked the Save query definition option in the External Data Range Properties dialog box, then Excel saves the query definition with the workbook. Simply move the cell pointer anywhere within the external data table in the worksheet and then use one of the following methods to refresh the query:

✦ Right-click and select Refresh Data from the shortcut menu

✦ Select Data ➪ Refresh Data

✦ Click the Refresh Data tool on the External Data toolbar

Excel launches Query and uses your original query to bring in the current data from the external database.

Tip   If you find that refreshing the query causes undesirable results, use Excel's Undo feature to "unrefresh" the data.

Making Multiple Queries

A single workbook can hold as many external data ranges as you need. Excel gives each query a unique name, and you can work with each query independently. Excel automatically keeps track of the query that produces each external data range.

Copying or Moving a Query

After performing a query, you may want to copy or move the external data range, which you can do by using the normal copy, cut, and paste techniques. However, make sure that you copy or cut the entire external data range—otherwise, the underlying query is not copied, and the copied data cannot be refreshed.

Deleting a Query

If you decide that you no longer need the data that is returned by a query, you can delete it by selecting the entire external data range and choosing Edit ➪ Delete.

Note   If you simply press Delete, the contents of the cells are erased, but the underlying query remains. Excel displays a dialog box asking whether you want to delete the query. If you choose No, you can refresh the query, and the deleted cells appear again, including any formatting that you applied to them.

When you refresh, Query returns only data that is retrieved from the external database. If you delete rows or columns that you inserted into the external data range, Query does not redisplay those rows and columns when you refresh.

Changing Your Query

If you bring the query results into your worksheet and discover that you don't have what you want, you can modify the query. Move the cell pointer anywhere within the external data table in the worksheet and then use one of the following methods to refresh the query:

✦ Right-click and select Edit Query from the shortcut menu

✦ Select Data ➪ Get External Data ➪ Edit Query

✦ Click the Edit Query tool on the External Data toolbar

Excel then launches (or activates) Query, and you can change the original query. After you finish, choose File ➪ Return Data to Microsoft Excel. Excel reactivates, executes the modified query, and updates the external data range.

Using Microsoft Query Without Query Wizard

Previous sections in this chapter describe how to use Query Wizard to create a database query. Query Wizard is essentially a "front end" for Microsoft Query. In some cases, you may want to use Query itself rather than Query Wizard.

When you select Data ➪ Get External Data ➪ Create New Query, the Choose Data Source dialog box gives you the option of whether to use Query Wizard. If you choose not to use Query Wizard, you work directly with Microsoft Query.

Creating a Query

Before you can create a query, you must display the Criteria pane. In Query, open the View menu and confirm that a check appears next to the Criteria command. If you don't see a check, choose View ➪ Criteria to display the Criteria pane in the middle of the window. (See Figure 24-11.)

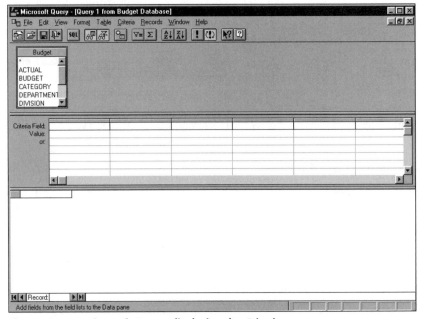

Figure 24-11: Microsoft Query, displaying the Criteria pane.

The Query window has three panes, which are split vertically:

✦ **Tables pane:** The top pane, which holds the data tables for the database. Each data table window has a list of the fields in the table.

✦ **Criteria pane:** The middle pane, which holds the criteria that determine the rows that the query returns.

✦ **Data pane:** The bottom pane, which holds the data that passes the criteria.

Creating a query consists of the following steps:

1. Drag fields from the Tables pane to the Data pane. You can drag as many fields as you want. These fields are the columns that the query will return. You can also double-click a field instead of dragging it.

2. Enter criteria in the Criteria pane. When you activate this pane, the first row (labeled Criteria Field) displays a drop-down list that contains all the field names. Select a field and enter the criteria below it. Query updates the Data pane automatically, treating each row like an OR operator.

3. Choose File ⇨ Return Data to Microsoft Excel to execute the query and place the data in a worksheet or pivot table.

Figure 24-12 shows how the query for the example presented earlier in this chapter appears in Query.

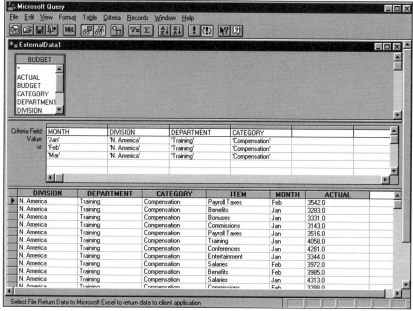

Figure 24-12: The center pane contains a query definition.

Running Microsoft Query by Itself

Normally, you run Query from Excel. But because Query is a standalone application, you also can run it directly. The executable file is named msqry32.exe and its location can vary (use the Windows Find File feature to locate this program on your system).

If you run Query by itself, you can't return the data to Excel automatically. You can, however, use the Clipboard to copy data from the data pane to any application that you want (including Excel).

Using Multiple Database Tables

The example in this chapter uses only one database table. Some databases, however, use multiple tables. These databases are known as *relational databases*, because a common field links the tables. Query lets you use any number of tables in your queries. To see an example of a relational database, load the sample database (called Northwind Traders) that's provided with Microsoft Query. This particular database has six tables.

Adding and Editing Records in External Database Tables

To add, delete, and edit data when you are using Query, make sure that a check appears next to the Records ➪ Allow Editing command. Of course, you can't edit a database file that's set up as read-only. In any case, you need to be careful with this feature, because your changes are saved to disk as soon as you move the cell pointer out of the record that you're editing (you do not need to choose File ➪ Save).

Formatting Data

If you don't like the data's appearance in the data pane, you can change the font used, by selecting Format ➪ Font. Be aware that selective formatting isn't allowed (unlike in Excel); changing the font affects all the data in the data pane.

Sorting Data

If you need to view the data in the data pane in a different order, choose Records ➪ Sort (or click the Sort Ascending or Sort Descending toolbar icon).

Learning More

This chapter isn't intended to cover every aspect of Microsoft Query. Rather, it discusses the basic features that are used most often. In fact, if you use Query Wizard, you may never need to interact with Query itself. But, if you do need to use Query, you can experiment and consult the online Help to learn more. As with anything related to Excel, the best way to master Query is to use it — preferably with data that's meaningful to you.

Summary

This chapter introduces Microsoft Query — a standalone application that can be executed by Excel. Use Query to retrieve data from external database files. You can specify the criteria, and Query returns the data to your Excel worksheet.

✦   ✦   ✦

Analyzing Data with Pivot Tables

Excel provides many data analysis tools, but the pivot table feature may be the most useful overall. Pivot tables are valuable for summarizing information that is contained in a database, which can be stored in a worksheet or in an external file.

This chapter demonstrates this innovative feature and suggests how you can use it to view your data in ways that you may not have imagined.

What Is a Pivot Table?

A *pivot table* provides a dynamic summary of data that is contained in a database or list. A pivot table enables you to create frequency distributions and cross-tabulations of several different data dimensions. In addition, you can display subtotals and any level of detail that you want. But, as explained later in this chapter, a pivot table *isn't* appropriate for all databases.

The best way to understand the concept of a pivot table is to see one. Start with Figure 25-1, which shows the data that is being used to create the pivot table in this chapter.

	A	B	C	D	E	F
1	Date	Amount	AcctType	OpenedBy	Branch	Customer
2	09/01/97	340	Checking	New Accts	Central	Existing
3	09/01/97	15,759	CD	Teller	Westside	Existing
4	09/01/97	15,276	CD	New Accts	North County	Existing
5	09/01/97	12,000	CD	New Accts	Westside	Existing
6	09/01/97	5,000	CD	New Accts	North County	Existing
7	09/01/97	7,000	Savings	New Accts	North County	New
8	09/01/97	90,000	CD	New Accts	Central	Existing
9	09/01/97	124	Checking	Teller	Central	Existing
10	09/01/97	400	Checking	Teller	Central	Existing
11	09/01/97	100	Checking	New Accts	Central	Existing
12	09/01/97	14,644	CD	New Accts	Westside	New
13	09/01/97	5,000	Savings	New Accts	Westside	Existing
14	09/01/97	4,623	Savings	New Accts	North County	Existing
15	09/01/97	5,879	Checking	New Accts	Central	Existing
16	09/01/97	3,171	Checking	New Accts	Westside	Existing
17	09/01/97	4,000	Savings	New Accts	Central	Existing
18	09/01/97	5,000	Checking	New Accts	Central	Existing
19	09/01/97	16,000	CD	New Accts	Central	New
20	09/01/97	50,000	Savings	New Accts	Central	Existing
21	09/01/97	13,636	CD	New Accts	North County	Existing

Banking.xls — Pivot Table / September

Figure 25-1: This database is used to create a pivot table.

This database consists of daily new-account information for a three-branch bank. The database contains 350 records and tracks:

✦ The date that each account was opened

✦ The opening amount

✦ The account type (CD, checking, savings, or IRA)

✦ Who opened the account (a teller or a new-account representative)

✦ The branch at which it was opened

✦ Whether a new customer or an existing customer opened the account

On the CD-ROM   You can find this workbook on this book's CD-ROM; it is used in many examples throughout the chapter.

The bank database contains a lot of information, but it's not all that revealing, because, in its present form, the information is difficult to understand. If the data were summarized, it would be more useful. Summarizing a database is essentially the process of answering questions about the data. Here are a few questions that may be of interest to the bank's management:

✦ What is the total deposit amount for each branch, broken down by account type?

✦ How many accounts were opened at each branch, broken down by account type?

✦ What's the dollar distribution of the different account types?

✦ What types of accounts do tellers most often open?

✦ How is the Central branch doing compared to the other two branches?

✦ Which branch opens the most accounts for new customers?

You can use a pivot table to answer questions like these. It takes only a few seconds and doesn't require a single formula.

Figure 25-2 shows a pivot table created from the database that is displayed in Figure 25-1. This pivot table shows the amount of new deposits, broken down by branch and account type. This summary is one of hundreds that you can produce from this data.

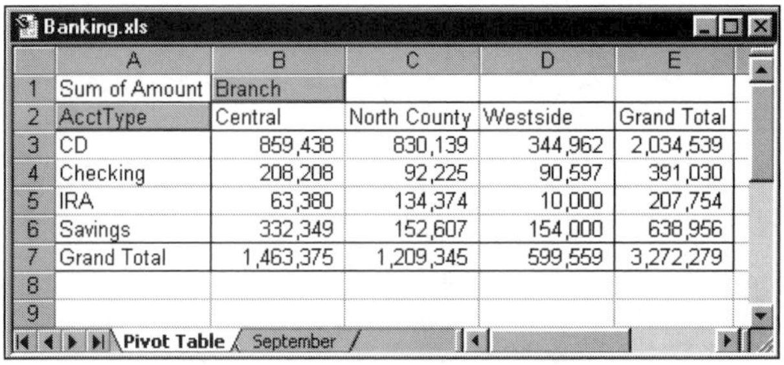

	A	B	C	D	E
1	Sum of Amount	Branch			
2	AcctType	Central	North County	Westside	Grand Total
3	CD	859,438	830,139	344,962	2,034,539
4	Checking	208,208	92,225	90,597	391,030
5	IRA	63,380	134,374	10,000	207,754
6	Savings	332,349	152,607	154,000	638,956
7	Grand Total	1,463,375	1,209,345	599,559	3,272,279
8					
9					

Banking.xls — Pivot Table / September

Figure 25-2: A simple pivot table.

Figure 25-3 shows another pivot table that is generated from the bank data. This pivot table uses a page field for the Customer item. In this case, the pivot table displays the data only for new customers. Notice that the orientation of the table is changed. (Branches appear in rows and AcctType appears in columns.)

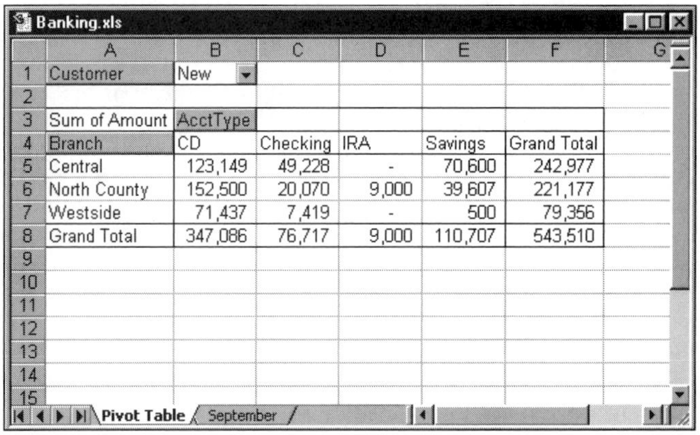

	A	B	C	D	E	F	G
1	Customer	New					
2							
3	Sum of Amount	AcctType					
4	Branch	CD	Checking	IRA	Savings	Grand Total	
5	Central	123,149	49,228	-	70,600	242,977	
6	North County	152,500	20,070	9,000	39,607	221,177	
7	Westside	71,437	7,419	-	500	79,356	
8	Grand Total	347,086	76,717	9,000	110,707	543,510	
9							
10							
11							
12							
13							
14							
15							

Banking.xls — Pivot Table / September

Figure 25-3: A pivot table that uses a page field.

Data Appropriate for a Pivot Table

Before getting into the details of pivot tables, you need to understand the type of data that's relevant to this feature. The data that you're summarizing must be in the form of a database (although an exception to this does exist, which is discussed later in the chapter). You can store the database in either a worksheet (such a database is sometimes known as a table) or an external database file. Although Excel can convert any database to a pivot table, not all databases benefit.

Generally speaking, fields in a database table can be one of two types:

✦ **Data:** Contains a value. In Figure 25-1, the Amount field is a data field.

✦ **Category:** Describes the data. In Figure 25-1, the Date, AcctType, OpenedBy, Branch, and Customer fields are category fields, because they describe the data in the Amount field.

Pivot Table Terminology

If you're new to Excel, the concept of a pivot table may be a bit baffling. As far as I know, Microsoft invented the name *pivot table.* Understanding the terminology associated with pivot tables is important. Refer to the accompanying figure to get your bearings.

✦ **Column field:** A field that has a column orientation in the pivot table. Each item in the field occupies a column. In the figure, Customer is a column field, and it has two items (Existing and New). Column fields can be nested.

✦ **Data area:** The cells in a pivot table that contain the summary data. Excel offers several ways to summarize the data (sum, average, count, and so on). In the figure, the Data area includes C5:E20.

✦ **Grand totals:** A row or column that displays totals for all cells in a row or column in a pivot table. You can specify that grand totals be calculated for rows, columns, or both (or neither). The pivot table in the figure has grand totals for rows and columns.

✦ **Group:** A collection of items that are treated as a single item. You can group items manually or automatically (group dates into months, for example).

✦ **Item:** An element in a field that appears as a row or column header in a pivot table. In the figure, Existing and New are items for the Customer field. The Branch field has three items: Central, North County, and Westside. AcctType has four items: CD, Checking, IRA, and Savings.

✦ **Page field:** A field that has a page orientation in the pivot table — similar to a slice of a three-dimensional cube. Only one item in a page field can be displayed at one time. In the figure, OpenedBy is a page field that's displaying the NewAccts item; the pivot table shows data only for NewAccts.

✦ **Refresh:** To recalculate the pivot table after changes to the source data have been made.

+ **Row field:** A field that has a row orientation in the pivot table. Each item in the field occupies a row. Row fields can be nested. In the figure, Branch and AcctType are both row fields.

+ **Source data:** The data used to create a pivot table. It can reside in a worksheet or an external database.

+ **Subtotals:** A row or column that displays subtotals for detail cells in a row or column in a pivot table.

	A	B	C	D	E	F	G	H
	Banking.xls							
		A	B	C	D	E	F	G	H
1	OpenedBy	New Accts ▾						
2								
3	Sum of Amount		Customer ▾					
4	Branch ▾	AcctType ▾	Existing	New	Grand Total			
5	Central	CD	671289	123149	794438			
6		Checking	156884	49228	206112			
7		IRA	27000		27000			
8		Savings	239347	70600	309947			
9	Central Total		1094520	242977	1337497			
10	North County	CD	646184	152500	798684			
11		Checking	55880	20070	75950			
12		IRA	35554	7000	42554			
13		Savings	87136	39607	126743			
14	North County Total		824754	219177	1043931			
15	Westside	CD	143766	71437	215203			
16		Checking	52978	7419	60397			
17		IRA	10000		10000			
18		Savings	153500	500	154000			
19	Westside Total		360244	79356	439600			
20	Grand Total		2279518	541510	2821028			
21								

Terminology / September / Central / North County

A single database table can have any number of data fields and category fields. When you create a pivot table, you usually want to summarize one or more of the data fields. The values in the category fields, on the other hand, appear in the pivot table as rows, columns, or pages.

Exceptions exist, however, and you may find that Excel's pivot table feature is useful even for databases that don't contain actual numerical data fields. The database in Figure 25-4, for example, doesn't contain numerical data fields, but you can create a useful pivot table that counts fields rather than sums them.

You can summarize information in pivot tables by using methods other than summing. For example, the pivot table that you see in Figure 25-5 cross-tabulates the Month Born field by the Sex field, and the intersecting cells show the count for each combination of city and sex.

	A	B	C	D
	Name List.xls			
1	**Employee**	**Month Born**	**Sex**	
2	Miller	September	Female	
3	Santos	February	Female	
4	Alios	June	Male	
5	Chan	December	Female	
6	Henderson	March	Male	
7	Klinger	July	Female	
8	Rosarita	June	Male	
9	Fuller	February	Male	
10	Wilson	January	Female	
11	Quigley	July	Male	
12	Ross-Jacobs	April	Male	
13	Ocarina	August	Female	
14	Yulanderpol	November	Female	
15	Franklin	June	Female	

Figure 25-4: This database doesn't have any numerical fields, but you can use it to generate a pivot table.

	A	B	C	D	E
	Name List.xls				
1	Count of Employee	Sex			
2	Month Born	Female	Male	Grand Total	
3	January	2	2	4	
4	February	2	2	4	
5	March	0	5	5	
6	April	1	2	3	
7	May	2	0	2	
8	June	3	3	6	
9	July	3	2	5	
10	August	3	2	5	
11	September	4	0	4	
12	October	2	2	4	
13	November	3	1	4	
14	December	2	2	4	
15	Grand Total	27	23	50	

Figure 25-5: This pivot table summarizes non-numeric fields by displaying a count rather than a sum.

Creating a Pivot Table

This section walks you through the steps to create a pivot table by using the PivotTable and PivotChart Wizard. You access the PivotTable and PivotChart Wizard by choosing Data ➪ PivotTable and PivotChart Report.

On the CD-ROM

This section uses the banking account workbook, which is available on this book's CD-ROM.

Identifying Where the Data Is Located

When you choose Data ➪ PivotTable and PivotChart Report, the first of several dialog boxes appears (see Figure 25-6).

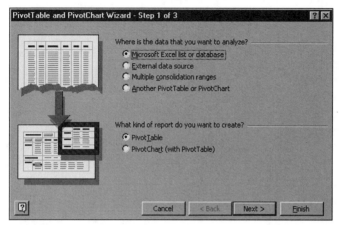

Figure 25-6: The first of three PivotTable and PivotChart Wizard dialog boxes.

In this step, you identify the data source. The possible data sources are described in the following sections.

Note   You see different dialog boxes while you work through the Wizard, depending on the location of the data that you want to analyze. The following sections present the Wizard dialog boxes for data located in an Excel list or database, in the context of describing the various possible data sources.

Excel list or database

Usually, the data that you analyze is stored in a worksheet database—which is also known as a *list*. Databases stored in a worksheet are limited to 65,535 records and 256 fields. Working with a database of this size isn't efficient, however (and memory may not even allow it). The first row in the database should be field names. No other rules exist. The data can consist of values, text, or formulas.

External data source

If you use the data in an external database for a pivot table, the data is retrieved by using Query (a separate application). You can use dBASE files, SQL server data, or other data that your system is set up to access. You are prompted for the data source in Step 2 of the PivotTable and PivotChart Wizard.

Pivot Tables and OLAP Cubes

In Chapter 24, the sidebar, "OLAP Databases" explains that OLAP (*online analytical processing*) presents a new way to organize large databases, to suit the way that you analyze and manage information. In an OLAP database, data is organized by level of detail, and the various aspects of data contained in an OLAP database are called *dimensions.* Because you combine dimensions to obtain information, OLAP databases are called *cubes.*

Generally, creating pivot tables in Excel from OLAP databases is faster than creating pivot tables from other types of external databases, because the OLAP server, not Excel, computes summarized values. Excel, therefore, receives less data from an OLAP cube when you create a pivot table or pivot chart.

Excel contains OLAP Cube Wizard, which helps you to organize data from external relational databases into OLAP cubes. Excel also contains Offline Cube Wizard, which enables you to create cube files that you can query even when you're not connected to your network. Distribute cube files over a network or on the Web to provide access to part, but not all, of a database.

You can create cube files only if you use an OLAP provider that supports creating cube files, such as Microsoft DSS Analysis server.

Chapter 24 discusses external database access, including Query. If you plan to create a pivot table by using data in an external database, you should consult Chapter 24 before proceeding.

Multiple consolidation ranges

You also can create a pivot table from multiple tables. This procedure is equivalent to consolidating the information in the tables. When you create a pivot table to consolidate information in tables, you have the added advantage of using all of the pivot table tools while you work with the consolidated data. (An example of this is presented later in the chapter.)

Chapter 19 discusses other consolidation techniques.

Another pivot table

Excel enables you to create a pivot table from an existing pivot table. Actually, this is a bit of a misnomer. The pivot table that you create is based on the *data* that the first pivot table uses (not the pivot table itself). If the active workbook has no pivot tables, this option is grayed, meaning you can't choose it.

Tip

If you need to create more than one pivot table from the same set of data, the procedure is more efficient (in terms of memory usage) if you create the first pivot table and then use that pivot table as the source for subsequent pivot tables.

Specifying the Data

To move on to the next step of the Wizard, click the Next button. Step 2 of the PivotTable and PivotChart Wizard prompts you for the data. Remember, the dialog box varies, depending on your choice in the first dialog box; Figure 25-7 shows the dialog box that appears when you select an Excel list or database in Step 1.

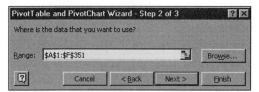

Figure 25-7: In Step 2, you specify the data range.

> **Tip** If you place the cell pointer anywhere within the worksheet database when you select Data ➪ PivotTable Report, Excel identifies the database range automatically in Step 2 of the PivotTable and PivotChart Wizard.

You can use the Browse button to open a different worksheet and select a range. To move on to Step 3, click the Next button.

Completing the Pivot Table

The following sections outline how to complete the pivot table. The first step is to determine the pivot table's location. The dialog box for the final step of the PivotTable and PivotChart Wizard is shown in Figure 25-8. In this step, you specify the location for the pivot table.

Figure 25-8: In Step 3, you specify the pivot table's location.

If you select the New worksheet option, Excel inserts a new worksheet for the pivot table. If you select the Existing worksheet option, the pivot table appears on the current worksheet (you can specify the starting cell location).

Pivot table options

You can click the Options button to select some options that determine how the table appears. Refer to the sidebar "Pivot Table Options," later in this chapter. Click OK to redisplay the PivotTable and PivotChart Wizard – Step 3 of 3 dialog box.

Setting up the layout of the pivot table

You can set up the layout of the pivot table in two different ways: either by using the PivotTable and PivotChart Wizard or by using the PivotTable toolbar directly on the worksheet.

Using a dialog box to lay out a pivot table

Click the Layout button of the last Wizard dialog box to see the dialog box shown in Figure 25-9. The fields in the database appear as buttons along the right side of the dialog box. Simply drag the buttons to the appropriate area of the pivot table diagram.

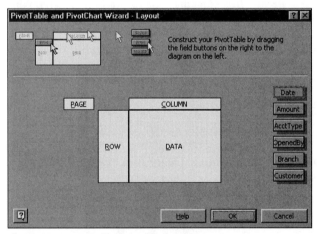

Figure 25-9: Specify the table layout.

The pivot table diagram has four areas

- ✦ **Page:** Values in the field appear as page items in the pivot table.
- ✦ **Row:** Values in the field appear as row items in the pivot table.
- ✦ **Data:** The field is summarized in the pivot table.
- ✦ **Column:** Values in the field appear as column items in the pivot table.

You can drag as many field buttons as you want to any of these locations, and you don't have to use all the fields. Any fields that you don't use simply don't appear in the pivot table.

When you drag a field button to the Data area, the PivotTable and PivotChart Wizard applies the Sum function if the field contains numeric values, and the Count function if the field contains non-numeric values.

While you're setting up the pivot table, you can double-click a field button to customize it. You can specify, for example, that a particular field be summarized as a Count or other function. You also can specify which items in a field to hide or omit. Be aware, however, that you can customize fields at any time after the pivot table is created; this is demonstrated later in this chapter.

If you drag a field button to an incorrect location, just drag it off the table diagram to get rid of it.

Figure 25-10 shows how the dialog box looks after some field buttons were dragged to the pivot table diagram. This pivot table displays the sum of the Amount field, broken down by AcctType (as rows) and Customer (as columns). In addition, the Branch field appears as a page field. Click OK to redisplay the PivotTable and PivotChart Wizard – Step 3 of 3 dialog box.

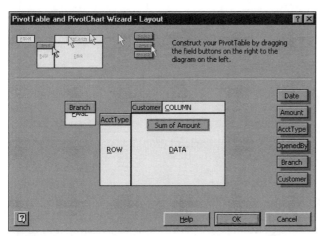

Figure 25-10: The table layout after dragging field buttons to the pivot table diagram.

Laying out a pivot table by using the PivotTable toolbar

Starting in Excel 2000, you can lay out a pivot table directly in a worksheet by using the PivotTable toolbar. The technique is very similar to the one just described, because you still drag and drop fields.

EXCEL 2000 The PivotTable toolbar is new to Excel 2000.

Complete the first two steps of the PivotTable and PivotChart Wizard. If you want, set options for the pivot table by using the Options button that appears in the third dialog box of the Wizard. Don't bother with the Layout button, however. Select a location for the pivot table and choose Finish. Excel displays a pivot table template similar to the one you see in Figure 25-11. The template provides you with hints about where to drop various types of fields.

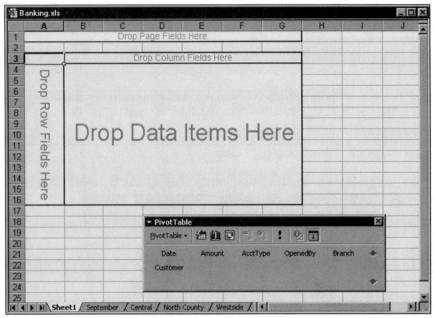

Figure 25-11: Use the PivotTable toolbar to drag and drop fields onto the pivot table template that Excel displays.

Drag and drop fields from the PivotTable toolbar onto the template. As you point at buttons on the toolbar, you'll see tool tips that instruct you to drag the field to the template. Excel continues to update the pivot table as you drag and drop fields; for this reason, you'll find this method easiest to use if you drag and drop data items last.

If you make a mistake, simply drag the field off the template and drop it anyplace on the worksheet — Excel removes it from the pivot table template. All fields remain on the PivotTable toolbar, even if you use them.

The finished product

When you click the Finish button in this last Wizard dialog box, Excel creates the PivotTable. Figure 25-12 shows the result of this example.

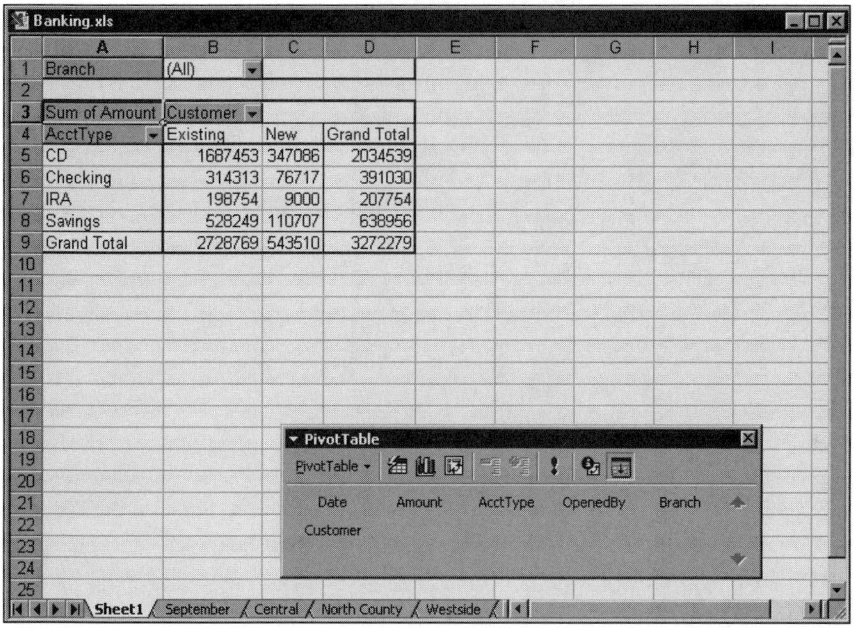

Figure 25-12: The pivot table that is created by the PivotTable and PivotChart Wizard.

Notice that the page field is displayed as a drop-down box. You can choose which item in the page field to display by choosing it from the list. You also can choose an item called All, which displays all the data.

Pivot Table Options

Excel provides plenty of options that determine how your pivot table looks and works. To access these options, click the Options button in the final step of the PivotTable and PivotChart Wizard. You can also access this dialog box after you create the pivot table. Right-click any cell in the pivot table and then select Options from the shortcut menu. The accompanying figure shows the PivotTable Options dialog box.

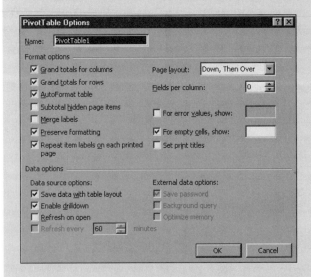

The PivotTable Options dialog box contains the following choices:

✦ **Name:** You can provide a name for the pivot table. Excel provides default names in the form of PivotTable1, PivotTable2, and so on.

✦ **Grand totals for columns:** Check this box if you want Excel to calculate grand totals for items that are displayed in columns.

✦ **Grand totals for rows:** Check this box if you want Excel to calculate grand totals for items that are displayed in rows.

✦ **AutoFormat table:** Check this box if you want Excel to apply one of its AutoFormats to the pivot table. Excel uses the AutoFormat even if you rearrange the table layout.

✦ **Subtotal hidden page items:** Check this box if you want Excel to include hidden items in the page fields in the subtotals.

✦ **Merge labels:** Check this box if you want Excel to merge the cells for outer row and column labels. Doing so may make the table more readable.

✦ **Preserve formatting:** Check this box if you want Excel, when it updates the pivot table, to keep any of the formatting that you applied.

✦ **Repeat item labels on each printed page:** Check this box to set row titles that appear on each page when you print a PivotTable report.

✦ **Page layout:** You can specify the order in which you want the page fields to appear.

✦ **Fields per column:** You can specify the number of page fields to show before starting another row of page fields.

✦ **For error values, show:** You can specify a value to show for pivot table cells that display an error.

✦ **For empty cells, show:** You can specify a value to show for pivot table cells that are empty.

✦ **Set print titles:** Check this box to set column titles that appear at the top of each page when you print a PivotTable report.

✦ **Save data with table layout:** If you check this option, Excel stores an additional copy of the data (called a *pivot table cache*), enabling Excel to recalculate the table more quickly when you change the layout. If memory is an issue, you should keep this option unchecked (updating is then a bit slower).

✦ **Enable drilldown:** If checked, you can double-click a cell in the pivot table to view details.

✦ **Refresh on open:** If checked, the pivot table is refreshed whenever you open the workbook.

✦ **Refresh every x minutes:** If you are connected to an external database, you can specify how often you want the pivot table refreshed while the workbook is open.

✦ **Save password:** If you use an external database that requires a password, you can store the password as part of the query, so that you don't have to reenter it.

✦ **Background query:** If checked, Excel runs the external database query in the background while you continue your work.

✦ **Optimize memory:** This option reduces the amount of memory that is used when you refresh an external database query.

Working with Pivot Tables

After you create a pivot table, it's not a static object. You can continue to modify and tweak it until it looks exactly how you want it to look. This section discusses modifications that you can make to a pivot table.

You'll find the PivotTable toolbar quite useful when you work with pivot tables. This toolbar appears automatically when you activate a worksheet that contains a pivot table.

Changing the Pivot Table Structure

Notice that a pivot table, when displayed in a worksheet, includes the field buttons. You can drag any of the field buttons to a new position in the pivot table (known as *pivoting*). For example, you can drag a column field to the row position. Excel immediately redisplays the pivot table to reflect your change. You also can change the order of the row fields or the column fields by dragging the buttons. This action affects how Excel nests the fields and can have a dramatic effect on the appearance of the table.

Figure 25-13 shows the pivot table that was created in the preceding example, after making a modification to the table's structure. The page field button (Branch) has been dragged to the row position. The pivot table now shows details for each item in the AcctType field for each branch.

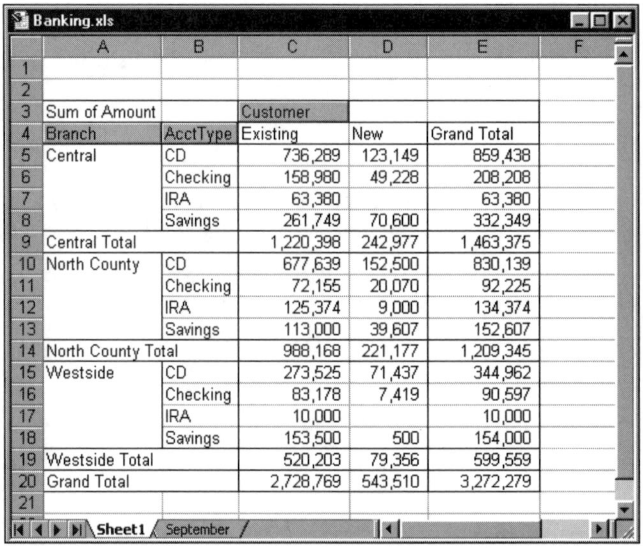

	A	B	C	D	E	F
1						
2						
3	Sum of Amount		Customer			
4	Branch	AcctType	Existing	New	Grand Total	
5	Central	CD	736,289	123,149	859,438	
6		Checking	158,980	49,228	208,208	
7		IRA	63,380		63,380	
8		Savings	261,749	70,600	332,349	
9	Central Total		1,220,398	242,977	1,463,375	
10	North County	CD	677,639	152,500	830,139	
11		Checking	72,155	20,070	92,225	
12		IRA	125,374	9,000	134,374	
13		Savings	113,000	39,607	152,607	
14	North County Total		988,168	221,177	1,209,345	
15	Westside	CD	273,525	71,437	344,962	
16		Checking	83,178	7,419	90,597	
17		IRA	10,000		10,000	
18		Savings	153,500	500	154,000	
19	Westside Total		520,203	79,356	599,559	
20	Grand Total		2,728,769	543,510	3,272,279	
21						

Figure 25-13: This pivot table has two row fields.

Describing how to change the layout of a pivot table is more difficult than doing it. I suggest that you create a pivot table and experiment by dragging around field buttons to see what happens.

Note

A pivot table is a special type of range, and (with a few exceptions) you can't make any changes to it. For example, you can't insert or delete rows, edit results, or move cells. If you attempt to do so, Excel displays an appropriate error message.

Removing a Field

To remove a field from a pivot table, click the field button and drag it away from the pivot table. The mouse pointer changes to include a button with an X across it. Release the mouse button, and Excel updates the table to exclude the field.

Adding a New Field

To add a new field to the pivot table, select any field in the pivot table. Then, drag the field that you want to add from the PivotTable toolbar onto the pivot table. Excel updates the pivot table with the new field.

You also can add fields from the PivotTable and PivotChart Wizard; choose Data ⇨ PivotTable and PivotChart Report to start the Wizard.

Refreshing a Pivot Table

Notice that pivot tables don't contain formulas. Rather, Excel recalculates the pivot table every time that you make a change to it. If the source database is large, some delay may occur while this recalculation takes place, but for small databases, the update is virtually instantaneous.

In some cases, you may change the source data. When this happens, Excel doesn't update the pivot table automatically. Rather, you must refresh it manually. To refresh a pivot table, you can use any of the following methods:

✦ Choose Data ⇨ Refresh Data

✦ Right-click anywhere in the pivot table and select Refresh Data from the short-cut menu

✦ Click the Refresh Data tool on the PivotTable toolbar

Customizing a Pivot Table Field

Several options are available for fields within a pivot table. To access these options, simply double-click a field button (or right-click and select Field from the shortcut menu). Excel displays a PivotTable Field dialog box, like the one shown in Figure 25-14.

You can modify any of the following items:

✦ **Name:** Changes the name that is displayed on the field button. You can also make this change directly by editing the cell that holds the field button.

✦ **Orientation:** Changes how the field's items are displayed. You can also take the more direct approach of dragging the field button to another location, as described previously.

✦ **Subtotals:** Lets you change the type of subtotaling that is displayed. Subtotaling is relevant only if you have more than one field displayed as rows or columns. You can make a multiple selection in the list box, which results in more than one line of subtotals. To eliminate subtotals, click the None option.

✦ **Hide items:** Enables you to hide (not display) one or more items from a field. Click the specific item names that you want to hide.

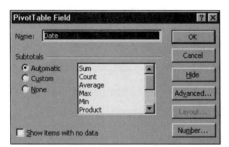

Figure 25-14: Double-clicking a PivotTable field button displays a dialog box like this one.

Excel includes some additional field options that you can specify by clicking the Advanced button in the PivotTable Field dialog box. These options let you specify how the field items are sorted and how many items to show (for example, just the top ten).

Formatting a Pivot Table

When you create a pivot table, Excel, by default, applies an AutoFormat to the table (you can change this by clicking the Options button in Step 3). After Excel creates the pivot table, you can always specify a different AutoFormat. Place the cell pointer in the pivot table and click the Format Report tool on the PivotTable toolbar. Excel displays the AutoFormat dialog box. Select an AutoFormat and click OK.

To change the number format for the pivot table data, use the following procedure:

1. Select any cell in the pivot table's Data area.

2. Right-click and choose PivotTable Field Settings from the shortcut menu. Excel displays its PivotTable Field dialog box.

3. Click the Number button.

4. Select the number format that you want to use.

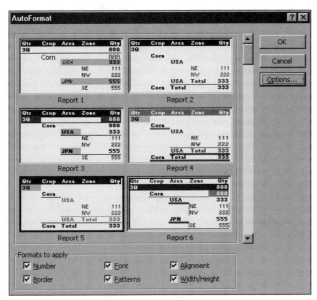

Figure 25-15: Change the formatting of a pivot table.

Tip If you want Excel to preserve all the formatting that you perform on individual cells, make sure that the Preserve formatting option is turned on. You do this in the PivotTable Options dialog box (right-click a cell and select Table Options from the shortcut menu). If this option is not turned on, Excel returns the formats to the default formats when you refresh the pivot table.

Grouping Pivot Table Items

Grouping pivot table items is a handy feature that enables you to group specific items in a field. If one of the fields in your database consists of dates, for example, the pivot table displays a separate row or column for every date. You may find that grouping the dates into months or quarters and then hiding the details is more useful. Fortunately, this is easy to do.

Figure 25-16 shows a pivot table that was created using the bank database. It shows total balances for each AcctType (column field) by the Branch (row field). To create a report that compares the Central branch to the other two branches combined, create a group that consists of the Westside and North County branches.

Banking.xls						
	A	B	C	D	E	F
1						
2						
3	Sum of Amount	AcctType				
4	Branch	CD	Checking	IRA	Savings	Grand Total
5	Central	859,438	208,208	63,380	332,349	1,463,375
6	North County	830,139	92,225	134,374	152,607	1,209,345
7	Westside	344,962	90,597	10,000	154,000	599,559
8	Grand Total	2,034,539	391,030	207,754	638,956	3,272,279
9						
10						
11						
12						
13						
14						

Sheet1 / September

Figure 25-16: This version of the pivot table shows balances for each account type, by branch.

To create the group, select the cells that you want to group — in this case, A6:A7. Then, choose Data ⇨ Group and Outline ⇨ GroupPivotTable. Excel creates a new field called Branch2, which has two items: Central and Group1 (see Figure 25-17). At this point, you can remove the original Branch field (drag away the field button) and change the names of the field and the items. Figure 25-18 shows the pivot table after making these modifications.

Banking.xls						
	A	B	C	D	E	F
1						
2						
3	Sum of Amount		AcctType			
4	Branch2	Branch	CD	Checking	IRA	Savings	G
5	Central	Central	859,438	208,208	63,380	332,349	
6	Group1	North County	830,139	92,225	134,374	152,607	
7		Westside	344,962	90,597	10,000	154,000	
8	Grand Total		2,034,539	391,030	207,754	638,956	
9						
10						
11						
12						

Sheet1 / September

Figure 25-17: The pivot table after grouping the North County and Westside branches.

Note   The new field name can't be an existing field name. If it is, Excel adds the field to the pivot table. In this example, you can't rename Branch2 to Branch.

Banking.xls

	A	B	C	D	E	F
1						
2						
3	Sum of Amount	AcctType				
4	Branch2	CD	Checking	IRA	Savings	Grand Total
5	Central	859,438	208,208	63,380	332,349	1,463,375
6	WS & NC	1,175,101	182,822	144,374	306,607	1,808,904
7	Grand Total	2,034,539	391,030	207,754	638,956	3,272,279
8						
9						
10						
11						
12						

Sheet1 / September /

Figure 25-18: The pivot table after removing the original Branch field and renaming the new field and items.

Tip

If the items that you want to group are not adjacent to each other, you can make a multiple selection by pressing Ctrl and selecting the items that make up the group.

If the field items that you want to group consist of values, dates, or times, you can let Excel do the grouping for you. Figure 25-19 shows part of another pivot table that was generated from the bank database. This time, Amount is used for the row field and AcctType for the column field. The Data area shows the count for each combination. This report isn't useful, because the Amount field contains so many different items. The report can be salvaged, however, by grouping the items into bins.

Banking.xls

	A	B	C	D	E	F
1						
2						
3	Count of Amount	AcctType				
4	Amount	CD	Checking	IRA	Savings	Grand Total
5	100	0	16	0	0	16
6	124	0	4	0	0	4
7	133	0	4	0	0	4
8	200	0	3	0	3	6
9	240	0	9	0	0	9
10	245	0	1	0	0	1
11	250	0	0	0	3	3
12	275	0	1	0	0	1
13	340	0	1	0	0	1
14	344	0	3	0	0	3
15	400	0	7	0	0	7
16	500	0	2	0	8	10
17	600	0	0	0	5	5
18	1,000	0	7	0	1	8
19	1,325	0	2	0	0	2
20	1,946	0	2	0	0	2
21	2,000	3	0	6	0	9
22	2,749	0	5	0	0	5

Sheet1 / September /

Figure 25-19: This isn't a useful pivot table report, because the Amount field contains too many different items.

To create groups automatically, select any item in the Amount field. Then, choose Data ➪ Group and Outline ➪ Group. Excel displays the Grouping dialog box, shown in Figure 25-20. By default, it shows the smallest and largest values — but you can change these to whatever you want. To create groups of $5,000 increments, enter **0** for the Starting at value, **100000** for the Ending at value, and **5000** for the By value (as shown in Figure 25-20). Click OK, and Excel creates the groups. Figure 25-21 shows the result, which is much more meaningful than the ungrouped data.

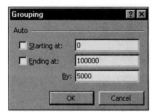

Figure 25-20: The Grouping dialog box instructs Excel to create groups automatically.

	A	B	C	D	E	F
1						
2						
3	Count of Amount	AcctType				
4	Amount	CD	Checking	IRA	Savings	Grand Total
5	0-4999	3	127	6	36	172
6	5000-9999	4	18	13	31	66
7	10000-14999	56	2	8	1	67
8	15000-19999	19	0	0	2	21
9	20000-24999	0	0	0	1	1
10	25000-29999	1	0	0	1	2
11	30000-34999	0	0	0	2	2
12	35000-39999	2	0	0	0	2
13	40000-44999	0	0	0	1	1
14	45000-49999	1	0	0	0	1
15	50000-54999	4	0	0	1	5
16	65000-69999	0	0	0	2	2
17	75000-79999	5	0	0	0	5
18	90000-94999	3	0	0	0	3
19	Grand Total	98	147	27	78	350
20						
21						

Banking.xls — Sheet1 / September

Figure 25-21: The pivot table after grouping the Amount field items.

Seeing the Details

Each cell in the Data area of a pivot table represents several records in the source database. You may be interested in seeing exactly which fields contribute to a summary value in the pivot table. Using the banking example, you may want to see a list of the records that constitute the total CD accounts in the Central branch. To do so, double-click the appropriate summary cell in the Data area. Excel creates a new worksheet with the records that were used to create the summary. Figure 25-22 shows an example.

Note   If double-clicking a cell doesn't work, make sure that the Enable drilldown option is turned on in the PivotTable Options dialog box (right-click a pivot table cell and select Options from the shortcut menu).

Displaying a Pivot Table on Different Sheets

If your pivot table displays a field in the Page position, you can see only one slice of the data at a time, by using the drop-down list box. Excel has an option, however, that puts each item from a page field on a separate sheet, creating a three-dimensional block of data. Click the PivotTable button on the PivotTable toolbar and choose Show Pages from the shortcut menu (or right-click the pivot table and select Show Pages from the shortcut menu). Excel displays the Show Pages dialog box, shown in Figure 25-23, which lists the page fields in your PivotTable. Select the fields that you want, and Excel inserts enough new sheets to accommodate each item in that field.

	Date	Amount	AcctType	OpenedBy	Branch	Customer	
1	Date	Amount	AcctType	OpenedBy	Branch	Customer	
2	09/29/97	2000	CD	New Accts	Central	New	
3	09/29/97	11000	CD	New Accts	Central	New	
4	09/01/97	90000	CD	New Accts	Central	Existing	
5	09/29/97	14548	CD	New Accts	Central	Existing	
6	09/29/97	15000	CD	New Accts	Central	Existing	
7	09/29/97	17000	CD	Teller	Central	Existing	
8	09/29/97	90000	CD	New Accts	Central	Existing	
9	09/29/97	15208	CD	New Accts	Central	Existing	
10	09/01/97	16000	CD	New Accts	Central	New	
11	09/04/97	13000	CD	New Accts	Central	Existing	
12	09/04/97	13519	CD	New Accts	Central	New	
13	09/28/97	15208	CD	New Accts	Central	Existing	
14	09/26/97	13519	CD	New Accts	Central	Existing	
15	09/26/97	13000	CD	New Accts	Central	Existing	
16	09/25/97	15208	CD	New Accts	Central	Existing	
17	09/04/97	14548	CD	New Accts	Central	Existing	
18	09/22/97	2000	CD	Teller	Central	Existing	
19	09/04/97	11000	CD	New Accts	Central	New	
20	09/04/97	35000	CD	New Accts	Central	Existing	
21	09/22/97	13519	CD	New Accts	Central	Existing	

Figure 25-22: Double-clicking a cell in the Data area of a pivot table generates a new worksheet with the underlying data.

Figure 25-23: The Show Pages dialog box enables you to display each page field item on a separate worksheet.

Inserting a Calculated Field into a Pivot Table

As previously noted, a pivot table is a special type of data range, and you can't insert new rows or columns into a pivot table. This means that you can't insert formulas to perform calculations with the data in a pivot table. However, you can create calculated fields for a pivot table. A *calculated field* consists of a calculation that can involve other fields.

Note   You cannot create a calculated field in a pivot table that is based on an OLAP database.

In the banking example, for instance, assume that management wants to increase deposits by 15 percent and wants to compare the projected deposits to the current deposits. In this situation, you can use a calculated field. Calculated fields must reside in the Data area of the pivot table (you can't use them in the Page, Row, or Column areas).

Use the following procedure to create a calculated field that consists of the Amount field multiplied by 1.15 (that is, a 15 percent increase):

1. Move the cell pointer anywhere within the pivot table.
2. Right-click and choose Formulas ➪ Calculated Field from the shortcut menu. Excel displays the Insert Calculated Field dialog box, shown in Figure 25-24.
3. Enter a descriptive name for the field and specify the formula. The formula can use other fields, but can't use worksheet functions. For this example, the name is Projected, and the formula is the following:

   ```
   =Amount*1.15
   ```

4. Click Add to add this new field.
5. To create additional calculated fields, repeat Steps 3 and 4. Click OK to close the dialog box.

After you create the field, Excel adds it to the Data area of the pivot table. You can treat it just like any other field, with one exception: you can't move it to the Page, Row, or Column area (it must remain in the Data area). Figure 25-25 shows a pivot table with a calculated field (called Projected).

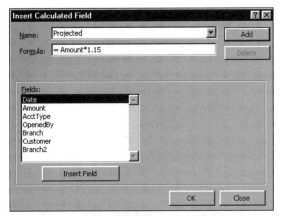

Figure 25-24: The Insert Calculated Field dialog box.

Figure 25-25: This pivot table uses a calculated field.

Tip
The formulas that you develop can also use worksheet functions, but the functions cannot refer to cells or named ranges.

Inserting a Calculated Item into a Pivot Table

The previous section explains how to create a calculated field. Excel also enables you to create *calculated items* for a pivot table field. For example, if you have a field named Months, you can create a calculated item (called Q1, for example) that displays the sum of January, February, and March. You can also do this by grouping the items — but using grouping hides the individual months and shows only the total of the group. Creating a calculated item for quarterly totals shows the total and the individual months. Calculated items must reside in the Page, Row, or Column area of a pivot table (you can't use calculated items in the Data area).

Note   You can't create a calculated item in a pivot table based on an OLAP database.

In the banking example, management may want to look at CD accounts combined with savings accounts; you can show this information by creating a calculated item. To create a calculated item, use these steps:

1. Move the cell pointer to a Row, Column, or Page area of the pivot table. The cell pointer cannot be in the Data area.

2. Right-click and choose Formulas ➪ Calculated Item from the shortcut menu. Excel displays the Insert Calculated Item dialog box, as shown in Figure 25-26.

3. Enter a name for the new item and specify the formula. The formula can use items in other fields, but can't use worksheet functions. For this example, the new item is named **CD & Savings**, and the formula is as follows:

   ```
   =CD + Savings
   ```

4. Click Add.

5. Repeat Steps 3 and 4 to create additional items. Click OK to close the dialog box.

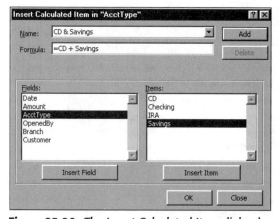

Figure 25-26: The Insert Calculated Item dialog box.

After you create the item, it appears in the pivot table. Figure 25-27 shows the pivot table after adding a calculated item.

If you use a calculated item in your pivot table, you may need to turn off the Grand Total display, to avoid double-counting.

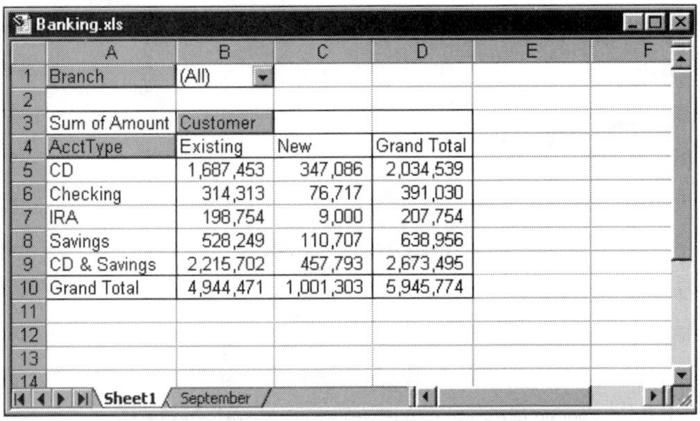
Banking.xls

Branch	(All)		
Sum of Amount	Customer		
AcctType	Existing	New	Grand Total
CD	1,687,453	347,086	2,034,539
Checking	314,313	76,717	391,030
IRA	198,754	9,000	207,754
Savings	528,249	110,707	638,956
CD & Savings	2,215,702	457,793	2,673,495
Grand Total	4,944,471	1,001,303	5,945,774

Figure 25-27: This pivot table uses a calculated item.

Pivot Table Examples

This section describes additional examples of pivot tables, to spark your creativity and help you apply some of these techniques to your own data.

The best way to master pivot tables is to work with them, using your own data—not just read about them.

On the CD-ROM

If you want to work with some prefab pivot tables, I've developed a few for you to use, which you can find on this book's CD-ROM.

Using a Pivot Table to Consolidate Sheets

Chapter 19 discusses several ways to consolidate data across different worksheets or workbooks. Excel's pivot table feature gives you yet another consolidation option. Figure 25-28 shows three worksheets, each containing monthly sales data for a store (three different stores) in a music store chain. The goal is to consolidate this information into a single pivot table. In this example, all the source data is in a single workbook, but you can consolidate data from different workbooks.

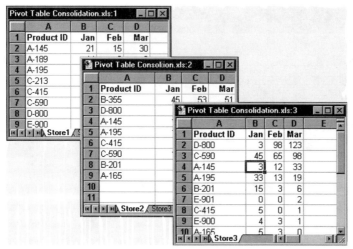

Figure 25-28: You can use a pivot table to consolidate these three worksheets.

You can find this workbook on this book's CD-ROM.

Use the following steps to create this pivot table:

1. Start with a new worksheet named **Summary**.

2. Choose Data ➪ PivotTable and PivotChart Report, to display the PivotTable and PivotChart Wizard.

3. Select the Multiple Consolidation Ranges option and then click Next.

4. In Step 2a of the PivotTable Wizard, select the option labeled Create a single page field for me. Click Next.

5. In Step 2b, specify the ranges to be consolidated. The first range is **Store1!$A$1:$D$12** (you can enter this directly or point to it). Click Add to add this range to the All Ranges list.

6. Repeat this for the other two ranges (see Figure 25-29). Click Next to continue to Step 3.

7. The dialog box in Step 3 of the PivotTable Wizard should look familiar. Click Finish.

Figure 25-30 shows the pivot table. It uses generic names, which you can change to more meaningful names.

In Step 2a of the PivotTable Wizard, you can choose the option labeled I will create the page fields. Doing so enables you to provide an item name for each item in the page field (rather than the generic Item1, Item2, and Item3).

Figure 25-29: Step 2b of the PivotTable Wizard.

	A	B	C	D	E	
1	Page1	(All)				
2						
3	Sum of Value	Column				
4	Row	Jan	Feb	Mar	Grand Total	
5	A-145	39	43	84	166	
6	A-165	8	3	1	12	
7	A-189	14	2	2	18	
8	A-195	45	23	36	104	
9	B-201	19	5	9	33	
10	B-355	45	53	51	149	
11	C-213	2	12	5	19	
12	C-415	15	11	18	44	
13	C-590	93	86	109	288	
14	D-800	12	196	257	465	
15	E-900	9	4	1	14	
16	E-901	0	0	2	2	
17	E-904	3	5	7	15	
18	E-912	0	0	2	2	
19	E-923	1	0	0	1	
20	Grand Total	305	443	584	1332	

Figure 25-30: This pivot table uses data from three ranges.

Creating Charts from a Pivot Table

A Pivot chart report is a chart that is linked to a pivot table. By using the PivotTable and PivotChart Wizard, you can create simultaneously both a pivot table and a linked chart; you can use the techniques described earlier to drag and drop fields onto the pivot chart or the pivot table. To simultaneously create a pivot table and a pivot chart, choose PivotChart (with PivotTable) in the first dialog box of the PivotTable and PivotChart Wizard. Excel creates a new worksheet and a new chart sheet; both will contain templates for the pivot table and the pivot chart, respectively. Drag fields from the PivotTable toolbar onto either the chart or the table—

simply switch between the sheets in the workbook to choose the sheet with which you want to work.

 EXCEL 2000   Pivot chart reports are a new feature of Excel 2000.

Although you can create a pivot chart by using the PivotTable and PivotChart Wizard, you'll find it easier to create the chart from an existing pivot table. While viewing the pivot table, click the Chart Wizard button on the PivotTable toolbar. Excel immediately creates a chart sheet in the workbook based on the pivot table. Figure 25-31 shows the pivot table used as the foundation for the pivot chart shown in Figure 25-32. Excel updates this chart whenever you make changes to the pivot table.

 Tip   A pivot chart is always created on a separate Chart sheet. To convert the chart to an embedded chart on a worksheet, activate the Chart sheet and select Chart ➪ Location. Select the second option (as object in) and specify a worksheet for the chart.

	A	B	C	D
1	Branch	(All)		
2				
3	Sum of Amount	Customer		
4	AcctType	Existing	New	Grand Total
5	CD	1687453	347086	2034539
6	Checking	314313	76717	391030
7	IRA	198754	9000	207754
8	Savings	528249	110707	638956
9	Grand Total	2728769	543510	3272279

Sheet1 / September / Central / North County / Westside

Figure 25-31: The pivot table from which the chart in Figure 25-32 was created.

Analyzing Survey Data

This example demonstrates how to use a pivot table to analyze survey data that was obtained via a questionnaire. Figure 25-33 shows part of the raw data that is typical of data collected from a survey questionnaire. Each record represents the responses for one respondent.

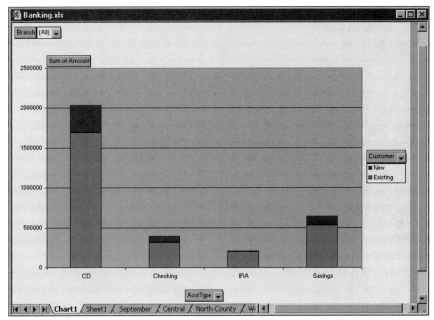

Figure 25-32: The chart changes based on the pivot table.

	A	B	C	D	E	F	G	H	I	J	
1	Name	Sex	Age	State	Item01	Item02	Item03	Item04	Item05	Item06	Iter
2	Subject1	Male	40	Illinois	1	4	4	4	1	1	
3	Subject2	Female	31	Illinois	2	5	1	1	4	2	
4	Subject3	Male	56	New York	1	1	4	2	3	3	
5	Subject4	Male	55	Illinois	2	1	3	5	1	2	
6	Subject5	Female	47	New York	2	2	5	5	4	2	
7	Subject6	Female	51	Illinois	2	4	3	3	1	1	
8	Subject7	Female	48	California	2	4	5	4	5	3	
9	Subject8	Male	39	New York	3	2	1	2	3	4	
10	Subject9	Female	37	California	3	4	4	4	5	1	
11	Subject10	Male	38	New York	2	1	5	5	5	1	
12	Subject11	Male	38	California	4	3	3	2	1	2	
13	Subject12	Female	46	California	2	1	4	5	5	5	
14	Subject13	Female	48	Illinois	4	3	4	3	2	5	
15	Subject14	Female	56	New York	2	3	4	2	1	1	

Figure 25-33: Use a pivot table to tabulate this survey data.

On the CD-ROM

You can find the workbook used in this example on this book's CD-ROM.

Figure 25-34 shows a pivot table that was created to calculate averages for each of the 12 survey items, broken down by sex. Additional page fields enable you to examine the results easily by an age group or a particular state. Or, for a more complex pivot table, you can drag one or both of the page fields to a row or column position.

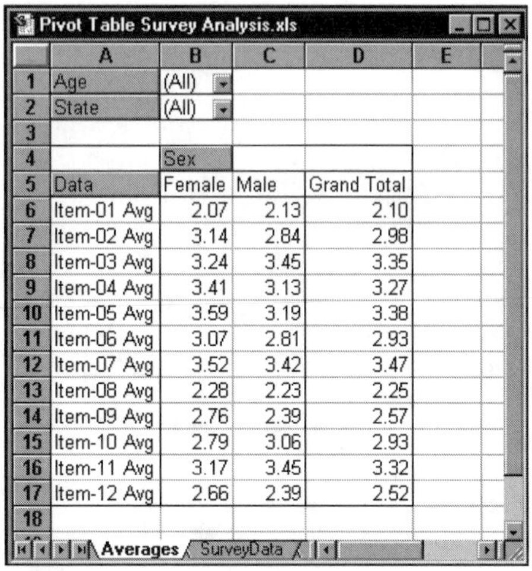

Pivot Table Survey Analysis.xls

	A	B	C	D
1	Age	(All)		
2	State	(All)		
3				
4		Sex		
5	Data	Female	Male	Grand Total
6	Item-01 Avg	2.07	2.13	2.10
7	Item-02 Avg	3.14	2.84	2.98
8	Item-03 Avg	3.24	3.45	3.35
9	Item-04 Avg	3.41	3.13	3.27
10	Item-05 Avg	3.59	3.19	3.38
11	Item-06 Avg	3.07	2.81	2.93
12	Item-07 Avg	3.52	3.42	3.47
13	Item-08 Avg	2.28	2.23	2.25
14	Item-09 Avg	2.76	2.39	2.57
15	Item-10 Avg	2.79	3.06	2.93
16	Item-11 Avg	3.17	3.45	3.32
17	Item-12 Avg	2.66	2.39	2.52
18				

Averages / SurveyData

Figure 25-34: This pivot table calculates averages for each item.

Figure 25-35 shows another sheet in the workbook. This sheet contains 12 separate pivot tables, one for each survey item. Each pivot table displays the frequency of responses and the percentage of responses. Although you could create each table manually, the workbook includes a macro that creates them all in just a few seconds.

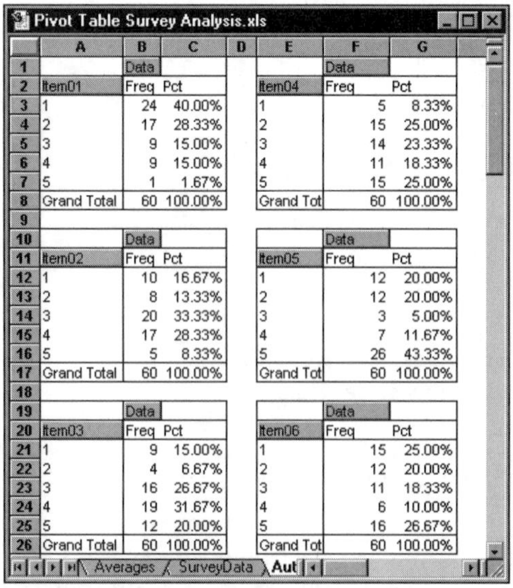

Pivot Table Survey Analysis.xls

	A	B	C	D	E	F	G
1		Data				Data	
2	Item01	Freq	Pct		Item04	Freq	Pct
3	1	24	40.00%		1	5	8.33%
4	2	17	28.33%		2	15	25.00%
5	3	9	15.00%		3	14	23.33%
6	4	9	15.00%		4	11	18.33%
7	5	1	1.67%		5	15	25.00%
8	Grand Total	60	100.00%		Grand Tot	60	100.00%
9							
10		Data				Data	
11	Item02	Freq	Pct		Item05	Freq	Pct
12	1	10	16.67%		1	12	20.00%
13	2	8	13.33%		2	12	20.00%
14	3	20	33.33%		3	3	5.00%
15	4	17	28.33%		4	7	11.67%
16	5	5	8.33%		5	26	43.33%
17	Grand Total	60	100.00%		Grand Tot	60	100.00%
18							
19		Data				Data	
20	Item03	Freq	Pct		Item06	Freq	Pct
21	1	9	15.00%		1	15	25.00%
22	2	4	6.67%		2	12	20.00%
23	3	16	26.67%		3	11	18.33%
24	4	19	31.67%		4	6	10.00%
25	5	12	20.00%		5	16	26.67%
26	Grand Total	60	100.00%		Grand Tot	60	100.00%

Averages / SurveyData / Aut

Figure 25-35: This sheet contains 12 pivot tables, created by a macro.

Customer Geographic Analysis

As a byproduct of creating a pivot table, you end up with a list of unique entries in a field. Figure 25-36 shows part of a database that tracks customers. The field of interest is the State field (which holds the country in the case of non-U.S. orders). The Type field contains a formula that returns either Foreign or Domestic, depending on the length of the entry in the State field. The goal of this example is to create a map that shows sales by state.

	C	D	E	F	G	H	I
1	City	State	Zip	HowPaid	Amount	Month	Type
56		Canada	L5A 3T5	Card	$49.95	Feb	Foreign
57	Neuendettelesau	Germany		Check	$49.95	Feb	Foreign
58	San Jose	CA	95126-4800	Check	$129.00	Feb	Domestic
59	Montreal Nord, Quebec	Canada	H1G 3L1	Card	$79.95	Feb	Foreign
60	Bellevue	WA	98008-2928	Card	$129.00	Feb	Domestic
61	Austin	TX	78745	Card	$49.95	Feb	Domestic
62	San Antonio	TX	78245	Check	$79.95	Feb	Domestic
63	Fords	NJ	08863	Card	$49.95	Feb	Domestic
64	Solana Beach	CA	92075	Card	$49.95	Feb	Domestic
65	Elkhart	IN	46514	Card	$79.95	Feb	Domestic
66	Omaha	NE	68127	Card	$129.00	Feb	Domestic
67	8036-Barcelona	Spain		Check	$49.95	Feb	Foreign
68	Miami	FL	33122	Card	$79.95	Feb	Domestic
69	Houston	TX	77002	Check	$49.95	Feb	Domestic
70	Great Falls	VA	22066	Check	$129.00	Feb	Domestic
71	Burlington	VT	05402	Check	$49.95	Feb	Domestic
72	Bolingbrook	IL	60440	Check	$49.95	Feb	Domestic

Pivot Table \ **Customers**

Figure 25-36: This customer database would make a good map, but the data is not in the proper format.

On the CD-ROM

You can find this workbook on the CD-ROM.

Figure 25-37 shows a pivot table created from the data displayed in Figure 25-36. It displays the data in terms of total amount, plus a count. Three page fields were used to filter the data.

Figure 25-38 shows the map that was created by using Excel's mapping feature (described fully in Chapter 17).

	A	B	C	D
	Pivot Table Geographic Analysis.xls			
1	HowPaid	(All)		
2	Type	Domestic		
3	Month	(All)		
4				
5		Data		
6	State	Sum of Amount	Count of Amount	
7	AK	$388	4	
8	AL	$50	1	
9	AR	$130	2	
10	AZ	$100	2	
11	CA	$6,556	68	
12	CO	$1,243	12	
13	CT	$1,047	12	
14	DC	$180	3	
15	FL	$1,343	14	
16	GA	$547	5	
17	HI	$129	1	
18	IA	$209	2	
19	IL	$1,553	17	
20	IN	$599	8	
21	KS	$129	1	

Pivot Table / Customers /

Figure 25-37: This pivot table contains perfect input for an Excel map.

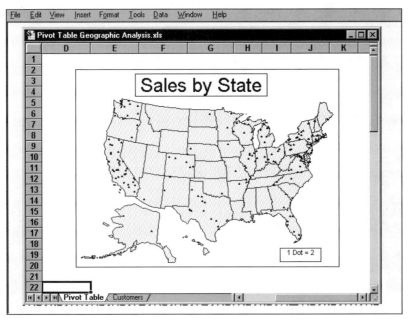

Figure 25-38: This map was created from the data in the pivot table.

Grouping by Month and Years

The final pivot table example (see Figure 25-39) demonstrates some techniques that involve grouping by dates. The worksheet contains daily pricing data for two years. I created a macro to change the grouping to days, weeks, months, quarters, or years. The macro also changes the range that is used in the chart.

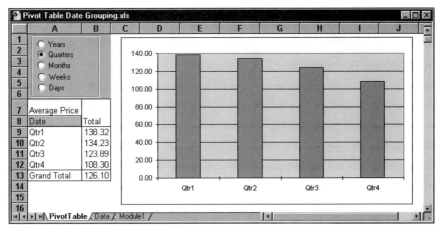

Figure 25-39: Clicking an option button executes a macro that changes the date grouping and updates the chart.

You can find this workbook on the CD-ROM.

Summary

This chapter discusses Excel's pivot table feature, which enables you to summarize data from a database that can be stored in a worksheet or in an external file. The examples in this chapter demonstrate some useful techniques. The best way to master this feature, however, is to use a database with which you're familiar and experiment until you understand how it works.

✦   ✦   ✦

Performing Spreadsheet What-If Analysis

One of the most appealing aspects of a spreadsheet program — including Excel — is that you can use formulas to create dynamic models that instantly recalculate when you change values in cells to which the formulas refer. When you change values in cells in a systematic manner and observe the effects on specific formula cells, you're performing a type of *what-if* analysis. What-if analysis is the process of asking questions such as, "What if the interest rate on the loan changes to 8.5 rather than 9.0 percent?" or "What if we raise the prices of our products by 5 percent?"

If you set up your spreadsheet properly, answering such questions is a matter of plugging in new values and observing the results of the recalculation. Excel provides useful tools to assist you in your what-if endeavors.

A What-If Example

Figure 26-1 shows a spreadsheet that calculates information pertaining to a mortgage loan. The worksheet is divided into two sections: the input cells and the result cells. Column D shows the formulas stored in column C.

With this worksheet, you can easily answer the following what-if questions:

✦ What if I can negotiate a lower purchase price on the property?

✦ What if the lender requires a 20-percent down payment?

✦ What if I can get a 40-year mortgage?

✦ What if the interest rate decreases to 7.5 percent?

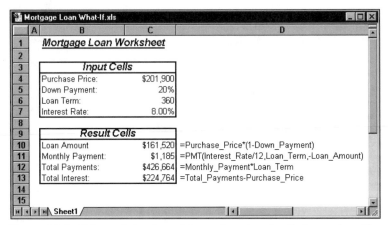

Figure 26-1: This worksheet model uses four input cells to produce the results in the formulas.

You can answer these questions simply by changing the values in the cells in range C4:C7 and observing the effects in the dependent cells (C10:C13). You can, of course, vary any number of input cells simultaneously.

Hard Code Values? No Way!

The mortgage calculation example, simple as it is, demonstrates an important point about spreadsheet design: You should always set up your worksheet so that you have maximum flexibility to make changes. Perhaps the most fundamental rule of spreadsheet design is the following:

Do not hard code (store) values in a formula. Rather, store the values in separate cells, and use cell references in the formula.

The term *hard code* refers to the use of actual values, or *constants,* in a formula. In the mortgage loan example, all the formulas use references to cells, not actual values.

You *could* use the value 360, for example, for the loan term argument of the PMT function in cell C11. Using a cell reference has two advantages. First, you have no doubt about the values that the formula uses (they aren't buried in the formula). Second, you can easily change the value.

Using values in formulas may not seem like much of an issue when only one formula is involved, but just imagine what would happen if this value were hard coded into several hundred formulas that were scattered throughout a worksheet.

Types of What-If Analyses

As you may expect, Excel can handle much more sophisticated models than the preceding example. To perform a what-if analysis using Excel, you have four basic options:

✦ **Manual what-if analysis:** Plug in new values and observe the effects on formula cells.

✦ **Macro-assisted what-if analysis:** Create macros to plug in variables for you.

✦ **Data tables:** Create a table that displays the results of selected formula cells as you systematically change one or two input cells.

✦ **Scenario Manager:** Create named scenarios and generate reports that use outlines or pivot tables.

Manual What-If Analysis

This method doesn't require too much explanation. In fact, the example that opens this chapter is a good one. It's based on the idea that you have one or more input cells that affect one or more key formula cells. You change the value in the input cells and see what happens to the formula cells. You may want to print the results or save each scenario to a new workbook. The term *scenario* refers to a specific set of values in one or more input cells.

This is how most people perform what-if analysis. Manual what-if analysis certainly has nothing wrong with it, but you should be aware of some other techniques.

Macro-Assisted What-If Analysis

A slightly more sophisticated form of manual what-if analysis uses macros. As is discussed in later chapters, a *macro* is a program that performs several operations automatically. Rather than change the input cells manually, you can create a macro to make the changes for you. For example, you may have three macros named BestCase, WorstCase, and MostLikelyCase. Running the BestCase macro enters the appropriate values into the input cells. Executing the WorstCase or MostLikelyCase macros enters other values.

If you understand how to create macros, this technique can be simple to set up. You can attach the macros to buttons to make running the macros as easy as clicking the button.

Figure 26-2 shows a worksheet designed for what-if analysis. This simple production model contains two input cells: the hourly cost of labor and the unit cost for materials. The company produces three products, and each product requires a different number of hours and a different amount of materials to produce. Excel calculates the combined total profit. Management is trying to predict the total profit but is uncertain what the hourly labor cost and material costs are going to be. They've identified three scenarios, as listed in Table 26-1.

	A	B	C	D	E	F	G	H
	What_if.xls							
1	Resource Cost Variables				Best Case			
2	Hourly Cost	34						
3	Materials Cost	59			Worst Case			
4	Total Profit	$13,008						
5					Most Likely			
6		Model A	Model B	Model C				
7	Hours per unit	12	14	24				
8	Materials per unit	6	9	14				
9	Cost to product	762	1,007	1,642				
10	Sales price	795	1,295	2,195				
11	Unit profit	33	288	553				
12	Units produced	36	18	12				
13	Total profit per model	1,188	5,184	6,636				
14								
	Sheet1							

Figure 26-2: This worksheet uses macros to display three different combinations of values for the input cells.

Table 26-1
Three Scenarios for the Production Model

Scenario	Hourly Cost	Materials Cost
Best Case	30	57
Worst Case	38	62
Most Likely	34	59

I developed three simple macros and attached one to each of the three buttons on the worksheet. Figure 26-3 shows the VBA macros (also known as subroutines) that Excel executes when you click a worksheet button. These macros simply place values into the named cells on the worksheet. To change the values that any one of the scenarios uses, you must edit the macros.

Note   If you like the idea of instantly displaying a particular scenario, you may be interested in learning about Excel's Scenario Manager, which is described later in this chapter. The Scenario Manager does not require macros.

```
 WHAT_IF.XLS - Module1 (Code)                    _ □ ✕

 (General)                  ▼   (Declarations)           ▼

    Sub BestCase()
        Range("Hourly_Cost") = 30
        Range("Materials_Cost") = 57
    End Sub

    Sub WorstCase()
        Range("Hourly_Cost") = 38
        Range("Materials_Cost") = 62
    End Sub

    Sub LikelyCase()
        Range("Hourly_Cost") = 34
        Range("Materials_Cost") = 59
    End Sub
```

Figure 26-3: These macros simply place different values in the input cells in the worksheet.

Creating Data Tables

When you're working with a what-if model, Excel displays only one scenario at a time. But you can compare the results of various scenarios by using any of the following techniques:

✦ Print multiple copies of the worksheet, each displaying a different scenario.

✦ Copy the model to other worksheets and set it up so that each worksheet displays a different scenario.

✦ Manually create a table that summarizes key formula cells for each scenario.

✦ Use Excel's Data ➪ Table command to create a summary table automatically.

This section discusses the last option — the Data ➪ Table command, which enables you to create a handy data table that summarizes formula cells for various values of either of the following:

✦ A single input cell

✦ Various combinations of two input cells

For example, in the production model example, you may want to create a table that shows the total profit for various combinations of hourly cost and materials cost. Figure 26-4 shows a two-input data table that shows these combinations.

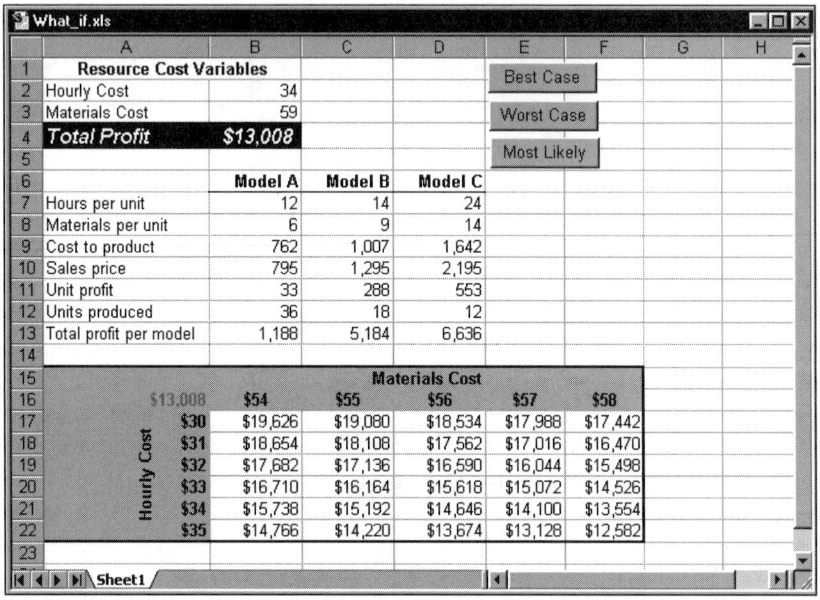

	A	B	C	D	E	F
1	Resource Cost Variables					
2	Hourly Cost	34				
3	Materials Cost	59				
4	*Total Profit*	*$13,008*				
5						
6		**Model A**	**Model B**	**Model C**		
7	Hours per unit	12	14	24		
8	Materials per unit	6	9	14		
9	Cost to product	762	1,007	1,642		
10	Sales price	795	1,295	2,195		
11	Unit profit	33	288	553		
12	Units produced	36	18	12		
13	Total profit per model	1,188	5,184	6,636		
14						
15				**Materials Cost**		
16	$13,008	**$54**	**$55**	**$56**	**$57**	**$58**
17	Hourly Cost **$30**	$19,626	$19,080	$18,534	$17,988	$17,442
18	**$31**	$18,654	$18,108	$17,562	$17,016	$16,470
19	**$32**	$17,682	$17,136	$16,590	$16,044	$15,498
20	**$33**	$16,710	$16,164	$15,618	$15,072	$14,526
21	**$34**	$15,738	$15,192	$14,646	$14,100	$13,554
22	**$35**	$14,766	$14,220	$13,674	$13,128	$12,582
23						

Figure 26-4: This data table summarizes the total profit for various combinations of the input values.

You can create a data table fairly easily, but data tables have some limitations. In particular, a data table can deal with only one or two input cells at a time. In other words, you can't create a data table that uses a combination of three or more input cells.

The Scenario Manager, discussed later in this chapter, can produce a report that summarizes any number of input cells and result cells.

Creating a One-Input Data Table

A one-input data table displays the results of one or more formulas when you use multiple values in a single input cell. Figure 26-5 shows the general layout for a one-input data table. You can place the table anywhere in the workbook. The left column contains various values for the single input cell. The top row contains formulas or, more often, references to formulas located elsewhere in the worksheet. You can use a single formula reference or any number of formula references. The upper-left cell of the table remains empty. Excel calculates the values that result from each level of the input cell and places them under each formula reference.

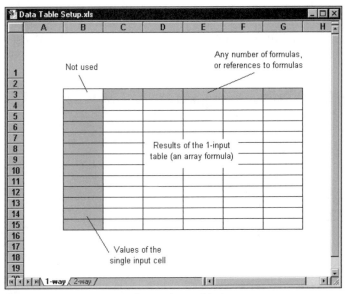

Figure 26-5: How a one-input data table is set up.

This example uses the mortgage loan worksheet from earlier in the chapter, which is shown again in Figure 26-6. The goal of this example is to create a table that shows the values of the four formula cells (loan amount, monthly payment, total payments, and total interest) for various interest rates ranging from 7 to 9 percent, in 0.25 percent increments.

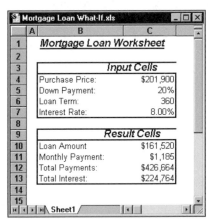

Figure 26-6: This example uses the mortgage loan worksheet to generate a one-input data table.

Figure 26-7 shows the setup for the data table area. Row 2 consists of references to the formulas in the worksheet. For example, cell F3 contains the formula =C10. Column E contains the values of the single input cell (interest rate) that Excel will use in the table. Borders also are added, to indicate where the calculated values go.

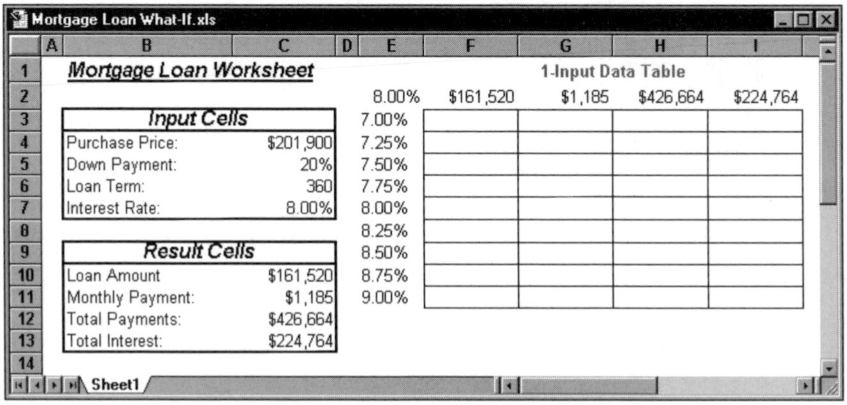

	A	B	C	D	E	F	G	H	I
		Mortgage Loan What-If.xls							
1		*Mortgage Loan Worksheet*				1-Input Data Table			
2					8.00%	$161,520	$1,185	$426,664	$224,764
3		*Input Cells*			7.00%				
4		Purchase Price:	$201,900		7.25%				
5		Down Payment:	20%		7.50%				
6		Loan Term:	360		7.75%				
7		Interest Rate:	8.00%		8.00%				
8					8.25%				
9		*Result Cells*			8.50%				
10		Loan Amount	$161,520		8.75%				
11		Monthly Payment:	$1,185		9.00%				
12		Total Payments:	$426,664						
13		Total Interest:	$224,764						
14									

Sheet1

Figure 26-7: Preparing to create a one-input data table.

To create the table, select the range (in this case, E2:I11) and then choose Data ✑ Table. Excel displays the Table dialog box, shown in Figure 26-8. You must specify the worksheet cell that contains the input value. Because variables for the input cell appear in a column in the data table rather than in a row, you place this cell reference in the text box called Column input cell. Enter **Interest_Rate** (the name for cell C7) or point to the cell in the worksheet. Leave the Row input cell field blank. Click OK, and Excel fills in the table with the appropriate results (see Figure 26-9).

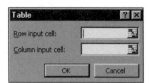

Figure 26-8: The Table dialog box.

Mortgage Loan What-If.xls									
	A	B	C	D	E	F	G	H	I
1	**Mortgage Loan Worksheet**					1-Input Data Table			
2					8.00%	$161,520	$1,185	$426,664	$224,764
3		*Input Cells*			7.00%	161,520	1,075	386,855	184,955
4	Purchase Price:		$201,900		7.25%	161,520	1,102	396,666	194,766
5	Down Payment:		20%		7.50%	161,520	1,129	406,574	204,674
6	Loan Term:		360		7.75%	161,520	1,157	416,574	214,674
7	Interest Rate:		8.00%		8.00%	161,520	1,185	426,664	224,764
8					8.25%	161,520	1,213	436,840	234,940
9		*Result Cells*			8.50%	161,520	1,242	447,102	245,202
10	Loan Amount		$161,520		8.75%	161,520	1,271	457,444	255,544
11	Monthly Payment:		$1,185		9.00%	161,520	1,300	467,866	265,966
12	Total Payments:		$426,664						
13	Total Interest:		$224,764						
14									

Sheet1

Figure 26-9: The result of the one-input data table.

Examine the contents of the cells that Excel entered as a result of this command, and notice that Excel filled in formulas — more specifically, array formulas that use the TABLE function. As discussed in Chapter 20, an array formula is a single formula that produces results in multiple cells. Because the table uses formulas, Excel updates the table that you produce if you change the cell references in the first row or plug in different interest rates in the first column.

Note

You can arrange a one-input table vertically (as in this example) or horizontally. If you place the values of the input cell in a row, you enter the input cell reference in the text box labeled Row input cell in the Table dialog box.

Creating a Two-Input Data Table

As the name implies, a two-input data table lets you vary *two* input cells. You can see the setup for this type of table in Figure 26-10. Although it looks similar to a one-input table, the two-input table has one critical difference: it can show the results of only one formula at a time. With a one-input table, you can place any number of formulas, or references to formulas, across the top row of the table. In a two-input table, this top row holds the values for the second input cell. The upper-left cell of the table contains a reference to the single result formula.

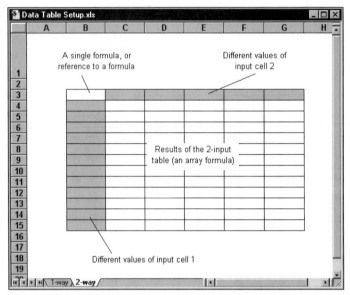

Figure 26-10: The setup for a two-input data table.

In the preceding example, you could create a two-input data table that shows the results of a formula (say, monthly payment) for various combinations of two input cells (such as interest rate and down-payment percent). To see the effects on other formulas, you simply create multiple data tables—one for each formula cell that you want to summarize.

The worksheet that is shown in Figure 26-11 demonstrates a two-input data table. In this example, a company wants to conduct a direct-mail promotion to sell its product. The worksheet calculates the net profit from the promotion.

This model uses two input cells: the number of promotional pieces mailed and the anticipated response rate. The following items appear in the results area:

✦ **Printing costs per unit:** The cost to print a single mailer. The unit cost varies with the quantity: $0.20 each for quantities less than 200,000; $0.15 each for quantities of 200,001 through 300,000; and $0.10 each for quantities of more than 300,000. The following formula is used:

```
=IF(Number_mailed<200000,0.2,IF(Number_mailed<300000,0.15,0.1))
```

✦ **Mailing costs per unit:** This is a fixed cost, $0.32 per unit mailed.

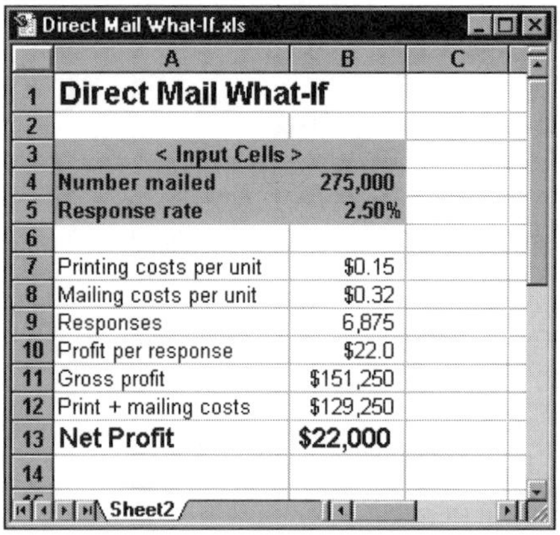

Direct Mail What-If.xls

	A	B	C
1	Direct Mail What-If		
2			
3	< Input Cells >		
4	Number mailed	275,000	
5	Response rate	2.50%	
6			
7	Printing costs per unit	$0.15	
8	Mailing costs per unit	$0.32	
9	Responses	6,875	
10	Profit per response	$22.0	
11	Gross profit	$151,250	
12	Print + mailing costs	$129,250	
13	Net Profit	$22,000	
14			

Sheet2

Figure 26-11: This worksheet calculates the net profit from a direct-mail promotion.

✦ **Responses:** This is the number of responses, calculated from the response rate and the number mailed. The formula in this cell is the following:

```
=Response_rate*Number_mailed
```

✦ **Profit per response:** This is a fixed value. The company knows that it will realize a profit of $22 per order.

✦ **Gross profit:** This is a simple formula that multiplies the profit per response by the number of responses:

```
=Profit_per_response*Responses
```

✦ **Print + mailing costs:** This formula calculates the total cost of the promotion:

```
=Number_mailed*(Printing_costs_per_unit+Mailing_costs_per_unit)
```

✦ **Net Profit:** This formula calculates the bottom line—the gross profit minus the printing and mailing costs.

If you plug in values for the two input cells, you see that the net profit varies widely—often going negative to produce a net loss.

Figure 26-12 shows the setup of a two-input data table that summarizes the net profit at various combinations of quantity and response rate; the table appears in the range A15:I25.

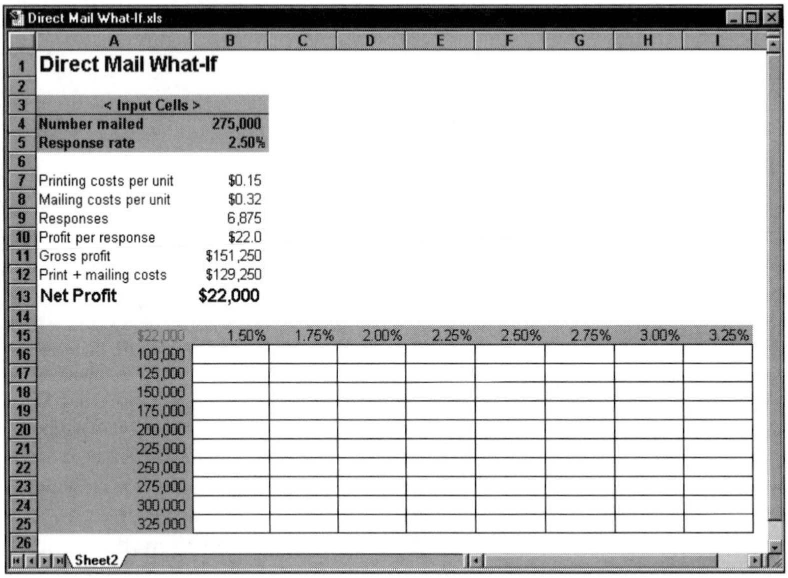

	A	B	C	D	E	F	G	H	I
1	Direct Mail What-If								
2									
3	< Input Cells >								
4	Number mailed	275,000							
5	Response rate	2.50%							
6									
7	Printing costs per unit	$0.15							
8	Mailing costs per unit	$0.32							
9	Responses	6,875							
10	Profit per response	$22.0							
11	Gross profit	$151,250							
12	Print + mailing costs	$129,250							
13	Net Profit	$22,000							
14									
15	$22,000	1.50%	1.75%	2.00%	2.25%	2.50%	2.75%	3.00%	3.25%
16	100,000								
17	125,000								
18	150,000								
19	175,000								
20	200,000								
21	225,000								
22	250,000								
23	275,000								
24	300,000								
25	325,000								
26									

Figure 26-12: Preparing to create a two-input data table.

To create the data table, select the range and choose Data ➪ Table. The Row input cell is Number_Mailed (the name for cell B4), and the Column input cell is Response_Rate (the name for cell B5). Figure 26-13 shows the result of this command.

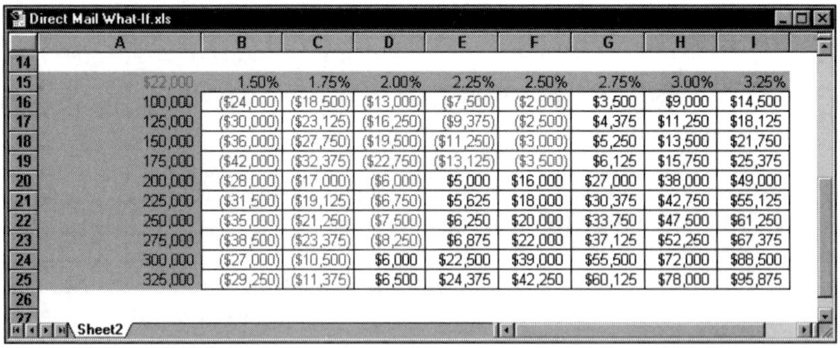

	A	B	C	D	E	F	G	H	I
14									
15	$22,000	1.50%	1.75%	2.00%	2.25%	2.50%	2.75%	3.00%	3.25%
16	100,000	($24,000)	($18,500)	($13,000)	($7,500)	($2,000)	$3,500	$9,000	$14,500
17	125,000	($30,000)	($23,125)	($16,250)	($9,375)	($2,500)	$4,375	$11,250	$18,125
18	150,000	($36,000)	($27,750)	($19,500)	($11,250)	($3,000)	$5,250	$13,500	$21,750
19	175,000	($42,000)	($32,375)	($22,750)	($13,125)	($3,500)	$6,125	$15,750	$25,375
20	200,000	($28,000)	($17,000)	($6,000)	$5,000	$16,000	$27,000	$38,000	$49,000
21	225,000	($31,500)	($19,125)	($6,750)	$5,625	$18,000	$30,375	$42,750	$55,125
22	250,000	($35,000)	($21,250)	($7,500)	$6,250	$20,000	$33,750	$47,500	$61,250
23	275,000	($38,500)	($23,375)	($8,250)	$6,875	$22,000	$37,125	$52,250	$67,375
24	300,000	($27,000)	($10,500)	$6,000	$22,500	$39,000	$55,500	$72,000	$88,500
25	325,000	($29,250)	($11,375)	$6,500	$24,375	$42,250	$60,125	$78,000	$95,875
26									
27									

Figure 26-13: The result of the two-input data table.

Two-input data tables often make good 3D charts. An example of such a chart for the direct-mail example appears in Figure 26-14.

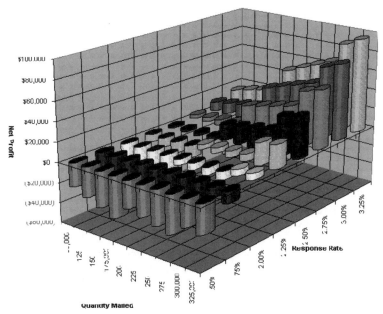

Figure 26-14: Viewing the two-input data table graphically.

Using Scenario Manager

Data tables are useful, but they have a few limitations:

✦ You can vary only one or two input cells at a time.

✦ The process of setting up a data table is not all that intuitive.

✦ A two-input table shows the results of only one formula cell (although you can create additional tables for more formulas).

✦ More often than not, you're interested in a few select combinations — not an entire table that shows all possible combinations of two input cells.

Excel's Scenario Manager feature makes it easy to automate your what-if models. You can store different sets of input values (called *changing cells* in the terminology of Scenario Manager) for any number of variables and give a name to each set. You can then select a set of values by name, and Excel displays the worksheet by using those values. You can also generate a summary report that shows the effect of various combinations of values on any number of result cells. These summary reports can be an outline or a pivot table.

Your sales forecast for the year, for example, may depend on several factors. Consequently, you can define three scenarios: best case, worst case, and most likely case. You then can switch to any of these scenarios by selecting the named scenario from a list. Excel substitutes the appropriate input values in your worksheet and recalculates the formulas. This process is similar, in some respects, to the macro-assisted what-if technique described earlier. The Scenario Manager is easier to use, however.

Defining Scenarios

To introduce you to the Scenario Manager, this section starts with a simple example: the production model used earlier in the chapter.

This example defines three scenarios, as depicted in Table 26-2. The Best Case scenario has the lowest hourly cost and materials cost. The Worst Case scenario has high values for both the hourly cost and the materials cost. The third scenario, Most Likely Case, has intermediate values for both of these input cells (this represents the management's best estimate). The managers need to be prepared for the worst case, however — and they are interested in what would happen under the Best Case scenario.

Table 26-2
Three Scenarios for the Production Model

Scenario	Hourly Cost	Materials Cost
Best Case	30	57
Worst Case	38	62
Most Likely Case	34	59

Access the Scenario Manager by selecting Tools ⇨ Scenarios to display the Scenario Manager dialog box, shown in Figure 26-15.

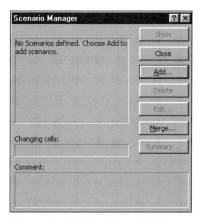

Figure 26-15: The Scenario Manager dialog box lets you assign names to different sets of assumptions.

When you first open this dialog box, it tells you that no scenarios are defined — which is not too surprising, because you're just starting. As you add named scenarios, they appear in this dialog box.

> **Tip** I strongly suggest that you create names for the changing cells and all the result cells that you want to examine. Excel uses these names in the dialog boxes and in the reports that it generates. If you use names, you'll find that keeping track of what's going on is much easier; names also make your reports more readable.

To add a scenario, click the Add button in the Scenario Manager dialog box. Excel displays its Add Scenario dialog box, shown in Figure 26-16.

Figure 26-16: The Add Scenario dialog box lets you create a named scenario.

This dialog box consists of four parts:

✦ **Scenario name:** The name for the scenario. You can give it any name that you like — preferably something meaningful.

✦ **Changing cells:** The input cells for the scenario. You can enter the cell addresses directly or point to them. Multiple selections are allowed, so the input cells need not be adjacent. Each named scenario can use the same set of changing cells or different changing cells. The number of changing cells for a scenario is limited to 32.

✦ **Comment:** By default, Excel displays the name of the person who created the scenario and the date that it was created. You can change this text, add new text to it, or delete it.

✦ **Protection:** The two options (preventing changes and hiding a scenario) are in effect only when you protect the worksheet and choose the Scenario option in the Protect Sheet dialog box. Protecting a scenario prevents anyone from modifying it; a hidden scenario doesn't appear in the Scenario Manager dialog box.

In this example, define the three scenarios that are listed in the preceding table. The changing cells are Hourly_Cost (B4) and Materials_Cost (B5).

After you enter the information in the Add Scenario dialog box, click OK. Excel then displays the Scenario Values dialog box, shown in Figure 26-17. This dialog box displays one field for each changing cell that you specified in the previous dialog box. Enter the values for each cell in the scenario. If you click OK, you return to the Scenario Manager dialog box — which then displays your named scenario in its list. If you have more scenarios to create, click the Add button to return to the Add Scenario dialog box.

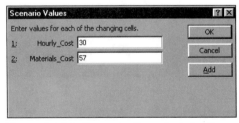

Figure 26-17: You enter the values for the scenario in the Scenario Values dialog box.

Using the Scenarios Tool

Excel has a Scenarios tool, which is a drop-down list that shows all the defined scenarios and enables you to display a scenario or create a new scenario. Oddly, this useful tool doesn't appear on any of the prebuilt toolbars. But, if you use the Scenario Manager, you may want to add the Scenarios tool to one of your toolbars, using the following procedure:

1. Choose Tools ⇨ Customize.

2. In the Customize dialog box, click the Commands tab.

3. Select the Tools category.

4. In the Commands tab, locate the Scenarios tool and drag it to any toolbar.

5. Click the Close button.

Refer to Chapter 33 for additional details on customizing toolbars.

Using the Scenarios tool may be more efficient than bringing up the Scenario Manager dialog box to create or view a different scenario.

To create a scenario by using the Scenarios tool, enter the scenario's values, select the changing cells, and then enter the name for the scenario in the Scenario drop-down box. To view a named scenario, just choose it from the list. Scenarios that you define in this manner also appear in the Scenario Manager dialog box. So, if you want to perform any operations on your scenarios (add comments, edit values, or generate reports), you need to select Tools ⇨ Scenarios, to display the Scenario Manager dialog box.

Displaying Scenarios

After you define all the scenarios and return to the Scenario Manager dialog box, the dialog box displays the names of your defined scenarios. Select one of the scenarios and then click the Show button. Excel inserts the corresponding values into the changing cells and calculates the worksheet to show the results for that scenario.

Modifying Scenarios

The Edit button in the Scenario Manager dialog box lets you change one or more of the values for the changing cells of a scenario. Select the scenario that you want to change, click the Edit button, choose OK to access the Scenario Values dialog box, and then make your changes. Notice that Excel automatically updates the Comments box with new text that indicates when the scenario was modified.

Merging Scenarios

In workgroup situations, you may have several people working on a spreadsheet model, and several people may have defined various scenarios. The marketing department, for example, may have its opinion of what the input cells should be, the finance department may have another opinion, and your CEO may have yet another opinion.

Excel makes it easy to merge these various scenarios into a single workbook by using the Merge button in the Scenario Manager dialog box. Clicking this button displays the dialog box shown in Figure 26-18.

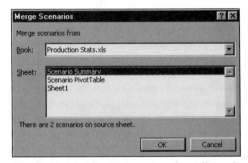

Figure 26-18: The Merge Scenarios dialog box lets you merge scenarios that are defined by others into your workbook.

Before you merge scenarios, make sure that the workbook from which you're merging is open. Then, click the Merge button in the Scenario Manager dialog box. Excel displays its Merge Scenarios dialog box. Choose the workbook from which you're merging in the Book drop-down list. Then, choose the sheet that contains the scenarios you want to merge from the Sheet list box (notice that the dialog box displays the number of scenarios in each sheet as you scroll through the Sheet list box). Click OK, and you return to the previous dialog box, which now displays the scenario names that you merged from the other workbook.

Generating a Scenario Report

You are ready to take the Scenario Manager through its final feat — generating a summary report. When you click the Summary button in the Scenario Manager dialog box, Excel displays the Scenario Summary dialog box, shown in Figure 26-19.

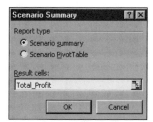

Figure 26-19: The Scenario Summary dialog box enables you to choose a report type and specify the result cells in which you're interested.

You have a choice of report types:

✦ **Scenario Summary:** The summary report appears in the form of an outline.

✦ **Scenario PivotTable:** The summary report appears in the form of a pivot table (see Chapter 25).

For simple cases of scenario management, a standard Scenario Summary report is usually sufficient. If you have many scenarios defined with multiple result cells, however, you may find that a Scenario Pivot Table provides more flexibility.

The Scenario Summary dialog box also asks you to specify the result cells (the cells that contain the formulas in which you're interested). For this example, select B15:D15 and B17 (a multiple selection) to make the report show the profit for each product, plus the total profit.

Excel creates a new worksheet to store the summary table. Figure 26-20 shows the Scenario Summary form of the report, and Figure 26-21 shows the Scenario Pivot Table form. If you gave names to the changing cells and result cells, the table uses these names. Otherwise, it lists the cell references.

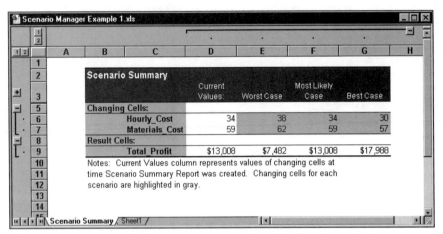

Figure 26-20: A Scenario Summary report produced by the Scenario Manager.

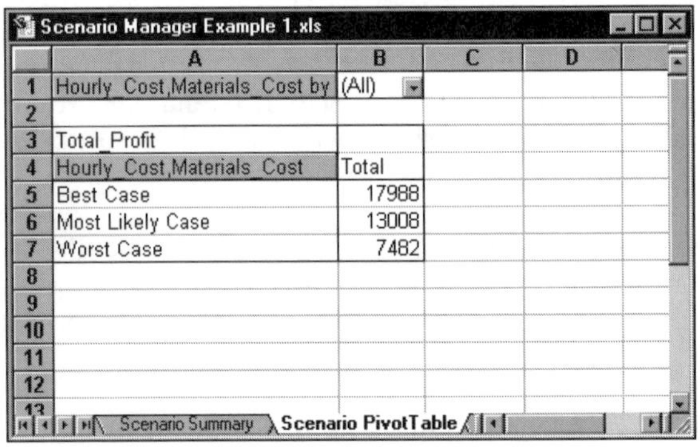

Figure 26-21: A Scenario Pivot Table report produced by the Scenario Manager.

Scenario Manager Limitations

As you work with the Scenario Manager, you may discover its main limitation: a scenario can use no more than 32 changing cells. If you attempt to use more, you get the message that is shown in Figure 26-22.

Figure 26-22: The Scenario Manager is limited to 32 changing cells.

You can get around this limitation by splitting your scenarios into parts. For example, assume that you have a worksheet with monthly sales projections for three years (36 changing cells). You may want to define various scenarios for these projections. But, because the number of changing cells exceeds the 32-cell limit, you can break it down into two or three scenarios — each of which uses a different set of changing cells. For example, you can define a scenario for the first 12 months, another for the second 12 months, and yet another for the third 12 months. Then, to display a particular scenario, you must display all three subscenarios. Writing simple macros makes this easy. If you use this technique, be aware that Excel includes superfluous information in summary reports.

Summary

This chapter discusses the concept of spreadsheet what-if analysis. What-if analysis is the process of systematically changing input cells and observing the effects on one or more formula cells. You can perform what-if analysis manually by plugging in different values. You also can use macros to automate this process. Excel's data table feature enables you to summarize the results of various values of a single input cell or various combinations of two input cells. The Scenario Manager feature makes it easy to create scenarios and generate summary reports.

✦ ✦ ✦

Analyzing Data Using Goal Seeking and Solver

The preceding chapter discusses *what-if analysis* — the process of changing input cells to observe the results on other dependent cells. This chapter looks at that process from the opposite perspective — finding the value of one or more input cells that produces a desired result in a formula cell.

What-If Analysis — In Reverse

Consider the following what-if question: "What is the total profit if sales increase by 20 percent?" If you set up your worksheet properly, you can change the value in one cell to see what happens to the profit cell. Goal seeking takes the opposite approach. If you know what a formula result *should* be, Excel can tell you the values that you need to enter in one or more input cells to produce that result. In other words, you can ask a question such as, "How much do sales need to increase to produce a profit of $1.2 million?" Excel provides two tools that are relevant:

   ✦ **Goal seeking:** Determines the value that you need to enter in a single input cell to produce a result that you want in a dependent (formula) cell.

   ✦ **Solver:** Determines the values that you need to enter in multiple input cells to produce a result that you want. Moreover, because you can specify certain constraints to the problem, you gain significant problem-solving ability.

Single-Cell Goal Seeking

Single-cell goal seeking (also known as *backsolving*) is a rather simple concept. Excel determines what value in an input cell produces a desired result in a formula cell. Walk through the following example to understand how single-cell goal seeking works.

A Goal-Seeking Example

Figure 27-1 shows the mortgage loan worksheet that was used in the preceding chapter. This worksheet has four input cells and four formula cells. Originally, this worksheet was used for a what-if analysis example. In this section, the opposite approach is taken — rather than supply different input cell values to look at the calculated formulas, this example lets Excel determine one of the input values.

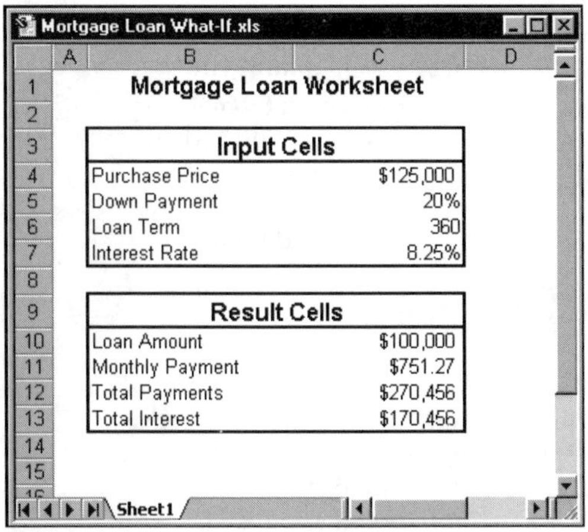

Figure 27-1: This worksheet is a good demonstration of goal seeking.

Assume that you're in the market for a new home and you know that you can afford $1,200 per month in mortgage payments. You also know that a lender can issue a fixed-rate mortgage loan for 8.25 percent, based on an 80 percent loan-to-value (that is, a 20-percent down payment). The question is, "What is the maximum purchase price I can handle?" In other words, what value in cell C4 causes the formula in cell C11 to result in $1,200? You could plug values into cell C4 until C11 displays $1,200; however, Excel can determine the answer much more efficiently.

To answer the question posed in the preceding paragraph, select Tools ➪ Goal Seek. Excel displays the dialog box shown in Figure 27-2. Completing this dialog box is similar to forming a sentence. You want to set cell C11 to 1200 by changing cell C4. Enter this information in the dialog box either by typing the cell references or by pointing with the mouse. Click OK to begin the goal-seeking process.

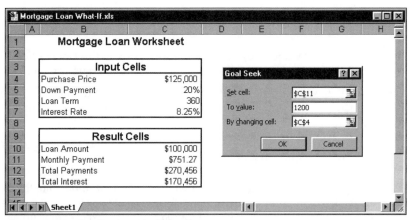

Figure 27-2: The Goal Seek dialog box.

In about a second, Excel announces that it has found the solution and displays the Goal Seek Status box, which shows the target value and the value that Excel calculated. In this case, Excel found an exact value. The worksheet now displays the found value in cell C4 ($199,663). As a result of this value, the monthly payment amount is $1,200. At this point, you have two options:

✦ Click OK to replace the original value with the found value.

✦ Click Cancel to restore your worksheet to the form that it had before you chose Tools ➪ Goal Seek.

More About Goal Seeking

Excel can't always find a value that produces the result for which you're looking — sometimes, a solution simply doesn't exist. In such a case, the Goal Seek Status box informs you of that fact (see Figure 27-3).

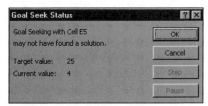

Figure 27-3: When Excel can't find a solution to your goal-seeking problem, it tells you so.

Other times, however, Excel may report that it can't find a solution, but you're pretty sure that one exists. If that's the case, you can try the following options:

✦ Change the current value of the By changing cell box in the Goal Seek dialog box to a value that is closer to the solution, and then reissue the command.

✦ Adjust the Maximum iterations setting in the Calculation tab of the Options dialog box. Increasing the number of iterations makes Excel try more possible solutions.

✦ Double-check your logic and make sure that the formula cell does, indeed, depend on the specified changing cell.

Note   Like all computer programs, Excel has limited precision. To demonstrate this limitation, enter **=A1^2** into cell A2. Then, select Tools ⇨ Goal Seek to find the value in cell A1 (which is empty) that makes the formula return 16. Excel comes up with a value of 4.00002269 (you may need to widen the column to see the complete value), which is close to the square root of 16, but certainly not exact. You can adjust the precision in the Calculation tab of the Options dialog box (make the Maximum change value smaller).

Note   In some cases, multiple values of the input cell produce the same desired result. For example, the formula =A1^2 returns 16 if cell A1 contains either –4 or +4. If you use goal seeking when two solutions are possible, Excel gives you the solution that has the same sign as the current value in the cell.

Perhaps the main limitation of the Tools ⇨ Goal Seek command is its inability to find the value for more than one input cell. For example, it can't tell you what purchase price *and* what down-payment percent will result in a particular monthly payment. If you want to change more than one variable at a time, use Solver (discussed later in this chapter).

Graphical Goal Seeking

Excel provides another way to perform goal seeking — by manipulating a graph. Figure 27-4 shows a worksheet that projects sales for a startup company. The CFO knows from experience that companies in this industry can grow exponentially according to a formula such as this one:

$$y*(b_x)$$

Table 27-1 lists and describes the variables.

Table 27-1
Variables Used in the Sales Growth Formula

Variable	Description
y	A constant equal to the first year's sales
b	A growth coefficient
x	A variable relating to time

The company managers know that sales during the first year are going to be $250,000, and they want to increase the company's sales to $10 million by the year 2005. The financial modelers want to know the exact growth coefficient that meets this goal. The worksheet that is shown in Figure 27-4 uses formulas to forecast the annual sales, based on the growth coefficient in cell B1. The worksheet has an embedded chart that plots the annual sales.

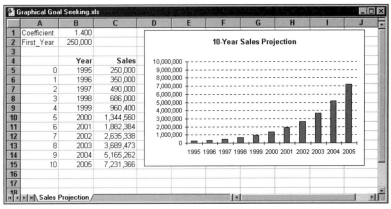

Figure 27-4: This sales projection predicts exponential growth, based on the growth coefficient in cell B1.

The initial guess for the growth coefficient is 1.40. As you can see, this number is too low—it results in sales of only $7.231 million for the year 2005. Although you can select Tools ➪ Goal Seek to arrive at the exact coefficient, you have another way to do it.

Click the chart so that you can edit it and then select the chart series. Now, click the last data column to select only that column in the series. Point to the top of the column, and the mouse pointer changes shape. Drag the column upward and watch the value change in the small box displayed next to the mouse pointer. When the value is exactly $10 million, release the mouse button.

Excel responds with the Goal Seek dialog box, with two fields completed, as shown in Figure 27-5. Excel just needs to know which cell to use for the input cell. Specify cell B1 or enter **Coefficient** in the By changing cell edit box. Excel calculates the value of Coefficient that is necessary to produce the result that you pointed out on the chart. If you want to keep that number (which, by the way, is 1.44612554959182), click OK. Excel replaces the current value of Coefficient with the new value, and the chart is updated automatically. You can probably appreciate the fact that it would take quite a while to arrive at this number by plugging in successive approximations.

Figure 27-5: The Goal Seek dialog box appears when you directly manipulate a point on a chart that contains a formula.

You don't want to use this graphical method all the time, however, because the normal Tools ➪ Goal Seek command is more efficient. But, it does demonstrate another way to approach problems that is helpful for those who are more visually oriented.

As you may expect, goal seeking can get much more impressive when it's used with complex worksheets that have many dependent cells. In any event, it sure beats trial and error.

Introducing Solver

Excel's goal-seeking feature is a useful tool, but it clearly has limitations. It can solve for only one adjustable cell, for example, and it returns only a single solution. Excel's powerful Solver tool extends this concept by enabling you to do the following:

✦ Specify multiple adjustable cells.

✦ Specify constraints on the values that the adjustable cells can have.

✦ Generate a solution that maximizes or minimizes a particular worksheet cell.

✦ Generate multiple solutions to a problem.

Although goal seeking is a relatively simple operation, using Solver can be much more complicated. In fact, Solver is probably one of the most difficult (and potentially frustrating) features in Excel. I'm the first to admit that Solver isn't for everyone. In fact, most Excel users have no use for this feature. However, many users find that having this much power is worth spending the extra time to learn about it.

Appropriate Problems for Solver

Problems that are appropriate for Solver fall into a relatively narrow range. They typically involve situations that meet the following criteria:

✦ A target cell depends on other cells and formulas. Typically, you want to maximize or minimize this target cell or set it equal to some value.

✦ The target cell depends on a group of cells (called *changing cells*) that Solver can adjust to affect the target cell.

✦ The solution must adhere to certain limitations, or *constraints*.

After you set up your worksheet appropriately, you can use Solver to adjust the changing cells and produce the result that you want in your target cell — and, simultaneously meet all the constraints that you have defined.

On the CD-ROM

You can find all the Solver examples in this chapter on this book's CD-ROM.

A Simple Solver Example

I start with a simple example to introduce Solver and then present some increasingly complex examples to demonstrate what it can do.

Figure 27-6 shows a worksheet that is set up to calculate the profit for three products. Column B shows the number of units of each product, column C shows the profit per unit for each product, and column C contains formulas that calculate the profit for each product by multiplying the units by the profit per unit.

	A	B	C	D	E
2		Units	Profit/Unit	Profit	
3	Product A	100	$13	$1,300	
4	Product B	100	$18	$1,800	
5	Product C	100	$22	$2,200	
6	Total	300		$5,300	

Solver Production Model.xls — Sheet1

Figure 27-6: Use Solver to determine the number of units to maximize the total profit.

It doesn't take an MBA degree to realize that the greatest profit per unit comes from Product C. Therefore, the logical solution is to produce only Product C. If things were really this simple, you wouldn't need tools such as Solver. As in most situations, this company has some constraints to which it must adhere:

✦ The combined production capacity is 300 total units per day.

✦ The company needs 50 units of Product A to fill an existing order.

✦ The company needs 40 units of Product B to fill an anticipated order.

✦ Because the market for Product C is relatively limited, the company doesn't want to produce more than 40 units of this product.

These four constraints make the problem more realistic and challenging. In fact, it's a perfect problem for Solver.

The basic procedure for using Solver is as follows:

1. Set up the worksheet with values and formulas. Make sure that you format cells logically; for example, if you cannot produce portions of your products, format those cells to contain numbers with no decimal values.

2. Bring up the Solver dialog box.

3. Specify the target cell.

4. Specify the changing cells.

5. Specify the constraints.

6. Change the Solver options, if necessary.

7. Let Solver solve the problem.

To start Solver, select Tools ➪ Solver. Excel displays its Solver Parameters dialog box, shown in Figure 27-7.

Figure 27-7: The Solver Parameters dialog box.

No Tools ⇨ Solver Command?

Solver is an add-in, so it's available only when the add-in is installed. If the Tools menu doesn't show a Solver command, you need to install the add-in before you can use it.

Select Tools ⇨ Add-Ins. Excel displays its Add-Ins dialog box. Scroll down the list of add-ins and place a check mark next to the item named Solver Add-In. Click OK, and Excel installs the add-in and makes the Tools ⇨ Solver command available. If Solver isn't available on your computer, you'll be asked if you want to install it.

In this example, the target cell is D6—the cell that calculates the total profit for three products. Enter (or point to) cell D6 in the Set Target Cell field of the Solver Parameters dialog box. Because the objective is to maximize this cell, click the Max option. Next, specify the changing cells, which are in the range B3:B5, in the By Changing Cells box.

The next step is to specify the constraints on the problem. The constraints are added one at a time and appear in the box labeled Subject to the Constraints. To add a constraint, click the Add button. Excel displays the Add Constraint dialog box, shown in Figure 27-8. This dialog box has three parts: a cell reference, an operator, and a value. To set the first constraint—that the total production capacity is 300 units—enter B6 as the Cell Reference, choose equal (=) from the drop-down list of operators, and enter 300 as the Constraint value. Click Add to add the remaining constraints. Table 27-2 summarizes the constraints for this problem.

Figure 27-8: The Add Constraint dialog box.

Table 27-2
Constraints Summary

Constraint	Expressed As
Capacity is 300 units	B6=300
At least 50 units of Product A	B3>=50
At least 40 units of Product B	B4>=40
No more than 40 units of Product C	B5<=40

After you enter the last constraint, click OK to return to the Solver Parameters dialog box—which now lists the four constraints.

At this point, Solver knows everything about the problem. Click the Solver button to start the solution process. You can watch the progress onscreen, and Excel soon announces that it has found a solution. The Solver Results dialog box is shown in Figure 27-9.

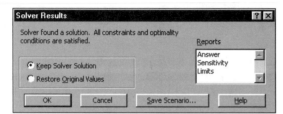

Figure 27-9: Solver displays this dialog box when it finds a solution to the problem.

At this point, you have the following options:

✦ Replace the original changing cell values with the values that Solver found

✦ Restore the original changing cell values

✦ Create any or all three reports that describe what Solver did (press Shift to select multiple reports from this list)

✦ Click the Save Scenario button to save the solution as a scenario, so that the Scenario Manager can use it (see Chapter 26)

If you specify any report options, Excel creates each report on a new worksheet, with an appropriate name. Figure 27-10 shows an Answer Report. In the Constraints section of the report, all the constraints except one are *binding*, which means that the constraint was satisfied at its limit, with no more room to change.

This simple example illustrates how Solver works. The fact is, you could probably solve this particular problem manually just as quickly. That, of course, isn't always the case.

	Cell	Name	Original Value	Final Value

Microsoft Excel 9.0 Answer Report
Worksheet: [Solver Production Model.xls]Sheet1
Report Created: 9/4/1998 11:52:06 AM

Target Cell (Max)

Cell	Name	Original Value	Final Value
$D$6	Profit	$ 5,300	$ 5,310

Adjustable Cells

Cell	Name	Original Value	Final Value
$B$3	Product A Units	100	50
$B$4	Product B Units	100	210
$B$5	Product C Units	100	40

Constraints

Cell	Name	Cell Value	Formula	Status	Slack
$B$6	Units	300	$B$6=300	Binding	0
$B$5	Product C Units	40	$B$5<=40	Binding	0
$B$3	Product A Units	50	$B$3>=50	Binding	0
$B$4	Product B Units	210	$B$4>=40	Not Binding	170

Figure 27-10: One of three reports that Solver can produce.

More About Solver

Before presenting complex examples, this section discusses the Solver Options
dialog box—one of the more feature-packed dialog boxes in Excel. From this dialog
box, you control many aspects of the solution process, as well as load and save
model specifications in a worksheet range.

Having Solver report to you that it can't find a solution isn't unusual—even when
you know that one should exist. Often, you can change one or more of the Solver
options and try again. When you choose the Options button in the Solver Parameters
dialog box, Excel displays the Solver Options dialog box shown in Figure 27-11.

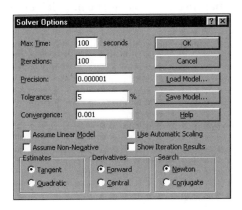

Figure 27-11: You can control
many aspects of how Solver
solves a problem.

This list describes Solver's options:

✦ **Max Time:** Specify the maximum amount of time (in seconds) that you want Solver to spend on a problem. If Solver reports that it exceeded the time limit, you can increase the amount of time that it spends searching for a solution.

✦ **Iterations:** Enter the maximum number of trial solutions that you want Solver to perform.

✦ **Precision:** Specify how close the Cell Reference and Constraint formulas must be to satisfy a constraint. Excel may solve the problem more quickly if you specify less precision.

✦ **Tolerance:** Designate the maximum percentage of error allowed for integer solutions (relevant only if an integer constraint is used).

✦ **Assume Linear Model:** Choose this option to speed the solution process, but you can use it only if all the relationships in the model are linear. You can't use this option if the adjustable cells are multiplied or divided, or if the problem uses exponents.

✦ **Use Automatic Scaling:** Use when the problem involves large differences in magnitude — when you attempt to maximize a percentage, for example, by varying cells that are very large.

✦ **Show Iteration Results:** Instruct Solver to pause and display the results after each iteration, by checking this box.

✦ **Estimates, Derivatives, and Search group boxes:** Use these options to control some technical aspects of the solution. In most cases, you don't need to change these settings.

✦ **Load Model:** Click this button to make Excel display the Load Model dialog box, in which you specify a range containing the model that you want to load.

✦ **Save Model:** Click this button to make Excel display the Save Model dialog box, in which you specify a range where Excel should save the model parameters.

Usually, you want to save a model only when you're using more than one set of Solver parameters with your worksheet, because Excel saves the first Solver model automatically with your worksheet (using hidden names). If you save additional models, Excel stores the information in the form of the formulas that correspond to the specification that you make (the last cell in the saved range is an array formula that holds the options settings).

Solver Examples

The remainder of this chapter consists of examples of using Solver for various types of problems.

Minimizing Shipping Costs

This example involves finding alternative options for shipping materials while keeping total shipping costs at a minimum (see Figure 27-12). A company has warehouses in Los Angeles, St. Louis, and Boston. Retail outlets throughout the United States place orders, which the company then ships from one of the warehouses. Ideally, the company wants to meet the product needs of all six retail outlets from available inventory in the warehouses—and keep total shipping charges as low as possible.

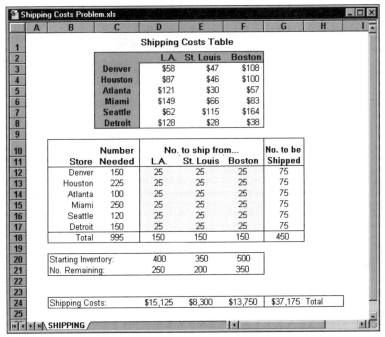

Figure 27-12: This worksheet determines the least expensive way to ship products from warehouses to retail outlets.

This workbook is rather complicated, so each part is explained individually:

✦ **Shipping Costs Table:** This table, at the top of the worksheet, contains per-unit shipping costs from each warehouse to each retail outlet. The cost to ship a unit from Los Angeles to Denver, for example, is $58.

✦ **Product needs of each retail store:** This information appears in C12:C17. For example, Denver needs 150 units, Houston needs 225, and so on. C18 holds the total needed.

✦ **Number to ship:** The shaded range (D12:F17) holds the adjustable cells that Solver varies (they are all initialized with a value of 25, to give Solver a starting value.) Column G contains formulas that total the number of units the company needs to ship to each retail outlet.

✦ **Warehouse inventory:** Row 20 contains the amount of inventory at each warehouse, and row 21 contains formulas that subtract the amount shipped (row 18) from the inventory. For example, cell D21 contains the following formula: =D20–D18.

✦ **Calculated shipping costs:** Row 24 contains formulas that calculate the shipping costs. Cell D24 contains the following formula, which is copied to the two cells to the right of cell D24:

```
=SUMPRODUCT(D3:D8,D12:D17)
```

This formula calculates the total shipping cost from each warehouse. Cell G24 is the bottom line, the total shipping costs for all orders.

Solver fills in values in the range D12:F17 in such a way that minimizes shipping costs while still supplying each retail outlet with the desired number of units. In other words, the solution minimizes the value in cell C24 by adjusting the cells in D12:F17, subject to the following constraints:

✦ The number of units needed by each retail outlet must equal the number shipped (in other words, all the orders are filled). These constraints are represented by the following specifications:

```
C12=G12    C14=G14    C16=G16
C13=G13    C15=G15    C17=G17
```

✦ The adjustable cells can't be negative, because shipping a negative number of units makes no sense. These constraints are represented by the following specifications:

```
D12>=0    E12>=0    F12>=0
D13>=0    E13>=0    F13>=0
D14>=0    E14>=0    F14>=0
D15>=0    E15>=0    F15>=0
D16>=0    E16>=0    F16>=0
D17>=0    E17>=0    F17>=0
```

✦ The number of units remaining in each warehouse's inventory must not be negative (that is, they can't ship more than what is available). This is represented by the following constraint specifications:

```
D21>=0    E21>=0    F21>=0
```

Note   Before you solve this problem with Solver, you may try your hand at minimizing the shipping cost manually by entering values in D12:F17. Don't forget to make sure that all the constraints are met. This is often a difficult task—and you can better appreciate the power behind Solver.

Setting up the problem is the difficult part. For example, you must enter 27 constraints. When you have specified all the necessary information, click the Solve button to put Solver to work. This process takes a while (Solver's speed depends on the speed of your computer and the amount of memory installed on your computer), but eventually Solver displays the solution that is shown in Figure 27-13.

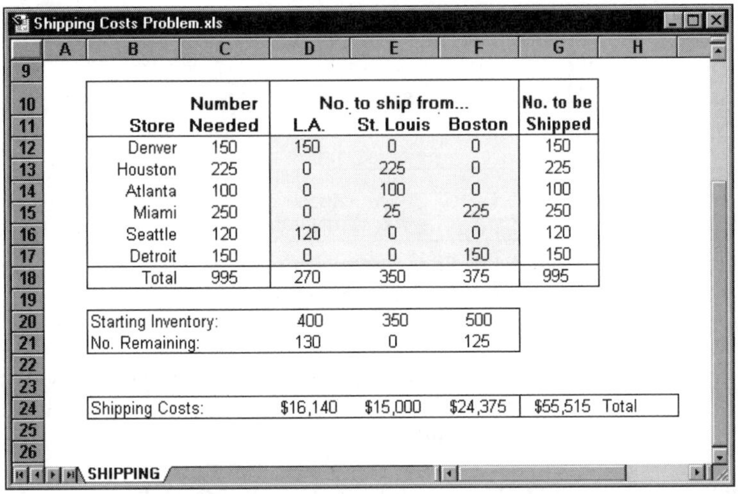

Store	Number Needed	No. to ship from... L.A.	St. Louis	Boston	No. to be Shipped
Denver	150	150	0	0	150
Houston	225	0	225	0	225
Atlanta	100	0	100	0	100
Miami	250	0	25	225	250
Seattle	120	120	0	0	120
Detroit	150	0	0	150	150
Total	995	270	350	375	995

Starting Inventory:	400	350	500
No. Remaining:	130	0	125

Shipping Costs:	$16,140	$15,000	$24,375	$55,515 Total

Figure 27-13: The solution that was created by Solver.

The total shipping cost is $55,515, and all the constraints are met. Notice that shipments to Miami come from both St. Louis and Boston.

Scheduling Staff

This example deals with staff scheduling. Such problems usually involve determining the minimum number of people that satisfy staffing needs on certain days or times of the day. The constraints typically involve such details as the number of consecutive days or hours that a person can work.

Figure 27-14 shows a worksheet that is set up to analyze a simple staffing problem. The question is, "What is the minimum number of employees required to meet daily staffing needs?" At this company, each person works five consecutive days. As a result, employees begin their five-day workweek on different days of the week.

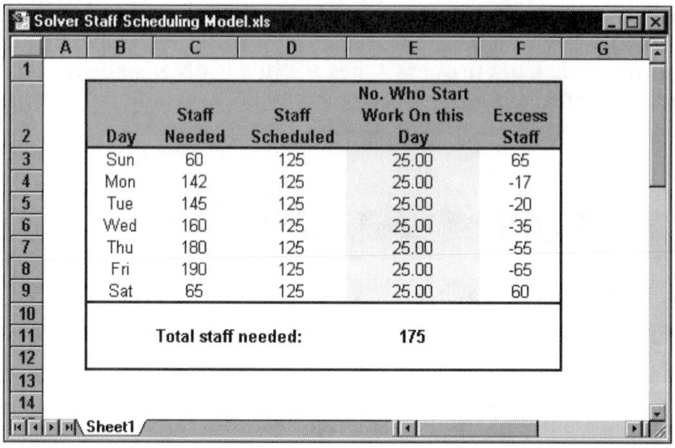

Day	Staff Needed	Staff Scheduled	No. Who Start Work On this Day	Excess Staff
Sun	60	125	25.00	65
Mon	142	125	25.00	-17
Tue	145	125	25.00	-20
Wed	160	125	25.00	-35
Thu	180	125	25.00	-55
Fri	190	125	25.00	-65
Sat	65	125	25.00	60
	Total staff needed:		175	

Figure 27-14: This staffing model determines the minimum number of staff members required to meet daily staffing needs.

The key to this problem, as with most Solver problems, is figuring out how to set up the worksheet. This example makes it clear that setting up your worksheet properly is critical to Solver. This worksheet is laid out as follows:

✦ **Day:** Column B consists of plain text for the days of the week.

✦ **Staff Needed:** The values in column C represent the number of employees needed on each day of the week. As you see, staffing needs vary quite a bit by the day of the week.

✦ **Staff Scheduled:** Column D holds formulas that use the values in column E. Each formula adds the number of people who start on that day to the number of people who started on the preceding four days. Because the week wraps around, you can't use a single formula and copy it. Consequently, each formula in column D is different:

```
D3:    =E3+E9+E8+E7+E6
D4:    =E4+E3+E9+E8+E7
D5:    =E5+E4+E10+E9+E8
D6:    =E6+E5+E4+E10+E9
D7:    =E7+E6+E5+E4+E10
D8:    =E8+E7+E6+E5+E4
D9:    =E9+E8+E7+E6+E5
```

✦ **Adjustable cells:** Column E holds the adjustable cells — the numbers to be determined by Solver. These cells are initialized with a value of 25, to give Solver a starting value. Generally, you should initialize the changing cells to values that are as close as possible to the anticipated answer.

✦ **Excess Staff:** Column F contains formulas that subtract the number of staff members needed from the number of staff members scheduled, to determine excess staff. Cell F3 contains =D3 – C3, which was copied to the six cells below it.

✦ **Total staff needed:** Cell E11 contains a formula that sums the number of people who start on each day. The formula is =SUM(E3:E9). This is the value that Solver minimizes.

This problem, of course, has constraints. The number of people scheduled each day must be greater than or equal to the number of people required. If each value in column F is greater than or equal to 0, the constraints are satisfied.

After the worksheet is set up, select Tools ➪ Solver and specify that you want to minimize cell E11 by changing cells E3:E9. Next, click the Add button to begin adding the following constraints:

```
F3>=0
F4>=0
F5>=0
F6>=0
F7>=0
F8>=0
F9>=0
```

Click Solve to start the process. The solution that Solver finds, shown in Figure 27-15, indicates that a staff of 188 meets the staffing needs and that no excess staffing exists on any day.

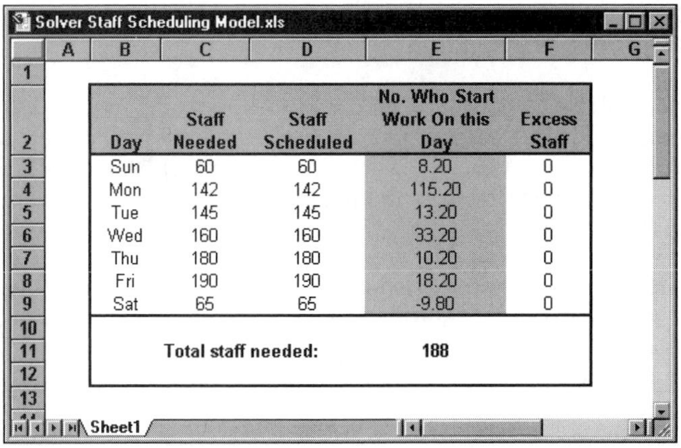

Day	Staff Needed	Staff Scheduled	No. Who Start Work On this Day	Excess Staff
Sun	60	60	8.20	0
Mon	142	142	115.20	0
Tue	145	145	13.20	0
Wed	160	160	33.20	0
Thu	180	180	10.20	0
Fri	190	190	18.20	0
Sat	65	65	-9.80	0
	Total staff needed:		188	

Figure 27-15: This solution offered by Solver isn't quite right—you have to add more constraints.

But wait! If you examine the results carefully, you notice that a few things are wrong here:

✦ Solver's solution involves partial people—who are difficult to find. For example, 8.2 people begin their workweek on Sunday.

✦ Even more critical is the suggestion that a negative number of people should begin their workweek on Saturday.

You can correct both of these problems easily by adding more constraints. Fortunately, Solver enables you to limit the solution to integers, by using the integer option in the Add Constraint dialog box. This means that you must add another constraint for each cell in E3:E9. Figure 27-16 shows how you can specify an integer constraint. Avoiding the negative people problem requires seven more constraints of the form **E3>=0**, one for each cell in E3:E9.

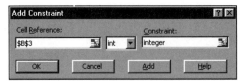

Figure 27-16: With many problems, you have to limit the solution to integers. You can do this by selecting the integer option in the Constraint box of the Add Constraint dialog box.

These two problems (integer solutions and negative numbers) are quite common when using Solver. They also demonstrate that checking the results is important, rather than relying only on Solver's solution.

Tip   If you find that adding these constraints is tedious, save the model to a worksheet range. Then, you can add new constraints to the range in the worksheet (and make sure that you don't overwrite the last cell in this range). Next, run Solver again and load the modified model from the range that you edited. The example workbook (available on this book's CD-ROM) has three Solver ranges stored in it.

After adding these constraints, run Solver again. This time it arrives at the solution shown in Figure 27-17. Notice that this solution requires 192 people and results in excess staffing on three days of the week. This solution is the best one possible that uses the fewest number of people—and almost certainly is better than what you would arrive at manually.

Solver Staff Scheduling Model.xls

Day	Staff Needed	Staff Scheduled	No. Who Start Work On this Day	Excess Staff
Sun	60	60	1.00	0
Mon	142	142	118.00	0
Tue	145	145	14.00	0
Wed	160	169	36.00	9
Thu	180	180	11.00	0
Fri	190	191	12.00	1
Sat	65	73	0.00	8
	Total staff needed:		192	

Sheet1

Figure 27-17: Rerunning Solver after adding more constraints produces a better solution to the staffing model problem.

Allocating Resources

The example in this section is a common type of problem that's ideal for Solver. Essentially, problems of this sort involve optimizing the volumes of individual production units that use varying amounts of fixed resources. Figure 27-18 shows an example for a toy company.

Solver Resource Allocation Model.xls

XYZ Toys Inc.

	Materials Needed							
Material	**Toy A**	**Toy B**	**Toy C**	**Toy D**	**Toy E**	**Amt. Avail.**	**Amt. Used**	**Amt. Left**
Red Paint	0	1	0	1	3	625	500	125
Blue Paint	3	1	0	1	0	640	500	140
White Paint	2	1	2	0	2	1,100	700	400
Plastic	1	5	2	2	1	875	1,100	-225
Wood	3	0	3	5	5	2,200	1,600	600
Glue	1	2	3	2	3	1,500	1,100	400
Unit Profit	$15	$30	$20	$25	$25			
No. to Make	100	100	100	100	100			
Profit	$1,500	$3,000	$2,000	$2,500	$2,500			
Total Profit	**$11,500**							

Sheet1

Figure 27-18: Using Solver to maximize profit when resources are limited.

This company makes five different toys, which use six different materials in varying amounts. For example, Toy A requires 3 units of blue paint, 2 units of white paint, 1 unit of plastic, 3 units of wood, and 1 unit of glue. Column G shows the current inventory of each type of material. Row 10 shows the unit profit for each toy. The number of toys to make is shown in the range B11:F11 — these are the values that Solver determines. The goal of this example is to determine how to allocate the resources to maximize the total profit (B13). In other words, Solver determines how many units of each toy to make. The constraints in this example are relatively simple:

✦ Ensure that production doesn't use more resources than are available. This can be accomplished by specifying that each cell in column F is greater than or equal to zero.

✦ Ensure that the quantities produced aren't negative. This can be accomplished by specifying that each cell in row 11 be greater than or equal to zero.

Figure 27-19 shows the results that are produced by Solver. It shows the product mix that generates $12,365 in profit and uses all resources in their entirety, except for glue.

	A	B	C	D	E	F	G	H	I
1				**XYZ Toys Inc.**					
2				Materials Needed					
3	Material	Toy A	Toy B	Toy C	Toy D	Toy E	Amt. Avail.	Amt. Used	Amt. Left
4	Red Paint	0	1	0	1	3	625	625	0
5	Blue Paint	3	1	0	1	0	640	640	0
6	White Paint	2	1	2	0	2	1,100	1,100	0
7	Plastic	1	5	2	2	1	875	875	0
8	Wood	3	0	3	5	5	2,200	2,200	0
9	Glue	1	2	3	2	3	1,500	1,353	147
10	Unit Profit	$15	$30	$20	$25	$25			
11	No. to Make	194	19	158	40	189			
12	Profit	$2,903	$573	$3,168	$1,008	$4,713			
13	Total Profit	$12,365							
14									
15									

Figure 27-19: Solver determined how to use the resources to maximize the total profit.

Optimizing an Investment Portfolio

This example demonstrates how to use Solver to help maximize the return on an investment portfolio. Portfolios consist of several investments, each of which has different yields. In addition, you may have some constraints that involve reducing risk and diversification goals. Without such constraints, a portfolio problem becomes a no-brainer: put all of your money in the investment with the highest yield.

This example involves a credit union, a financial institution that takes members' deposits and invests them in loans to other members, bank CDs, and other types of investments. The credit union distributes part of the return on these investments to the members in the form of *dividends*, or interest on their deposits. This hypothetical credit union must adhere to some regulations regarding its investments, and the board of directors has imposed some other restrictions. These regulations and restrictions comprise the problem's constraints. Figure 27-20 shows a workbook set up for this problem.

Solver Investment Optimization.xls

	A	B	C	D	E
1	Portfolio Amount:	$5,000,000			
2					
3					
4	Investment	Pct Yield	Amount Invested	Yield	Pct. of Portfolio
5	New Car Loans	6.90%	1,000,000	69,000	20.00%
6	Used Car Loans	8.25%	1,000,000	82,500	20.00%
7	Real Estate Loans	8.90%	1,000,000	89,000	20.00%
8	Unsecured Loans	13.00%	1,000,000	130,000	20.00%
9	Bank CDs	4.60%	1,000,000	46,000	20.00%
10	TOTAL		$5,000,000	$416,500	100.00%
11					
12			Total Yield:	8.33%	
13					
14			Auto Loans	40.00%	
15					

Sheet1

Figure 27-20: This worksheet is set up to maximize a credit union's investments, given some constraints.

The following constraints are the ones to which you must adhere in allocating the $5 million portfolio:

✦ The amount that the credit union invests in new-car loans must be at least three times the amount that the credit union invests in used-car loans (used-car loans are riskier investments). This constraint is represented as C5>=C6*3.

✦ Car loans should make up at least 15 percent of the portfolio. This constraint is represented as D14>=.15.

✦ Unsecured loans should make up no more than 25 percent of the portfolio. This constraint is represented as E8<=.25.

✦ At least 10 percent of the portfolio should be in bank CDs. This constraint is represented as E9>=.10.

✦ All investments should be positive or zero. In other words, the problem requires five additional constraints to ensure that none of the changing cells go below zero.

The changing cells are C5:C9, and the goal is to maximize the total yield in cell D12. Starting values of 1,000,000 have been entered in the changing cells. When you run Solver with these parameters, it produces the solution that is shown in Figure 27-21, which has a total yield of 9.25 percent.

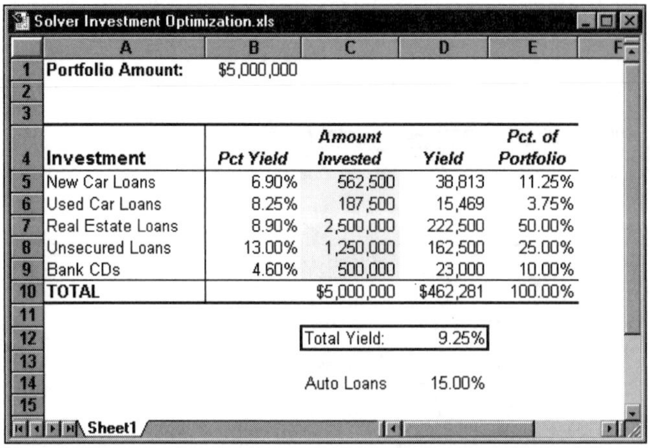

Figure 27-21: The results of the portfolio optimization.

In this example, the starting values of the changing cells are very important. For example, if you use smaller numbers as the starting values (such as 10) and rerun Solver, you find that it doesn't do as well. In fact, it produces a total yield of only 8.35 percent. This demonstrates that you can't always trust Solver to arrive at the optimal solution with one try—even when the Solver Results dialog box tells you that *All constraints and optimality conditions are satisfied.* Usually, the best approach is to use starting values that are as close as possible to the final solution.

The best advice? Make sure that you understand Solver well before you entrust it with helping you make major decisions. Try different starting values, and adjust the options to see whether Solver can do better.

Summary

This chapter discusses two Excel commands: Tools ➪ Goal Seek and Tools ➪ Solver. The latter command is available only if the Solver add-in is installed. Goal seeking is used to determine the value in a single input cell that produces a result that you want in a formula cell. Solver determines values in multiple input cells that produce a result that you want, given certain constraints. Using Solver can be challenging, because it has many options and the result that it produces isn't always the best one.

✦   ✦   ✦

Analyzing Data with Analysis ToolPak

Although spreadsheets such as Excel are designed primarily with business users in mind, these products can be found in other disciplines, including education, research, statistics, and engineering. One way that Excel addresses these nonbusiness users is with its Analysis ToolPak add-in. Many of the features and functions in the Analysis ToolPak are valuable for business applications as well.

The Analysis ToolPak: An Overview

The Analysis ToolPak is an add-in that provides analytical capability that normally is not available. The Analysis ToolPak consists of two parts:

✦ Analytical procedures

✦ Additional worksheet functions

These analysis tools offer many features that may be useful to those in the scientific, engineering, and educational communities — not to mention business users whose needs extend beyond the normal spreadsheet fare.

This section provides a quick overview of the types of analyses that you can perform with the Analysis ToolPak. Each of the following tools are discussed in detail in the course of this chapter:

✦ Analysis of variance (three types)

✦ Correlation

✦ Covariance

✦ Descriptive statistics

✦ Exponential smoothing

✦ F-test

✦ Fourier analysis

✦ Histogram

✦ Moving average

✦ Random number generation

✦ Rank and percentile

✦ Regression

✦ Sampling

✦ t-test (three types)

✦ z-test

As you can see, the Analysis ToolPak add-in brings a great deal of new functionality to Excel. These procedures have limitations, however, and in some cases, you may prefer to create your own formulas to do some calculations.

Besides the procedures just listed, the Analysis ToolPak provides many additional worksheet functions. These functions cover mathematics, engineering, unit conversions, financial analysis, and dates. These functions are listed at the end of the chapter.

Using the Analysis ToolPak

This section discusses the two components of the Analysis ToolPak: its tools and its functions.

Using the Analysis Tools

The procedures in the Analysis ToolPak add-in are relatively straightforward. To use any of these tools, you select Tools ➪ Data Analysis, which displays the dialog box shown in Figure 28-1. Scroll through the list until you find the analysis tool that you want to use and then click OK. Excel displays a new dialog box that's specific to the procedure that you select.

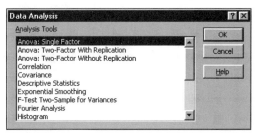

Figure 28-1: The Data Analysis dialog box enables you to select the tool in which you're interested.

Usually, you need to specify one or more input ranges, plus an output range (one cell is sufficient). Alternatively, you can choose to place the results on a new worksheet or in a new workbook. The procedures vary in the amount of additional information that is required. In many dialog boxes, you may be able to indicate whether your data range includes labels. If so, you can specify the entire range, including the labels, and indicate to Excel that the first column (or row) contains labels. Excel then uses these labels in the tables that it produces. Most tools also provide different output options that you can select, based on your needs.

Caution In some cases, the procedures produce their results by using formulas. Consequently, you can change your data, and the results update automatically. In other procedures, Excel stores the results as values, so if you change your data, the results don't reflect your changes. Make sure that you understand what Excel is doing.

Using the Analysis ToolPak Functions

After you install the Analysis ToolPak, you have access to all the additional functions (which are described fully in the online Help system). You access these functions just like any other functions, and they appear in the Function Wizard dialog box, intermixed with Excel's standard functions.

Note If you plan to share worksheets that use these functions, make sure that the other user has access to the add-in functions. If the other user doesn't install the Analysis ToolPak add-in, formulas that use any of the Analysis ToolPak functions will return #VALUE.

The Analysis ToolPak Tools

This section describes each tool and provides an example. Space limitations prevent a discussion of every available option in these procedures. However, if you need to use some of these advanced analysis tools, then you probably already know how to use most of the options not covered here.

The Analysis of Variance Tool

Analysis of variance is a statistical test that determines whether two or more samples were drawn from the same population. Using tools in the Analysis ToolPak, you can perform three types of analysis of variance:

✦ **Single-factor:** A one-way analysis of variance, with only one sample for each group of data.

✦ **Two-factor with replication:** A two-way analysis of variance, with multiple samples (or replications) for each group of data.

✦ **Two-factor without replication:** A two-way analysis of variance, with a single sample (or replication) for each group of data.

Figure 28-2 shows the dialog box for a single-factor analysis of variance. Alpha represents the statistical confidence level for the test.

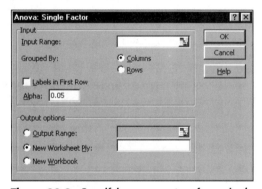

Figure 28-2: Specifying parameters for a single-factor analysis of variance.

Figure 28-3 shows the results of an analysis of variance. The output for this test consists of the means and variances for each of the four samples, the value of F, the critical value of F, and the significance of F (P-value). Because the probability is greater than the Alpha value, the conclusion is that the samples were drawn from the same population.

	F	G	H	I	J	K	L
1	Anova: Single Factor						
2							
3	SUMMARY						
4	*Groups*	*Count*	*Sum*	*Average*	*Variance*		
5	Low	8	538	67.25	6680.214		
6	Medium	8	578	72.25	7700.214		
7	High	8	636	79.5	9397.714		
8	Control	8	544	68	6845.714		
9							
10							
11	ANOVA						
12	*Source of Variation*	*SS*	*df*	*MS*	*F*	*P-value*	*F crit*
13	Between Groups	757	3	252.3333	0.032959	0.991785	2.946685
14	Within Groups	214367	28	7655.964			
15							

Read_Me ╲ **Anova** ╱ Correlation ╱ Covariance ╱ Descriptive

Figure 28-3: The results of the analysis of variance.

The Correlation Tool

Correlation is a widely used statistic that measures the degree to which two sets of data vary together. For example, if higher values in one data set are typically associated with higher values in the second data set, the two data sets have a positive correlation. The degree of correlation is expressed as a coefficient that ranges from –1.0 (a perfect negative correlation) to +1.0 (a perfect positive correlation). A correlation coefficient of 0 indicates that the two variables are not correlated.

Figure 28-4 shows the Correlation dialog box. Specify the input range, which can include any number of variables, arranged in rows or columns.

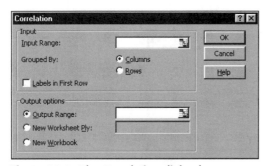

Figure 28-4: The Correlation dialog box.

Figure 28-5 shows the results of a correlation analysis for eight variables. The output consists of a correlation matrix that shows the correlation coefficient for each variable paired with every other variable.

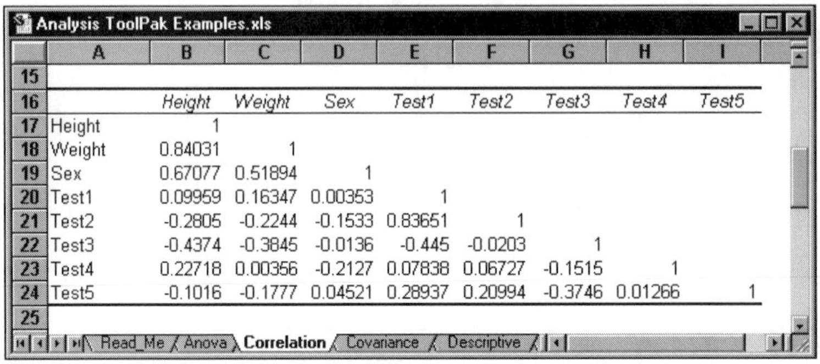

	Height	Weight	Sex	Test1	Test2	Test3	Test4	Test5
Height	1							
Weight	0.84031	1						
Sex	0.67077	0.51894	1					
Test1	0.09959	0.16347	0.00353	1				
Test2	-0.2805	-0.2244	-0.1533	0.83651	1			
Test3	-0.4374	-0.3845	-0.0136	-0.445	-0.0203	1		
Test4	0.22718	0.00356	-0.2127	0.07838	0.06727	-0.1515	1	
Test5	-0.1016	-0.1777	0.04521	0.28937	0.20994	-0.3746	0.01266	1

Figure 28-5: The results of a correlation analysis.

Note

Notice that the resulting correlation matrix doesn't use formulas to calculate the results. Therefore, if any data changes, the correlation matrix isn't valid. You can use Excel's CORREL function to create a correlation matrix that changes automatically when you change data.

The Covariance Tool

The Covariance tool produces a matrix that is similar to the one generated by the Correlation tool. *Covariance*, like correlation, measures the degree to which two variables vary together. Specifically, covariance is the average of the product of the deviations of each data point pair from their respective means.

Figure 28-6 shows a covariance matrix. Notice that the values along the diagonal (where the variables are the same) are the variances for the variable.

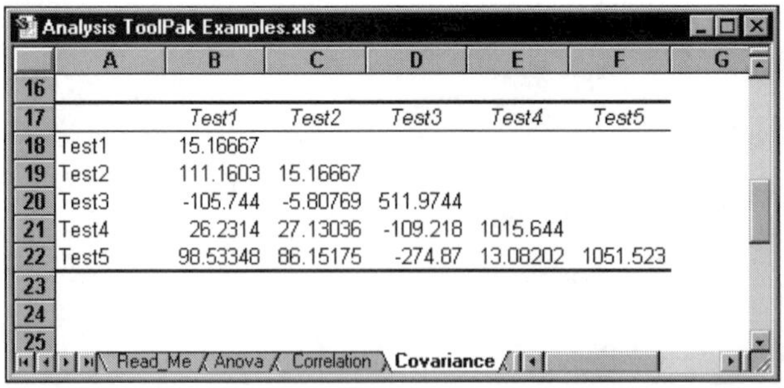

	Test1	Test2	Test3	Test4	Test5
Test1	15.16667				
Test2	111.1603	15.16667			
Test3	-105.744	-5.80769	511.9744		
Test4	26.2314	27.13036	-109.218	1015.644	
Test5	98.53348	86.15175	-274.87	13.08202	1051.523

Figure 28-6: The results of a covariance analysis.

You can use the COVAR function to create a covariance matrix that uses formulas. The values that are generated by the Analysis ToolPak are *not* the same values that you would get if you used the COVAR function.

The Descriptive Statistics Tool

This tool produces a table that describes your data with some standard statistics. It uses the dialog box that is shown in Figure 28-7. The Kth Largest option and Kth Smallest option each display the data value that corresponds to a rank that you specify. For example, if you check Kth Largest and specify a value of 2, the output shows the second-largest value in the input range (the standard output already includes the minimum and maximum values).

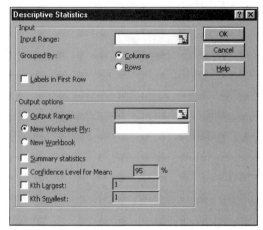

Figure 28-7: The Descriptive Statistics dialog box.

Sample output for the Descriptive Statistics tool appears in Figure 28-8. This example has three groups. Because the output for this procedure consists of values (not formulas), you should use this procedure only when you're certain that your data isn't going to change; otherwise, you will need to re-execute the procedure. You can generate all of these statistics by using formulas.

Analysis ToolPak Examples.xls

	E	F	G	H	I	J
1	*W. Coast Sample*		*Midwest Sample*		*E. Coast Sample*	
2						
3	Mean	39.25	Mean	46	Mean	41.35
4	Standard Error	1.84801	Standard Error	2.10763	Standard Error	1.56487
5	Median	37.5	Median	45.5	Median	41.5
6	Mode	37	Mode	52	Mode	37
7	Standard Deviation	8.26454	Standard Deviation	9.42561	Standard Deviation	6.99831
8	Sample Variance	68.3026	Sample Variance	88.8421	Sample Variance	48.9763
9	Kurtosis	1.47266	Kurtosis	-0.47699	Kurtosis	-0.28025
10	Skewness	1.18011	Skewness	0.14121	Skewness	-0.24858
11	Range	32	Range	34	Range	26
12	Minimum	28	Minimum	28	Minimum	28
13	Maximum	60	Maximum	62	Maximum	54
14	Sum	785	Sum	920	Sum	827
15	Count	20	Count	20	Count	20
16	Confidence Level(95.0%)	3.86793	Confidence Level(95.0%)	4.41132	Confidence Level(95.0%)	3.27531

Correlation / Covariance / **Descriptive** / Exponential Smoothing

Figure 28-8: Output from the Descriptive Statistics tool.

The Exponential Smoothing Tool

Exponential smoothing is a technique for predicting data that is based on the previous data point and the previously predicted data point. You can specify the *damping factor* (also known as a *smoothing constant*), which can range from 0 to 1. This determines the relative weighting of the previous data point and the previously predicted data point. You also can request standard errors and a chart.

The exponential smoothing procedure generates formulas that use the damping factor that you specify. Therefore, if the data changes, Excel updates the formulas. Figure 28-9 shows sample output from the Exponential Smoothing tool.

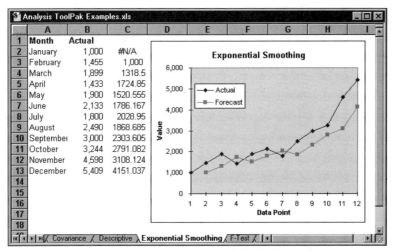

Figure 28-9: Output from the Exponential Smoothing tool.

The F-Test (Two-Sample Test for Variance) Tool

The *F-test* is a commonly used statistical test that enables you to compare two population variances. Figure 28-10 shows the dialog box for this tool.

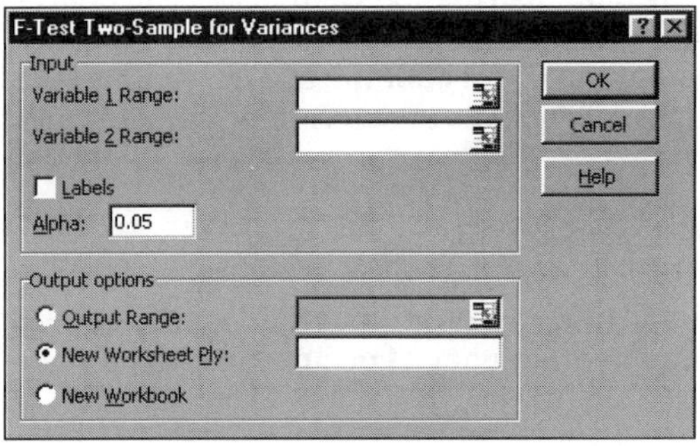

Figure 28-10: The F-Test dialog box.

The output for this test consists of the means and variances for each of the two samples, the value of F, the critical value of F, and the significance of F. Sample output appears in Figure 28-11.

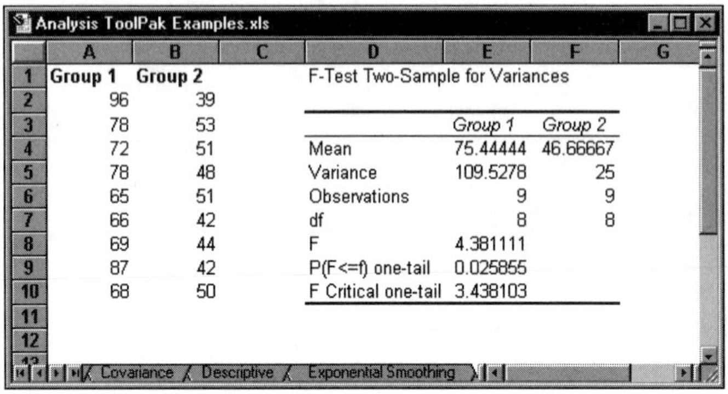

Figure 28-11: Sample output for the F-test.

The Fourier Analysis Tool

This tool performs a "fast Fourier" transformation of a range of data. Using the Fourier Analysis tool, you can transform a range limited to the following sizes: 1, 2, 4, 8, 16, 32, 64, 128, 256, 512, or 1,024 data points. This procedure accepts and generates complex numbers, which are represented as labels (not values).

The Histogram Tool

This procedure is useful for producing data distributions and histogram charts. It accepts an input range and a bin range. A *bin* range is a range of values that specifies the limits for each column of the histogram. If you omit the bin range, Excel creates ten equal-interval bins for you. The size of each bin is determined by a formula of the following form:

```
=(MAX(input_range)-MIN(input_range))/10
```

The Histogram dialog box appears in Figure 28-12. As an option, you can specify that the resulting histogram be sorted by frequency of occurrence in each bin.

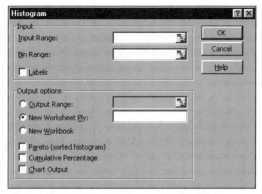

Figure 28-12: The Histogram tool enables you to generate distributions and graphical output.

If you specify the Pareto (sorted histogram) option, the bin range must contain values and can't contain formulas. If formulas appear in the bin range, Excel doesn't sort properly, and your worksheet displays error values.

Figure 28-13 shows a chart generated from this procedure. The Histogram tool doesn't use formulas, so if you change any of the input data, you need to repeat the histogram procedure to update the results.

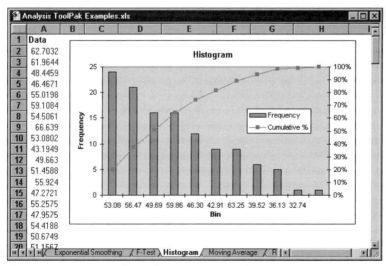

Figure 28-13: Output from the Histogram tool.

The Moving Average Tool

The Moving Average tool helps you to smooth out a data series that has a lot of variability. This is best done in conjunction with a chart. Excel does the smoothing by computing a moving average of a specified number of values. In many cases, a moving average enables you to spot trends that otherwise would be obscured by noise in the data.

Figure 28-14 shows the Moving Average dialog box. You can, of course, specify the number of values that you want Excel to use for each average. If you place a check in the Standard Errors check box, Excel calculates standard errors and places formulas for these calculations next to the moving average formulas. The standard error values indicate the degree of variability between the actual values and the calculated moving averages. When you close this dialog box, Excel creates formulas that reference the input range that you specify.

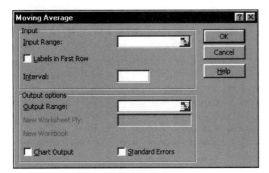

Figure 28-14: The Moving Average dialog box.

Figure 28-15 shows the results of using this tool. The first few cells in the output are #N/A because not enough data points exist to calculate the average for these initial values.

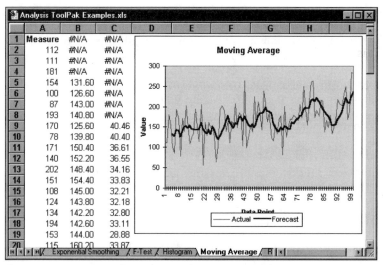

Figure 28-15: Output from the Moving Average tool.

The Random Number Generation Tool

Although Excel contains a built-in function to calculate random numbers, the Random Number Generation tool is much more flexible, because you can specify what type of distribution you want the random numbers to have. Figure 28-16 shows the Random Number Generation dialog box. The Parameters box varies, depending on the type of distribution that you select.

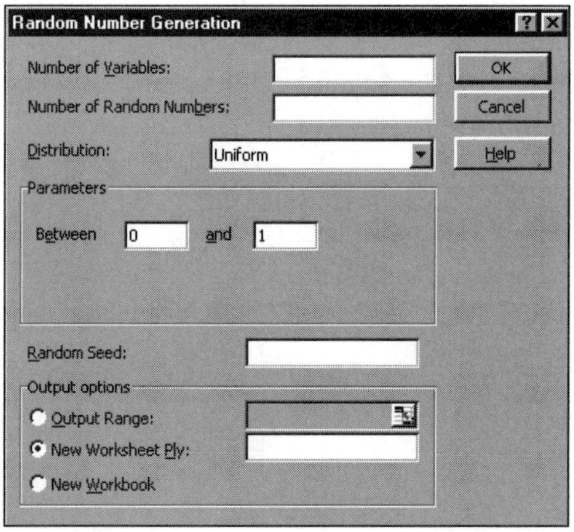

Figure 28-16: This dialog box enables you to generate a wide variety of random numbers.

The Number of Variables refers to the number of columns that you want, and the Number of Random Numbers refers to the number of rows that you want. For example, if you want 200 random numbers arranged in 10 columns of 20 rows, you specify 10 and 20, respectively, in these text boxes.

The Random Seed box enables you to specify a starting value that Excel uses in its random number-generating algorithm. Usually, you leave this blank. If you want to generate the same random number sequence, however, you can specify a seed between 1 and 32,767 (integer values only). You can create the following types of distributions:

✦ **Uniform:** Every random number has an equal chance of being selected. You specify the upper and lower limits.

✦ **Normal:** The random numbers correspond to a normal distribution. You specify the mean and standard deviation of the distribution.

✦ **Bernoulli:** The random numbers are either 0 or 1, determined by the probability of success that you specify.

✦ **Binomial:** This returns random numbers based on a Bernoulli distribution over a specific number of trials, given a probability of success that you specify.

✦ **Poisson:** This option generates values in a Poisson distribution. This is characterized by discrete events that occur in an interval, where the probability of a single occurrence is proportional to the size of the interval. The *lambda* parameter is the expected number of occurrences in an interval. In a Poisson distribution, lambda is equal to the mean, which also is equal to the variance.

✦ **Patterned:** This option doesn't generate random numbers. Rather, it repeats a series of numbers in steps that you specify.

✦ **Discrete:** This option enables you to specify the probability that specific values are chosen. It requires a two-column input range; the first column holds the values, and the second column holds the probability of each value being chosen. The sum of the probabilities in the second column must equal 100 percent.

The Rank and Percentile Tool

This tool creates a table that shows the ordinal and percentile ranking for each value in a range. Figure 28-17 shows the results of this procedure. You can also generate ranks and percentiles by using formulas.

SalesRep	Sales		Point	Sales	Rank	Percent
Allen	137,676		4	197,107	1	100.00%
Brandon	155,449		3	180,414	2	94.40%
Campaigne	180,414		17	170,538	3	88.80%
Dufenberg	197,107		14	161,750	4	83.30%
Fox	130,814		2	155,449	5	77.70%
Giles	133,283		11	151,466	6	72.20%
Haflich	116,943		19	149,627	7	66.60%
Hosaka	107,684		12	145,088	8	61.10%
Jenson	128,060		1	137,676	9	55.50%
Larson	121,336		18	134,395	10	50.00%
Leitch	151,466		6	133,283	11	44.40%
Miller	145,088		5	130,814	12	38.80%
Peterson	127,995		9	128,060	13	33.30%
Richards	161,750		13	127,995	14	27.70%
Richardson	117,203		10	121,336	15	22.20%
Ryan	102,571		15	117,203	16	16.60%
Serrano	170,538		7	116,943	17	11.10%
Struyk	134,395		8	107,684	18	5.50%
Winfrey	149,627		16	102,571	19	.00%

Figure 28-17: Output from the rank and percentile procedure.

The Regression Tool

The Regression tool calculates a regression analysis from worksheet data. Use regression to analyze trends, forecast the future, build predictive models, and, often, to make sense out of a series of seemingly unrelated numbers.

Regression analysis enables you to determine the extent to which one range of data (the dependent variable) varies as a function of the values of one or more other ranges of data (the independent variables). This relationship is expressed mathematically, using values that Excel calculates. You can use these calculations to create a mathematical model of the data and predict the dependent variable by using different values of one or more independent variables. This tool can perform simple and multiple linear regressions and calculate and standardize residuals automatically.

Figure 28-18 shows the Regression dialog box.

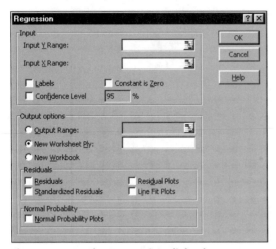

Figure 28-18: The Regression dialog box.

As you can see, the Regression dialog box offers many options:

✦ **Input Y Range:** The range that contains the dependent variable.

✦ **Input X Range:** One or more ranges that contain independent variables.

✦ **Confidence Level:** The confidence level for the regression.

✦ **Constant is Zero:** If checked, this forces the regression to have a constant of zero (which means that the regression line passes through the origin; when the X values are 0, the predicted Y value is 0).

✦ **Residuals:** These options specify whether to include residuals in the output. *Residuals* are the differences between observed and predicted values.

✦ **Normal Probability:** This generates a chart for normal probability plots.

The results of a regression analysis appear in Figure 28-19. If you understand regression analysis, the output from this procedure is familiar.

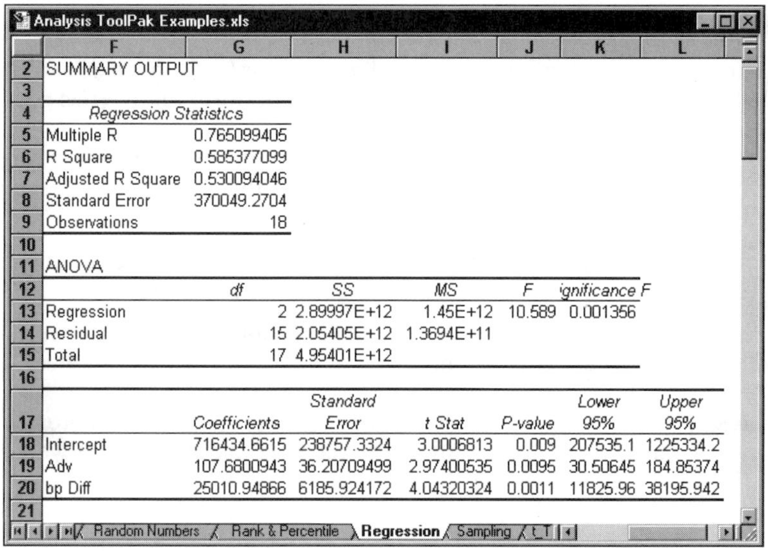

Analysis ToolPak Examples.xls

	F	G	H	I	J	K	L
2	SUMMARY OUTPUT						
3							
4	*Regression Statistics*						
5	Multiple R	0.765099405					
6	R Square	0.585377099					
7	Adjusted R Square	0.530094046					
8	Standard Error	370049.2704					
9	Observations	18					
10							
11	ANOVA						
12		*df*	*SS*	*MS*	*F*	*ignificance F*	
13	Regression	2	2.89997E+12	1.45E+12	10.589	0.001356	
14	Residual	15	2.05405E+12	1.3694E+11			
15	Total	17	4.95401E+12				
16							
17		*Coefficients*	*Standard Error*	*t Stat*	*P-value*	*Lower 95%*	*Upper 95%*
18	Intercept	716434.6615	238757.3324	3.0006813	0.009	207535.1	1225334.2
19	Adv	107.6800943	36.20709499	2.97400535	0.0095	30.50645	184.85374
20	bp Diff	25010.94866	6185.924172	4.04320324	0.0011	11825.96	38195.942
21							

Random Numbers / Rank & Percentile / Regression / Sampling / t_T

Figure 28-19: Sample output from the Regression tool.

The Sampling Tool

The Sampling tool generates a random sample from a range of input values. The Sampling tool can help you to work with a large database by creating a subset of it. The Sampling dialog box appears in Figure 28-20. This procedure has two options: periodic and random. If you choose a periodic sample, Excel selects every *n*th value from the input range, where *n* equals the period that you specify. With a random sample, you simply specify the size of the sample you want Excel to select, and every value has an equal probability of being chosen.

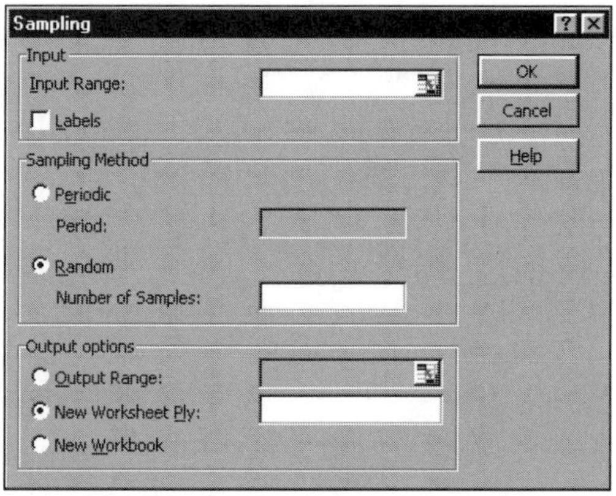

Figure 28-20: The Sampling dialog box is useful for selecting random samples.

The t-Test Tool

Use the *t-test* to determine whether a statistically significant difference exists between two small samples. The Analysis ToolPak can perform three types of t-tests:

✦ **Paired two-sample for means:** For paired samples in which you have two observations on each subject (such as a pretest and a posttest). The samples must be the same size.

✦ **Two-sample assuming equal variances:** For independent, rather than paired, samples. Excel assumes equal variances for the two samples.

✦ **Two-sample assuming unequal variances:** For independent, rather than paired, samples. Excel assumes unequal variances for the two samples.

Figure 28-21 shows the dialog box for the Paired Two Sample for Means t-test. You specify the significance level (alpha) and the hypothesized difference between the two means (that is, the *null hypothesis*).

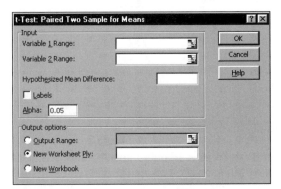

Figure 28-21: The paired t-Test dialog box.

Figure 28-22 shows sample output for the paired two sample for means t-test. Excel calculates *t* for both a one-tailed and two-tailed test.

The z-Test (Two-Sample Test for Means) Tool

The t-test is used for small samples; the z-test is used for larger samples or populations. You must know the variances for both input ranges.

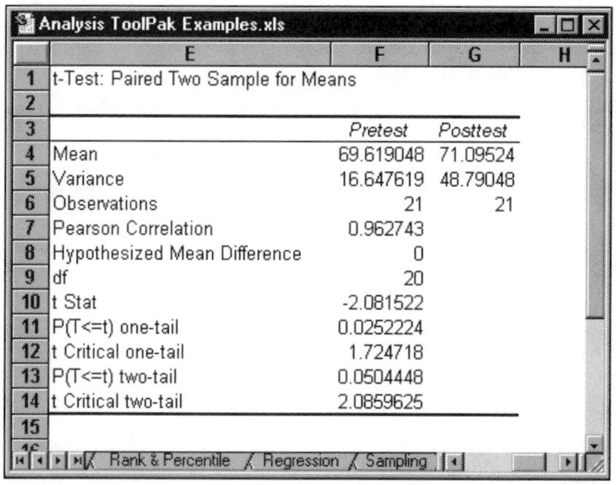

t-Test: Paired Two Sample for Means		
	Pretest	*Posttest*
Mean	69.619048	71.09524
Variance	16.647619	48.79048
Observations	21	21
Pearson Correlation	0.962743	
Hypothesized Mean Difference	0	
df	20	
t Stat	-2.081522	
P(T<=t) one-tail	0.0252224	
t Critical one-tail	1.724718	
P(T<=t) two-tail	0.0504448	
t Critical two-tail	2.0859625	

Figure 28-22: Results of a paired two sample for means t-test.

Analysis ToolPak Worksheet Functions

This section lists the worksheet functions that are available in the Analysis ToolPak. For specific information about the arguments required, click the Help button in the Paste Function dialog box.

Remember, the Analysis ToolPak add-in must be installed to use these functions in your worksheet. If you use any of these functions in a workbook that you distribute to a colleague, make clear to your colleague that the workbook requires the Analysis ToolPak.

These functions appear in the Paste Function dialog box in the following categories:

- ✦ Date & Time
- ✦ Engineering (a new category that appears when you install the Analysis ToolPak)
- ✦ Financial
- ✦ Information
- ✦ Math & Trig

Date & Time Category

Table 28-1 lists the Analysis ToolPak worksheet functions that you'll find in the Date & Time category.

Table 28-1
Date & Time Category Functions

Function	Purpose
EDATE	Returns the serial number of the date that is the indicated number of months before or after the start date
EOMONTH	Returns the serial number of the last day of the month before or after a specified number of months
NETWORKDAYS	Returns the number of whole workdays between two dates
WEEKNUM	Returns the week number in the year
WORKDAY	Returns the serial number of the date before or after a specified number of workdays
YEARFRAC	Returns the year fraction representing the number of whole days between start_date and end_date

Engineering Category

Table 28-2 lists the Analysis ToolPak worksheet functions that you'll find in the Engineering category. Some of these functions are quite useful for nonengineers as well. For example, the CONVERT function converts a wide variety of measurement units.

Table 28-2
Engineering Category Functions

Function	Purpose
BESSELI	Returns the modified Bessel function $In(x)$
BESSELJ	Returns the Bessel function $Jn(x)$
BESSELK	Returns the modified Bessel function $Kn(x)$
BESSELY	Returns the Bessel function $Yn(x)$
BIN2DEC	Converts a binary number to decimal
BIN2HEX	Converts a binary number to hexadecimal
BIN2OCT	Converts a binary number to octal
COMPLEX	Converts real and imaginary coefficients into a complex number
CONVERT	Converts a number from one measurement system to another

Function	Purpose
DEC2BIN	Converts a decimal number to binary
DEC2HEX	Converts a decimal number to hexadecimal
DEC2OCT	Converts a decimal number to octal
DELTA	Tests whether two numbers are equal
ERF	Returns the error function
ERFC	Returns the complementary error function
FACTDOUBLE	Returns the double factorial of a number
GESTEP	Tests whether a number is greater than a threshold value
HEX2BIN	Converts a hexadecimal number to binary
HEX2DEC	Converts a hexadecimal number to decimal
HEX2OCT	Converts a hexadecimal number to octal
IMABS	Returns the absolute value (modulus) of a complex number
IMAGINARY	Returns the imaginary coefficient of a complex number
IMARGUMENT	Returns the argument q, an angle expressed in radians
IMCONJUGATE	Returns the complex conjugate of a complex number
IMCOS	Returns the cosine of a complex number
IMDIV	Returns the quotient of two complex numbers
IMEXP	Returns the exponential of a complex number
IMLN	Returns the natural logarithm of a complex number
IMLOG10	Returns the base-10 logarithm of a complex number
IMLOG2	Returns the base-2 logarithm of a complex number
IMPOWER	Returns a complex number raised to an integer power
IMPRODUCT	Returns the product of two complex numbers
IMREAL	Returns the real coefficient of a complex number
IMSIN	Returns the sine of a complex number
IMSQRT	Returns the square root of a complex number
IMSUB	Returns the difference of two complex numbers
IMSUM	Returns the sum of complex numbers
OCT2BIN	Converts an octal number to binary
OCT2DEC	Converts an octal number to decimal
OCT2HEX	Converts an octal number to hexadecimal

Financial Category

Table 28-3 lists the Analysis ToolPak worksheet functions that you'll find in the Financial category.

Table 28-3	
Financial Category Functions	

Function	Purpose
ACCRINT	Returns the accrued interest for a security that pays periodic interest
ACCRINTM	Returns the accrued interest for a security that pays interest at maturity
AMORDEGRC	Returns the prorated linear depreciation of an asset for each accounting period. Similar to the AMORLINC function, except that this function uses a depreciation coefficient that depends on the life of the assets
AMORLINC	Returns the prorated linear depreciation of an asset for each accounting period
COUPDAYBS	Returns the number of days from the beginning of the coupon period to the settlement date
COUPDAYS	Returns the number of days in the coupon period that contain the settlement date
COUPDAYSNC	Returns the number of days from the settlement date to the next coupon date
COUPNCD	Returns the next coupon date after the settlement date
COUPNUM	Returns the number of coupons payable between the settlement date and maturity date
COUPPCD	Returns the previous coupon date before the settlement date
CUMIPMT	Returns the cumulative interest paid between two periods
CUMPRINC	Returns the cumulative principal paid on a loan between two periods
DISC	Returns the discount rate for a security
DOLLARDE	Converts a dollar price, expressed as a fraction, into a dollar price, expressed as a decimal number
DOLLARFR	Converts a dollar price, expressed as a decimal number, into a dollar price, expressed as a fraction
DURATION	Returns the annual duration of a security with periodic interest payments
EFFECT	Returns the effective annual interest rate

Function	Purpose
FVSCHEDULE	Returns the future value of an initial principal after applying a series of compound interest rates
INTRATE	Returns the interest rate for a fully invested security
MDURATION	Returns the Macauley modified duration for a security with an assumed par value of $100
NOMINAL	Returns the annual nominal interest rate
ODDFPRICE	Returns the price per $100 face value of a security with an odd first period
ODDFYIELD	Returns the yield of a security with an odd first period
ODDLPRICE	Returns the price per $100 face value of a security with an odd last period
ODDLYIELD	Returns the yield of a security with an odd last period
PRICE	Returns the price per $100 face value of a security that pays periodic interest
PRICEDISC	Returns the price per $100 face value of a discounted security
PRICEMAT	Returns the price per $100 face value of a security that pays interest at maturity
RECEIVED	Returns the amount received at maturity for a fully invested security
TBILLEQ	Returns the bond-equivalent yield for a Treasury bill
TBILLPRICE	Returns the price per $100 face value for a Treasury bill
TBILLYIELD	Returns the yield for a Treasury bill
XIRR	Returns the internal rate of return for a schedule of cash flows
XNPV	Returns the net present value for a schedule of cash flows
YIELD	Returns the yield on a security that pays periodic interest
YIELDDISC	Returns the annual yield for a discounted security (for example, a Treasury bill)
YIELDMAT	Returns the annual yield of a security that pays interest at maturity

Information Category

Table 28-4 lists the two Analysis ToolPak worksheet functions that you'll find in the Information category.

	Table 28-4 Information Category Functions	
Function	**Purpose**	
ISEVEN	Returns TRUE if the number is even	
ISODD	Returns TRUE if the number is odd	

Math & Trig Category

Table 28-5 lists the Analysis ToolPak worksheet functions that you'll find in the Math & Trig category.

	Table 28-5 Math & Trig Category Functions	
Function	**Purpose**	
GCD	Returns the greatest common divisor	
LCM	Returns the least common multiple	
MROUND	Returns a number rounded to the desired multiple	
MULTINOMIAL	Returns the multinomial of a set of numbers	
QUOTIENT	Returns the integer portion of a division	
RANDBETWEEN	Returns a random number between the numbers that you specify	
SERIESSUM	Returns the sum of a power series based on the formula	
SQRTPI	Returns the square root of pi	

Summary

This chapter discusses the Analysis ToolPak, an add-in that extends the analytical powers of Excel. It includes 19 analytical procedures and 93 functions. Many of the tools are useful for general business applications, but many are for more specialized uses, such as statistical tests.

✦   ✦   ✦

Other Topics

Sharing Data with Other Applications

Windows applications are designed to work together. The applications in Microsoft Office are an excellent example. These programs have a common look and feel, and sharing data among these applications is quite easy. This chapter explores some ways that you can make use of other applications while working with Excel, as well as some ways that you can use Excel while working with other applications.

Sharing Data with Other Windows Applications

Besides importing and exporting files, the following are the essential three ways in which you can transfer data to and from other Windows applications:

✦ Copy and paste, using either the Windows Clipboard or the Office Clipboard. Copying and pasting information creates a static copy of the data.

✦ Create a link so that changes in the source data are reflected in the destination document.

✦ Embed an entire object from one application into another application's document.

The following sections discuss these techniques and present an example for each one.

Using the Windows or Office Clipboards

As you probably know, whenever Windows is running, you have access to the Windows Clipboard — an area of your computer's memory that acts as a shared holding area for information that you have cut or copied from an application. The Windows Clipboard works behind the scenes, and you usually aren't aware of it. Whenever you select data and then choose either Edit ⇨ Copy or Edit ⇨ Cut, the application places the selected data on the Windows Clipboard. Like most other Windows applications, Excel can then access the Clipboard data if you choose the Edit ⇨ Paste command (or the Edit ⇨ Paste Special command).

EXCEL 2000

If you copy or cut information while working in an Office application, the application places the copied information on both the Windows Clipboard and the Office Clipboard.

Note

Once you copy information to the Windows Clipboard, it remains on the Windows Clipboard even after you paste it, so you can use it multiple times. However, because the Windows Clipboard can hold only one item at a time, when you copy or cut something else, the information previously stored on the Windows Clipboard is replaced. The Office Clipboard, unlike the Windows Clipboard, can hold up to 12 separate selections. The Office Clipboard operates in all Office applications; for example, you can copy two selections from Word and three from Excel and paste any or all of them in PowerPoint.

Copying information from one Windows application to another is quite easy. The application that contains the information that you're copying is called the *source application,* and the application to which you're copying the information is called the *destination application.*

The general steps that are required to copy from one application to another are as follows. These steps apply to copying from Excel to another application and to copying from another application to Excel.

1. Activate the source document window that contains the information that you want to copy.

2. Select the information by using the mouse or the keyboard. If Excel is the source application, this information can be a cell, range, chart, or drawn object.

3. Select Edit ⇨ Copy. Excel places a copy of the information onto the Windows Clipboard and the Office Clipboard.

4. Activate the destination application. If the program isn't running, you can start it without affecting the contents of the Clipboard.

5. Move to the appropriate position in the destination application (where you want to paste the copied material).

6. Select Edit ⇨ Paste from the menu in the destination application. If the Clipboard contents are not appropriate for pasting, the Paste command is grayed (not available).

In Step 3 in the preceding steps, you also can select Edit ➪ Cut from the source application menu. This step erases your selection from the source application after placing the selection on the Clipboard.

EXCEL 2000 If you repeat Step 3 in any Office application, the Office Clipboard toolbar appears automatically. It continues to appear if the destination application that you activate in Step 4 is another Office application.

Note In Step 6 in the preceding steps, you can sometimes select the Edit ➪ Paste Special command, which displays a dialog box that presents different pasting options.

If you're copying a graphics image, you may have to resize or crop it. If you're copying text, you may have to reformat it by using tools that are available in the destination application. The information that you copy from the source application remains intact, and a copy remains on the Clipboard until you copy or cut something else. Figure 29-1 shows an embedded Excel chart. You can easily insert a copy of this chart into a Microsoft Word report. First, select the chart in Excel by clicking it once. Then, copy it to the Clipboard by choosing Edit ➪ Copy. Next, activate the Word document into which you want to paste the copy of the chart, and move the insertion point to the place where you want the chart to appear. When you select Edit ➪ Paste from the Word menu bar, the chart is pasted from the Clipboard and appears in your document (see Figure 29-2).

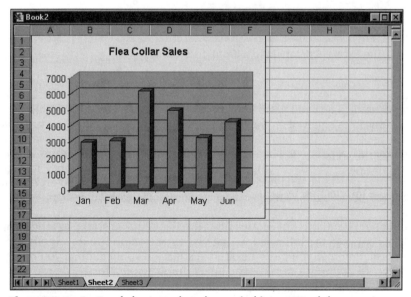

Figure 29-1: An Excel chart, ready to be copied into a Word document.

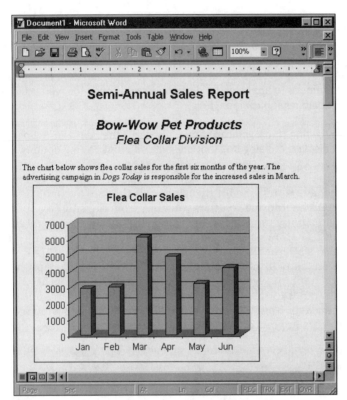

Figure 29-2: The Excel chart copied to a Word document.

Note   You need to understand that Windows applications vary in the way that they respond to data that you paste from the Clipboard. If the Edit ➪ Paste command is not available (is grayed on the menu) in the destination application, the application can't accept the information from the Clipboard. If you copy a range of data from Excel to the Clipboard and paste it into Word, Word creates a table when you paste the data. Other applications may respond differently to Excel data. If you plan to do a lot of copying and pasting, I suggest that you experiment until you understand how the two applications handle each other's data.

You should understand that this copy-and-paste technique is static. In other words, no link exists between the information that you copy from the source application and the information that you paste into the destination application. If you're copying from Excel to a word processing document, for example, the word processing document *will not* reflect any subsequent changes that you make in your Excel worksheet or charts. Consequently, you have to repeat the copy-and-paste procedure to update the destination document with the source document changes. The next topic presents a way to get around this limitation.

Linking Data

If you want to share data that may change, the static copy-and-paste procedure described in the preceding section isn't your best choice. Instead, create a dynamic link between the data that you copy from one Windows application to another. In this way, if you change the data in the source document, you don't *also* need to make the changes in the destination document, because the link automatically updates the destination document.

When would you want to use this technique? If you generate proposals by using a word processor, for example, you may need to refer to pricing information that you store in an Excel worksheet. If you set up a link between your word processing document and the Excel worksheet, you can be sure that your proposals always quote the latest prices. Not all Windows applications support dynamic linking, so you must make sure that the application to which you are copying is capable of handling such a link.

Creating Links

Setting up a link from one Windows application to another isn't difficult, although the process varies slightly from application to application. The following are the general steps to take:

1. Activate the window in the source application that contains the information that you want to copy.

2. Select the information by using the mouse or the keyboard. If Excel is the source application, you can select a cell, range, or entire chart.

3. Select Edit ➪ Copy from the source application's menu. The source application copies the information to the Windows Clipboard.

4. Activate the destination application. If it isn't open, you can start it without affecting the contents of the Clipboard.

5. Move to the appropriate position in the destination application.

6. Select the appropriate command in the destination application to paste a link. The command varies, depending on the application. In Microsoft Office applications, the command is Edit ➪ Paste Special.

7. A dialog box will probably appear, letting you specify the type of link that you want to create. The following section provides more details.

More About Links

Keep in mind the following information when you're using links between two applications:

✦ Not all Windows applications support linking. Furthermore, you can link *from* but not *to* some programs. When in doubt, consult the documentation for the application with which you're dealing.

✦ When you save an Excel file that has a link, you save the most recent values with the document. When you reopen this document, Excel asks whether you want to update the links.

✦ Links can be broken rather easily. If you move the source document to another directory or save it under a different name, for example, the destination document's application won't be able to update the link. You can usually reestablish the link manually, if you understand how the application manages the links. In Excel, you use the Edit ➪ Links command, which displays the Links dialog box, shown in Figure 29-3.

✦ You also can use the Edit ➪ Links command to break a link. After breaking a link, the data remains in the destination document, but is no longer linked to the source document.

✦ In Excel, external links are stored in array formulas. If you know what you're doing, you can modify a link by editing the array formula.

✦ When Excel is running, it responds to link requests from other applications, unless you have disabled remote requests. If you don't want Excel to respond to link-update requests from other applications, choose Tools ➪ Options, select the General tab, and then place a check in the Ignore other applications check box.

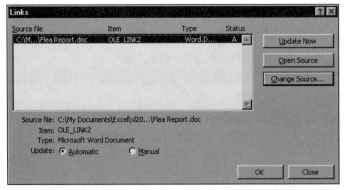

Figure 29-3: The Links dialog box lets you work with links to other applications.

Copying Excel Data to Word

One of the most frequently used software combinations is a spreadsheet and a word processor. This section discusses the types of links that you can create by using Microsoft Word.

Note   Most information in this section also applies to other word processors, such as Corel's WordPerfect for Windows and Lotus Word Pro. The exact techniques vary, however. I use Word in the examples because readers who acquired Excel as part of the Microsoft Office have Word installed on their systems. If you don't have a word processor installed on your system, you can use the WordPad application that comes with Windows. The manner in which WordPad handles links is very similar to that for Word.

Figure 29-4 shows the Paste Special dialog box from Microsoft Word after a range of data has been copied from Excel to the Clipboard. The result that you get depends on whether you select the Paste or the Paste link option, and on your choice of the type of item to paste. If you select the Paste link option, you can choose to have the information pasted as an icon. If you do so, you can double-click this icon to activate the source worksheet.

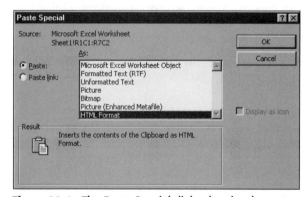

Figure 29-4: The Paste Special dialog box is where you specify the type of link to create.

Pasting Without a Link

Often, you don't need a link when you copy data. For example, if you're preparing a report in your word processor and you simply want to include a range of data from an Excel worksheet, you probably don't need to create a link.

Table 29-1 describes the effect of choosing the various paste choices when you select the Paste option—the option that *doesn't* create a link to the source data.

Table 29-1
Result of Using the Paste Special Command in Word
(Paste Option)

Paste Type	Result
Microsoft Excel Worksheet Object	An object that includes the Excel formatting. This creates an *embedded object*, described in the next section.
Formatted Text (RTF)	A Word table that is formatted as the original Excel range. No link to the source exists. This produces the same result as using Edit ➪ Paste.
Unformatted Text	Text (not a table) that corresponds to Word's Normal style. Formatting from Excel is not transferred, and no link to the source exists.
Picture	A picture object that retains the formatting from Excel. No link to the source exists. This usually produces better results than the Bitmap option. Double-clicking the object after you paste it enables you to edit the picture.
Bitmap	A bitmap object that retains the formatting from Excel. No link exists to the source. Double-clicking the object after you paste it enables you to edit the bitmap.
HTML Format	A table that is formatted as the original Excel range. No link to the source exists. Use this format when you expect to publish the document as a Web page.

Figure 29-5 shows how a copied range from Excel appears in Word, using each of the paste special formats.

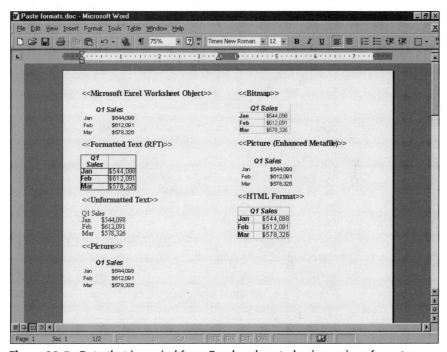

Figure 29-5: Data that is copied from Excel and pasted using various formats.

The pasted data *looks* the same regardless of whether the Paste or Paste link option is selected.

Some Excel formatting does not transfer when pasted to Word as formatted text. For example, Word doesn't support vertical alignment for table cells (but you can use Word's paragraph formatting commands to apply vertical alignment).

Pasting with a Link

If you think the data that you're copying will change, you may want to paste a link. If you paste the data by using the Paste link option in the Paste Special dialog box, you can make changes to the source document, and the changes appear in the destination application (a few seconds of delay may occur). You can test these changes by displaying both applications onscreen, making changes to the source document, and watching for them to appear in the destination document.

Table 29-2 describes the effect of choosing the various paste choices in Word's Paste Special dialog box when the Paste link option is selected.

Table 29-2
Result of Using the Paste Special Command in Word
(Paste Link Option)

Paste Type	Result
Microsoft Excel Worksheet Object	A linked object that includes the Excel formatting. Double-click the object after pasting it to edit the source data in Excel.
Formatted Text (RTF)	A Word table that is formatted as the original Excel range. Changes in the source are reflected automatically.
Unformatted Text	Text (not a table) that corresponds to Word's Normal style. Formatting from Excel is not transferred. Changes in the source are reflected automatically.
Picture	A picture object that retains the formatting from Excel. Changes in the source are reflected automatically. This usually produces better results than the Bitmap option. Double-click the object after pasting it to edit the source data in Excel.
Bitmap	A bitmap object that retains the formatting from Excel. Changes in the source are reflected automatically. Double-click the object after pasting it to edit the source data in Excel.
HTML Format	A table that is formatted as the original Excel range. Use this format when you expect to publish the document as a Web page.

Embedding Objects

Using *Object Linking and Embedding* (OLE), you can also embed an object to share information between Windows applications. This technique enables you to insert an object from another program and use that program's editing tools to manipulate it. The OLE objects can be items such as those in the following list:

✦ Text documents from other products, such as word processors

✦ Drawings or pictures from other products

✦ Information from special OLE server applications, such as Microsoft Equation

✦ Sound files

✦ Video or animation files

Most of the major Windows applications support OLE. You can embed an object into your document in either of two ways:

Remember that no link is involved here. If you make changes to the embedded object in Word, these changes do not appear in the original Excel worksheet. The embedded object is completely independent from the original source.

Using this technique, you have access to all of Excel's features while you are still in Word. Microsoft's ultimate goal is to enable users to focus on their documents — not on the application that produces the document.

Tip You can accomplish the embedding previously described by selecting the range in Excel and then dragging it to your Word document. In fact, you can use the Windows desktop as an intermediary storage location. For example, you can drag a range from Excel to the desktop and create a *scrap*. Then, you can drag this scrap into your Word document. The result is an embedded Excel object.

Creating a New Excel Object in Word

The preceding example embeds a range from an existing Excel worksheet into a Word document. This section demonstrates how to create a new (empty) Excel object in Word. This may be useful if you're creating a report and need to insert a table of values that doesn't exist in a worksheet. You *could* insert a normal Word table, but you can take advantage of Excel's formulas and functions to make this task much easier.

To create a new Excel object in a Word document, choose Insert ➪ Object in Word. Word responds with the Object dialog box, shown in Figure 29-9. The Create New tab lists the types of objects that you can create (the contents of the list depends on the applications that you have installed on your system). Choose the Microsoft Excel Worksheet option and click OK.

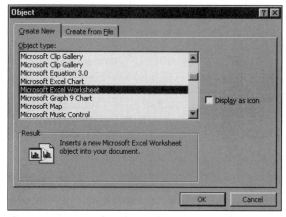

Figure 29-9: Word's Object dialog box enables you to create a new object.

Word inserts an empty Excel worksheet object into the document and activates it for you, as shown in Figure 29-10. You have full access to Excel commands, so you can enter whatever you want into the worksheet object. After you finish, click anywhere in the Word document. You can, of course, double-click this object at any time to make changes or additions.

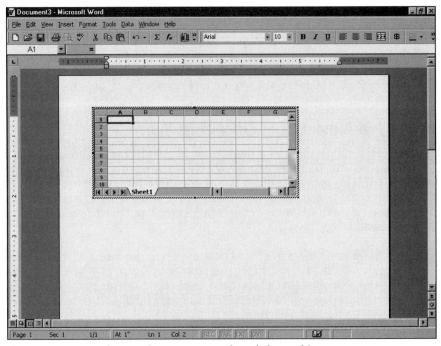

Figure 29-10: Word created an empty Excel worksheet object.

You can change the size of the object while it's activated by dragging any of the sizing handles that appear on the borders of the object. You also can crop the object, so that when it isn't activated, the object displays only cells that contain information. To crop an object in Word, select the object so that you can see sizing handles. Then, display Word's Picture toolbar (right-click any toolbar button and choose Picture). Click the Cropping tool (it looks like a pair of plus signs) and then drag any sizing handle on the object.

Note   Even if you crop an Excel worksheet object in Word, when you double-click the object, you have access to all rows and columns in Excel. Cropping changes only the *displayed* area of the object.

Embedding an Existing Workbook in Word

Yet another option is to embed an existing workbook into a Word document. Use Word's Insert ➪ Object command. In the Object dialog box, click the tab labeled Create from File (see Figure 29-11). Click the Browse button and locate the Excel workbook that you want to embed.

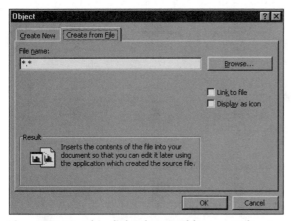

Figure 29-11: This dialog box enables you to locate a file to embed in the active document.

When you use this technique, you embed a *copy* of the selected workbook in the Word document. You can either use it as is or double-click it to make changes. Note that any changes that you make to this copy of the document are not reflected in the original workbook.

Embedding Objects in an Excel Worksheet

The preceding examples involve embedding Excel objects in a Word document. The same procedures can be used to embed other objects into an Excel worksheet.

For example, if you have an Excel workbook that requires a great amount of explanatory text, you have several choices:

✦ You can enter the text into cells. This is tedious and doesn't allow much formatting.

✦ You can use a text box. This is a good alternative, but it doesn't offer many formatting features.

✦ You can embed a Word document in your worksheet. This gives you full access to all of Word's formatting features.

To embed an empty Word document into an Excel worksheet, choose Excel's Insert ➪ Object command. In the Object dialog box, click the Create New tab and select Microsoft Word Document from the Object type list.

The result is a blank Word document, activated and ready for you to enter text. Notice that Word's menus and toolbars replace Excel's menus and toolbars. You can resize the document as you like, and the words wrap accordingly. Figure 29-12 shows an example of a Word document embedded in an Excel worksheet.

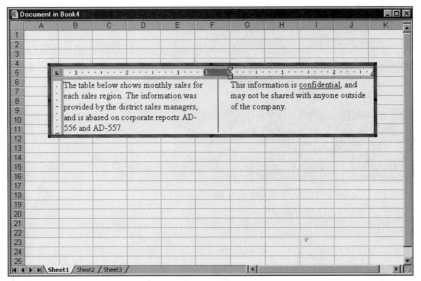

Figure 29-12: A Word document that is embedded in an Excel worksheet.

You can embed many other types of objects, including audio clips, video clips, MIDI sequences, and even an entire Microsoft PowerPoint presentation.

When you embed a video clip, Excel doesn't store the actual video clip file in the Excel document. Rather, Excel stores a pointer to the original file. If, for some reason, you want to embed the complete video clip file, you can use the Object Packager application. Be aware, however, that video clip files are typically quite large, and opening and saving the workbook will take a lot of time.

Microsoft Office includes a few additional applications that you may find useful. These all can be embedded in Excel documents:

✦ **Microsoft Equation:** Create equations, such as the one shown in Figure 29-13.

✦ **Microsoft WordArt:** Modify text in some interesting ways, as in Figure 29-14.

✦ **MS Organization Chart:** Create attractive organizational charts, as shown in Figure 29-15.

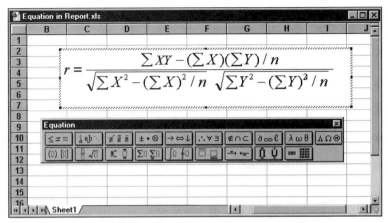

Figure 29-13: This object was created with Microsoft Equation.

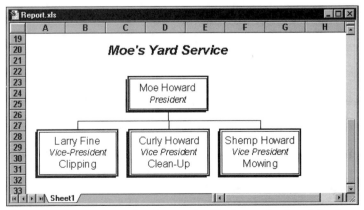

Figure 29-14: An example of Microsoft WordArt.

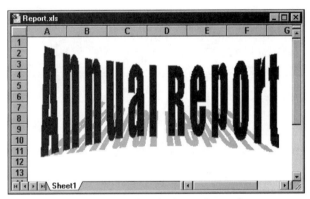

Figure 29-15: An example of an embedded organizational chart.

Using Office Binders

If you have Microsoft Office installed, you may take advantage of its binder feature. A *binder* is a container that can hold documents from different applications: Excel, Word, and PowerPoint.

You may find that a binder is useful when you are working on a project that involves documents from different applications. For example, you may be preparing a sales presentation that uses charts and tables from Excel, reports and memos from Word, and slides prepared with PowerPoint. You can store all the information in a single file. And, when you print the entire binder, pages are numbered sequentially.

To use a binder, start the Binder application, and an empty binder appears. You then can add existing documents to the binder or create new documents in the binder. Figure 29-16 shows a binder that contains Word, Excel, and PowerPoint documents. Consult the online Help for complete details on using this application.

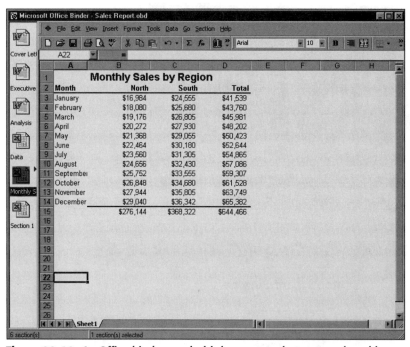

Figure 29-16: An Office binder can hold documents that are produced by different applications.

Note   You may need to rerun Office setup if Binder isn't installed on your computer. You'll find it under a category called Office Tools.

Summary

This chapter describes techniques that enable you to use data from other applications. These techniques include standard copy-and-paste options using the Windows and Office Clipboards, dynamic linking between applications, and embedding objects. This chapter concludes with a note on Microsoft Office's binder application, which enables you to work with documents that are produced by different applications.

✦   ✦   ✦

Excel and the Internet

Chances are, you're already involved in the Internet in
some way. This technology seems to have taken the
world by storm. The World Wide Web (WWW) is probably the
most exciting thing happening these days in the world of computing. In fact, the Web reaches well beyond the computer
community and is a pervasive force in our lives. It's now quite
common to see Web site addresses listed in TV commercials,
in magazine ads, and even on billboards.

The applications in Microsoft Office 2000 — including Excel —
have all been revamped to put them on a better footing with
the Internet. This chapter provides an introduction to the
Internet (for those who have yet to discover this resource) and
discusses the Internet features that are available in Excel 2000.

What Is the Internet?

The *Internet,* in a nutshell, is a collection of computers that are
located all around the world. These computers are all connected to each other, and they can pass information back and
forth. Strange as it may seem, the Internet is essentially a non-
commercial system, and no single entity "runs" the Internet.

Most people don't think of the Internet as a collection of
computers. Rather, the Internet is a *resource* that contains
information — and you use a computer to access that information. The computers that are connected to the Internet
simply do the grunt work of passing the information from
point A (which could be a computer in Hamburg, Germany)
to point B (which could be the computer in your cubicle).

Internet Terminology for Newcomers

If you're just starting to explore the Internet, you'll encounter many new terms (many of which are acronyms). The following is a list of a few common Internet terms and their definitions:

✦ **Browser:** Software that is designed to download HTML documents, interpret them, and display their contents. You can also use a browser to download files from an FTP site. The two leading Web browsers are Microsoft Internet Explorer and Netscape Navigator.

✦ **Download:** To transfer a file from another computer to your computer.

✦ **E-mail:** A method of sending messages to others electronically. You may be able to send and receive e-mail only within your company, or you may be able to send and receive e-mail all over the world by using the Internet.

✦ **FTP:** An acronym for *File Transfer Protocol*. This is one method by which a file is transferred from one computer to another.

✦ **FTP site:** An area of a computer that contains files that can be downloaded. For example, Microsoft maintains several FTP sites that have files that you can download.

✦ **HTML document:** A computer file that contains information that is viewable in a browser. The file includes embedded "tags" that describe how the information is displayed and formatted. Browser software is designed to interpret these tags and display the information. Sometimes known as a *Web document* or a *Web page*.

✦ **HTTP:** An acronym for Hypertext Transfer Protocol. This is the method by which documents are transferred over the WWW.

✦ **Hyperlink:** A clickable object (or text) that opens another document. Most Web pages include hyperlinks, to allow the user to jump to another topic or Web site.

✦ **Internet:** A network of computers throughout the world that can communicate with each other and pass information back and forth.

✦ **Intranet:** A company-wide network of computers that uses Internet protocols to allow access to information. An intranet can be accessed only by users who have permission.

✦ **URL:** An acronym for *Uniform Resource Locator*. A URL uniquely describes an Internet resource, such as a WWW document or a file. For example, the URL for the opening page of Microsoft's Web site is `http://www.microsoft.com`.

✦ **Web site:** A collection of HTML documents and other files located on a particular computer. The files on a Web site are available to anyone in the world. For example, Microsoft maintains a Web site that contains information about its products, technical support, and other resources.

✦ **WWW:** The World Wide Web, which is a part of the Internet that supports the transfer of information between computers throughout the world.

What's Available on the Internet?

The amount and variety of information that's available on the Internet is simply mind-boggling. You can think of virtually any topic in the world, and an excellent chance exists that at least some information on that topic can be found on the Internet. Not unexpectedly, computer-related information is especially abundant.

So, where do you get this information? The following are the four primary sources for information on the Internet:

✦ **Web sites:** The Web has rapidly become the most popular part of the Internet. Hundreds of thousands of Web sites are available that you can access with your Web browser software. For example, my own Web site (The Spreadsheet Page) has the following URL: `http://www.j-walk.com/ss/`

✦ **FTP sites:** These are computers that have files available for download. You can download these files by using Web browser software or other software that is designed specifically to download files from FTP sites. The following is the URL for Microsoft's FTP site: `ftp://ftp.microsoft.com`

✦ **Newsgroups:** These are essentially electronic bulletin boards. People post messages or questions, and others respond to the messages or answer their questions. Thousands of newsgroups are available for just about any topic that you can think of. You need special "news reader" software to read or post messages to a newsgroup (although most Web browsers also include this feature). For more information, see the sidebar "Excel Newsgroups."

✦ **Mailing lists:** If you have access to Internet e-mail, you can subscribe to any of several thousand mailing lists that address a broad array of topics. Subscribers send e-mail to the mailing list, and then every other subscriber to the list receives that e-mail. There are two popular mailing lists that deal with Excel (refer to the "Excel Mailing Lists" sidebar for details).

How Do You Get on the Internet?

You can access the Internet in a number of ways. Here are some of the most common ways:

✦ **Through your company:** Your company may already be connected to the Internet. If so, just fire up your Web browser and you're there!

✦ **Through an Internet Service Provider (ISP):** Most communities have several companies that can set up an Internet account for you. For a small monthly fee (usually around $20) you can have unlimited (or almost unlimited) access to the Internet. All that's required on your part is a computer, a modem, and a phone line.

✦ **Through an online service:** If you subscribe to any of the following online services, you can access the Internet through that service: America Online, CompuServe, Microsoft Network, or Prodigy.

Excel Newsgroups

Newsgroups are perhaps the best source for help with Excel. Typically, questions posed on a newsgroup are answered within 24 hours—assuming, of course, that the question is asked in a manner that makes others want to reply. The following is a list of newsgroups that deal with Excel:

✦ `comp.apps.spreadsheets` Covers all spreadsheets, but about 90 percent of the posts deal with Excel.

✦ `microsoft.public.excel.programming` Covers Excel programming issues, including VBA and XLM macros.

✦ `microsoft.public.excel.123quattro` Covers issues concerning conversion of 1-2-3 or Quattro Pro files to Excel.

✦ `microsoft.public.excel.worksheet.functions` Covers worksheet functions.

✦ `microsoft.public.excel.charting` Covers topics related to charts.

✦ `microsoft.public.excel.printing` Covers topics that deal with printing.

✦ `microsoft.public.excel.queryDAO` Discussion area about using the Microsoft Query and Data Access Objects (DAO) in Excel.

✦ `microsoft.public.excel.datamap` Covers the Data Map feature in Excel.

✦ `microsoft.public.excel.crashesGPFs` Covers General Protection Faults and other system failures.

✦ `microsoft.public.excel.misc` A catch-all group for topics that do not fit one of the other categories.

✦ `microsoft.public.excel.links` Covers topics related to using links in Excel.

✦ `microsoft.public.excel.interopoledde` Discussion area for Object Linking and Embedding (OLE), Dynamic Data Exchange (DDE), and other cross-application issues.

✦ `microsoft.public.excel.setup` Covers problems dealing with setup and installation of Excel.

✦ `microsoft.public.excel.templates` Discussion area for the Spreadsheet Solutions templates and other XLT files.

Note If your ISP doesn't carry the `microsoft.public.excel.*` groups, you can access them directly from Microsoft's news server. You need to configure your newsreader software or Web browser to access Microsoft's news server, which is `msnews.microsoft.com`.

Excel Mailing Lists

If you like the idea of communicating with other Excel users, you may want to join one of the Excel mailing lists. You can read messages, questions, and answers posted by others and eventually contribute your own messages to the list. If you find that the amount of mail is overwhelming, it's easy to "unsubscribe."

The EXCEL-G mailing list. For Excel users of all levels. To subscribe to the list, send e-mail to the following: LISTSERV@PEACH.EASE.LSOFT.COM.

In the body of the message, enter the following:

```
SUB EXCEL-G YourFirstName YourLastName
```

You'll receive complete instructions via e-mail.

The EXCEL-L mailing list. Primarily for Excel developers who discuss more advanced topics. To subscribe to the list, send e-mail to the following: LISTSERV@PEACH.EASE.LSOFT.COM

In the body of the message, enter the following:

```
SUB EXCEL-L YourFirstName YourLastName
```

You'll receive complete instructions via e-mail.

Where to Find Out More About the Internet

The best place to find out more about the Internet is — you guessed it — the Internet. A good starting place is the IDG Books Web site. To access it, open the following URL in your Web browser: http://www.idgbooks.com.

IDG Books Worldwide publishes numerous Internet books for users of all levels, and you can find these listed and described on the IDG Web site.

Excel's Internet Tools

The remainder of this chapter describes the Internet-related features available in Excel 2000. These features include:

✦ Using HTML as a native file format (instead of the XLS file format).

✦ Saving a worksheet as an interactive Web page.

✦ Using Excel's Web toolbar.

✦ Inserting hyperlinks into a worksheet.

✦ Creating and using Web queries.

✦ Scheduling and conducting online meetings.

✦ Creating discussion groups.

Using HTML As a Native File Format

 Excel's standard file format is, of course, an XLS file. Excel 2000, however, has the ability to use HTML as a native file format. This means that you can create a workbook and save it in HTML format. Then, you can reopen the file without losing any information. In other words, your Excel-specific information (such as formulas, charts, pivot tables, and macros) survive the translation to HTML.

If you've used the "save as HTML" feature in Excel 97, you probably know that the HTML file that's created works fine in Web browsers — but if you reopen the file in Excel, all of your formulas (as well as other Excel-specific features) will be gone. With Excel 2000, this problem no longer exists, because the HTML file contains lots of proprietary tags that are ignored by browsers but that enable Excel to re-create the workbook.

To save a workbook in HTML format, select File ➪ Save As. You'll see the familiar Save As dialog box — but with some new options (see Figure 30-1). In the field labeled Save as type, make sure Web Page (*.htm, *.html) is selected. Provide a filename, and click Save. To reopen the file, use the normal File ➪ Open command.

Figure 30-1: Use the Save As dialog box to save a workbook in HTML format.

Caution   Unless your workbook is very simple, saving it in HTML format generates additional "supporting" files, because the HTML file format can't handle Excel-specific items, such as macros, charts, and pivot tables. The supporting files are stored in a separate subdirectory within the directory where you save the file. The directory name consists of the file's name, followed by a space and the word "files." Therefore, if you need to transfer the file to another computer, make sure that you also transfer the supporting files in the subdirectory.

If you save your work in HTML format, you should be aware of some additional options. Select Tools ➪ Options, click the General tab, and then click the Web Options button. You'll see the dialog box shown in Figure 30-2. Most of the time, the default settings work just fine. However, familiarizing yourself with the options available is worthwhile (these are described in the online Help). You can also access the Web Options dialog box from the Tools menu in the Save As dialog box.

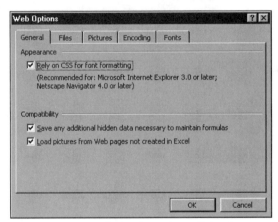

Figure 30-2: Use the Web Options dialog box to set various options for working with HTML files.

When you save a workbook in HTML format, by default, it will not be interactive when it's opened in a browser. The browser displays a good rendition of the worksheet, but it's essentially a "dead" workbook, because the user can't change any cells. The next section describes how to save your Excel workbook in a way that provides interactivity within a Web browser.

Providing Interactivity in Your Web Documents

When you save an Excel workbook in HTML format, you can select an option that makes the file interactive within the browser. This means that the user can perform standard Excel operations directly in the browser. For example, the user can change cells or manipulate data in a pivot table. Saving an Excel file with interactivity is limited to a single sheet.

Note   To take advantage of this interactivity, the user must have Office 2000 installed, or have a licensed copy of the Office Client Pak. The Office Client Pak consists of the ActiveX controls necessary to work with interactive Office documents in a Web browser. Currently, the only browser that supports this technology is Microsoft Internet Explorer.

Figure 30-3 shows an example of an Excel workbook displayed in Internet Explorer. The user can change the values, and the formulas display the calculated results.

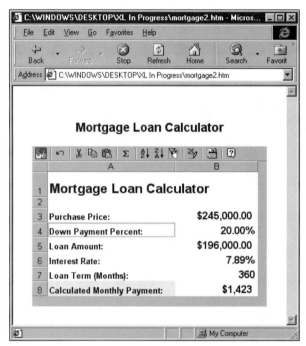

Figure 30-3: An interactive Excel workbook opened in Internet Explorer.

You need to understand that the interactivity is limited. For example, you can't execute macros when an interactive Excel file is displayed in a browser.

Using the Web Toolbar

Use the Web toolbar (shown in Figure 30-4) to move among files (Excel files and HTML documents); this is similar to using a Web browser. You can jump forward or backward among the workbooks and other files that you've visited, and add the ones that you may use frequently to a "favorites" list.

Figure 30-4: The Web toolbar.

Working with Hyperlinks

Hyperlinks are shortcuts that provide a quick way to jump to other workbooks and files. You can jump to files on your own computer, your network, and the Internet and Web.

Inserting a hyperlink

You can create hyperlinks from cell text or graphic objects, such as shapes and pictures. To create a text hyperlink, choose the Insert ➪ Hyperlink command (or press Ctrl+K). Excel responds with the dialog box shown in Figure 30-5.

Select an icon in the Link to column that represents the type of hyperlink you want to create. Then, specify the location for the file that you want to link to. The dialog box will change, depending on the icon selected. Click OK, and Excel creates the hyperlink in the active cell.

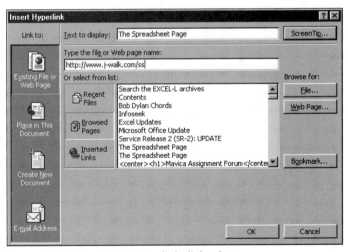

Figure 30-5: The Insert Hyperlink dialog box.

Adding a hyperlink to a graphic object works the same way. Add an object to your worksheet by using the Drawing toolbar. Select the object and then choose the Insert ➪ Hyperlink command. Specify the required information as outlined in the previous paragraph.

Using hyperlinks

When you work with hyperlinks, remember that Excel attempts to mimic a Web browser. For example, when you click a hyperlink, the hyperlinked document replaces the current document — it takes on the same window size and position. The document that contains the hyperlink is hidden. You can use the Back and Forward buttons on the Web toolbar to activate the documents.

Web Queries

Excel enables you to pull in data contained in an HTML file by performing a Web query. The data is transferred to a worksheet, where you can manipulate it any way you like. You need to understand that performing a Web query does not actually open the HTML file in Excel.

Note   The Web query feature is very similar to performing a normal database query (see Chapter 24). The only difference is that the data is coming from a Web page rather than a database file. Figure 30-6 shows a Web page that's a good candidate for a Web query.

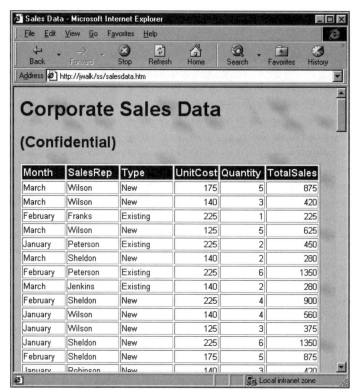

Figure 30-6: The table in this Web page will be brought into a worksheet as a Web query.

The best part about a Web query is that Excel remembers where the data came from. Therefore, after you create a Web query, you can "refresh" the query to pull in the most recent data.

To create a Web query, select Data ⇨ Get External Data ⇨ New Web Query. Excel displays the New Web Query dialog box, shown in Figure 30-7. In part 1, specify the HTML file, using the Browse button if you like. The HTML file can be on the Internet, a corporate intranet, or on a local or network drive. In part 2, select how much of the file you want to use. Most of the time, you'll just want to bring in a particular table. In part 3, specify the type of formatting that you'd like to see. Click the Advanced button for some additional options — these options might be necessary if the data in the HTML file is not in the form of a table. Click OK and you get another dialog box asking where you want to place the data.

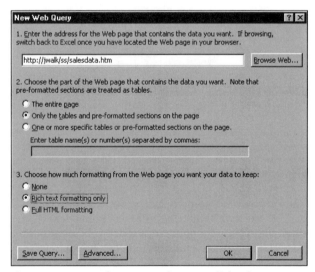

Figure 30-7: Use the New Web Query dialog box to specify the source of the data.

Figure 30-8 shows an Excel workbook, after performing a Web query.

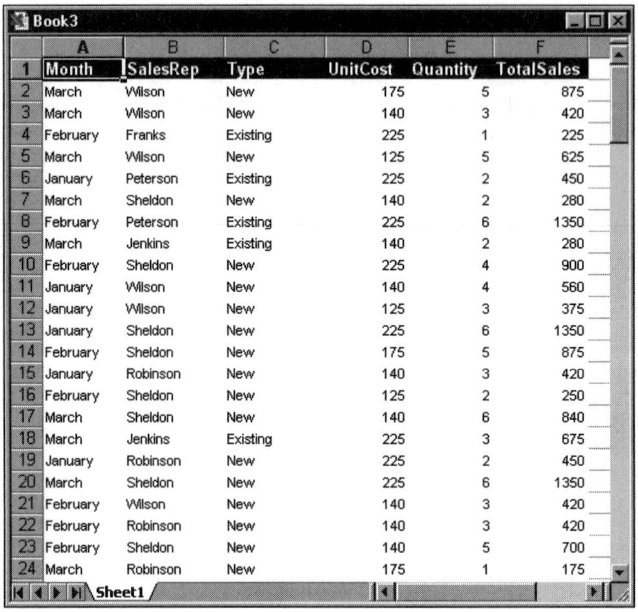

Month	SalesRep	Type	UnitCost	Quantity	TotalSales
March	Wilson	New	175	5	875
March	Wilson	New	140	3	420
February	Franks	Existing	225	1	225
March	Wilson	New	125	5	625
January	Peterson	Existing	225	2	450
March	Sheldon	New	140	2	280
February	Peterson	Existing	225	6	1350
March	Jenkins	Existing	140	2	280
February	Sheldon	New	225	4	900
January	Wilson	New	140	4	560
January	Wilson	New	125	3	375
January	Sheldon	New	225	6	1350
February	Sheldon	New	175	5	875
January	Robinson	New	140	3	420
February	Sheldon	New	125	2	250
March	Sheldon	New	140	6	840
March	Jenkins	Existing	225	3	675
January	Robinson	New	225	2	450
March	Sheldon	New	225	6	1350
February	Wilson	New	140	3	420
February	Robinson	New	140	3	420
February	Sheldon	New	140	5	700
March	Robinson	New	175	1	175

Figure 30-8: The data in this workbook resulted from a Web query.

After you create your Web query, you have some options. Activate any cell in the data range and select Data ➪ Get External Data ➪ Data Range Properties. Or, you can right-click and select the command from the shortcut menu. Either method displays the dialog box shown in Figure 30-9. Adjust the settings to your liking.

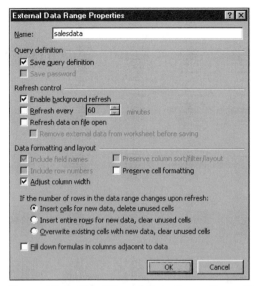

Figure 30-9: The External Data Range Properties dialog box provides you with some options regarding your Web query.

Summary

This chapter provides a brief introduction to the Internet and describes several Internet tools that are available in Excel. It explains how to use HTML as a native file format, use the Web toolbar, work with hyperlinks, and use Web queries.

✦　　✦　　✦

Making Your Worksheets Error-Free

T he ultimate goal in developing a spreadsheet solution is to generate accurate results. For simple worksheets, this isn't difficult, and you can usually tell whether the results are correct. But when your worksheets are large or complex, ensuring accuracy becomes more difficult. This chapter provides you with tools and techniques to help you identify and correct errors.

Types of Worksheet Problems

Making a change in a worksheet — even a relatively minor change — may produce a ripple effect that introduces errors in other cells. For example, accidentally entering a value into a cell that formerly held a formula is all too easy to do. This can have a major impact on other formulas, and you may not discover the problem until long after you make the change. Or, you may *never* discover the problem.

An Excel worksheet can have many types of problems. Some problems — such as a formula that returns an error value — are immediately apparent. Other problems are more subtle. For example, if a formula was constructed using faulty logic, it may never return an error value — it simply returns the wrong values. If you're lucky, you can discover the problem and correct it.

Common problems that occur in worksheets are the following:

✦ Incorrect approach to a problem

✦ Faulty logic in a formula

✦ Formulas that return error values

✦ Circular references

✦ Spelling mistakes

✦ A worksheet is new to you, and you can't figure out how it works

Excel provides tools to help you identify and correct some of these problems. In the remaining sections, I discuss these tools along with others that I've developed.

Formula AutoCorrect

When you enter a formula that has a syntax error, Excel attempts to determine the problem and offers a suggested correction.

For example, if you enter the following formula (which has a syntax error), Excel displays the dialog box that is shown in Figure 31-1:

```
=SUM(A1:A12)/3B
```

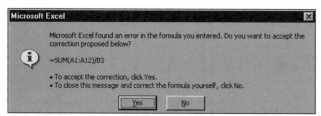

Figure 31-1: Excel can often offer a suggestion to correct a formula.

Caution   Be careful about accepting corrections for your formulas from Excel, because it doesn't always guess correctly. For example, I entered the following formula (which has mismatched parentheses):

```
=AVERAGE(SUM(A1:A12,SUM(B1:B12))
```

Excel proposed the following correction to the formula:

```
=AVERAGE(SUM(A1:A12,SUM(B1:B12)))
```

You may be tempted to accept the suggestion without even thinking. In this case, the proposed formula is syntactically correct—but not what I intended.

Tracing Cell Relationships

Excel has several useful tools that can help you track down errors and logical flaws in your worksheets. This section discusses the following items:

✦ Go To Special dialog box

✦ Excel's built-in auditing tools

These tools are useful for debugging formulas. As you probably realize by now, the formulas in a worksheet can become complicated and refer (directly or indirectly) to hundreds or thousands of other cells. Trying to isolate a problem in a tangled web of formulas can be frustrating.

Before discussing these features, you need to be familiar with the following two concepts:

✦ **Cell precedents:** Applicable only to cells that contain a formula. A formula cell's precedents are all the cells that contribute to the formula's result. A *direct precedent* is a cell that you use directly in the formula. An *indirect precedent* is a cell that isn't used directly in the formula, but is used by a cell to which you refer in the formula.

✦ **Cell dependents:** Formula cells that depend on a particular cell. Again, the formula cell can be a direct dependent or an indirect dependent.

Often, identifying cell precedents for a formula cell sheds light on why the formula isn't working correctly. On the other hand, knowing which formula cells depend on a particular cell is often helpful. For example, if you're about to delete a formula, you may want to check whether it has any dependents.

The Go To Special Dialog Box

The Go To Special dialog box can be useful, because it enables you to specify the type of cells that you want Excel to select. To display this dialog box, choose Edit ➪ Go To (or press F5). The Go To dialog box appears. Click the Special button, which displays the Go To Special dialog box, as shown in Figure 31-2.

Figure 31-2: The Go To Special dialog box.

If you select a range before choosing Edit ➪ Go To, the command looks only at the selected cells. If only a single cell is selected, the command operates on the entire worksheet.

You can use this dialog box to select cells of a certain type—which can often be helpful in identifying errors. For example, if you choose the Formulas option, Excel selects all the cells that contain a formula. If you zoom the worksheet out to a small size, you can get a good idea of the worksheet's organization (see Figure 31-3). It may also help you spot a common error: a formula that you overwrote with a value. If you find a cell that's not selected amid a group of selected formula cells, chances are good that the cell formerly contained a formula that has been replaced by a value.

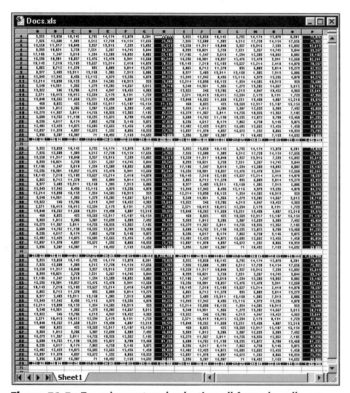

Figure 31-3: Zooming out and selecting all formula cells can give you a good overview of how the worksheet is designed.

You can also use the Go To Special dialog box to identify cell precedents and dependents. In this case, Excel selects all cells that qualify. In either case, you can choose whether to display direct or all levels.

Excel has shortcut keys that you can use to select precedents and dependents. These are listed in Table 31-1.

Table 31-1 Shortcut Keys to Select Precedents and Dependents	
Key Combination	**What It Selects**
Ctrl+[	Direct precedents
Ctrl+Shift+[	All precedents
Ctrl+]	Direct dependents
Ctrl+Shift+]	All dependents

You also can select a formula cell's direct dependents by double-clicking the cell. This technique, however, works only when you turn off the Edit directly in the cell option on the Edit tab of the Options dialog box.

Excel's Auditing Tools

Excel provides a set of interactive auditing tools that you may find helpful. Access these tools either by selecting Tools ➪ Auditing (which results in a submenu with additional choices) or by using the Auditing toolbar, shown in Figure 31-4.

Figure 31-4: The Auditing toolbar.

Pay Attention to the Colors

When you edit a cell that contains a formula, Excel color-codes the cell and range references in the formula. Excel also outlines the cells and ranges used in the formula by using corresponding colors. Therefore, you can see at a glance the cells that are used in the formula.

You can also manipulate the colored outline to change the cell or range reference. To change the references that are used, drag the outline's border or drag the outline's fill handle (at the lower-right corner of the outline).

The tools on the Auditing toolbar, from left to right, are as follows:

✦ **Trace Precedents:** Draws arrows to indicate a formula cell's precedents. Click this multiple times to see additional levels of precedents.

✦ **Remove Precedent Arrows:** Removes the most recently placed set of precedent arrows.

✦ **Trace Dependents:** Draws arrows to indicate a cell's dependents. Click this multiple times to see additional levels of dependents.

✦ **Remove Dependent Arrows:** Removes the most recently placed set of dependent arrows.

✦ **Remove All Arrows:** Removes all precedent and dependent arrows from the worksheet.

✦ **Trace Error:** Draws arrows from a cell that contains an error to the cells that may have caused the error.

✦ **New Comment:** Inserts a comment for the active cell. This really doesn't have much to do with auditing. It lets you attach a comment to a cell.

✦ **Circle Invalid Data:** Draws a circle around all the cells that contain invalid data. This applies only to cells that have validation criteria specified with the Data ⇨ Validation command.

✦ **Clear Validation Circles:** Removes the circles that are drawn around cells that contain invalid data.

These tools can identify precedents and dependents by drawing arrows (known as *cell tracers*) on the worksheet, as shown in Figure 31-5. In this case, cell G11 was selected and then the Trace Precedents toolbar button was clicked. Excel drew lines to identify the cells used by the formula in G11 (direct precedents).

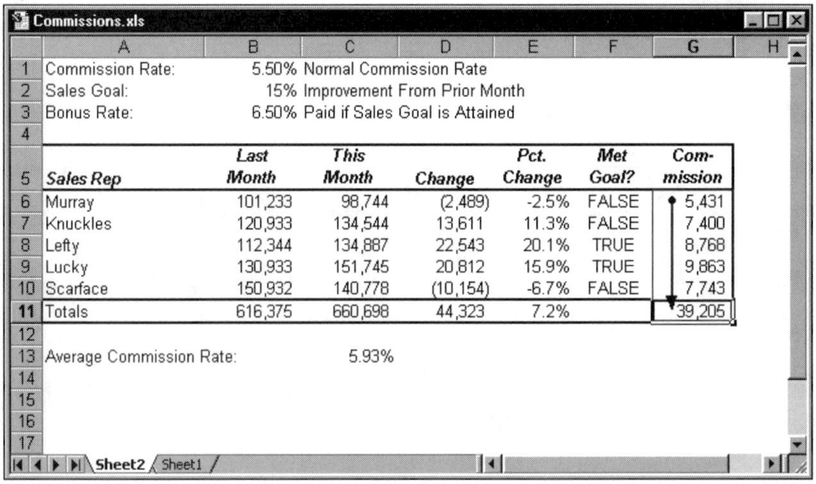

	A	B	C	D	E	F	G	H
	Commissions.xls							
1	Commission Rate:	5.50%	Normal Commission Rate					
2	Sales Goal:	15%	Improvement From Prior Month					
3	Bonus Rate:	6.50%	Paid if Sales Goal is Attained					
4								
5	*Sales Rep*	*Last Month*	*This Month*	*Change*	*Pct. Change*	*Met Goal?*	*Com- mission*	
6	Murray	101,233	98,744	(2,489)	-2.5%	FALSE	5,431	
7	Knuckles	120,933	134,544	13,611	11.3%	FALSE	7,400	
8	Lefty	112,344	134,887	22,543	20.1%	TRUE	8,768	
9	Lucky	130,933	151,745	20,812	15.9%	TRUE	9,863	
10	Scarface	150,932	140,778	(10,154)	-6.7%	FALSE	7,743	
11	Totals	616,375	660,698	44,323	7.2%		39,205	
12								
13	Average Commission Rate:		5.93%					
14								
15								
16								
17								

Sheet2 / Sheet1

Figure 31-5: Excel draws lines to indicate a cell's precedents.

Figure 31-6 shows what happens when the Trace Precedents button is clicked again. This time, Excel adds more lines to show the indirect precedents. The result is a graphical representation of the cells that are used (directly or indirectly) by the formula in cell G11.

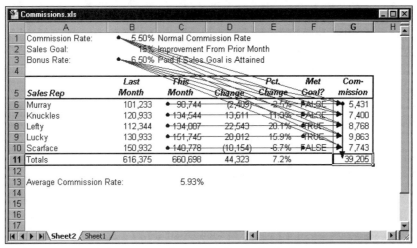

Figure 31-6: Excel draws more lines to indicate the indirect precedents.

Tip
This type of interactive tracing is often more revealing when the worksheet is zoomed out to display a larger area.

The best way to learn about these tools is to use them. Start with a worksheet that has formulas and experiment with the various buttons on the Auditing toolbar.

Tracing Error Values

The Trace Error button on the Auditing toolbar helps you to identify the cell that is causing an error value to appear. Often, an error in one cell is the result of an error in a precedent cell. Activate a cell that contains an error, and click the Trace Error button. Excel draws arrows to indicate the error source.

Table 31-2 lists the types of error values that may appear in a cell that has a formula. The Trace Error button works with all of these errors.

<table>
<tr><td colspan="2" align="center">Table 31-2
Excel Error Values</td></tr>
</table>

Error Value	Explanation
#DIV/0!	The formula is trying to divide by zero (an operation that's not allowed on this planet). This also occurs when the formula attempts to divide by a cell that is empty.
#NAME?	The formula uses a name that Excel doesn't recognize. This can happen if you delete a name that's used in the formula or if you have unmatched quotation marks when using text.
#N/A	The formula refers to an empty cell range.
#NULL!	The formula uses an intersection of two ranges that do not intersect (this concept is described later in the chapter).
#NUM!	A problem with a value exists—for example, you specified a negative number where a positive number is expected.
#REF!	The formula refers to a cell that is not valid. This can happen if the cell has been deleted from the worksheet.
#VALUE!	The formula includes an argument or operand of the wrong type.

Circular References

A *circular reference* occurs when a formula refers to its own cell—either directly or indirectly. Usually, this is the result of an error (although some circular references are intentional). When a worksheet has a circular reference, Excel displays the cell reference in the status bar.

Cross-Reference   Refer to the discussion of circular references in Chapter 9.

Other Auditing Tools

The registered version of the Power Utility Pak includes a utility named Auditing Tools. The dialog box for this utility is shown in Figure 31-7.

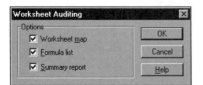

Figure 31-7: The Worksheet Auditing dialog box from the Power Utility Pak.

This utility works with the active worksheet and can generate any or all of the following items:

✦ **Worksheet map:** A color-coded graphical map of the worksheet that shows the type of contents for each cell — value, text, formula, logical value, or error. See Figure 31-8.

✦ **Formula list:** A list of all formulas in the worksheet, including their current values.

✦ **Summary report:** An informative report that includes details about the worksheet, the workbook that it's in, and a list of all defined names.

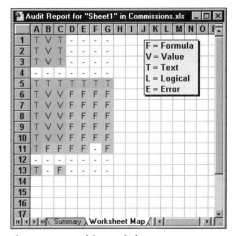

Figure 31-8: This worksheet map was produced by the Auditing Tools utility from the Power Utility Pak.

On the CD-ROM

You can find the shareware version of the Power Utility Pak on this book's CD-ROM. Owners of this book can purchase the Power Utility Pak at a significant discount. Use the coupon in the back of the book to order your copy.

Spelling and Word-Related Options

Excel includes several handy tools to help you with the non-numeric problems — those related to spelling and words.

Spell Checking

If you use a word processing program, you probably run its spelling checker before printing an important document. Spelling mistakes can be just as embarrassing when they appear in a spreadsheet. Fortunately, Microsoft includes a spelling checker with Excel. You can access the spelling checker by using any of these methods:

✦ Select Tools ➪ Spelling

✦ Click the Spelling button on the Standard toolbar

✦ Press F7

The result of using any one of these methods is the Spelling dialog box that is shown in Figure 31-9.

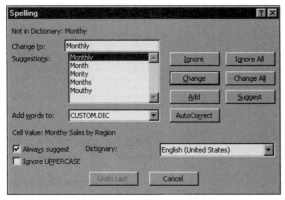

Figure 31-9: The Spelling dialog box.

The extent of the spell checking depends on what you selected before you opened the Spelling dialog box. If you selected a single cell, Excel checks the entire worksheet, including cell contents, notes, text in graphic objects and charts, and page headers and footers. Even the contents of hidden rows and columns are checked. If you select a range of cells, Excel checks only that range. If you select a group of characters in the formula bar, Excel checks only those characters.

The Spelling dialog box works similarly to other spelling checkers with which you may be familiar. If Excel encounters a word that isn't in the current dictionary or is misspelled, it offers a list of suggestions. You can respond by clicking one of the following buttons:

✦ **Ignore:** Ignores the word and continues the spell check.

✦ **Ignore All:** Ignores the word and all subsequent occurrences of it.

✦ **Change:** Changes the word to the selected word in the Change to edit box.

✦ **Change All:** Changes the word to the selected word in the Change to edit box and changes all subsequent occurrences of it without asking.

✦ **Add:** Adds the word to the dictionary.

✦ **Suggest:** Displays a list of replacement words. This button is grayed if the Always suggest check box is checked.

✦ **AutoCorrect:** Adds the misspelled word and its correct spelling to the list:

```
=SUM(A1:A12)/3B
```

Using AutoCorrect

AutoCorrect is a handy feature that automatically corrects common typing mistakes. You also can add words to the list that Excel corrects automatically. The AutoCorrect dialog box appears in Figure 31-10. You access this feature by choosing Tools ➪ AutoCorrect.

Figure 31-10: The AutoCorrect dialog box.

This dialog box has several options:

✦ **Correct TWo INitial CApitals:** Automatically corrects words with two initial uppercase letters. For example, *BUdget* is converted to *Budget*. This is a common mistake among fast typists. You can click on the Exceptions button to specify a list of exceptions to this rule. For example, my company name is *JWalk and Associates,* so I created an exception for *JWalk.*

✦ **Capitalize first letter of sentence:** Capitalizes the first letter in a sentence.

✦ **Capitalize names of days:** Capitalizes the days of the week. If you enter *monday,* Excel converts it to *Monday.*

✦ **Correct accidental use of cAPS LOCK key:** Corrects errors caused if you accidentally hit the CapsLock key while typing.

✦ **Replace text as you type:** AutoCorrect automatically changes incorrect words as you type them.

Excel includes a long list of AutoCorrect entries for commonly misspelled words. In addition, it has AutoCorrect entries for some symbols. For example, *(c)* is replaced with © and *(r)* is replaced with ® You can also add your own AutoCorrect entries. For example, if you find that you frequently misspell the word *January* as *Janruary,* you can create an AutoCorrect entry so that it's changed automatically. To create a new AutoCorrect entry, enter the misspelled word in the Replace box and the correctly spelled word in the With box. As I noted previously, you also can do this in the Spelling dialog box.

You also can use the AutoCorrect feature to create shortcuts for commonly used words or phrases. For example, if you work for a company named Consolidated Data Processing Corporation, you can create an AutoCorrect entry for an abbreviation, such as cdp. Then, whenever you type *cdp,* Excel automatically changes it to *Consolidated Data Processing Corporation.*

Using AutoComplete

AutoComplete automatically finishes a word as soon as Excel recognizes it. For Excel to recognize the word, it must appear elsewhere in the same column. This feature is most useful when you're entering a list that contains repeated text in a column. For example, assume that you're entering customer data in a list, and one of the fields is City. Whenever you start typing, Excel searches the other entries in the column. If it finds a match, it completes the entry for you. Press Enter to accept it. If Excel guesses incorrectly, keep typing to ignore the suggestion.

If AutoComplete isn't working, select Tools ➪ Options, click on the Edit tab, and check the box labeled Enable AutoComplete for cell values.

You also can display a list of all items in a column by right-clicking and choosing Pick from list from the shortcut menu. Excel then displays a list box of all entries that are in the column (see Figure 31-11). Click on the one that you want, and Excel enters it into the cell for you.

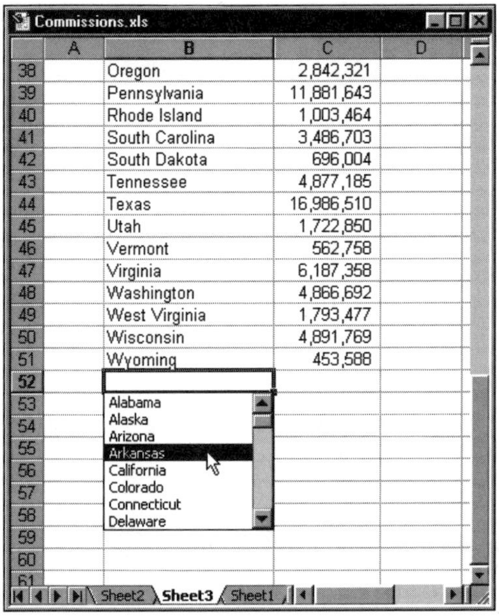

Figure 31-11: Choosing the Pick from list option from the shortcut menu gives you a list of entries from which to choose.

Learning About an Unfamiliar Spreadsheet

When you develop a workbook yourself, you have a thorough understanding of how it's put together. But if you receive an unfamiliar workbook from someone, it may be difficult to understand how it all fits together — especially if it's large.

First, identify the bottom-line cell or cells. Often, a worksheet is designed to produce results in a single cell or in a range of cells. After you identify this cell or range, you should be able to use the cell-tracing techniques described earlier in this chapter to determine the cell relationships.

Although every worksheet is different, a few techniques can help you become familiar with an unfamiliar workbook. I discuss these techniques in the following sections.

Zooming Out for the Big Picture

I find that it's often helpful to use Excel's zoom feature to zoom out to get an overview of the worksheet's layout. You can select View ➪ Full Screen to see even more of the worksheet. When a workbook is zoomed out, you can use all of the normal commands. For example, you can use the Edit ➪ Go To command to select a name range. Or, you can use the options that are available in the Go To Special dialog box (explained previously in this chapter) to select formula cells, constants, or other special cell types.

Viewing Formulas

You can become familiar with an unfamiliar workbook by displaying the formulas rather than the results of the formulas. Select Tools ➪ Options, and check the box labeled Formulas on the View tab. You may want to create a new window for the workbook before issuing this command. That way, you can see the formulas in one window and the results in the other.

Figure 31-12 shows an example. The window on the top shows the normal view (formula results). The window on the bottom displays the formulas.

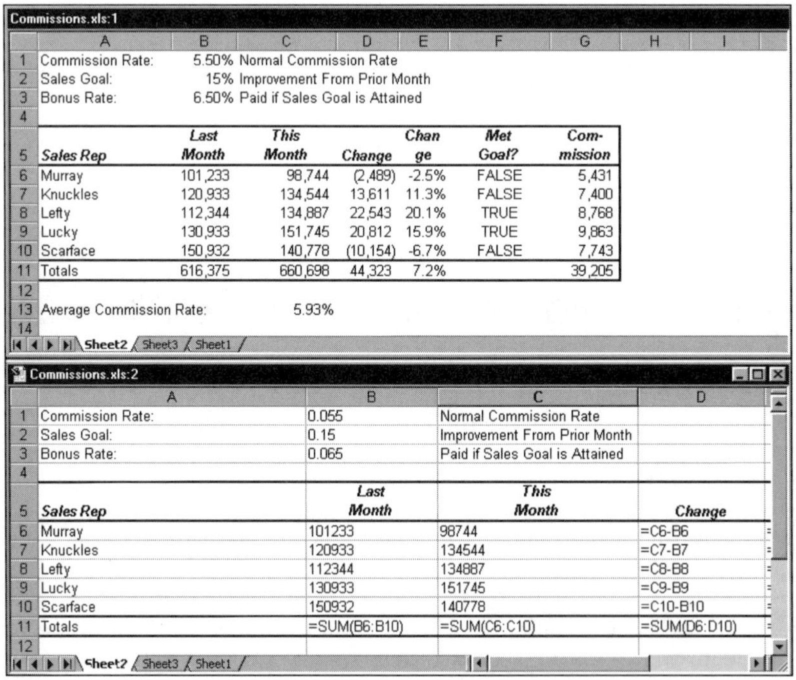

Commissions.xls:1

	A	B	C	D	E	F	G	H	I
1	Commission Rate:	5.50%	Normal Commission Rate						
2	Sales Goal:	15%	Improvement From Prior Month						
3	Bonus Rate:	6.50%	Paid if Sales Goal is Attained						
4									
5	*Sales Rep*	*Last Month*	*This Month*	*Change*	*Chan ge*	*Met Goal?*	*Com-mission*		
6	Murray	101,233	98,744	(2,489)	-2.5%	FALSE	5,431		
7	Knuckles	120,933	134,544	13,611	11.3%	FALSE	7,400		
8	Lefty	112,344	134,887	22,543	20.1%	TRUE	8,768		
9	Lucky	130,933	151,745	20,812	15.9%	TRUE	9,863		
10	Scarface	150,932	140,778	(10,154)	-6.7%	FALSE	7,743		
11	Totals	616,375	660,698	44,323	7.2%		39,205		
12									
13	Average Commission Rate:		5.93%						
14									

Sheet2 / Sheet3 / Sheet1

Commissions.xls:2

	A	B	C	D
1	Commission Rate:	0.055	Normal Commission Rate	
2	Sales Goal:	0.15	Improvement From Prior Month	
3	Bonus Rate:	0.065	Paid if Sales Goal is Attained	
4				
5	*Sales Rep*	*Last Month*	*This Month*	*Change*
6	Murray	101233	98744	=C6-B6
7	Knuckles	120933	134544	=C7-B7
8	Lefty	112344	134887	=C8-B8
9	Lucky	130933	151745	=C9-B9
10	Scarface	150932	140778	=C10-B10
11	Totals	=SUM(B6:B10)	=SUM(C6:C10)	=SUM(D6:D10)
12				

Sheet2 / Sheet3 / Sheet1

Figure 31-12: The underlying formulas are shown in the bottom window.

Pasting a List of Names

If the worksheet uses named ranges, create a list of the names and their references. Move the cell pointer to an empty area of the worksheet and choose Insert ➪ Name ➪ Paste. Excel responds with its Paste Name dialog box. Click on the Paste List button to paste a list of the names and their references into the workbook. Figure 31-13 shows an example.

	A	B	C	D	E
6	Murray	101,233	98,744	(2,489)	-2.5%
7	Knuckles	120,933	134,544	13,611	11.3%
8	Lefty	112,344	134,887	22,543	20.1%
9	Lucky	130,933	151,745	20,812	15.9%
10	Scarface	150,932	140,778	(10,154)	-6.7%
11	Totals	616,375	660,698	44,323	7.2%
12					
13	Average Commission Rate:		5.93%		
14					
15	BonusRate	=Sheet1!$B$3			
16	CommissionRate	=Sheet1!$B$1			
17	Last_Month	=Sheet1!$B$6:$B$11			
18	SalesGoal	=Sheet1!$B$2			
19	This_Month	=Sheet1!$C$6:$C$11			
20	Totals	=Sheet1!$B$11:$G$11			
21					
22					

Figure 31-13: Pasting a list of names (in A15:B20) can sometimes help you understand how a worksheet is constructed.

Summary

In this chapter, I discuss tools that can help you make your worksheets error-free. I identify the types of errors that you're likely to encounter. I also cover three tools that Excel provides, which can help you trace the relationships between cells: the Info window, the Go To Special dialog box, and Excel's interactive auditing tools. I go over text-related features, including spell checking, AutoCorrect, and AutoComplete. I conclude the chapter with general tips that can help you understand how an unfamiliar worksheet is put together.

✦　　✦　　✦

Fun Stuff

Although Excel is used primarily for serious applications, many users discover that this product has a lighter side. This chapter is devoted to the less-serious applications of Excel, including games and interesting diversions.

Games

Excel certainly wasn't designed as a platform for games. Nevertheless, I've developed a few games using Excel and have downloaded several others from various Internet sites. I've found that the key ingredient in developing these games is creativity. In almost every case, I had to invent one or more workarounds to compensate for Excel's lack of game-making features. In this section, I show you a few of my own creations.

The examples in this chapter are either available on the companion CD-ROM or included with the registered version of my Power Utility Pak (see the coupon at the back of the book).

Tick-Tack-Toe

Although Tick-Tack-Toe is not the most mentally stimulating game, everyone knows how to play it. Figure 32-1 shows the Tick-Tack-Toe game that I developed using Excel. In this implementation, the user plays against the computer. I wrote some formulas and VBA macros to determine the computer's moves, and it plays a reasonably good game — about on par with a three-year-old child. I'm embarrassed to admit that the program has even beaten me a few times (OK, so I was distracted!).

This workbook is available on the companion CD-ROM.

You can choose who makes the first move (you or the computer) and which marker you want to use (X or O). The winning games and ties are tallied in cells at the bottom of the window.

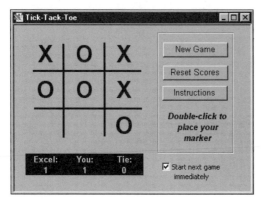

Figure 32-1: My Tick-Tack-Toe game.

Moving Tile Puzzle

At some time in your life, you've probably played one of those moving tile puzzles. They come in several variations, but the goal is always the same: rearrange the tiles so that they are in order.

This workbook is available on the companion CD-ROM.

Figure 32-2 shows a version of this game that I wrote using VBA. This version lets you choose the number of tiles (from a simple 3×3 matrix up to a challenging 6×6 matrix).

When you click the tile, it appears to move to the empty position. Actually, no movement is taking place. The program is simply changing the text on the buttons and making the button in the empty position invisible.

Figure 32-2: My Moving Tile puzzle.

Keno

If you've ever spent any time in a casino, you may be familiar with Keno (see Figure 32-3). If you're smart, you probably know to avoid this game like the plague, because it has the lowest return of any casino game. With my Keno for Excel, you don't have to worry about losing any money: all the action takes place on a worksheet, and no money changes hands. And, it's a lot faster than the casino version.

This workbook is available on the companion CD-ROM. In addition, I've included another workbook that calculates the various odds associated with Keno. Take a look at this workbook and you may never play casino Keno again!

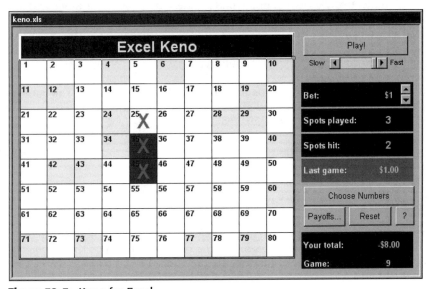

Figure 32-3: Keno for Excel.

Power Utility Pak Games

The four games listed in this section are included with my Power Utility Pak. Use the coupon in the back of the book to order your copy at a huge discount.

Video Poker

Developing my Video Poker game for Excel (see Figure 32-4) was quite a challenge. I was forced to spend many hours performing research at a local casino to perfect this game so that it captures the excitement of a real poker machine. The only problem is that I haven't figured out a way to dispense the winnings. Oh well, maybe in the next version.

Figure 32-4: My Video Poker game.

This version has two games: Joker's Wild (a joker can be used for any card) and Jacks or Better (a pair of jacks or better is required to win). You select which cards to discard by clicking the card face. You can change the game (or the bet) at any time while playing. You can also request a graph that shows your cumulative winnings (or, more typically, your cumulative losses).

Identifying the various poker hands is done using VBA procedures. The game also has a Hide button that temporarily hides the game (pressing Esc has the same effect). You can then resume the game when your boss leaves the room.

This game is included with the registered version of the Power Utility Pak. See the coupon in the back of the book for details on how to get your copy.

Dice Game

The goal of the Dice Game (shown in Figure 32-5) is to obtain a high score by assigning dice rolls to various categories. You get to roll the dice three times on each turn, and you can keep or discard the dice before rolling again. Everything is done using VBA.

This game is included with the registered version of the Power Utility Pak. See the coupon in the back of the book for details on how to get your copy.

Bomb Hunt

Windows comes with a game called Minesweeper. I developed a version of this game for Excel and named it Bomb Hunt (see Figure 32-6). The goal is to discover the hidden bombs in the grid. Double-clicking a cell reveals a bomb (you lose) or a number that indicates the number of bombs in the surrounding cells. You use logic to determine where the bombs are located.

This game is included with the registered version of the Power Utility Pak. See the coupon in the back of the book for details on how to get your copy.

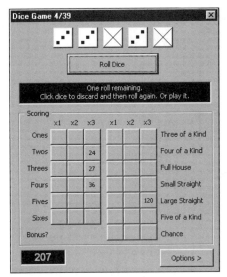

Figure 32-5: My Dice Game.

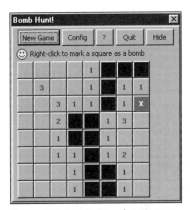

Figure 32-6: My Bomb Hunt game.

Hangman

Hangman is another game that almost everyone has played. Figure 32-7 shows a version that I developed for Excel. The objective is to identify a word by guessing letters. Correctly guessed letters appear in their proper position. Every incorrectly guessed letter adds a new body part to the person being hanged (to reduce gratuitous violence, I substituted a skeleton for the hanged gentleman). Ten incorrect guesses and the skeleton is completed — that is, the game is over.

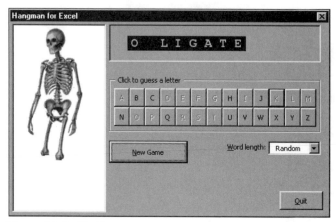

Figure 32-7: My Hangman game.

The workbook includes 1,400 words, ranging in length from 6 to 12 letters. You can either choose how many letters you want in the word or have the number of letters determined randomly. The entire game takes place in a dialog box.

Animated Shapes

With a bit of imagination (and lots of help from VBA), you can create some simple animations in a workbook. I've put together a few examples to demonstrate how it's done. Figure 32-8 shows an example (use your imagination—it really is animated).

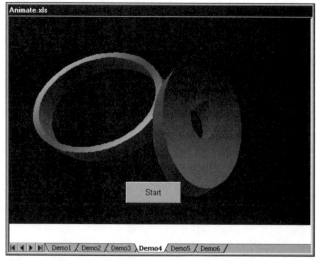

Figure 32-8: Animated Shapes.

This workbook is available on the companion CD-ROM.

Symmetrical Pattern Drawing

I must admit, this program is rather addictive — especially for doodlers. It lets you create colorful symmetrical patterns by using the arrow keys on the keyboard. Figure 32-9 shows an example. As you draw, the drawing is reproduced as mirror images in the other three quadrants. When you move the cursor to the edge of the drawing area, it wraps around and appears on the other side. This workbook is great for passing the time on the telephone when you're put on hold.

The drawing is all done with VBA macros. I used the OnKey method to trap the following key presses: left, right, up, and down. Each of these keystrokes executes a macro that shades a cell. The cells in the drawing area are very tiny, so the shading appears as lines.

This workbook is available on the companion CD-ROM

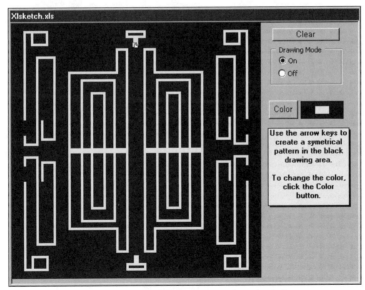

Figure 32-9: My Symmetrical Pattern Drawing worksheet.

For Guitar Players

If you play guitar, check out this workbook. As you see in Figure 32-10, this workbook has a graphic depiction of a guitar's fret board. It displays the notes (and fret positions) of the selected scale or mode in any key. You can even change the tuning of the guitar, and the formulas automatically recalculate.

On the CD-ROM

This workbook is available on the companion CD-ROM.

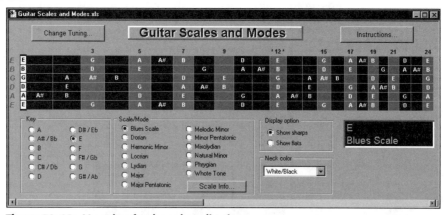

Figure 32-10: My guitar fret board application.

Other options include the choice to display half-notes as sharps or flats, to pop up information about the selected scale or mode, and to change the color of the guitar neck. This workbook uses formulas to do the calculation, and VBA plays only a minor role. This file was designated a "top pick" on America Online, and I've received positive feedback from fellow pickers all over the world.

An April Fool's Prank

Here's a good April Fool's trick to play on an office mate (with luck, one with a sense of humor). When he or she is out of the office, load this workbook and click the button to reverse the menus. For example, the Insert ⇨ Name ⇨ Define command becomes the Tresni ⇨ Eman ⇨ Enifed command. Excel's menus look like they're in a strange language. Figure 32-11 shows how this looks.

On the CD-ROM

This workbook is available on the companion CD-ROM.

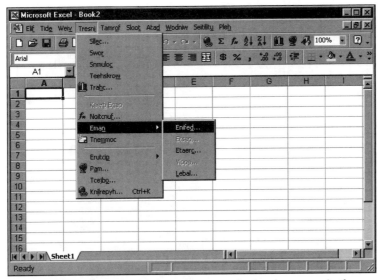

Figure 32-11: Excel with backward menus. The hot keys remain the same.

The routine performs its mischief by calling a custom function that reverses the text in the captions (except for the ellipses), converts the new text to proper case, and maintains the original hot keys. The net effect is a worksheet menu system that works exactly like the original (and is even keystroke-compatible) but looks very odd.

Clicking the Reset menu button returns the menus to normal.

Creating Word Search Puzzles

Most daily newspapers feature a word search puzzle. These puzzles contain words that are hidden in a grid. The words can be vertical, diagonal, horizontal, forwards, or backwards. If you've ever had the urge to create your own word search puzzle, this workbook can make your job a lot easier by doing it for you. You supply the words; the program places them in the grid and fills in the empty squares with random letters. Figure 32-12 shows the puzzle creation sheet plus a sample puzzle that was created with this application.

This is all done with VBA, and randomness plays a major role. Therefore, you can create multiple puzzles using the same words.

This workbook is available on the companion CD-ROM.

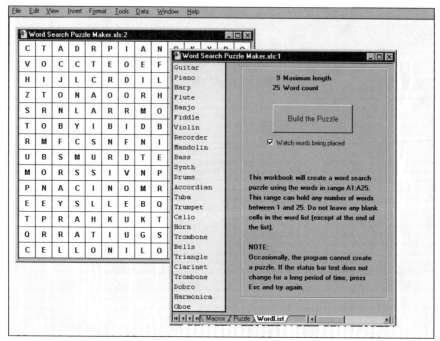

Figure 32-12: My Word Search Puzzle Maker.

ASCII Art

ASCII art consists of pictures made up of simple ASCII characters. The Internet is filled with thousands of examples of ASCII art. I created a workbook with a few examples that I picked up from the public domain. Figure 32-13 shows an example.

This workbook is available on the companion CD-ROM.

For the image to look correct, you must view ASCII art using a fixed-width font, such as Courier New.

Sound File Player

Excel doesn't have to be quiet. I created a simple macro that lets you play any WAV or MIDI file on your system.

This workbook is available on the companion CD-ROM.

Figure 32-13: An example of ASCII art.

Fun with Charts

Excel's charting feature has the potential to be fun. In this section, I provide examples of some nonserious charting applications.

Plotting Trigonometric Functions

Although I don't know too much about trigonometry, I've always enjoyed plotting various trigonometric functions as XY charts. Sometimes you can come up with attractive images. Figure 32-14 shows an example of a trigonometric plot. Clicking the button changes a random number that makes a new chart.

This workbook is available on the companion CD-ROM.

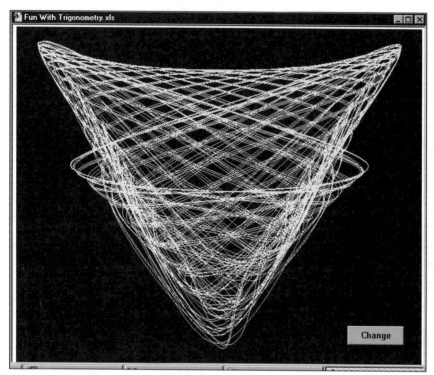

Figure 32-14: This chart plots trigonometric functions.

XY-Sketch

In this workbook, you use the controls to draw an XY chart (see Figure 32-15). Clicking a directional button adds a new X and Y value to the chart's data range, which is then plotted on the chart. You can change the step size, adjust the color, and choose between smooth and normal lines. I include a multilevel Undo button that successively removes data points that you added.

On the CD-ROM

This workbook is available on the companion CD-ROM.

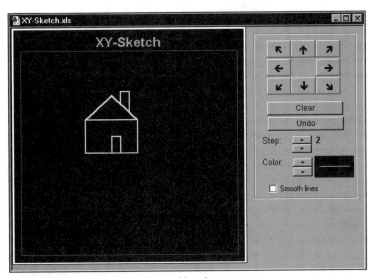

Figure 32-15: My XY-Sketch workbook.

Summary

In this chapter, I present several examples of nonserious applications for Excel. Some of these examples can most likely be adapted and used in more serious applications (well, maybe not).

✦   ✦   ✦

Customizing Excel

✦ ✦ ✦ ✦

✦ ✦ ✦ ✦

Customizing Toolbars and Menus

You're probably familiar with many of Excel's built-in toolbars, and you have most likely thoroughly explored the menu system. Excel lets you modify both toolbars and menus. This chapter explains how to customize the built-in toolbars, create new toolbars, and change the menus that Excel displays. Although many of these customizations are most useful when you create macros (discussed in subsequent chapters), even nonmacro users may find these techniques helpful.

Menu Bar = Toolbar

Beginning with Excel 97, virtually no distinction exists between a menu bar and a toolbar. In fact, the menu bar that you see at the top of Excel's window is actually a toolbar that is named Worksheet Menu Bar. As with any toolbar, you can move it to a new location by dragging it (see Figure 33-1).

Many of the menu items display icons in addition to text — a good sign that Excel's menus are not "real" menus. To further demonstrate that Excel's menu bars are different from those used in other programs, note that if you change the colors or fonts used for menus (using the Windows Control panel), these changes do not appear in Excel's menus.

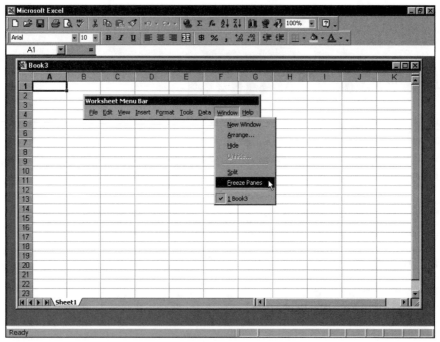

Figure 33-1: Excel's menu bar is actually a toolbar, and you can move it to any location that you want.

Customizing Toolbars

The official term for toolbars, menu bars, and shortcut menus is a *CommandBar*. All told, Excel comes with nearly 100 built-in CommandBars, made up of the following:

✦ Two menu bars (one for worksheets and one for chart sheets)

✦ 40 traditional style toolbars

✦ 51 shortcut menus (the menus that appear when you right-click a selection)

Each CommandBar consists of one or more "commands." A command can take the form of an icon, text, or both. Some additional commands don't appear on any of the prebuilt toolbars.

Many users like to create custom toolbars that contain the commands that they use most often.

How Excel Keeps Track of Toolbars

When you start Excel, it displays the same toolbar configuration that was in effect the last time that you used it. Did you ever wonder how Excel keeps track of this information? When you exit Excel, it updates a file in your Windows folder. This file stores your custom toolbars, as well as information about which toolbars are visible and the onscreen location of each. The file is stored in your Windows directory, and has an XLB extension (the actual filename will vary).

To restore the toolbars to their previous configuration, select File ⇨ Open to open this XLB file. This restores your toolbar configuration to the way that it was when you started Excel. You can also make a copy of the XLB file and give it a different name, which enables you to store multiple toolbar configurations that you can load at any time.

Types of Customizations

The following list is a summary of the types of customizations that you can make when working with toolbars (which also include menu bars):

✦ **Move toolbars.** Any toolbar can be moved to another location .

✦ **Remove buttons from built-in toolbars.** You may want to do this to eliminate buttons that you never use.

✦ **Add buttons to built-in toolbars.** You can add as many buttons as you want to any toolbar.

✦ **Create new toolbars.** You can create as many new toolbars as you like, with as many buttons as you like.

✦ **Change the functionality of a button.** You make such a change by attaching your own macro to a built-in toolbar button.

✦ **Change the image that appears on any toolbar button.** A rudimentary but functional toolbar-button editor is included with Excel.

Shortcut Menus

The casual user cannot modify Excel's shortcut menus (the menus that appear when you right-click an object). Doing so requires the use of VBA macros.

Moving Toolbars

A toolbar can be either floating or docked. A *docked* toolbar is fixed in place at the top, bottom, left, or right edge of Excel's workspace. *Floating* toolbars appear in an "always-on-top" window, and you can drag them wherever you like.

To move a toolbar, just click its border and drag it to its new position. If you drag it to one of the edges of Excel's window, it attaches itself to the edge and becomes docked. You can create several layers of docked toolbars. For example, the Standard and Formatting toolbars are (normally) both docked along the upper edge.

If a toolbar is floating, you can change its dimensions by dragging a border. For example, you can transform a horizontal toolbar to a vertical toolbar by dragging one of its corners.

Using the Customize Dialog Box

To make any changes to toolbars, you need to be in "customization mode." In customization mode, the Customize dialog box is displayed, and you can manipulate the toolbars in a number of ways. To get into customization mode, perform either of the following actions:

✦ Select View ➪ Toolbars ➪ Customize

✦ Select Customize from the shortcut menu that appears when you right-click a toolbar

Either of these methods displays the Customize dialog box that is shown in Figure 33-2. This dialog box lists all the available toolbars, including custom toolbars that you have created.

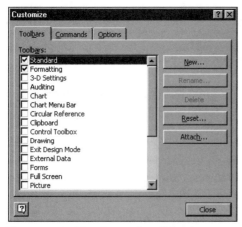

Figure 33-2: The Customize dialog box.

The Customize dialog box has three tabs, each of which is described in the following sections.

The Toolbars Tab

Figure 33-2 shows the Toolbars tab of the Customize dialog box. The following sections describe how to perform various procedures that involve toolbars.

 Caution Operations that you perform by using the Customize dialog box cannot be undone.

Hiding or displaying a toolbar

The Toolbars tab displays every toolbar (built-in toolbars and custom toolbars). Add a check mark to display a toolbar; remove the check mark to hide it. The changes take effect immediately.

Creating a new toolbar

Click the New button and then enter a name in the New Toolbar dialog box. Excel creates and displays an empty toolbar. You can then add buttons to the new toolbar. See "Adding or Removing Toolbar Buttons" later in this chapter.

Renaming a custom toolbar

Select a custom toolbar from the list and click the Rename button. Enter a new name in the Rename Toolbar dialog box. You cannot rename a built-in toolbar.

Deleting a custom toolbar

Select a custom toolbar from the list and click the Delete button. You cannot delete a built-in toolbar.

Resetting a built-in toolbar

Select a built-in toolbar from the list and click the Reset button. The toolbar is restored to its default state. If you've added any custom tools to the toolbar, they are removed. If you've removed any of the default tools, they are restored.

The Reset button is not available when a custom toolbar is selected.

Attaching a toolbar to a workbook

If you create a custom toolbar that you want to share with someone else, you can "attach" it to a workbook. To attach a custom toolbar to a workbook, click the Attach button, which presents the Attach Toolbars dialog box. Select the toolbars that you want to attach to a workbook (see Figure 33-3). You can attach any number of toolbars to a workbook.

A toolbar that's attached to a workbook appears automatically when the workbook is opened, unless the workspace already has a toolbar by the same name.

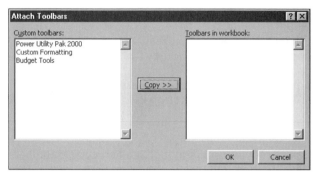

Figure 33-3: You can attach custom toolbars to a workbook in the Attach Toolbars menu.

The toolbar that's stored in the workbook is an exact copy of the toolbar at the time that you attach it. If you modify the toolbar after attaching it, the changed version is not stored in the workbook automatically. You must manually remove the old toolbar and then add the edited toolbar.

The Commands Tab

The Commands tab of the Customize dialog box contains a list of every tool that's available. Use this tab when you customize a toolbar. This feature is described later in the chapter (see "Adding or Removing Toolbar Buttons").

The Options Tab

The Options tab of the Customize dialog box, shown in Figure 33-4, gives you several choices of ways to customize your menus, toolbars, icons, and the like. The following list explains these options.

✦ **Personalized Menus and Toolbars:** On the Options tab, the new options of Excel 2000 are Personalized Menus and Toolbars and, in the Other area, List font names in their font.

• These options provide you with some control over how the menus and toolbars work. Set these options according to your personal preferences.

✦ **Large icons:** To change the size of the icons used in toolbars, select or deselect the Large icons check box. This option only affects the images that are in buttons. Buttons that contain only text (such as buttons in a menu) don't change.

✦ **List font names in their font:** This new feature displays the font names using the actual font. The advantage is that you can preview the font before you select it. The disadvantage is that it's a bit slower.

✦ **Show ScreenTips on toolbar:** ScreenTips are the pop-up messages that display the button names when you pause the mouse pointer over a button. If you find the ScreenTips distracting, remove the check mark from the Show ScreenTips on toolbars check box. The status bar still displays a description of the button when you move the mouse pointer over it.

✦ **Menu animations:** When you select a menu, Excel animates the display of the menu as it is dropping down. You can select the type of animation that you want:

- **Slide:** The menu drops down with a sliding motion

- **Unfold:** The menu unfolds as it drops down

- **Random:** The menu either slides or unfolds randomly

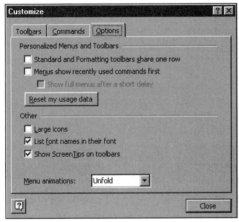

Figure 33-4: The Options tab of the Customize dialog box.

Toolbar Autosensing

Normally, Excel displays a particular toolbar automatically when you change contexts; this is called *autosensing*. For example, when you activate a chart, the Chart toolbar appears. When you activate a sheet that contains a pivot table, the PivotTable toolbar appears.

You can easily defeat autosensing by hiding the toolbar. After you do so, Excel no longer displays that toolbar when you switch to its former context. You can restore this automatic behavior, however, by displaying the appropriate toolbar when you're in the appropriate context. Thereafter, Excel reverts to its normal automatic toolbar display when you switch to that context.

Adding or Removing Toolbar Buttons

As noted earlier in this chapter, you can put Excel into customization mode by displaying the Customize dialog box. When Excel is in customization mode, you have access to all the commands and options in the Customize dialog box. In addition, you can perform the following actions:

✦ Reposition a button on a toolbar

✦ Move a button to a different toolbar

✦ Copy a button from one toolbar to another

✦ Add new buttons to a toolbar by using the Commands tab of the Customize dialog box

Moving and Copying Buttons

When the Customize dialog box is displayed, you can copy and move buttons freely among any visible toolbars. To move a button, drag it to its new location (the new location can be within the current toolbar or on a different toolbar).

To copy a button, press Ctrl while you drag the button to another toolbar. You can also copy a toolbar button within the same toolbar, but no reason really exists to have multiple copies of a button the same toolbar.

Inserting a New Button

To add a new button to a toolbar, you use the Commands tab of the Customize dialog box (see Figure 33-5).

Figure 33-5: The Commands tab contains a list of every available button.

New in Excel 2000: An Easier Way to Add or Remove Buttons

Excel 2000 provides a much simpler way to add or remove buttons from a toolbar. Just click the arrow at the end of the toolbar and select Add or Remove Buttons. You'll see a list of all the buttons for the toolbar (see the accompanying figure).

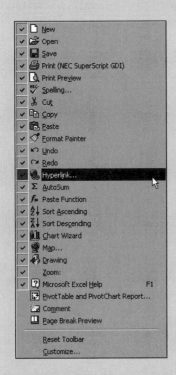

Buttons displayed with a check mark are visible in the toolbar; those without a check mark are not visible in the toolbar. Simply add or remove the check marks according to your preferences. For additional types of customization, you need to use the Customize dialog box.

The buttons are arranged in 16 categories. When you select a category, the buttons in that category appear to the right in the Commands list box. To determine a button's function, select it and click the Description button.

To add a button to a toolbar, locate it in the Commands tab and then click and drag it to the toolbar.

Other Toolbar Button Operations

When Excel is in customization mode (that is, the Customize dialog box is displayed), you can right-click a toolbar button to get a shortcut menu of additional actions for the tool. Figure 33-6 shows the shortcut menu that appears when you right-click a button in customization mode.

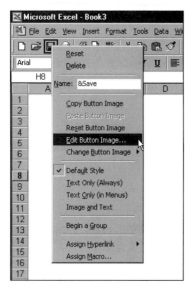

Figure 33-6: In customization mode, right-clicking a button displays this shortcut menu.

These commands are described in the following list (note that some of these commands are not available for certain toolbar tools):

✦ **Reset:** Resets the tool to its original state.

✦ **Delete:** Deletes the tool.

✦ **Name:** Lets you change the name of the tool.

✦ **Copy Button Image:** Makes a copy of the button's image and places it on the Clipboard.

✦ **Paste Button Image:** Pastes the image from the Clipboard to the button.

✦ **Reset Button Image:** Restores the button's original image.

✦ **Edit Button Image:** Lets you edit the button's image, using Excel's button editor.

✦ **Change Button Image:** Lets you change the image by selecting from a list of 42 button images.

✦ **Default Style:** Displays the tool with its default style (either text only or image and text).

✦ **Text Only (Always):** Always displays text (no image) for the tool.

✦ **Text Only (In Menus):** Displays text (no image) if the tool is in a menu bar.

✦ **Image and Text:** Displays the tool's image and text.

✦ **Begin a Group:** Inserts a divider in the toolbar. In a drop-down menu, a separator bar appears as a horizontal line between commands. In a toolbar, a separator bar appears as a vertical line.

✦ **Assign Hyperlink:** Lets you assign a hyperlink that will activate a Web page.

✦ **Assign Macro:** Lets you assign a macro that is executed when the button is clicked.

 Assign Hyperlink is a new feature of Excel 2000.

Creating a Custom Toolbar: An Example

This section walks you through the steps that are used to create a custom toolbar. This toolbar is an enhanced Formatting toolbar that contains many additional formatting tools that aren't found on Excel's built-in Formatting toolbar. You may want to replace the built-in Formatting toolbar with this new custom toolbar.

 If you don't want to create this toolbar yourself, this workbook is available on this book's CD-ROM.

Adding the First Button

The following steps are required to create this new toolbar and add one button (which has five subcommands):

1. Right-click any toolbar and select Customize from the shortcut menu.

   Excel displays its Customize dialog box.

2. Click the Toolbars tab and then click New.

   Excel displays its New Toolbar dialog box.

3. Enter a name for the toolbar: **Custom Formatting**. Click OK.

   Excel creates a new (empty) toolbar.

4. In the Customize dialog box, click the Commands tab.

5. In the Categories list, scroll down and select New Menu.

   The New Menu category has only one command (New Menu), which appears in the Commands list.

6. Drag the New Menu command from the Commands list to the new toolbar.

   This creates a menu button in the new toolbar.

7. Right-click the New Menu button in the new toolbar and change the name to **Font**.

8. In the Customize dialog box, select Format from the Categories list.

9. Scroll down through the Commands list and drag the Bold command to the Font button in your new toolbar.

   This step makes the Font button display a submenu (Bold) when the button is clicked.

10. Repeat Step 9, adding the following buttons from the Format category: Italic, Underline, Font Size, and Font.

At this point, you may want to click the Close button in the Customize dialog box to try out your new toolbar. The new toolbar contains only one button, but this button expands to show five font-related commands. Figure 33-7 shows the Custom Formatting toolbar at this stage.

Figure 33-7: A new Custom Formatting toolbar after adding a menu button with five commands. In this example, Underline is selected.

Adding More Buttons

If you followed the steps in the previous section, you should understand how toolbar customization works, and you can now add additional buttons by following the procedures that you learned. To finish the toolbar, right-click a toolbar button and select Customize. Then, add additional tools.

Figure 33-8 shows the final version of the Custom Formatting toolbar, and Table 33-1 describes the tools on this toolbar. This customized toolbar includes all the tools that are on the built-in Formatting toolbar — plus quite a few more (38 tools in all). But, because the Custom Formatting toolbar uses five menus (which expand to show more commands), the toolbar takes up a relatively small amount of space.

You can, of course, customize the toolbar any way that you like. The tools that are listed in the table are my preferences. You may prefer to omit tools that you never use — or add other tools that you use frequently.

With two exceptions, all the tools are found in the Formatting category. The Clear Formatting tool is in the Edit category, and the Format Cells tool is in the Built-In Menus category.

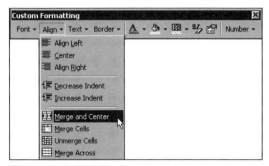

Figure 33-8: The final version of the Custom Formatting toolbar.

Table 33-1 Tools in the Custom Formatting Toolbar	
Tool	**Subcommands**
New Menu (renamed Font)	Bold, Italic, Underline, Font Size, Font
New Menu (renamed Align)	Align Left, Center, Align Right, Decrease Indent, Increase Indent, Merge and Center, Merge Cells, Unmerge Cells, Merge Across
New Menu (renamed Text)	Vertical Text, Rotate Text Up, Rotate Text Down, Angle Text Downward, Angle Text Upward
New Menu (renamed Border)	Clear Border, Apply Outline Borders, Apply Inside Border, Left Border, Right Border, Top Border, Bottom Border, Inside Vertical Border, Inside Horizontal Border, Bottom Double Border
Font Color	(none)
Fill Color	(none)
Pattern	(none)
Clear Formatting	(none)
Format Cells	(none)
New Menu (renamed Number)	Currency Style, Percent Style, Comma Style, Decrease Decimal, Increase Decimal

Saving the Custom Toolbar

Excel doesn't have a command to save a toolbar. Rather, the new toolbar is saved when you exit Excel. Refer to the sidebar "How Excel Keeps Track of Toolbars," earlier in this chapter.

Caution You need to remember that if Excel shuts down by non-normal means (that is, it crashes!), your custom toolbar will be lost. Therefore, if you invest a lot of time creating a new toolbar, you should close Excel to force the new toolbar to be saved.

Changing a Toolbar Button's Image

To change the image that is displayed on a toolbar button, you have several options:

✦ Choose 1 of the 42 images that are provided by Excel

✦ Modify or create the image by using Excel's Button Editor dialog box

✦ Copy an image from another toolbar button

Each of these methods is discussed in the following sections.

To make any changes to a button image, you must be in toolbar customization mode (the Customize dialog box must be visible). Right-click any toolbar button and select Customize from the shortcut menu.

Using a Built-in Image

To change the image on a toolbar button, right-click the button and select Change Button Image from the shortcut menu. As you can see in Figure 33-9, this menu expands to show 42 images from which you can choose. Just click the image that you want, and the selected button's image changes.

Editing a Button Image

If none of the 42 built-in images suits your tastes, you can edit an existing image or create a new image by using Excel's Button Editor.

To begin editing, right-click the button that you want to edit and then choose Edit Button Image from the shortcut menu. The image appears in the Button Editor dialog box (see Figure 33-10), in which you can change individual pixels and shift the entire image up, down, to the left, or to the right. If you've never worked with icons before, you may be surprised at how difficult it is to create attractive images in such a small area.

The Edit Button Image dialog box is straightforward. Just click a color and then click a pixel (or drag across pixels). When it looks good, click OK. Or, if you don't like what you've done, click Cancel, and the button keeps its original image.

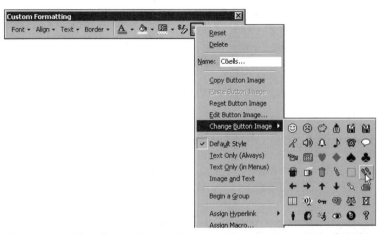

Figure 33-9: The Change Button Image option gives you 42 built-in button images to choose from.

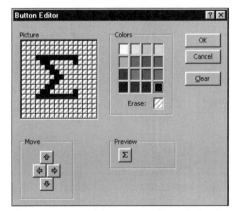

Figure 33-10: The Button Editor dialog box, in which you can design your own button image or edit an existing one.

Copying Another Button Image

Another way to get a button image on a custom toolbar is to copy it from another toolbar button. Right-click a toolbar button, and it displays a shortcut menu that enables you to copy a button image to the Clipboard or paste the Clipboard contents to the selected button.

Activating a Web Page from a Toolbar Button

You might want to create a button that activates your Web browser and loads a Web page.

 EXCEL 2000   This feature is available only in Excel 2000.

To add a new button and attach a hyperlink, make sure that you're in toolbar customization mode. Use the procedure previously described to add a new button and (optionally) specify a button image. Then, right-click the button and select Assign Hyperlink ➪ Open. You'll see the Assign Hyperlink: Open dialog box, shown in Figure 33-11. Type a URL or select one from the list.

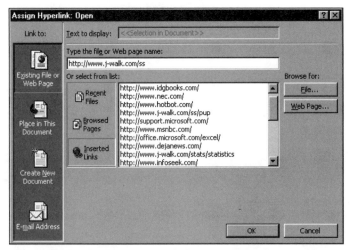

Figure 33-11: The Assign Hyperlink: Open dialog box enables you to assign a hyperlink to a toolbar button.

Summary

This chapter discusses how to modify two components of Excel's user interface: toolbars and menus. Users of all levels can benefit from creating custom toolbars. To create new commands that are executed by toolbar buttons, however, you need to write macros. This chapter also discusses how to change the image that appears on a toolbar button, and then introduces Excel's menu editor, which is most useful for macro writers.

✦   ✦   ✦

Using and Creating Templates

This chapter covers one of the most potentially useful features in Excel — template files. Templates can be used for a variety of purposes, ranging from custom "fill-in-the-blanks" workbooks to a way to change Excel's defaults for new workbooks or new worksheets.

An Overview of Templates

A *template* is essentially a model that serves as the basis for something else. An Excel template is a workbook that's used to create other workbooks. If you understand this concept, you may save yourself a lot of work. For example, you may always use a particular header on your printouts. Consequently, every time that you print a worksheet, you need to select File ➪ Page Setup to add your page header. The solution is to create a new workbook by modifying the template that Excel uses. In this case, you modify the template file by inserting your header into the template. Save the template file, and then every new workbook that you create has your customized page header.

Excel supports three types of templates:

✦ **The default workbook template:** Used as the basis for new workbooks.

✦ **The default worksheet template:** Used as the basis for new worksheets that are inserted into a workbook.

✦ **Custom workbook templates:** Usually, ready-to-run workbooks that include formulas. Typically, these templates are set up so that a user can simply plug in values and get immediate results. The Spreadsheet Solutions templates (included with Excel) are examples of this type of template.

Each template type is discussed in the following sections.

The Default Workbook Template

Every new workbook that you create starts out with some default settings. For example, the workbook's worksheets have gridlines, text appears in Arial 10-point font, values that are entered display in the General number format, and so on. If you're not happy with any of the default workbook settings, you can change them.

Changing the Workbook Defaults

Making changes to Excel's default workbook is fairly easy to do, and it can save you lots of time in the long run. Take the following steps to change Excel's workbook defaults:

1. Start with a new workbook.

2. Add or delete sheets to give the workbook the number of worksheets that you want.

3. Make any other changes that you want to make, which can include column widths, named styles, page setup options, and many of the settings that are available in the Options dialog box.

 Tip
To change the default formatting for cells, choose Format ➪ Style, and then modify the settings for the Normal style. For example, you can change the default font, size, or number format. Refer to "Using Named Styles" in Chapter 11 for details.

4. When your workbook is set up to your liking, select File ➪ Save As.

5. In the Save As dialog box, select Template (*.xlt) from the Save as type box.

6. Enter **book.xlt** for the filename.

7. Save the file in your \XLStart folder. This folder is probably located within your c:\Program Files\Microsoft Office\Office folder.

   You can also save your book.xlt template file in the folder that is specified as an alternate startup folder. You specify an alternate startup folder in the General tab of the Options dialog box.

8. Close the file.

After you perform the preceding steps, the new default workbook is based on the book.xlt workbook template. You can create a workbook based on your template by using any of the following methods:

✦ Click the New button on the Standard toolbar

✦ Press Ctrl+N

✦ Choose File ➪ New and then select the Workbook icon in the General tab of the New dialog box (see Figure 34-1)

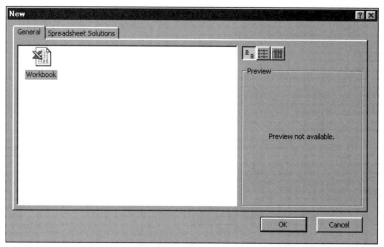

Figure 34-1: After you create a book.xlt template, clicking the Workbook icon creates a new workbook that is based on your template.

Note Normally, the Xlstart folder does not contain a file named book.xlt. If a file with this name is not present, Excel creates new workbooks using built-in default settings.

Editing the book.xlt Template

After you create your book.xlt template, you may discover that you need to change it. You can open the book.xlt template file and edit it just like any other workbook. After you finish with your edits, save the workbook and close it.

Resetting the Default Workbook

If you create a book.xlt file and then decide that you would rather use the standard default workbook settings, simply delete the book.xlt template file from the Xlstart folder. Excel then resorts to its built-in default settings for new workbooks.

The Default Worksheet Template

When you insert a new worksheet into a workbook, Excel uses its built-in worksheet defaults for the worksheet. This includes items such as column width, row height, and so on.

Note Versions of Excel prior to Excel 97 also use other sheet templates (dialog.xlt and macro.xlt). These templates are not used in Excel 97 or later versions.

If you don't like the default settings for a new worksheet, you can change them by using the following procedure:

1. Start with a new workbook, deleting all the sheets except one.

2. Make any changes that you want to make, which can include column widths, named styles, page setup options, and many of the settings that are available in the Options dialog box.

3. When your workbook is set up to your liking, select File ➪ Save As.

4. In the Save As dialog box, select Template (*.xlt) from the Save as type box.

5. Enter **sheet.xlt** for the filename.

6. Save the file in your \XLStart folder. This folder is probably located within your c:\Program Files\Microsoft Office\Office folder.

    You can also save your book.xlt template file in the folder that is specified as an alternate startup folder. You specify an alternate startup folder in the General tab of the Options dialog box.

7. Close the file.

After performing this procedure, all new sheets that you insert with the Insert ➪ Worksheet command are formatted like your sheet.xlt template.

When you right-click a sheet tab and choose Insert from the shortcut menu, Excel displays its Insert dialog box (which looks just like the New dialog box). If you've created a template named sheet.xlt, you can select it by clicking the icon labeled Worksheet.

Editing the sheet.xlt Template

After you create your sheet.xlt template, you may discover that you need to change it. You can open the sheet.xlt template file and edit it just like any other workbook. After you make your changes, save the file and close it.

Resetting the Default New Worksheet

If you create a sheet.xlt template and then decide that you would rather use the standard default new worksheet settings, simply delete the sheet.xlt template file from the Xlstart folder. Excel then resorts to its built-in default settings for new worksheets.

Custom Workbook Templates

The book.xlt and sheet.xlt templates discussed in the previous section are two special types of templates that determine default settings for new workbooks and new worksheets. This section discusses other types of templates, referred to as *workbook templates,* which are simply workbooks that are set up to be used as the basis for new workbooks.

Why use a workbook template? The simple answer is that it saves you from repeating work. Assume that you create a monthly sales report that consists of your company's sales by region, plus several summary calculations and charts. You can create a template file that consists of everything except the input values. Then, when it's time to create your report, you can open a workbook based on the template, fill in the blanks, and you're finished.

You could, of course, just use the previous month's workbook and save it with a different name. This is prone to errors, however, because you easily can forget to use the Save As command and accidentally overwrite the previous month's file.

How Templates Work

When you create a workbook that is based on a template, Excel creates a copy of the template in memory so that the original template remains intact. The default workbook name is the template name with a number appended. For example, if you create a new workbook based on a template named Sales Report.xlt, the workbook's default name is Sales Report1.xls. The first time that you save a workbook that is created from a template, Excel displays its Save As dialog box, so that you can give the template a new name if you want to.

Templates That Are Included with Excel

Excel ships with three workbook templates (called Spreadsheet Solutions templates), which were developed by Village Software. When you select File ➪ New, you can select one of these templates from the New dialog box. Click the tab labeled Spreadsheet Solutions to choose one of the following templates upon which to base your new workbook (see Figure 34-2).

EXCEL 2000 These templates are included with Excel 2000.

✦ **Expense Statement:** Helps you to create expense report forms and a log to track them

✦ **Invoice:** Helps you to create invoices

✦ **Purchase Order:** Helps you to create purchase orders to send to vendors

 Note A fourth template, named Village Software.xlt, describes additional templates that you can obtain from Village Software.

 Tip You can also download some additional templates from Microsoft's Web site: http://www.microsoft.com/excel.

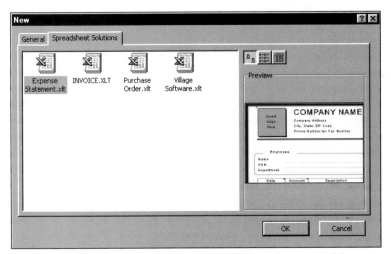

Figure 34-2: You can create a new workbook based on one of the Spreadsheet Solutions templates.

Creating Custom Templates

This section describes how to create workbook templates, which is really quite simple.

A *custom template* is essentially a normal workbook, and it can use any of Excel's features, such as charts, formulas, and macros. Usually, a template is set up so that the user can enter values and get immediate results. In other words, most templates include everything but the data—which is entered by the user.

If the template is going to be used by novices, you may consider locking all the cells except the input cells (use the Protection panel of the Format Cells dialog box for this). Then, protect the worksheet by choosing Tools ➪ Protection ➪ Protect Sheet.

To save the workbook as a template, choose File ➪ Save As and select Template (*.xlt) from the drop-down list labeled Save as type. Save the template in your Microsoft Office\Templates folder (or a folder within that Templates folder).

Before you save the template, you may want to specify that the file be saved with a preview image. Select File ➪ Properties, and check the box that is labeled Save Preview Picture. That way, the New dialog box displays the preview when the template's icon is selected.

Where to Store Your Templates

Template files can be stored anywhere. When you open a template file (by selecting File ➪ New), you don't actually open the template. Rather, Excel creates a new workbook that's based on the template that you specify. However, your templates are easier to access if you store them in one of the following locations:

✦ **Your \XLStart folder:** This is probably located within c:\Program Files\Microsoft Office\Office. If you create a default workbook template (book.xlt) or a default worksheet template (sheet.xlt), you store these templates in this folder.

✦ **Your \Templates folder:** This is probably located within your c:\Program Files\Microsoft Office\Office folder. Custom templates that are stored here appear in the New dialog box.

✦ **A folder located in your \Templates folder:** If you create a new folder within this folder, its name appears as a tab in the New dialog box. Clicking the tab displays the templates that are stored in that folder. The accompanying figure shows how the New dialog box looks when a new folder (named John's Templates) is in the Templates folder.

If you've specified an alternate startup folder (using the General panel of the Options dialog box), templates that are stored in that location also appear in the New dialog box.

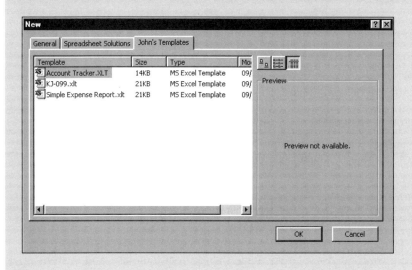

If you later discover that you want to modify the template, choose File ➪ Open to open and edit the template (don't use the File ➪ New command, which creates a workbook that is based on the template).

Ideas for Creating Templates

This section provides a few ideas that may spark your imagination for creating templates. A partial list of the settings that you can adjust and use in your custom templates is as follows:

✦ **Multiple formatted worksheets:** You can, for example, create a workbook template that has two worksheets: one formatted to print in landscape mode and one formatted to print in portrait mode.

✦ **Workbook properties:** You can set one or more workbook properties. For example, Excel doesn't store a preview picture of your workbook. Select File ⇨ Properties and then change the Save Preview Picture option in the Summary panel.

✦ **Several settings in the View panel of the Options dialog box:** For example, you may not like to see sheet tabs, so you can turn off this setting.

✦ **Color palette:** Use the Color panel of the Options dialog box to create a custom color palette for a workbook.

✦ **Style:** The best approach is to choose Format ⇨ Style and modify the attributes of the Normal style. For example, you can change the font or size, the alignment, and so on.

✦ **Custom number formats:** If you create number formats that you use frequently, these can be stored in a template.

✦ **Column widths and row heights:** You may prefer that columns be wider or narrower, or you may want the rows to be taller.

✦ **Print settings:** Change these settings in the Page Setup dialog box. You can adjust the page orientation, paper size, margins, header and footer, and several other attributes.

✦ **Sheet settings:** These are options in the Options dialog box. They include gridlines, automatic page break display, and row and column headers.

Summary

This chapter introduces the concept of templates. Excel supports three template types: a default workbook template, a default worksheet template, and custom workbook templates. This chapter describes how to create such templates and where to store them. It also discusses the Template Wizard, a tool that helps you to create templates that can store data in a central database.

✦ ✦ ✦

Using Visual Basic for Applications

This chapter is an introduction to the Visual Basic for Applications (VBA) macro language — perhaps the key component for users who want to customize Excel. A complete discussion of VBA would require an entire book. This chapter teaches you how to record macros and create simple macro subroutines. Subsequent chapters expand upon the topics in this chapter.

Introducing VBA Macros

In its broadest sense, a *macro* is a sequence of instructions that automates some aspect of Excel so that you can work more efficiently and with fewer errors. You may create a macro, for example, to format and print your month-end sales report. After the macro is developed and debugged, you can invoke the macro — with a single command — to perform many time-consuming procedures automatically.

Macros are usually considered to be one of the advanced features of Excel, because you must have a pretty thorough understanding of Excel to put them to good use. The truth is that the majority of Excel users have never created a macro and probably never will. If you want to explore one of the most powerful aspects of Excel, however, you should know about macros. This chapter is designed to acquaint you with VBA, which enables you to develop simple macros and execute macros that are developed by others.

Are Macros for You?

You need not be a power user to create and use simple VBA macros. Casual users can simply turn on Excel's macro recorder: Excel records and then converts your subsequent actions into a VBA macro — which is essentially a program. When you execute this program, Excel performs the actions again. More advanced users, though, can write code that tells Excel to perform tasks that can't be recorded. For example, you can write procedures that display custom dialog boxes, add new commands to Excel's menus, or process data in a series of workbooks.

VBA: One of Two Macro Languages in Excel

VBA was introduced in Excel 5. Prior to that version, Excel used an entirely different macro system, known as *XLM* (that is, the Excel 4 macro language). VBA is far superior in terms of both power and ease of use. For compatibility reasons, however, the XLM language is still supported in Excel 2000. This means that you can load an older Excel file and still execute the macros that are stored in it. However, Excel 2000 does not let you record XLM macros — and you really have no reason to do so.

What You Can Do with VBA

VBA is an extremely rich programming language with thousands of uses. The following list contains just a few things that you can do with VBA macros:

✦ **Insert a text string or formula:** If you need to enter your company name into worksheets frequently, you can create a macro to do the typing for you. The AutoCorrect feature can also do this.

✦ **Automate a procedure that you perform frequently:** For example, you may need to prepare a month-end summary. If the task is straightforward, you can develop a macro to do it for you.

✦ **Automate repetitive operations:** If you need to perform the same action in 12 different workbooks, you can record a macro while you perform the task once — and then let the macro repeat your action in the other workbooks.

✦ **Create a custom command:** For example, you can combine several of Excel's menu commands so that they are executed from a single keystroke or from a single mouse click.

✦ **Create a custom toolbar button:** You can customize Excel's toolbars with your own buttons to execute macros that you write.

✦ **Create a simplified "front end" for users who don't know much about Excel:** For example, you can set up a foolproof data entry template.

✦ **Develop a new worksheet function:** Although Excel includes a wide assortment of built-in functions, you can create custom functions that greatly simplify your formulas.

✦ **Create complete, turnkey, macro-driven applications:** Excel macros can display custom dialog boxes and add new commands to the menu bar.

✦ **Create custom add-ins for Excel:** Most of the add-ins that are shipped with Excel were created with Excel macros. I used VBA exclusively to create my Power Utility Pak.

Two Types of VBA Macros

Before getting into the details of creating macros, you need to understand a key distinction. A VBA macro (or procedure) can be one of two types: a *subroutine* or a *function*. The next two sections discuss the difference.

VBA Subroutines

You can think of a *subroutine macro* as a new command that can be executed by either the user or another macro. You can have any number of subroutines in an Excel workbook.

Figure 35-1 shows a simple VBA subroutine. When this subroutine is executed, VBA inserts the current date into the active cell, formats it, and then adjusts the column width.

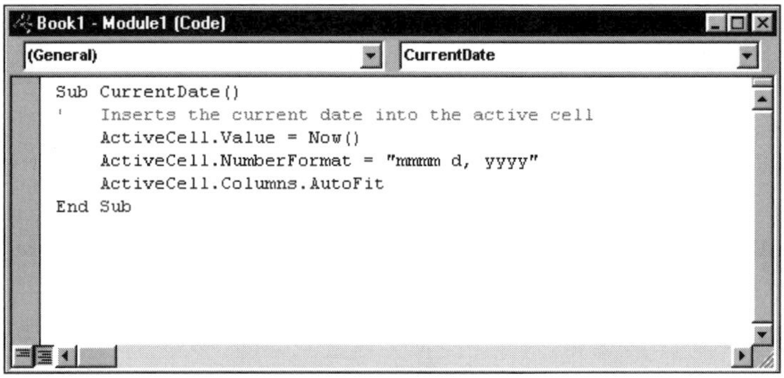

```
Sub CurrentDate()
'    Inserts the current date into the active cell
     ActiveCell.Value = Now()
     ActiveCell.NumberFormat = "mmmm d, yyyy"
     ActiveCell.Columns.AutoFit
End Sub
```

Figure 35-1: A simple VBA subroutine.

Subroutines always start with the keyword Sub, the macro's name (every macro must have a unique name), and then a pair of parentheses. (The parentheses are required; they are empty unless the procedure uses one or more arguments.) The End Sub statement signals the end of a subroutine. The lines in between comprise the procedure's code.

Using VBA in Excel 2000

If you've used VBA in an Excel version prior to Excel 97, you should be aware that Excel 2000 handles VBA very differently than do previous versions. The following is a list of a few of the key areas in which Excel 2000 differs from Excel 95 and Excel 5:

✦ Excel 2000 does not display module sheets in a workbook. To view or edit VBA code, you must activate the Visual Basic Editor (Alt+F11 toggles between Excel and the Visual Basic Editor).

✦ Excel 2000 makes use of UserForms rather than dialog sheets. You create and edit UserForms in the Visual Basic Editor. A UserForm also contains the VBA code that works with the objects in the form. This feature is discussed in Chapter 37.

✦ Excel 2000 includes many new objects and methods, providing the macro programmer with a great deal of new capability.

Excel 5 and Excel 95 macros and dialog boxes continue to work in Excel 2000. However, the compatibility is not perfect, and you may notice a few problems due to changes.

The subroutine shown in Figure 35-1 also includes a comment. *Comments* are simply notes to yourself, and they are ignored by VBA. A comment line begins with an apostrophe. You can also put a comment after a statement. In other words, when VBA encounters an apostrophe, it ignores the rest of the text in the line.

You execute a subroutine in any of the following ways:

✦ Choose Tools ⇨ Macro and then select the subroutine's name from the list.

✦ Press the subroutine's shortcut key combination (if it has one).

✦ If the Visual Basic Editor is active, move the cursor anywhere within the subroutine and press F5.

✦ Refer to the subroutine in another VBA procedure.

Subroutines are covered in detail later in this chapter.

VBA Functions

The second type of VBA procedure is a function. A *function* always returns a single value (just as a worksheet function always returns a single value). A VBA function can be executed by other VBA procedures or used in worksheet formulas, just as you would use Excel's built-in worksheet functions.

Some Definitions

VBA newcomers are often overwhelmed by the terminology that is used in VBA. I've put together some key definitions to help you keep the terms straight. These terms cover VBA and UserForms (custom dialog boxes) — two important elements that are used to customize Excel:

✦ **Code:** VBA instructions that are produced in a module sheet when you record a macro. You also can enter VBA code manually.

✦ **Controls:** Objects on a UserForm (or in a worksheet) that you manipulate. Examples include buttons, check boxes, and list boxes.

✦ **Function:** One of two types of VBA macros that you can create (the other is a subroutine). A function returns a single value. You can use VBA functions in other VBA macros or in your worksheets.

✦ **Macro:** A set of Excel instructions that are performed automatically. Excel macros can be XLM macros or VBA macros. This book focuses exclusively on VBA macros, which are also known as *procedures.*

✦ **Method:** An action that is taken on an object. For example, applying the Clear method to a range object erases the contents of the cells.

✦ **Module:** A container for VBA code.

✦ **Object:** An element that you manipulate with VBA. Examples include ranges, charts, drawing objects, and so on.

✦ **Procedure:** Another name for a macro. A VBA procedure can be a subroutine or a function.

✦ **Property:** A particular aspect of an object. For example, a range object has properties such as Height, Style, and Name.

✦ **Subroutine:** One of two types of Visual Basic macros that you can create. The other is a function.

✦ **UserForm**: A container that holds controls for a custom dialog box, and holds VBA code to manipulate the controls. (Custom dialog boxes are explained in depth in Chapter 36).

✦ **VBA:** Visual Basic for Applications. The macro language that is available in Excel as well as in the other applications in Microsoft Office 2000.

✦ **VBE:** Visual Basic Editor. The window (separate from Excel) that you use to create VBA macros and UserForms.

Figure 35-2 shows the listing of a custom worksheet function and shows the function in use in a worksheet. This function is named CubeRoot and requires a single argument. CubeRoot calculates the cube root of its argument. A function looks much like a subroutine. Notice, however, that function procedures begin with the keyword, Function, and end with an End Function statement.

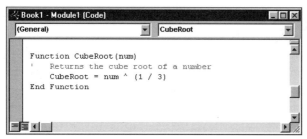

Figure 35-2: This VBA function returns the cube root of its argument.

Creating VBA functions that you use in worksheet formulas can simplify your formulas and enable you to perform calculations that otherwise may be impossible. VBA functions are discussed in greater detail in Chapter 36.

Creating VBA Macros

Excel provides two ways to create macros:

✦ Turn on the macro recorder and record your actions

✦ Enter the code directly into a VBA module

The following sections describe both of these methods.

Recording VBA Macros

The basic steps that you take to record a VBA macro are described in this section. In most cases, you can record your actions as a macro and then simply replay the macro; you needn't look at the code that's generated. If this is as far as you go with VBA, you don't need to be concerned with the language itself (although a basic understanding of how things work doesn't do any harm).

Recording Your Actions to Create VBA Code: The Basics

Excel's macro recorder translates your actions into VBA code. To start the macro recorder, choose Tools ➪ Macro ➪ Record New Macro. Excel displays the Record Macro dialog box, shown in Figure 35-3.

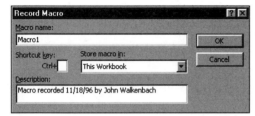

Figure 35-3: The Record Macro dialog box.

The Record Macro dialog box presents several options:

✦ **Macro name:** The name of the macro. By default, Excel proposes names such as Macro1, Macro2, and so on.

✦ **Shortcut key:** You can specify a key combination that executes the macro. You can also press Shift when you enter a letter. For example, pressing Shift while you enter the letter H makes the shortcut key combination Ctrl+Shift+H.

✦ **Store macro in:** The location for the macro. Your choices are the current workbook, your Personal Macro Workbook (described later in this chapter), or a new workbook.

✦ **Description:** A description of the macro. By default, Excel inserts the date and your name. You can add additional information if you like.

To begin recording your actions, click OK. Excel displays the Stop Recording toolbar, which contains two buttons: Stop Recording and Relative Reference. After you finish recording the macro, choose Tools ➪ Macro ➪ Stop Recording (or click the Stop Recording button on the toolbar).

Note   Recording your actions always results in a new subroutine procedure. You can't create a function procedure by using the macro recorder. Function procedures must be created manually.

Recording a Macro: An Example

This example demonstrates how to record a macro that changes the formatting for the current range selection. The macro makes the selected range use Arial 16-point type, boldface, and the color red. To create the macro, follow these steps:

1. Enter a value or text into a cell — anything is okay. This gives you something to start with.

2. Select the cell that contains the value or text that you entered in the preceding step.

3. Select Tools ➪ Macro ➪ Record New Macro. Excel displays the Record Macro dialog box.

4. Enter a new name for the macro, to replace the default Macro1 name. A good name is **FormattingMacro**.

5. Assign this macro to the shortcut key Ctrl+Shift+F by entering **F** in the edit box labeled Shortcut key.

6. Click OK. This closes the Record Macro dialog box. Excel displays a toolbar called Stop Recording.

7. Select Format ➪ Cells and then click the Font tab. Choose Arial font, Bold, and 16-point type, and make the color red. Click OK to close the Format Cells dialog box.

8. The macro is finished, so click the Stop Recording button on the Stop Recording toolbar (or select Tools ➪ Macro ➪ Stop Recording).

Examining the Macro

The macro was recorded in a new module named Module1. To view the code in this module, you must activate the Visual Basic Editor (VBE). You can activate the VBE in either of two ways:

✦ Press Alt+F11

✦ Choose Tools ➪ Macro ➪ Visual Basic Editor

Figure 35-4 shows the VBE window. Although the module is stored in the Excel workbook, you can view the module only in the VBE window.

The Project window displays a list of all open workbooks and add-ins. This list is displayed as a tree diagram, which can be expanded or collapsed. The code that you recorded previously is stored in Module1 in the current workbook. When you double-click Module1, the code in the module is displayed in the Code window.

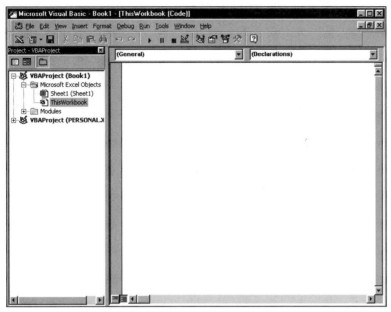

Figure 35-4: The VBE window.

Figure 35-5 shows the recorded macro, as displayed in the Code window.

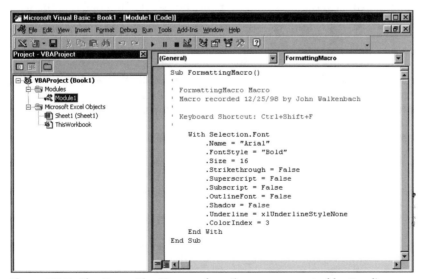

Figure 35-5: The FormattingMacro subroutine was generated by Excel's macro recorder.

Activate the module and examine the macro. It should consist of the following code:

```
Sub FormattingMacro Macro()
'
' FormatCells Macro
' Macro recorded by John Walkenbach
'
' Keyboard Shortcut: Ctrl+Shift+F
'
    With Selection.Font
        .Name = "Arial"
        .FontStyle = "Bold"
        .Size = 16
        .Strikethrough = False
        .Superscript = False
        .Subscript = False
        .OutlineFont = False
        .Shadow = False
        .Underline = xlUnderlineStyleNone
        .ColorIndex = 3
    End With
End Sub
```

The macro recorded is a subroutine (it begins with a Sub statement) that is named FormattingMacro. The statements tell Excel what to do when the macro is executed.

Notice that Excel inserted some comments at the top of the subroutine. This is the information that appeared in the Record Macro dialog box. These comment lines (which begin with an apostrophe) aren't really necessary, and deleting them has no effect on how the macro runs.

Note   You may notice that the macro recorded some actions that you didn't take. For example, it sets the Strikethrough, Superscript, and Subscript properties to False. This is just a byproduct of the method that Excel uses to translate actions into code. Excel sets the properties for every option in the Font tab of the Format Cells dialog box, even though you didn't change all of them.

Testing the Macro

Before you recorded this macro, you set an option that assigned the macro to the Ctrl+Shift+F shortcut key combination. To test the macro, return to Excel by using either of the following methods:

✦ Press Alt+F11

✦ Click the View Microsoft Excel button on the VBE toolbar

When Excel is active, activate a worksheet (it can be in the workbook that contains the VBA module or in any other workbook). Select a cell or range, and press Ctrl+Shift+F. The macro immediately changes the formatting of the selected cell(s).

Continue testing the macro with other selections. You'll find that the macro always applies exactly the same formatting.

> **Note**
>
> In the preceding example, notice that you selected the cell to be formatted *before* you started recording your macro. This is important. If you select a cell while the macro recorder is turned on, the actual cell that you selected will be recorded into the macro. In such a case, the macro would always format that particular cell, and it would not be a "general-purpose" macro.

Editing the Macro

After you record a macro, you can change it (although you must know what you're doing). Assume that you discover that you really want to make the text 14 point rather than 16 point. You could rerecord the macro, but this is a simple modification, so editing the code is more efficient. Just activate Module1, locate the statement that sets the font size, and change 16 to **14**. You can also remove the following lines:

```
.Strikethrough = False
.Superscript = False
.Subscript = False
.OutlineFont = False
.Shadow = False
.Underline = xlNone
```

Removing these lines causes the macro to ignore the properties that are referred to in the statements. For example, if the cell has underlining, the underlining isn't affected by the macro.

The edited macro appears as follows:

```
Sub FormattingMacro()
  With Selection.Font
    .Name = "Arial"
    .FontStyle = "Bold"
    .Size = 14
    .ColorIndex = 3
  End With
End Sub
```

Test this new macro, and you see that it performs as it should. Also, notice that it doesn't remove a cell's underlining, which occurred in the original version of the macro.

Another Example

This example shows you how to record a slightly more complicated VBA macro that converts formulas into values. Converting formulas into values is usually a two-step process in Excel:

1. Copy the range to the Clipboard.
2. Choose Edit ➪ Paste Special (with the Values option selected) to paste the values over the formulas.

This macro combines these steps into a single command.

Furthermore, you want to be able to access this command by pressing a shortcut key combination (Ctrl+Shift+V). Take the following steps to create this macro:

1. Enter a formula into a cell. Any formula will do.
2. Select the cell that contains the formula.
3. Choose Tools ➪ Macro ➪ Record New Macro. Excel displays the Record Macro dialog box.
4. Complete the New Macro dialog box so that it looks like Figure 35-6. This assigns the macro the name **FormulaConvert**. It also gives it a Ctrl+Shift+V shortcut key.

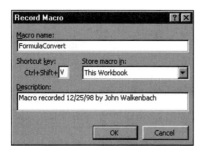

Figure 35-6: How the Record Macro dialog box should look when recording the sample macro.

5. Click OK to begin recording.
6. With the range still selected, choose Edit ➪ Copy to copy the range to the Clipboard.
7. Select Edit ➪ Paste Special, click the Values option, and then click OK to close the dialog box.
8. Press Esc to cancel Paste mode. (Excel removes the moving border around the selected range.)
9. Click the Stop Recording button (or choose Tools ➪ Macro ➪ Stop Recording).

To test the macro, activate a worksheet, enter some formulas, and then select the formulas. You can execute the macro in two ways:

✦ Press Ctrl+Shift+V

✦ Choose Tools ⇨ Macro ⇨ Macros command and double-click the macro name (FormulaConvert)

Excel converts the formulas in the selected range to their values — in a single step instead of two.

Caution   Be careful when you use this macro, because you can't undo the conversion of formulas to values. Actually, you can edit the macro so that its results can be undone, but the procedure is beyond the scope of this discussion.

Note   The shortcut key combination (Ctrl+Shift+V) is valid only when the workbook is open. When you close the workbook, pressing Ctrl+Shift+V has no effect.

The recorded macro appears as follows:

```
' FormulaConvert Macro
' Macro recorded by John Walkenbach
'
' Keyboard Shortcut: Ctrl+Shift+V
'
Sub ConvertFormulas()
   Selection.Copy
   Selection.PasteSpecial Paste:=xlValues, Operation:=xlNone, _
      SkipBlanks:=False, Transpose:=False
   Application.CutCopyMode = False
End Sub
```

Again, Excel added some comment lines that describe the macro. The actual macro begins with the Sub statement. The subroutine has three statements. The first simply copies the selected range. The second statement, which is displayed on two lines (the underscore character means that the statement continues on the next line), pastes the Clipboard contents to the current selection. The second statement has several arguments, representing the options in the Paste Special dialog box. The third statement cancels the moving border around the selected range. (I generated the statement by pressing Esc after the paste operation.)

If you prefer, you can delete the underscore character in the second statement and combine the two lines into one (a VBA statement can be any length). This action may make the macro easier to read.

More About Recording VBA Macros

If you followed along with the preceding examples, you should have a better feel for how to record macros. If you find the VBA code confusing, don't worry — you don't really have to be concerned with it as long as the macro that you record works correctly. If the macro doesn't work, rerecording the macro rather than editing the code often is easier.

A good way to learn about what gets recorded is to set up your screen so that you can see the code that is being generated in the Visual Basic Editor windows. Figure 35-7 shows an example of such a setup. While you're recording your actions, make sure that the VBE window is displaying the module in which the code is being recorded (you may have to double-click the module name in the Project window).

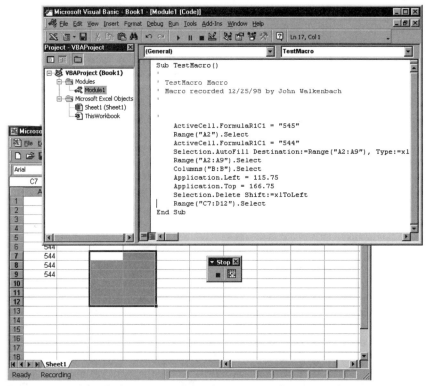

Figure 35-7: This window arrangement lets you see the VBA code as you record your actions.

Tip   If you want to view the code as it's being recorded, using a high-resolution video display really helps, such as 1024 x 768. Otherwise, you may find that fitting the windows of both Excel and VBE onscreen is very difficult.

Absolute Versus Relative Recording

If you're going to work with macros, you need to understand the concept of *relative* versus *absolute* recording. Normally, when you record a macro, Excel stores exact references to the cells that you select (that is, it performs *absolute* recording). If you select the range B1:B10 while you're recording a macro, for example, Excel records this selection as

```
Range("B1:B10").Select
```

This means exactly what it says: "Select the cells in the range B1:B10." When you invoke this macro, the same cells are always selected, regardless of where the active cell is located.

You may have noticed that the Stop Recording toolbar has a tool named Relative Recording. When you click this tool while recording a macro, Excel changes its recording mode from absolute (the default) to relative. When recording in relative mode, selecting a range of cells is translated differently, depending on where the active cell is located. For example, if you're recording in relative mode and cell A1 is active, selecting the range B1:B10 generates the following statement:

```
ActiveCell.Offset(0, 1).Range("A1:A10").Select
```

This statement can be translated as "From the active cell, move 0 rows and 1 column, and then treat this new cell as if it were cell A1. Now select what would be A1:A10." In other words, a macro that is recorded in relative mode starts out by using the active cell as its base and then stores relative references to this cell. As a result, you get different results, depending on the location of the active cell. When you replay this macro, the cells that are selected depend on the active cell. It selects a range that is 10 rows by 1 column, offset from the active cell by 0 rows and 1 column.

When Excel is recording in relative mode, the Relative Reference toolbar button appears depressed. To return to absolute recording, click the Relative Reference button again (and it displays its normal, undepressed state).

Note The recording mode — either absolute or relative — can make a *major* difference in how your macro performs. Therefore, understanding the distinction is important.

EXCEL 2000 In previous version of Excel, recording commands such as Shift+Ctrl+right-arrow key or Shift+Ctrl+down-arrow key (commands that extend the selection to the end of a block of cells) were not recorded correctly. The macro recorder always recorded the exact cells that were selected. The problem is fixed in Excel 2000, so recording these types of selection commands produces macros that work properly.

Storing Macros in the Personal Macro Workbook

Most macros that are created by users are designed for use in a specific workbook, but you may want to use some macros in all of your work. You can store these general-purpose macros in the Personal Macro Workbook, so that they are always available to you. The Personal Macro Workbook is loaded whenever you start Excel. The file, personal.xls, is stored in the XlStart folder, which is in your Excel folder. This file doesn't exist until you record a macro, using Personal Macro Workbook as the destination.

Note   The Personal Macro Workbook normally is in a hidden window (to keep it out of the way).

To record the macro in your Personal Macro Workbook, select the Personal Macro Workbook option in the Record Macro dialog box before you start recording.

If you store macros in the Personal Macro Workbook, you don't have to remember to open the Personal Macro Workbook when you load a workbook that uses macros. When you want to exit, Excel asks whether you want to save changes to the Personal Macro Workbook.

Assigning a Macro to a Toolbar Button

When you record a macro, you can assign it to a shortcut key combination. After you record the macro and test it, you may want to assign the macro to a toolbar button. You can follow these steps to do so:

1. If the macro is a general-purpose macro that you plan to use in more than one workbook, make sure that the macro is stored in your Personal Macro Workbook.

2. Select View ➪ Toolbars ➪ Customize. Excel displays its Customize dialog box.

3. Click the Toolbars tab in the Customize dialog box and make sure that the toolbar is visible that is to contain the new button.

4. Click the Commands tab in the Customize dialog box.

5. Click the Macros category.

6. In the Commands list, drag the Custom Button icon to the toolbar.

7. Right-click the toolbar button and select Assign Macro from the shortcut menu. Excel displays its Assign Macro dialog box.

8. Select the macro name from the list and click OK.

9. At this point, you can right-click the button again to change its name and button image.

10. Click Close to exit the Customize dialog box.

Cross-Reference   See Chapter 33 for details about customizing toolbars.

Writing VBA Code

As demonstrated in the preceding sections, the easiest way to create a simple macro is to record your actions. To develop more complex macros, however, you have to enter the VBA code manually — in other words, *write a program*. To save time, you can often combine recording with manual code entry.

Before you can begin writing VBA code, you must have a good understanding of topics such as objects, properties, and methods—and it doesn't hurt to be familiar with common programming constructs, such as looping and If-Then statements.

This section is an introduction to VBA programming, which is essential if you want to write (rather than record) VBA macros. This is not intended to be a complete instructional guide. My book titled *Excel 2000 Power Programming with VBA* (IDG Books Worldwide, Inc.) covers all aspects of VBA and advanced spreadsheet application development.

The Basics: Entering and Editing Code

Before you can enter code, you must insert a module into the workbook. If the workbook already has a module sheet, you can use the existing module sheet for your new code.

Use the following steps to insert a new module:

1. Press Alt+F11 to activate the Visual Basic Editor window. The Visual Basic Editor window is a separate application, although it works very closely with Excel.

2. The Project window displays a list of all open workbooks and add-ins. Locate the workbook that you are currently working in, and select it (see Figure 35-8).

3. Choose Insert ⇨ Module. VBA inserts a new (empty) module into the workbook and displays it in the Code window.

A VBA module, which is displayed in a separate window, works like a text editor. You can move through the sheet, select text, insert, copy, cut, paste, and so on.

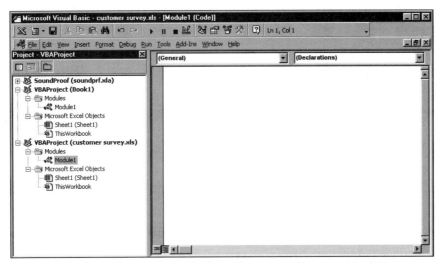

Figure 35-8: The Project window displays all open workbooks and add-ins.

VBA Coding Tips

When you enter code in a module sheet, you're free to use indenting and blank lines to make the code more readable (in fact, this is an excellent habit).

After you enter a line of code (by pressing Enter), it is evaluated for syntax errors. If none are found, the line of code is reformatted, and colors are added to keywords and identifiers. This automatic reformatting adds consistent spaces (before and after an equal sign, for example) and removes extra spaces that aren't needed. If a syntax error is found, you receive a pop-up message, and the line is displayed in a different color (red, by default). You need to correct your error before you can execute the macro.

A single statement can be as long as needed. However, you might want to break the statement into two or more lines. To do so, insert a space followed by an underscore(_). The following code, although written as two lines, is actually a single VBA statement:

```
Sheets("Sheet1").Range("B1").Value = _
Sheets("Sheet1").Range("A1").Value
```

You also can put two or more statements in a single line. You do this by using a colon (:) to separate the statements. The following line consists of three statements:

```
x = 4: y = 6: z = 12
```

You can insert comments freely into your VBA code. The comment indicator is an apostrophe singe quote character ('). Any text that follows a single quote is ignored. A comment can be a line by itself, or inserted after a statement. The following examples show two comments:

```
' Assign the values to the variables
Rate = .085   'Rate as of November 16
```

How VBA Works

VBA is by far the most complex feature in Excel, and you can easily get overwhelmed. To set the stage for the details of VBA, here is a concise summary of how VBA works:

✦ You perform actions in VBA by writing (or recording) code in a VBA module sheet and then executing the macro in any one of various ways. VBA modules are stored in an Excel workbook, and a workbook can hold any number of VBA modules. To view or edit a VBA module, you must activate the Visual Basic Editor window (press Alt+F11 to toggle between Excel and the VBE window).

✦ A VBA module consists of subroutine procedures. A *subroutine procedure* is basically computer code that performs some action with objects. The following is an example of a simple subroutine called ShowSum (it adds 1 + 1 and displays the result):

```
Sub ShowSum()
  Sum = 1 + 1
  MsgBox "The answer is " & Sum
End Sub
```

✦ A VBA module also can store function procedures. A *function procedure* performs some calculations and returns a single value. A function can be called from another VBA procedure or can even be used in a worksheet formula. Here's an example of a function named AddTwo (it adds two values, which are supplied as arguments):

```
Function AddTwo(arg1, arg2)
  AddTwo = arg1 + arg2
End Function
```

✦ VBA manipulates objects. Excel provides well over 100 objects that you can manipulate. Examples of objects include a workbook, a worksheet, a range on a worksheet, a chart, and a drawn rectangle.

✦ Objects are arranged in a hierarchy, and can act as containers for other objects. For example, Excel itself is an object called Application, and it contains other objects such as Workbook objects. The Workbook object can contain other objects, such as Worksheet objects and Chart objects. A Worksheet object can contain objects such as Range objects, PivotTable objects, and so on. The arrangement of these objects is referred to as an *object model*. Excel's object model is depicted in the online Help system (see Figure 35-9).

✦ Objects that are alike form a *collection*. For example, the Worksheets collection consists of all worksheets in a particular workbook. The CommandBars collection consists of all CommandBar objects (that is, menu bars and toolbars). Collections are objects in themselves.

✦ You refer to an object in your VBA code by specifying its position in the object hierarchy, using a period as a separator.

For example, you can refer to a workbook named Book1.xls as

```
Application.Workbooks("Book1")
```

This refers to the Book1.xls workbook in the Workbooks collection. The Workbooks collection is contained in the Application object (that is, Excel). Extending this to another level, you can refer to Sheet1 in Book1 as follows:

```
Application.Workbooks("Book1").Worksheets("Sheet1")
```

You can take it to still another level and refer to a specific cell as follows:

```
Application.Workbooks("Book1").Worksheets("Sheet1").
Range("A1")
```

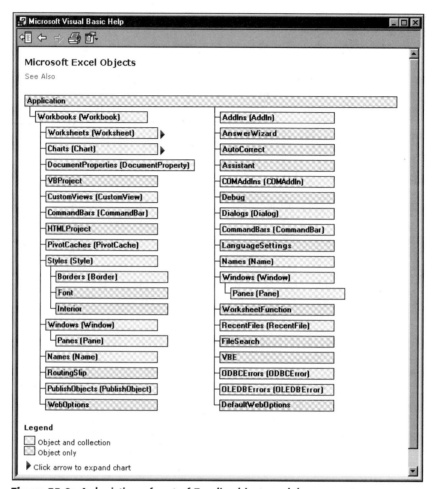

Figure 35-9: A depiction of part of Excel's object model.

✦ If you omit specific references, Excel uses the *active* objects. If Book1 is the active workbook, the preceding reference can be simplified as follows:

```
Worksheets("Sheet1").Range("A1")
```

If you know that Sheet1 is the active sheet, you can simplify the reference even more:

```
Range("A1")
```

✦ Objects have properties. A *property* can be thought of as a setting for an object. For example, a range object has properties such as Value and Name. A chart object has properties such as HasTitle and Type. You can use VBA both to determine object properties and to change them.

✦ You refer to properties by combining the object with the property, separated by a period. For example, you can refer to the value in cell A1 on Sheet1 as follows:

```
Worksheets("Sheet1").Range("A1").Value
```

✦ You can assign values to variables. To assign the value in cell A1 on Sheet1 to a variable called Interest, use the following VBA statement:

```
Interest = Worksheets("Sheet1").Range("A1").Value
```

✦ Objects have methods. A *method* is an action that is performed with the object. For example, one of the methods for a range object is ClearContents. This method clears the contents of the range.

✦ You specify methods by combining the object with the method, separated by a period. For example, to clear the contents of cell A1, use the following statement:

```
Worksheets("Sheet1").Range("A1:C12").ClearContents
```

✦ VBA also includes all the constructs of modern programming languages, including arrays, looping, and so on.

Believe it or not, this describes VBA in a nutshell. Now you just have to learn the details, some of which are covered in the rest of this chapter.

Objects and Collections

VBA is an *object-oriented language,* which means that it manipulates *objects,* such as ranges, charts, drawing objects, and so on. These objects are arranged in a hierarchy. The Application object (which is Excel) contains other objects. For example, the Application object contains a number of objects, including the following:

✦ AddIns (a collection of AddIn objects)

✦ Windows (a collection of Window objects)

✦ WorksheetFunction

✦ Workbooks (a collection of Workbook objects)

Most of these objects can contain other objects. For example, a Workbook object can contain the following objects:

✦ Charts (a collection of Chart objects)

✦ Names (a collection of Name objects)

✦ Styles (a collection of Style objects)

✦ Windows (a collection of Window objects in the workbook)

✦ Worksheets (a collection of Worksheet objects)

Each of these objects, in turn, can contain other objects. A `Worksheet` object, for example, can contain the following objects:

  ✦ `ChartObjects` (a collection of all `ChartObject` objects)
  ✦ `PageSetup`
  ✦ `PivotTables` (a collection of all `PivotTable` objects)
  ✦ `Range`

A *collection* consists of all like objects. For example, the collection of all `Workbook` objects is known as the `Workbooks` collection. You can refer to an individual object in a collection by using an index number, or a reference. For example, if a workbook has three worksheets (named Sheet1, Sheet2, and Sheet3), you can refer to the first object in the `Worksheets` collection in either of these ways:

```
Worksheets(1)
Worksheets("Sheet1")
```

Properties

The objects that you work with have *properties,* which you can think of as attributes of the objects. For example, a range object has properties such as `Column`, `Row`, `Width`, and `Value`. A chart object has properties such as `Legend`, `ChartTitle`, and so on. `ChartTitle` is also an object, with properties such as `Font`, `Orientation`, and `Text`. Excel has many objects, and each has its own set of properties. You can write VBA code to do the following:

  ✦ Examine an object's current property setting and take some action based on it
  ✦ Change an object's property setting

You refer to a property in your VBA code by placing a period and the property name after the object's name. For example, the following VBA statement sets the `Value` property of a range named frequency to 15 (that is, it causes the number 15 to appear in the range's cells):

```
Range("frequency").Value = 15
```

Some properties are *read-only,* which means that you can examine the property, but you can't change the property. For a single-cell range object, the `Row` and `Column` properties are read-only properties: You can determine where a cell is located (in which row and column), but you can't change the cell's location by changing these properties.

A range object also has a `Formula` property, which is *not* read-only; that is, you can insert a formula into a cell by changing its `Formula` property. The following statement inserts a formula into a cell named total by changing the cell's `Formula` property:

```
Range("total").Formula = "=SUM(A1:A10)"
```

Note   Contrary to what you may think, Excel doesn't have a `Cell` object. When you want to manipulate a single cell, you use the `Range` object (with only one cell in it).

You need to be aware of the `Application` object, which is actually Excel, the program. The `Application` object has several useful properties:

✦ `Application.ActiveWorkbook`: Returns the active workbook (a `Workbook` object) in Excel.

✦ `Application.ActiveSheet`: Returns the active sheet (a `Sheet` object) of the active workbook.

✦ `Application.ActiveCell`: Returns the active cell (a `Range` object) object of the active window.

✦ `Application.Selection`: Returns the object that is currently selected in the active window of the `Application` object. This can be a range, a chart, a shape, or some other selectable object.

You also should understand that properties can return objects. In fact, that's exactly what the preceding examples do. The result of `Application.ActiveCell`, for example, is a `Range` object. Therefore, you can access properties by using a statement such as the following:

```
Application.ActiveCell.Font.Size = 15
```

In this case, `Application.ActiveCell.Font` is an object, and `Size` is a property of the object. The preceding statement sets the `Size` property to 15; that is, it causes the font in the currently selected cell to have a size of 15 points.

Tip   Because `Application` properties are so commonly used, you can omit the object qualifier (`Application`). For example, to get the row of the active cell, you can use a statement such as the following:

```
ActiveCell.Row
```

Many different ways to refer to the same object may exist. Assume that you have a workbook named Sales.xls and it's the only workbook open. Furthermore, assume that this workbook has one worksheet, named Summary. Your VBA code can refer to the Summary sheet in any of the following ways:

```
Workbooks("Sales.xls").Worksheets("Summary")
Workbooks(1).Worksheets(1)
Workbooks(1).Sheets(1)
Application.ActiveWorkbook.ActiveSheet
ActiveWorkbook.ActiveSheet
ActiveSheet
```

The method that you use is determined by how much you know about the workspace. For example, if more than one workbook is open, the second or third method is not reliable. If you want to work with the active sheet (whatever it may be), either of the last three methods would work. To be absolutely sure that you're referring to a specific sheet on a specific workbook, the first method is your best choice.

Methods

Objects also have *methods*. You can think of a method as an action taken with an object. For example, range objects have a `Clear` method. The following VBA statement clears the range named total, an action that is equivalent to selecting the range and then choosing Edit ➪ Clear ➪ All:

```
Range("total").Clear
```

In VBA code, methods *look* like properties, because they are connected to the object with a "dot." However, methods and properties are different concepts.

Variables

Like all programming languages, VBA enables you to work with variables. In VBA (unlike in some languages), you don't need to declare variables explicitly before you use them in your code (although it's definitely a good practice).

In the following example, the value in cell A1 on Sheet1 is assigned to a variable named `rate`:

```
rate = Worksheets("Sheet1").Range("A1").Value
```

You then can work with the variable `rate` in other parts of your VBA code. Note that the variable `rate` is not a named range, which means that you can't use it as such in a worksheet formula.

Controlling Execution

VBA uses many constructs that are found in most other programming languages. These constructs are used to control the flow of execution. This section introduces a few of the more common programming constructs.

The If-Then construct

One of the most important control structures in VBA is the `If-Then` construct. This common command gives your applications decision-making capability. The basic syntax of the `If-Then` structure is as follows:

```
If condition Then statements [Else elsestatements]
```

The following is an example (which doesn't use the optional Else clause). This subroutine checks the active cell. If it contains a negative value, the cell's color is changed to red. Otherwise, nothing happens.

```
Sub CheckCell()
   If ActiveCell.Value < 0 Then ActiveCell.Font.ColorIndex = 3
End Sub
```

For-Next loops

For example, you can use a For-Next loop to process a series of items. Its syntax is as follows:

```
For counter = start To end [Step stepval]
   [statements]
   [Exit For]
   [statements]
Next [counter]
```

The following is an example of a For-Next loop:

```
Sub SumSquared()
   Total = 0
   For Num = 1 To 10
      Total = Total + (Num ^ 2)
   Next Num
   MsgBox Total
End Sub
```

This example has one statement between the For statement and the Next statement. This single statement is executed ten times. The variable Num takes on successive values of 1, 2, 3, and so on, up to 10. The variable Total stores the sum of Num squared, added to the previous value of Total. The result is a value that represents the sum of the first ten integers squared. This result is displayed in a message box.

The With-End With construct

Another construct that you encounter if you record macros is the With-End With construct. This is a shortcut way of dealing with several properties or methods of the same object. The following is an example:

```
Sub AlignCells()
   With Selection
      .HorizontalAlignment = xlCenter
      .VerticalAlignment = xlCenter
      .WrapText = False
      .Orientation = xlHorizontal
   End With
End Sub
```

The following subroutine performs exactly the same operations, but doesn't use the With-End With construct:

```
Sub AlignCells()
    Selection.HorizontalAlignment = xlCenter
    Selection.VerticalAlignment = xlCenter
    Selection.WrapText = False
    Selection.Orientation = xlHorizontal
End Sub
```

The Select Case construct

The Select Case construct is useful for choosing among two or more options. The syntax for the Select Case structure is as follows:

```
Select Case testexpression
    [Case expressionlist-n
            [statements-n]] . . .
    [Case Else
            [elsestatements]]
End Select
```

The following example demonstrates the use of a Select Case construct. In this example, the active cell is checked. If its value is less than 0, it's colored red. If it's equal to 0, it's colored blue. If the value is greater than 0, it's colored black.

```
Sub CheckCell()
    Select Case ActiveCell.Value
        Case Is < 0
            ActiveCell.Font.ColorIndex = 3 'Red
        Case 0
            ActiveCell.Font.ColorIndex = 5 'Blue
        Case Is > 0
            ActiveCell.Font.ColorIndex = 1 'Black
    End Select
End Sub
```

Any number of statements can go below each Case statement, and they all get executed if the case is true. If you use only one statement, as in the preceding example, you may want to put the statement on the same line as the Case statement.

A Macro That Can't Be Recorded

The following is a VBA macro that can't be recorded, because it uses an If-Then structure. This macro enables you to identify quickly cells that exceed a certain value. When you run this macro, it prompts the user for a value and then evaluates every cell in the selection. If the cell's value is greater than the value that is entered by the user, the macro makes the cell bold and red.

```
Sub SelectiveFormat()
'This procedure selectively shades cells greater than
'a specified target value
'Get target value from user
  Message = "Change attributes of values greater than or
equal_to..."
  Target = InputBox(Message)
  Target=Val(Target)

'Evaluate each cell in the selection
  For Each Item In Selection
    If IsNumeric(Item) Then
      If Item.Value >= Target Then
        With Item
          .Font.Bold = True
          .Font.ColorIndex = 3 'Red
        End With
      End If
    End If
  Next Item
End Sub
```

Although this macro may look complicated, it's fairly simple when you break it down.

First, the macro assigns text to a variable named Message. It then uses the InputBox function to solicit a value from the user. The InputBox function has a single argument (which is the Message variable), and returns a string — which is assigned to the Target variable. Next, the Val function is used to convert this string to a value.

The For-Next loop checks every cell in the selected range. The first statement within the loop uses the IsNumeric function to determine whether the cell can be evaluated as a number. This is important, because a cell without a value would generate an error when the Value property is accessed in the next statement. If the cell is numeric, it is checked against the target value. If it's greater than or equal to the target value, the Bold and ColorIndex properties are changed. Otherwise, nothing happens and the loop is incremented.

After entering this macro, named SelectiveFormat, into a module sheet, you can provide a shortcut key to access it. Choose Tools ➪ Macro ➪ Macros to display the Macros dialog box. Select the macro from the list, and click Options. Excel displays a new dialog box (see Figure 35-10) that enables you to specify a shortcut key combination to execute the macro.

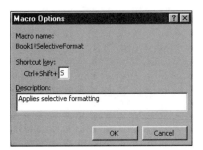

Figure 35-10: You can execute this macro by pressing Ctrl+S.

Figure 35-11 shows the macro in action. Note that you must select the range before you execute the macro.

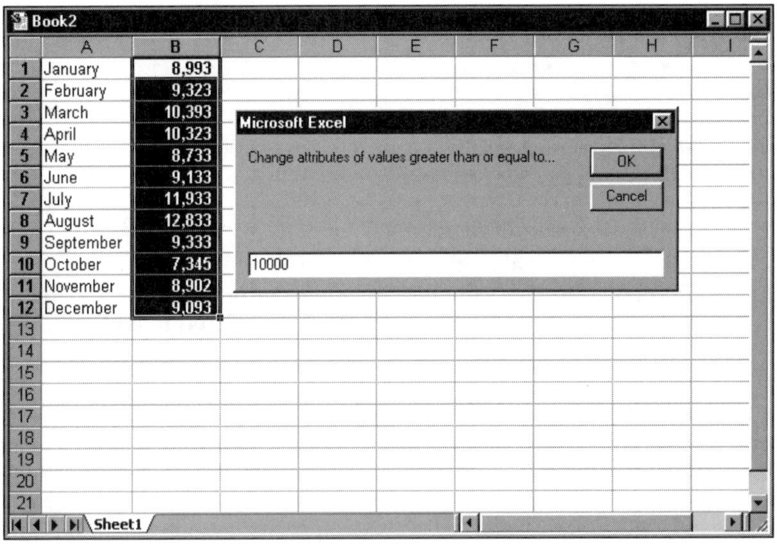

Figure 35-11: The macro uses the InputBox function to prompt the user for a value.

As macros go, this example is not very good. It's not very flexible and doesn't include any error handling. For example, if a nonrange object (such as a graphic object) is selected, the macro halts and displays an error message. To avoid this error message and abort the macro if anything except a range is selected, you can insert the following statement as the first statement in the procedure (directly below the Sub statement):

```
If TypeName(Selection) <> "Range" Then Exit Sub
```

This causes the macro to halt if the selection is not a Range object.

Notice also that the macro is executed even if you click Cancel in the input box. To avoid this problem, enter the following statement directly above the `Target=Val(Target)` statement:

    If Target = "" then Exit Sub

This aborts the subroutine if `Target` is empty.

A much more versatile version of this utility is part of the Power Utility Pak (see Figure 35-12). The shareware version is available from this book's Web site.

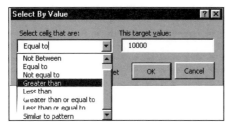

Figure 35-12: The Select By Value utility in the Power Utility Pak is a more versatile version of this macro.

Learning More

This chapter barely scratches the surface of what you can do with VBA. If this is your first exposure to VBA, you're probably a bit overwhelmed by objects, properties, and methods. I don't blame you. If you try to access a property that an object doesn't have, you get a run-time error, and your VBA code grinds to a screeching halt until you correct the problem. Fortunately, several good ways are available to learn about objects, properties, and methods.

Read the Rest of the Book

This book has three more chapters that are devoted to VBA. Chapter 36 covers VBA functions, Chapter 37 describes custom dialog boxes, and Chapter 38 consists of useful (and informative) VBA examples.

Record Your Actions

The best way—without question—to become familiar with VBA is to turn on the macro recorder and record actions that you make in Excel. This learning technique is even better if the VBA module in which the code is being recorded is visible while you're recording.

Use the Online Help System

The main source of detailed information about Excel's objects, methods, and procedures is the online Help system. Help is very thorough and easy to access. When you're in a VBA module, just move the cursor to a property or method and press F1. You get help that describes the word that is under the cursor.

Buy Another Book

Okay, I promise. This is the last plug for my other book, *Excel 2000 Power Programming With VBA*. I've received feedback from hundreds of previous-edition readers who claim that it's the best Excel/VBA book available. You be the judge.

Summary

This chapter introduces VBA, one of two macro languages included with Excel. If you want to learn macro programming, VBA is the language to use. In this chapter, you learn that a VBA module can contain subroutine procedures and function procedures, and that VBA is based on objects, properties, and methods. You also learn how to use the macro recorder to translate your actions into VBA code and write simple code directly in a VBA module. Three other chapters in this book provide additional information about VBA.

✦   ✦   ✦

Creating Custom Worksheet Functions

As mentioned in the preceding chapter, you can create two types of VBA procedures: subroutines and functions. This chapter focuses on function procedures.

Overview of VBA Functions

Function procedures that you write in VBA are quite versatile. You can use these functions in two situations:

  ✦ As part of an expression in a different VBA procedure

  ✦ On formulas that you create in a worksheet

In fact, you can use a function procedure anywhere that you can use an Excel worksheet function or a VBA built-in function. Custom functions also appear in the Paste Function dialog box, so they appear to be part of Excel.

Excel contains hundreds of predefined worksheet functions. With so many from which to choose, you may be curious as to why anyone would need to develop additional functions. The main reason is that creating a custom function can greatly simplify your formulas by making them shorter—and shorter formulas are more readable and easier to work with. For example, you can often replace a complex formula with a single function. Another reason is that you can write functions to perform operations that would otherwise be impossible.

Note   This chapter assumes that you are familiar with entering and editing VBA code in the Visual Basic Editor (VBE). Refer to Chapter 35 for an overview of the VBE.

An Introductory Example

The process of creating custom functions is relatively easy, once you understand VBA. Without further ado, here's an example of a VBA function procedure. This function is stored in a VBA module, which is accessible from the VBE.

A Custom Function

This example function, named NumSign, uses one argument. The function returns a text string of Positive if its argument is greater than zero, Negative if the argument is less than zero, and Zero if the argument is equal to zero. The function is shown in Figure 36-1.

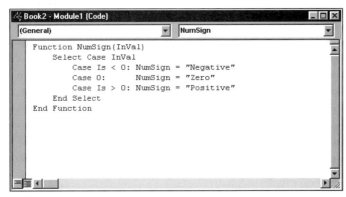

```
Function NumSign(InVal)
    Select Case InVal
        Case Is < 0: NumSign = "Negative"
        Case 0:      NumSign = "Zero"
        Case Is > 0: NumSign = "Positive"
    End Select
End Function
```

Figure 36-1: A custom function.

You could, of course, accomplish the same effect with the following worksheet formula, which uses a nested IF function:

```
=IF(A1=0,"Zero",IF(A1>0,"Positive","Negative"))
```

Many would agree that the custom function solution is easier to understand and to edit than the worksheet formula.

Using the Function in a Worksheet

When you enter a formula that uses the NumSign function, Excel executes the function to get the result (see Figure 36-2). This custom function works just like any built-in worksheet function. You can insert it in a formula by using the Insert ⇨ Function command, which displays the Paste Function dialog box (custom functions are located in the User Defined category). You also can nest custom functions and combine them with other elements in your formulas.

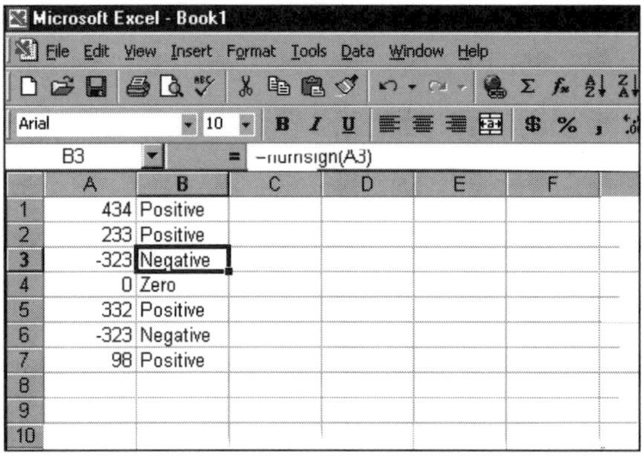

Figure 36-2: Using a custom function in a worksheet formula.

Using the Function in a VBA Subroutine

The following VBA subroutine procedure, which is defined in the same module as the custom NumSign function, uses the built-in MsgBox function to display the result of the NumSign function:

```
Sub ShowSign()
  CellValue = ActiveCell.Value
  MsgBox NumSign(CellValue)
End Sub
```

In this example, the variable CellValue contains the value in the active cell (this variable could contain any value, not necessarily obtained from a cell). CellValue is then passed to the function as its argument. Figure 36-3 shows the result of executing the NumSign subroutine.

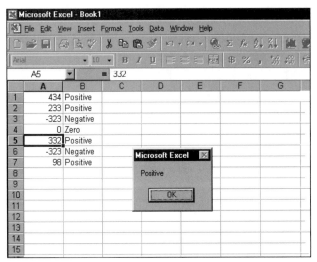

Figure 36-3: Using a custom function in a VBA subroutine.

Analyzing the Custom Function

This section describes the NumSign function. Here again is the code:

```
Function NumSign(InVal)
  Select Case InVal
    Case Is < 0: NumSign = "Negative"
    Case 0:    NumSign = "Zero"
    Case Is > 0: NumSign = "Positive"
  End Select
End Function
```

Notice that the procedure starts with the keyword Function rather than Sub, followed by the name of the function (NumSign). This custom function uses one argument (InVal); the argument's name is enclosed in parentheses. InVal is the cell or variable that is to be processed. When the function is used in a worksheet, the argument can be a cell reference (such as A1) or a literal value (such as –123). When the function is used in another procedure, the argument can be a numeric variable, a literal number, or a value that is obtained from a cell.

The NumSign function uses the Select Case construct (described in Chapter 35) to take a different action, depending on the value of InVal. If InVal is less than zero, NumSign is assigned the text Negative. If InVal is equal to zero, NumSign is Zero. If InVal is greater than zero, NumSign is Positive. The value returned by a function is always assigned to the function's name.

The procedure ends with an End Function statement.

About Function Procedures

A custom function procedure has a lot in common with a subroutine procedure, covered in the preceding chapter. Function procedures have some important differences, however, which are discussed in this section.

Declaring a Function

The syntax for declaring a function is as follows:

```
[Public | Private][Static] Function name [(arglist)][As type]
   [statements]
   [name = expression]
   [Exit Function]
   [statements]
   [name = expression]
End Function
```

These elements are defined as follows:

✦ `Public`: Indicates that the function is accessible to all other procedures in all other modules in the workbook. (Optional)

✦ `Private`: Indicates that the function is accessible only to other procedures in the same module. `Private` functions can't be used in worksheet formulas and do not appear in the Paste Function dialog box. (Optional)

✦ `Static`: Indicates that the values of variables declared in the function are preserved between calls, rather than being reset. (Optional)

✦ `Function`: A keyword that indicates the beginning of a function procedure. (Required)

✦ `name`: Any valid variable name. When the function finishes, the single-value result is assigned to the function's name. (Required)

✦ `arglist`: A list (one or more) of variables that represent arguments passed to the function. The arguments are enclosed in parentheses. Use a comma to separate arguments. (Optional)

✦ `type`: The data type that is returned by the function. (Optional)

✦ `statements`: Valid VBA statements. (Optional)

✦ `Exit Function`: A statement that causes an immediate exit from the function. (Optional)

✦ `End Function`: A keyword that indicates the end of the function. (Required)

Keep in mind that a value is assigned to the function's name when a function is finished executing.

To create a custom function, follow these steps:

1. Activate the Visual Basic Editor (or press Alt+F11).

2. Select the workbook in the Project window.

3. Choose Insert ➪ Module to insert a VBA module (or you can use an existing module).

4. Enter the keyword `Function` followed by the function's name and a list of the arguments (if any) in parentheses.

5. Insert the VBA code that performs the work — and make sure that the variable corresponding to the function's name has the appropriate value (this is the value that the function returns).

6. End the function with an `End Function` statement.

Function names must adhere to the same rules as variable names, and you can't use a name that looks like a worksheet cell (for example, a function named J21 isn't accepted).

What a Function Can't Do

Almost everyone who starts creating custom worksheet functions using VBA makes a fatal mistake: They try to get the function to do more than is possible.

A worksheet function returns a value, and it must be completely "passive." In other words, the function cannot change anything on the worksheet. For example, it's impossible to develop a worksheet function that changes the formatting of a cell (every VBA programmer has tried this, and not one of them has been successful!). If your function attempts to perform an action that is not allowed, the function simply returns an error.

VBA functions that are not used in worksheet formulas can do anything that a regular subroutine can do — including changing cell formatting.

Executing Function Procedures

Although many ways exist to execute a *subroutine* procedure, you can execute a *function* procedure in just two ways:

✦ Call it from another procedure

✦ Use it in a worksheet formula

Calling custom functions from a procedure

You can call custom functions from a procedure just as you call built-in VBA functions. For example, after you define a function called `CalcTax`, you can enter a statement such as the following:

```
Tax = CalcTax(Amount, Rate)
```

This statement executes the `CalcTax` custom function with `Amount` and `Rate` as its arguments. The function's result is assigned to the `Tax` variable.

Using custom functions in a worksheet formula

Using a custom function in a worksheet formula is like using built-in functions. You must ensure that Excel can locate the function procedure, however. If the function procedure is in the same workbook, you don't have to do anything special. If the function is defined in a different workbook, you may have to tell Excel where to find the function. The following are the three ways in which you can do this:

✦ **Precede the function's name with a file reference.** For example, if you want to use a function called `CountNames` that's defined in a workbook named MyFunctions, you can use a reference such as the following:

```
=MyFunctions.xls!CountNames(A1:A1000)
```

If you insert the function with the Paste Function dialog box, the workbook reference is inserted automatically.

✦ **Set up a reference to the workbook.** If the custom function is defined in a reference workbook, you don't need to precede the function name with the workbook name. You establish a reference to another workbook with the Tools ➪ References command (in the Visual Basic Editor). You are presented with a list of references that includes all open workbooks. Place a check mark in the item that refers to the workbook that contains the custom function (use the Browse button if the workbook isn't open).

Create an add-in. When you create an add-in from a workbook that has function procedures, you don't need to use the file reference when you use one of the functions in a formula; the add-in must be installed, however. Chapter 40 discusses add-ins.

Note

If you plan on developing custom worksheet functions, make sure that you heed the warning in the sidebar, "What a Function Can't Do."

Your function procedures don't appear in the Macros dialog box when you select Tools ➪ Macro, because you can't execute a function directly. As a result, you need to do extra, up-front work to test your functions as you're developing them. One approach is to set up a simple subroutine that calls the function. If the function is designed to be used in worksheet formulas, you can enter a simple formula to test it as you're developing the function.

Function Procedure Arguments

Keep in mind the following about function procedure arguments:

✦ Arguments can be variables (including arrays), constants, literals, or expressions.

✦ Some functions do not have arguments.

✦ Some functions have a fixed number of required arguments (from 1 to 60).

✦ Some functions have a combination of required and optional arguments.

The following section presents a series of examples that demonstrate how to use arguments effectively with functions. Coverage of optional arguments is beyond the scope of this book.

Example: A Function with No Argument

Like subroutines, functions don't necessarily have to use arguments. Excel, for example, has a few built-in worksheet functions that don't use arguments. These include RAND, TODAY, and NOW.

The following is a simple example of a function that has no arguments. This function returns the UserName property of the Application object, which is the name that appears in the Options dialog box (General tab). This example is simple, but it can be useful, because no other way is available to get the user's name to appear in a worksheet formula.

```
Function User()
' Returns the name of the current user
  User = Application.UserName
End Function
```

When you enter the following formula into a worksheet cell, the cell displays the name of the current user:

```
=User()
```

As with Excel's built-in functions, when you use a function with no arguments, you must include a set of empty parentheses.

The following example is a simple subroutine that uses the User custom function as an argument for the MsgBox function. The concatenation operator (&) joins the literal string with the result of the User function.

```
Sub ShowUser()
  MsgBox ("The user is " & User())
End Sub
```

Example: A Function with One Argument

This section contains a more complex function that is designed for a sales manager who needs to calculate the commissions that are earned by the sales force. The commission rate is based on the amount sold — those who sell more earn a higher commission rate. The function returns the commission amount, based on the sales made (which is the function's only argument — a required argument). The calculations in this example are based on the following table:

Monthly Sales	Commission Rate
0 – $9,999	8.0%
$10,000 – $19,999	10.5%
$20,000 – $39,999	12.0%
$40,000+	14.0%

Several ways exist to calculate commissions for various sales amounts that are entered into a worksheet. You could write a formula such as the following:

```
=IF(AND(A1>=0,A1<=9999.99),A1*0.08,IF(AND(A1>=10000,A1<=19999.9
9), A1*0.105
,IF(AND(A1>=20000,A1<=39999.99),A1*0.12,IF(A1>=40000,A1*0.14,0)
)))
```

This is not the best approach, for a couple of reasons. First, the formula is overly complex and difficult to understand. Second, the values are hard coded into the formula, making the formula difficult to modify if the commission structure changes.

A better approach is to use a lookup table function to compute the commissions; for example:

```
=VLOOKUP(A1,Table,2)*A1
```

Using the VLOOKUP function requires that you have a table of commission rates set up in your worksheet.

An even better approach is to create a custom function, such as the following:

```
Function Commission(Sales)
' Calculates sales commissions
  Tier1 = 0.08
  Tier2 = 0.105
  Tier3 = 0.12
  Tier4 = 0.14
  Select Case Sales
      Case 0 To 9999.99: Commission = Sales * Tier1
      Case 1000 To 19999.99: Commission = Sales * Tier2
      Case 20000 To 39999.99: Commission = Sales * Tier3
      Case Is >= 40000: Commission = Sales * Tier4
  End Select
End Function
```

After you define the `Commission` function in a VBA module, you can use it in a worksheet formula or call it from other VBA procedures.

Entering the following formula into a cell produces a result of 3,000 (the amount, 25,000, qualifies for a commission rate of 12 percent):

```
=Commission(25000)
```

Even if you don't need custom functions in a worksheet, creating function procedures can make your VBA coding much simpler. If your VBA procedure calculates sales commissions, for example, you can use the `Commission` function and call it from a VBA subroutine. The following is a tiny subroutine that asks the user for a sales amount and then uses the `Commission` function to calculate the commission due and to display it:

```
Sub CalcComm()
    Sales = InputBox("Enter Sales:")
    MsgBox "The commission is " & Commission(Sales)
End Sub
```

The subroutine starts by displaying an input box that asks for the sales amount. Then, the procedure displays a message box with the calculated sales commission for that amount. The `Commission` function must be available in the active workbook; otherwise, Excel displays a message saying that the function is not defined.

Example: A Function with Two Arguments

This example builds on the previous one. Imagine that the sales manager implements a new policy: The total commission paid is increased by one percent for every year that the salesperson has been with the company. For this example, the custom `Commission` function (defined in the preceding section) has been modified so that it takes two arguments—both of which are required arguments. Call this new function `Commission2`:

```
Function Commission2(Sales, Years)
'  Calculates sales commissions based on years in service
    Tier1 = 0.08
    Tier2 = 0.105
    Tier3 = 0.12
    Tier4 = 0.14
    Select Case Sales
       Case 0 To 9999.99: Commission2 = Sales * Tier1
       Case 1000 To 19999.99: Commission2 = Sales * Tier2
       Case 20000 To 39999.99: Commission2 = Sales * Tier3
       Case Is >= 40000: Commission2 = Sales * Tier4
    End Select
    Commission2 = Commission2 + (Commission2 * Years / 100)
End Function
```

The modification was quite simple. The second argument (Years) was added to the Function statement and an additional computation was included that adjusts the commission, before exiting the function.

The following is an example of how you write a formula by using this function (it assumes that the sales amount is in cell A1, and the number of years that the salesperson has worked is in cell B1):

```
=Commission2(A1,B1)
```

Example: A Function with a Range Argument

The example in this section demonstrates how to use a worksheet range as an argument. Actually, it's not at all tricky; Excel takes care of the details behind the scenes.

Assume that you want to calculate the average of the five largest values in a range named Data. Excel doesn't have a function that can do this, so you can write the following formula:

```
=(LARGE(Data,1)+LARGE(Data,2)+LARGE(Data,3)+LARGE(Data,4)+LARGE
(Data,5))/5
```

This formula uses Excel's LARGE function, which returns the *n*th largest value in a range. The preceding formula adds the five largest values in the range named Data and then divides the result by 5. The formula works fine, but it's rather unwieldy. And, what if you need to compute the average of the top *six* values? You would need to rewrite the formula—and make sure that all copies of the formula also get updated.

Wouldn't it be easier if Excel had a function named TopAvg? For example, you could use the following (nonexistent) function to compute the average:

```
=TopAvg(Data,5)
```

This is an example of when a custom function can make things much easier for you. The following is a custom VBA function, named TopAvg, which returns the average of the top *n* values in a range:

```
Function TopAvg(InRange, Num)
' Returns the average of the highest Num values in InRange
  Sum = 0
  For i = 1 To Num
    Sum = Sum + WorksheetFunction.Large(InRange, i)
  Next i
  TopAvg = Sum / Num
End Function
```

This function takes two arguments: InRange (which is a worksheet range) and Num (the number of values to average). The code starts by initializing the Sum variable to 0. It then uses a For-Next loop to calculate the sum of the *n*th largest values in the range. Note that Excel's LARGE function is used within the loop. You can use an Excel worksheet function in VBA if you precede the function with WorksheetFunction and a period. Finally, TopAvg is assigned the value of Sum divided by Num.

You can use all of Excel's worksheet functions in your VBA procedures, *except* those that have equivalents in VBA. For example, VBA has a Rnd function that returns a random number. Therefore, you can't use Excel's RAND function in a VBA procedure.

Debugging Custom Functions

Debugging a function procedure can be a bit more challenging than debugging a subroutine procedure. If you develop a function to use in worksheet formulas, an error in the function procedure simply results in an error display in the formula cell (usually #VALUE!). In other words, you don't receive the normal run-time error message that helps you to locate the offending statement.

When you are debugging a worksheet formula, using only one instance of the function in your worksheet is the best technique. The following are three methods that you may want to use in your debugging:

✦ **Place MsgBox functions at strategic locations to monitor the value of specific variables.** Fortunately, message boxes in function procedures pop up when the procedure is executed. But, make sure that you have only one formula in the worksheet that uses your function; otherwise, the message boxes appear for each formula that's evaluated.

✦ **Test the procedure by calling it from a subroutine procedure.** Run-time errors display normally, and you can either fix the problem (if you know what it is) or jump right into the debugger.

✦ **Set a breakpoint in the function and then use Excel's debugger to step through the function.** You then can access all the normal debugging tools.

Pasting Custom Functions

Excel's Paste Function dialog box is a handy tool that enables you to choose a worksheet function; you even can choose one of your custom worksheet functions. The Formula Palette prompts you for the function's arguments.

Function procedures that are defined with the `Private` keyword do not appear in the Paste Function dialog box.

You also can display a description of your custom function in the Paste Function dialog box. To do so, follow these steps:

1. Create the function in a module by using the VBE.

2. Activate Excel.

3. Choose the Tools ⇨ Macro ⇨ Macros command.

   Excel displays its Macro dialog box (see Figure 36-4).

Figure 36-4: Excel's Macro dialog box doesn't list functions, so you must enter the function name yourself.

4. In the Macro dialog box, type the name of the function in the box labeled Macro Name. Notice that functions do not normally appear in this dialog box, so you must enter the function name yourself.

5. Click the Options button.

   Excel displays its Macro Options dialog box. (See Figure 36-5.)

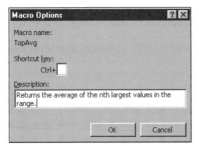

Figure 36-5: Entering a description
for a custom function. This description
appears in the Paste Function
dialog box.

6. Enter a description of the function and then click OK. The Shortcut key field is
   irrelevant for functions.

The description that you enter appears in the Paste Function dialog box.

Custom functions are listed under the User Defined category, and no straightforward way exists to create a new function category for your custom functions.

Figure 36-6 shows the Paste Function dialog box, listing the custom functions that
are in the User Defined category. In the second Function Wizard dialog box, the user
is prompted to enter arguments for a custom function—just as in using a built-in
worksheet function.

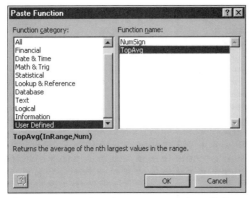

Figure 36-6: Using the Paste Function dialog
box to insert a custom function.

When you access a *built-in* function from the Paste Function dialog box, the Formula Palette displays a description of each argument. Unfortunately, you can't provide such descriptions for custom functions.

Learning More

The information in this chapter only scratches the surface when it comes to creating custom functions. It should be enough to get you started, however, if you're interested in this topic. Refer to Chapter 38 for more examples of useful VBA functions. You may be able to use the examples directly or adapt them for your needs.

Summary

In this chapter, you read about how to create and use custom VBA functions. These functions can be used in worksheet formulas and in other VBA procedures. Several examples are provided, and you can refer to Chapter 38 for more examples.

✦   ✦   ✦

Creating Custom Dialog Boxes

You can't use Excel very long without being exposed to dialog boxes. Excel, like most Windows programs, uses dialog boxes to obtain information, clarify commands, and display messages. If you develop VBA macros, you can create your own dialog boxes that work just like those that are built into Excel. This chapter introduces you to custom dialog boxes.

Note   Beginning with Excel 97, Microsoft introduced a new method for creating custom dialog boxes. Therefore, the information in this chapter does not apply to versions of Excel prior to Excel 97.

Why Create Custom Dialog Boxes?

Some macros that you create behave exactly the same every time that you execute them. For example, you may develop a macro that enters a list of your employees into a worksheet range. This macro always produces the same result and requires no additional user input. You may develop other macros, however, that you want to behave differently under different circumstances, or that offer some options for the user. In such cases, the macro may benefit from a custom dialog box.

The following is an example of a simple macro that makes each cell in the selected range uppercase (but it skips cells that have a formula). The subroutine uses VBA's built-in StrConv function.

```
Sub ChangeCase()
  For Each cell In Selection
    If Not cell.HasFormula Then
      cell.Value = StrConv(cell.Value,
vbUpperCase)
    End If
  Next cell
End Sub
```

This macro is useful, but it could be even more useful. For example, the macro would be more helpful if it could also change the cells to lowercase or initial capitals (only the first letter of each word is uppercase). This modification is not difficult to make, but if you make this change to the macro, you need some method of asking the user what type of change to make to the cells. The solution is to present a dialog box like the one shown in Figure 37-1. This dialog box is a UserForm that was created by using the Visual Basic Editor, and it is displayed by a VBA macro.

Figure 37-1: A custom dialog box that asks the user for an option.

Another solution would be to develop three macros — one for each type of text case change. Combining these three operations into a single macro and using a dialog box represents a more efficient approach, however. This example, including how to create the dialog box, is discussed later in the chapter.

Custom Dialog Box Alternatives

Although developing custom dialog boxes isn't difficult, sometimes using the tools that are built into VBA is easier. For example, VBA includes two functions (InputBox and MsgBox) that enable you to display simple dialog boxes, without having to create a UserForm in the VBE. These dialog boxes can be customized in some ways, but they certainly don't offer the options that are available in a custom dialog box.

The InputBox Function

The InputBox function is useful for obtaining a single input from the user. A simplified version of the function's syntax follows:

```
InputBox(prompt[,title][,default])
```

The elements are defined as follows:

✦ prompt: Text that is displayed in the input box. (Required)

✦ title: Text that appears in the input box's title bar. (Optional)

✦ default: The default value. (Optional)

The following is an example of how you can use the InputBox function:

```
Rate = InputBox("Commission rate?","Commission Worksheet")
```

When this VBA statement is executed, Excel displays the dialog box that is shown in Figure 37-2. Notice that this example uses only the first two arguments and does not supply a default value. When the user enters a value and clicks OK, the value is assigned to the variable Rate.

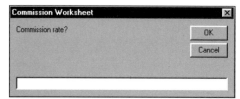

Figure 37-2: This dialog box is displayed by VBA's InputBox function.

VBA's InputBox function always returns a string, so you may need to convert the results to a value. You can use the Val function to convert a string to a value, as follows:

```
Rate = Val(InputBox("Commission rate?","Commission Worksheet"))
```

The MsgBox Function

VBA's MsgBox function is a handy way to display information and to solicit simple input from users. I use VBA's MsgBox function in many of this book's examples, to display a variable's value. A simplified version of the MsgBox syntax is as follows:

```
MsgBox(prompt[,buttons][,title])
```

The elements are defined as follows:

✦ prompt: Text that is displayed in the message box. (Required)

✦ buttons: The code for the buttons that are to appear in the message box. (Optional)

✦ title: Text that appears in the message box's title bar. (Optional)

You can use the MsgBox function by itself or assign its result to a variable. If you use it by itself, don't include parentheses around the arguments. The following example displays a message and does not return a result:

```
Sub MsgBoxDemo()
  MsgBox "Click OK to continue"
End Sub
```

Figure 37-3 shows how this message box appears.

Figure 37-3: A simple message box, displayed with VBA's `MsgBox` function.

To get a response from a message box, you can assign the result of the `MsgBox` function to a variable. The following code uses some built-in constants (described later) to make it easier to work with the values that are returned by `MsgBox`:

```
Sub GetAnswer()
  Ans = MsgBox("Continue?", vbYesNo)
  Select Case Ans
   Case vbYes
' ...[code if Ans is Yes]...
   Case vbNo
' ...[code if Ans is No]...
  End Select
End Sub
```

When this procedure is executed, the `Ans` variable contains a value that corresponds to `vbYes` or `vbNo`. The `Select Case` statement determines the action to take based on the value of `Ans`.

You can easily customize your message boxes, because of the flexibility of the buttons argument. Table 37-1 lists the built-in constants that you can use for the button argument. You can specify which buttons to display, whether an icon appears, and which button is the default.

Table 37-1
Constants That Are Used in the MsgBox Function

Constant	Value	Description
vbOKOnly	0	Display OK button
vbOKCancel	1	Display OK and Cancel buttons
vbAbortRetryIgnore	2	Display Abort, Retry, and Ignore buttons
vbYesNoCancel	3	Display Yes, No, and Cancel buttons
vbYesNo	4	Display Yes and No buttons
vbRetryCancel	5	Display Retry and Cancel buttons
vbCritical	16	Display Critical Message icon

Constant	Value	Description
vbQuestion	32	Display Warning Query icon
vbExclamation	48	Display Warning Message icon
vbInformation	64	Display Information Message icon
vbDefaultButton1	0	First button is default
vbDefaultButton2	256	Second button is default
vbDefaultButton3	512	Third button is default
vbSystemModal	4096	System modal; all applications are suspended until the user responds to the message box

The following example uses a combination of constants to display a message box with a Yes button, a No button (vbYesNo), and a question mark icon (vbQuestion); the second button is designated as the default button (vbDefaultButton2) — which is the button that is executed if the user presses Enter. For simplicity, these constants are assigned to the Config variable and Config is then used as the second argument in the MsgBox function.

```
Sub GetAnswer()
   Config = vbYesNo + vbQuestion + vbDefaultButton2
   Ans = MsgBox("Process the monthly report?", Config)
   If Ans = vbYes Then RunReport
   If Ans = vbNo Then End
End Sub
```

Figure 37-4 shows how this message box appears when the GetAnswer subroutine is executed. If the user clicks the Yes button (or presses Enter), the routine executes the procedure named RunReport (which is not shown). If the user clicks the No button, the routine is ended with no action. Because the title argument was omitted in the MsgBox function, Excel uses the default title ("Microsoft Excel").

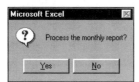

Figure 37-4: The second argument of the MsgBox function determines what appears in the message box.

The routine that follows is another example of using the MsgBox function:

```
Sub GetAnswer2()
  Msg = "Do you want to process the monthly report?"
  Msg = Msg & vbLf & vbLf
  Msg = Msg & "Processing the monthly report will take
approximately "
  Msg = Msg & "15 minutes. It will generate a 30-page report
for all "
  Msg = Msg & "sales offices for the current month."
  Title = "XYZ Marketing Company"
  Config = vbYesNo + vbQuestion
  Ans = MsgBox(Msg, Config, Title)
  If Ans = vbYes Then RunReport
  If Ans = vbNo Then End
End Sub
```

This example demonstrates an efficient way to specify a longer message in a message box. A variable (Msg) and the concatenation operator (&) are used to build the message in a series of statements. In the second statement, vbLf is a constant that represents a line feed character (using two line feeds inserts a blank line). The title argument is also used to display a different title in the message box. Figure 37-5 shows how this message box appears when the procedure is executed.

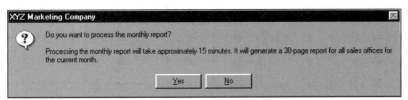

Figure 37-5: A message box with a longer message and a title.

Creating Custom Dialog Boxes: An Overview

The InputBox and MsgBox functions do just fine for many cases, but if you need to obtain more information, then you need to create a custom dialog box. A custom dialog box is created on a UserForm in the Visual Basic Editor.

The following is a list of the general steps that you typically take to create a custom dialog box:

1. Determine exactly how the dialog box is going to be used and where it is to fit into your VBA macro.

2. Activate the Visual Basic Editor and insert a new UserForm (select Insert ➪ UserForm).

3. Add the appropriate controls to the dialog box.

4. Create a macro to display the dialog box.

5. Create "event-handler" VBA subroutines that are executed when the user manipulates the controls (for example, clicks the OK button).

The following sections provide more details on creating a custom dialog box.

Working with UserForms

Excel stores custom dialog boxes on UserForms (one dialog box per form). To create a dialog box, you must first insert a new UserForm in the Visual Basic Editor window.

To activate the Visual Basic Editor, select Tools ➪ Macro ➪ Visual Basic Editor (or press Alt+F11). Make sure that the current workbook is selected in the Project window and then select Insert ➪ UserForm. The Visual Basic Editor displays an empty form, as shown in Figure 37-6. When you activate a form, the Visual Basic editor displays the Toolbox, which is used to add controls to the dialog box.

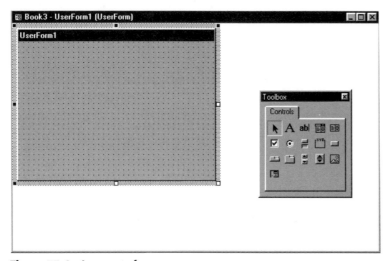

Figure 37-6: An empty form.

Adding Controls

The Toolbox, shown in Figure 37-7, contains various ActiveX controls that you can add to your dialog box.

Figure 37-7: The Toolbox contains the controls that you add to your dialog box.

When you move the mouse pointer over a control in the Toolbox, the control's name is displayed. To add a control, click and drag it in the form. After adding a control, you can move it or change its size.

Table 37-2 lists the Toolbox controls.

Table 37-2 Toolbox Controls	
Control	*Description*
Select Objects	Lets you select other controls by dragging
Label	Adds a label
TextBox	Adds a text box
ComboBox	Adds a combo box
ListBox	Adds a list box
CheckBox	Adds a check box
OptionButton	Adds an option button
ToggleButton	Adds a toggle button
Frame	Adds a frame (a container for other objects)
CommandButton	Adds a command button
TabStrip	Adds a tab strip
MultiPage	Adds a multipage control (a container for other objects)
ScrollBar	Adds a scrollbar
SpinButton	Adds a spin button
Image	Adds a control that can contain an image
RefEdit	Adds a reference edit control (lets the user select a range)

Cross-Reference   You can also place some of these controls directly on your worksheet. Refer to Chapter 38 for details.

Changing the Properties of a Control

Every control that you add to a UserForm has several properties that determine how the control looks and behaves. You can change some of these properties (such as `Height` and `Width`) by clicking and dragging the control's border. To change other properties, use the Properties window.

To display the Properties window, select View ⇨ Properties Window (or press F4). The Properties window displays a list of properties for the selected control (each control has a different set of properties). If you click the form itself, the Properties window displays properties for the form. Figure 37-8 shows the Properties window for a CommandButton control.

Figure 37-8: The Properties window for a CommandButton control.

To change a property, select the property in the Property window and then enter a new value. Some properties (such as `BackColor`) enable you to select a property from a list. The top of the Properties window contains a drop-down list that enables you to select a control to work with. You can also click a control to select it and display its properties.

When you set properties by using the Property window, you're setting properties at *design time*. You can also use VBA to change the properties of controls while the dialog box is displayed (that is, at *run time*).

A complete discussion of all the properties is well beyond the scope of this book. To find out about a particular property, select it in the Property window and press F1. The online Help for UserForm controls is extremely thorough.

Handling Events

When you insert a UserForm, that form can also hold VBA subroutines to handle the events that are generated by the form. An *event* is something that occurs when the user manipulates a control. For example, clicking a button is an event. Selecting an item in a list box control is an event. To make a dialog box useful, you must write VBA code to do something when an event occurs.

Event-handler subroutines have names that combine the control with the event. The general form is the control's name, followed by an underscore, and then the event name. For example, the subroutine that is executed when the user clicks a button named MyButton is `MyButton_Click`.

Displaying Custom Dialog Boxes

You also need to write a subroutine to display a custom dialog box. You use the `Show` method of the UserForm object. The following procedure displays the dialog box that is located on the UserForm1 form:

```
Sub ShowDialog()
    UserForm1.Show
End Sub
```

This subroutine should be stored in a regular VBA module (not the code module for the UserForm).

When this subroutine is executed, the dialog box is displayed. What happens next depends on the event-handler subroutines that you create.

A Custom Dialog Box Example

The preceding section is, admittedly, rudimentary. However, this section demonstrates how to develop a custom dialog box. This example is rather simple. The UserForm displays a message to the user — something that could be accomplished more easily by using the `MsgBox` function. However, the custom dialog box gives you a lot more flexibility in terms of formatting and layout of the message.

Creating the Dialog Box

If you're following along on your computer, start with a new workbook. Then, follow these steps:

1. Choose Tools ➪ Macro ➪ Visual Basic Editor (or press Alt+F11) to activate the VBE window.

2. In the VBE window, choose Insert ➪ UserForm.

   The VBE adds an empty form named UserForm1 and displays the Toolbox.

3. Press F4 to display the Properties window and then change the following properties of the UserForm object:

Property	Change To
Name	AboutBox
Caption	About This Workbook

4. Use the toolbar to add a Label object to the dialog box.

5. Select the Label object. In the Properties window, enter any text that you want for the label's Caption.

6. In the Properties window, click the Font property and adjust the font. You can change the typeface, size, and so on. The changes then appear in the form. Figure 37-9 shows an example of a formatted Label control.

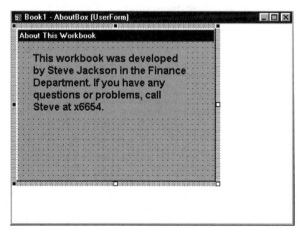

Figure 37-9: A Label control, after changing its Font properties.

7. Add a CommandButton object to the dialog box, and change the following properties for the CommandButton:

Property	Change To
Name	OKButton
Caption	OK
Default	True

8. Make other adjustments so that the form looks good to you. You can change the size of the form, or move or resize the controls.

Testing the Dialog Box

At this point, the dialog box has all the necessary controls. What's missing is a way to display the dialog box. This section explains how to write a VBA subroutine to display the custom dialog box.

1. Insert a module by selecting Insert ➪ Module.

2. In the empty module, enter the following code:

```
Sub ShowAboutBox()
 AboutBox.Show
End Sub
```

3. Activate Excel.

4. Choose Tools ➪ Macro ➪ Macros (or press Alt+F8).

5. In the Macros dialog box, select ShowAboutBox from the list of macros and click OK.

   The custom dialog box then appears.

If you click the OK button, notice that it doesn't close the dialog box as you may expect. This button needs to have an event-handler subroutine. You can dismiss the dialog box by clicking the close button in its title box.

Creating an Event-Handler Subroutine

An event-handler subroutine is executed when an event occurs. In this case, you need a subroutine to handle the Click event that's generated when the user clicks the OK button.

1. Activate the Visual Basic Editor (pressing Alt+F11 is the fastest way).

2. Activate the AboutBox form by double-clicking its name in the Project window.

3. Double-click the OKButton control.

4. VBE activates the module for the UserForm and inserts some code, as shown in Figure 37-10.

Figure 37-10: The module for the UserForm.

5. Insert the following statement before the End Sub statement:

```
Unload AboutBox
```

This statement simply dismisses the UserForm. The complete event-handler subroutine is listed below:

```
Private Sub OKButton_Click()
 Unload AboutBox
End Sub
```

Attaching the Macro to a Button

This section describes how to attach the ShowAboutBox subroutine to a Button object on a worksheet. Follow these steps:

1. Activate Excel.

2. Right-click any toolbar and select Forms from the shortcut menu.

   The Forms toolbar is displayed.

3. Click the Button tool on the Forms toolbar.

4. Drag the Button tool into the worksheet to create a Button object.

   When you release the mouse button, Excel displays its Assign Macro dialog box (see Figure 37-11).

Figure 37-11: The Assign Macro dialog box.

5. Select the ShowAboutBox macro from the list.

6. Click OK to close the Assign Macro dialog box.

7. Change the caption of the button to **About...**

After you perform these steps, click the button to execute the ShowAboutBox subroutine—which displays your custom dialog box.

Another Custom Dialog Box Example

The example in this section is an enhanced version of the ChangeCase example presented at the beginning of the chapter. Recall that the original version of this macro changes the text in the selected cells to uppercase characters. This modified version asks the user what type of case change to make: uppercase, lowercase, or initial capitals.

This workbook is available on the companion CD-ROM.

Creating the Dialog Box

This dialog box needs one piece of information from the user: the type of change to make to the text. Because only one option can be selected, OptionButton controls are appropriate. Follow these steps to create the custom dialog box. Start with an empty workbook:

1. Choose Tools ➪ Macro ➪ Visual Basic Editor (or press Alt+F11) to activate the VBE window.

2. In the VBE window, choose Insert ➪ UserForm.

   VBE adds an empty form named UserForm1 and displays the Toolbox.

3. Press F4 to display the Properties window and then change the following properties of the UserForm object:

Property	Change To
Name	CaseChangerDialog
Caption	Case Changer

4. Add a CommandButton object to the dialog box and then change the following properties for the CommandButton:

Property	Change To
Name	OKButton
Caption	OK
Default	True

5. Add another CommandButton object and then change the following properties:

Property	Change To
Name	CancelButton
Caption	Cancel
Cancel	True

6. Add an OptionButton control and then change the following properties (this option is the default, so its Value property should be set to True):

Property	Change To
Name	OptionUpper
Caption	Upper Case
Value	True

7. Add a second OptionButton control and then change the following properties:

Property	Change To
Name	OptionLower
Caption	Lower Case

8. Add a third OptionButton control and then change the following properties:

Property	Change To
Name	OptionProper
Caption	Proper Case

9. Adjust the size and position of the controls and the form until your screen resembles Figure 37-12. Make sure that the controls do not overlap.

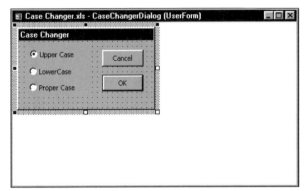

Figure 37-12: The dialog box after adding controls and adjusting some properties.

Tip

The Visual Basic Editor provides several useful commands to help you size and align the controls. Select the controls that you want to work with, and then choose a command from the Format menu. These commands are fairly self-explanatory, and the online Help has complete details.

Testing the Dialog Box

At this point, the dialog box has all the necessary controls. What's missing is a way to display the dialog box. This section explains how to write a VBA subroutine to display the custom dialog box. Make sure that the VBE window is activated.

1. Insert a module by selecting Insert ➪ Module.

2. In the empty module, enter the following code:

```
Sub ChangeCase()
 CaseChangerDialog.Show
End Sub
```

3. Select Run ➪ Sub/UserForm (or press F5).

The Excel window is then activated, and the new dialog box is displayed, as shown in Figure 37-13. The OptionButtons work, but clicking the OK and Cancel buttons has no effect. These two buttons need to have event-handler subroutines. Click the Close button in the title bar to dismiss the dialog box.

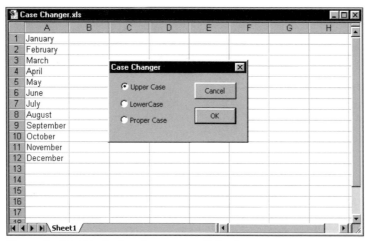

Figure 37-13: Displaying the custom dialog box.

Creating Event-Handler Subroutines

This section explains how to create two event-handler subroutines: one to handle the Click event for the CancelButton CommandButton and the other to handle the Click event for the OKButton CommandButton. Event handlers for the OptionButtons are not necessary. The VBA code can determine which of the three OptionButtons is selected.

Event-handler subroutines are stored in the form module. To create the subroutine to handle the Click event for the CancelButton, follow these steps:

1. Activate the CaseChangerDialog form by double-clicking its name in the Project window.

2. Double-click the CancelButton control.

3. VBE activates the module for the form and inserts some code, as shown in Figure 37-14.

4. Insert the following statement before the `End Sub` statement:

```
Unload CaseChangerDialog
```

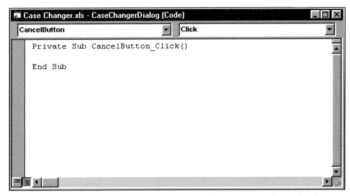

Figure 37-14: VBE sets up an empty subroutine to handle the Click event for the CancelButton control.

That's all there is to it. The following is a listing of the entire subroutine:

```
Private Sub CancelButton_Click()
  Unload CaseChangerDialog
End Sub
```

This subroutine is executed when the CancelButton is clicked. It consists of a single statement that unloads the CaseChangerDialog form.

The next step is to add the code to handle the Click event for the OKButton control. Follow these steps:

1. Select OKButton from the drop-down list at the top of the module. VBE begins a new subroutine called `OKButton_Click`.

2. Enter the following code (the first and last statements have already been entered for you by VBE):

```
Private Sub OKButton_Click()
    Application.ScreenUpdating = False
'   Exit if a range is not selected
    If TypeName(Selection) <> "Range" Then Exit Sub
'      Upper case
    If OptionUpper Then
        For Each cell In Selection
        If Not cell.HasFormula Then
            cell.Value = StrConv(cell.Value, vbUpperCase)
        End If
        Next cell
    End If
'   Lower case
    If OptionLower Then
        For Each cell In Selection
        If Not cell.HasFormula Then
```

```
                cell.Value = StrConv(cell.Value, vbLowerCase)
            End If
            Next cell
        End If
'    Proper case
    If OptionProper Then
        For Each cell In Selection
        If Not cell.HasFormula Then
            cell.Value = StrConv(cell.Value, bProperCase)
        End If
        Next cell
    End If
Unload CaseChangerDialog
End Sub
```

The macro starts by turning off screen updating (this makes the macro run faster). Next, the code checks the type of the selection. If a range is not selected, the procedure ends. The remainder of the subroutine consists of three separate blocks. Only one block is executed, determined by which OptionButton is selected. The selected OptionButton has a value of True. Finally, the UserForm is unloaded (dismissed).

Testing the Dialog Box

To try out the dialog box, follow these steps:

1. Activate Excel.

2. Enter some text into some cells.

3. Select the range with the text.

4. Choose Tools ➪ Macro ➪ Macros (or press Alt+F8).

5. In the Macros dialog box, select ChangeCase from the list of macros and then click OK. The custom dialog box appears.

6. Make your choice, and click OK.

Try it with a few more selections. Notice that if you click Cancel, the dialog box is dismissed and no changes are made.

Making the Macro Available from a Toolbar Button

At this point, everything should be working properly. However, you have no quick and easy way to execute the macro. A good way to execute this macro would be from a toolbar button. You can use the following steps:

1. Right-click any toolbar, and select Customize from the shortcut menu.

   Excel displays its Customize dialog box.

2. Click the Commands tab and then select Macros from the Categories list.

3. Click the Custom Button in the Commands list and drag it to a toolbar.

4. Right-click the new toolbar button and then select Assign Macro from the shortcut menu.

5. Choose ChangeCase from the list of macros, and click OK.

   You can also change the button image and add a tool tip by using other commands that are on the shortcut menu.

6. Click Close to close the Customize dialog box.

After performing the preceding steps, clicking the toolbar button executes the macro and displays the dialog box.

Note   If the workbook that contains the macro is not open already, it is opened. You may want to hide the workbook window (select Window ➪ Hide) so that it isn't displayed. Another option is to create an add-in. See Chapter 40 for specifics.

More on Creating Custom Dialog Boxes

Creating custom dialog boxes can make your macros much more versatile. You can create custom commands that display dialog boxes that look exactly like those that Excel uses. This section contains some additional information to help you develop custom dialog boxes that work like those that are built into Excel.

Adding Accelerator Keys

Dialog boxes should not discriminate against those who want to use the keyboard rather than a mouse. All of Excel's dialog boxes work equally well with a mouse and a keyboard, because each control has an associated accelerator key. The user can press Alt plus the accelerator key to work with a specific dialog box control.

Adding accelerator keys to your custom dialog boxes is a good idea. You do this in the Properties window by entering a character for the Accelerator property.

Obviously, the letter that you enter as the accelerator key must be a letter that is contained in the caption of the object. It can be any letter in the text (not necessarily the first letter). You should make sure that an accelerator key is not duplicated in a dialog box. If you have duplicate accelerator keys, the accelerator key acts on the first control in the "tab order" of the dialog box (explained shortly).

Some controls (such as edit boxes) don't have a caption property. You can assign an accelerator key to a label that describes the control. Pressing the accelerator key then activates the next control in the tab order (which should be the edit box).

Controlling Tab Order

The previous section refers to a dialog box's *tab order*. When you're working with a dialog box, pressing Tab and Shift+Tab cycles through the dialog box's controls. When you create a custom dialog box, you should make sure that the tab order is correct. Usually, this means that tabbing should move to the controls in a logical sequence.

To view or change the tab order in a custom dialog box, use the Properties window. If the TabStop property is True, the selected control is selectable when the user clicks Tab. Change the value of the TabIndex property. These values range from 0 (first in the tab order) to 1 less than the number of controls that have a TabIndex property. When you change the TabIndex, VBE automatically adjusts the TabIndex of all subsequent controls in the tab order.

Learning More

Mastering custom dialog boxes takes practice. You should closely examine the dialog boxes that Excel uses; these are examples of well-designed dialog boxes. You can duplicate nearly every dialog box that Excel uses.

The best way to learn more about creating dialog boxes is by using the online Help system.

Summary

This chapter describes how to create dialog boxes and use them with your VBA macros. It also covers two VBA functions — InputBox and MsgBox — which can sometimes take the place of a custom dialog box. The chapter includes several examples to help you understand how to use this feature.

✦   ✦   ✦

Using Dialog Box Controls in Your Worksheet

Chapter 37 presented an introduction to custom dialog boxes. If you like the idea of using dialog box controls — but don't like the idea of creating a dialog box — this chapter is for you. It explains how to enhance your worksheet with a variety of interactive controls, such as buttons, ListBoxes, and OptionButtons.

Why Use Controls on a Worksheet?

The main reason to use dialog box controls on a worksheet is to make it easier for the user to provide input. For example, if you create a model that uses one or more input cells, you can create controls to allow the user to select values for the input cells.

Adding controls to a worksheet requires much less effort than creating a dialog box. In addition, you may not have to create any macros, because you can link a control to a worksheet cell. For example, if you insert a CheckBox control on a worksheet, you can link it to a particular cell. When the CheckBox is selected, the linked cell displays TRUE. When the CheckBox is not selected, the linked cell displays FALSE.

Figure 38-1 shows a simple example that uses OptionButtons and a ScrollBar control.

Figure 38-1: This worksheet uses dialog box controls.

Controls That Are Available to You

Adding controls to a worksheet can be a bit confusing, because these controls have two sources. The controls that you can insert on a worksheet come from two toolbars:

✦ **Forms toolbar:** These controls are insertable objects (and are compatible with Excel 5 and Excel 95).

✦ **Control Toolbox toolbar:** These are ActiveX controls. These controls are a subset of those that are available for use on UserForms. These controls work only with Excel 97 and Excel 2000, and are not compatible with Excel 5 and Excel 95.

To add to the confusion, most of the controls are available on both toolbars. For example, the Forms toolbar and the Control Toolbox toolbar both have a control named ListBox. However, these are two entirely different controls. In general, the ActiveX controls (those on the Control Toolbox toolbar) provide more flexibility, and you should use those controls. However, if you need to save your workbook so that it can be opened by Excel 5 or Excel 95, you should use the controls that are on the Forms toolbar.

Note   This chapter focuses exclusively on the controls that are available in the Control Toolbox toolbar, as shown in Figure 38-2.

Figure 38-2: The
Control Toolbox toolbar.

A description of the buttons in the Control Toolbox appears in Table 38-1.

Table 38-1
Buttons on the Control Toolbox Toolbar

Button	What It Does
Design Mode	Toggles design mode
Properties	Displays the Properties window
View Code	Switches to the Visual Basic Editor so that you can write or edit VBA code for the selected control
CheckBox	Inserts a CheckBox control
TextBox	Inserts a TextBox control
CommandButton	Inserts a CommandButton control
OptionButton	Inserts an OptionButton control
ListBox	Inserts a ListBox control
ComboBox	Inserts a ComboBox control
ToggleButton	Inserts a ToggleButton control
SpinButton	Inserts a SpinButton control
ScrollBar	Inserts a ScrollBar control
Label	Inserts a Label control
Image	Inserts an Image control
More Controls	Displays a list of other ActiveX controls that are installed on your system

Using Controls

Adding ActiveX controls in a worksheet is easy. After you add a control, you can
adjust its properties to modify the way that the control looks and works.

Adding a Control

To add a control to a worksheet, make sure that the Control Toolbox toolbar is displayed — and don't confuse it with the Forms toolbar. Then, click and drag the control that you want to use into the worksheet to create the control. You don't need to be too concerned about the exact size or position, because you can modify these properties at any time.

About Design Mode

When you add a control to a worksheet, Excel goes into *design mode*. In this mode, you can adjust the properties of any controls on your worksheet, add or edit macros for the control, or change the control's size or position.

When Excel is in design mode, you can't try out the controls. To test the controls, you must exit design mode by clicking the Exit Design Mode button on the Control Toolbox toolbar.

Adjusting Properties

Every control that you add has various properties that determine how it looks and behaves. You can adjust these properties only when Excel is in design mode. When you add a control to a worksheet, Excel enters design mode automatically. If you need to change a control after you exit design mode, simply click the Design Mode button on the Control Toolbox toolbar.

To change the properties for a control, select the control and then click the Properties button on the Control Toolbox toolbar. Excel displays its Properties window, as shown in Figure 38-3. The Properties window has two tabs. The Alphabetic tab displays the properties in alphabetical order. The Categorized tab displays the properties by category. Both tabs show the same properties; only the order is different.

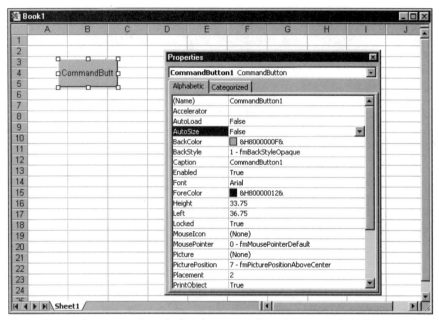

Figure 38-3: The Properties window lets you adjust the properties of a control.

To change a property, select it in the Properties window and then make the change. The manner in which you change a property depends on the property. Some properties display a drop-down list that lets you select from a list of options. Others (such as Font) provide a button that, when clicked, displays a dialog box. Other properties require you to type the property value. When you change a property, the change takes effect immediately.

Tip   To learn about a particular property, select the property in the Properties window and press F1.

Common Properties

Each control has its own unique set of properties. However, many controls share properties. This section describes some of the properties that are common to all or many controls, as set forth in Table 38-2.

Table 38-2
Properties Shared by Multiple Controls

Property	Description
Accelerator	The letter underlined in the control's caption.
AutoSize	If True, the control resizes itself automatically, based on the text in its caption.
BackColor	The background color of the control.
BackStyle	The style of the background (either transparent or opaque).
Caption	The text that appears on the control.
LinkedCell	A worksheet cell that contains the current value of a control.
ListFillRange	A worksheet range that contains items displayed in a ListBox or ComboBox control.
Value	The control's value.
Left and Top	Values that determine the control's position.
Width and Height	Values that determine the control's width and height.
Visible	If False, the control is hidden.
Name	The name of the control. By default, a control's name is based on the control type. You can change the name to any valid name. However, each control's name must be unique on the worksheet.
Picture	Enables you to specify a graphic image to display. The image must be contained in a file (it can't be copied from the Clipboard).

Linking Controls to Cells

Often, you can use ActiveX controls in a worksheet, without using any macros. Many of the controls have a LinkedCell property, which specifies a worksheet cell that is "linked" to the control.

For example, you might add a SpinButton control and specify B1 as its LinkedCell property. After doing so, cell B1 contains the value of the SpinButton, and clicking the SpinButton changes the value in cell B1 (see Figure 38-4). You can, of course, use the value contained in the linked cell in your formulas.

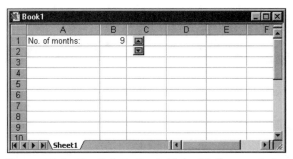

Figure 38-4: The SpinButton's LinkedCell property is set to cell B1, enabling the user to change the cell's value by using the SpinButton control.

Creating Macros for Controls

To create a macro for a control, you must use the Visual Basic Editor (VBE). The macros are stored in the code module for the sheet that contains the control. Each control can have a macro to handle any of its events. For example, a CommandButton control can have a macro for its `Click` event, its `DblClick` event, and various other events.

Tip The easiest way to access the code module for a control is to double-click the control while in design mode. Excel displays the VBE and creates an empty macro for the control's `Click` event. (See Figure 38-5.)

The control's name appears in the upper-left portion of the code window, and the event appears in the upper-right area. If you want to create a macro that executes when a different event occurs, select the event from the list in the upper-right area.

The following steps demonstrate how to insert a CommandButton and create a simple macro that displays a message when the button is clicked:

1. Make sure that the Control Toolbox toolbar is displayed.
2. Click the CommandButton tool in the Control Toolbox.
3. Click and drag in the worksheet to create the button.
4. Double-click the button. The VBE window is activated, and an empty subroutine is created.
5. Enter the following VBA statement before the `End Sub` statement:

   `MsgBox "You clicked on the command button."`

6. Press Alt+F11 to return to Excel.
7. Adjust any other properties for the CommandButton.
8. Click the Exit Design Mode button in the Control Toolbox toolbar.

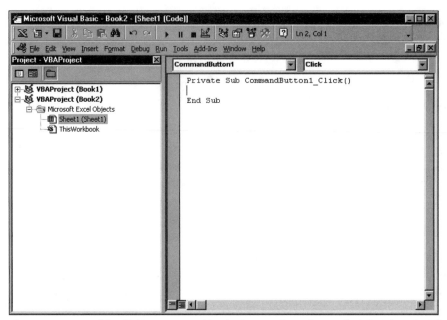

Figure 38-5: Double-clicking a control in design mode activates the Visual Basic Editor.

After performing the preceding steps, click the CommandButton to display the message box that is shown in Figure 38-6.

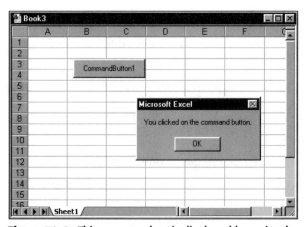

Figure 38-6: This message box is displayed by a simple macro.

Note

When you use a CommandButton on a worksheet, setting its TakeFocus-OnClick property to False is recommended. Otherwise, you may run into problems if the macro tries to select cells on the worksheet. If the CommandButton has the focus, the cells can't be selected!

The Controls Toolbox Controls

The sections that follow describe the ActiveX controls that are available on the Controls Toolbox toolbar.

On the CD-ROM The companion CD-ROM contains a file that includes examples of all the ActiveX controls.

CheckBox Control

A CheckBox control is useful for getting a binary choice: yes or no, true or false, on or off, and so on. Figure 38-7 shows some examples of CheckBox controls. Each of these controls displays its value in a cell (in A1:A4).

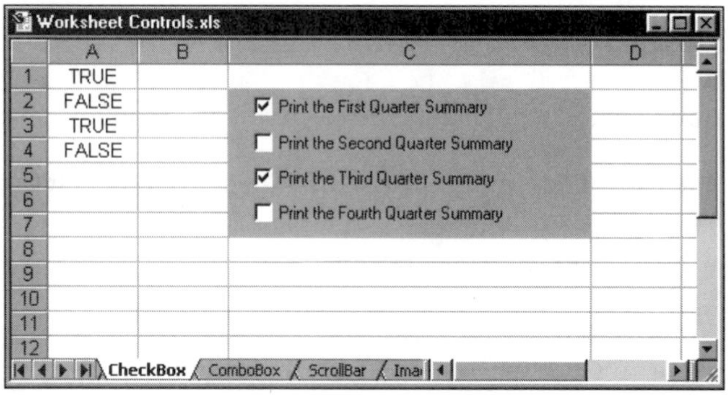

Figure 38-7: CheckBox controls on a worksheet.

The following is a description of the most useful properties of a CheckBox control:

✦ **Accelerator:** A letter that enables the user to change the value of the control by using the keyboard. For example, if the accelerator is A, pressing Alt+A changes the value of the CheckBox control.

✦ **LinkedCell:** The worksheet cell that's linked to the CheckBox. The cell displays TRUE if the control is checked or FALSE if the control is not checked.

ComboBox Control

A ComboBox control is similar to a ListBox control. A ComboBox, however, is a drop-down box, and it displays only one item at a time. Another difference is that the user may be allowed to enter a value that does not appear in the list of items.

Figure 38-8 shows a few ComboBox controls. One of these controls uses two columns for its ListFill range.

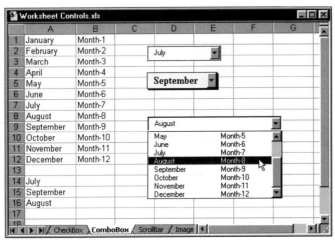

Figure 38-8: ComboBox controls.

The following is a description of the most useful properties of a ComboBox control:

✦ **BoundColumn:** If the list contains multiple columns, this property determines which column contains the returned value.

✦ **ColumnCount:** The number of columns in the list.

✦ **LinkedCell:** The worksheet cell that displays the selected item.

✦ **ListFillRange:** The worksheet range that contains the list items.

✦ **ListRows:** The number of items to display when the list drops down.

✦ **ListStyle:** Determines the appearance of the list items.

✦ **MultiSelect:** Determines whether the user can select multiple items from the list.

✦ **Style:** Determines whether the control acts like a drop-down list or a ComboBox. A drop-down list doesn't allow the user to enter a new value.

Note   If you use a multiselect ListBox, you cannot specify a LinkedCell; you need to write a macro to determine which items are selected.

CommandButton Control

A CommandButton is useless if you don't provide a macro to execute when the button is clicked. Figure 38-9 shows a worksheet that uses several CommandButtons. One of these CommandButtons uses a picture.

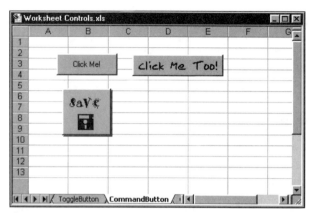

Figure 38-9: CommandButtons on a worksheet.

When a button is clicked, it executes a macro with a name that is made up of the CommandButton's name, an underscore, and the word *Click*. For example, if a CommandButton is named MyButton, clicking it executes the macro named MyButton_Click.

Image Control

An Image control is used to display an image that is contained in a file. This control offers no significant advantages over using standard imported images (as described in Chapter 14).

Label Control

A Label control simply displays text. This is not a useful control for use on worksheets, and a standard TextBox AutoShape gives you more versatility.

ListBox Controls

The ListBox control presents a list of items, and the user can select an item (or multiple items). Figure 38-10 shows a worksheet with several ListBox controls. As you can see, you have a great deal of control over the appearance of ListBox controls. One of the ListBoxes uses two columns as its ListFill range.

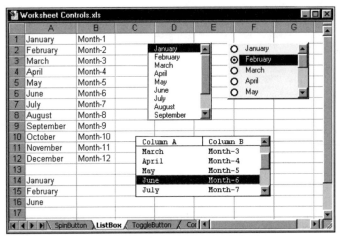

Figure 38-10: ListBox controls on a worksheet.

You can specify a range that holds the ListBox items, and this range can consist of multiple columns.

The following is a description of the most useful properties of a ListBox control:

✦ **BoundColumn:** If the list contains multiple columns, this property determines which column contains the returned value.

✦ **ColumnCount:** The number of columns in the list.

✦ **IntegralHeight:** This is True if the height of the ListBox adjusts automatically to display full lines of text when the list is scrolled vertically. If False, the ListBox may display partial lines of text when it is scrolled vertically.

✦ **LinkedCell:** The worksheet cell that displays the selected item.

✦ **ListFillRange:** The worksheet range that contains the list items.

✦ **ListStyle:** Determines the appearance of the list items.

✦ **MultiSelect:** Determines whether the user can select multiple items from the list.

Note

If you use a multiselect ListBox, you cannot specify a LinkedCell; you need to write a macro to determine which items are selected.

OptionButton Controls

OptionButtons are useful when the user needs to select from a small number of items. OptionButtons are always used in groups of at least two. Figure 38-11 shows two sets of OptionButtons. One set uses graphic images (set with the Picture property).

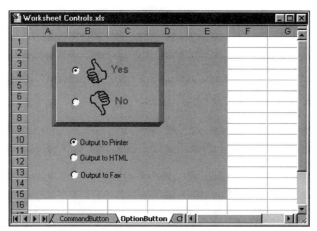

Figure 38-11: Two sets of OptionButtons.

The following is a description of the most useful properties of an OptionButton control:

✦ **Accelerator:** A letter that lets the user select the option by using the keyboard. For example, if the accelerator for an OptionButton is C, pressing Alt+C selects the control.

✦ **GroupName:** A name that identifies an OptionButton as being associated with other OptionButtons with the same GroupName property.

✦ **LinkedCell:** The worksheet cell that's linked to the OptionButton. The cell displays TRUE if the control is selected or FALSE if the control is not selected.

Note

If your worksheet contains more than one set of OptionButtons, you *must* change the GroupName property for all OptionButtons in a particular set. Otherwise, all OptionButtons become part of the same set.

ScrollBar Control

The ScrollBar control is similar to a SpinButton control (discussed next). The difference is that the user can drag the ScrollBar's button to change the control's value in larger increments. Figure 38-12 shows a worksheet with three ScrollBar controls. These ScrollBars are used to change the color in the rectangle objects. The value of the ScrollBars determines the red, green, or blue component of the rectangle's color. This example uses a few simple macros to change the colors.

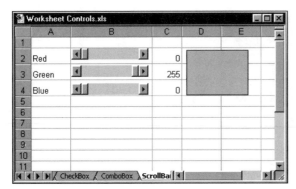

Figure 38-12: This worksheet has several ScrollBar controls.

The following is a description of the most useful properties of a ScrollBar control:

✦ **Value:** The current value of the control.

✦ **Min:** The minimum value for the control.

✦ **Max:** The maximum value for the control.

✦ **LinkedCell:** The worksheet cell that displays the value of the control.

✦ **SmallChange:** The amount that the control's value is changed by a click.

✦ **LargeChange:** The amount that the control's value is changed by clicking either side of the button.

The ScrollBar control is most useful for selecting a value that extends across a wide range of possible values.

SpinButton Control

The SpinButton control lets the user select a value by clicking the control, which has two arrows (one to increase the value and the other to decrease the value). Figure 38-13 shows a worksheet that uses several SpinButton controls. Each control is linked to the cell to the right. As you can see, a SpinButton can display either horizontally or vertically.

The following is a description of the most useful properties of a SpinButton control:

✦ **Value:** The current value of the control.

✦ **Min:** The minimum value of the control.

✦ **Max:** The maximum value of the control.

✦ **LinkedCell:** The worksheet cell that displays the value of the control.

✦ **SmallChange:** The amount that the control's value is changed by a click. Usually, this property is set to 1, but you can make it any value.

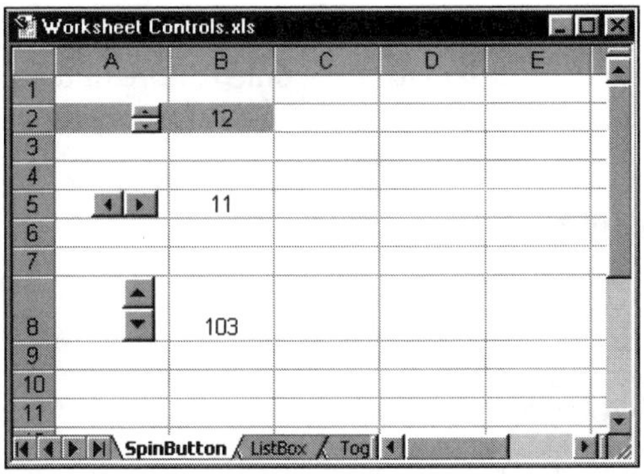

Figure 38-13: SpinButton controls in a worksheet.

If you use a linked cell for a SpinButton, you need to understand that the worksheet is recalculated every time the value of the control is changed. Therefore, if the user changes the value from 0 to 12, the worksheet gets calculated 12 times. If your worksheet takes a long time to calculate, you may want to reconsider using this control.

TextBox Controls

On the surface, a TextBox control may not seem useful. After all, it simply contains text — you can usually use worksheet cells to get text input. In fact, TextBox controls are useful not so much for input control but for output control. Because a TextBox can have ScrollBars, you can use a TextBox to display a great deal of information in a small area.

Figure 38-14 shows an example of a TextBox that is used to provide help information. The user can use the ScrollBar to read the text. The advantage is that the text uses only a small amount of screen space. The example in this figure uses three controls: the TextBox, a Label control, and a disabled CommandButton control (which provides a backdrop for the other two controls).

The following is a description of the most useful properties of a TextBox control:

✦ **AutoSize:** Determines whether the control adjusts its size automatically, depending on the amount of text.

✦ **IntegralHeight:** If True, the height of the TextBox adjusts automatically to display full lines of text when the list is scrolled vertically. If False, the ListBox may display partial lines of text when it is scrolled vertically.

✦ **MaxLength:** The maximum number of characters allowed in the TextBox. If 0, no limit exists on the number of characters.

✦ **MultiLine:** If True, the TextBox can display more than one line of text.

✦ **TextAlign:** Determines how the text is aligned in the TextBox.

✦ **WordWrap:** Determines whether the control allows word wrap.

✦ **ScrollBars:** Determines the type of ScrollBars for the control: horizontal, vertical, both, or none.

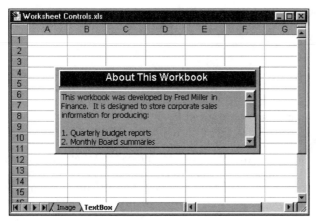

Figure 38-14: This worksheet uses a TextBox to display help information.

ToggleButton Control

A ToggleButton control has two states: on or off. Clicking the button toggles between these two states, and the button changes its appearance. Its value is either True (pressed) or False (not pressed). You can often use a ToggleButton in place of a CheckBox control.

Summary

This chapter describes how to add ActiveX controls to a worksheet and how to use these controls to enable users easily to provide data that's used in a worksheet.

✦   ✦   ✦

VBA
Programming
Examples

My philosophy about learning to write Excel macros
places heavy emphasis on examples. I've found that
a well-thought-out example often communicates a concept
much better than a lengthy description of the underlying the-
ory. In this book, I chose to avoid a painstaking description
of every nuance of VBA. I take this approach for two reasons.
First, space limitations prohibit such a discussion. But more
to the point, the VBA language is described very well in
Excel's online Help system.

This chapter consists of several examples that demonstrate
common VBA techniques. You may be able to use some of the
examples directly, but in most cases, you must adapt them to
your own needs. These examples are organized into the following categories:

+ Working with ranges
+ Changing Excel's settings
+ Working with graphic objects
+ Working with charts
+ Learning ways to speed your VBA code

All subroutines and functions in this chapter can be found in a
workbook that's included on the companion CD-ROM.

Working with Ranges

Most of what you do in VBA probably involves worksheet
ranges. When you work with range objects, keep the following points in mind:

✦ Your VBA code doesn't need to select a range to do something with the range.

✦ If your code does select a range, its worksheet must be active.

✦ The macro recorder doesn't always generate the most efficient code. Often, you can use the recorder to create your macro and then edit the code to make it more efficient.

✦ Using named ranges in your VBA code is recommended. For example, a reference such as Range ("Total") is better than Range ("D45"). In the latter case, you need to modify the macro if you add a row above row 45.

✦ When you record macros that select ranges, pay close attention to "relative vs. absolute" recording mode. The recording mode that you choose can drastically affect the way the macro operates.

✦ If you create a macro that loops through each cell in the current range selection, be aware that the user can select entire columns or rows. In most cases, you don't want to loop through every cell in the selection. You need to create a subset of the selection that consists only of nonblank cells.

✦ Be aware that Excel allows multiple selections. For example, you can select a range, press Ctrl, and then select another range. You can test for this in your macro and take appropriate actions.

The examples in the following sections demonstrate these points.

Copying a Range

Copying a range is a frequent activity in macros. When you turn on the macro recorder (using absolute recording mode) and copy a range from A1:A5 to B1:B5, you get a VBA macro like this:

```
Sub CopyRange()
    Range("A1:A5").Select
    Selection.Copy
    Range("B1").Select
    ActiveSheet.Paste
    Application.CutCopyMode = False
End Sub
```

This macro works, but it's not the most efficient way to copy a range. You can accomplish exactly the same result with the following one-line macro:

```
Sub CopyRange2()
    Range("A1:A5").Copy Range("B1")
End Sub
```

This takes advantage of the fact that the Copy method can use an argument that specifies the destination. Information such as this is available in the online Help system.

The example demonstrates that the macro recorder doesn't always generate the most efficient code. As you see, you don't have to select an object to work with it. Note that Macro2 doesn't select a range; therefore, the active cell doesn't change when this macro is executed.

Copying a Variable-Size Range

Often, you want to copy a range of cells in which the exact row and column dimensions are unknown.

Figure 39-1 shows a range on a worksheet. This range consists of a number of rows, and the number of rows can change daily. Because the exact range address is unknown at any given time, writing a macro to copy the range can be challenging.

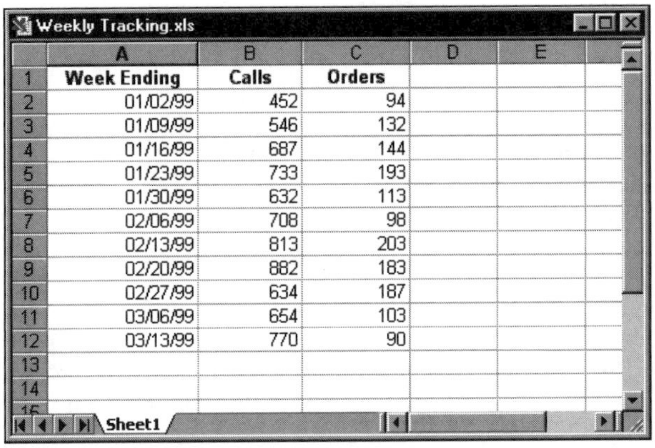

Figure 39-1: This range can consist of any number of rows.

The macro that follows demonstrates how to copy this range from Sheet1 to Sheet2 (beginning at cell A1). It uses the CurrentRegion property, which returns a Range object that corresponds to the active block of cells. This is equivalent to choosing Edit ➪ Go To, clicking the Special button, and then selecting the Current Region option.

```
Sub CopyCurrentRegion()
    Range("A1").CurrentRegion.Copy
    Sheets("Sheet2").Select
    Range("A1").Select
    ActiveSheet.Paste
    Sheets("Sheet1").Select
    Application.CutCopyMode = False
End Sub
```

Selecting to the End of a Row or Column

You probably are in the habit of using key combinations, such as Ctrl+Shift+right-arrow key and Ctrl+Shift+down-arrow key, to select from the active cell to the end of a row or column. When you record these actions in Excel (using relative recording mode), you'll find that the resulting code works as you would expect it to.

 In previous versions of Excel, the macro recorder always recorded absolute cell addresses when making these types of selections. This problem has been fixed in Excel 2000.

The following VBA subroutine selects the range that begins at the active cell and extends down to the last cell in the column (or to the first empty cell, whichever comes first). When the range is selected, you can do whatever you want with it — copy it, move it, format it, and so on.

```
Sub SelectDown()
    Range(ActiveCell, ActiveCell.End(xlDown)).Select
End Sub
```

This example uses the End method of the Range object, which returns a Range object. The End method takes one argument, which can be any of the following constants: xlUp, xlDown, xlToLeft, or xlToRight.

Selecting a Row or Column

The macro that follows demonstrates how to select the column of the active cell. It uses the EntireColumn property, which returns a range that consists of a column.

```
Sub SelectColumn()
    ActiveCell.EntireColumn.Select
End Sub
```

As you may suspect, an EntireRow property also is available, which returns a range that consists of a row.

If you want to perform an operation on all cells in the selected column, you don't need to select the column. For example, the following subroutine makes all cells bold in the row that contains the active cell:

```
Sub MakeRowBold()
    ActiveCell.EntireRow.Font.Bold = True
End Sub
```

Moving a Range

Moving a range consists of cutting it to the Clipboard and then pasting it to another area. If you record your actions while performing a move operation, the macro recorder generates code as follows:

```
Sub MoveRange()
    Range("A1:C6").Select
    Selection.Cut
    Range("A10").Select
    ActiveSheet.Paste
End Sub
```

As demonstrated with copying earlier in this chapter, this is not the most efficient way to move a range of cells. In fact, you can do it with a single VBA statement, as follows:

```
Sub MoveRange2()
    Range("A1:C6").Cut Range("A10")
End Sub
```

This statement takes advantage of the fact that the Cut method can use an argument that specifies the destination.

Looping Through a Range Efficiently

Many macros perform an operation on each cell in a range, or they may perform selective actions based on the content of each cell. These operations usually involve a For-Next loop that processes each cell in the range.

The following example demonstrates how to loop through all the cells in a range. In this case, the range is the current selection. In this example, Cell is a variable name that refers to the cell being processed. Within the For-Next loop, the single statement evaluates the cell and changes its font color if the cell value is negative (vbRed is a built-in constant that represents the color red).

```
Sub ProcessCells()
    For Each Cell In Selection
    If Cell.Value < 0 Then Cell.Font.Color = vbRed
    Next Cell
End Sub
```

The preceding example works, but what if the selection consists of an entire column or an entire range? This is not uncommon, because Excel lets you perform operations on entire columns or rows. But in this case, the macro seems to take forever, because it loops through each cell — even those that are blank. What's needed is a way to process only the nonblank cells.

This can be accomplished by using the SelectSpecial method. In the following example, the SelectSpecial method is used to create two new objects: the subset of the selection that consists of cells with constants, and the subset of the selection that consists of cells with formulas. Each of these subsets is processed, with the net effect of skipping all blank cells.

```
Sub SkipBlanks()
' Ignore errors
  On Error Resume Next

' Process the constants
  Set ConstantCells = Selection.SpecialCells(xlConstants, 23)
  For Each cell In ConstantCells
    If cell.Value > 0 Then cell.Font.Color = vbRed
  Next cell

' Process the formulas
  Set FormulaCells = Selection.SpecialCells(xlFormulas, 23)
  For Each cell In FormulaCells
    If cell.Value > 0 Then cell.Font.Color = vbRed
  Next cell
End Sub
```

The SkipBlanks subroutine works fast, regardless of what is selected. For example, you can select the range, select all columns in the range, select all rows in the range, or even select the entire worksheet. In all of these cases, only the cells that contain constants or values are processed. This is a vast improvement over the ProcessCells subroutine presented earlier.

Notice that the following statement is used in the subroutine:

```
On Error Resume Next
```

This statement causes Excel to ignore any errors that occur and simply to process the next statement. This is necessary because the SpecialCells method produces an error if no cells qualify. Normal error checking is resumed when the subroutine ends. To tell Excel explicitly to return to normal error-checking mode, use the following statement:

```
On Error GoTo 0
```

Prompting for a Cell Value

As discussed in Chapter 37, you can take advantage of VBA's InputBox function to solicit a value from the user. Figure 39-2 shows an example.

You can assign this value to a variable and use it in your subroutine. Often, however, you want to place the value into a cell. The following subroutine demonstrates how to ask the user for a value and place it into cell A1 of the active worksheet, using only one statement:

```
Sub GetValue()
  Range("A1").Value = InputBox("Enter the value for cell A1")
End Sub
```

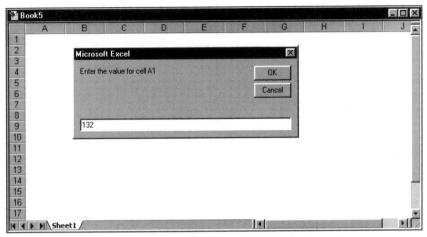

Figure 39-2: Using VBA's InputBox function to get a value from the user.

Determining the Type of Selection

If your macro is designed to work with a range selection, you need to determine that a range is actually selected. Otherwise, the macro most likely fails. The following subroutine identifies the type of object that is currently selected:

```
Sub SelectionType()
  MsgBox TypeName(Selection)
End Sub
```

If a Range object is selected, the MsgBox displays *Range*. If your macro is designed to work only with ranges, you can use an If statement to ensure that a range is actually selected. The following is an example that beeps, displays a message, and exits the subroutine if the current selection is not a Range object:

```
Sub CheckSelection()
  If TypeName(Selection) <> "Range" Then
    Beep
    MsgBox "Select a range."
    Exit Sub
  End If
' ... [Other statements go here]
End Sub
```

Another way to approach this is to define a custom function that returns True if the selection is a Range object, and False otherwise. The following function does just that:

```
Function IsRange(sel) As Boolean
 IsRange = False
 If TypeName(sel) = "Range" Then IsRange = True
End Function
```

If you enter the IsRange function in your module, you can rewrite the CheckSelection subroutine as follows:

```
Sub CheckSelection()
 If IsRange(Selection) Then
 ' ... [Other statements go here]
 Else
 Beep
 MsgBox "Select a range."
 Exit Sub
 End If
End Sub
```

Identifying a Multiple Selection

As you know, Excel enables you to make a multiple selection by pressing Ctrl while you select objects or ranges. This can cause problems with some macros; for example, you can't copy a multiple selection that consists of nonadjacent ranges. The following macro demonstrates how to determine whether the user has made a multiple selection:

```
Sub MultipleSelection()
   If Selection.Areas.Count > 1 Then
   MsgBox "Multiple selections not allowed."
   Exit Sub
   End If
 ' ... [Other statements go here]
End Sub
```

This example uses the Areas method, which returns a collection of all objects in the selection. The Count property returns the number of objects that are in the collection.

The following is a VBA function that returns True if the selection is a multiple selection:

```
Function IsMultiple(sel) As Boolean
   IsMultiple = False
   If Selection.Areas.Count > 1 Then IsMultiple = True
End Function
```

Changing Excel's Settings

Some of the most useful macros are simple subroutines that change one or more of Excel's settings. For example, it takes quite a few actions simply to change the Recalculation mode from automatic to manual.

This section contains two examples that demonstrate how to change settings in Excel. These examples can be generalized to other operations.

Boolean Settings

A Boolean setting is one that is either on or off. For example, you may want to create a macro that turns on and off the row and column headings. If you record your actions while you access the Options dialog box, you find that Excel generates the following code if you turn off the headings:

```
ActiveWindow.DisplayHeadings = False
```

It generates the following code if you turn on the headings:

```
ActiveWindow.DisplayHeadings = True
```

This may lead you to suspect that the heading display requires two macros: one to turn on the headings and one to turn them off. Actually, this isn't true. The following subroutine uses the `Not` operator effectively to toggle the heading display from `True` to `False` and from `False` to `True`:

```
Sub ToggleHeadings()
   If TypeName(ActiveSheet) <> "Worksheet" Then Exit Sub
   ActiveWindow.DisplayHeadings = Not
ActiveWindow.DisplayHeadings
End Sub
```

The first statement ensures that the active sheet is a worksheet; otherwise, an error occurs (chart sheets don't have row and column headers). This technique can be used with any other settings that take on Boolean (`True` or `False`) values. For example, you can create macros to toggle sheet tab display, gridlines, and so on. The best way to find out which properties control these items is to turn on the macro recorder while you change them. Then, examine the VBA code.

Non-Boolean Settings

For non-Boolean settings, you can use the following `Select Case` structure. This example toggles the `Calculation` mode and displays a message indicating the current mode:

```
Sub ToggleCalcMode()
  Select Case Application.Calculation
    Case xlManual
      Application.Calculation = xlAutomatic
      MsgBox "Automatic Calculation Mode"
    Case xlAutomatic
      Application.Calculation = xlManual
      MsgBox "Manual Calculation Mode"
  End Select
End Sub
```

Working with Graphic Objects (Shapes)

VBA subroutines can work with any type of Excel object, including graphic objects that are embedded on a worksheet's draw layer. This section provides a few examples of using VBA to manipulate graphic objects.

Creating a Text Box to Match a Range

The following example creates a text box that is positioned precisely over the selected range of cells. This is useful if you want to make a text box that covers up a range of data.

```
Sub CreateTextBox()
  If TypeName(Selection) <> "Range" Then Exit Sub
  Set RangeSelection = Selection
' Get coordinates of range selection
  SelLeft = Selection.Left
  SelTop = Selection.Top
  SelWidth = Selection.Width
  SelHeight = Selection.Height
' Create a text box

  ActiveSheet.Shapes.AddTextbox(msoTextOrientationHorizontal, _
    SelLeft, SelTop, SelWidth, SelHeight).Select
  RangeSelection.Select
End Sub
```

The macro first checks to make sure that a range is selected. If not, the subroutine is exited with no further action. If a range is selected, the coordinates (Left, Top, Width, and Height) are assigned to four variables. These variables are then used as the arguments for the AddTextbox method of the Shapes collection.

The following is a more sophisticated version of this macro that works with a multiple selection of cells. The subroutine creates a text box for each area in the multiple selection. It uses a For-Next loop to cycle through each area in the range selection. If the range has only one area (not a multiple selection), the For-Next loop is activated only one time.

```
Sub CreateTextBox2()
  If TypeName(Selection) <> "Range" Then Exit Sub
  Set RangeSelection = Selection
  For Each Part In Selection.Areas
'    Get coordinates of range selection
    SelLeft = Part.Left
    SelTop = Part.Top
    SelWidth = Part.Width
    SelHeight = Part.Height
'   Create a text box

    ActiveSheet.Shapes.AddTextbox(msoTextOrientationHorizontal,
_
      SelLeft, SelTop, SelWidth, SelHeight).Select
  Next Part
  RangeSelection.Select
End Sub
```

Drawing Attention to a Range

The example in this section is a macro that draws an AutoShape around the selected range. Figure 39-3 shows an example.

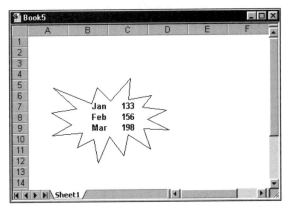

Figure 39-3: A macro draws the AutoShape around a selected range of cells.

```
Sub AddExplosion()
If TypeName(Selection) <> "Range" Then Exit Sub
  SelLeft = Selection.Left - (Selection.Width * 0.2)
  SelTop = Selection.Top - (Selection.Height * 0.5)
  SelWidth = Selection.Width + (Selection.Width * 0.4)
  SelHeight = Selection.Height + Selection.Height
  ActiveSheet.Shapes.AddShape (msoShapeExplosion1, _
    SelLeft, SelTop, SelWidth, SelHeight).Select
  Selection.ShapeRange.Fill.Visible = msoFalse
End Sub
```

The macro begins by determining the location and size of the shape, using the selected range. The shape needs to be larger than the selected range and must be offset to the left and to the top. Therefore, the macro performs some calculations to determine the left, top, width, and height of the shape. In this example, the shape's height is twice as large as the height of the selection and 40 percent wider than the width of the selection. These calculations were determined by trial and error. In most cases, the shape is drawn in such a way that the contents of the underlying cells are completely visible. In other cases, slight adjustments are required.

After the parameters are calculated, the AutoShape is added to the active sheet. The AutoShape that's drawn by the macro is identified by a constant (msoShapeExplosion1). The final statement makes the shape transparent.

Working with Charts

Manipulating charts with VBA can be confusing, mainly because of the large number of objects involved. To get a feel for this, turn on the macro recorder, create a chart, and perform some routine chart editing. You may be surprised by the amount of code that's generated.

After you understand the objects in a chart, however, you can create some useful macros. This section presents a few macros that deal with charts. When you write macros that manipulate charts, you need to understand some terminology. An embedded chart on a worksheet is a ChartObject object. Before you can do anything to a ChartObject, you must activate it. The following statement activates the ChartObject named Chart 1.

```
ActiveSheet.ChartObjects("Chart 1").Activate
```

After you activate the ChartObject, you can refer to it in your VBA code as the ActiveChart. If the chart is on a separate chart sheet, it becomes the active chart as soon as the chart sheet is activated.

Modifying the Chart Type

The following example changes the chart type of every embedded chart on the active sheet. It makes each chart an area chart by adjusting the Type property of the ActiveChart object. A built-in constant, xlArea, represents an area chart.

```
Sub ChartType()
  For Each cht In ActiveSheet.ChartObjects
    cht.Activate
    ActiveChart.Type = xlArea
  Next cht
End Sub
```

The preceding example uses a `For-Next` loop to cycle through all the `ChartObject` objects on the active sheet. Within the loop, the chart is activated and then the chart type is assigned a new value.

The following macro performs the same function but works on all chart sheets in the active workbook:

```
Sub ChartType2()
  For Each cht In ThisWorkbook.Charts
    cht.Activate
    ActiveChart.Type = xlArea
  Next cht
End Sub
```

Modifying Properties

The following example changes the legend font for all charts that are on the active sheet. It uses a `For-Next` loop to process all `ChartObject` objects, and uses the `On Error` statement to ignore the error that occurs if a chart does not have a legend.

```
Sub LegendMod()
  On Error Resume Next
  For Each cht In ActiveSheet.ChartObjects
    cht.Activate
    With ActiveChart.Legend.Font
      .Name = "Arial"
      .FontStyle = "Bold"
      .Size = 8
    End With
  Next cht
End Sub
```

Applying Chart Formatting

This example applies several different formatting types to the active chart. A chart must be activated before executing this macro. You activate an embedded chart by selecting it. Activate a chart on a chart sheet by activating the chart sheet.

```
Sub ChartMods()
  On Error Resume Next
  With ActiveChart
    .Type = xlArea
    .ChartArea.Font.Name = "Arial"
    .ChartArea.Font.FontStyle = "Regular"
    .ChartArea.Font.Size = 9
    .PlotArea.Interior.ColorIndex = xlNone
    .Axes(xlValue).TickLabels.Font.Bold = True
    .Axes(xlCategory).TickLabels.Font.Bold = True
    .Legend.Position = xlBottom
  End With
End Sub
```

I created this macro by recording my actions as I formatted a chart. Then, I cleaned up the recorded code by removing irrelevant lines.

VBA Speed Tips

VBA is fast, but it's often not fast enough. This section presents some programming examples that you can use to help speed your macros.

Turning Off Screen Updating

You've probably noticed that when you execute a macro, you can watch everything that occurs in the macro. Sometimes this is instructive, but after you get the macro working properly, it can be annoying and slow things considerably.

Fortunately, a way exists to disable the normal screen updating that occurs when you execute a macro. Insert the following statement to turn off screen updating:

```
Application.ScreenUpdating = False
```

If, at any point during the macro, you want the user to see the results of the macro, use the following statement to turn back on screen updating:

```
Application.ScreenUpdating = True
```

Preventing Alert Messages

One of the benefits of using a macro is that you can perform a series of actions automatically. You can start a macro and then get a cup of coffee while Excel does its thing. Some operations cause Excel to display messages that must be attended to, however. For example, if your macro deletes a sheet, you see the message that is shown in the dialog box in Figure 39-4. These types of messages mean that you can't execute your macro unattended.

Figure 39-4: You can instruct Excel not to display these types of alerts while a macro is running.

To avoid these alert messages, insert the following VBA statement:

```
Application.DisplayAlerts = False
```

When the subroutine ends, the `DisplayAlerts` property is automatically reset to `True` (its normal state).

Simplifying Object References

As you probably have discovered, references to objects can get very lengthy—especially if your code refers to an object that's not on the active sheet or in the active workbook. For example, a fully qualified reference to a `Range` object may look like this:

```
Workbooks("MyBook").Worksheets("Sheet1").Range("IntRate")
```

If your macro uses this range frequently, you may want to create an object variable by using the `Set` command. For example, to assign this `Range` object to an object variable named `Rate`, use the following statement:

```
Set Rate = Workbooks("MyBook").Worksheets("Sheet1"). _
    Range("IntRate")
```

After this variable is defined, you can use the variable `Rate` instead of the lengthy reference.

Besides simplifying your coding, using object variables also speeds your macros quite a bit. I've seen some macros execute twice as fast after creating object variables.

Declaring Variable Types

Usually, you don't have to worry about the type of data that's assigned to a variable. Excel handles all these details behind the scenes. For example, if you have a variable named `MyVar`, you can assign a number or any type to it. You can even assign a text string to it later in the procedure.

But if you want your procedures to execute as fast as possible, you should tell Excel in advance what type of data is going be assigned to each of your variables. This is known as *declaring* a variables type.

Table 39-1 lists all the data types that are supported by VBA. This table also lists the number of bytes that each type uses and the approximate range of possible values.

Table 39-1
Data Types

Data Type	Bytes Used	Approximate Range of Values
Byte	1	0 to 255
Boolean	2	True or False
Integer	2	−32,768 to 32,767
Long (long integer)	4	−2,147,483,648 to 2,147,483,647
Single (single-precision floating-point)	4 3	−3.4E38 to −1.4E−45 for negative values; 1.4E−45 to 4E38 for positive values
Double (double-precision floating-point)	8 1	−1.7E308 to −4.9E−324 for negative values; 4.9E−324 to .7E308 for positive values
Currency (scaled integer)	8	−9.2E14 to 9.2E14
Decimal	14	+/−7.9E28 with no decimal point
Date	8	January 1, 100, to December 31, 9999
Object	4	Any Object reference
String (variable-length)	10 + string length	0 to approximately 2 billion
String (fixed-length)	Length of string	1 to approximately 65,400
Variant (with numbers)	16	Any numeric value up to the range of a Double
Variant (with characters)	22 + string length	Same range as for variable-length String
User-defined (using Type)	Number required by elements	The range of each element is the same as the range of its data type

If you don't declare a variable, Excel uses the Variant data type. In general, the best technique is to use the data type that uses the smallest number of bytes yet can still handle all the data assigned to it. When VBA works with data, execution speed is a function of the number of bytes that VBA has at its disposal. In other words, the fewer bytes that are used by data, the faster VBA can access and manipulate the data.

To declare a variable, use the Dim statement before you use the variable for the first time. For example, to declare the variable Units as an integer, use the following statement:

```
Dim Units as Integer
```

To declare the variable UserName as a string, use the following statement:

```
Dim UserName as String
```

If you know that UserName can never exceed 20 characters, you can declare it as a fixed-length string, as follows:

```
Dim UserName as String * 20
```

If you declare a variable within a procedure, the declaration is valid only within that procedure. If you declare a variable outside of any procedures (but before the first procedure), the variable is valid in all procedures in the module.

If you use an object variable (as described previously), you can declare the variable as an object data type. The following is an example:

```
Dim Rate as Range
Set Rate = Workbooks("MyBook").Worksheets("Sheet1").
Range("IntRate")
```

To force yourself to declare all the variables that you use, insert the following statement at the top of your module:

```
Option Explicit
```

If you use this statement, Excel displays an error message if it encounters a variable that hasn't been declared.

Summary

This chapter presents several examples of VBA code that work with ranges, Excel's settings, graphic objects, and charts. It also discusses techniques that you can use to make your VBA macros run faster.

✦　　✦　　✦

Creating Custom Excel Add-Ins

For developers, one of the most useful features in Excel is the capability to create add-ins. This chapter discusses this concept and provides a practical example of creating an add-in.

What Is an Add-In?

Generally speaking, a spreadsheet *add-in* is something that's added to the spreadsheet to give it additional functionality. Excel 2000 has several add-ins, including the Analysis ToolPak, AutoSave, and Solver. Some add-ins (such as the Analysis ToolPak, discussed in Chapter 28) provide new worksheet functions that can be used in formulas. Usually, the new features blend in well with the original interface, so they appear to be part of the program.

Excel's approach to add-ins is quite powerful, because any knowledgeable Excel user can create add-ins from XLS workbooks. An Excel add-in is basically a different form of an XLS workbook file. Any XLS file can be converted into an add-in, but not every workbook is a good candidate for an add-in. Add-ins are always hidden, so you can't display worksheets or chart sheets that are contained in an add-in. But, you can access its VBA subroutines and functions and display dialog boxes that are contained on dialog sheets.

The following are some typical uses for Excel add-ins:

+ **To store one or more custom worksheet functions.** When the add-in is loaded, the functions can be used like any built-in worksheet function.

+ **To store Excel utilities.** VBA is ideal for creating general-purpose utilities that extend the power of Excel. The Power Utility Pak that I created is an example of such a function.

✦ **To store proprietary macros.** If you don't want end users to see (or modify) your macros, store the macros in an add-in. The macros can be used, but they can't be viewed or changed.

As previously noted, Excel ships with several useful add-ins (see the sidebar "Add-Ins That Are Included with Excel"), and you can acquire other add-ins from third-party vendors or the Internet. In addition, Excel includes the tools that enable you to create your own add-ins. This process is explained later in the chapter, but first, some background is required.

Working with Add-Ins

The best way to work with add-ins is to use Excel's add-in manager, which you access by selecting Tools ➪ Add-Ins. This command displays the Add-Ins dialog box, shown in Figure 40-1. The list box contains all the add-ins that Excel knows about. Those that are checked are currently open. You can open and close add-ins from this dialog box by selecting or deselecting the check boxes.

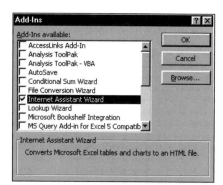

Figure 40-1: The Add-Ins dialog box.

Note   Most add-in files can also be opened by selecting File ➪ Open. You'll find that after an add-in is opened, however, you can't choose File ➪ Close to close it. The only way to remove the add-in is to exit and restart Excel or to write a macro to close the add-in.

When an add-in is opened, you may or may not notice anything different. In nearly every case, however, some change is made to the menu — either a new menu or one or more new menu items on an existing menu. For example, when you open the Analysis ToolPak add-in, a new menu item appears on the Tools menu: Data Analysis. When you open my Power Utility Pak add-in, you get a new Utilities menu, which is located between the Data and Window menus.

Add-Ins That Are Included with Excel

The following is a list of the add-ins that are included with Excel. Some of these add-ins may not have been installed. If you try to use one of these add-ins and it's not installed, you receive a prompt asking whether you want to install it.

✦ **Analysis ToolPak:** Statistical and engineering tools, plus new worksheet functions.

✦ **Analysis ToolPak – VBA:** VBA functions for the Analysis ToolPak.

✦ **AutoSave:** Automatically saves your workbook at a time interval that you specify.

✦ **Conditional Sum Wizard:** Helps you to create formulas that add values based on a condition.

✦ **File Conversion Wizard:** Converts a group of files to Excel format.

✦ **Lookup Wizard:** Helps you to create formulas that look up data in a list.

✦ **Microsoft AccessLinks Add-In:** Lets you use Microsoft Access forms and reports with Excel worksheets (Access 97 must be installed on your system).

✦ **Microsoft Bookshelf Integration:** Lets you access Microsoft Bookshelf from Excel

✦ **MS Query Add-In for Excel 5 Compatibility:** Works with Microsoft Query to bring external data into a worksheet.

✦ **ODBC Add-In:** Lets you use ODBC functions to connect to external data sources directly.

✦ **Report Manager:** Prints reports that consist of a set sequence of views and scenarios.

✦ **Solver Add-In:** A tool that helps you to use a variety of numeric methods for equation solving and optimization.

✦ **Template Utilities:** Utilities that are used by the Spreadsheet Solutions templates. This is loaded automatically when you use one of these templates.

✦ **Template Wizard with Data Tracking:** Helps you to create custom templates.

✦ **Update Add-in Links:** Updates links to MS Excel 4.0 add-ins to directly access the new built-in functionality.

✦ **Web Form Wizard**: Sets up a form on a Web server to send data to a database.

The Internet Assistant Wizard, included with Excel 97, is no longer necessary, because Excel 2000 can use HTML as a native file format.

Why Create Add-Ins?

Most Excel users have no need to create add-ins. But if you develop spreadsheets for others — or if you simply want to get the most out of Excel — you may be interested in pursuing this topic further.

The following are several reasons why you may want to convert your XLS application to an add-in:

✦ **To prevent access to your VBA code.** When you distribute an application as an add-in, the end users can't view the sheets in the workbook. If you use proprietary techniques in your VBA code, this can prevent it from being copied (or at least make it more difficult to copy).

✦ **To avoid confusion.** If an end user loads your application as an add-in, the file is not visible and, therefore, is less likely to confuse novice users or get in the way. Unlike a hidden XLS workbook, an add-in can't be unhidden.

✦ **To simplify access to worksheet functions.** Custom worksheet functions that are stored in an add-in don't require the workbook name qualifier. For example, if you have a custom function named MOVAVG stored in a workbook named Newfunc.xls, you would have to use a syntax such as the following to use this function in a different workbook:

```
=NEWFUNC.XLS!MOVAVG(A1:A50)
```

But if this function is stored in an add-in file that's open, the syntax is much simpler, because you don't need to include the file reference:

```
=MOVAVG(A1:A50)
```

✦ **To provide easier access.** After you identify the location of your add-in, it appears in the Add-Ins dialog box with a friendly name and a description of what it does.

✦ **To permit better control over loading.** Add-ins can be opened automatically when Excel starts, regardless of the directory in which they are stored.

✦ **To omit prompts when unloading.** When an add-in is closed, the user never sees the *Save change in...?* prompt.

Creating Add-Ins

Although any workbook can be converted to an add-in, not all workbooks benefit by this. In fact, workbooks that consist only of worksheets (that is, not macros or custom dialog boxes) become unusable, because add-ins are hidden.

Note   To convert a workbook to an add-in, the workbook must have at least one worksheet. Therefore, if your workbook consists only of Excel 5/95 dialog sheets or Excel 4 macro sheets, you can't convert it to an add-in.

The only types of workbooks that benefit from conversion to an add-in are those with macros. For example, you may have a workbook that consists of general-purpose macros (subroutines and functions). This type of workbook makes an ideal add-in.

Creating an add-in is quite simple. These steps describe how to create an add-in from a normal workbook file:

1. Develop your application and make sure that everything works properly. Don't forget to include a method to execute the macro or macros. You may want to add a new menu item (described later in the chapter).

2. Test the application by executing it when a *different* workbook is active. This simulates its behavior when it's an add-in, because an add-in is never the active workbook. You may find that some references no longer work. For example, the following statement works fine when the code resides in the active workbook, but fails when a different workbook is active:

```
x = Worksheets("Data").Range("A1")
```

You could qualify the reference with the name of the workbook object, like this:

```
x = Workbooks("MYBOOK.XLS").Worksheets("Data").Range("A1")
```

This method is not recommended, because the name of the workbook changes when it's converted to an add-in. The solution is to use the ThisWorkbook qualifier, as follows

```
x = ThisWorkbook.Worksheets("Data").Range("A1")
```

3. Select File ➪ Summary Info, enter a brief descriptive title in the Title field, and then enter a longer description in the Comments field. This step is not required, but it makes using the add-in easier.

4. Lock the project. This is an optional step that protects the VBA code and UserForms from being viewed. You do this in the Visual Basic Editor, using the Tools ➪ Properties command. Click the Protection tab and make the appropriate choices.

5. Save the workbook as an XLA file by selecting File ➪ Save As. Select Microsoft Excel Add-In from the Save as type drop-down list.

After you create the add-in, you need to test it. Select Tools ➪ Add-Ins and use the Browse button in the Add-Ins dialog box to locate the XLA file that you created in Step 5. This installs the add-in. The Add-Ins dialog box uses the descriptive title that you provided in Step 3.

Note   You can continue to modify the macros and UserForms in the XLA version of your file, and save your changes in the Visual Basic Editor. In versions prior to Excel 97, the changes have to be made to the XLS version and then the workbook has to be resaved as an add-in.

An Add-In Example

This section discusses the steps that are used to create a useful add-in that displays a dialog box (see Figure 40-2) in which the user can quickly change several Excel settings. Although these settings can be changed in the Options dialog box, the add-in makes these changes interactively. For example, if the Grid Lines check box is deselected, the gridlines are removed immediately.

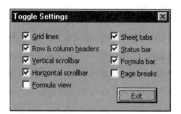

Figure 40-2: This dialog box enables the user to change various Excel settings interactively.

This file is available on the companion CD-ROM. The file is not locked, so you have full access to the VBA code and UserForm.

Setting Up the Workbook

This workbook consists of one worksheet, which is empty. Although the worksheet is not used, it must be present, because every workbook must have at least one sheet.

Use the Visual Basic Editor to insert a VBA module (named Module1) and a UserForm (named UserForm1).

Module1

The following macro is contained in the Module1 module. This subroutine ensures that a worksheet is active. If the active sheet is not a worksheet, a message box is displayed and nothing else happens. If a worksheet is active, the subroutine displays the dialog box that is contained in UserForm1.

```
Sub ShowToggleSettingsDialog()
  If TypeName(ActiveSheet) <> "Worksheet" Then
    MsgBox "A worksheet must be active.", vbInformation
  Else
    UserForm1.Show
  End If
End Sub
```

ThisWorkbook

The `ThisWorkbook` object contains a macro that adds a menu item to the Tools menu when the workbook (add-in) is opened. Another macro removes the menu item when the workbook (add-in) is closed. These two subroutines, which appear in the following syntax, are explained next:

```
Private Sub Workbook_Open()
  Set NewMenuItem = Application.CommandBars _
    ("Worksheet Menu Bar").Controls("Tools").Controls.Add
  With NewMenuItem
    .Caption = "Toggle Settings..."
    .BeginGroup = True
    .OnAction = "ShowToggleSettingsDialog"
  End With
End Sub

Private Sub Workbook_BeforeClose(Cancel As Boolean)
  On Error Resume Next
  Application.CommandBars("Worksheet Menu Bar"). _
    Controls("Tools").Controls("Toggle Settings...").Delete
End Sub
```

The `Workbook_Open` subroutine adds a menu item (Toggle Settings) to the bottom of the Tools menu on the Worksheet Menu Bar. This subroutine is executed when the workbook (or add-in) is opened.

The `Workbook_BeforeClose` subroutine is executed when the add-in is closed. This subroutine removes the Toggle Settings menu item from the Tools menu.

UserForm1

Figure 40-3 shows the UserForm1 form, which has ten controls: nine check boxes and one command button. The controls have descriptive names, and the `Accelerator` property is set so that the controls display an accelerator key (for keyboard users).

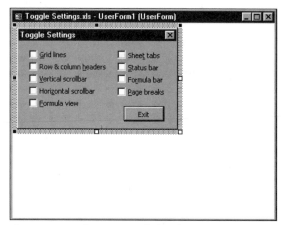

Figure 40-3: The custom dialog box.

The UserForm1 object contains the event-handler subroutines for the objects that are on the form. The following subroutine is executed before the dialog box is displayed:

```
Private Sub UserForm_Initialize()
    cbGridlines = ActiveWindow.DisplayGridlines
    cbHeaders = ActiveWindow.DisplayHeadings
    cbVerticalScrollbar = ActiveWindow.DisplayVerticalScrollBar
    cbHorizontalScrollbar =
ActiveWindow.DisplayHorizontalScrollBar
    cbFormulaView = ActiveWindow.DisplayFormulas
    cbSheetTabs = ActiveWindow.DisplayWorkbookTabs
    cbStatusBar = Application.DisplayStatusBar
    cbFormulaBar = Application.DisplayFormulaBar
    cbPageBreaks = ActiveSheet.DisplayPageBreaks
End Sub
```

The UserForm_Initialize subroutine adjusts the settings of the CheckBox controls in the dialog box to correspond to the current settings. For example, if the worksheet is displaying gridlines, ActiveWindow.DisplayGridlines returns True. This value is assigned to the cbGridlines CheckBox — which means that the CheckBox is displayed with a check mark.

Each CheckBox also has an event-handler subroutine, listed in the following code, that is executed when the control is clicked. Each subroutine makes the appropriate changes. For example, if the Grid lines CheckBox is selected, the DisplayGridlines property is set to correspond to the CheckBox.

```
Private Sub cbGridlines_Click on()
  ActiveWindow.DisplayGridlines = cbGridlines
End Sub

Private Sub cbHeaders_Click on()
  ActiveWindow.DisplayHeadings = cbHeaders
End Sub

Private Sub cbVerticalScrollbar_Click on()
  ActiveWindow.DisplayVerticalScrollBar = cbVerticalScrollbar
End Sub

Private Sub cbHorizontalScrollbar_Click on()
  ActiveWindow.DisplayHorizontalScrollBar =
cbHorizontalScrollbar
End Sub

Private Sub cbFormulaView_Click on()
  ActiveWindow.DisplayFormulas = cbFormulaView
End Sub

Private Sub cbSheetTabs_Click on()
  ActiveWindow.DisplayWorkbookTabs = cbSheetTabs
End Sub

Private Sub cbStatusBar_Click on()
  Application.DisplayStatusBar = cbStatusBar
End Sub

Private Sub cbFormulaBar_Click on()
  Application.DisplayFormulaBar = cbFormulaBar
End Sub

Private Sub cbPageBreaks_Click on()
  ActiveSheet.DisplayPageBreaks = cbPageBreaks
End Sub
```

The UserForm1 object has one additional event-handler subroutine for the Exit
button. This subroutine, listed as follows, simply closes the dialog box:

```
Private Sub ExitButton_Click on()
  Unload UserForm1
End Sub
```

Testing the Workbook

Before you convert this workbook to an add-in, you need to test it. You should test it
when a different workbook is active, to simulate what happens when the workbook
is an add-in. Remember, an add-in is never the active workbook and it never displays
any of its worksheets.

To test it, I saved the workbook, closed it, and then reopened it. When the workbook was opened, the Workbook_Open subroutine was executed. This subroutine added the new menu item to the Tools menu. Figure 40-4 shows how this looks.

Figure 40-4: The Tools menu displays a new menu item, Toggle Settings.

Selecting Tools ⇨ Toggle Setting displays the dialog box that is shown in Figure 40-5.

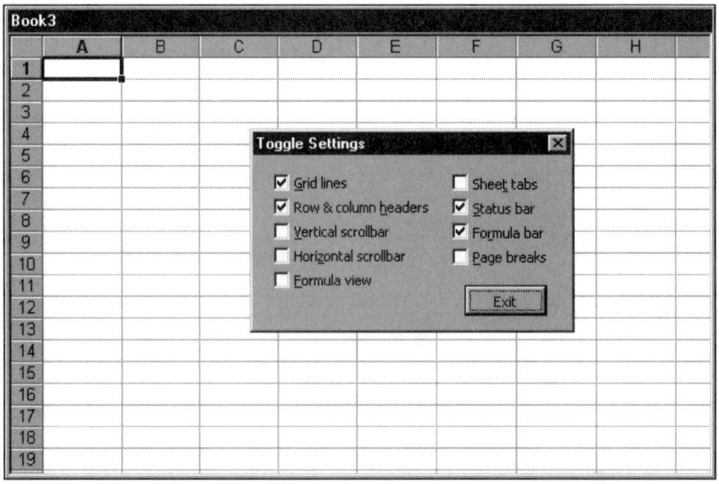

Figure 40-5: The custom dialog box, in action.

Adding Descriptive Information

This step is recommended but not necessary. Choose File ➪ Properties to bring up the Properties dialog box. Then, click the Summary tab, as shown in Figure 40-6.

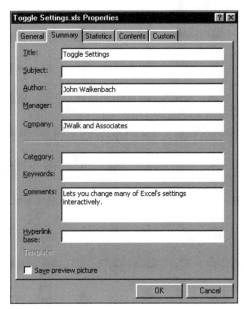

Figure 40-6: Use the Properties dialog box to enter descriptive information about your add-in.

Enter a title for the add-in in the Title field. This is the text that appears in the Add-Ins dialog box. In the Comments field, enter a description. This information appears at the bottom of the Add-Ins dialog box when the add-in is selected.

Protecting the Project

One advantage of an add-in is that it can be protected so that others can't see the source code. If you want to protect the project, follow these steps:

1. Activate the Visual Basic Editor.

2. In the Project window, click the project.

3. Select Tools ➪ [*project name*] Properties.

   VBE displays its Project Properties dialog box.

4. Click the Protection tab (see Figure 40-7).

5. Select the Lock project for viewing check box.

6. Enter a password (twice) for the project.

7. Click OK.

Figure 40-7: The Project Properties dialog box.

Creating the Add-In

To save the workbook as an add-in, activate Excel, make sure the workbook is active, and then choose File ➪ Save As. Select Microsoft Excel Add-In (*.xla) from the Save as Type drop-down list. Enter a name for the add-in file and then click OK.

Opening the Add-In

To avoid confusion, close the XLS workbook before you open the add-in that was created from it. Then, select Tools ➪ Add-Ins. Excel displays its Add-Ins dialog box. Click the Browse button and locate the add-in that you just created. After you do so, the Add-Ins dialog box displays the add-in in its list. Notice that the information that you provided in the Properties dialog box appears here (see Figure 40-8). Click OK to close the dialog box and open the add-in.

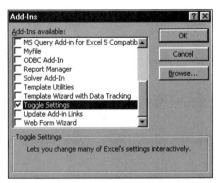

Figure 40-8: The Add-Ins dialog box, with the new add-in selected.

When the add-in is open, the Tools menu displays a new menu item (Toggle Settings) that executes the `ShowToggleSettingsDialog` subroutine in the add-in.

If you activate the VBE window, you find that the add-in is listed in the Project window. However, you can't make any modifications unless you provide the password.

Summary

This chapter discusses the concept of add-ins — files that add new capabilities to Excel — and explains how to work with add-ins and why you may want to create custom add-ins. The chapter closes with an example of an add-in that enables users easily to toggle on and off several Excel settings.

✦   ✦   ✦

Using Online Help: A Primer

Excel's online Help system has always been good. But the Help available with Excel 2000 is better than ever. However, the online Help system can be a bit intimidating for beginners, because you can get help in many ways. This appendix assists you in getting the most out of this valuable resource.

Why Online Help?

In the early days of personal computing, software programs usually came bundled with bulky manuals that described how to use the product. Some products included rudimentary help that could be accessed online. Over the years, that situation gradually changed. Now, online help is usually the *primary* source of documentation, which may be augmented by a written manual.

After you become accustomed to it, you'll find that online help (if it's done well) offers many advantages over written manuals:

+ You don't have to lug around a manual — especially important for laptop users who do their work on the road.

+ You don't have to thumb through a separate manual, which often has a confusing index.

+ You can search for specific words and then select a topic that's appropriate to your question.

+ In some cases (for example, writing VBA code), you can copy examples from the Help window and paste them into your application.

+ Help sometimes includes embedded buttons that you can click to go directly to the command that you need.

Types of Help

Excel offers several types of online Help:

✦ **Tooltips:** Move the mouse pointer over a toolbar button and the button's name appears.

✦ **Office Assistant:** The animated Office Assistant monitors your actions while you work. If a more efficient way to perform an operation exists, the Assistant can tell you about it.

✦ **Dialog box help:** When a dialog box is displayed, click the Help button in the title bar (it has a question mark on it) and then click any part of the dialog box. Excel pops up a description of the selected control. Figure A-1 shows an example.

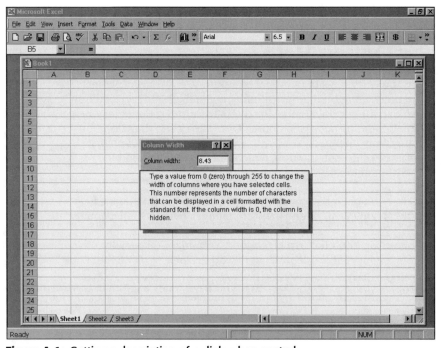

Figure A-1: Getting a description of a dialog box control.

✦ **"What's This" help:** Press Shift+F1, and the mouse pointer turns into a question mark. You can then click virtually any part of the screen to get a description of the object.

✦ **1-2-3 help:** The Help ⇨ Lotus 1-2-3 Help command provides help designed for those who are familiar with 1-2-3's commands.

✦ **Internet-based help:** You can access a variety of Internet resources directly from Excel.

✦ **Detailed help:** This is what's usually considered online help. As you'll see, you have several ways to locate a particular Help topic.

Accessing Help

When you work with Excel 2000, you can access the online Help system by using the Help menu, shown in Figure A-2. The various options are described in the sections that follow.

Figure A-2: The Help menu.

The Office Assistant

Selecting Microsoft Excel Help displays the Office Assistant, shown in Figure A-3. Type a brief description of the subject about which you want help, and the Assistant displays a list of Help topics. Chances are good that one of these topics will lead to the help that you need; click a list item to view a Help topic.

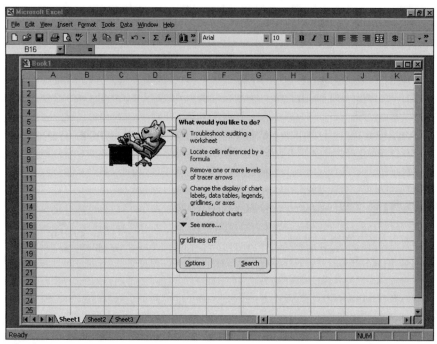

Figure A-3: The Office Assistant.

The information that you type doesn't have to be in the form of a question. Rather, you can simply enter one or more keywords that describe the topic. For example, if you want to find out how to turn off gridlines, you can type **gridlines off**.

Tip

You have a great deal of control over the Office Assistant. Right-click the Assistant and select Options from the shortcut menu. Excel displays the dialog box shown in Figure A-4. The Gallery tab lets you select a new character for the Assistant. The Options tab lets you determine whether to use the Assistant and, if you do, how the Assistant behaves. If you find that the Office Assistant is distracting, remove the check from the Use the Office Assistant check box. You can turn on the Office Assistant again by choosing the Show the Office Assistant command on the Help menu.

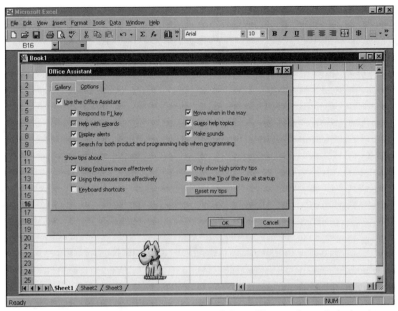

Figure A-4: Use this dialog box to control the Office Assistant's behavior.

The Help Window

EXCEL 2000 Whether you use the Office Assistant or turn it off, the Help window appears tiled to the right of the Excel window (see Figure A-5); all Office 2000 products allow the Help window to share your monitor space with an Office product.

Tip On most Help topics, you'll find links to related Help topics that look like Web links (they appear underlined). You'll also see links to the Web. Help text for all Office products is written in HTML. As you'll read in a moment, navigating through Help topics is like using a browser.

If you click the Show button in the Help window, the Help window expands to include two panes; in the right pane, Help topics continue to appear, but in the left pane, you'll see three tabs. Each of the following tabs provides a different way to find the information that you need.

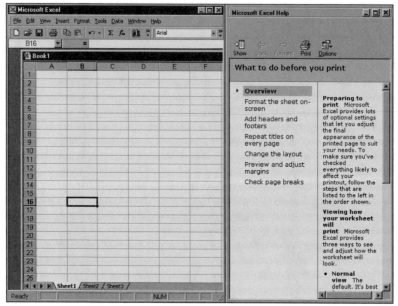

Figure A-5: The Help window tiles to the right of the program window so that you can view Help while working.

Contents Tab

Figure A-6 shows the Contents tab. This tab is arranged alphabetically by subject; you can compare the Contents tab to the table of contents in a book, because they both organize information by similar topic. When you double-click a book icon (or single-click the plus sign to the left of the book icon), the book expands to show Help topics (each with a question-mark icon). To close a book, double-click it again or single-click the minus sign to the left of the book. To display a Help topic, single-click the topic title.

The Help topic remains onscreen until you either close Help or select another Help topic.

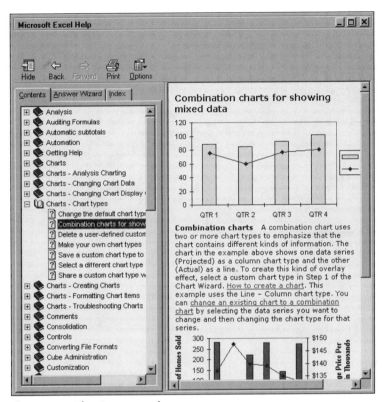

Figure A-6: The Contents tab.

Answer Wizard Tab

The Answer Wizard tab works in much the same way as the Office Assistant works. Type a question or some words related to the subject about which you want help, and then click the Search button (see Figure A-7). Topics appear at the bottom of the window. Double-click a topic in the bottom of the window and the Help topic appears in the right pane of the Help window.

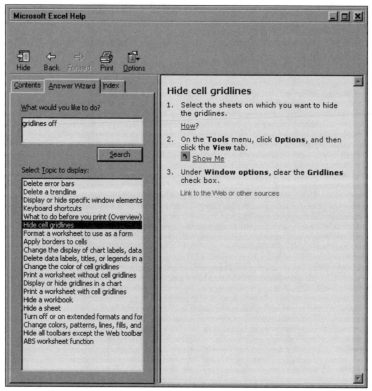

Figure A-7: The Answer Wizard tab of the Help window.

Index Tab

Figure A-8 shows the Index tab of the Help Topics dialog box. The keywords are arranged alphabetically, much like an index for a book. You can enter in the box at the top the first few letters of a keyword for which you'd like to search. Click the Search button to display related topics at the bottom of the box. Double-click a topic at the bottom of the box to display it in the right pane of the Help window.

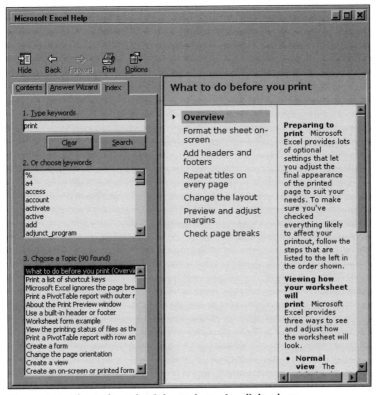

Figure A-8: The Index tab of the Help topics dialog box.

Mastering Help

After you select a Help topic, you can navigate through Help in the same way that you use a browser to navigate on the Web. The Back and Forward buttons let you view Help topics that you previously viewed, in the order that you viewed them. Use the Print button to print a Help topic. Click the Options button to display a drop-down menu that contains commands that perform the same functions as the Show, Hide, Back, Forward, and Print buttons. You'll also find a Stop command and a Refresh command; you can use these if you connect to the Web for Help and want to stop loading a page or refresh the Web page you're viewing.

The information provided in this appendix gets you started using Excel's online Help. Everyone develops his or her own style for using this help, and I urge you to explore this resource. Even if you think you understand a topic in Excel fairly well, you can often discover one or two subtle features that you didn't know about. A thorough understanding of how to use the online Help system will definitely make you a more productive Excel user.

✦ ✦ ✦

Worksheet Function Reference

This appendix contains a complete listing of Excel's worksheet functions. The functions are arranged alphabetically by categories used by the Paste Function dialog box. Some of these functions (indicated in the lists that follow) are available only when a particular add-in is attached.

For more information about a particular function, including its arguments, select the function in the Function Wizard and click the Help button.

Table B-1 Database Category Functions	
Function	**What It Does**
DAVERAGE	Returns the average of selected database entries
DCOUNT	Counts the cells containing numbers from a specified database and criteria
DCOUNTA	Counts nonblank cells from a specified database and criteria
DGET	Extracts from a database a single record that matches the specified criteria
DMAX	Returns the maximum value from selected database entries

Continued

Table B-1 *(continued)*

Function	What It Does
DMIN	Returns the minimum value from selected database entries
DPRODUCT	Multiplies the values in a particular field of records that match the criteria in a database
DSTDEV	Estimates the standard deviation based on a sample of selected database entries
DSTDEVP	Calculates the standard deviation based on the entire population of selected database entries
DSUM	Adds the numbers in the field column of records in the database that match the criteria
DVAR	Estimates variance based on a sample from selected database entries
DVARP	Calculates variance based on the entire population of selected database entries
SQL.CLOSE**	Terminates a SQL.OPEN connection
SQL.BIND**	Specifies where to place SQL.EXEC.QUERY results
SQL.ERROR**	Returns error information on SQL* functions
SQL.EXEC.QUERY**	Executes a SQL statement on a SQL.OPEN connection
QUERYGETDATA***	Gets external data using Microsoft Query
QUERYGETDATADIALOG***	Displays a dialog box to get data using Microsoft Query
SQL.GET.SCHEMA**	Returns information on a SQL.OPEN connection
SQL.OPEN**	Makes a connection to a data source via ODBC
QUERYREFRESH***	Updates a data range using Microsoft Query
SQL.REQUEST**	Requests a connection and executes a SQL query
SQL.RETRIEVE**	Retrieves SQL.EXEC.QUERY results
SQL.RETRIEVE.TO.FILE**	Retrieves SQL.EXEC.QUERY results to a file

* Available only when the Analysis ToolPak add-in is attached

** Available only when the ODBC add-in is attached

*** Available only when the MS Query add-in is attached

Table B-2
Date and Time Category Functions

Function	What It Does
DATE	Returns the serial number of a particular date
DATEVALUE	Converts a date in the form of text to a serial number
DAY	Converts a serial number to a day of the month
DAYS360	Calculates the number of days between two dates, based on a 360-day year
EDATE*	Returns the serial number of the date that is the indicated number of months before or after the start date
EOMONTH*	Returns the serial number of the last day of the month before or after a specified number of months
HOUR	Converts a serial number to an hour
MINUTE	Converts a serial number to a minute
MONTH	Converts a serial number to a month
NETWORKDAYS*	Returns the number of whole workdays between two dates
NOW	Returns the serial number of the current date and time
SECOND	Converts a serial number to a second
TIME	Returns the serial number of a particular time
TIMEVALUE	Converts a time in the form of text to a serial number
TODAY	Returns the serial number of today's date
WEEKDAY	Converts a serial number to a day of the week
WEEKNUM*	Returns the week number in the year
WORKDAY*	Returns the serial number of the date before or after a specified number of workdays
YEAR	Converts a serial number to a year
YEARFRAC*	Returns the year fraction representing the number of whole days between start_date and end_date

* Available only when the Analysis ToolPak add-in is attached

Table B-3
Engineering Category Functions

Function	What It Does
BESSELI*	Returns the modified Bessel function In(x)
BESSELJ*	Returns the Bessel function Jn(x)
BESSELK*	Returns the modified Bessel function Kn(x)
BESSELY*	Returns the Bessel function Yn(x)
BIN2DEC*	Converts a binary number to decimal
BIN2HEX*	Converts a binary number to hexadecimal
BIN2OCT*	Converts a binary number to octal
COMPLEX*	Converts real and imaginary coefficients into a complex number
CONVERT*	Converts a number from one measurement system to another
DEC2BIN*	Converts a decimal number to binary
DEC2HEX*	Converts a decimal number to hexadecimal
DEC2OCT*	Converts a decimal number to octal
DELTA*	Tests whether two values are equal
ERF*	Returns the error function
ERFC*	Returns the complementary error function
GESTEP*	Tests whether a number is greater than a threshold value
HEX2BIN*	Converts a hexadecimal number to binary
HEX2DEC*	Converts a hexadecimal number to decimal
HEX2OCT*	Converts a hexadecimal number to octal
IMABS*	Returns the absolute value (modulus) of a complex number
IMAGINARY*	Returns the imaginary coefficient of a complex number
IMARGUMENT*	Returns the argument theta, an angle expressed in radians
IMCONJUGATE*	Returns the complex conjugate of a complex number
IMCOS*	Returns the cosine of a complex number
IMDIV*	Returns the quotient of two complex numbers
IMEXP*	Returns the exponential of a complex number
IMLN*	Returns the natural logarithm of a complex number
IMLOG2*	Returns the base-2 logarithm of a complex number
IMLOG10*	Returns the base-10 logarithm of a complex number

Function	What It Does
IMPOWER*	Returns a complex number raised to an integer power
IMPRODUCT*	Returns the product of two complex numbers
IMREAL*	Returns the real coefficient of a complex number
IMSIN*	Returns the sine of a complex number
IMSQRT*	Returns the square root of a complex number
IMSUB*	Returns the difference of two complex numbers
IMSUM*	Returns the sum of complex numbers
OCT2BIN*	Converts an octal number to binary
OCT2DEC*	Converts an octal number to decimal
OCT2HEX*	Converts an octal number to hexadecimal

* Available only when the Analysis ToolPak add-in is attached

Table B-4
Financial Category Functions

Function	What It Does
ACCRINT*	Returns the accrued interest for a security that pays periodic interest
ACCRINTM*	Returns the accrued interest for a security that pays interest at maturity
AMORDEGRC*	Returns the depreciation for each accounting period
AMORLINC*	Returns the depreciation for each accounting period
COUPDAYBS*	Returns the number of days from the beginning of the coupon period to the settlement date
COUPDAYS*	Returns the number of days in the coupon period that contains the settlement date
COUPDAYSNC*	Returns the number of days from the settlement date to the next coupon date
COUPNCD*	Returns the next coupon date after the settlement date
COUPNUM*	Returns the number of coupons payable between the settlement date and maturity date
COUPPCD*	Returns the previous coupon date before the settlement date
CUMIPMT*	Returns the cumulative interest paid between two periods

Continued

Table B-4 *(continued)*

Function	What It Does
CUMPRINC*	Returns the cumulative principal paid on a loan between two periods
DB	Returns the depreciation of an asset for a specified period, using the fixed-declining balance method
DDB	Returns the depreciation of an asset for a specified period, using the double-declining balance method or some other method that you specify
DISC*	Returns the discount rate for a security
DOLLARDE*	Converts a dollar price, expressed as a fraction, into a dollar price, expressed as a decimal number
DOLLARFR*	Converts a dollar price, expressed as a decimal number, into a dollar price, expressed as a fraction
DURATION*	Returns the annual duration of a security with periodic interest payments
EFFECT*	Returns the effective annual interest rate
FV	Returns the future value of an investment
FVSCHEDULE*	Returns the future value of an initial principal after applying a series of compound interest rates
INTRATE*	Returns the interest rate for a fully invested security
IPMT	Returns the interest payment for an investment for a given period
IRR	Returns the internal rate of return for a series of cash flows
ISPMT	Returns the interest associated with a specific loan payment.
MDURATION*	Returns the Macauley modified duration for a security with an assumed par value of $100
MIRR	Returns the internal rate of return where positive and negative cash flows are financed at different rates
NOMINAL*	Returns the annual nominal interest rate
NPER	Returns the number of periods for an investment
NPV	Returns the net present value of an investment based on a series of periodic cash flows and a discount rate
ODDFPRICE*	Returns the price per $100 face value of a security with an odd first period
ODDFYIELD*	Returns the yield of a security with an odd first period

Function	What It Does
ODDLPRICE*	Returns the price per $100 face value of a security with an odd last period
ODDLYIELD*	Returns the yield of a security with an odd last period
PMT	Returns the periodic payment for an annuity
PPMT	Returns the payment on the principal for an investment for a given period
PRICE*	Returns the price per $100 face value of a security that pays periodic interest
PRICEDISC*	Returns the price per $100 face value of a discounted security
PRICEMAT*	Returns the price per $100 face value of a security that pays interest at maturity
PV	Returns the present value of an investment
RATE	Returns the interest rate per period of an annuity
RECEIVED*	Returns the amount received at maturity for a fully invested security
SLN	Returns the straight-line depreciation of an asset for one period
SYD	Returns the sum-of-years' digits depreciation of an asset for a specified period
TBILLEQ*	Returns the bond-equivalent yield for a Treasury bill
TBILLPRICE*	Returns the price per $100 face value for a Treasury bill
TBILLYIELD*	Returns the yield for a Treasury bill
VDB	Returns the depreciation of an asset for a specified or partial period using a declining balance method
XIRR*	Returns the internal rate of return for a schedule of cash flows that is not necessarily periodic
XNPV*	Returns the net present value for a schedule of cash flows that is not necessarily periodic
YIELD*	Returns the yield on a security that pays periodic interest
YIELDDISC*	Returns the annual yield for a discounted security; for example, a Treasury bill
YIELDMAT*	Returns the annual yield of a security that pays interest at maturity

* Available only when the Analysis ToolPak add-in is attached

Table B-5
Information Category Functions

Function	What It Does
CELL	Returns information about the formatting, location, or contents of a cell
COUNTBLANK	Counts the number of blank cells within a range
ERROR.TYPE	Returns a number corresponding to an error type
INFO	Returns information about the current operating environment
ISBLANK	Returns TRUE if the value is blank
ISERR	Returns TRUE if the value is any error value except #N/A
ISERROR	Returns TRUE if the value is any error value
ISEVEN*	Returns TRUE if the number is even
ISLOGICAL	Returns TRUE if the value is a logical value
ISNA	Returns TRUE if the value is the #N/A error value
ISNONTEXT	Returns TRUE if the value is not text
ISNUMBER	Returns TRUE if the value is a number
ISODD*	Returns TRUE if the number is odd
ISREF	Returns TRUE if the value is a reference
ISTEXT	Returns TRUE if the value is text
N	Returns a value converted to a number
NA	Returns the error value #N/A
TYPE	Returns a number indicating the data type of a value

* Available only when the Analysis ToolPak add-in is attached

Table B-6
Logical Category Functions

Function	What It Does
AND	Returns TRUE if all of its arguments are TRUE
FALSE	Returns the logical value FALSE
IF	Specifies a logical test to perform
NOT	Reverses the logic of its argument
OR	Returns TRUE if any argument is TRUE
TRUE	Returns the logical value TRUE

Table B-7
Lookup and Reference Category Functions

Function	What It Does
ADDRESS	Returns a reference as text to a single cell in a worksheet
AREAS	Returns the number of areas in a reference
CHOOSE	Chooses a value from a list of values
COLUMN	Returns the column number of a reference
COLUMNS	Returns the number of columns in a reference
GETPIVOTDATA	Returns data stored in a PivotTable
HLOOKUP	Looks in the top row of an array and returns the value of the indicated cell
HYPERLINK	Creates a shortcut that opens a document on your hard drive, a server, or the Internet
INDEX	Uses an index to choose a value from a reference or array
INDIRECT	Returns a reference indicated by a text value
LOOKUP	Looks up values in a vector or array
MATCH	Looks up values in a reference or array
OFFSET	Returns a reference offset from a given reference
ROW	Returns the row number of a reference
ROWS	Returns the number of rows in a reference
TRANSPOSE	Returns the transpose of an array
VLOOKUP	Looks in the first column of an array and moves across the row to return the value of a cell

Table B-8
Math and Trig Category Functions

Function	What It Does
ABS	Returns the absolute value of a number
ACOS	Returns the arccosine of a number
ACOSH	Returns the inverse hyperbolic cosine of a number
ASIN	Returns the arcsine of a number
ASINH	Returns the inverse hyperbolic sine of a number

Continued

Table B-8 *(continued)*

Function	What It Does
ATAN	Returns the arctangent of a number
ATAN2	Returns the arctangent from x and y coordinates
ATANH	Returns the inverse hyperbolic tangent of a number
CEILING	Rounds a number to the nearest integer or to the nearest multiple of significance
COMBIN	Returns the number of combinations for a given number of objects
COS	Returns the cosine of a number
COSH	Returns the hyperbolic cosine of a number
COUNTIF	Counts the number of nonblank cells within a range that meets the given criteria
DEGREES	Converts radians to degrees
EVEN	Rounds a number up to the nearest even integer
EXP	Returns e raised to the power of a given number
FACT	Returns the factorial of a number
FACTDOUBLE	Returns the double factorial of a number
FLOOR	Rounds a number down, toward 0
GCD*	Returns the greatest common divisor
INT	Rounds a number down to the nearest integer
LCM*	Returns the least common multiple
LN	Returns the natural logarithm of a number
LOG	Returns the logarithm of a number to a specified base
LOG10	Returns the base-10 logarithm of a number
MDETERM	Returns the matrix determinant of an array
MINVERSE	Returns the matrix inverse of an array
MMULT	Returns the matrix product of two arrays
MOD	Returns the remainder from division
MROUND*	Returns a number rounded to the desired multiple
MULTINOMIAL*	Returns the multinomial of a set of numbers
ODD	Rounds a number up to the nearest odd integer

Function	What It Does
PI	Returns the value of pi
POWER	Returns the result of a number raised to a power
PRODUCT	Multiplies its arguments
QUOTIENT*	Returns the integer portion of a division
RADIANS	Converts degrees to radians
RAND	Returns a random number between 0 and 1
RANDBETWEEN*	Returns a random number between the numbers that you specify
ROMAN	Converts an Arabic numeral to Roman, as text
ROUND	Rounds a number to a specified number of digits
ROUNDDOWN	Rounds a number down, toward 0
ROUNDUP	Rounds a number up, away from 0
SERIESSUM*	Returns the sum of a power series based on the formula
SIGN	Returns the sign of a number
SIN	Returns the sine of the given angle
SINH	Returns the hyperbolic sine of a number
SQRT	Returns a positive square root
SQRTPI*	Returns the square root of (*number* * pi)
SUBTOTAL	Returns a subtotal in a list or database
SUM	Adds its arguments
SUMIF	Adds the cells specified by a given criteria
SUMPRODUCT	Returns the sum of the products of corresponding array components
SUMSQ	Returns the sum of the squares of the arguments
SUMX2MY2	Returns the sum of the difference of squares of corresponding values in two arrays
SUMX2PY2	Returns the sum of the sum of squares of corresponding values in two arrays
SUMXMY2	Returns the sum of squares of differences of corresponding values in two arrays
TAN	Returns the tangent of a number
TANH	Returns the hyperbolic tangent of a number
TRUNC	Truncates a number to an integer

* Available only when the Analysis ToolPak add-in is attached

Table B-9
Statistical Category Functions

Function	What It Does
AVEDEV	Returns the average of the absolute deviations of data points from their mean
AVERAGE	Returns the average of its arguments
AVERAGEA	Returns the average of its arguments and includes evaluation of text and logical values
BETADIST	Returns the cumulative beta probability density function
BETAINV	Returns the inverse of the cumulative beta probability density function
BINOMDIST	Returns the individual term binomial distribution probability
CHIDIST	Returns the one-tailed probability of the chi-squared distribution
CHIINV	Returns the inverse of the one-tailed probability of the chi-squared distribution
CHITEST	Returns the test for independence
CONFIDENCE	Returns the confidence interval for a population mean
CORREL	Returns the correlation coefficient between two data sets
COUNT	Counts how many numbers are in the list of arguments
COUNTA	Counts how many values are in the list of arguments
COUNTBLANK	Counts the number of blank cells in the argument range
COUNTIF	Counts the number of cells that meet the criteria you specify in the argument
COVAR	Returns covariance, the average of the products of paired deviations
CRITBINOM	Returns the smallest value for which the cumulative binomial distribution is less than or equal to a criterion value
DEVSQ	Returns the sum of squares of deviations
EXPONDIST	Returns the exponential distribution
FDIST	Returns the F probability distribution
FINV	Returns the inverse of the F probability distribution
FISHER	Returns the Fisher transformation
FISHERINV	Returns the inverse of the Fisher transformation
FORECAST	Returns a value along a linear trend
FREQUENCY	Returns a frequency distribution as a vertical array
FTEST	Returns the result of an F-test

Function	What It Does
GAMMADIST	Returns the gamma distribution
GAMMAINV	Returns the inverse of the gamma cumulative distribution
GAMMALN	Returns the natural logarithm of the gamma function, $G(x)$
GEOMEAN	Returns the geometric mean
GROWTH	Returns values along an exponential trend
HARMEAN	Returns the harmonic mean
HYPGEOMDIST	Returns the hypergeometric distribution
INTERCEPT	Returns the intercept of the linear regression line
KURT	Returns the kurtosis of a data set
LARGE	Returns the kth largest value in a data set
LINEST	Returns the parameters of a linear trend
LOGEST	Returns the parameters of an exponential trend
LOGINV	Returns the inverse of the lognormal distribution
LOGNORMDIST	Returns the cumulative lognormal distribution
MAX	Returns the maximum value in a list of arguments, ignoring logical values and text
MAXA	Returns the maximum value in a list of arguments, including logical values and text
MEDIAN	Returns the median of the given numbers
MIN	Returns the minimum value in a list of arguments, ignoring logical values and text
MINA	Returns the minimum value in a list of arguments, including logical values and text
MODE	Returns the most common value in a data set
NEGBINOMDIST	Returns the negative binomial distribution
NORMDIST	Returns the normal cumulative distribution
NORMINV	Returns the inverse of the normal cumulative distribution
NORMSDIST	Returns the standard normal cumulative distribution
NORMSINV	Returns the inverse of the standard normal cumulative distribution
PEARSON	Returns the Pearson product moment correlation coefficient
PERCENTILE	Returns the kth percentile of values in a range
PERCENTRANK	Returns the percentage rank of a value in a data set

Continued

Table B-9 *(continued)*

Function	What It Does
PERMUT	Returns the number of permutations for a given number of objects
POISSON	Returns the Poisson distribution
PROB	Returns the probability that values in a range are between two limits
QUARTILE	Returns the quartile of a data set
RANK	Returns the rank of a number in a list of numbers
RSQ	Returns the square of the Pearson product moment correlation coefficient
SKEW	Returns the skewness of a distribution
SLOPE	Returns the slope of the linear regression line
SMALL	Returns the kth smallest value in a data set
STANDARDIZE	Returns a normalized value
STDEV	Estimates standard deviation based on a sample, ignoring text and logical values
STDEVA	Estimates standard deviation based on a sample, including text and logical values
STDEVP	Calculates standard deviation based on the entire population, ignoring text and logical values
STDEVPA	Calculates standard deviation based on the entire population, including text and logical values
STEYX	Returns the standard error of the predicted y-value for each x in the regression
TDIST	Returns the student's t-distribution
TINV	Returns the inverse of the student's t-distribution
TREND	Returns values along a linear trend
TRIMMEAN	Returns the mean of the interior of a data set
TTEST	Returns the probability associated with a *student's t-Test*
VAR	Estimates variance based on a sample, ignoring logical values and text
VARA	Estimates variance based on a sample, including logical values and text
VARP	Calculates variance based on the entire population, ignoring logical values and text
VARPA	Calculates variance based on the entire population, including logical values and text
WEIBULL	Returns the Weibull distribution
ZTEST	Returns the two-tailed P-value of a z-test

Table B-10
Text Category Functions

Function	*What It Does*
CHAR	Returns the character specified by the code number
CLEAN	Removes all nonprintable characters from text
CODE	Returns a numeric code for the first character in a text string
CONCATENATE	Joins several text items into one text item
DOLLAR	Converts a number to text, using currency format
EXACT	Checks to see whether two text values are identical
FIND	Finds one text value within another (case-sensitive)
FIXED	Formats a number as text with a fixed number of decimals
LEFT	Returns the leftmost characters from a text value
LEN	Returns the number of characters in a text string
LOWER	Converts text to lowercase
MID	Returns a specific number of characters from a text string, starting at the position that you specify
PROPER	Capitalizes the first letter in each word of a text value
REPLACE	Replaces characters within text
REPT	Repeats text a given number of times
RIGHT	Returns the rightmost characters from a text value
SEARCH	Finds one text value within another (not case-sensitive)
SUBSTITUTE	Substitutes new text for old text in a text string
T	Converts its arguments to text
TEXT	Formats a number and converts it to text
TRIM	Removes spaces from text
UPPER	Converts text to uppercase
VALUE	Converts a text argument to a number

✦　　✦　　✦

Excel's Shortcut Keys

This appendix lists the most useful shortcut keys that are available in Excel. The shortcuts are arranged by context.

The keys listed assume that you are not using the Transition Navigation Keys, which are designed to emulate Lotus 1-2-3. You can select this option in the Transition tab of the Options dialog box.

Table C-1 Moving Through a Worksheet	
Key(s)	What It Does
Arrow keys	Move left, right, up, or down one cell
Home	Moves to the beginning of the row
Home*	Moves to the upper-left cell displayed in the window
End*	Moves to the lower-left cell displayed in the window
Arrow keys*	Scrolls left, right, up, or down one cell
PgUp	Moves up one screen
Ctrl+PgUp	Moves to the previous sheet
PgDn	Moves down one screen
Ctrl+PgDn	Moves to the next sheet
Alt+PgUp	Moves one screen to the left
Alt+PgDn	Moves one screen to the right
Ctrl+Home	Moves to the first cell in the worksheet (A1)
Ctrl+End	Moves to the last active cell of the worksheet

Continued

Table C-1 *(continued)*

Key(s)	What It Does
Ctrl+arrow key	Moves to the edge of a data block; if the cell is blank, moves to the first nonblank cell
Ctrl+Backspace	Scrolls to display the active cell
End+Home	Moves to the last nonempty cell on the worksheet
F5	Prompts for a cell address to go to
F6	Moves to the next pane of a workbook that has been split
Shift+F6	Moves to the previous pane of a workbook that has been split
Ctrl+Tab	Moves to the next window
Ctrl+Shift+Tab	Moves to the previous window

* With Scroll Lock on

Table C-2
Selecting Cells in the Worksheet

Key(s)	What It Does
Shift+arrow key	Expands the selection in the direction indicated
Shift+spacebar	Selects the entire row
Ctrl+spacebar	Selects the entire column
Ctrl+Shift+	Selects the entire worksheet spacebar
Shift+Home	Expands the selection to the beginning of the current row
Ctrl+*	Selects the block of data surrounding the active cell
F8	Extends the selection as you use navigation keys
Shift+F8	Adds other nonadjacent cells or ranges to the selection; pressing Shift+F8 again ends Add mode
F5	Prompts for a range or range name to select
Ctrl+G	Prompts for a range or range name to select
Ctrl+A	Selects the entire worksheet
Shift+Backspace	Selects the active cell in a range selection

Table C-3
Moving Within a Range Selection

Key(s)	What It Does
Enter	Moves the cell pointer down to the next cell in the selection
Shift+Enter	Moves the cell pointer up to the preceding cell in the selection
Tab	Moves the cell pointer right to the next cell in the selection
Shift+Tab	Moves the cell pointer left to the preceding cell in the selection
Ctrl+period (.)	Moves the cell pointer to the next corner of the current cell range
Ctrl+Tab	Moves the cell pointer to the next cell range in a nonadjacent selection
Ctrl+Shift+Tab	Moves the cell pointer to the previous cell range in a nonadjacent selection
Shift+Backspace	Collapses the cell selection to just the active cell

Table C-4
Editing Keys in the Formula Bar

Key(s)	What It Does
F2	Begins editing the active cell
F3	Pastes a name into a formula
Arrow keys	Moves the cursor one character in the direction of the arrow
Home	Moves the cursor to the beginning of the line
Esc	Cancels the editing
End	Moves the cursor to the end of the line
Ctrl+right arrow	Moves the cursor one word to the right
Ctrl+left arrow	Moves the cursor one word to the left
Del	Deletes the character to the right of the cursor
Ctrl+Del	Deletes all characters from the cursor to the end of the line
Backspace	Deletes the character to the left of the cursor

Table C-5
Formatting Keys

Key(s)	What It Does
Ctrl+1	Format ⇨ [Selected Object]
Ctrl+B	Sets or removes boldface
Ctrl+I	Sets or removes italic
Ctrl+U	Sets or removes underlining
Ctrl+5	Sets or removes strikethrough
Ctrl+Shift+~	Applies the general number format
Ctrl+Shift+!	Applies the comma format with two decimal places
Ctrl+Shift+#	Applies the date format (day, month, year)
Ctrl+Shift+@	Applies the time format (hour, minute, a.m./p.m.)
Ctrl+Shift+$	Applies the currency format with two decimal places
Ctrl+Shift+%	Applies the percent format with no decimal places
Ctrl+Shift+&	Applies border to outline
Ctrl+Shift+_	Removes all borders
Alt+'	Selects Format ⇨ Style

Table C-6
Other Shortcut Keys

Key(s)	What It Does
Alt+=	Inserts the AutoSum formula
Alt+Backspace	Selects Edit ⇨ Undo
Alt+Enter	Starts a new line in the current cell
Ctrl+;	Enters the current date
Ctrl+0 (zero)	Hides columns
Ctrl+1	Displays the Format dialog box for the selected object
Ctrl+6	Cycles among various ways of displaying objects

Key(s)	What It Does
Ctrl+7	Toggles the display of the standard toolbar
Ctrl+8	Toggles the display of outline symbols
Ctrl+9	Hides rows
Ctrl+A	After typing a function name in a formula, displays the Formula Palette
Ctrl+C	Selects Edit ➪ Copy
Ctrl+D	Selects Edit ➪ Fill Left
Ctrl+Delete	Selects Edit ➪ Cut
Ctrl+F	Selects Edit ➪ Find
Ctrl+H	Selects Edit ➪ Replace
Ctrl+Insert	Selects Edit ➪ Copy
Ctrl+K	Selects Insert ➪ Hyperlink
Ctrl+N	Selects File ➪ New
Ctrl+O	Selects File ➪ Open
Ctrl+P	Selects File ➪ Print
Ctrl+R	Selects Edit ➪ Fill Right
Ctrl+S	Selects File ➪ Save
Ctrl+Shift+(	Unhides rows
Ctrl+Shift+)	Unhides columns
Ctrl+Shift+:	Enters the current time
Ctrl+Shift+A	After typing a valid function name in a formula, inserts the argument names and parentheses for the function
Ctrl+V	Selects Edit ➪ Paste
Ctrl+X	Selects Edit ➪ Cut
Ctrl+Z	Selects Edit ➪ Undo
Delete	Selects Edit ➪ Clear
Shift+Insert	Selects Edit ➪ Paste

Table C-7 Function Keys	
Key(s)	**What It Does**
F1	Displays Help or the Office Assistant
Shift+F1	Displays the What's This cursor
Alt+F1	Inserts a chart sheet
Alt+Shift+ F1	Inserts a new worksheet
F2	Edits the active cell
Shift+F2	Edits a cell comment
Alt+F2	Issues Save As command
Alt+Shift+F2	Issues Save command
F3	Pastes a name into a formula
Shift+F3	Pastes a function into a formula
Ctrl+F3	Defines a name
Ctrl+Shift+F3	Displays the Creates Names dialog box, to create names using row and column labels
F4	Repeats the last action
Shift+F4	Repeats the last Find (Find Next)
Ctrl+F4	Closes the window
Alt+F4	Exits the program
F5	Displays the Go To dialog box
Shift+F5	Displays the Find dialog box
Ctrl+F5	Restores the window size
F6	Moves to the next pane
Shift+F6	Moves to the previous pane
Ctrl+F6	Moves to the next workbook window
Ctrl+Shift+F6	Moves to the previous workbook window
F7	Issues Spelling command
Ctrl+F7	Moves the window
F8	Extends a selection
Shift+F8	Adds to the selection
Ctrl+F8	Resizes the window
Alt+F8	Displays the Macro dialog box

Key(s)	What It Does
F9	Calculates all sheets in all open workbooks
Shift+F9	Calculates the active worksheet
Ctrl+F9	Minimizes the workbook
F10	Makes the menu bar active
Shift+F10	Displays a shortcut menu
Ctrl+F10	Maximizes or restores the workbook window
F11	Creates a chart
Shift+F11	Inserts a new worksheet
Ctrl+F11	Inserts an Excel 4.0 macro sheet
Alt+F11	Displays Visual Basic Editor
F12	Issues Save As command
Shift+F12	Issues Save command
Ctrl+F12	Issues Open command
Ctrl+Shift+F12	Issues Print command

✦　　✦　　✦

What's on the CD-ROM

This appendix describes the contents of the companion CD-ROM.

CD-ROM Overview

The CD-ROM consists of four components:

+ **Chapter Examples:** Excel workbooks that were discussed in the chapter of this book.

+ **Bonus Files:** Additional Excel workbooks and add-ins that you may find useful or instructive. These were all developed by the author

+ **Power Utility Pak:** The shareware version of the author's popular Excel add-in. Use the coupon in this book to order the full version, and save $30.

+ **Sound-Proof:** The demo version of the author's audio proofreader add-in.

Chapter Examples

Each chapter of this book that contains example workbooks has its own subdirectory on the CD-ROM. For example, the example files for Chapter 32 will be found in the following directory:

```
chapters\chap32\
```

Following is a list of the chapter examples that follow a brief description of each.

Chapter 3

This workbook contains the end result of the hands on exercise.

handson.xls

Chapter 6

This workbook contains a variety of custom number formats.

formats.xls

Chapter 10

This workbook demonstrates the use of PMT, PPMT< and IPMP functions to calculate a fixed-rate amortization schedule.

amortize.xls

This workbook demonstrates the use of the INDEX and MATCH functions to display the mileage between various cities.

mileage.xls

This workbook demonstrates the use of the INDIRECT function.

indirect.xls

This workbook demonstrates the use of a lengthy "megaformula" to remove the middle names and middle initials from a list of names.

megaform.xls

Chapter 11

This workbook contains many examples of cell and range formatting.

fmtexamp.xls

This workbook contains custom style examples.

styles.xls

Chapter 16

This workbook demonstrates how to create a Gantt chart.

gantt.xls

This workbook demonstrates how to create a comparative histogram.

```
comphist.xls
```

This workbook contains a chart that updates automatically when you add new data to the data range.

```
autochart.xls
```

Chapter 18

This budgeting workbook demonstrates the use of row and column outlining.

```
outline.xls
```

This workbook demonstrates the use of an outline to display various levels of text.

```
textout.xls
```

Chapter 20

This workbook demonstrates some uses for array formulas.

```
arrays.xls
```

Chapter 24

The dBASE file is used for the examples in this chapter.

```
budget.dbf
```

Chapter 25

This workbook is used for several pivot table examples.

```
banking.xls
```

These four files are used in the pivot table consolidation example.

```
consolid.xls, file1.xls, file2.xls, file3.xls
```

This workbook demonstrates pivot charts.

```
pivchart.xls
```

This workbook demonstrates a survey data analysis using pivot tables.

```
survey.xls
```

This workbook demonstrates a geographic analysis using a pivot table.

```
geog.xls
```

This workbook demonstrates how to group pivot table data by dates.

```
pivdates.xls
```

Chapter 27

This workbook is set up to demonstrate the shipping costs example using Solver.

```
shipping.xls
```

This workbook is set up to demonstrate the staff scheduling example using Solver.

```
schedule.xls
```

This workbook is set up to demonstrate the resource allocation example using Solver.

```
allocate.xls
```

This workbook is set up to demonstrate the investment portfolio example using Solver.

```
invest.xls
```

Chapter 32

An Excel version of tick-tack-toe.

```
tictac.xls
```

An Excel version of the common moving tile puzzle.

```
movetile.xls
```

An Excel version of Keno.

```
keno.xls
```

This workbook calculates the odds of winning in Keno.

```
kenoodds.xls
```

This workbook contains some animated Shape objects.

```
animshap.xls
```

Create colorful symmetrical patterns in Excel.

```
pattern.xls
```

This workbook displays a guitar fretboard and the notes in various scales and keys.

```
guitar.xls
```

This workbook contains a macro which reverses the text in Excel's menus.

```
menushen.xls
```

This workbook creates word search puzzles.

```
wordsrch.xls
```

This workbook contains examples of ASCII art.

```
asciiart.xls
```

This workbook lets you play sound files (WAV or MID format).

```
sounder.xls
```

This workbook displays interesting charts that use trigonometric functions.

```
trigfun.xls
```

This workbook lets you draw simple figures that are actually *X-Y* charts.

```
xysketch.xls
```

Chapter 33

This workbook contains a custom toolbar to assist with formatting.

```
toolbar.xls
```

Chapter 36

This workbook contains several examples of custom worksheet functions written in VBA.

```
funcs.xls
```

Chapter 37

This workbook contains a utility (with a custom dialog box) to make it easy to change the case of text in cells.

    chngcase.xls

Chapter 38

This workbook contains examples of Excel's ActiveX controls.

    activex.xls

Chapter 39

This is VBA macros that demonstrate how to copy a range of cells.

    rngcopy.xls

This is VBA macros that demonstrate various ways to select a range of cells.

    select.xls

This is VBA macros that demonstrate how to loop though a range of cells.

    loop.xls

This is VBA macros that demonstrate how to prompt for a value and insert the value into a cell.

    Prompt.xls

This is VBA macros that demonstrate how to determine the type of object that is selected.

    seltype.xls

This is VBA macros that demonstrate how to create a text box.

    textbox.xls

This is VBA macros that demonstrate how to call attention to a particular cell.

    explode.xls

This is VBA macros that work with chart objects.

    chartmacs.xls

Chapter 40

This add-in contains a utility to make it easy to toggle various settings in Excel. This add-in is not protected, so you can view or modify the code.

    toggles.xla

Bonus Files

The files contained in the Bonus directory aren't discussed in the book, but you may find them helpful. These files consists of Excel add-ins and standard Excel workbooks. On the CD-ROM, they appear in the following directories:

    bonus\addins\
    bonus\wkbooks\

Add-Ins

This section contains a list of the add-ins on the companion CD-ROM, with a brief description of each.

Note To install an add-in, first copy it to a directory on your local hard drive. Then, in Excel, select Tools ⇨ Add-Ins. In the Add-Ins dialog box, click Browse and locate the *.xla file that you want to install.

Caution The Add-Ins dialog box lists all add-ins that Excel knows about. The add-ins that are checked will be loaded each time Excel starts. To reduce the startup time for Excel, remove the checkmark from any add-ins that you don't use.

    daterept.xla

An add-in that generates a useful report that describes all date cells in a worksheet. This may help you identify potential Year 2000 problems.

    faceid.xla

An add-in that makes it very easy for developers to determine the FaceID value for a CommandBar image. Useful if you develop custom menus in Excel.

    dataform.xla

An add-in that provides an alternative to Excel's Data ⇨ Form command.

Workbooks

Below is a list of workbooks that follow a brief description of each.

This workbook demonstrates a technique that makes it very easy to create a custom menu for an Excel workbook or add-in. VBA programming not required!

```
menumakr.xls
```

This workbook demonstrates a technique to display help topics in Excel.

```
helpmakr.xls
```

This workbook contains an easy-to-use time sheet for tracking daily hours worked.

```
timesht.xls
```

This workbook lets you generate and print daily appointment calendar pages.

```
apptcal.xls
```

This macro generates all possible permutations of a string. Uses a recursive VBA subroutine.

```
permute.xls
```

Power Utility Pak

Power Utility Pak is a collection of Excel add-ins developed by the author of this book. The companion CD-ROM contains a copy of the shareware version of this product. The shareware version contains a subset of the features.

Note   The CD-ROM contains PUP97. PUP97 works with both Excel 97 and Excel 2000. A significantly enhanced version, PUP2000, was being finalized as this book went to press. If you would like to try the shareware version of PUP2000, download a copy from:

```
http://www.j-walk.com/ss/pup
```

Registering Power Utility Pak

The normal registration fee for Power Utility Pak is $39.95. However, you can use the coupon in this book to get the full version for only $9.95.

Installing the shareware version

To install the shareware version of Power Utility Pak:

   1. Make sure Excel is not running.

2. Locate the pup97r3.exe file on the CD-ROM. This file is located in the pup\ directory.

3. Double-click pup97r3.exe. This will expand the files to a directory you specify on your hard drive.

4. Start Excel.

5. Select Tools ➪ Add-Ins and click the Browse button. Locate the power97.xla file in the directory you specified in Step 3.

6. Make sure Power Utility Pak 97 is checked in the add-ins list.

7. Click OK to close the Add-Ins dialog box.

The procedure described above will install Power Utility Pak, and it will be available whenever you start Excel. When the product is installed, you'll have a new menu: Utilities. Access the Power Utility Pak features from the Utilities menu.

Note Power utility Pak includes extensive on-line help. Select Utilities ➪ Help to view the Help file.

To uninstall Power Utility Pak

If you decide that you don't want Power Utility Pak, follow these instructions to remove it:

1. In Excel, select Tools ➪ Add-Ins

2. In the Add-Ins dialog box, remove the checkmark from Power Utility Pak 97.

3. Click OK to close the Add-Ins dialog box

After performing these steps, you can re-install Power Utility Pak at any time by placing a checkmark next to the Power Utility Pak 97 item in the Add-Ins dialog box.

Note To permanently remove Power Utility Pak from your system, delete the directory into which you originally installed it.

Sound-Proof

Sound-Proof is an Excel add-in, developed by the author of this book. Sound-Proof uses a synthesized voice to read the contents of selected cells. It's the perfect proof-reading tool for anyone who does data entry in Excel.

Cells are read back using natural language format. For example, 154.78 is read as "One hundred fifty-four point seven eight." Date values are read as actual dates (for example, "June fourteen, nineteen ninety-eight") and time values are read as actual times (for example, "Six forty-five AM").

The companion CD-ROM contains a demo version of Sound-Proof. The full version is available for $19.95. Ordering instructions are provided in the online Help file.

Note

The only limitation in the demo version is that it reads no more than 12 cells at a time.

Installing the demo version

To install the demo version of Sound-Proof:

1. Make sure Excel is not running.
2. Locate the sp.exe file on the CD-ROM. This file is located in the sp\ directory.
3. Double-click sp.exe. This will expand the files to a directory you specify on your hard drive.
4. Start Excel.
5. Select Tools ⇨ Add-Ins, and click the Browse button. Locate the soundprf.xla file in the directory you specified in Step 3.
6. Make sure Sound-Proof is checked in the add-ins list.
7. Click OK to close the Add-Ins dialog box.

The procedure described above will install Sound-Proof, and it will be available whenever you start Excel. When the product is installed, you'll have a new menu command: Tools ⇨ Sound-Proof. This command will display the Sound-Proof toolbar.

To uninstall Sound-Proof

If you decide that you don't want Sound-Proof, follow these instructions to remove it:

1. In Excel, select Tools ⇨ Add-Ins
2. In the Add-Ins dialog box, remove the checkmark from Sound-Proof.
3. Click OK to close the Add-Ins dialog box

After performing these steps, you can re-install Sound-Proof at any time by placing a checkmark next to the Sound-Proof item in the Add-Ins dialog box.

Note

To permanently remove Sound-Proof from your system, delete the directory into which you originally installed it.

◆   ◆   ◆

Index

continued

continued

IDG BOOKS WORLDWIDE, INC.
END-USER LICENSE AGREEMENT

<u>READ THIS.</u> You should carefully read these terms and conditions before opening the software packet(s) included with this book ("Book"). This is a license agreement ("Agreement") between you and IDG Books Worldwide, Inc. ("IDGB"). By opening the accompanying software packet(s), you acknowledge that you have read and accept the following terms and conditions. If you do not agree and do not want to be bound by such terms and conditions, promptly return the Book and the unopened software packet(s) to the place you obtained them for a full refund.

1. <u>License Grant.</u> IDGB grants to you (either an individual or entity) a nonexclusive license to use one copy of the enclosed software program(s) (collectively, the "Software") solely for your own personal or business purposes on a single computer (whether a standard computer or a workstation component of a multiuser network). The Software is in use on a computer when it is loaded into temporary memory (RAM) or installed into permanent memory (hard disk, CD-ROM, or other storage device). IDGB reserves all rights not expressly granted herein.

2. <u>Ownership.</u> IDGB is the owner of all right, title, and interest, including copyright, in and to the compilation of the Software recorded on the disk(s) or CD-ROM ("Software Media"). Copyright to the individual programs recorded on the Software Media is owned by the author or other authorized copyright owner of each program. Ownership of the Software and all proprietary rights relating thereto remain with IDGB and its licensers.

3. <u>Restrictions on Use and Transfer.</u>

   (a) You may only (i) make one copy of the Software for backup or archival purposes, or (ii) transfer the Software to a single hard disk, provided that you keep the original for backup or archival purposes. You may not (i) rent or lease the Software, (ii) copy or reproduce the Software through a LAN or other network system or through any computer subscriber system or bulletin-board system, or (iii) modify, adapt, or create derivative works based on the Software.

   (b) You may not reverse engineer, decompile, or disassemble the Software. You may transfer the Software and user documentation on a permanent basis, provided that the transferee agrees to accept the terms and conditions of this Agreement and you retain no copies. If the Software is an update or has been updated, any transfer must include the most recent update and all prior versions.

4. <u>Restrictions on Use of Individual Programs.</u> You must follow the individual requirements and restrictions detailed for each individual program in Appendix D, "What's on the CD-ROM," of this Book. These limitations are also contained in the individual license agreements recorded on the Software Media. These limitations may include a requirement that after using the program for a specified period of time, the user must pay a registration fee

or discontinue use. By opening the Software packet(s), you will be agreeing to abide by the licenses and restrictions for these individual programs that are detailed in Appendix D, "What's on the CD-ROM," and on the Software Media. None of the material on this Software Media or listed in this Book may ever be redistributed, in original or modified form, for commercial purposes.

5. **Limited Warranty**.

   (a) IDGB warrants that the Software and Software Media are free from defects in materials and workmanship under normal use for a period of sixty (60) days from the date of purchase of this Book. If IDGB receives notification within the warranty period of defects in materials or workmanship, IDGB will replace the defective Software Media.

   (b) IDGB AND THE AUTHORS OF THE BOOK DISCLAIM ALL OTHER WARRANTIES, EXPRESS OR IMPLIED, INCLUDING WITHOUT LIMITATION IMPLIED WARRANTIES OF MERCHANTABILITY AND FITNESS FOR A PARTICULAR PURPOSE, WITH RESPECT TO THE SOFTWARE, THE PROGRAMS, THE SOURCE CODE CONTAINED THEREIN, AND/OR THE TECHNIQUES DESCRIBED IN THIS BOOK. IDGB DOES NOT WARRANT THAT THE FUNCTIONS CONTAINED IN THE SOFTWARE WILL MEET YOUR REQUIREMENTS OR THAT THE OPERATION OF THE SOFTWARE WILL BE ERROR FREE.

   (c) This limited warranty gives you specific legal rights, and you may have other rights that vary from jurisdiction to jurisdiction.

6. **Remedies**.

   (a) IDGB's entire liability and your exclusive remedy for defects in materials and workmanship shall be limited to replacement of the Software Media, which may be returned to IDGB with a copy of your receipt at the following address: Software Media Fulfillment Department, Attn.: *Microsoft Excel 2000 Bible*, IDG Books Worldwide, Inc., 7260 Shadeland Station, Ste. 100, Indianapolis, IN 46256, or call 1-800-762-2974. Please allow three to four weeks for delivery. This Limited Warranty is void if failure of the Software Media has resulted from accident, abuse, or misapplication. Any replacement Software Media will be warranted for the remainder of the original warranty period or thirty (30) days, whichever is longer.

   (b) In no event shall IDGB or the authors be liable for any damages whatsoever (including without limitation damages for loss of business profits, business interruption, loss of business information, or any other pecuniary loss) arising from the use of or inability to use the Book or the Software, even if IDGB has been advised of the possibility of such damages.

   (c) Because some jurisdictions do not allow the exclusion or limitation of liability for consequential or incidental damages, the above limitation or exclusion may not apply to you.

7. **U.S. Government Restricted Rights.** Use, duplication, or disclosure of the Software by the U.S. Government is subject to restrictions stated in paragraph (c)(1)(ii) of the Rights in Technical Data and Computer Software clause of DFARS 252.227-7013, and in subparagraphs (a) through (d) of the Commercial Computer — Restricted Rights clause at FAR 52.227-19, and in similar clauses in the NASA FAR supplement, when applicable.

8. **General.** This Agreement constitutes the entire understanding of the parties and revokes and supersedes all prior agreements, oral or written, between them and may not be modified or amended except in a writing signed by both parties hereto that specifically refers to this Agreement. This Agreement shall take precedence over any other documents that may be in conflict herewith. If any one or more provisions contained in this Agreement are held by any court or tribunal to be invalid, illegal, or otherwise unenforceable, each and every other provision shall remain in full force and effect.

my2cents.idgbooks.com

Register This Book — And Win!

Visit **http://my2cents.idgbooks.com** to register this book and we'll automatically enter you in our fantastic monthly prize giveaway. It's also your opportunity to give us feedback: let us know what you thought of this book and how you would like to see other topics covered.

Discover IDG Books Online!

The IDG Books Online Web site is your online resource for tackling technology — at home and at the office. Frequently updated, the IDG Books Online Web site features exclusive software, insider information, online books, and live events!

10 Productive & Career-Enhancing Things You Can Do at www.idgbooks.com

- Nab source code for your own programming projects.

- Download software.

- Read Web exclusives: special articles and book excerpts by IDG Books Worldwide authors.

- Take advantage of resources to help you advance your career as a Novell or Microsoft professional.

- Buy IDG Books Worldwide titles or find a convenient bookstore that carries them.

- Register your book and win a prize.

- Chat live online with authors.

- Sign up for regular e-mail updates about our latest books.

- Suggest a book you'd like to read or write.

- Give us your 2¢ about our books and about our Web site.

You say you're not on the Web yet? It's easy to get started with IDG Books' *Discover the Internet,* available at local retailers everywhere.

CD-ROM Installation Instructions

The Microsoft Excel 2000 Bible CD-ROM contains all of the example chapters referenced in this books along with a set of outstanding free software, demos, on-line catalogs, product brochures, and more.

Most of the directories or subdirectories contain installation files with an .EXE file extension. You can simply display the directories and files using your Windows Explorer and then double click on any .EXE file to launch the install program for the file you want to copy to your hard drive. Each installation file will ask if you want a Start menu shortcut created for you.

Please read Appendix D for a complete guide to installing and using the CD-ROM.